Fundamentals of College Admission Counseling

A Textbook for Graduate Students and Practicing Counselors

Fourth Edition

Jonathan D. Mathis, PhD, Raquel M. Rall, PhD & Todd M. Laudino, Editors

Visit NACAC's website for additional resources associated with this text:

www.nacacnet.org/Fundamentals4th

NACAC

Images: *http://www.istockphoto.com/*

Copyright © 2015 by National Association for College Admission Counseling (NACAC)

ISBN 978-0-9862863-0-8.

Printed in the United States of America
10 9 8 7 6 5 4 3 2 1

Contents

Acknowledgments

The fourth edition of the National Association for College Admission Counseling (NACAC)'s *Fundamentals of College Counseling: A Textbook for Graduate Students and Practicing Counselors,* advances the organization's commitment to offer relevant, rigorous, timely and industry-recognized resources to support professionals who help students and families transition to and through postsecondary education.

The previous editions commenced a tradition of blending reflections from practitioners and the voice of faculty in the same text. The most recent edition offered even further connections to research informing and shaping the work of college admission counseling professionals. The text was noted for its ability to make connections between practice and literature still shaping the industry.

As NACAC remains responsive to the needs of the field—including pre-service, novice and continuing counseling professionals—this text is structured such that it opens with a foundation, with proceeding sections building and enhancing a knowledge base. We thank faculty members who contributed insight into the scope and sequence of the fourth edition, thereby best serving those who will use this text to direct instruction.

NACAC would also like to thank the contributors to this edition, as well as previous versions. Our forthcoming authors and contributors for our online supplement, too, are thanked for their efforts and expertise. We are grateful for each author and their diligence in our efforts to move from conceptual design to publication. To the content editors, thank you for the vision and execution of this book. To our designer, IconoGraph Designs, and our copy editor Julie Bogart, thank you for your assistance in preparing the text for publication.

NACAC would also like to acknowledge the dedicated staff who were instrumental in the design and preparation of the fourth edition. It is without question the delivery of this text includes a significant commitment from colleagues across the national office. In particular, we extend our deepest gratitude to the directors and staff members of the following NACAC departments: Education and Training; Communications, Publications and Technology; Public Policy and Research; Membership and Affiliate Relations; and Information Systems.

NACAC Staff

Shanda Ivory

David Hawkins

Crystal Newby

Kristen Garman

Melissa E. Clinedinst

Kelly Ferrante

National Association for College Admission Counseling 2014–2015 Board of Directors

Letter from the Editors

The fourth edition of *Fundamentals of College Admission Counseling: A Textbook for Graduate Students and Practicing Counselors* stands as an imperative resource for novice and continuing professionals. This text is comprised of thoughtful reflections, conceptual and theoretical frameworks informing research, policy and practice, as well as discussions from researchers and faculty at universities across the United States. In total, the text represents a comprehensive view of the considerations for leadership and practice in the field of college admission counseling.

The collection of chapters in this text maintains a variety of voices and communities to be served. As editors, we are grateful for the diverse collection of authors, as well as the variance in approaches utilized in the presentation of material. The authors use a range of tones: anecdotal, conceptual and research-focused. The discussions here are poised to promote continued learning and growth in facilitating college access and success. Authors have also thought of additional resources and topics to further the conversation beyond the text and gear its application toward practice. We offer tremendous gratitude for the dedication and sacrifice of our colleagues—those contributing to both print and the online supplement—for their service and expertise shared within the field.

The design of this text is in response to the needs of both faculty members and their constituents. Content featured in the fourth edition is organized into five distinct areas:

I.   **Framing the Field of College Counseling**

II.   **Defining the Work of College Counselors**

III. **Identifying Pathways and Options**

IV.   **Serving Our Students and Families**

V.   **Advancing Our Work**

Content offered in the **Framing the Field of College Counseling** section focuses on the foundational understandings needed for college counselors, including conceptual, theoretical and ethical frameworks governing the work of professionals in the field of college admission. Offering both a historical and organizational context, the chapters here establish a foundation for proceeding content.

Our second section, **Defining the Work of College Counselors,** moves the reader closer to considerations of practice. From designing the counseling suite and facilitating application processes to managing data and large caseloads, the authors offer conceptual frameworks and field-based best practices to guide the work of novice professionals and revitalize the work of seasoned professionals.

Identifying Pathways and Options, the third section, explores the various routes to and through college, while also considering the available options and pathways for financing higher education. Authors in this section offer insight on the academic experience, data supporting students' transition through the enrollment process, as well as considerations for standardized tests.

The final two sections are designed to assist varying student demographic communities, as well as offer forthcoming thoughts for advancing access and the successful work of college admission counseling professionals. **Serving Our Students and Families** includes content that supports those professionals working with first-generation, low-income and other marginalized student populations and their families, as well as college-bound students with learning disabilities. This section closes with resources for counselors serving diverse student populations, as well as content to help counselors cultivate student-based advocacy. Lastly, **Advancing Our Work** encourages professionals to maintain a future-orientation while thinking about pipelines and pathways to and through college. Conversations about building early awareness efforts, partnerships among varying social and educational institutions, and a propensity for foreshadowed occurrences in the field are all incorporated in the final chapters of this edition.

We do acknowledge that each chapter, and author, for that matter, has unique perspectives and insights to offer. Therefore, this text maintains a fluidity of tone and reflection. Each chapter has been carefully crafted by professionals within the field, and those scholars and faculty who have research interests in the topics featured. To remain responsive to the demands aligning to praxis—the ability to effectively move research into practice—we, as editors, remain cognizant of the unique marrying of theory, practice and reflection that is this fourth edition. We have also been intentional about the grouping of content, both in this text, and what will remain a living online repository for those utilizing this text. That said, we present this text as a springboard of ideas and resources that we hope benefits the readers and those communities they work in and for in efforts to address some of the most pressing issues facing college admission practitioners today.

Consumers of the fourth edition will have access to contemporary, dynamic and even conceptual chapters through the online resource: *www.nacacnet.org/Fundamentals4th*. Upon the release of this text, our online supplement includes the following content and chapters: NACAC's Statement of Principles of Good Practice and its companion guide, Education, Monitoring Procedures and Penalties document; *The 21st Century College Counselor,* written by graduate school faculty and school counselor Eileen Houlihan; *Mind the Gap: Gap Years and the Growing Trend in Higher Education,* written by the executive director of the American Gap Association, Ethan Knight; and forthcoming texts on topics such as serving undocumented students, the college transition for internationally-mobile students and financing higher education.

We encourage you to join the **Fundamentals 4th Edition List-Serve** as a way to stay abreast of new content, relevant articles and professional development opportunities provided by NACAC. To register your text, visit our online resource: *www.nacacnet.org/Fundamentals4th*. Lastly, we also encourage your continued engagement with the authors of this text via social media. A few of our authors have provided means for direct contact, via social media, encouraging continuous engagement in the conversation. We are confident that this text will be a great resource for both novice and continuing professionals.

Sincerely,

Jonathan D. Mathis, PhD
Director of Education and Training,
NACAC

Raquel M. Rall, PhD
Adjunct Assistant Professor,
University of Southern California

Todd M. Laudino
Education and Training
Coordinator, NACAC

I.   Framing the Field of College Counseling

Chapter 1:   The Counseling Landscape*

Cheryl Holcomb-McCoy, PhD

* This chapter was originally printed in *Fundamentals of College Admission Counseling (Third Edition)*. The reprint from the original author includes additional updates for the fourth edition.

INTRODUCTION

For educators, the challenge of preparing a future workforce that is ready to compete in a global economy is daunting. Although the national high school graduation rate has increased to 75.5 percent, the US still suffers from a high school "dropout problem" and an overall achievement gap based on students' ethnic and income backgrounds (Balfanz et al., 2011). Essentially, the achievement gap in the US has resulted in a college enrollment gap—low-income students and students of color (primarily African-American and Latino/Hispanic students) attend and graduate from college disproportionately compared to their white, Asian and affluent peers (Baum & Payea, 2003; National Center of Education Statistics, 2010). This is a critical problem, given that many of the fastest growing jobs in the US require some form of post-

and students of color (Castleman & Page, 2014; Gandara & Bial, 2001; Plank & Jordan, 2001; McDonough, 2004). However, the empirical examination of college counseling is relatively new. Major questions that arise when discussing counseling to enhance K–12 students' college and career readiness have to do with the accessibility of counseling, who conducts the counseling, to whom counseling will be available, and the impact of counseling on actual student behavior and progress (e.g, rate of college going, college retention). Additionally, with the increasingly diverse student population in today's K–12 schools, it's imperative that counseling professionals ask, "What constitutes effective or good college counseling with diverse populations of students and families?" This is a critical question that warrants examination if equitable access is the goal (Holcomb-McCoy, 2007).

In response to the need for an increased number of college graduates, there has been an unparalleled development of college and career readiness initiatives across the US.

secondary education (e.g., an associate degree, bachelor's degree) (US Chamber of Commerce, 2012). As such, a key factor in our nation's ability to compete in an increasingly global economy is the rate at which we can prepare students for entry into postsecondary institutions. President Obama has even made "investments in education" (college-going and completion), one of the five pillars of the country's new economic foundation. He stated that "by 2020, America will once again have the highest proportion of college graduates in the world" (Obama, 2009).

In response to the need for an increased number of college graduates, there has been an unparalleled development of college and career readiness initiatives across the US. Recently, First Lady Michelle Obama's *Reach Higher* initiative has highlighted what students need to be ready for either college and/or careers. Namely, her initiative focuses on the need to expose students to college and career opportunities, financial aid eligibility, academic planning and effective high school counseling (Obama, M., 2014). Repeated studies have shown that counseling (if accessible) can improve college-going rates, particularly for low-income students, first-generation college students

Given the urgency to address the aforementioned issues, a variety of contextual factors influence the efficacy of counseling, particularly college counseling conducted in schools. The remainder of this chapter will provide a historical overview of counseling, followed by a discussion of contextual factors that possibly impede effective college counseling. Trends and future directions will also be discussed. As a note, most private schools and some public high schools have designated college counselors. The typical public high school has a guidance department, consisting of school counselors who all perform college counseling tasks in addition to other counseling-related duties (e.g., scheduling, crisis counseling, dropout prevention programming). There are also community-based college counselors and college preparation organizations that provide college counseling and/or coaching. For the sake of clarity, in this chapter, college counseling refers to all of these scenarios.

HISTORICAL OVERVIEW OF COUNSELING

Professional counseling continues to evolve in response to social, educational, political, and economic trends. In October 2010, the American Counseling Association (ACA) Governing Council approved the following definition of counseling:

> Counseling is a professional relationship that empowers diverse individuals, families, and groups to accomplish mental health, wellness, education, and career goals.

Several researchers have cited the evolution of vocational guidance and psychology to transformative school counseling (ASCA, 1999; Cobia and Henderson, 2003; Coy, 1999a; Education Trust, 1997; House, & Martin, 1998; Schmidt, 2003). However, college counseling as it relates to school counseling has a less defined path. The most notable and frequently cited influence that initially heightened postsecondary awareness was the passing of the National Defense Education Act (NDEA) in 1958. Enacted by the federal government, the NDEA provided funding to improve secondary school counseling, with emphases on high school counselor preparation, subsidized training programs and professional institutes for guidance personnel. It was also in the 1950s that the American Psychological Association and the American Personnel and Guidance Association (APGA) introduced distinct standards and requirements for pupil personnel workers (e.g., psychologists, guidance counselors, social workers).

In the 1970s, 1980s and early 1990s, focus turned to education initiatives, such as High Schools That Work and The School Development Program, which were student-centered and developed to increase academic achievement and postsecondary student preparedness (Board, 1999a; Comer, 1996). The High Schools That Work research visibly placed school counselor roles in the practice of vocational guidance (Board, 1999a, 1999b). Evidence-based research in The School Development Program demonstrated consistent and continuous student improvement, especially in urban settings; however, direct linkage to school counseling services was vague (Smylie, Wenzel, & Fendt, 2003). During the concurrent era, state department of education personnel and counselor educators began to evaluate the impact or absence of school counseling interventions on education reform models, instructional environments and college counseling. Inharmonious discussions centered on the role of the school counselor and

postsecondary advisement. Also during this time, graduate counselor education programs were grounded in clinical and community mental health models that viewed college counseling and academic advisement as conflicting role identities for school counselors (McDonough, 2004). As a result, school counselors were being trained to be highly skilled mental health counselors without an educational framework or perspective from which to guide their practice (Kaplan, 1995).

During the 1990s, community agency partnerships and federally funded opportunity programs were downsized, and some educators began to question if college counseling services were necessary to inform and empower students on the path to college. Prior to the 1990s, a significant segment of college counseling was absorbed through self-help modalities as a guiding principle (McDonough, 2004). That same focus continued during the early 1990s, as widening achievement gaps, astounding dropout rates and declining test scores gave rise to the rethinking and evaluation of school counselor roles and responsibilities in educational settings. Social challenges such as violence, teen pregnancy, peer pressure, poverty, hunger, and homelessness suggested a need for school counselors to use systemic approaches as an integral part of their counseling services (Capuzzi & Gross, 2000; Hossler, Schmidt, & Vesper, 1999).

The literature suggests that the aforementioned history led to the DeWitt Wallace-Education Trust's national initiative to transform school counseling in 1997. Both organizations were convinced that school counselors were not prepared to contribute to equitable learning and college access for all students. Yet, they postulated that professional school counselors were in the best position to identify barriers that impede academic success for all students. ASCA supported the Education Trust's initiative and principles (e.g., leadership, advocacy, collaboration) and consequently, introduced the *ASCA National Model: A Framework for School Counseling Programs* in 2003, as a guide for school counselors' development of data-driven comprehensive school counseling programs. Currently, the Education Trust's New Vision for School Counseling promotes school counseling in which "school counselors advocate for educational equity, access to a rigorous college and career-readiness curriculum, and academic success for all students" (Education Trust, 2012). The Education Trust's Web site lists 23 "Transforming School Counselor Preparation" programs. These programs are committed to training school counselors in skills that are needed to remove barriers that impede student achievement (e.g., collaboration, use of data). The number of practicing school counselors who ascribe to the principles of the Education Trust's New Vision is unknown.

FACTORS INFLUENCING COLLEGE COUNSELING IN SCHOOLS

There are multiple indicators that suggest a need for a possible shift in the foundational principles and practices of counseling in school settings. First and foremost, there are stark disparities in college enrollments across groups of students. Low-income students, students whose parents have never attended college and students of color (i.e., African-American, Latino/Hispanic) are less likely to attend college when compared to their more affluent white and Asian peers (Baum & Payea, 2003; Perna et al., 2008). Although college enrollments have increased across all groups, there is still a persistent enrollment gap. Also, according to the National Center for Education Statistics, when students from underrepresented groups do enroll in college, they tend to enroll in public two-year colleges and less-selective and less-resourced four-year colleges and universities. The lack of college counseling in high schools has been noted as an explanation for these disparities in college access and choice; consequently, school counselors have been blamed for their lack of engagement and gate-keeping practices related to college advising (Rosenbaum, Miller, & Krei, 1996). Obviously, school-based counselors are a logical source of assistance for African Americans, Latinos, low-income students, and students whose parents do not have direct experience with college (Perna, 2004; Horn, Chen, & Chapman, 2003). Chapter 17 outlines working with marginalized communities including these student populations.

Recent studies on the efficacy and long-term effects of school counseling services have highlighted contextual factors (e.g., non-unity among professional associations) that can ultimately shape the extent to which college counseling is offered in schools. Not only do these factors affect the nature of college counseling services offered to students and parents, but they also affect college choice,

preparation for college, transition to college, and adjustment to the college environment.

NON-UNIFIED PROFESSIONAL COMMITMENT TO COLLEGE COUNSELING

Counseling professionals and organizations have always embraced career and academic development as dimensions of the counselor's role or practice. In recent years, counseling professional organizations have increasingly become more overt in their recognition of college counseling as a significant role for counselors. However, these professional associations very rarely work together, providing unified and organized college counseling efforts and professional development in communities and regions of the country (McDonough, 2004). Below are short descriptions of associations that focus on college/career readiness.

The American School Counselor Association (ASCA): The only professional organization specifically designed for school counselors, ASCA provides national standards and a framework for school counseling programs. Inclusive of comprehensive counseling programs, the ASCA standards attempt to address accountability in counseling, particularly in relation to achievement and attainment gaps among students. ASCA addresses the need of school counselors to develop programs that are aligned with student needs illustrated by data. Additionally, in 2006, ASCA created a position statement on academic and career planning that states the following: "Professional school counselors implement academic and career planning based on students' abilities, interests, and goals with the hope of reducing inequities based on stereotypes or special needs and is an important step towards equal access to postsecondary opportunities" (ASCA, p. 1). The ASCA framework and positions, however, have few linkages to other professional associations and college-based organizations.

The National Association for College Admission Counseling (NACAC): A professional association that includes members from schools, communities and organizations, NACAC compiles a by-state report highlighting student-to-counselor ratios and conducts yearly surveys of issues relevant to school counselors. NACAC has recently developed a series of professional development activities for school-based counselors and other college counselors. Nevertheless, most school-based counselors are not members of NACAC and are unaware of its resources. Chapters four and five, however, highlight NACAC resources.

The College Board: As far back as 1992, the College Board published the book, *From Gatekeeper to Advocate,* which challenged the role of school counselors within the context of school reform and restructuring. More recently, the College Board's National Office of School Counselor Advocacy (NOSCA) provides leadership, as well as college counseling training, for school-based counselors. According to its Web site, NOSCA's overall mission is to advance equitable educational access and rigorous academic preparation necessary for college readiness for all students. In 2011, NOSCA published findings from its National Survey of School Counselors. The findings highlighted counselors' concerns within the profession and in the context of preparing students for college and other postsecondary opportunities (Bridgeland & Bruse, 2011). Based on the findings, the following actions were suggested for schools and communities:

1. Align the mission of counselors with the needs of students.

2. Focus counselors' work on activities that accelerate student success.

3. Target professional development dollars.

4. Schools should pilot test measures of accountability.

5. Coordinate initiatives with community-based organizations.

The Education Trust's National Center for Transforming School Counseling (NCTSC): In its New Vision for School Counseling (2009), the NCTSC advocates for educational equity, access to a rigorous college and career-readiness curriculum and academic success for all students. The NCTSC, established by the Education Trust and MetLife, provides professional development, program reviews and state department collaborative activities that promote school counselor involvement in school reform initiatives.

Again, although the aforementioned professional associations have demonstrated a commitment to college counseling, they have historically worked separately with little collaboration. Future efforts to increase counselors'

knowledge and skills in college counseling will be dependent upon how well these organizations work together to provide professional development and training for pre-service and existing college counselors.

CURRENT EDUCATION REFORM INITIATIVES

Counselors have been largely left out of the education reform agenda until recently. And, recently, most of the attention they've received has challenged the value of school counseling. For instance, the recent Gates Foundation Public Agenda report, Can I Get a Little Advice Here, highlighted college students' perceptions of school counselors' roles in the college going process (Johnson et. al, 2010). Using a complex sampling design, Johnson, Rochkind, Ott, & Dupont surveyed 614 individuals between 22–30 years old who had some postsecondary education experience. Between 54 and 67 percent of the young adults rated school counselors as only poor or fair in helping them decide what school was right for them, finding ways to pay for college, such as financial aid and scholarships, thinking about different careers, and in explaining and helping with the college application process. Almost 50 percent of the young adults felt that school counselors merely saw them as "just another face in the crowd," while 47 percent felt that school counselors made an effort to get to know them as an individual. In addition, out of those who felt like a face in the crowd, 18 percent delayed going to college, as opposed to 13 percent who felt like counselors made an effort to get to know them.

Despite the clear national mandate for college and career readiness for all students, school counselors are not mentioned in central education reform mandates (e.g., Race to the Top). Though Secretary of Education Arne Duncan voiced commitment in a 2009 American Counseling Association interview, school counseling was not included in the President's Blueprint for Reform or the Race to the Top proposal guidelines. The Race to the Top and Blueprint for Reform both focus on four core areas that guide the reauthorization of the Elementary and Secondary Education Act:

1. Enhance and reward principal and teacher effectiveness.

2. Build data systems that inform parents and educators about student achievement and guide instruction.

3. Develop college- and career-ready standards and assessments aligned to those standards.

4. Implement effective interventions and support that will improve academic achievement in the lowest performing schools.

In particular, the Blueprint for Reform emphasizes the importance of meeting the needs of students with the highest learning needs, (i.e., culturally diverse learners, diverse English learners, children with disabilities, students of migrant families and workers, homeless students, underprivileged children in rural and highest-need districts). Indeed, Title I, a central component of the Elementary and Secondary Education Act (ESEA), may tie funding for high poverty schools to their ability to articulate and measure college and career readiness for students. The omission of counselors from these reform initiatives is concerning, and counseling associations have begun to respond. For instance, the ACA developed a School Counseling Task Force to specifically address the unique needs of school counselors and to develop ways in which ACA can partner and collaborate with school-reform organizations.

Pre-Service Training of School Counselors

The Council for the Accreditation of Counseling and Related Educational Programs (CACREP) is an accrediting body of pre-service counselor training programs. All pre-service school counselor training programs occur at the graduate or master's level and include coursework and supervised field work. Programs are generally designed to comply with state and/or national counselor certification and licensure requirements.

Programs accredited by CACREP include coursework in the following areas: professional orientation and ethical practice, social and cultural diversity, human growth and development, career development, helping relationships, group work, assessment, and research and program evaluation. School counseling programs accredited by CACREP also must align their program to meet standards that specifically address school-based issues and client populations. The 2009 CACREP School Counseling standards includes college counseling as a training requirement. A graduate of a CACREP program: "Knows how to design, implement, manage, and evaluate transition programs including

school-to work, postsecondary planning, and college admissions counseling" (CACREP, 2009, p. 40).

Programs that are not CACREP-accredited do not have to meet the above standard; thus, many practicing school counselors may not have received college counseling training at all during the pre-service period.

School Counselor Identity

There continues to be role ambiguity in professional school counseling, which ultimately influences the extent to which college counseling occurs in secondary schools. According to Lambie and Williamson (2004), there is incongruence between what is learned in pre-service training and the actual duties most professional school counselors perform. In addition, the literature is replete with illustrations of how school counselors are perceived as ancillary professionals in school districts and remain on the "outside" of important decision-making and policy development.

For many years, counselors have advocated for a stronger identity and a desire for others to understand their role and capabilities (Johnson, 2001). Administrators, parents, community members, teachers, and other stakeholders consistently view the role of school counselors differently. While ASCA's focus is on the counselor as educator, the Association for Counselor Education and Supervision (ACES), along with other counseling organizations, call for a unified professional counselor identity.

Another professional identity issue is that some school counseling professionals have found that school counselors are too often involved in non-counseling related activities (e.g., clerical work, scheduling, lunch duty) (Burnham & Jackson, 2000). These non-counseling related activities, in turn, take counselors away from direct ser-

While ASCA's focus is on the counselor as educator, the Association for Counselor Education and Supervision (ACES), along with other counseling organizations, call for a unified professional counselor identity.

vices, such as college counseling. In a recent study conducted by the College Board, school counselors reported that they would like to spend more time on targeted activities pertaining to career and college counseling, academic planning and building a college-going culture.

COUNSELOR-TO-STUDENT RATIOS

Although there is no simple solution to increasing college and career readiness, numerous case studies indicate that school counselors can play an instrumental role in increasing college enrollment rates. Sink and Stroh (2003) have even found a linkage between comprehensive school counseling programs and academic performance. Lapan, Gysbers and Sun (1997) found that schools with more fully implemented guidance programs had positive effects on high school students' self-reporting of grades, preparation for the future, career and college resources, and perceptions of school climate. Carrell and Carrell (2006), using data provided by Florida's Alachua County School District, found that lower-school counselor-to-student ratios decrease both the recurrence of student disciplinary problems and the share of students involved in a disciplinary incident. Given these studies, albeit limited, the ASCA recommends that there be no more than 250 students to each school counselor. However, a majority of school districts do not adhere to this recommendation. From 2009 to 2010, the student-to-school-counselor ratio increased slightly from the previous year to 459-to-1. According to ASCA, the previous year's ratio was 457-to-1. The College Board recently discovered that, on average, counselors in schools with higher rates of students on free or reduced-price lunches, or higher rates of minority students, also face larger caseloads. There are ways that counselors can still work to meet the needs of a large number of students and these recommendations are discussed in chapter seven.

FURTHER CONSIDERATIONS

Research clearly shows that counselors, when accessible and able to provide direct college counseling to students and their families, can be highly influential in the college admission process. Nevertheless, several school reform groups paint a picture of school counselors as being untrained, inaccessible and unhelpful when it comes to college information sharing, financial aid knowledge and

overall college counseling. The Gates Foundation Public Agenda report, *Can I Get a Little Advice Here,* highlights this fact (Johnson, Rochkind, Ott, & DuPont, 2010).

Research even suggests that access to college information and counseling is a significant benefit in the college application process, particularly for prospective first-generation college students (discussed in chapter 18). Nonetheless, a review of the literature suggests extensive structural constraints that impede the availability of high school counselors (McDonough, 2004a). Counselors are few in number, often have large student caseloads and are limited in the amount of time they have to implement college counseling. According to the National Association for College Admission Counseling (2011), in 2010, public school counselors spent 23 percent of their time on postsecondary counseling, while their private school counterparts spent 55 percent of their time on college counseling. This inequitable focus on college counseling in schools is directly linked to inequitable achievement gains and overall economic and wealth attainment.

In recent years, higher education researchers and professionals have recognized the influence that a strong college-going culture in schools has on students' college-going rates (Govan, 2011; MacDonald & Dorr, 2006; McDonough, 2006). College-going culture theory is a developing theory introduced by McClafferty, McDonough and Nunez in 2002. The idea of a school with a "college-going culture" evolved from partnerships between UCLA and a group of urban schools that wanted to create a college culture in their schools. A college-going culture can start with a college counseling office and, as chapter six highlights, it is up to counselors to create that space and provide students with access to vital college information. Since 2002, the principles, conditions and assessment of college-going culture has grown, and the College Board has endorsed it, giving it credibility in the field. McClafferty et al. (2002) suggest that there are nine principles of a college-going culture: college talk, clear expectations, information and resources, comprehensive counseling model, testing and curriculum, faculty involvement, family involvement, college partnerships, and articulation. Despite the inclusion of a "comprehensive counseling model" as one of the principles, counselors, for the most part, have not fully embraced a role in developing college-going cultures in schools. This is evident by the lack of counseling literature on college-going culture theory, practice and/or assessment.

SUMMARY

In spite of the many contributions of counselors, there may be dire consequences for counselors if they do not show their contributions toward helping students with postsecondary planning and college counseling. In this era of economic recession and a need for a new, more educated workforce, research, such as the Public Agenda report, that points to counselors' lack of engagement in the college-going process could mean a cut in funding for school counseling programs and positions. This may account for the recent proposal before the Senate to consolidate funding from the Elementary and Secondary School Counseling Program (ESSCP) and other similar programs into one funding stream called "Successful, Safe and Healthy Students," which would focus on school-climate issues. This move would severely compromise school counseling programs, because ESSCP is the only program that provides funds to local education agencies (LEAs) to expand or create district-wide comprehensive school counseling services.

Unless school counselors across the nation are able to show that they attend to and effectively facilitate college and career readiness for all students, especially those with the highest learning needs, school counseling programs in some states may risk extinction. For instance, in many districts, counselors have been replaced with other models of student support (e.g., a dean's model). Clearly, the need for counselors to be advocates for their profession is needed. The College Board has coined the term, "own the turf," which will be applied to a national campaign to mobilize counselors to own the knowledge and skills related to college and career counseling and to take the lead in establishing a college-going culture in their schools, districts and communities.

Thus, the arena of college counseling represents one of the most dynamic areas of contemporary education reform and policy. This book, including a wide array of writings by thought leaders in college counseling, reflects the current movements and discourse of the field. Several chapters of the book examine the ways in which a college-going culture can be created in PK–12 school settings, including the cultivation of school-family-community part-

nerships. Another group of chapters present overviews of counselor-specific responsibilities and skills that enhance college readiness and college-going. And the remaining chapters offer research, recommendations and resources related to the practice of college counseling (e.g., use of non-cognitive variables, standardized testing). Rather than providing definitive solutions, the chapters are intended to stimulate discussion about the kinds of practices and strategies that can be implemented in order to increase the diversity of students who are ready to pursue a postsecondary education.

ABOUT THE AUTHOR

Dr. Cheryl Holcomb-McCoy is currently the vice provost for faculty affairs at Johns Hopkins University (MD) and a professor of counseling and human development at the School of Education. As vice provost, Dr. Holcomb-McCoy works closely with the vice deans of faculty and with faculty across the university to advance and promote their important work. In concert with her colleagues in the schools, she concentrates her efforts on ensuring the continued excellence of Johns Hopkins faculty by enhancing faculty development initiatives, increasing faculty diversity and improving the quality of faculty life.

Previous to this role, Dr. Holcomb-McCoy served as the vice dean of academic affairs and chair of the Department of Counseling and Human Services at the School of Education. She has held appointments as associate professor of counselor education at the University of Maryland, College Park and assistant professor and director of the School Counseling Program at Brooklyn College of the City University of New York (NY). Her areas of research specialization include the measurement of multicultural self-efficacy and cultural competence in counseling, the evaluation of urban school counselor preparation and training, and school counselors' influence on low-income students' college readiness.

Dr. Holcomb-McCoy is currently an associate editor of the *Journal for Counseling and Development,* and she has served on numerous journal editorial boards, including the *Professional School Counseling* journal, *Journal for Specialists in Group Work* and *Journal for Social Action in Counseling and Psychology.*

Professional colleagues have recognized her with awards for outstanding multicultural/diversity research, excellence in teaching and exemplar service. She served as a Faculty Lilly Fellow at the University of Maryland and in 2009, she was awarded the Mary Smith Arnold Anti-Oppression Award at the American Counseling Association conference. Because of her expertise in college counseling, Dr. Holcomb-McCoy was selected to participate as a consultant to the Obama Administration's Reach Higher Initiative. In July 2014, she was one of the plenary speakers at the White House's Summit on Higher Education held at Harvard University (MA).

REFERENCES

Bowers, J., & Hatch, T. (2005). *The ASCA national model: A framework for school counseling programs.* Alexandria: American School Counselor Association.

American School Counselor Association. (2006). *ASCA position statements.* Alexandria: American School Counselor Association.

Balfanz, R., Bridgeland, J.M., Bruce, M., and Fox, J.H. (2012). *Building a grad nation: Progress and challenge in ending the high school dropout epidemic.* Civic Enterprises, Everyone Graduates Center at Johns Hopkins University, America's Promise Alliance, and Alliance for Excellent Education.

Baum, S., & Payea, K. (2004). *Education pays 2004: The benefits of higher education for individuals and society.* New York, NY: College Board.

Board, S.R.E. (1999). Improving teachers, parents, and the community in guiding all students into a challenging program of study. *Site Development Guide,* 5. 1–25.

Board, S.R.E. (1999). School strategies: Motivating students to work hard to meet high performance standards. High Schools That Work Site Development Guide: Extra Help and Time, 6. 381–698.

Bridgeland, J., & Bruce, M. (2011). *2011 National Survey of School Counselors: Counseling at a Crossroads.* Washington, DC: College Board Advocacy and Policy Center.

Burnham, J.J., & Jackson, C.M. (2000). School counselor roles: Discrepancies between actual practice and existing models. *Professional School Counseling,* 4, 41–49.

Capuzzi, D., & Gross, D. (2000). Approaches to prevention. In D. Capuzzi & D. Gross (Eds.) *Youth at risk: A prevention resource for counselors, teachers, and parents, 3rd Edition* (pp. 23–40). Alexandria, VA: American Counseling Association..

Carrell, S.E., & Carrell, S.A. (2006). Do lower student to counselor ratios reduce school disciplinary problems? *Contributions to Economic Analysis and Policy,* 5, 1–24.

Castleman, B. L., & Page, L.C. (2014). A trickle or a torrent? Understanding the extent of summer "melt" among college-intending high school graduates. *Social Science Quarterly,* 95(1), 202–220.

Clinedist, M., Hurley, S., & Hawkins, D. (2011). *The state of college admission.* Arlington, VA: National Association for College Admission Counseling.

Cobia, D., & Henderson, D. (2003). *Handbook for school counseling.* Upper Saddle: Merrill-Prentice Hall.

Council for Accreditation of Counseling and Related Educational Programs (CACREP). (2009). 2009 CACREP Standards. Retrieved from *www.cacrep. org/wp-content/uploads/2013/12/2009-Standards.pdf.* Alexandria, VA: CACREP.

Coy, D. (1999). The role and training of the school counselor: Background and purpose. *NASSP Bulletin,* 83, 2–8.

The Education Trust. (2012, April 10). The new vision for school counseling. *The Education Trust.*

The Education Trust. (1997). *Working definition of school counseling.* Washington, DC: Unpublished manuscript.

Fast Facts. (2012, April 10). *Institute of Education Sciences.*

Gandara, P., & Bial, D. (2001). *Paving the way to postsecondary education: K–12 intervention programs for underrepresented youth.* Washington, DC: National Postsecondary Education Cooperative Working Group on Access to Postsecondary Education.

Govan, R.H. (2011). *The soul of a school: An ethnographic study of college-going culture at an u high school.* New Orleans: University of New Orleans.

Holcomb-McCoy, C. (2007). *School counseling to close the achievement gap: A social justice framework for success.* Thousand Oaks: Corwin Press.

Horn, L.J., Chen, X., & Chapman, C. (2003). *Getting ready to pay for college: What students and their parents know about the cost of college tuition and what they are doing to find out.* Washington, DC: National Center for Education.

House, R., & Martin, P. (1998). Advocating for better futures for all students: A new vision for school counselors. *Education,* 119, 284–291.

Hossler, D., Schmidt, J., & Vesper, N. (1999). *Going to college:How social, economic, and educational factors influence the decisions students make.* Baltimore: Johns HopkinsPress.

Johnson, L. (2000). Promoting professional identity in an era of educational reform. *Professional School Counseling,* 4, 31–40.

Johnson, J., Rochkind, J., Ott, A., & DuPoint, S. (2009). *With their whole lives ahead of them: Myths and realities about why so many students fail to finish college.* New York: Public Agenda.

Kaplan, L.S. (1995). Principals versus counselors: Resolving tension from different practice models. *The School Counselor,* 42, 261–267.

Lambie, G.W., & Williamson, L.L. (2004). The challenge to change from guidance counseling to professional school counseling: A historical proposition. *Professional School Counseling,* 8, 124–131.

Lapan, R.T., Gysbers, N.C., & Sun, Y. (1997). The impact of more fully implemented guidance programs on the school experiences of high school students: A statewide evaluation study. *Journal of Counseling and Development,* 75(4), 292–302.

MacDonald, M.F., & Dorr, A. (2006). *Creating a college-going culture: A resource guide.* Los Angeles, CA: Building Educational Success Through Collaboration in Los Angeles County.

McClafferty, K.A., McDonough, P.M., & Nunez, A.M. (2002). *What is a college-going culture? Facilitating college preparation through organizational change.* Los Angeles, CA: UCLA Graduate School of Education and Information Studies.

McDonough, P. (2006). *Overview of college going culture theory.* Los Angeles, CA: UCLA Graduate School of Education and Information Studies.

McDonough, P. (2004). *Counseling matters: Knowledge, assistance, and organizational commitment in college preparation.* In W. Tierney, Z. Corwin, & J. Colyar, Preparing for college: Nine elements of effective outreach (pp. 69–88). Albany, NY: State University of New York Press.

National Office for School Counselor Advocacy. (2012, April 10). College Board Advocacy & Policy Center.

New Ratios Released. (2012, April 10). American School Counselor Association.

Obama, B. (2009). *Remarks by the President on the economy.* Georgetown University.

Obama, M. (2014, May 7). *Remarks by the First Lady at San Antonio signing day Reach Higher event.* Retrieved from *http://beforeitsnews.com/obama/2014/05/ remarks-by-the-first-lady-at-san-antonio-signing-day-reach-higher-event-2-2463146.html.*

Perna, L. (2004). Understanding the decision to enroll in graduate school: Sex and racial/ethnic group differences. *Journal of Higher Education,* 75(5), (487–527.

Perna, L., Rowan-Kenyon, H., Thomas, S., Bell, A., Anderson, R., & Li, C. (2008). The role of college counseling in shaping college opportunity: Variations across high schools. *Review of Higher Education,* 31(2), 131–159.

Plank, S.B., & Jordan, W.J. (2001). Effects of information, guidance, and actions on postsecondary destinations: A study of talent loss. *American Educational Research Journal,* 38(4), 947–979.

Resources—Definition of Counseling. (2012, April 10). American Counseling Association.

Rosenbaum, J.E., Miller, S.R, & Krei, M.S. (1996). Gatekeeping in an era of more open gates: High school counselors' views of their influence on students' college plans. *American Journal of Education,* 104, 257–279.

Schmidt, J.J. (2003). *Counseling in schools: Essential services and comprehensive programs* (4th ed.).Boston: Pearson Education, Inc.

Sink, C.A., & Stroh, H.R. (2003). Raising achievement test scores of early elementary school studentsthrough comprehensive school counseling programs. *Professional School Counseling,* 6(5), 352–364.

Smylie, M., Wenzel, S., & Fendt, C. (2003). The Chicago *Annenberg Challenge: Lessons on leadership for school development.* In J.M.A. Datnow (Ed.) Leadership lessons from comprehensive school reforms. . Thousand Oaks: Sage.

US Chamber of Commerce. (2012, April 10). *Jobs agenda: Education and workforce.*

Wingfield, R.J., Reese, R.F., & West-Olatunji, C.A. (2010). *Counselors as Leaders in Schools,* 4, 114-130.

Chapter 2:

Framework for College Counseling: Considerations for Novice and Continuing Professionals

LaVerne Ware, PhD
@lyware

Jonathan D. Mathis, PhD
@NACACedu

The landscape of college counseling continues to evolve in response to many factors: federal and state initiatives to increase college participation, federal and local funding programs, and philanthropic efforts and private donations. These conditions have, in many ways, made pursuing postsecondary education a realistic option for many students. Due to the previously mentioned environmental factors, school counselors are even more pressed to ensure that their students are adequately prepared to graduate from high school and transition to college (Conley, 2010). If the goal is to promote college readiness of students, it is imperative that educators—counselors, teachers and leaders—work to address the needs of all students. However, this is no easy feat and comes with its own unique set of challenges and professional needs regarding content and training.

Counseling professionals in secondary schools are chiefly responsible for leading critical areas of student development. We know that school counselors are not

ment: academic; personal, social and emotional; career; and postsecondary engagement and outcomes. This chapter does not set out to cover all facets of these ideas; instead, it serves as a platform for future reading and areas for further training and development for college admission professionals and their colleagues.

The discussion begins with a look at elements of academic development, followed by conceptual and theoretical considerations for personal, social and emotional development for college-bound students. The second segment of this conversation focuses on frameworks informing college choice, career aspirations and development, with a closing review of considerations highlighting affordability and financial resources supporting access and success.

To begin, it might be best to frame the conversation with the work of Kuh and colleagues (2006) in regard to the research literature informing student success. Kuh and colleagues (2006) offer six variables defining stu-

If the goal is to promote college readiness of students, it is imperative that educators—counselors, teachers and leaders—work to address the needs of all students.

only responsible for guiding students through the college search process, but also are known to be the resource person who assists students with their class schedules and supports them in times of crisis and even more. The American School Counselor Association (ASCA) recommends a student-to-counselor ratio of 250 to 1. The national average is 471 students to every one counselor. Given this number and school counselors' myriad of responsibilities, it is clear that one professional cannot carry a school's college resource infrastructure (Lombana, 1985; McDonough & Perez, 1998; Monson & Brown, 1985). However, as this counseling professional provides leadership for the infrastructure, it is important for the counselor to be well-equipped with the frameworks and considerations that might inform the professional development of self and others serving students throughout the college application process.

With college access and success as goals for all students, this work includes several domains of develop-

dents' pre-college experiences: academic preparation; aptitude and college readiness; family and peer support; motivation to learn; enrollment choices; and student background characteristics and demographics. In what follows, the authors highlight and draw connections among conceptual, theoretical and practical frameworks, and the proceeding chapters. First, the frameworks that help understand academic development.

ACADEMIC FRAMEWORKS

A suggested outcome of secondary education is the college readiness of students. Conley (2010) writes, "high schools should be considered successful in proportion to the degree to which they prepare their students to continue to learn beyond high school" (p. 9). High school graduation, completion of required courses necessary for college admission and demonstration of basic literacy skills are used to define college readiness (Greene & Forster, 2003). Academics matter, therefore, the assistance counselors provide to students in course selection, study skills, time management, among many other supports, is crucial to college access and success. As it pertains to access, Perna (2004) concludes that students' academic preparation is among the most important predictors of a predisposition toward, interest in and actual college enrollment.

Yet, as we extend beyond simply college access, scholars suggest that "the quality of the academic experience and intensity of the high school curriculum affect almost every dimension of success in postsecondary education" (Kuh, et al., 2006, p. 19). Other scholarship speaks to "college knowledge"—cognitive strategies, contextual skills and knowledge, academic behaviors, all in addition to content knowledge (Conley, 2005; 2008). Of particular interest for further discussion are the following two concepts: key content knowledge and academic behaviors. Although these two concepts will be explored further in chapter 11, it is helpful to offer a brief overview of these two elements of Conley's conceptual framework highlighting college and career readiness.

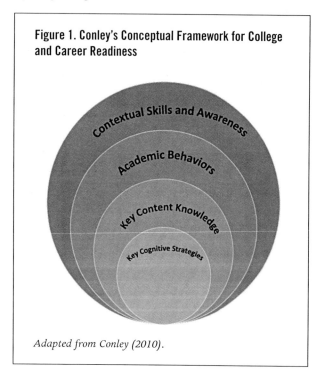

Figure 1. Conley's Conceptual Framework for College and Career Readiness

Adapted from Conley (2010).

Key content knowledge includes a student's ability to acquire a deep "understanding of academic disciplines," thus supporting mastery and application of core academic subjects beyond high school (Conley, 2010, p. 35). The academic content knowledge then might accelerate student's ability to fully utilize cognitive strategies to support critical thinking and analysis. Academic behaviors, on the other hand, speak to the ability to self-manage. Within this concept, Conley (2010) suggests that with exemplary display of academic behaviors, students exhibit greater "self-awareness, self-monitoring, and self-control of a series of processes and behaviors necessary for academic success" (p. 39). These behaviors promote higher ideals of metacognition, which Conley describes as "the ability to think about how one is thinking" (p. 39). The role and influence of counselors, especially those supporting the transition to college, is heightened in the area of ensuring students' self-awareness of their content knowledge and cultivation of academic behaviors.

Conley (2010) presents a powerful reflection that is an important consideration for educators, which then can inform the advocacy efforts of counseling professionals:

> Although no one wants to be accused of closing off opportunities to young people, many educators observe that their students do not seem interested in doing the work necessary to be ready for postsecondary studies. Perhaps it makes more sense to help these students prepare for productive lives in endeavors that may not necessarily require education beyond a high school diploma. The dilemma that this point of view highlights is that a choice is being made about a student's life and future…The real underlying issue is whether a decision of this nature should be left solely or primarily to students in the first place and whether the adults really know enough about student potential and capabilities to make such choices for them (Conley, 2010, p. 2).

The academic aptitude of students is often associated with grade point average and scores from standardized assessments. However, a counselor's understanding of students' academic self-concept and promotion of self-authorship might empower even greater aspirations and outcomes.

Academic Self-Concept

The construct of self-concept informs dimensions of an individual's perception of their personal abilities and identity; it articulates a self-assessment and internalized statement of ability. Specifically, academic self-concept is described "as a person's perception about himself or herself related to his or her academic endeavors" (Rinn & Cunningham, 2008, p. 232). These perceptions are suggested to be the result of actual and perceived social status of parents, as well as interactions within institutions and peer groups (Orr & Dinur, 1995). Bandura and colleagues suggest:

> self-efficacious parents hold high academic
> aspirations for their children. Parental perceived
> academic efficacy and educational aspirations
> are both consistently related to their children's
> perceived academic efficacy and aspirations
> (Bandura et al., 1996, p. 1,213).

In the school setting, how might counselors create conditions where these ideas regarding self-concept might be directed to college participation—both access and success in postsecondary educational pursuits?

Self-Authorship

As counseling professionals, we have all witnessed various stages of adolescent development, including the physiological and hormonal changes students demonstrate in our learning communities—in and outside of the classroom setting. But, how students come to know themselves and their academic abilities is of great importance in moments of change and growth. Scholars write about adolescents' belief that knowledge resides and is possessed by authority figures. This belief reinforces an idea that limits students' ability to see themselves as active consumers of knowledge from multiple perspectives (Baxter Magolda & King, 2008). It is from this viewpoint that self-authorship is suggested to enhance academic development in late adolescent students.

As a theoretical framework, self-authorship suggests the intrapersonal, interpersonal and cognitive development of students as they begin to "own" their postsecondary identity, acquisition and creation of knowledge. Intrapersonal development includes the manner in which students acquire, articulate and nurture the evolution of their identity. Within intrapersonal development, an individual might ask, "Who am I?" (Baxter Magolda, 2005, p. 820). This dimension includes "an internally generated belief system that regulates one's interpretations of expe-

rience and guides one's choice" (King & Baxter Magolda, 2005, p. 103).

Interpersonal development focuses on the construction of relationships among students and members of the educational environment. This area of development considers the maintenance of previously established relationships prior to college enrollment, as well as those created in the postsecondary environment. Specifically, the ability to take "others' perspective into account rather than being consumed by them" highlights students' appreciation for varying opinions, while also honoring the student's own understanding (King & Baxter Magolda, 2005, p. 103).

Lastly, cognitive development includes identity and the aforementioned academic self-concept. Scholars suggest that this area of development is seen when students ask a very critical question: "How do I know?" (Baxter Magolda, 2005, p. 82) When an individual is able to assess "one's own views in light of existing evidence and construction [of] a reasonable perspective based on available evidence," it represents a core element of cognitive development (King & Baxter Magolda, 2005, p. 103).

The bridge between academic and identity development frameworks is of importance—an ever-present phenomenon of which counselors need to be aware. Academic content knowledge and behaviors might be enhanced or re-directed given a student's self-concept and self-authorship. The question arises, how might professionals take these conceptual considerations forward to inform the practice of college admission counseling? One suggestion offered here aligns with the work of Baxter Magolda and King (2008):

> reflective conversations are one approach in
> educators' overall efforts to guide students
> through the transformation from external
> definition to self-authorship…[these conversations]
> are one way to construct learning partnerships
> that intentionally combine challenge, reflection
> and support to help students develop increasingly
> complex frames of reference to guide their
> academic decisions. (para. 13).

The use of reflection is not only important for academic frameworks, it is also useful to understand and promote personal, social and emotional development.

PERSONAL, SOCIAL AND EMOTIONAL DEVELOPMENT

Within the last section of this chapter, we provided a cursory overview of frameworks and concepts defining academic identity and achievement platforms. Here, we look to provide considerations for both personal and social development concepts that might influence or moderate the work of college admission counseling professionals. Personal and social development of adolescent students is a major factor in the college preparation process. Specifically, this section highlights the following concepts: self-esteem, autonomy and resiliency; peers and motivation; and self-efficacy.

Self-esteem, Autonomy and Resiliency

A discussion of self-esteem first requires an acknowledgement of the interchangeability of the term with another: self-concept. As noted in the previous section, one's self-concept is aligned with a personal belief of one's abilities and attitudes, which might be informed or reinforced by familial or institutional contexts. Self-esteem, however, is described as reactionary to self-concept (Pintrich & Schunk, 1996). At its core, scholars point to self-esteem as a dual concept—"as a means of enhancing inclusion and as a means of avoiding exclusion" (Leary, Tambor, Terdal, & Downs, 1995, p. 528). Birkeland, Melkerik, Holsen, and Wold's (2012) discussion of self-esteem includes the following argument: "global self-esteem may act as an indicator of how the adolescents face and manage [physical, psychological and contextual] changes" (p. 43). These scholars acknowledge that from the age of 14 years old to 23 years old, "the mean level of global self-esteem is quite stable and increases slowly" (Birkeland et al., 2012, p. 50). This finding heightens the impact and influences of educators and counselors assisting students in their transition to and through college.

Adolescence is often highlighted by scholars as a phase of development during which there is particular tension between the struggle for autonomy and the strong attachment that teens have to their parents. It is the highly autonomous teen who is suggested to adapt relatively well to one particular stressor: adjustment to college (McElhaney et al, 2009). This knowledge helps counselors to position their work in multiple ways, in-

cluding the encouragement of students to step beyond and expand their comfort zone. It is in this phase of transition students might learn new and challenging things, take on leadership roles, and develop autonomy and self-confidence. Fergus and Zimmerman (2005) suggests that youth who have self-confidence and social skills also are somewhat predisposed to being resilient regardless of the risk or outcome. Therefore, we hope this confidence extends beyond the challenges of transition through the application process and into the pursuit of postsecondary educational opportunities.

Often postsecondary planning includes the possibility of the teen moving out of his parents' home and far away from friends and family. This can cause major anxiety and apprehension for the student. Vultaggio and Friedfeld (2013) discuss the various stressors throughout the college application and enrollment process. The authors share survey data in which some students describe the admission process as stressful, given the potential and perceived outcomes: acceptances versus denial; success versus failure. The lack of knowledge of the process, outcomes or understanding of relevant information all were suggested to contribute to the anxiety of students. Vultaggio and Friedfeld (2013) offer recommendations to college admission professionals that might both promote autonomy and restore resiliency among students. These recommendations include: helping students to understand the admission process; providing exposure to information outlets and college options; providing access to information; addressing stress; and promoting time management. It is here that we suggest for the counseling professional to be patient and honest with the student and members of the family to ensure that they are well informed and know what to expect throughout the process. As an outcome, counselors promote the furthered autonomy of students. Belsky and Cassidy (1994) suggest that secure adolescents might be better able to use their parents as a base from which to confidently and autonomously explore the world around them, returning to parents for comfort, support and advice when the limits of their competence are reached.

Peers and Motivation

In adolescence, peer groups mediate important links between cultural values and individual development (Chen

& Jensen, 2013). As noted in both Chapman (1981) and Perna's (2006) frameworks regarding college choice, members of one's peer groups, "friends" for the sake of argument here, might contribute immensely to the decision to attend college and often the selection of the college. Fletcher and Tienda (2009) found that those who possess "larger high school peer groups upon entering college outperform their counterparts with fewer coenrolled classmates and are more likely to remain enrolled after successfully execute the behavior required to produce outcomes" (p. 193). When we consider the college admission process, there are varying data points and information that might be communicated to students that might impact self-efficacy tremendously. In the prior sections, attention to anxiety and resiliency highlight two viewpoints that might emerge from similar situations: possible avoidance or internalization of challenges versus possible coping strategies to advance aspirations.

When we consider the college admission process, there are varying data points and information that might be communicated to students that might impact self-efficacy tremendously.

four semesters" (p. 307). Additionally, these scholars found that "minority students who enter college with sizable cohorts reap larger academic benefits than do their white counterparts" (Fletcher & Tienda, 2009, p. 309). The creation of cohort groups entering college has been seen among philanthropic efforts and scholarships, but this transition type might not be the norm among secondary students.

From the *What Works Clearinghouse,* scholars suggest that secondary-level educators should "surround students with adults and peers who build and support their college-going aspirations" (Tierney et al., 2009, p. 26). In action, the authors point to peer-mentors—possibly local college students and/or graduates of the high school—to assist in communicating college-going aspirations. Specifically, the authors mention four roles mentors might fulfill: serve as college-going role models; assist with the college entry process; monitor academic progress; and listen to and advise students (Tierney et al., 2009).

Self-efficacy

Scholars recognize that the concept of self-efficacy takes shape across various perspectives. In general, Gecas (1989) suggests that self-efficacy "refers to people's assessments of their effectiveness, competence, and causal agency" (p. 292). The nuances of self-efficacy draw further attention to an individual's experiences, beliefs and their self-evaluation. Focusing on the latter, Bandura (1977) writes that "an efficacy expectation is the conviction that one can

Counseling professionals who work to address students who demonstrate low levels of self-efficacy might best serve students by assisting in their development of "competencies and expectations of personal effectiveness" (Bandura, 1977, p. 205). Pajares (1996) takes into consideration the value of the research informing intervention strategies, despite these suggested practices being slow to action. In particular, a summary of research findings suggests that educators might give as much attention to perceptions of competence as to demonstrated competency and performance. Student-held beliefs, then, can be challenged, and aspirations might even be increased through dialogue, information and exposure.

CAREER FRAMEWORKS AND ASPIRATIONS

Postsecondary planning often includes intentional conversations about career aspiration and choice. It is through this focus that counselors might employ interest assessments, career day and job shadowing programs, in addition to the cultivation of business etiquette. These elements of exposure can aid in career awareness and selection. As such, counseling professionals are encouraged to become familiar with a variety of career opportunities and those skills needed to perform professional roles.

Integral to the aforementioned statement is "opportunities," which is the centerpiece to Furlong and Cartmel's scholarship informing career aspirations. Furlong and Cartmel (1997) present the idea of "opportunity structures," which encompass the experiences and programs fostering exposure to career awareness, ultimately leading to informed aspirations. Within these opportunities, it is helpful for counselors to consider the manner in which ideas and aspirations might align with one's self-efficacy. Bandura (1993) reminds us that self-efficacy, described in the previous section, also has substantial impact on students' career aspirations and development. As a choice-related process, career development is believed to maintain the following argument:

> The stronger people's belief in their efficacy, the more career options they consider possible, the greater the interest they show in them, the better they prepare themselves educationally for different occupations, and the greater their staying power and success in difficult occupational pursuits (p. 135).

The question then becomes, how might admission counseling professionals take these ideas into account as conversations about careers, as an outcome of college, take place?

There are numerous tools available to assist students with becoming aware of their learning style, character traits, job readiness skills, and career choices. We offer just a brief description for four of the tools used among counselors. *Big Future,* by the College Board, provides students with interactive tools and guidance to understand college options and opportunities. This program also allows students to explore interests and career options, thereby informing their decisions for the future (*bigfuture.collegeboard.org*). Second, *ACT Aspire,* a computer-based assessment system functioning with a longitudinal design—connects student progress from elementary grades through high school in the context of college and career readiness. Aspire utilizes reporting categories that are based on the ACT® College Readiness Standards (*discoveractaspire.org*). Third, *EducationPlanner* functions as a career and college planning Web site and provides students with advice as they prepare to make decisions about their futures. This Web site utilizes interactive exercises, easy-to-use search tools, and information for students, parents and counselors (*educationplanner.org*).

Lastly, *Mapping Your Future* provides students, families and schools with resources and tools to assist students in navigating the college planning, career selection and financial aid processes (*http://mappingyourfuture.org*). Each of the four resources briefly defined here are virtual, free and readily available for students and parents to learn more about postsecondary planning and careers.

We do know that various inventories exist and acknowledge their utility. The question remains, how might counseling professionals cultivate greater self-efficacy among their students? How might we suggest students utilize this information to compete with or inform elements of college access and career-engagement as a success measure of college?

College Choice

Conversations regarding access to and enrolling in college often look back to dimensions of choice. Our purpose here is not to explore multiple options situated in the research. However, in a forthcoming chapter on college search and choice, the author highlights additional frameworks informing practice (see chapter eight). We agree, first, that "ensuring that all individuals have the opportunity to enroll in college is a critical step toward maximizing the private and public benefits that result from higher education, including state and national prosperity" (Perna, 2006, p. 105).

Second, we offer essential considerations for counselors, followed by two frameworks considered foundational in the canon access literature: Chapman (1981) and Perna (2006). We begin with Chapman's (1981) conceptual framework of student college choice, which takes a longitudinal approach suggesting:

> to understand a student's choice of which college to attend, it is necessary to take into account both background and current characteristics of the student, the student's family, and the characteristics of the college (p. 492).

Second, Perna (2006) offers a conceptual model that:

> integrates aspects of economic and sociological approaches. The model assumes that an individual's assessment of the benefits and costs of an investment in college is shaped by the individual's habitus, as well as the school and community context, the higher education context, and the social, economic, and policy context (p. 101).

Both Chapman's (1981) and Perna's (2006) work will be explored in greater detail, following the considerations that begin with the work and support of counselors to students.

Counselor Agreements and Considerations

When making a college selection, there are some standard considerations for college admission professionals. The route to college is continuous throughout the student's educational journey; the student should not wait until the senior year to begin. An early start is most advantageous when deciding where he or she will spend the next four years of life, which is further discussed in chapter 22. College visits, virtual tours and attending college fairs all provide students with the information and tools needed to make the best college selection.

As students commence the journey, they should be encouraged to consider their strengths, qualities and desires when selecting a college. There must also be some sort of acknowledgement of the external environment influencing college choice. A review of prior research suggests that four kinds of state public policies may influence the type of college that individuals in the state attend: (a) direct appropriations to higher education institutions, (b) financial aid to students, (c) tuition, and (d) policies related to academic preparation at the elementary- and secondary-school levels (Perna & Titus, 2004). Both individual and external influences—examples of which are stated above—are included in the works of Chapman (1981) and Perna (2006).

Chapman (1981) and College Choice

It is important to note that Chapman (1981) positions his contribution for understanding the "traditional age (18–21) prospective students," acknowledging the inability to capture and define the "special pressures and influences on older adults" as it pertains to choice (p. 492).

Chapman (1981) offers three categories that best generalize the influences on students' college choice: (1) influences of significant persons; (2) fixed characteristics of the institution; and (3) an individual institution's efforts to communicate with prospective students. Chapman also acknowledges that both "student characteristics and the external influences to and, in turn, are shaped by students' generalized expectations of college life" (p. 492). The characteristics and external influences discussed

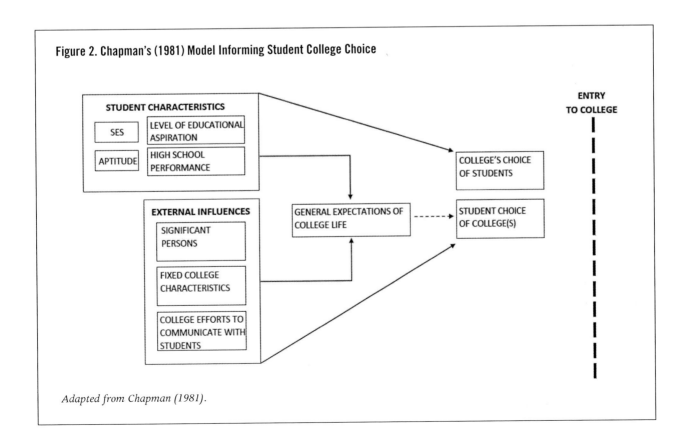

Figure 2. Chapman's (1981) Model Informing Student College Choice

Adapted from Chapman (1981).

here by Chapman (1981) are later described by Kuh and colleagues' work, as discussed at the start of this chapter, pre-college experiences: aptitude; motivation to learn; student demographics; family support; and peer support (Kuh et al., 2006).

Influences of significant persons. Why this model is discussed here in this chapter, versus other frameworks, is largely due to this component of the model and its seminal contribution to the field. Chapman (1981) suggests that as students are selecting a college they "are strongly persuaded by the comments and advice of their friends and family" (p. 494). However, it is how these groups influence the student that suggests the approach of the college admission counseling professional:

1. Their comments shape the student's expectations of what a particular college is like.

2. They may offer direct advice as to where the student should go to college.

3. In the case of close friends, where the friends themselves go to college will influence the student's decision (Chapman, 1981).

We offer the following argument: Following the influence of peers and families, counselors are likely faced with the challenge of redirecting or re-educating students on options. These professionals might be tasked with a number of actions: (1) trying to extend students' awareness of options beyond those suggested by family and friends; (2) providing accurate information that verifies or refutes perceived "truths"; and (3) advising students where to further inform their search, and how they might best compose their listing of potential colleges and universities.

Fixed characteristics of the institution. When college choice and college search are topics of discussion, there are several factors that become increasingly familiar to navigating several options down to a short list. Chapman (1981) writes, "location, costs, campus environment, and the availability of desired programs" define the fixed characteristics that help to inform choice (p. 495). The scholar acknowledges that institutions have the ability to modify much of these factors, with the exception, in general, to location. But, as noted in the last component of the model, the manner in which this information is communicated to students becomes the challenge.

College efforts to communicate with students. Enrollment will continue to be at the forefront of institutional efforts and planning. Accordingly, colleges and universities are suggested to systematically consider marketing principles and research to best inform modes operating to connect to and share information and attract students (Chapman, 1981). We, too, suggest that this component of the model could include the manner in which information is shared with counseling professionals who are largely responsible for the school-based dissemination of college-related processes and resources.

Understanding Cultural Capital and Habitus

Before beginning to describe this model in greater detail, it is helpful to add a bit of clarity to the idea of "habitus" mentioned in the outline of this section. French sociologist Pierre Bourdieu (1986) provides seminal works defining cultural capital as existing in three facets: embodied—"in the form of long-lasting dispositions of the mind and body,"; objectified—"in the form of cultural goods"; and institutionalized—"a form of objectification which must be set apart because, as will be seen in the case of education qualifications, it confers entirely original properties on the cultural capital which it is presumed to guarantee" (p. 243). Embodied cultural capital might include understanding and performing the nuances of dining etiquette, whereas objectified cultural capital might include appreciating the designer of the fine chinaware from which one might eat. Institutionalized cultural capital, however, might include the perceived value, both intrinsic and extrinsic, of one's degree and the granting university or college. Habitus, in short, might be described as embodied cultural capital embedded and replicated within one's own familial and environmental context. It represents accepted, reproduced and socialized norms informing action.

Bourdieu (1973) writes that habitus represents a "system of dispositions which as a mediation between structures and practice...structures...[which] reproduce themselves by producing agents endowed with the system of predispositions" (p. 72). Thus, habitus becomes akin to schema—fundamental building blocks of knowing or performing activities—as it is all one might know or understand, from which all else is established.

Perna (2006) and College Choice

Perna's (2006) conceptual model informing student college choice "draws on an economic model of human capital investment as well as the sociological concepts of habitus, cultural and social capital, and organizational context" (p. 116).

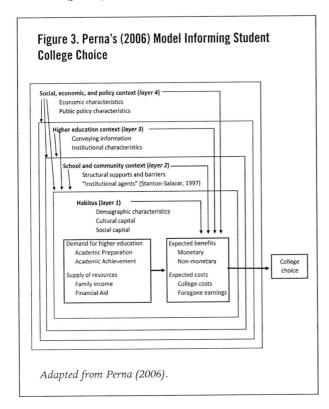

Figure 3. Perna's (2006) Model Informing Student College Choice

Adapted from Perna (2006).

The positioning of human capital investment is seen at the center of the first layer of this model. Perna (2006) begins by framing this component as a comparison of both the expected benefits and costs. "The expected benefits include both monetary and nonmonetary benefits, while the expected costs include the costs of attendance and foregone earnings" (p. 116). Perna adds that the perceived academic preparation and ability to pay also influence choice in this area. From this starting point we see four contextual layers, superimposed on one another, assumed to shape college-choice decisions: (1) the individual's habitus; (2) school and community context; (3) the higher education context; and (4) the broader social, economic, and policy context (Perna, 2006).

Individual's habitus. As highlighted at the start of this discussion, habitus represents the idea of structuring norms that are argued to inform predispositions, actions and, in this case, future-oriented aspirations. Within this layer, Perna highlights how habitus "is expected to reflect an individual's demographic characteristic…as well as cultural and social capital" (2006, pp. 116–117).

School and community context. This layer represents the impact and influence of the local contextual environment on student's college choice. Here is where the norms and expectations of the school community might "facilitate or impede" choice (Perna, 2006, p. 117); it is here, too, that college admission counseling professionals might operate in a capacity to combat norms that might stand to undervalue college enrollment. Perna connects this argument with the work of Stanton-Salazar's (1997) articulation of institutional agents, which is further discussed in the fourth chapter of this textbook. We also see tenets of the impact of counselor-created, school-based, college-going culture, as discussed in the seventh chapter of this textbook.

Higher education context. Perna (2006) reviews the multiple ways in which higher education institutions might inform or shape students' choice. Similar to the argument presented by Chapman (1981), the aforementioned avenues colleges might take to correspond with or market to students become of paramount interest around enrollment efforts. Perna (2006) adds that the manner in which college and university admission professionals might convey information, discuss environmental attributes and institutional selectivity all impact choice.

Social, economic and policy context. The fourth layer of Perna's (2006) model "recognizes that college choice is also influenced directly and indirectly through other contextual layers, by changes in social forces…economic conditions…and public policies" (p. 119). These factors impact not only students, but arguably, these factors also begin to define some of the stressors and/or concerns of parents.

The layers, both separate and as a composite, help to frame the individual efforts, institutionally-based programming, and culture-shaping activities of college admission professionals serving students and families.

AFFORDABILITY PLANNING AND CONSIDERATIONS

The financial aid process can be daunting for students and their parents, especially for those who do not have funds readily available to cover the cost of entrance exams, admission fees and college tuition. School counselors are charged with providing students and their families with scholarship opportunities, as well as educating them on loan options (for further reading on this topic, see chapters 15 and 16). Completion of the Free Application for Federal Student Aid (FAFSA) is required by many colleges, universities and numerous scholarship providers. School counselors can assist families with this process by organizing a scholarship or financial aid night. Many community-based organizations, banks and lending institutions will assist families with completing the FAFSA.

A growing number of states are devoting resources to merit-based financial aid programs (Heller, 2002). While need-based programs award financial aid to the most economically disadvantaged students, merit-based programs award financial aid to students who meet a specified threshold of academic achievement, a criterion that is positively correlated with family income. Following the lead of Georgia's HOPE Scholarship Program and Florida's Bright Futures Scholarship Program, the two largest state-administered, merit-based student aid programs, other states (e.g., Alabama, Kentucky, Louisiana, Maryland, Michigan, New Mexico, Texas, and Washington) have recently implemented such programs (Heller, 2002). Since the mid-1990s, state funding for merit-based financial aid programs has increased at a faster rate than state funding for need-based programs (Heller, 2002).

Closing Thoughts

Adolescent students are faced with many challenges during their pre-college years. Elements of their academic, personal, social, and emotional development are paramount to their pre-college experiences. It is also during this time that students spend a great deal of their time and energy planning life after high school. During this period, counselors are encouraged to be aware of familial and contextual conditions that might inform or hinder a student's self-concept, efficacy, college choice, and career aspirations.

Today's social environment, both familial and contextual, is one that is multi-faceted and multicultural, thus warranting the use of culturally focused, evidence-based practices to meet the needs of consumers seeking assistance with problem behaviors in a variety of environmental settings and disciplines (Chavis, 2012). As we consider the frameworks mentioned in this chapter, counselors are charged with learning and implementing culturally diverse

tactics and skills to motivate students when they lose hope or want to give up. Counselors represent the possibility of college as a reality; they transition students to and through the high-school-graduation-to-college journey.

Certainly, the work of counselors already consumes multiple roles, considerations and best practices. What we set out to do in this chapter was to offer a foundation for practice, highlighting theoretical and conceptual considerations that might best explain what is seen throughout the college enrollment process, and ultimately, career aspirations and development. This chapter should leave counseling professionals with the desire to learn and know more about the frameworks. Take this energy forth to create professional development experiences for those who will assist in the choice process, including teachers, paraprofessionals, volunteers, and even parents. Consider the frameworks presented here as opportunities for future conversations and even strategies to promote the development of college-bound students.

School counselors, parents, guardians, and community members are a student's best resource when navigating the college admission process. Students need encouragement, training, exposure, and guidance when making critical decisions and planning for their future academic endeavors. It is imperative that the professionals charged with guiding, advocating and supporting them have an overabundance of tools and the required knowledge to aid students in making the best college choice.

About the Authors

LaVerne Ware, PhD has served as the coordinator of secondary counseling in Atlanta Public Schools (GA) for the past six years. She entered the field of counseling nearly 20 years ago and has experience in both middle and high school counseling. She was also recognized as Georgia's 2003 Region 3 Counselor of the Year. Dr. Ware is passionate about school counseling and training counselors to provide comprehensive, data driven programs that equip students to become college and career ready.

Jonathan D. Mathis, PhD serves as director of education and training for the National Association for College Admission Counseling (NACAC). Prior to joining NACAC, Dr. Mathis was a postdoctoral scholar for research and practice, and regional director for PUC Schools, in Los Angeles. In this role, Dr. Mathis has created a pilot program that re-conceptualizes the way in which high schools cultivate college readiness for students. He supported high school leaders and college counselors, as well as a team of interns, in the development, implementation, and evaluation of this innovative college identity development model. In addition to his work in the K–12 schools, Dr. Mathis was appointed as an adjunct assistant professor in Rossier School of Education, for both masters and educational doctorate programs. Dr. Mathis earned his Doctor of Philosophy (PhD) from the University of Southern California (CA) under the advisement of Dr. William G. Tierney. While at USC, he served as a mentor for the I AM College Access mentoring program, facilitator for Pullias Center's SummerTIME program, and a graduate assistant for the McNair Scholars Program. He completed a bachelor's of science in business administration at American University (DC), and a master's of science in administration, for K–12 educational administration at Trinity Washington University (DC).

REFERENCES

ACT Aspire LLC. (2014). *ACT Aspire—exceptional college & career readiness.* Retrieved from *http://www.discoveractaspire.org.*

Bandura, A. (1977). Self-efficacy: Toward a unifying theory of behavioral change. *Psychological Review, 84*(2), 191–215.

Bandura, A. (1993). Perceived self-efficacy in cognitive development and functioning. *Educational Psychologist, 28*(2), 117–148.

Bandura, A., Barbaranelli, C., Caprara, G.V., & Pastorelli, C. (1996). Multifaceted impact of self-efficacy beliefs on academic functioning. *Child Development, 67*(3), 1206–1222.

Baxter Magolda, M.B. (2005). Complex lives. In M.E. Wilson & L.E. Wolf-Wendel (Eds.), *ASHE reader on college student development theory* (pp. 81–100). Boston: Pearson.

Baxter Magolda, M.B., & King, P.M. (2008). Toward reflective conversations: An advising approach that promotes self-authorship. *Peer Review, 10*(1). Retrieved from *http://www.aacu.org/publications-research/periodicals/toward-reflective-conversations-advising-approach-promotes-self*

Belsky, J., & Cassidy, J. (1994). Attachment: Theory and evidence. In M. Rutter & D. Hay (Eds.), *Development through life: A handbook for clinicians* (pp. 373–402). Oxford, UK: Blackwell.

Birkeland, M.S., Melkevik, O., Holsen, I., & Wold, B. (2012). Trajectories of global self-esteem development during adolescence. *Journal of Adolescence, 35*, 43–54.

Bourdieu, P. (1973). Cultural reproduction and social reproduction. In R. Brown (Ed.), *Knowledge, education and cultural change: Papers in the sociology of education* (pp. 71–112). London: Tavistock Publications.

Bourdieu, P. (1986). The forms of capital. In J.G. Richardson (Ed.), *Handbook of theory and research for the sociology of education* (pp. 241–258). New York: Greenwood Press.

Chapman, D.W. (1981). A model of student college choice. *The Journal of Higher Education, 52*(5), 490–505.

Chavis, A.M. (2012). Social learning theory and behavioral therapy: Considering human behaviors within the social and cultural context of individuals and families. *Journal of Human Behavior in the Social Environment 22*, 54–64.

Chen, X., & Jensen, L.A. (2013). Adolescent development in a diverse and changing world: Introduction. *Journal of Research on Adolescence, 23*(2), 197–200.

College Board, The. (2014). *BigFuture—get ready for college—college planning, financial aid, educator resources.* Retrieved from *https://bigfuture.collegeboard.org.*

Conley, D.T. (2008). Rethinking college readiness. *New Directions for Higher Education, 2008*(144), 3–13. Retrieved from *http://files.eric.ed.gov/fulltext/EJ794245.pdf.*

Conley, D.T. (2010). *College and career ready: Helping all students succeed beyond high school.* San Francisco: Jossey-Bass.

EducationPlanner. (2014). *EducationPlanner.org.* Retrieved from *http://www.educationplanner.org.*

Fergus, S., & Zimmerman, M. (2005). Adolescent resilience: A framework for understanding healthy development in the face of risk. *Annual Review of Public Health,* 26, 399–419.

Fletcher, J.M., & Tienda, M. (2009). High school classmates and college success. *Sociology of Education,* 82, 287–314.

Furlong, A., & Cartmel, F. (1997). Aspirations and opportunity structures: 13-year olds in areas with restricted opportunities. *British Journal of Guidance and Counseling,* 23(3), 361–376.

Gecas, V. (1989). The social psychology of self-efficacy. *Annual review of sociology,* 15(1989), 291–316.

Heller, D. E., & Marin, P. (Eds.). (2002). *Who should we help? The negative social consequences of merit scholarships.* Cambridge, MA: The Civil Rights Project at Harvard University.

King, P.M., & Baxter Magolda, M.B. (2005). Toward a developmental model of intercultural maturity: An holistic approach to collegiate education. In M.E. Wilson & L.E. Wolf-Wendel (Eds.), *ASHE reader on college student development theory* (pp. 101–113). Boston: Pearson.

Leary, M.R., Terdal, S.K., Tambor, E.S., & Downs, D.L. (1995). Self-esteem as an interpersonal monitor: The sociometer hypothesis. *Journal of Personality and Social Psychology,* 68(3), 518–530.

Lombana, J.H. (1985). Guidance accountability: A new look at an old problem. *The School Counselor,* 340–346.

Mapping Your Future. Inc. (2014). *Mapping Your Future.* Retrieved from *http://mappingyourfuture.org.*

McDonough, P.M., & L. Perez. (1998). *High School Counseling: A Confused Profession.* Under review.

McElhaney, K.B., Allen, J.P., Stephenson, J.C., & Hare, A.L. (2009). Attachment and autonomy during adolescence. In *Handbook of Adolescent Psychology* (11). Retrieved from *http://onlinelibrary.wiley.com/ doi/10.1002/9780470479193.adlpsy001012/full.*

Monson, R., & Brown, D. (1985). Secondary school counseling: A time for reassessment and revitalization. *NASSP Bulletin,* December, 32–35. Retrieved from *http://bul.sagepub.com/ content/69/485/32?patientinform-links=yes&legid=spbul;69/485/32.*

National Education Association (2003). *A parent's guide to testing at your child's school.* Washington, DC: Author.

Orr, E., & Dinur, B. (1995). Actual and perceived parental social status: Effects on adolescent self-concept. *Adolescence,* 30(119).

Pajares, F. (1996). Self-efficacy beliefs in academic settings. *Review of Educational Research,* 66(4), 543–578.

Perna, L.W. (2006). Studying college access and choice: A proposed conceptual model. In J.C. Smart (Ed.), *Higher education: handbook of theory and research,* Vol. XXI (pp. 99–157). Netherlands: Springer.

Perna, L.W., & Titus, M.A. (2004). Understanding differences in the choice of college attended: The role of state public policies. *Review of Higher Education,* 27(4), 501–524.

Pintrich, P.R., & Schunk, D.H. (1996). *Motivation in education: Theory, research, and applications.* Columbus, OH: Merrill.

Rinn, A.N., & Cunningham, L.G. (2008). Using self-concept instruments with high-ability college students: Reliability and validity evidence. *The Gifted Child Quarterly,* 52(3), 232–242.

Tierney, W.G., Bailey, T., Constantine, J., Finkelstein, N., & Hurd, N. (2009). *Helping students navigate the path to college: What high schools can do: A practical guide* (NCEE #2009-4066). Washington, DC: National Center for Education Evaluation and Regional Assistance, Institute of Education Sciences, U.S. Department of Education. Retrieved from *http://ies.ed.gov/ncee/wwc/ publications/practiceguides.*

Vultaggio, J., & Friedfeld, S. (2013, Fall). Stressors in college choice, application and decision-making. *Journal of College Admission,* 221, 6–12.

Chapter 3: Increasing College Access and Success

Ronald E. Hallett, PhD

Tenisha Tevis, PhD

INTRODUCTION

Juan and Isaac grew up in Los Angeles and had aspirations to attend college. At 17 years old, Isaac dreamed of playing basketball in college and then becoming a firefighter. At the same age, Juan intended to become a doctor in order to serve people living in poverty. They both lived in low-income communities and attended low-performing schools in South Central Los Angeles. Isaac, a black male, lived with a foster parent. After running away from several group homes, he was placed with a friend of the family. Isaac shifted to several different high schools, which negatively impacted his grades and ability to play on an athletic team. Juan immigrated with his family to the United States prior to the start of high school. He struggled for several years to learn English and relied on soccer to make friends. Isaac and Juan were both motivated and had promise when they began high school. They believed that education could be their path out of poverty. For one that dream came true. The other slowly lost hope.

workforce have college and advanced degrees. In a review of research on the benefits of college, Torche (2011) found that individuals with bachelor's degrees experience a host of additional benefits beyond wage increases, including better health, longer life expectancy and greater happiness. College graduates tend to be more personally satisfied with their career and work in fields that have been more resistant to job loss or long-term unemployment during the most recent recession (Pew Research Center, 2014). Increasing the percentage of adults with college degrees has been a priority of the president and federal government for the past few decades. The only way to reach this goal is to target traditionally underrepresented student groups.

While a degree has clear benefits, some individuals may opt out of pursuing postsecondary education. For many reasons, an individual may choose a different pathway, including military service, directly entering the workforce or apprenticeships. Each person graduating

We do not argue that every person needs a four-year college degree to have a good life. We make the case for ensuring all students have opportunities to pursue and achieve their aspirations.

Earning a college degree has been associated with many positive outcomes. The value of a high school diploma has decreased over the past three decades; a college degree is now needed to achieve middle-class status and lifestyle (Deming & Dynarski, 2009). Individuals with a postsecondary degree earn on average about one million dollars more over the course of a lifetime than those with a high school diploma or less (College Board, 2007). The potential of achieving a postsecondary degree or credential differs depending upon family economic status. By the time they turn 26 years old, only 7 percent of low-income individuals complete a degree, as compared to 51 percent of their peers in the highest economic quartile (Haveman & Smeeding, 2006). The earning power of a college degree can be a dramatic shift from poverty to middle-class standing for marginalized communities.

Society also benefits. Tax revenues increase, and reliance on social services decrease. Countries become more internationally competitive when larger numbers of the

from high school should be afforded the opportunity to choose from a range of options. Unfortunately, many students have constrained choices. Isaac, for example, moved so frequently that he could not maintain social or academic connections that would have supported his educational pursuits. Four years after he began high school, he had only completed a year's worth of course credit. Many students do not have the requisite skills and supports to be successful upon entering postsecondary institutions. Even though Juan entered a prestigious four-year university, he struggled academically and needed remediation. Fortunately, he had access to a mentor and college bridge programs that offered assistance.

We do not argue that every person needs a four-year college degree to have a good life. We make the case for ensuring all students have opportunities to pursue and achieve their aspirations. Low-income, first-generation students and students of color often get funneled out of the postsecondary pipeline. These students frequently lack knowledge of the complex and fluid requirements related to the college application and financial aid processes (Burleson, Hallett, & Park, 2008; Conley, 2008).

Scholars and practitioners explore different ways to provide access to this information and guidance for transitioning to college campuses. Gaining access to college is important, but only really matters if individuals succeed once enrolled. A large number of students from underserved and marginalized backgrounds do not continue after the first semester of college (Engle & Tinto, 2008). Dropping out of college can result in many negative outcomes for the individual and community (Pew Research Institute, 2014). In addition to having possibly accrued debt, the lack of success can reaffirm notions within marginalized groups that postsecondary education is unattainable.

Many marginalized students and families face challenges throughout the college preparation and application processes. Applying to college may seem straightforward—particularly for middle-class professionals who were raised by families with postsecondary experience and in school systems with a culture of college-going. Preparing for college in these settings feels intuitive; however, many lower income schools may be better at preparing students for prison or welfare than college (Bahena et al., 2012). The design of the current educational system in the United States emerged from a system intended to educate only the privileged elite. As such, those who do not fit into that category often face many challenges. This chapter provides an overview of the multifaceted challenges that limit equity in educational access and success.

We focus primarily on students pursuing a degree at a four-year institution. Although students may opt for community college degrees or trade school certificate programs, the vast majority of students aspire to earn at least a bachelor's degree. As will become evident, not all students have the same opportunities. In particular, low-income students, first-generation students and students of color face numerous barriers that can result in abandoning aspirations. These issues can seem so daunting that a professional educator may not know where to begin to address these constraints. There is hope. These injustices can be unearthed and undone.

Our hope is to provide enough background knowledge to equip professionals to identify and articulate the problem. The role of college counselors is to increase access and facilitate opportunity for all students. This can be a significant challenge when working with students like Isaac and Juan who faced multiple barriers. However, steps can then be taken to increase opportunity within the local context. This chapter provides some guidance.

Understanding Readiness, Enrollment and Achievement

Professionals hired to help students navigate the educational pipeline need to be aware of the interconnectedness of the entire educational process, from preschool education through college completion and then employment and advanced degree pursuit. While hyper-focusing on the specific tasks of a specific position may seem prudent (e.g., recruiting students), the lack of an overarching perspective maintains inequity. The complexity and ambiguity of each step creates multiple barriers for students without guidance and frames how they engage in the educational process once admitted to college. Further, improving students' pathway through the entire system makes the specific professional tasks easier to manage. For example, college recruitment becomes easier when more students are academically prepared and understand the financial aid process. As will be seen by looking at the pipeline, there is not one specific problem that keeps marginalized students from being successful. The cumulative process of navigating a system that seems to be against these individuals results in the status quo.

One point is worth noting before discussing the multilayered challenges these students endure. While aspects of their life differ, students from low-income backgrounds tend to be more similar than different from their middle-class peers. They want to make their families proud. They go on dates and experience breakups. Midterms and finals make them nervous and, like most students, they pull all-nighters to get papers done. The transition to adulthood is both exciting and scary. We hyper-focus on the challenges they experience in achieving their postsecondary goals only because those barriers may limit their ability to be a college student—not because they intrinsically differ from a "typical" student. Program development should involve theory and research on college student experiences, while also considering the sociological barriers particular marginalized groups experience. However, marginalized student groups should not be treated as anomalies or different than the overall student body. Students will resent such categorizations. Rather, professionals working with these students should be aware of the systemic barriers that have been put in place that disadvantage some individuals while advantaging others. Being aware of these challenges allows educational professionals to both recognize injustices within the system while also meeting the needs of marginalized students without making them feel like these barriers define who they are as a person.

We focus much of our discussion on low-income students. These individuals include the working poor who secure employment that does not fully cover the costs of basic needs (McSwain & Davis, 2007). These families can rarely financially contribute to covering the costs of higher education. Latina/o, black and first-generation students tend to be overrepresented in low-income communities (DeNavas-Walt & Proctor, 2014). Students who have delayed enrollment often do so for lack of socioeconomic resources (Bozick & DeLuca, 2005). In addition, these individuals may be parents and in need of childcare in order to attend class (McSwain & Davis, 2007). Conversations about college access often involve the intersection of many social issues that marginalize specific groups. This should not be considered an exhaustive review of research on this topic. Continued discussion of invisible and marginalized student subgroups is warranted (e.g., LGBTQ, veteran, undocumented, homeless, and foster students).

We consider *success* as enrolling in college and completing a degree. Navigating the P—20 educational systems requires concerted effort. Laura Perna and Scott Thomas (2008) identify four transitions that frame student success in the educational process: college readiness, college enrollment, college achievement, and post-college attainment. Using these broad categories, we discuss how marginalized students may struggle to successfully navigate the educational process.

COLLEGE READINESS

Most students aspire to earn a four-year degree, but lack knowledge of the academic and social aspects of preparing for the transition to college (Hooker & Brand, 2010). College readiness involves how prepared an individual is for the transition to college, as well as the increased rigor

of postsecondary coursework. Conley (2008) defines college readiness as "the level of preparation a student needs in order to enroll and succeed, without remediation, in a credit-bearing general education course at a postsecondary institution that offers a baccalaureate degree or transfer to a baccalaureate program" (p. 4). He identifies four components of college readiness that frame whether an individual student is prepared for the college transition: cognitive strategies; academic knowledge and skills; academic behaviors; and contextual skills (see Table 1).

Table 1. Facets of College Readiness

Cognitive Strategies	Problem formulation and solving Research Reasoning, argument and proof Interpretation Precision and accuracy
Academic Knowledge and Skills	English Math Science Social Sciences World Languages Arts
Academic behaviors	Self-awareness Self-monitoring Self-control
Contextual skills	"[T]he information students need to apply successfully to college, gain necessary financial aid, and then, subsequent to matriculation, understand how college operates as a system and culture." (Conley, 2008, p. 10)

See Conley (2008) for a full discussion.

College readiness begins long before the senior year of high school. The educational system is a cumulative process where each grade and experience builds upon the previous one. As a result, preparation for college involves preschool through high school, as well as experiences outside of the traditional school day. While involving elementary-age students in college preparation would be ideal, scholars generally agree that concerted college preparation efforts should begin no later than middle school (Pell Institute, 2008; Standing, Judkins, Keller, & Shimshak, 2008; Wimberly & Noeth, 2005). Waiting to focus on college knowledge and preparation with 11th and 12th graders results in "creaming off the top" of students who managed to take the steps necessary to be successful in the college application process, but does little to institute more dramatic change that would enable a larger number of marginalized student groups to be prepared for postsecondary education.

Although beyond the scope of this chapter, it is worth noting that earning a high school diploma can be a significant barrier to accessing postsecondary education. More than 7,000 students in the United States drop out of school each day, which translates to about 1.2 million students not finishing high school each year (Hooker & Brand, 2010). Students tend to drop out of the educational process because they do not feel the classes are relevant to their lives, and they feel unsupported by educational institutions (Cammarota, 2007; Stanton-Salazar, 2011). Therefore, college access is not limited to just getting students into college, but a major component of it is getting students through high school and earning a diploma. In what follows, we highlight aspects of college preparation to frame the experiences and aspirations of traditionally underserved student groups: rigorous curriculum, college knowledge, high school counselors, and social connections.

A number of modes of increasing rigor have emerged, particularly at the high-school level. Comprehensive college preparation curriculums exist, such as International Baccalaureate (Mayer, 2008), Gear Up and AVID programs (Engle, 2007). These programs intentionally offer rigorous classroom experiences designed to prepare low-income and potentially first-generation college students for higher education coursework. Typically, a select group of high-achieving students with academic potential get the opportunity to participate in these learning environments. As a result, a college-going culture gets created for only a subset of the overall student body.

Advanced placement courses may be offered in conjunction with these college-preparation programs. While the aforementioned programs specifically target marginalized students, advanced placement (AP) and honors coursework are more general programming that offer students higher level coursework in order to prepare for college. These courses, overseen by the College Board, have standardized exams that can be used for college credit at some postsecondary institutions. The lack of universal rigor in these programs has led some selective universi-

Therefore, college access is not limited to just getting students into college, but a major component of it is getting students through high school and earning a diploma.

Rigorous coursework. College achievement starts with high school achievement. Degree completion, the ultimate measure of college achievement, is correlated with high school coursework, students' grades and senior-year test scores (Adelman 1999, 2006). However, high school curriculum and class rankings are subjective concepts; some schools offer an inferior curriculum leading to students being underprepared for college. Moreover, students of color, as compared to whites, are less likely to have access to challenging coursework and may be reluctant to enroll in courses where the class does not look like them (Viadero, 2000). High school grades, a key indicator of students' academic performance, may be reflective of the students' ability, as well as the opportunities and support available.

ties to stop giving bonus points (i.e., increasing grade point average by half to a full point for advanced placement class) to students who took AP courses or exams. In order for students to benefit from rigorous coursework, the classes need to actually be rigorous. Often, advanced placement and honors course content and experiences may be dramatically less rigorous in low-income and underperforming schools (Hallett & Venegas, 2011).

Universities tend to favorably view students who are involved in college-preparation programs and advanced placement courses. Even if the level of rigor may differ, engaging in the most challenging academic opportunities available demonstrates initiative and engagement. These students are also more likely to gain access to college knowledge.

College knowledge and aspirations. Before students will engage in rigorous academic coursework and other aspects of college preparation, they must aspire to college and believe that attending a postsecondary institution is a realistic possibility. Educational and professional aspirations can begin well before high school. By exposing young people to different career possibilities and college experiences in elementary and pre-school, teachers and administrators lay the groundwork for future educational aspirations and pursuits. This is particularly important for low-income and future first-generation college students who tend to have less exposure to college and professional experiences in their homes or communities. Some postsecondary institutions provide programming targeting these younger students by offering tours, summer academies or other college-access-related programming. While many low-income students may have narrow views of college majors, the vast majority aspires to earn at least a bachelor degree (McKillip, Rawls, & Barry, 2012).

Even vague aspirations to attend college provide a foundation. Students then need to acquire "college knowledge" that creates a blueprint for accessing postsecondary education. Hooker and Brand (2010) define college knowledge as having "an understanding of the complex college admission and selection processes, that options available to help pay for postsecondary education, the academic requirements for college-level work, and the cultural differences between secondary and postsecondary education" (p. 77). College knowledge involves helping students understand the complex and dynamic institutional processes involved with gaining access to college and attaining procedural knowledge of how to navigate compasses once admitted (Burleson, Hallett, & Park, 2008).

Information about college and how to apply is often presented passively in low-income schools. Teachers and counselors may pass out information about financial aid opportunities or a college fair without going over the information in detail or spending time with students individually discussing their interests and personal situations. Students consistently mention that they would prefer to have more time spent going over information about college because they do not fully understand the information when reading through materials independently (Bell, Rowan-Kenyon, & Perna, 2009; Venezia & Kirst, 2005).

In addition to relying on counselors and teachers for guidance, many students use the Internet to locate resources and information. Over the past few decades, the amount of information available about college preparation has exponentially increased each year. In an age of information overload, students may be unsure where to begin sifting through the Web sites. They also have a difficult time distinguishing between helpful and inaccurate information. Students need support from a knowledgeable adult who can recommend Web sites and assist with the process of choosing which information to rely upon when making individual decisions about college preparation.

Utilizing out-of-school time to engage students in college-access programming has been one solution to limited college knowledge among low-income and first-generation college students. Often, these programs occur during the summer months. Out-of-school time can also be used to provide students the opportunity to engage in supplemental curricular experiences. Some of these programs specifically target academic and professional fields where low-income and minority students are underrepresented to encourage more involvement, including science, technology, engineering, and math (STEM) fields (e.g., Carnegie Mellon's Summer Academy for Math and Science). Additionally, programming can focus on remediation, such as summer school. The amount of time and rigor of support programs influences student success in college (Tierney, Hallett, & Venegas, 2007). Simply designing a program that is fun or feels good is not enough; college access programs need to involve considerable time to allow students to fully develop skills and resources needed to overcome complex barriers and experience success in college.

High school counselors. In low-income communities where many students will be first-generation college students, high school counselors play a critical role in providing college knowledge. Some high schools designate a college counselor. These designated college counselors can work with administration and teachers to develop a college-going culture within the high school, as well as shape the perceptions and expectations of college options among the parents, family members and community (McDonough, 1997, 2005; Roderick, Coca, & Nagaoka, 2011). A college-going culture is a setting where all students expect (and are expected) to pursue postsecondary education; administrators and educators work to create programming that reinforces high educational expectations, along with the needed resources to achieve those goals (Schneider, 2007). The shared sense of aspiration creates momentum for all students to pursue a college education and encourages students to support one another through positive peer pressure (Nagaoka, Roderick, & Coca, 2009). These students develop a college-going identity (Roderick, Coca, & Nagaoka, 2011). Venezia and Kirst (2005) found that "clear, consistent, and reinforced signals will enhance the college knowledge of prospective students in secondary schools" (p. 288). The presence of a college counselor or a college support center at the high school dramatically increases the students' access to information about the higher education process, as well as their confidence that the advice given will improve their success in college (Bell, Rowan-Keynon, & Perna, 2009).

Not all students have adequate access to college counselors. In order to provide the necessary information and guidance to all students pursuing college acceptance, the American School Counselor Association (ASCA) recommends that student-to-counselor ratios not exceed 100:1. According to the United States Department of Education (2012), the national average is 471:1, with seven states exceeding 600:1—Indiana (620:1), Illinois (655:1), Michigan (706:1), Utah (726:1), Minnesota (782:1), Arizona (861:1), and California (1,016:1). Wyoming, Vermont and New Hampshire have the lowest ratios, but still exceed the ASCA's recommendation by at least double. Taking a more nuanced look, students in large public schools typically have less access to counselors than those attending smaller or independent schools (NACAC, 2006). Most middle schools do not have counselors—particularly college counselors—even though research consistently stresses the importance of starting college access programming earlier than high school.

Most high school counselors experience "role confusion" because they have been trained to deal with mental-health-related issues, are assigned administrative tasks, are expected to know about college and financial aid applications, and have large numbers of students assigned to their caseloads (McKillip, Rawls, & Barry, 2012). College-access programming is regularly pushed aside for other priorities. Most counselor preparation programs focus on mental health counseling and time-sensitive responsibilities like class scheduling. This prioritization can adversely affect students with higher education aspiration (Perna et al., 2008). When college conversations do happen, often counselors opt to do group presentations in classes or grade-level assemblies because they lack time and resources to engage with students individually. The limited resources in most high schools restrict low-income and first-generation students' access to college knowledge.

Social connections. Underserved student groups need to either reconfirm their social networks to support their college aspirations or create alternative networks (Rios-Aguilar & Deil-Amen, 2012). Unlike their more advantaged peers with networks that shepherd them into postsecondary education, low-income and first-generation college students may experience challenges within their familial and community networks that are further complicated if the students attend a low-performing school. As discussed in chapter 23, parents and families should be considered partners in the college preparation processes. Culturally responsive programs attempt to leverage the knowledge, expertise and strengths of parents and families by avoiding a hyper-focus on perceived deficits in procedural knowledge about college access or success (Kirshner, Saldivar, & Tracy, 2011). Reaching out to community leaders and organizations that people trust and utilize (e.g., places of worship and community centers) increases the likelihood of reaching low-income and minority students (Bryan et al., 2011).

COLLEGE ENROLLMENT

Moving from college aspirations to enrollment tends to be a significant barrier. Transitioning between high school and college requires concerted effort. Unlike transitions within the K–12 system (e.g., from middle school to high school), transitioning to college is a complex process. This is particularly difficult when considering four-year universities. As previously mentioned, students must take specific high school classes and achieve a minimum grade point average in order to apply. Selective universities require additional qualifications and reject some percentage of applicants—most four-year universities fall into this category. Students will need to take either the ACT or SAT exam. If a student is interested in moderately or highly selective universities, the process becomes more nuanced and complex. Students must be able to "sell" themselves to the university. Students may need to write college application essays (see chapter 21) explaining their involvement in school activities, leadership and community service. Letters of recommendation, as discussed in chapter 12, may need to be included in the application packet. These institutions may also have mandatory interviews as part of the application process.

High schools and postsecondary institutions play important roles in the college preparation and transition process. The final step of beginning the first week of class represents successfully navigating many obstacles. While many of these students demonstrate high levels of motivation and resilience, institutional agents play a critical role in helping them navigate the transition between two disjointed educational systems. The following sections illustrate both the challenges students face, as well as the roles educators can play.

Researching choices. Many underserved students are unaware of the diversity of postsecondary institutions or the differing requirements. Assuming all postsecond-

quirements, taken entrance exams, chosen a potential major, and narrowed a list of universities to which to apply. To be competitive in the application process, preparation typically takes years. Unfortunately, many first-generation students in low-income areas are unaware of the need to begin the college choice and application process early in high school. Another student we worked with planned to "worry about what college to go to after graduation." Her assumption that she could apply to college in June and begin the following fall constricted her choices to a community college and, even though community colleges are open-access in California, she was unable to enroll in a full load of classes because she waited too long.

Given the complexity of the application process, students need guidance. Large group sessions that present general information about applying to college and financial aid may be conducted by local and national organizations, as well as colleges and universities. While these sessions can be useful in giving general information, they do little to offer specific information to low-income families

The college application process takes at least six months—students need to have met minimal academic requirements, taken entrance exams, chosen a potential major, and narrowed a list of universities to which to apply.

ary institutions are the same can be problematic. For example, a low-income, first-generation student we worked with explained how he hoped "to attend CSU-LA, but if I don't get in there, I will just go to USC." Not understanding the difference between California State University Los Angeles—a minimally selective university—and the University of Southern California—a highly selective private university—demonstrates limited exposure to postsecondary educational systems. Low-income, first-generation students tend to be less likely than their more privileged peers to conduct a thorough college search to find campuses and programs that would best suit their needs and goals (Perez & McDonough, 2008). They may be more likely to attend campuses close to home or where a close family member or friend attended.

The college application process takes at least six months—students need to have met minimal academic re-

that may have complex financial, personal and academic situations that may frame decisions about where (or if) to apply. Single-seminar-type events have limited utility, because students and families often need guidance making sense out of how the policies relate to their individual situations (Venegas & Hallett, 2008). Individual meetings where people can ask questions about their particular situation and get information are needed, like the Increasing Access via Mentoring program at the University of Southern California.

Choosing where to apply. College choice involves if and where students decide to attend (Bergerson, 2009). The majority of marginalized students who graduate from high school have the ability to attend some form of postsecondary institution, but they may avoid the application process to avoid presumed rejection (Roderick, Coca, & Nagoaka, 2011). Before students can negotiate the process of choosing which institutions to submit applications, they need access to conversations about the different postsecondary options and how their goals and skills match what is required to attend these institutions. Once students and families understand that attending college could be a realistic option, they are prepared to begin making a choice of where to attend.

As aforementioned, choices of where to go to college are constrained by the places where the student applies, where the student gets accepted and where the student chooses to attend. "Under match" involves attending a college or university that is less selective than a student's skills and achievements would suggest. Personal, professional and familial reasons frame why individuals choose a specific institution. An alarming trend has emerged. Low-income, first-generation students and students of color experience under match at significantly higher rates than their middle-class and white peers (Perez & McDonough, 2008). Students from low-income backgrounds who do enroll frequently attend postsecondary institutions that are of lower quality, prestige and cost, which influences their rates of persistence to degree, as well as limits access to labor market advantages associated with higher ranked institutions (Thomas & Perna, 2004). Students involved in extracurricular activities and sports while in high school have an increased likelihood of attending a postsecondary institution that matches their skills and achievement, whereas the number of hours an individual works increases the likelihood of under match (Roderick, Coca, & Nagaoka, 2011).

Influence of financial aid. For most low-income and middle-class students, financial aid is an essential component of attending college. Financial aid covers a larger number of different funding sources and involves both merit-based and need-based sources of funding. Grants (federal, state and institutional), scholarships, and student loans represent a large portion of financial aid. Low-income students rely heavily on need-based aid, including Pell Grants, state-level grants, institutional grants and scholarships, and student loans. Each of these has a specific application process and deadlines, but most require completion of the FASFA. Students and families may find these applications difficult to navigate.

Financial aid conversations are often considered important once a student gets admitted to a university. However, research demonstrates that financial aid information plays an important role throughout the college access process, including college choice (Tierney & Venegas, 2009). Assumptions about how much a college, housing and related expenses cost have a dramatic impact on where students apply and how many applications are submitted. In addition, the access to information about financial aid prior to entering high school frames how students and families understand the viability of pursuing a college education. Families may feel more confident in encouraging students to attend college once they believe that financial opportunities exist, even if they do not begin the financial applications for many years (Hallett & Griffen, forthcoming).

The increasing gap between family income and need-based funding, along with rising tuition cost has led to students either opting out of postsecondary education or incurring significant student loan debt. Many students have unmet costs that are not covered by financial aid, such as traveling to school and trips back home. Students and families from low-income and minority backgrounds may have aversions to debt and borrowing against uncertain future earnings (McDonough, Calderone, & Venegas, forthcoming; Rothstein & Rouse, 2010). McDonough and colleagues (forthcoming) argue that institutions and institutional agents need to establish trust with marginalized communities in order to have conversations about financing a college education and the potential benefits of modest borrowing in the form of student loans. These trusting relationships take time. Waiting until the senior year of high school for a high school counselor or admission officer to begin building these connections is often too late. Institutions need to carefully consider how their policies either encourage or inhibit access to financial aid information. And institutional agents need to reach out to marginalized students and communities to help reestablish the belief that educational achievement can be a pathway out of poverty.

The complexity of the current college choice, application and financial aid processes make it very difficult for teenagers to navigate all of the information and forms without guidance from a trusted source. Unfortunately, simplification of these processes is unlikely to happen in the near future. As a result, educational institutions need to consider ways to help students—particularly those who are low-income and first-generation students.

Transition to college. The summer between high school and college tends to be a time when students have no direct connection to institutional agents. These three months involve many crucial decisions, including selecting housing, making deposits, accepting financial aid packages, arranging the move to campus, and enrolling in classes. Students and families may also be struggling with the emotional aspects of actually taking the risk of entering postsecondary education. Casteman and Page (2013) found that "nearly 40% of students intending on a community college and nearly 20% of students intending on a four-year institution fail to matriculate in the fall after high school graduation" (p. 212). This "summer melt" occurs so frequently that most postsecondary institutions factor it into the number of students accepted for enrollment. First-generation college students tend to be the most susceptible to dropping out before college begins (Castleman, Arnold, & Wartman, 2012). For these students, a significant gap exists between college acceptance and enrollment (Arnold et al., 2009). The summer becomes a period when students reconsider where or *if* to attend college (see chapter 24).

Some postsecondary institutions offer "summer bridge" programs that provide different forms of support for marginalized students as they transition to college. Participation in summer bridge programs has the potential to increase students' academic self-efficacy and academic skills, which frequently result in better grades the first semester of college (Strayhorn, 2011). These programs have various goals, including building connections for students of color or first-generation students, completing remedial classes before the semester begins, or offering an expanded orientation to the campus community. Not all universities have these programs and students may be unaware of the opportunities or their value. In addition, bridge programs frequently invite students to campus a week or two before the semester begins. Students may have decided not to attend before these programs begin.

While some opportunities exist to "start early" at the college, few high schools allow students to "stay late" (Castleman, Arnold, & Wartman, 2012). Although high school teachers and college counselors may have helped students through the entire college preparation process, those connections get broken upon high school graduation, and the students have not yet developed bonds with the postsecondary institution. A significant challenge for students is that they do not know the specifics of their financial aid package until after high school graduation (Arnold et al., 2009). A few programs exist that provide support for students during this critical time, but they are rare (see Tierney, 2013, for an example of a university initiative with local high schools). The Big Picture Longitudinal Study (BPLS) conducted a thorough evaluation of innovate high school programs that provide extended support for low-income students (Arnold et al., 2009; Castle, Arnold, & Wartman, 2012). High schools in the BPLS program often extended the contract of a counselor through the summer, who then became the "transition counselor" for students planning to begin college the following fall. The success of the program led to the following recommendations:

- Make sure college access experts at the high school and college remain available to support students through the summer transition to college.

- Continue a dialogue with students concerning the relationship between their skills, interests and postsecondary education goals.

- Provide ongoing support for families and students to help them cope with the social and emotional challenges associated with the college transition.

- Ensure students and families have access to intensive and consistent guidance as they review financial aid packages, sign contracts and make deposits.

- Consider expanding current college-preparation programs at local school sites (e.g., GEAR UP and AVID) to cover the summer transition.

- Develop summer bridge programs at all postsecondary institutions that are intentionally designed to deal with issues that lead to summer attrition for low-income and first-generation students.

- Utilize social media as a means of continued dialogue with students about resources available, as well as information about important deadlines.

COLLEGE ACHIEVEMENT

College achievement focuses on issues of persistence during enrollment in a postsecondary institution that result in degree completion (Perna & Thomas, 2008). Earning a college degree has similar economic benefits for all students, regardless of their family background (Torche, 2011).

While enrollment in college has steadily risen over the past 40 years, the percentage of students earning a degree has only modestly increased (Turner, 2006). Improving retention and completion rates has proven challenging for postsecondary institutions of all types. Approximately 20 percent of students leave postsecondary institutions within the first year and almost 40 percent have not completed a degree within six years of beginning college (College Board, 2005).

In particular, low-income and first-generation students are overrepresented among those who do not complete a degree (Torche, 2011). The attrition rates tend to be significantly higher at non-selective schools that primarily serve students from low-income backgrounds and have high numbers of students who work at least part-time and commute from home (Deming & Dynarski, 2009; Roderick, Coca, & Nagaoka, 2011). Increasing the rates of college completion should be an important aspect of initiatives and policies intended to increase college access for underserved and marginalized student groups (Deming & Dynarski, 2009).

Placement exams and remedial education. Most colleges and universities require students to take placement exams to determine the appropriate English and math levels for incoming students (Deil-Amen & Tevis, 2010). Students may confuse these with the entrance exams (i.e., SAT and ACT) which may be used as a determinant of college enrollment, predictor of who will attend college, and measure of students' academic ability and college preparedness. Entrance exams tend to be reflective of high school attendance and family socioeconomic status, which may further exclude or discourage marginalized student populations. Placement exams, on the other hand, occur after a student has been admitted to the postsecondary institution and constrain the options for English and math courses. Students planning to attend community colleges and nonselective four-year universities often assume that these institutions do not have academic standards; however, almost all postsecondary institutions use placement tests that determine access to credit-level—non-remedial—coursework (Venezia & Kirst, 2005).

Many marginalized groups from low-performing schools end up using their aid to enroll in remedial courses at postsecondary institutions. Nonselective institutions tend to have high rates of remediation because they have open access policies that enable almost all students who apply to enroll (Venezia & Kirst, 2005). The bulk of students entering at the community-college level, where the majority are low-income and underrepresented (Morrice, 2011), are required to take remedial courses (Kuh, Kinzie, Buckley, Bridges, & Hayek, 2006). At the four-year level, approximately a quarter of the incoming class takes remedial courses. Taking remedial courses can be beneficial; resources are typically built into the curriculum and students have greater access to support than their peers. Students who participate in remedial curriculum are more likely to persist than those who need support and do not participate in remediation; however, as the number of remedial courses students are required to take increases, their odds of dropping out also increases (Kuh, Kinzie, Buckley, Bridges, & Hayek, 2006; Silvernail, Sloan, & Johnson, 2013). This can greatly impact students' academic trajectory.

At the community-college level, this epidemic is referred to as *cooling out* (Clark, 1960), affecting students' ability to transfer and reducing their academic career options and aspirations. For those students at a four-year institution, enrollment in remedial courses may increase their time to degree, possibly leading to students getting frustrated and dropping out. To remedy the need to take remedial courses and help students prepare for their first year of college and beyond, some institutions have developed summer opportunities to catch-up academically in the form of bridge programs. These programs allow for students to complete some of their developmental coursework prior to the start of classes and may continue through the first year.

Students in remedial education courses face challenges. However, postsecondary institutions should not avoid accepting these students. Until high school and college curriculum become more seamlessly connected, rejecting students who need remedial education will only perpetuate inequalities in society. Higher education institutions do need to carefully consider how to integrate remedial education with coursework in ways that do not discourage students or significantly increase their time to degree. In addition, colleges and universities can work more closely with local high schools to ease the transition between K–12 and college curriculum.

First year. Academic performance once students arrive on campus frames their success. The first semester or year of school, in particular, is a critical period of achievement. Generally speaking, students drop out at the highest rate after the first semester and with the second highest percentage occurring after completion of the first year (Engle & Tinto, 2008). The odds of completing a degree significantly increase if students can successfully complete the first year of college. However, if we look at underserved populations and those whose first year includes remediation, some students face significant barriers.

Academic performance can also be closely associated with financial aid. Need-based financial aid typically has a minimum GPA requirement, as do scholarships. Merit-based funding typically has even higher GPA expectations. Deming and Dynarski (2009) found that financial aid is important, but has the greatest impact when coupled with supportive services that help students persist through college. They argue that services alone have little impact. In this regard, academic performance can

pecially for underserved groups who may lack the social and cultural capital necessary for college acclimation. Institutions of higher education may not explicitly exclude marginalized students. However, not providing the support structures and services these students may need to persist through graduation attests to the limited value these institutions may place on these students as part of the campus community (Engstrom & Tinto, 2008). Further, Engstrom and Tinto explain that postsecondary institutions interested in increasing student success need to believe students have the ability to succeed and they (the institutions) have the responsibility to create the conditions for student success. It is imperative that administrators and organizations develop and highlight resources and opportunities for continued learning outside of the classroom to ensure the success of their student body. Many of these resources can be used to remedy students' prior academic performance and experiences.

Educational psychologists suggest that educational institutions are not meeting the needs of their marginalized population (Ormrod, 2006). Ormrod further explains that a possible explanation for this divergence could be

Students who do not adjust or have not developed the necessary capital to acclimate to the college environment often drop out.

be closely associated with the continued financial viability of persisting through to degree completion. Institutional agents need to consider how students navigate the process of "completing entry-level courses at a level of understanding and proficiency that makes it possible for the student to consider taking the next course in the sequence or the next level of course in the subject area" (Conley, 2008, p. 4).

Social acclimation. In addition to academic preparation and the variability in institutional resources, another critical element of college achievement is social acclimation (Tinto, 1993). Tinto explains that, in order to be successful in college, students must acclimate both academically and socially. This can be challenging, es-

attributed to a cultural mismatch between the students and the school—leading to culture shock. Students from various cultural backgrounds may find school a confusing space to contend with, leaving them void of the social and cultural capital necessary for academic success. Ormrod cites "any such cultural mismatch between home and school cultures can interfere with students' adjustment to the school setting, and ultimately with their academic achievement as well" (p. 137). Students from underserved and marginalized backgrounds may also experience culture shock when starting college; hence the need for social acclimation. Students who do not adjust or have not developed the necessary capital to acclimate to the college environment often drop out.

Some scholars have critiqued institutions that have embraced college acclimation and integration without considering the social context of higher education (Melguizo, 2011). Attending college involves navigating complex social structures that frame the students' experiences and opportunities. In addition to the aforementioned culture shock, these students may face hidden challenges—for example, homeless or foster students may have nowhere to go when residence halls close for winter break (Hallett, 2010). Institutions that primarily serve commuter students or have a significant online component of coursework may also find the integration process difficult—or irrelevant—to students. And minority students may face different issues that tend to not be accounted for within this model (Melguizo, 2011). Attempting to connect the student to the campus clearly improves their potential outcomes; however, integration programs are important and cannot be devoid of the sociological realities of life outside the college campus or oppressive structures that impact student groups differently.

Postsecondary institutions can take steps to make the campus environment more conducive to success. Venezia and Kirst (2005) argue that "[t]he current fractured systems send students, their parents, and K–12 educators conflicting and vague messages about what students need to know and be able to do to enter and succeed in college" (p. 284). Although changing college requirements may be difficult, institutional agents can work more closely with local high schools to limit the disconnect between the two systems. In particular, high school educators and students need more information about how their coursework relates to their entrance and placement exams that will determine where they begin taking classes in college. Further, institutional agents should critically consider what it means to create a supportive environment for marginalized students who may feel out of place or unsupported on campus. While increasing college access remains a goal of many educational advocates, improving outcomes once students enter campus is essential.

Post-College Achievement

Gaining knowledge and experience in order to become a learned and informed citizen was once the main mission of educational institutions. Such ideas seem trite and archaic in the modern era, particularly for low-income individuals attempting to use higher education as a pathway to middle-class standing and stability. Access to gainful employment tends to be the primary motivation for low-income students pursuing a college degree (McSwain & Davis, 2007; Pew Research Center, 2014); all other benefits are secondary.

Due to the changing economic landscape and the need to adapt to a shifting workforce from manual labor to professional occupations, it is imperative to have a highly educated workforce. According to Conley (2013), "entirely new categories of work have rapidly emerged with the shift from agricultural and industrial jobs to service jobs. Knowledge workers and the creative class have become increasingly prevalent in the workforce" (p. 21). Now that a high school diploma will not afford middle class standing in the current economy, it is imperative that students continue to learn far beyond secondary school, "first in formal settings and then in the workplace throughout their careers" (Conley, 2013, p. 25).

Less attention has been given to the transition out of college and into the workforce. The assumption seems to be that earning an undergraduate degree involves all the skills and connections needed to be career ready and successful. The mission of institutions of higher education may or may not focus on preparing students for life after college. A few aspects of the transition out of college are worth consideration, including preparation for advanced degree programs, entering the workforce and personal challenges associated with entering the middle class.

Advanced degrees. College education has traditionally been an essential component of professional preparation (Bisconti & Kessler, 1980); however, more careers now require an advanced degree. Whereas only 5 percent of men and 1 percent of women earned a degree beyond a bachelor's in 1970, the rates reached 11 percent of men and 10 percent of women in 2005 (Torche, 2011). Graduate school involves undergoing both formalized training and professional socialization that may yield social connections. First-generation college students may be completely unaware of advanced degree programs prior to beginning their undergraduate careers. Many first-generation students may not believe they are capable—either academically or financially—of pursuing a graduate degree. First-generation students often feel like "imposters" when they enter graduate programs and fear not being able to meet the expectations, which negatively impacts their engagement (Craddock et al., 2011). These students may experience social isolation, financial constraints and have a difficult time adjusting to the program expectations and culture (Gardner & Holley, 2011). Clearly, not all students completing an undergraduate degree will need an advanced degree. However, marginalized students with academic potential or career goals warranting a graduate degree will likely need additional guidance and support. They may, for example, benefit from being told that they should explore graduate programs. Having a respected person with knowledge of the profession say, "I think you would really do well in a graduate program" can have a dramatic impact on a student's belief that such an opportunity is possible.

As previously stated, most students graduate from college with student loan debt. An inverse relationship exists between student loan debt and choice profession: the higher the debt, the lower the likelihood of choosing a public service career (Rothstein & Rouse, 2010). Debt may also discourage individuals from responsibilities associated with adulthood, such as purchasing a home, getting married or having children (Chiteji, 2007). Debt may also discourage individuals from pursuing advanced degrees that could encourage their professional advancement. First-generation college graduates may not have access to an advisor who can help them weigh the cost-benefit analysis of continuing education.

Transition to career. A lot of research and programming has focused on college access and success. Much less attention has been given to the transition out of college. Although career readiness often assumes academic content, students from low-income backgrounds may also find the transition to a professional setting financially difficult. Working in an office often involves professional attire. A student who accesses college through student loans and grants may have few resources to expend to purchase clothing, move out of campus housing and begin life in a middle-class environment. Many students experience a gap between college graduation and fulltime employment. On average, individuals with a college degree take about 27 weeks to find a job (Pew Research Center, 2014). Given the limited financial resources of these students and their families, colleges may need to assist students in starting the job search process early in the final year to minimize the time between degree and gainful employment. While we do not think postsecondary institutions should guarantee employment, they do have a responsibility to provide some assistance in helping students who perceive the degree is an investment in their future.

First-generation college graduates frequently come from families that have limited access to earning money beyond the labor market. They may be the first in their family to make decisions about retirement plans or investing in homeownership. Further, these individuals may be completely unaware of the "extra-occupational" resources available through the stock market or other forms of public and private assets (Torche, 2011). These individuals may not know how to navigate these complex, and potentially risky, systems or how to gain access to a reliable financial advisor. Postsecondary institutions may consider developing "bridge out" programs similar to the programs that transition between high school and college. These initiatives could involve resources that will assist students in being successful once they leave a structured educational system and could include guidance building social connections that will benefit them as they navigate life.

CONCLUDING THOUGHTS AND APPLICATIONS

The college access and success processes are not fair or easy. Educators and educational professions can be change agents who assist marginalized students through multiple and complex steps that lead to a college degree and transition to a career. However, these forms of intervention need to be intentional, require concerted effort and involve thinking critically about the entire educational process. For example, Juan graduating from a selective four-year institution can be attributed to access to institutional agents who served as mentors, whereas Isaac experienced social isolation. High school and college educators and administrators can provide resources and guidance that enable all students to have hope and success.

Some scholars have come to critique the idea of an achievement gap. By focusing on achievement, the individual student is held responsible for performance without critically considering the systemic structures that constrain the opportunity to achieve. Framing the issue as "opportunity" gaps holds the educational and political systems accountable. Instead of simply focusing on broken students that do not achieve, the systematic exclusion of marginalized students from educational opportunities is held under the microscope and critiqued. Since an overhaul of the system is unlikely, the role of advocates is to find ways to adjust the system in ways that provide space and support for marginalized groups. This is no small feat.

In this chapter, we discussed many of the challenges that marginalized students may experience when navigating educational institutions. Resolving these barriers will take concerted effort and creativity. No simple fix exists. And institutional context will frame the challenges students face, as well as the supportive structures that will be needed. We encourage educational professionals to be aware of the sociological aspects of higher education that advantage some student groups and marginalize others. Using this information, interventions and policy reforms can be developed that create opportunities for underrepresented students to gain access to college and achieve success. Social change happens when persons in power make it happen.

DISCUSSION QUESTIONS AND ACTION ITEMS

In the above discussion, we speak about challenges that exist within the abstract. We want you to think more critically about the local context and your role in resolving inequality. While you may be tempted to give a quick response, we encourage taking time to really think through each of these issues and be honest with yourself. Not everyone can be a change agent. But those who choose this path need to be intentional and persistent. Here are a few steps to get you started:

- Consider the job you have or plan to pursue. How does this position fit within the entire educational pipeline? What aspects of this career traditionally create opportunities for marginalized students? What aspects create barriers?

- Evaluate your current institution. What connections exist between the local high school and postsecondary institutions? How well do the curriculums match? Do local students attend selective and highly selective institutions in the area? How well do they fair at those institutions? How can these systems be more aligned?

- Reflect on your role in removing sociological barriers. Do you feel it is your charge to deal with these issues? Are there particular issues that motivate you? Are there also marginalized groups that you have a difficult time approaching with empathy?

- Look at the enrollment and graduation data for your institution. What groups attend your institutions in large numbers? What groups attend in small numbers? Who is excluded? What groups graduate? What groups do not or take a longer time to achieve degree completion? Does this match the public mission of your institution? What changes need to be made?

- Graduate students and early career professionals may feel that change needs to be made, but feel disempowered. However, they do have some control over systems and may be able to voice concerns to persons in power. What changes can you institute this semester to make your institution more equitable? Will you actually take steps to bring about change?

- Identify an issue related to the educational success of marginalized students at your institution (including the potential absence of this group). Who are the institutional and community stakeholders that may be interested in working toward resolving the issue? Are there researchers at your institution who may be interested in studying a potential pilot program? What would it take to get all of these individuals in a room together? Consider if this is something you are willing to do.

ABOUT THE AUTHOR

Ronald E. Hallett, PhD is an associate professor at University of the Pacific (CA). His work focuses on increasing educational access to underserved and marginalized student groups. He frequently employs action-oriented research that involves developing college access programming with schools and districts.

Tenisha Tevis, PhD is an assistant professor at University of the Pacific (CA). Her research is most concerned with students' transition to postsecondary education and the impact both college entrance exams and high school composition has on the choices students make about higher education. She is more likely to utilize quantitative methods, however, she open to the methodology that best leads to the answer to the overarching research question.

For more detailed information about the authors, please visit: *http://www.pacific.edu/Academics/Schools-and-Colleges/Gladys-L-Benerd-School-of-Education/Faculty/Meet-Our-Faculty.html*

REFERENCES

Adelman, C. (1999). *Answers in the toolbox: Academic intensity, attendance patterns, and bachelor's degree attainment.* Jessup, MD: Ed Pubs.

Adelman, C. (2006). *The toolbox revisited: Paths to degree completion from high school through college.* Jessup, MD: Ed Pubs.

Arnold, K., Fleming, S., DeAnda, M., Castleman, B., & Wartman, K.L. (2009). The summer flood: The invisible gap among low-income students. *Thought & Action,* Fall 2009, 23–34.

Bahena, S., Cooc, N., Currie-Rubin, R., Kuttner, & Ng, M. (2012). *Disrupting the school-to-prison pipeline.* Cambridge, MA: Harvard Educational Review.

Bell, A.D., Rowan-Kenyon, H.T., Perna, L.W. (2009). College knowledge of 9th and 11th grade students: Variation by school and state context. *Journal of Higher Education,* 80(6), 663–685.

Bergerson, A.A. (2009). Introduction to college choice. *ASHE Higher Education Report,* 35(4), 1–10.

Bisconti, A.S., & Kessler, J.G. (1980). *College and other stepping stones: A study of learning experiences that contribute to effective performance in early and long-run jobs.* Bethlehem, PA: The College Placement Council.

Bozick, R., & DeLuca, S. (2005). Better late than never? Delayed enrollment in the high school to college transition. *Social Forces,* 84(1), 531–554.

Bryan, J., Moore-Thomas, C., Day-Vines, N.L., & Holcomb-McCoy, C. (2011). School counselors as social capital: The effects of high school college counseling on college application rates. *Journal of Counseling & Development,* 89(2), 190–199.

Burleson, D.A., Hallett, R.E., & Park, D.K. (2008). College knowledge: An assessment of urban students' awareness of college processes. *College and University,* 84(2), 10–17.

Cammarota, J. (2007). A social justice approach to achievement: Guiding Latina/o students toward educational attainment with a challenging, socially relevant curriculum. *Equity & Excellence in Education,* 40, 87–96.

Castleman, B.L., Arnold, K., & Wartman, K.L. (2012). Stemming the tide of summer melt: An experimental study of the effects of post-high school summer intervention on low-income students' college enrollment. *Journal of Research on Educational Effectiveness,* 5, 1–17.

Casteman, B.L., & Page, L.C. (2014). A trickle or a torrent? Understanding the extent of summer "melt" among college-intending high school graduates. *Social Science Quarterly,* 95(1), 202–220.

Chiteji, N.S. (2007). To have and to hold: An analysis of young adult debt. In S. Danziger & C.E. Rouse (Eds.), *The price of independence: The economics of early adulthood.* New York: Russell Sage Foundation.

Clark, B.R. (1960). The "cooling-out" function in higher education. *The American Journal of Sociology,* 65(6), 569–576.

College Board (2005). *Education Pays 2005.* New York: Author.

College Board (2007). *Education pays 2007: The benefits of higher education for individuals and society.* New York: Author.

Conley, D.T. (2008). Rethinking college readiness. *New Directions for Higher Education,* 144, 3–13.

Conley, D.T. (2013). *Getting ready for college, careers, and the common core: What every educator needs to know.* San Francisco, CA: Jossey-Bass.

Craddock, S., Birnbaum, M., Rodriguez, K., Cobb, C., & Zeeh, S. (2011). Doctoral students and the impostor phenomenon: Am I smart enough to be here? *Journal of Student Affairs Research and Practice,* 48(4), 429–442.

Deil-Amen, R., & Tevis, T. (2010). Circumscribed agency: The relevance of standardized college entrance exams for low SES high school students. *Review of Higher Education,* 33(2), 141–175.

Deming, D., & Dynarski, S. (2009). *Into college, out of poverty? Policies to increase the postsecondary attainment of poor.* Cambridge, MA: National Bureau of Economic Research.

DeNavas-Walt, C. & Proctor, B.D. (2014). *Income and poverty in the United States: 2013.* Washington, DC: US Census Bureau.

Engle, J. (2007). Postsecondary access and success for first-generation college students. *American Academic, 3*(1), 25–48.

Engle, J., & Tinto, V. (2008). *Moving Beyond Access: College Success for Low-Income, First-Generation Students.* Washington, DC: Pell Institute for the Study of Opportunity in Higher Education.

Engstrom, C., & Tinto, V. (2008). Access without support is not opportunity. *Change: The Magazine of Higher Learning, 40*(1), 46–50.

Hallett, R.E. (2010). Homeless: How residential instability complicates students' lives. *About Campus, 15*(3), 11–16.

Hallett, R.E., & Griffen, J. (forthcoming). Empowering parents in the college planning process: An action inquiry case study. *Journal of Education for Students Placed At Risk.*

Hallett, R.E., & Venegas, K.M. (2011). Is increased access enough? Advanced placement courses, quality, and success in low-income urban schools. *Journal for the Education of the Gifted, 34*(3), 468–487.

Hooker, S., & Brand, B. (2010). College knowledge: A critical component of college and career readiness. *New Directions for Youth Development, 127,* 75–85.

Gardner, S.K., & Holley, K.A. (2011). "Those invisible barriers are real": The progression of first-generation students through doctoral education. *Equity and Excellence in Education, 44*(1), 77–92.

Kirshner, B., Saldivar, M.G., & Tracy, R. (2011). How first-generation students learn to navigate education systems: A case study of First Graduate. *New directions for youth development, 2011*(S1), 107–122.

Kuh, G.D., Kinzie, J., Buckley, J.A., Bridges, B.K., & Hayek, J.C. (2006). *What matters to student success: A review of the literature commissioned report for the national symposium on postsecondary student success: Spearheading a dialog on student success.* Washington DC: National Postsecondary Education Cooperative.

National Association for College Admission Counseling. (2006). *State of college admission, 2006.* Washington, DC: Author.

Mayer, A.P. (2008). Expanding opportunities for high academic achievement: An international baccalaureate diploma program in an urban high school. *Journal of Advanced Academics, 19*(2), 202–235.

McDonough, P.M. (1997). *Choosing colleges: How social class and schools structure opportunity.* Albany: State University of New York Press.

McDonough, P.M. (2005). Counseling matters: Knowledge, assistance, and organizational commitment in college preparation. In W.G. Tierney, Z.B. Corwin, & J.E. Colyar (Eds.), *Preparing for college: Nine elements of effective outreach* (pp. 69–88). Albany, NY: State University of New York Press.

McDonough, P.M., Calderone, S., & Venegas, K. (forthcoming). The role of social trust in low-income Latino/a college financing decision. *Journal of Latino and Latin American Studies.*

McKillip, M.E.M, Rawls, A., & Barry, C. (2012). Improving college access: A review of research on the role of the high school counselors. *Professional School Counseling, 16*(1), 49–58.

McSwain, C., & Davis, R. (2007). *College access for the working poor: Overcoming burdens to succeed in higher education.* Washington, DC: Institute for Higher Education Policy.

Melguizo, T. (2011). A review of the theories developed to describe the process of college persistence and attainment. In J.C. Smart & M.B. Paulson (Eds.), *Higher education: Handbook of theory and research* (pp. 395–424). Netherlands: Springer.

Morrice, P.I. (2011). *"It's the Perfect Baby Step": African American Students' Community College Choice and Transfer to Four-Year Colleges and Universities.* Doctoral dissertation, The University of Michigan.

Nagaoka, J., Roderick, M., & Coca, V. (2009). *Barriers to college attainment: Lessons from Chicago.* Washington, DC: Center for American Progress.

Perez, P.A., & McDonough, P.M. (2008). Understanding Latina and Latino college choice: A social capital and chain migration analysis. *Journal of Hispanic Higher Education, 7*(3), 249–265.

Perna, L.W., Rowan-Kenyon, H.T., Thomas, S.L., Bell, A., Anderson, R., & Li, C. (2008). The role of college counseling in shaping college opportunity: Variations across high school. *The Review of Higher Education, 31*(2), 131–159.

Perna, L.W., & Thomas, S.L. (2008). *Theoretical perspectives on student success: Understanding the contributions of the disciplines.* ASHE Higher Education Report.

Pew Research Center (2014). *The rising cost of not going to college.* Washington, DC: Author.

Ormrod, J.E. (2006). *Essentials of educational psychology.* Upper Saddle River, NJ: Prentice Hall.

Rios-Aguilar, C., & Deil-Amen, R. (2012). Beyond getting in and fitting in: An examination of social networks and professionally relevant social capital among Latina/o university students. *Journal of Hispanic Higher Education,* 11(2), 179–196.

Roderick, M., Coca, V., & Nagaoka, J. (2011). Potholes on the road to college: High school effects in shaping urban students' participation in college application, four-year college enrollment and college match. *Sociology of Education,* 84(3), 178–211.

Rothstein, J., & Rouse, C.E. (2010). Constrained after college: Student loans and early-career occupational choices. *Journal of Public Economics,* 95, 149–163.

Schneider, B. (2007). *Forming a college-going community in US public high schools.* Lancing, MI: Michigan State University.

Standing, K., Judkins, D., Keller, B., & Shimshak, A. (2008). *Early outcomes of the GEAR UP program: Final report.* Rockville, MD: US Department of Education.

Stanton-Salazar, R. (2011). A social capital framework for study of institutional agents and their role in the empowerment of low-status students and youth. *Youth & Society,* 43, 1066–1109.

Silvernail, D.L., Sloan, J.E., & Johnson, A.F. (2013). *College participation rates of Maine's recent high school graduates: Examining the claims.* University of Southern Maine: Center for Education Policy, Applied Research, and Evaluation.

St. John, E. (2013). *Research, actionable knowledge, and social change: Reclaiming social responsibility through research partnerships.* Sterling, VA: Stylus Press.

Strayhorn, T.L. (2011). Bridging the pipeline: Increasing underrepresented students' preparation for college through a summer bridge program. *American Behavioral Scientist,* 55(2), 142–159.

Thomas, S.L., & Perna, L.W. (2004). The opportunity agenda: A reexamination of postsecondary reward and opportunity. In J.C. Smart (Ed.), *Higher education: Handbook of theory and research* (Vol. 19, pp. 43–84). Dordrecht, NL: Kluwer Academic Publishers.

Tierney, W.G. (2013). *The summer before: Improving college writing before freshman year.* Los Angeles, CA: Pullias Center for Higher Education.

Tierney, W.G., Hallett, R.E., & Venegas, K.M. (2007). It's about time: Temporal dimensions of college preparation programs. *Metropolitan Universities Journal,* 18(4), 102–121.

Tierney, W.G., & Venegas, K.M. (2009). Finding money on the table: Information, financial aid, and access to college. *The Journal of Higher Education,* 80(4), 363–388.

Tinto, V. (1993). *Leaving college: Rethinking the causes and cures of student attrition (second edition).* Chicago, IL: University of Chicago Press.

Torche, F. (2011). Is a college degree still the great equalizer? Intergenerational mobility across levels of schooling in the United States. *American Journal of Sociology,* 117(3), 763–807.

Turner, S. (2007). Higher education: Policies generating the 21st century workforce. In H. Holzer & D. Nightingale (Eds.), *Workforce policies for a changing economy* (pp. 91–16). Washington, DC: Urban Institute Press.

United States Department of Education (2012). *Public elementary and secondary school student enrollment and staff counts from the Common Core data: School year 2010–2011.* Washington, DC: National Center for Education Statistics.

Venegas, K.M., & Hallett, R.E. (2008). When a group presentation isn't enough: Financial aid advising for low-income urban college bound students. *College and University,* 83(4), 16–25.

Venezia, A., & Kirst, M.W. (2005). Inequitable opportunities: How current education systems and policies undermine the chances for student persistence and success in college. *Educational Policy,* 19(2), 283–307.

Viadero, D., & Johnston, R.C. (2000). Lags in minority achievement defy traditional explanations: The achievement gap. *Education Week,* 19, n2818.

Wimberly, G.L., & Noeth, R.J. (2005). College readiness begins in middle school: ACT policy report. Retrieved from *http://www.act.org/research/policymakers/reports/index.html.*

Chapter 4:   Purpose, Ethics and Practice: Values, Competencies and Impact of NACAC

Jonathan D. Mathis, PhD
@NACACedu

Todd M. Laudino
@NACACedu

"We remain convinced—are more certain than ever, in fact—that significantly increasing college attainment is the key to ensuring a bright future for our nation and its citizens."

Jamie P. Merisotis,
President and CEO, Lumina Foundation
(Lumina Foundation, 2014, p. 1)

Scholars and policymakers often link the success of a knowledge-based economy to the postsecondary educational attainment of its citizenry. Reports evaluating or informing participation in systems of education, from the Organisation of Economic Co-operation and Development (OECD), the Lumina Foundation, and Jobs for the Future, as well as state-based and nationally situated entities, all speak to the importance of college access and success. In essence, these data points and efforts continue to refine and heighten the impact of organizations such as the National Association for College Admission Counseling (NACAC). This chapter opens with examples of global, national and local efforts informing the work of college admission counseling professionals.

DEVELOPING AN AWARENESS OF CONTEXT AND PURPOSE

First, a global perspective suggests that "education and skills hold the key to future wellbeing and will be critical to restoring long-term growth, tackling unemployment, promoting competitiveness, and nurturing more inclusive and cohesive societies" (OECD, 2014, p. 15). OECD (2014) encourages attention to systems of education as a means of increasing the social mobility, meritocracy and productivity of society:

Education and skills have thus become increasingly important dimensions of social inequality; but they are also an indispensable part of the solution to this problem. Education can lift people out of poverty and social exclusion, but in order to do so, educational attainment has to translate into social mobility (p. 14).

On a global front, OECD (2014) reports rapid increases in postsecondary educational attainment across OECD countries in comparison to the US. In fact, the US is reported 34th of 41 countries with regard to the percentage of adults, ages 25–64 years old, with postsecondary education in 2000 and 2012 (OECD, 2014). In 2012, The US was 14th of 37 countries in the attainment of postsecondary education for a subsection of the population: 25–34 year olds (OECD, 2012). These data points ignite much of President Obama's (2009) call for greater educational attainment, as well as the Lumina Foundation's Goal 2025 (Lumina Foundation, 2013). As such, postsecondary participation—both access and success—continues to drive much of the work of national and state-based initiatives.

Initiatives. The White House launched the Reach Higher initiative as a vehicle to achieve what has been described as President Obama's "North Star" goal—for the US to again have the highest percentage of population with postsecondary educational attainment in the world, by 2020 (The White House, n.d.). The Reach Higher initiative was first announced by First Lady Michelle Obama at San Antonio Signing Day at the University of Texas at San Antonio. In her message, Michelle Obama (2014) shared that the initiative came about to inspire "every student in America to take charge of their future by completing their education past high school—whether at a professional training program, or a community college, or a four-year university or college." The efforts of The White House include collaboration across many organizational entities to provide access and resources to ensure college participation.

The Lumina Foundation highlights the urgency of postsecondary educational attainment as a part of the Goal 2025 initiative: "to increase the proportion of Americans with high-quality degrees, certificates and other credentials to 60% by the year 2025" (Lumina Foundation, 2012). The Lumina Foundation (2012) writes:

For many years, the main reason many people went to college was to gain access to better-paying jobs that allowed them to earn more throughout their lives. But earnings potential is no longer the only driver. In this economy, the issue is whether you even *have* a job (p. 2).

The work of the Lumina Foundation continues to influence the work of organizations, institutions and individuals in the college access and success realm. Postsecondary outcomes become central to the conversation to include gainful employment and societal engagement: "increasing the number of college graduates will not only bolster our economy, it will also strengthen our democracy and communities throughout the nation. These social and cultural reasons for increasing educational attainment are, at times, undervalued" (Lumina Foundation, 2012, p. 3).

Scholars at Jobs for the Future (JFF) investigated the manner and structure by which states author initiatives or commitments to access and success: "many states have begun to seek ways to drive improvements in higher education outcomes and productivity as a result of both budgetary constraints and the pressures of global competition" (Collins, 2006). States such as Kentucky and Texas, along with the District of Columbia, have all designed plans to increase postsecondary educational access and success among residents.

The Kentucky Council on Postsecondary Education (KCPE) (2007) authored a plan to increase the number of college graduates, focusing on bachelor's degree attainment. Core to this plan is the following understanding: "the link between economic prosperity and educational attainment is most dramatic at the bachelor's-degree level, both for states and individuals" (KCPE, 2007, p. 8). Five strategies are offered in hopes to achieve Kentucky's goal of doubling the number of bachelor degree earners by 2020: (1) raise high school graduation rates; (2) increase the number of GED graduates and transition more to college; (3) enroll more first-time students in the Kentucky Community and Technical College System and transfer them to four-year programs; (4) increase the number of Kentuckians going to and completing college; and (5) attract college-educated workers to the state and create new jobs for them (KCPE, 2007, pp. 10—14). Of these strategies, the second, third and fourth align with the professional work of college admission professionals.

In *Closing the Gaps: The Texas Higher Education Plan,* officials recognize the import of active participants in a knowledge-based economy: "Texas is profiting from a diverse, vibrant and growing economy. Yet this prosperity could turn to crisis if steps are not taken quickly to ensure an educated population and workforce for the future" (THECB, n.d., p. 4). The Texas Higher Education Coordinating Board (THECB) authors four goals, each with their respective desired outcomes. Of particular interest to the professionals serving in the college admission counseling community is the third strategy under the first goal, "close the gaps in participation": "ensure that all students and their parents understand the benefits of higher education and the necessary steps to prepare academically and financially for college" and "establish coordinated P—16+ informational, motivational and academic programs to prepare students for college" (THECB, n.d., p. 1). The additional goals include attention to the following: "success," defined by the completion of postsecondary degree programs; "excellence," measured by increases in notoriety of postsecondary degree programs offered in Texas; and "research," assessed by federal research dollars awarded to Texas postsecondary institutions.

Lastly, the District of Columbia, too, has an initiative to increase college access and success for its residents. *Double the Numbers for College Success* (2006), similar to the two states previously mentioned, first takes account of its residents while also considering the interplay with the entire nation and world:

> In the District of Columbia, the situation is even bleaker. Only 9 percent of incoming 9th graders complete college "on time"…The remainder— the more than 90 percent who leave the high school system, never start college or fail to finish their degree—will face a future of diminished opportunities and low-wage jobs (Kernan-Schloss & Potapchuk, 2006, p. 2)

The data served as impetus for greater attention to college access and success efforts. The collaborative effort of the DC College Access Program, DC Education Compact, DC Public Schools, and DC State Education Office resulted in a comprehensive plan to steward commitments for college access and success. These partners acknowledge:

> Doubling the number of students who graduate from high school and college requires focused and strategic work at multiple levels. Each student needs support throughout the education process…

whether it is passing 9th grade, graduating from high school, learning about college or other high-quality postsecondary options, navigating scholarships and aid programs, or getting help in a tough subject in college. This level of individualized attention will require the combined efforts of program, school, district and community leaders (Kernan-Schloss & Potapchuk, 2006, p. 6).

Within this 10-point plan, there are several specific contributions aligned with the work of college admission counseling professionals. In particular, the following points are of interest to colleagues in the college admission profession: "strengthen and support the expansion of proven systemic and school-level college access programs"; "educate DC students and families about the prerequisites of college and the value of a degree"; "overhaul the student support system so that counselors, teachers, and principals focus on helping students and their families better understand and prepare for their postsecondary options"; "expand DC students' options by working closely with additional four-year colleges and strengthening the pathways from two-year community colleges to four-year degrees" (Kernan-Schloss & Potapchuk, 2006, p. 7).

Each report, whether global, national and/or state-based, articulates a call for action that speaks to college access and success. Within each of these efforts, we read of a need for greater collaboration and intentionality among those who promote and ease transitions to and through postsecondary educational pursuits. The purpose of this chapter is to, first and foremost, situate the National Association for College Admission Counseling (NACAC) at the core of these efforts. Secondly, this chapter serves as the first in a two-segment block: Purpose, Ethics and Practice.

The emphasis here is on the origin and structure of the organization—a discussion that includes further articulation of the purpose, leadership and values governing NACAC. Accordingly, the discussion here will highlight competencies produced by the association, as a means to inform practice at both the individual and institutional levels. Tenets of social capital provide for a rich contextual and conceptual framing of the power of the association and its impact among constituents and across communities. In its entirety, this chapter is the ideal preamble to the proceeding content, which highlights ethical principles and practices agreed upon by members of NACAC.

Brief Historical Overview of NACAC

The National Association for College Admission Counseling believes that college admission counseling makes a powerful difference both for individual students and society. Effective transition to postsecondary education requires secondary school and college readiness preparation, holistic and ethical practices in guiding students, and knowledge and skills for continued success.

—*NACAC Vision Statement*

The National Association for College Admission Counseling (NACAC) began in 1937 as a convening of admission representatives from colleges and universities in the Midwest to discuss the pending and forthcoming needs of postsecondary enrollment (NACACa, n.d.). During the celebration of the 75th anniversary of the association, former NACAC President Mary Lee Hoganson (2012) penned a historical account. She wrote, "for 75 years the National Association for College Admission Counseling has guided the evolution of admission counseling into a recognized profession" (p. 1). She continued:

In reviewing the history of the association, from founding years to the current era, many common themes emerge. Over its history, NACAC has defined and promoted the highest ethical practices and professional standards. The association has become the premiere organization for professional admission counseling training and networking. Legislative advocacy has had an impact on educational policy at both the national and state levels. (p. 1)

Included in this publication, Hoganson (2012) provides a historical overview of the inception and growth of the association, for which a few highlights are offered in Table 1.

Table 1. Historical Overview of NACAC, by Decade

Date	Progression of NACAC
1937—39	Distinctions between scholarships and financial aid were defined; a member code of ethics was adopted; the issue of equity in college admission was raised; it was first suggested that application fees be charged; parameters for "College Days" and high school visitations were set; a national presence was deemed essential through regional accrediting agencies and the media.
1940—49	A first constitution for The Association of College Admission Counselors was adopted in March of 1942. In the summer of 1944, members convened for a two-day "Camp College," which, by 1947, grew into the first full association conference.
1950—59	Full voting, institutional membership was extended to high schools in October of 1955. At this time, the Executive Board was expanded to include three members from the secondary sector.
1960—69	The first national office opened in 1960 in Evanston, IL. In 1966, members voted sweeping governance changes, and the first NACAC Assembly convened in 1967. The Association became the National Association for College Admission Counselors in 1968.
1970—79	1972 saw the advent of the first NACAC College Fairs, an innovation that became pivotal to NACAC's financial solvency. But, without a doubt, deliberations regarding a move from the Midwest to Washington, DC, to assume an advocacy role of national prominence, became *the* issue of the 70s.
1980—89	By the beginning of the 80s, NACAC had established a DC satellite office and was active in federal advocacy. In 1984, voting membership was granted to independent counselors. The 1985 Assembly made a final decision that NACAC would relocate, and, in 1987, NACAC finally made the move to the nation's capital, opening an office in Alexandria, VA.
1990—1999	The 90s were largely centered on debate over member-institutional prerogatives vs. students' needs. The SPGP was amended to reflect compromises on standards regarding need-blind admission and merit vs. need-based aid. May 1 was affirmed as the uniform reply date. A 1995 name change to the National Association for College Admission Counseling reflected the growing diversity of roles of association members. The NACAC Listserv created instant member interaction in 1996.
2000 and Beyond	The first *State of College Admission* report appeared in 2003. The SPGP was substantively revised in 2005 to reflect changes in the admission world, while maintaining an unchanged commitment to this long-standing code of ethics. A new headquarters building was purchased in 2007, anticipating continuing association growth.

Adapted from Hoganson (2012).

The 1937 convening set out to discuss issues pertaining to college admission procedures—financial aid, in particular—while also establishing the origins of the national association and early statements detailing ethics of practice. It was here, too, that early conversations about application fees, suggested practices for high school visits and other college-exposure programs were discussed (Hoganson, 2012).

In the following decades, as highlighted in Table 1, several advances were made to solidify the purpose and functions of what is known today as NACAC. Some examples include the following: a constitution; a central clearinghouse for college applications; a resolution to provide support for disadvantaged students; an outcry for affirmative action in admission and financial aid; as well as establishing current programmatic efforts and policy considerations (Hoganson, 2012). The efforts and advances of the association are shared and assessed through its current strategic plan, the framework for which is readily available on the NACAC Web site.

The National Association for College Admission Counseling advocates and supports ethical and professional practice in helping students transition to postsecondary education. NACAC promotes high professional standards and social responsibility through collaboration, knowledge and education.

—*NACAC Mission Statement*

Today, NACAC is comprised of more than 13,000 admission professionals, serving students and families around the world. At the very core of this work is a clear, consistent commitment to "high standards that foster ethical and social responsibility among those involved in the transition process, as outlined in the NACAC Statement of Principles of Good Practice" (NACACb, n.d.).

NACAC's Governance and Leadership

The bylaws of NACAC offer a comprehensive description of the governance structure and leadership of the association.

Office of the President. The executive officers of the association include the following three roles: president, president-elect and immediate past president. Each office maintains a one-year term duration. The president serves as "the principal elected officer of the Association" and performs multiple roles, including: calling to order Assembly, Board and Executive Committee meetings; serving as official spokesperson of the association in concert with the chief executive officer; and appointing eligible individuals to various vacancies on committees or within leadership positions, when necessary. The president-elect is elected at the National Conference and succeeds to the Office of President. In this role, the elected individual fulfills many expectations, some of which include: assuming duties of president if he/she is unavailable and appointing chairs and/or members to committees prior to commencing term as president. The immediate past president serves in an advisory capacity, offering continuity of efforts and execution of strategic plans. In addition, this individual serves as a member, then chair, of the Governance and Nominating Committee (NACAC, 2011).

Chief Executive Officer (CEO). The role of CEO includes duality of leadership between the national staff and the Board of Directors. This individual "shall be employed by the Board of Directors to conduct business of NACAC and to administer its headquarters office in accordance with policies and procedures established by the Board of Directors" (NACAC, 2011). Along with the national staff, the CEO and Board of Directors articulate strategic plans—current and future activities of the association.

Board of Directors. As a charitable and educational organization, a Board of Directors is instrumental in safeguarding and advancing the work of any organization. Along with the president and CEO, directors are instrumental in developing policies and procedures informing the work of staff, volunteer and elected leaders within NACAC. In particular, directors are responsible for the following: overseeing the administration; exercising financial stewardship of the association; and determining annual budget and membership dues. Members of the Board of Directors bring diverse professional experiences and insights and are elected by members of the Assembly. Up to three directors can also be appointed by the Office of President and other members of the Board of Directors (NACAC, 2011).

Assembly. The Assembly is chiefly responsible for the electing of association officers, amending both Mandatory and Best Practices of the Statement of Principles of Good Practice (SPGP), and recommending matters to the Board (NACAC, 2011). Members serving in the Assembly include delegates who are elected by voting members; the delegates represent each affiliate and members of the Board (NACAC, 2011). At the time of this text, there are 23 affiliates (affiliated associations)—"separately incorporated... [operating] within a defined geographic territory... recognized by the Board of Directors" (NACAC, 2011).

NACAC Standing Committees. Within the bylaws, there is specific mention of three committees: Admission Practices, Finance, and Governance and Nominating (NACAC, 2011). The Admission Practices Committee is discussed in the following chapter, given their role in the maintenance and enforcement of the Statement of Principles of Good Practice (SPGP). Members of the finance committee offer the Board of Directors guidance on issues of financial and budgetary policy. Lastly, the Governance and Nominating Committee is responsible for recommending amendments to the association's bylaws and for nominating a slate of candidates for elected positions. The committees, many of which are not mentioned here, provide expertise and assist in the execution of the efforts of the national staff.

Values and Belief Systems

Of utmost importance to the association and its members is the commitment to students and their families. As seen in the expressed ethics agreed upon by all members, further described in NACAC's Statement of Principles of Good Practice (SPGP) (NACAC, 2014), and the proceeding chapter, integrity and assistance throughout the college enrollment process is paramount for NACAC members specifically, and required for professionals in the field.

Core Values. This section of the chapter highlights the six core values of the association, as well as member conventions established to assist in the framing of NACAC's code of ethics. Beginning with the core values, which are found at the start of the SPGP, professionals are exposed to the vision and belief structure of the association.

Professionalism: We believe our work in counseling, admission and enrollment management is professional only to the extent that we subscribe to and practice ethical behavior, as stated in our Member Conventions. We are responsible for the integrity of our actions and, insofar as we can affect them, the actions of our member institutions and organizations.

Collaboration: We believe the effectiveness of our profession, college counseling, admission and enrollment management is enhanced when we work together to promote and protect students and their best interests.

Trust: We believe our profession, college counseling, admission and enrollment management is based upon trust, mutual respect and honesty, with one another and with students.

Education: We believe in and are committed to educating students, their families, the public, fellow education professionals, and ourselves about the transition to and within postsecondary education.

Fairness and Equity: We believe our members have a responsibility to treat one another and students in a fundamentally fair and equitable manner.

Social Responsibility: We believe we have a duty to serve students responsibly, by safeguarding their rights and their access to and within postsecondary education.

Across these core values, with specific attention to "social responsibility," NACAC calls for its members to be conduits for students in their pursuit of higher education. In many ways, members are considered to be institutional agents—a concept that emerges from a social capi-

tal theoretical perspective. Stanton-Salazar (1997) defines institutional agents as "those individuals who have the capacity and commitment to transmit directly, or negotiate the transmission of, institutional resources and opportunities" (p. 6).

These individuals are suggested to "have the power to create change through their attitudes and actions. The combination of the desire to act and the know-how to act effectively makes these people institutional agents" (Stanton-Salazar, 2010, p. 1). Further discussion of Stanton-Salazar's (2010; 1997) conceptualization of institutional agents is included in Chapter 24. A brief aside is warranted here to further explore the concepts of social capital, with a narrow focus on the efforts and expectations of NACAC and its individual and organizational members.

CORE VALUES AND SOCIAL CAPITAL

Social capital, as a theoretical concept, is often considered to make the seemingly impossible, possible: "Like other forms of capital, social capital is productive in making possible the achievement of certain ends that would not be attainable in its absence" (Coleman, 1990, p. 302). This concept, as explained by sociologist James Coleman, includes discussion of functionality and categorization. Coleman (1990) suggests this form of capital finds its value in the social structure and resource available to actors who then perform actions "to realize their interests" (p. 305). Here, the argument is being presented that college admission professionals, as defined and described by the core values of NACAC, act in the interest of students and their families, by functioning within social structures and activating resources to ensure students' access and success in postsecondary educational pursuits.

To further our understanding here, it is helpful to see the linkages between the core values and Coleman's conceptualization of social capital, as captured in the table below.

The last concept of social capital, *norms and effective sanctions,* furthers the import and power of NACAC's Member Conventions. These ideas serve almost as the preamble to the Statement of Principles of Good Practice (SPGP), thus framing a shared agreement among all members. These agreements further the ideas put forth by Coleman (1990): social capital "not only facilitates certain actions but also constrains others" (p. 311).

Table 2. Interpretations of Social Capital Tenets and NACAC Values and Practices

Coleman's (1990) Social Capital	Interpretations of Social Capital Tenets	Examples from NACAC's Core Values
Obligations and Expectations	Describes commitments between actor and recipient; builds largely on trustworthiness in repayment and/or reciprocity	• "responsibility to treat one another and students in a fundamentally fair and equitable manner"; "our profession…is enhanced when we work together to promote and protect students" (NACAC, 2014)
Information Potential	Heightens the importance and basis for action; recognizes there is a cost for information, confirming network strength and value	• "committed to educating students, their families, the public, fellow education professionals, and ourselves about the transition to and within postsecondary education" (NACAC, 2014)
Norms and Effective Sanctions	Creates common beliefs and practices; "facilitates certain actions but also constrains others" (Coleman, 1990, p. 311)	• "subscribe to and practice ethical behavior"; "integrity in our actions and, insofar as we can affect them, the actions of our member institutions" (NACAC, 2014)

MEMBER CONVENTIONS

The member conventions are also an extension of the *norms and effective sanctions* tenet of social capital. It is within these statements that members of the association come to an agreement about shared purpose, organizational affiliation and ethical practices. The table below states each of these mandates.

As noted in the final convention, these ideas permeate the core of the Statement of Principles of Good Practice, which are discussed in the following chapter. In lieu of providing those details here, this chapter concludes with a closer look at the competencies attached to pre-service, novice and continuing secondary counseling professionals.

COMPETENCIES OF COUNSELING PROFESSIONALS SERVING IN SECONDARY SCHOOLS

The final component of this chapter highlights the professional competencies posed for secondary school admission counseling professionals.

Table 3. NACAC Member Conventions from Statement of Principles of Good Practice (2014)

Members will make protecting the best interests of all students a primary concern in the admission process.
Members will evaluate students on the basis of their individual qualifications and strive for inclusion of all members of society in the admission process.
Members will provide accurate admission and financial aid information to students, empowering all participants in the process to act responsibly.
Members will honor students' decisions regarding where they apply and choose to enroll.
Members will be ethical and respectful in their counseling, recruiting and enrollment practices.
Members will strive to provide equal access for qualified students through education about financial aid processes and institutional financial aid policies.
Members will abide by local, state and federal laws regarding the treatment of students and confidential information.
Members will support a common set of admission-related definitions and deadlines.
Members will support and enforce the Statement of Principles of Good Practice.

Table 4. Summary of NACAC Counselor Competencies and Associated Practices (NACAC, 2000)

Counselor Competencies	Selected Examples of Practices
The possession and demonstration of exemplary counseling and communication skills	• Assist students in the development of a sense of self-awareness and worth, and an exploration of goals • "Establish productive linkages with college admission representatives"
The ability to understand and promote student development and achievement	• "Possess a knowledge of the psychology of children, adolescence and young adults, human growth and development and learning needs" • "Assist students in the assessment of their individual strengths, weaknesses and differences"
The ability to facilitate transitions and counsel students toward the realization of their full educational potential	• "Provide information appropriate to the particular educational transition…and assist students in understanding the relationship that their curricular experiences and academic achievements will have on subsequent educational opportunities"
The ability to recognize, appreciate, and serve cultural differences and the special needs of students and families	• "Demonstrate an awareness of and sensitivity to the unique social, cultural and economic circumstances of students and their racial/ethnic, gender, age, physical, and learning differences" • "Seek to improve and extend services to underserved students"
The demonstration of appropriate ethical behavior and professional conduct in the fulfillment of roles and responsibilities	• "Recognize the interests and well-being of the student as paramount in the counseling relationship and place student interests above those of the institution" • "Demonstrate an understanding of and ability to counsel students in accordance with [NACAC's] Statement of Principles of Good Practice"
The ability to develop, collect, analyze, and interpret data	• "Establish effective systems for conveying important data and information about students between educational levels"
The demonstration of advocacy and leadership in advancing the concerns of students	• "Advocate the educational needs of students" • "Provide training…to school officials to assist them in responding to the educational development and precollege guidance and counseling needs of students"
The ability to organize and integrate the precollege guidance and counseling component into the total school guidance program	• "Conduct appropriate planning, design, research, and evaluation activities to ensure that all precollege guidance and counseling services are maintained at an effective and relevant level"

CLOSING

The conversation regarding the success of a knowledge-based economy circles back to college participation—access and success—among its citizenry. Colleagues in this work remain aware of the potential impact and further define respective contributions of all stakeholders.

> Without question, there is a growing sense of urgency—both inside and outside the higher education community—to increase student success rates, close attainment gaps and ensure high-quality learning. More and more stakeholders—from faculty members and administrators to employers to policymakers to growing numbers of students and families—are embracing the change agenda. In fact, each day seems to bring more evidence that fundamental redesign is already under way (Lumina Foundation, 2014, p.1)

Professional associations have the potential to impact practice, provide resources and information, and simultaneously create opportunities for service and leadership. NACAC, since 1937, continues to be an integral leader in the college access and success work of the nation, and around the world. One of the greatest strengths of the association is its positioning at the forefront of college admission. NACAC forges networks and opportunities that support the development of professionals who serve students, families and institutions. The vision, mission and ethical practices of the association exemplify several tenets of social capital; by embodying the core ideas suggested for institutional agents, NACAC demonstrates commitment to empowering practitioners with the knowledge and resources necessary to get their students to and through college.

ABOUT THE AUTHORS

Jonathan D. Mathis, PhD serves as director of education and training for the National Association for College Admission Counseling (NACAC). Prior to joining NACAC, Dr. Mathis was a postdoctoral scholar for research and practice, and regional director for PUC Schools, in Los Angeles. In this role, Dr. Mathis has created a pilot program that re-conceptualizes the way in which high schools cultivate college readiness for students. He supported high school leaders and college counselors, as well as a team of interns, in the development, implementation, and evaluation of this innovative college identity development model. In addition to his work in the K–12 schools, Dr. Mathis was appointed as an adjunct assistant professor in Rossier School of Education, for both masters and educational doctorate programs. Dr. Mathis earned his Doctor of Philosophy (PhD) from the University of Southern California (CA) under the advisement of Dr. William G. Tierney. While at USC, he served as a mentor for the I AM College Access mentoring program, facilitator for Pullias Center's SummerTIME program, and a graduate assistant for the McNair Scholars Program. He completed a bachelor's of science in business administration at American University (DC), and a master's of science in administration, for K–12 educational administration at Trinity Washington University (DC).

Todd M. Laudino is an education and training coordinator for the National Association for College Admission Counseling (NACAC), focusing on research and social media. Before joining NACAC, Todd was as an education volunteer with the Peace Corps, serving in a rural community in Rwanda as an English teacher and teacher trainer. This was not his first experience working in a school, though, as he had previously taught history and psychology at a public high school in New Jersey. Todd studied history as an undergraduate before earning his master's in social studies education at the Rutgers Graduate School of Education in 2009.

REFERENCES

Coleman, J.S. (1990). Social capital. In *Foundations of social theory* (pp. 300–321). Cambridge, MA: Harvard University Press.

Collins, M. (2006). *By the numbers: State goals for increasing postsecondary attainment*. Boston: Jobs for the Future.

Hoganson, M.L. (2012). *National Association for College Admission Counseling: Looking back as NACAC turns 75*. Arlington, VA: National Association for College Admission Counseling.

Kentucky Council on Postsecondary Education (KCPE). (2007). *Double the numbers: Kentucky's plan to increase college graduates*. Frankfort, KY: Author.

Kernan-Schloss, A., & Potapchuk, B. (2006). *Double the numbers for college success: A call for action for the District of Columbia*. Washington, DC: Office of the State Superintendent of Education.

Lumina Foundation. (2012). *Strategic plan 2013 to 2016*. Indianapolis, IN: Author. Retrieved from *http://luminafoundation.org/goal_2025*.

Lumina Foundation. (2014). *A stronger nation through higher education*. Indianapolis, IN: Author. Retrieved: *http://www.luminafoundation.org/stronger_nation*.

National Association for College Admission Counseling (NACAC). (2000). *Statement on counselor competencies*. Arlington, VA: Author. Retrieved from *http://www.nacacnet.org/about/Governance/Policies/Documents/CounselorCompetencies.pdf*.

National Association for College Admission Counseling (NACAC). (2011). *Bylaws of the National Association for College Admission Counseling*. Arlington, VA: Author.

National Association for College Admission Counseling (NACAC). (2014). *Statement of principles of good practice*. Arlington, VA: Author. Retrieved from *http://www.nacacnet.org/about/Governance/Policies*.

National Association for College Admission Counseling (NACACa). (n.d.). *NACAC History*. Arlington, VA: Author. Retrieved from *http://www.nacacnet.org/about/history/Pages/default.aspx*.

National Association for College Admission Counseling (NACACb). (n.d.). *About NACAC.* Arlington, VA: Author. Retrieved from *http://www.nacacnet.org/about/Pages/default.aspx.*

Obama, B. (2009, February 24). *Remarks of President Barack Obama, address to joint session of Congress.* Retrieved from *http://www.whitehouse.gov/the_press_office/Remarks-of-President-Barack-Obama-Address-to-Joint-Session-of-Congress.*

Obama, M. (2014, May 2). *Remarks by the First Lady at San Antonio signing day Reach Higher event.* San Antonio, TX: University of Texas, San Antonio. The White House Press Office.

OECD. (2012). *Education at a Glance 2012: OECD Indicators.* OECD Publishing. Retrieved from DOI: 10.1787/eag-2012-en.

OECD. (2014). *Education at a Glance 2014: OECD Indicators.* OECD Publishing. Retrieved from *http://dx.doi.org/10.1787/eag-2014-en.*

Stanton-Salazar, R.D. (1997). *A social capital framework for understanding the socialization of racial minority children and youths.* Harvard Educational Review, 67(1), p. 1–40.

Stanton-Salazar, R.D. (2010). *A social capital framework for the study of institutional agent & their role in the empowerment of low-status students & youth.* University of Southern California. Retrieved from *http://cue.usc.edu/tools/publications.*

Texas Higher Education Coordinating Board (THECB). (n.d.). *Closing the gaps: The Texas higher education plan.* Austin, TX: Author.

The White House. (n.d.). Reach Higher. Retrieved from *http://www.whitehouse.gov/reach-higher.*

Chapter 5: Purpose, Ethics and Practice: Statement of Principles of Good Practice

Peggy Hock, PhD
@phockmccalley

Katy Murphy

Central to the mission of the National Association for College Admission Counseling (NACAC), since its beginning, has been the need to determine and promote ethical practices and professional standards. These principles guide all professionals who work with students in the transition to postsecondary education, as noted in the previous chapter. NACAC's Statement of Principles of Good Practice (SPGP) defines both Mandatory and Best Practices for all professionals in the field of college admission counseling. These professionals include those who recruit students for postsecondary institutions, as well as those working in high schools, independent practice, community colleges, and community-based organizations helping students plan for the transition to or within postsecondary educational institutions. The goal of this chapter is to provide counseling practitioners with the knowledge and skills to perform professional college admission counseling in accordance with current ethical standards and best practices.

Depending on the professional setting, individuals may need to be conversant with other ethical guidelines, such as those established by the following: American Association of Collegiate Registrars and Admission Officers (AACRAO), the American School Counselor Association (ASCA), the Higher Education Consultants Association (HECA), the Independent Educational Consultants Association (IECA), and NAFSA: Association of International Educators (NAFSA). In addition, all education professionals need to understand and follow state and federal or national laws that govern their actions. In the United States, this mandate includes the requirements of the Family Educational Rights and Privacy Act (FERPA). A brief overview of these guidelines and legal considerations is offered in the supplemental discussion at the close of this chapter.

While specific coverage of these ideas is beyond the scope of this chapter, school-based professionals must operate within the regulations and policies of the employing school and/or school district, but are expected to challenge those policies if they conflict with Mandatory Practices in the SPGP.

Before continuing with this chapter, you are expected to read the SPGP in its entirety, which can be found in the supplemental section at the close of this chapter; note carefully Mandatory Practices and their Interpretations

and Best Practices. Best Practices are to be followed to the extent permitted by the setting in which the professional is employed. Integrity in all interactions with students, parents and other professionals is fundamental to our work, as is the principle of putting the needs of students first.

HOW ETHICS FRAMES OUR WORK AS COUNSELORS

While there are many codes of ethics that guide college counseling professionals, all of these codes emphasize that we are working on behalf of our students and must respect their rights and responsibilities. College counseling professionals have the responsibility to represent themselves and their institutions in an ethical manner as they engage students, families, schools, and colleges and universities.

- **College counseling professionals in school settings** are expected to provide accurate information to students, to assist each student in completing processes and representing him or herself accurately, to provide accurate information about students to school officials and college admission officers, and to stay current with the requirements of the SPGP. Professionals in the school setting are also expected to protect students' privacy within legal guidelines and to follow those policies adopted by the school and/or school district.

- **College counseling professionals working within community-based organizations** are expected to work on behalf of each student in assisting him or her in defining choices, in completing processes accurately, and to interact with college admission officers on behalf of students within legal and professional guidelines.

- **Independent college counselors** are expected to provide accurate information to students, to support students in completing processes accurately and to keep the student at the center of the work. Independent college counselors must learn about college opportunities, but it is not their role to advocate on behalf of the student with college admission officers, and the independent counselor is expected always to support the work of the school counselor on behalf of the student.

The balance of this section of the chapter will give specific information on how to provide students and institutions the best professional service possible.

Specific Tenets Within The SPGP

The preamble of the SPGP outlines our core values and member conventions. The SPGP itself contains three important sections: Mandatory Practices, Interpretations and Best Practices.

Mandatory Practices are those that are at the core of our profession and are reviewed and updated through NACAC's Admission Practices Committee and by vote of the NACAC Assembly. This section outlines the "musts" within our work together. Violation of these practices is cause for removal from privileges of membership and community.

The Interpretations section gives further information on how the Mandatory Practices work, detailing definitions or specifics related to a requirement. These Interpretations are not musts, but clarify the musts.

Best Practices further define the best ethical and responsible ways to work with students, parents and institutions. These Best Practices are not mandatory, but actually reflect the ways in which skilled and ethical college admission professionals should work with students and one another.

What happens when you believe you have encountered a violation of our code of ethics by an individual or institution? If that individual or institution is a member of NACAC or a regional affiliated association (ACAC), working within a school, college or organization, you must first contact the Admission Practices (AP) Committee within your affiliate (your own regional ACAC). You will provide specific information and documentation on what you believe violates a Mandatory Practice of the SPGP. All communications, including information provided by you in this case, remains confidential, and the alleged violator will not know who has reported the activity. It is possible that what you believe to be a violation is not actually a violation of a Mandatory Practice, but might go against Best Practices. In any case, the affiliate AP Committee will contact the individual or college and discuss the problem. This outreach usually results in the refining of practice at the individual and/or institutional level.

The majority of the time, violations are a case of the person or college official not understanding the requirements of the SPGP. If the person or institution is unwilling to change and it is a Mandatory Practice violation, then the affiliate AP Committee refers the allegation to the NACAC AP Committee for action. As stated in the *Education, Monitoring Procedures, and Penalties* companion to the SPGP:

> The national Admission Practices Committee may impose penalties, including a Statement of Non-compliance or exclusion from NACAC-sponsored events. In accordance with NACAC Bylaws, Article V, Discipline, only the NACAC Board of Directors may censure, suspend or expel any NACAC member. Therefore, the national Admission Practices Committee may only recommend such action to the Board of Directors (NACAC, 2012, p. 3)

If the violation is being made by an institution that is not a member of NACAC, you should report the activity to the chief executive officer of NACAC, who will work with the AP Committee to resolve the issue. Again, your role as a reporter will remain confidential. A full discussion of the educational consequences and penalties associated with alleged violations committed against the SPGP are also discussed in length in the supplemental section of this chapter.

Working Ethically With Students And Their Families

The key components of the SPGP and our professional code of ethics relate to how we work within our professional settings to provide the best possible environment for current students and future students as they apply, are accepted to and choose colleges.

The following topics and descriptions are taken from the SPGP and professional practices and should answer your most frequent questions. Not all topics are covered below, and every college counseling professional should read the SPGP and reflect upon his/her behavior and work in the areas outlined. Note: More specific information is available in the Interpretations section of the SPGP. Clauses of the SPGP that have offered Interpretations are denoted by an asterisk.

Section III. B. of the SPGP provides Mandatory Practices specifically for those college admission professionals who work directly with students. This section details that we provide documentation and work with students to represent themselves with the most accurate information possible about their accomplishments in the classroom, in activities and testing. This requires counselors in school settings to:

- provide accurate transcripts reflecting all of the grades the students have earned

- work with students to teach them to provide accurate information on their activities and accomplishments

- inform students about using Score Choice, etc., to report their test scores according to individual colleges' test acceptance policy

- support only one Early Decision/Restrictive Early Application for a student, and provide the information and support for the student to submit only one enrollment deposit, unless a student accepts admission from a wait list (NACAC, 2014, p. 5).

Again, within the Mandatory Practices, counseling professionals provide students and their families the best information possible, but do not guarantee admission or receive remuneration from any source for placement. Clauses I.A.3. and I.B.2. in Mandatory Practices detail these provisions, requiring counselors to:

- provide accurate information to families

- refrain from guaranteeing admission to a college

- not publicize the admission status of individuals they work with without those individuals' specific permission

- not receive payment for placement of students. International admission agents may receive remuneration from a college in accordance with NACAC's policies (NACAC, 2014, p. 3).

The SPGP continues to require counselors, who work in school settings, to provide information on students' individual personal information according to school policies and legal guidelines, noted in sections I.B. and III.B. (NACAC, 2014, pp. 3,5). As the authors of this chapter, we offer this important consideration:

Several factors are important in guiding counselors when providing students' personal information. First of all, it is important that counselors and school officials understand the legalities of personal information and what is protected, and the implications for those under and over the age of 18. Disciplinary issues and the reporting of poor academic or personal behavior to colleges is a matter of school policy. We suggest every school have a written policy distributed to parents and students and adhere consistently to that policy with all students in reporting probation or suspension on counseling documents provided in the application process. If a student has a learning disability and/or medical or mental health issues, it is important to work with the student and family and reach agreement on how or whether that information is shared with colleges.

WORKING ETHICALLY WITH COLLEGE ADMISSION OFFICERS

The following topics and descriptions are taken from the NACAC SPGP and professional Best Practices and should answer your most frequent questions. Not all topics are covered below, and every college counseling professional should read the SPGP and reflect upon his/her behavior and work in the areas outlined. Note: More specific information is available in the Interpretations section of the SPGP.

Counselors' professional relationships with college admission officers span many years, not just one admission cycle. It is essential to establish a good and trusting working relationship with college admission officers and offices to enable your students to continue to be reviewed in the best light possible. Your professional reputation can significantly impact the process for your students.

Specifically, as college admission professionals working in school settings, we provide colleges and universities accurate and timely data on transcripts (initial, mid-year and final) to provide our colleagues the best information possible about the student. As detailed in Mandatory Practices section I.B.8., all members will "provide, in a timely manner, accurate, legible and complete transcripts for all students for admission and scholarships" (NACAC, 2014, p. 3)

As noted in Mandatory Practices section III.B.7., counselors working in school settings are expected to provide colleges and universities accurate high school profiles to provide our colleagues the best information possible about the student and the context of the school the student attends. In support of the student's transcript, an accurate high school profile helps college admission officers understand the context of the school within which the student earned his/her grades, as well as engaged in other activities. This information should include all students in reporting averages of grades, ranking systems and test scores (NACAC, 2014, p. 5).

School-based counselors also are required to provide colleges and universities accurate depictions of the student and his/her accomplishments on counselor forms and in counselor letters, and provide information on your school's policies on reporting discipline infractions, as described in Mandatory Practices section III.B.2. (NACAC, 2014, p. 5). It is important to include information relevant to a student's potential to contribute in and out of the classroom to the college or university that he or she is applying to in order for the college admission officer to understand a student's preference, as that may affect admission and indeed may not be accurate information at any given time. It is the individual student's decision, not the counselor's. Also, colleges should be making decisions based on the qualities of the student, not based on his/her likelihood to attend based on information received from the counselor.

It is expected that counseling professionals provide accurate information on the college and university and do not disparage any institution, as noted in Mandatory Practices sections I.A.2. and I.B.2. (NACAC, 2014). It is important, as counselors, to give accurate information about colleges and universities to our students, as each institution is a "good" institution for some, regardless of whether you personally value that institution's values and opportunities or not. We are seen by our students and their families as experts and must project an unbiased attitude toward the qualities of the colleges and universities our students are considering. As professionals, we must base our work on objective and valid information, rather than rumor and stereotype.

Counseling professionals do not promise a student's acceptance of an offer of admission nor provide specific information on other students whose cases may impact the acceptance of the student in question.

she is applying to in order for the college admission officer to understand how that student might "fit" into that educational environment. This information should include only accurate facts about accomplishments, etc., and, as permitted by the school's policies on disclosing disciplinary actions, should include that information as appropriate.

Counseling professionals do not promise a student's acceptance of an offer of admission nor provide specific information on other students whose cases may impact the acceptance of the student in question. These mandates are described in Mandatory Practices sections II.B.2. and III.B.5. (NACAC, 2014). As counselors are advocates for students with colleges, it is important to remember that students' and families' ideas and priorities change over time, and it is not ethical to indicate to a col-

While working in a school setting, counseling professionals do not sign more than one Early Decision or Restrictive Early Action agreement for any student, as maintained in Mandatory Practices sections I.B.10 and III.B.3. (NACAC, 2014). In order to maintain positive relationships with colleges and ethical relationships with students and their families, it is our responsibility to explain "early" programs and to uphold the rules about them. Early applicants are often given more consideration in the admission process, and thus, if a student is allowed to submit multiple applications against the rules, that student will receive unfair advantage in the process. Colleges are entitled to accurate information when making admission decisions. It is our responsibility to educate students to understand their rights and responsibilities and to engage in an ethical process.

While working in any setting, counseling professionals should support the student's right to take a reasonable amount of time to respond to a college's offer of admission from a wait list, and that student's rights to learn about financial aid and housing availability before having to respond to an offer of admission. These recommendations are found in Best Practices section II.B.2. (NACAC, 2014). Students seeking admission from an institution's wait list may be in situations where financial aid, housing and other considerations will affect their decisions to accept a place in the entering class. While this is not a Mandatory Practice, we can coach students to request the time (up to 72 hours or May 1 for freshmen, whichever is later) to make their informed decisions.

Across the board, counselors should support a student's final decision about the college he/she wants to attend and encourage each student to report that decision to all of the colleges/universities to which that student was admitted—and to intervene if a college wants to recruit that student after being informed of the student's final decision, as noted in Mandatory Practices sections I.B.9. and II.A.2. (NACAC, 2014). It is our role as counselors to support a student's final decision once that decision has been made. We should encourage each student to report their decisions to all colleges to which he/she was admitted and to honor that commitment. It is as unethical for a student to send a deposit to two or more institutions as it is for a college to try to recruit a student away from a college to which that student has already committed.

It is expected that all counselors should support a student's right to a transparent application process, including the opportunity to apply to any institution after October 15 without penalty and to expect the same consideration for a place in the class, institutional scholarships, etc., as noted in Mandatory Practices sections II.B.12. and II.B.4. (NACAC, 2014). Regardless of the increasingly competitive environment, colleges need to give students the information and opportunities to apply in a reasonable time frame and to have expectations of how applications and scholarships, etc., will be considered given that reasonable time frame. This is important to give high school students an opportunity to discuss choices and the process with their counselors during the school year to help them reach a mature decision.

As noted in the Best Practices section II.B.19 counselors working in any setting should support a transfer student's opportunities to learn about all of their college acceptances before making a decision (NACAC, 2014). While this is not a Mandatory Practice, we as counselors should support transfer students' requests for extensions of deadlines for replies about admission if they have not received all of their acceptances.

ETHICS IN PRACTICE

For each of the following situations, identify which part of the SPGP guides the school counselor's behavior, note whether it is a Mandatory Practice or a Best Practice, and identify the ethical response.

1. A high school counselor is scheduling a school visit from his alma mater, a highly selective institution. The admission counselor requests that only juniors and seniors enrolled in honors and/or AP classes be informed of the visit. How should the school counselor respond?

2. A student has been admitted early decision to a college. She has requested that her high school counselor still send mid-year reports to the other colleges she applied to. How should the school counselor respond?

3. A high school counselor receives a phone call from an admission counselor who wants to discuss the high school's applicants. He asks whether any of the students have accepted offers of admission from other colleges. He then asks the school counselor which of the students who have not committed is most likely to attend the college if admitted. He says he can offer a scholarship if he is certain a student will attend if admitted. How should the school counselor respond?

DISCUSSION QUESTIONS

For each question, note the section of the NACAC SPGP that applies to the situation. Is it a Mandatory Practice or a Best Practice?

1. The most frequent question we encounter is about reporting disciplinary action. If a school policy prohibits reporting a student's infractions, would a counselor be held responsible for not reporting that fraction?

2. School counselors are often under pressure from other school officials and parents, etc., about reporting information about individual students or the school. Should a counselor be held responsible for eliminating a group of students' grades or test scores from those reported on the school profile?

3. Should a counselor inform a student about another student's reportedly bad experience at a college or university?

4. If a counselor knows that an admitted student will not be attending a college, should that counselor "bargain" with the college admission officer with that information in order to promote another student's admission?

5. Should a counselor advise a student against reporting his/her grades earned during a summer program at another school if those grades were subpar?

6. What is the counselor's responsibility if he/she learns that a college is actively recruiting a student who has already committed elsewhere?

7. What advice should a counselor give a transfer student who has a deadline for a commitment but has not heard about admission from other colleges?

8. Should a counselor accept valuable merchandise or money from a college that is interested in recruiting students? What are acceptable gifts from a college to a counselor?

9. If a student has a learning disability or has been diagnosed with depression, is it the counselor's responsibility to report that to the colleges to which that student is applying?

10. Should a counselor promote or reveal the value of scholarships an individual student has received and include the name of the student in the information?

About the Authors

Peggy Hock earned her PhD in psychology from Columbia University. She is the vice principal of academics and director of college counseling at Saint Lawrence Academy in Santa Clara, CA and an instructor in the UC Berkeley Extension certificate program in College Admissions Advising. Previously, Peggy was the director of college counseling at two other California independent high schools for 18 years. She has also been the disabilities coordinator at a high school and a college and a professor and research scientist at two universities. Peggy is the president of the Western Association for College Admissions Counseling and a NACAC assembly delegate. Her previous WACAC service includes three terms as a delegate and chair of the technology committee. Her passion is focused on professional development for high school counselors and programs to support students with learning disabilities in the transition to college.

Katy Murphy is the director of college counseling at Bellarmine College Preparatory in San Jose, California. Previously, Katy was a director / dean of admissions and enrollment for 28 years at four different private colleges in California. She is also an instructor in the UC Berkeley Extension College Advising Program. Katy has served as the president of the National Association for College Admission Counseling and twice as president of the Western Association for College Admission Counseling, in addition to other national and regional positions within NACAC and the College Board. Katy's passion is focused upon advocacy and professional development for public high school counselors and new admission officers.

. . . .

Chapter Supplemental and Discussion NACAC Staff

Statement of Principles of Good Practice (SPGP)

Throughout the chapter, the authors provide insight into the SPGP, its structure and importance to the field of college admission counseling. As you become familiar with this document in its entirety, an important reminder is that the SPGP is very much a living document, for which annual updates are made, as the dynamic nature of the field presents considerations necessary for ethical guidance and best practices for professionals. To access the most current version of this document, you are highly encouraged to visit the National Association for College Admission Counseling Web site (*www.nacacnet.org*).

Statement of Principles of Good Practice
Approved by the 2014 Assembly

Introduction

Ethical college admission is the cornerstone of the National Association for College Admission Counseling (NACAC). Since its founding in 1937, when a select number of college and university professionals and high school counselors came together to create a Code of Ethics within the admission-counseling profession, NACAC has striven to ensure principled conduct among professionals in the recruitment of students and the transition to postsecondary education.

This code of conduct is known today as the Statement of Principles of Good Practice (SPGP).

Historically, NACAC added principles to the SPGP cumulatively, as ethical issues arose each year. In more recent years, however, the application process has become increasingly influenced by marketplace forces that raise new and complex ethical questions. In this rapidly-changing admission landscape, it is imperative for NACAC to maintain a document that includes practices and policies reflecting these new concerns for the ethical treatment of students in the admission process. As the recognized leader in college admission counseling, NACAC willingly carries the responsibility of being the only association that protects students' rights in the transition to postsecondary education process, through monitoring and enforcing ethical standards and practices.

Member schools, colleges and universities, as well as other institutions, organizations and individuals dedicated to the pursuit of higher education, believe in the dignity, worth and potential of each and every student. To enable all students to make the dream of higher education a reality, these institutions and individuals develop and provide programs and services in postsecondary counseling, admission and financial aid. They strive to eliminate bias within the education system based on ethnicity, creed, gender, sexual orientation, socio-economic status, age, political affiliation, national origin, and disability. They understand and value the importance of college counseling and view it as a fundamental aspect of their job as educators.

They support, therefore, the following Statement of Principles of Good Practice of the National Association for College Admission Counseling.

October 4, 2014

Statement of Principles of Good Practice Introduction

Core Values

Core Values represent statements of the association's vision and beliefs and are the purview of the Board of Directors.

Professionalism
We believe our work in counseling, admission and enrollment management is professional only to the extent that we subscribe to and practice ethical behavior, as stated in our Member Conventions. We are responsible for the integrity of our actions and, insofar as we can affect them, the actions of our member institutions and organizations.

Collaboration
We believe the effectiveness of our profession, college counseling, admission, and enrollment management is enhanced when we work together to promote and protect students and their best interests.

Trust
We believe our profession, college counseling, admission, and enrollment management is based upon trust, mutual respect and honesty, with one another and with students.

Education
We believe in and are committed to educating students, their families, the public, fellow education professionals, and ourselves about the transition to and within postsecondary education.

Fairness and Equity
We believe our members have a responsibility to treat one another and students in a fundamentally fair and equitable manner.

Social Responsibility
We believe we have a duty to serve students responsibly, by safeguarding their rights and their access to and within postsecondary education.

Member Conventions

Member conventions represent a set of understandings or agreements to frame our code of ethics. These statements are the purview of the Board of Directors.

All members of NACAC agree to abide by the following:
1. Members will make protecting the best interests of all students a primary concern in the admission process.
2. Members will evaluate students on the basis of their individual qualifications and strive for inclusion of all members of society in the admission process.
3. Members will provide accurate admission and financial aid information to students, empowering all participants in the process to act responsibly.
4. Members will honor students' decisions regarding where they apply and choose to enroll.
5. Members will be ethical and respectful in their counseling, recruiting and enrollment practices.
6. Members will strive to provide equal access for qualified students through education about financial aid processes and institutional financial aid policies.
7. Members will abide by local, state and federal laws regarding the treatment of students and confidential information.
8. Members will support a common set of admission-related definitions and deadlines.
9. Members will support and enforce the Statement of Principles of Good Practice.

Statement of Principles of Good Practice
Mandatory Practices

(* Refers the reader to Interpretations of Mandatory Practices, pages 6 – 12, for an expanded clarification)

I. All Members—Mandatory Practices
A. Promotion and Recruitment
All members agree they will:

* 1. accurately represent and promote their schools, institutions, organizations, and services;

* 2. not use disparaging comparisons of secondary or postsecondary institutions;

* 3. not offer or accept any reward or remuneration from a secondary school, college, university, agency, or organization for placement or recruitment of students in the United States.

* 4. not employ agents who are compensated on a per capita basis[1] when recruiting students outside the United States, unless ensuring they and their agents conduct themselves with accountability, transparency, and integrity[2];

* 5. be responsible for compliance with applicable laws and regulations with respect to students' rights to privacy.

B. Admission, Financial Aid and Testing Policies and Procedures
All members agree they will:

* 1. not publicly announce the amount of need-based aid awarded to any student without his/her permission;

2. not guarantee admission or specific college placement or make guarantees of any institutionally-affiliated financial aid or scholarship awards prior to an application being submitted, except when pre-existing criteria are stated in official publications;

* 3. not make unethical or unprofessional requests of other admission counseling professionals;

* 4. send and receive information about candidates in confidence;

* 5. consider transcripts official only when transmitted in a confidential manner, from the secondary or postsecondary institution(s) attended by the applicant;

* 6. not use minimum test scores as the sole criterion for admission, advising or for the awarding of financial aid;

7. be responsible for ensuring the accurate representation and promotion of their institutions in recruitment materials, presentations and scholarship materials;

* 8. provide, in a timely manner, accurate, legible and complete transcripts for all students for admission or scholarships;

* 9. counsel students to abide by the application requirements and restrictions when they file;

* 10. permit pending Early Action, Restrictive Early Action and Early Decision candidates to initiate any Regular or Rolling Decision applications.

[1] Footnote:
Per capita compensation means that agents are compensated based on each student recruited. This is also referred to as "commission-based" recruiting.

[2] Footnote: NACAC will honor a moratorium on enforcement until September 2015.

3

Statement of Principles of Good Practice *Mandatory Practices*

II. Postsecondary Members—Mandatory Practices

A. Promotion and Recruitment

All postsecondary members agree they will:

* 1. state clearly the requirements for the first-year and transfer admission and enrollment processes, including secondary school preparation, standardized testing, financial aid, housing and notification deadlines, and refund procedures;

2. not knowingly recruit students who are enrolled or registered or have initiated deferred admission, declared their intent or submitted contractual deposits to other institutions, unless the students initiate inquiries themselves or unless cooperation is sought from institutions that provide transfer programs.

B. Admission, Financial Aid and Testing Policies and Procedures

All postsecondary members agree they will:

1. accept full responsibility for admission and financial aid decisions and for proper notification of those decisions to candidates;

* 2. not require or ask candidates or the secondary schools to indicate the order of the candidates' college or university preferences, except under Early Decision;

* 3. permit first-year candidates for fall admission to choose among offers of admission and institutionally-affiliated financial aid and scholarships until May 1 and state this deadline explicitly in their offers of admission;

* 4. not offer exclusive incentives that provide opportunities for students applying or admitted Early Decision that are not available to students admitted under other admission options;

* 5. work with their institutions' senior administrative officers to ensure that institutionally-affiliated financial aid and scholarship offers and housing options are not used to manipulate commitments prior to May 1;

* 6. establish wait list procedures that ensure that no student on any wait list is asked for a deposit to remain on the wait list or for a commitment to enroll prior to receiving an official written offer of admission written notification may include mail or electronic communications;

* 7. state the specific relationship among admission and financial aid practices and policies;

8. notify accepted aid applicants of financial aid decisions before the enrollment confirmation deadline, assuming all requested application forms are received on time;

9. clearly state policies on renewal of financial aid that typically include a review of students' current financial circumstances;

* 10. not knowingly offer financial aid packages to students committed to attend other institutions, unless the students initiate such inquiries. Athletic scholarships, which adhere to nationally-established signing periods, are a recognized exception to this provision;

* 11. initially report on all first-year admitted or enrolled students, including special subgroups in the reporting of test scores. If data on subgroup populations are also provided, clear explanations of who is included in the subgroup population will be made;

Statement of Principles of Good Practice *Mandatory Practices*

    * 12. not establish any application deadlines for first-year candidates for fall admission prior to October 15 and will give equal consideration to all applications received by that date;

    13. not notify first-year candidates for fall admission prior to the receipt of a transcript that reflects completion of the final semester of the junior year of high school or the equivalent. Institutions that require only an application prior to extending an offer of admission, including many community colleges, may accept students at the time of application.

III. Counseling Members—Mandatory Practices

A. Promotion and Recruitment

All counseling members agree they will:

    * 1. establish a policy for the release of students' names and other confidential information consistent with applicable laws and regulations.

B. Admission, Financial Aid and Testing Policies and Procedures

All counseling members agree they will:

    * 1. provide colleges and universities with a description of the school's marking system, if available, that will provide some indication of grade distribution that may include the rank in class and/or grade point average;

    * 2. provide, as permissible by law, accurate descriptions of the candidates' personal qualities relevant to the admission process;

    3. sign only one pending Early Decision or Restricted Early Action agreement, when applicable, for any student;

    4. follow, when applicable, the process used by the candidates' high schools for filing college applications;

    5. not reveal, unless authorized, candidates' college or university preferences

    * 6. work with school officials and other relevant individuals to keep test results confidential as governed by law and local regulations;

    7. report on all students within a distinct class (freshman, sophomore, junior, and senior) and subgroups, including non-native speakers, in the reporting of standardized test scores.

Statement of Principles of Good Practice
Interpretations of Mandatory Practices

The following statements correspond with the same statement number in the Mandatory Practices section.

I. All Members—Interpretations and Monitoring
A. Promotion and Recruitment
All members agree they will:

1. accurately represent and promote their schools, institutions, organizations or services by:
    a. having and maintaining an official policy regarding the collection, calculation and reporting of institutional statistics. This must include a process for validating all institutional data;
    b. providing precise information about their academic majors and degree programs. Such information shall include a factual and accurate; description of majors, minors, concentrations, and/or interdisciplinary offerings that apply toward the completion of the undergraduate degree;
    c. describing in detail any special programs, including overseas study, credit by examination or advanced placement.

2. not use disparaging comparisons of secondary or postsecondary institutions.
    a. Members will refrain from publicly disseminating biased, unflattering and/or potentially inaccurate information about secondary or postsecondary institutions, their admission criteria and/or their curricular offerings.

3. not offer or accept any reward or remuneration from a secondary school, college, university, agency, or organization for placement or recruitment of students in the United States.
   Members will:
    a. be compensated in the form of a fixed salary, rather than commissions or bonuses based on the number of students recruited;
    b. not contract with secondary school personnel for remunerations for referred students.

4. not employ agents who are compensated on a per capita basis[1] when recruiting students outside the United States, unless ensuring they and their agents conduct themselves with accountability, transparency, and integrity[2];
   Members will:
    a. ensure institutional accountability by monitoring the actions of those commission-based agents acting on the institution's behalf;

[1] Footnote:
   Per capita compensation means that agents are compensated based on each student recruited. This is also referred to as "commission-based" recruiting.

[2] Footnote: NACAC will honor a moratorium on enforcement until September 2015.

6

b.   ensure transparency with a conspicuous statement on their website that indicates their institution uses agents who are compensated on a per capita basis;

c.   ensure integrity by dealing ethically and impartially with applicants and other stakeholders, honoring commitments and acting in a manner that respects the trust and confidence placed in the institutions and the individuals representing them;

d.   adhere to US recruitment and remuneration laws (US Higher Education Act) for US citizens, where applicable;

e.   not contract with secondary school personnel for remunerations for referred students.

5.   be responsible for compliance with applicable laws and regulations with respect to students' rights to privacy by:

a.   establishing policies with respect to secondary school and college and university representatives for the release of students' names. Any policy that authorizes the release of students' names should indicate that the release be made only with the students' permission and be consistent with applicable laws and regulations;

b.   recognizing that permission may take the form of a general consent to release of the students' names;

c.   abiding by regulations in the *Family Educational Rights and Privacy Act* (FERPA), when applicable.

B. Admission, Financial Aid and Testing Policies and Procedures
All members agree they will:

1.   not publicly announce the amount of need-based aid awarded to any student without his/her permission.

a.   Given the complexity of aid packaging and the possibility that merit-based scholarships may also have some basis in financial need, members must take great care in publishing or posting, electronically or in print, the scholarship amounts of individual students when doing so may inadvertently reveal information about need-based awards.

3.   not make unethical or unprofessional requests of other admission counseling professionals.
Examples of unprofessional or unethical requests could include:

a.   making disparaging remarks about the services of school-based counselors or independent counselors when responding to requests from parents or students;

b.   independent counselors contacting school officials directly, instead of working through their clients for academic or personal information;

7

Statement of Principles of Good Practice *Interpretations of Mandatory Practices*

    c.   coercing or demeaning postsecondary institutional representatives if such institutions are unable to participate or attend local school events;

    d.   offering favors in return for counselors' listings of their best or strongest students for recruitment purposes;

    e.   creating an expectation of entitlement with regard to admission to specific institutions.

4.   send and receive information about candidates in confidence by honoring all applicable laws and regulations with respect to the confidential nature of such data. Members will honor applicable school policies, laws, regulations including the Family Education Rights and Privacy Act (FERPA).

Examples include:

    a.   admission officers not revealing the admission or denial status of applicants when using website or group email announcements;

    b.   secondary school personnel should not post lists of admitted students to specific colleges when doing so reveals applicants denied admission.

5.   consider transcripts official only when transmitted in a confidential manner, from the secondary or postsecondary institution(s) attended by the applicant.

    a.   The receiving institution will have full discretion in determining preferred and/or acceptable methods of transmission.

6.   not use minimum test scores as the sole criterion for admission, advising or for the awarding of financial aid.

    a.   Financial aid is defined as grants, loans, work-study, and scholarships. This practice does not apply to scholarship and financial aid programs that fall under state mandates.

8.   provide in a timely manner, accurate, legible, and complete transcripts for all students for admission or scholarships.

    a.   A complete transcript includes all attempted courses. However, when school and/or district policy prohibits the inclusion of all coursework, the transcript or school profile must state the institutional policies on recording repeated courses and indicate whether grades from all courses attempted are included in the cumulative GPA calculation.

9.   counsel students to abide by the application requirements and restrictions when they file.

    a.   The use of multiple admission plans by colleges and universities often results in confusion among students, parents and college admission counseling

8

professionals. NACAC believes institutions must clearly state policies, and counselors are advised to assist students with their understanding of the various admission decision options. The following outlines agreed-upon definitions and conditions.

10. **Non-Restrictive Application Plans:** All of these plans allow students to wait until May 1 to confirm enrollment.

Regular Decision is the application process in which a student submits an application to an institution by a specified date and receives a decision within a reasonable and clearly stated period of time. A student may apply to other institutions without restriction.

Rolling Admission is the application process in which an institution reviews applications as they are completed and renders admission decisions to students throughout the admission cycle. A student may apply to other institutions without restriction.

Early Action (EA) is the application process in which students apply to an institution of preference and receive a decision well in advance of the institution's regular response date. Students admitted under Early Action are not obligated to accept the institution's offer of admission or to submit a deposit prior to May 1. Under non-restrictive Early Action, a student may apply to other colleges.

Restrictive Application Plans: These are plans that allow institutions to limit students from applying to other early plans.

Early Decision (ED) is the application process in which students make a commitment to a first-choice institution where, if admitted, they definitely will enroll. While pursuing admission under an Early Decision plan, students may apply to other institutions, but may have only one Early Decision application pending at any time. Should a student who applies for financial aid not be offered an award that makes attendance possible, the student may decline the offer of admission and be released from the Early Decision commitment. The institution must notify the applicant of the decision within a reasonable and clearly stated period of time after the Early Decision deadline. Usually, a nonrefundable deposit must be made well in advance of May 1. The institution will respond to an application for financial aid at or near the time of an offer of admission.

Institutions with Early Decision plans may restrict students from applying to other early plans. Institutions will clearly articulate their specific policies in their Early Decision agreement.

Statement of Principles of Good Practice *Interpretations of Mandatory Practices*

Restrictive Early Action (REA) is the application process in which students make application to an institution of preference and receive a decision well in advance of the institution's regular response date. Institutions with Restrictive Early Action plans place restrictions on student applications to other early plans. Institutions will clearly articulate these restrictions in their Early Action policies and agreements with students. Students admitted under Restrictive Early Action are not obligated to accept the institution's offer of admission or to submit a deposit prior to May 1.

II. Postsecondary Members—Interpretations and Monitoring
A. Promotion and Recruitment
All postsecondary members agree they will:

1. state clearly the requirements for the first-year and transfer admission and enrollment processes, including secondary school preparation, standardized testing, financial aid, housing and notification deadlines, and refund procedures by:

    a. being responsible for the accurate representation and promotion of their admission calendar, academic offerings, housing application and deposit deadlines and campus and community descriptions written and electronic communications and presentations for students, parents and counseling personnel;

    b. being responsible for the development of publications, written communications presentations, i.e., college nights, college days and college fairs, used for their institutions' promotional and recruitment activities;

    c. stating clearly and precisely the requirements for secondary preparation, admission tests and transfer student admission;

    d. providing students, families and secondary schools with the most comprehensive information about costs of attendance and opportunities for all types of financial aid, and state the specific relationship between and among admission and financial aid practices and policies;

    e. providing accurate information about opportunities/selection for institutional housing, deadline dates for housing deposits, housing deposit refunds, and describing policies for renewal availability of such institutional housing;

    f. speaking forthrightly, accurately and comprehensively when presenting their institutions to counseling personnel, prospective students and their families;

    g. identifying the source and year of study when institutional publications and/or media communications cite published academic programs, academic rigor or reputations, or athletic rankings;

    h. providing accurate and specific descriptions of any special programs or support services available to students with handicapping conditions, physical and/or learning disabilities and/or other special needs;

    i. clearly stating all deadlines (including time zone) for application, notification, housing, and candidates' reply requirements for both admission and financial aid;

    j. clearly publicizing policies relating to placement by tests, awarding of credit and other policies based on test results.

Statement of Principles of Good Practice *Interpretations of Mandatory Practices*

B.   Admission, Financial Aid and Testing Policies and Procedures
All postsecondary members agree they will:

2. not require or ask candidates or the secondary schools to indicate the order of the candidates' college or university preferences, except under Early Decision.
    a. postsecondary members can assess the students' level of interest, but not through any type of rank order or question about first choice.

3. permit first-year candidates for fall admission to choose among offers of admission and institutionally-affiliated financial aid and scholarships until May 1 and state this deadline explicitly in their offers of admission.
    a. It is understood that May 1 will be viewed as the postmark and/or submission date for electronic submissions. When May 1 falls on a Sunday or holiday, May 2 becomes the recognized date;
    b. offers of admission must clearly state whether deposits submitted by students prior to May 1 are refundable or non-refundable. Making a deposit refundable, however, still obligates an institution to abide by the May 1 Candidates Reply Date;
    c. colleges will neither retract nor adversely alter their offers of admission and/or financial aid prior to May 1 for candidates who choose not to reply until that date, nor will they state or imply that candidates might incur such a penalty by waiting until May 1 (including time zone) to submit an enrollment deposit;
    d. the May 1 deadline also applies to any academic major or special program to which the candidate has been offered admission. Examples of special programs can include, but are not limited to, honors programs, dual-enrollment master's, or professional-degree programs;
    e. candidates admitted under an Early Decision program are a recognized exception to this practice.

4. not offer exclusive incentives that provide opportunities for students applying or admitted Early Decision that are not available to students admitted under other admission options.
    a. Examples of exclusive incentives include special dorms for ED admits, honors programs only for ED admits, full, need-based financial aid packages for ED admits only, special scholarships for ED admits only, any promise of an advantage in the admission process if student(s) convert from Regular Admission to Early Decision.

5. work with their institutions' senior administrative offices to ensure institutionally-affiliated financial aid and scholarship offers and housing are not used to manipulate commitments prior to May 1.
    a. While it is understood that institutions with limited housing may need to adopt a first-come, first-served policy for assigning on-campus housing, it is recommended that any enrollment or housing deposits they require to secure on-campus housing should be fully refundable if the student cancels

11

Statement of Principles of Good Practice *Interpretations of Mandatory Practices*

admission by May 1. It is at the discretion of each institution whether to refund fees associated with applications/contracts, but deposits should be refunded.

6. establish wait list procedures that ensure that no student on any wait list is asked for a deposit to remain on the wait list or for a commitment to enroll prior to receiving an official written offer of admission. Written notification may include mail or electronic communications.
   a. Wait list is an admission decision option utilized by institutions to protect against shortfalls in enrollment, in light of fluctuations in yields. By placing a student on the wait list, an institution does not initially offer or deny admission, but extends to the candidate the possibility of admission not later than August 1;
   b. institutions should state if they are recognizing the time zone for the institution's location or student's location.

7. state the specific relationship among admission and financial aid practices and policies. Colleges and universities may apply enrollment strategies to decisions to admit, wait list or deny students on the basis of stated or unstated financial need. Examples include:
   a. colleges that might prioritize wait lists by students' level of financial need;
   b. institutions that employ "need aware" admission for the bottom 10 percent of the class.

10. not knowingly offer financial aid packages to students committed to attend other institutions, unless the students initiate such inquiries. Athletic scholarships, which adhere to nationally-established signing periods, are a recognized exception to this provision.

   a. The National Collegiate Athletic Association (NCAA) has established bylaws, operational manuals and legislative directives guiding Division I, II, and III sports for men and women. Each NCAA division has its own set of rules and bylaws that govern intercollegiate athletics. In addition to divisional regulations, there are playing rules committees that set rules for specific sports. Each sport includes calendars regulating quiet periods, dead periods, evaluation periods,

   contact periods, and eventually, National Letter of Intent signing dates that occur in November, February and April. All such dates are in advance of May 1, the National Candidates Reply Date for admission. NACAC will continue to work with the NCAA to recognize May 1 as a critical date on the admission calendar. *For more information on NCAA deadlines, dates and requirements, visit www.NCAA.org.*

Statement of Principles of Good Practice *Interpretations of Mandatory Practices*

11. initially report on all first-year admitted or enrolled students, including subgroups in the reporting of test scores. If data on subgroup populations are also provided, clear explanations of who is included in the subgroup population will be made.

    a. Postsecondary members will furnish data describing the currently enrolled freshman class and will describe in published profiles all members of the enrolling freshman class;

    b. subgroups within the profile may be presented separately because of their unique character or special circumstances.

12. not establish any application deadlines for first-year candidates for fall admission prior to October 15 and will give equal consideration to all applications received by that date.

    a. Colleges and universities may welcome the initiation of applications from first-year students prior to the notification date and earliest application deadlines. Any incentives offered, including but not limited to application fee waivers, essay waivers, scholarships, housing, etc., must be honored at least through October 15;

    b. the earliest application deadline does not apply to juniors who have completed their requirements for high school graduation and are seeking early admission or joint opportunities to attend high school and community or postsecondary institutions. Admission officers should advise secondary school counselors of their policies to ensure compliance.

III. Counseling Members—Interpretations and Monitoring

A. Promotion and Recruitment

All counseling members agree they will:

1. establish a policy for the release of students' names and other confidential information, consistent with applicable laws and regulations.

    a. permission may be a general consent to any release of the students' names;

    b. secondary school members should be sensitive to the students' academic, athletic or other abilities, when releasing students' names.

B. Admission, Financial Aid and Testing Policies and Procedures

All counseling members agree they will:

1. provide colleges and universities with a description of the school's marking system, if available, that will provide some indication of grade distribution that may include the rank in class and/or grade point average.

    a. Members will disclose and clearly explain any type of weighing system that is used in determining class rank, grade point average and/or individual grades.

Statement of Principles of Good Practice *Interpretations of Mandatory Practices*

2.   provide, as permissible by law, accurate descriptions of the candidates' personal qualities relevant to the admission process.
     a.   The phrase "permissible by law" includes school policies as well as state or local regulations governing the release of student information;
     b.   counselors or school personnel will provide as much information as permitted by the Family Education Rights and Privacy Act (FERPA) and/or applicable school, local or state policies with the understanding that permission may take the form of a general consent to any release of student information.

6.   work with school officials and other relevant individuals to keep test results confidential as governed by law and local regulations.
     a.   School personnel should recognize that individual test scores are the property of the student and should not be revealed for any purpose without prior permission;
     b.   if individual test score information is requested or required by a postsecondary institution or third party, counselors and school personnel will honor the Family Educational Rights and Privacy Act (FERPA) and/or applicable school, local or state policies and regulations. Permission may take the form of a general consent to any release of student information.

Statement of Principles of Good Practice
Best Practices

I. All Members—Best Practices
All members should:

    A. indicate that their institutions are NACAC members and have endorsed the principles contained in the association's Statement of Principles of Good Practice (SPGP);

    B. inform those involved in counseling students in the postsecondary process about the content of the SPGP;

    C. be sensitive to students applying for admission to postsecondary institutions in other countries that may have different deadlines and timelines than those in the United States;

    D. familiarize themselves with published inter-association standards for educational and psychological testing, particularly with respect to test score use and interpretation, test bias and score differences between subgroups;

    E. educate staff in understanding the concepts of test measurement, test interpretation, and test use so they may consider standardized tests in their appropriate context. Such education may be obtained from NACAC, institutions of higher education, or other associations independent of companies that sponsor the test or test preparation activities or have stated positions for or against test usage. In addition, all members that make use of admission tests should acquire education and/or training in the appropriate use of specific tests from the sponsoring agencies.

II. Postsecondary Members—Best Practices
    A. Promotion and Recruitment
    All postsecondary members should:

        1. exercise appropriate responsibility for all people whom the institution involves in admission, promotional and recruitment activities (including alumni, coaches, students, faculty, and other institutional representatives);

        2. be responsible for assuring that admission consulting or management firms engaged by the institution adhere to the principles of the SPGP.

    B. Admission, Financial Aid and Testing Policies and Procedures
    All postsecondary members should:

        1. provide in the notification letter or electronic communication of those applicants offered a place on the wait list a history that describes the number of students offered places on the wait lists, the number accepting places, the number offered admission, and the availability of financial aid and housing;

        2. allow students a reasonable amount of time (at least 72 hours or May 1, whichever is later) to respond to an offer of admission from that institution's wait list and gain admission to that institution's incoming class. This offer of admission should be a written or electronic communication to the student. Postsecondary institutions should also strive to fully inform wait list students of their financial aid and housing opportunities, if different from their normal policies. Postsecondary institutions should not require a commitment from a student until the financial aid award and housing options, if any, have been provided;

Statement of Principles of Good Practice *Best Practices*

3. make applicants aware, in official communications, of summer or mid-year admission if such programs are available;

4. not apply newly-revised requirements to the disadvantage of candidates whose secondary school courses were established in accordance with earlier requirements;

5. not discriminate in the admission selection process against applicants based on the particular application form they use, provided that the college or university has agreed explicitly to accept the particular version of the application;

6. admit candidates on the basis of academic and personal criteria rather than financial need. This provision does not apply to international students ineligible for federal student assistance;

7. conduct institutional research to inquire into the most effective use of tests for admission decisions;

8. refrain from the public reporting of mean and median admission test scores and, instead, report scores by the middle 50 percent of the scores of all first-year applicants, admitted and/or enrolled students ;

9. view financial aid as supplementary to the efforts of students' families when students are not self-supporting;

10. meet the full need of accepted students to the extent possible, within the institutions' capabilities;

11. state that eligibility for, and packaging of, need-based and merit aid will be comparable for students admitted under Early and Regular programs;

12. refrain from asking students where else they have applied;

13. utilize an equitable process of needs analysis methodology in making expected estimates or awards of the amount of financial aid that may be available to students after documentation is provided;

14. include a current and accurate admission calendar in publications and websites. If the institution offers special admission options, such as Early Admission, Early Action, Early Decision, wait lists, or Restrictive Early Admission, the publication should define these programs and state deadline dates (including time zone), notification dates, required deposits, refund policies, and the date when the candidates must reply;

15. notify secondary schools, when possible, of admission decisions in a timely and proper manner;

16. report test scores for special subgroups that may include athletes or non-native speakers. Universities with more than one undergraduate division may report first by division and then by special subgroups within divisions. Clear explanations of who is included in the subgroup should be made. Those institutions that do not require tests or for which tests are optional will only report scores if the institution clearly and emphatically states the limits of the scores being reported;

17. clearly publicize policies, such as placement and awarding of credit, based on test results;

Statement of Principles of Good Practice *Best Practices*

18. issue a statement of disclosure as to how demonstration of student interest is used in the application process. Demonstration of student interest includes such measures as evaluating students on whether they visited campus, contacted admission representatives before or during a school visit or the frequency of email or mail contacts initiated by the students;

19. on a case-by-case basis, and when requested, grant flexibility on the institutional response deadline to admitted transfer students awaiting additional admission notifications.

III. Counseling Members—Best Practices
A. Admission, Financial Aid and Testing Policies and Procedures
All counseling members should:

1. provide programs of counseling that introduce a broad range of postsecondary opportunities to students;

2. encourage students and their families to take initiative in learning about colleges and universities;

3. provide information about opportunities and requirements for financial aid;

4. urge students to understand and discharge their responsibilities in the admission process in a timely manner;

5. counsel students and their families to notify and withdraw applications from other institutions when they have accepted an admission offer;

6. encourage students to be the sole authors of their applications and essays and counsel against inappropriate assistance on the parts of others;

7. report any significant change in a candidate's academic status or qualifications, including personal school conduct record between the time of recommendation and graduation, where permitted by applicable law;

8. establish a written policy on disclosure of disciplinary infractions in their communications to colleges;

9. provide a school profile, when applicable, that clearly describes special curricular opportunities (e.g., honors, advanced placement courses, seminars) and a comprehensive listing of all courses with an explanation of unusual abbreviations and any information required for proper understanding;

10. inform students about the tests needed for admission, where students may take them, how to interpret the results, and how test results are used for admission;

11. report, in the case of secondary schools, the middle 50 percent of all students tested by discrete grade level;

12. refrain from encouraging students to apply to particular colleges and universities to enhance the high schools' statistical records regarding the number or amount of scholarship awards received;

13. counsel students not to submit more than one admission deposit, which indicates their intent to enroll at more than one institution;

14. work with school officials and other relevant individuals to keep test results in perspective;

Statement of Principles of Good Practice *Best Practices*

15. counsel students to comply with requests for information in a timely manner;
16. counsel students who have deferred admission that they should follow any conditions imposed by the deferring institution.

Companion Guide: Statement of Principles of Good Practice: Education Monitoring Procedures and Penalties

As you have read, the SPGP includes both required and recommended practices designed to protect students in the college admission process (NACAC, 2012). The following companion guide articulates processes and penalties assigned to individual or institutional members who choose not to abide by the principles and ethical guidelines for college admission counseling. The document also provides guidance for allegations presented against individuals or institutions who are not members of NACAC or affiliate organizations. With these allegations, it is important to note that "the presiding committee shall hold in strict confidence the identities of both the original complainant and the alleged noncompliant party" (NACAC, 2012, p. 2).

STATEMENT OF PRINCIPLES OF GOOD PRACTICE:
Education, Monitoring Procedures, and Penalties

Approved by the Assembly, October 2012

Ethical college counseling and admission have been the cornerstones of the National Association for College Admission Counseling (NACAC) since its founding in 1937. The association strives to ensure principled conduct among professionals in the counseling and recruitment of students and throughout the students' consideration of their transition to postsecondary education options. The Statement of Principles of Good Practice (SPGP) was created by our founding institutions and continues to be maintained to articulate the association's preferred and recommended code of conduct. It includes practices and policies reflecting principled concerns for the ethical treatment of students and relationships among professionals in the admission process. All NACAC members agree to abide by the SPGP in the execution of their work.

The Admission Practices Committee of NACAC, together with the Admission Practices Committees of the affiliates, are responsible for promoting awareness of and compliance with the Statement of Principles of Good Practice (SPGP). The Admission Practices Committee primarily seeks to educate admission and counseling professionals and their institutions on ethical college admission standards and to assist them in fully integrating similar policies and procedures into their practices. The goal of the Admission Practices Committee is to seek full compliance with all provisions of the SPGP on a voluntary basis. Believing that member professionals and institutions wish to practice high ethical standards, one of the committee's chief functions is that of education. In addition, the committee monitors compliance with the SPGP, investigates alleged infractions, and recommends the application of penalties when necessary. Penalties may include issuance of a Statement of Noncompliance, exclusion from NACAC-sponsored events, suspension of membership and membership privileges, or termination of membership.

The Statement of Principles of Good Practice (SPGP) is a complex document comprised of both required and recommended practices designed to protect students in the college admission process. The SPGP's format includes the following:

The **Mandatory Practices** of the SPGP section outlines required practices and, as such, these practices will be monitored and enforced by the national and affiliate Admission Practices Committees.

The **Interpretations of Mandatory Practices** section includes further explanations or examples to enhance understanding of the Mandatory statements. A statement with an asterisk in the Mandatory section will have a corresponding statement in the Interpretations section.

The final section, **Best Practices**, offers recommended behaviors or guidelines for good practice but will not be strictly monitored or enforced. They represent how admission counseling professionals should function in the execution of their professional business.

Statement of Principles of Good Practice: Education, Monitoring Procedures, and Penalties

A. *Procedures*

Any allegation of noncompliance with the Mandatory Practices of the Statement of Principles of Good Practice shall be referred to the appropriate Admission Practices Committee as follows:

NACAC members who hold membership with an affiliate:

The allegation shall be referred to the affiliate's Admission Practices Committee. If adequate investigation or resolution cannot be made at the affiliate level, the allegation shall be referred to the national Admission Practices Committee for further action.

NACAC members who do not hold membership with an affiliate:

The allegation shall be referred directly to the national Admission Practices Committee

Parties who are neither NACAC nor affiliate members:

The allegation shall be referred to NACAC's Chief Executive Officer or designated staff member who will consult with the national Admission Practices Committee on the appropriate response. To preserve the anonymity of all parties involved in the allegation process, the complainant and the presiding committee shall hold in strict confidence the identities of both the original complainant and the alleged noncompliant party.

1. Allegations of infractions against a member of NACAC who is also a member of an affiliate shall be reported to the chairperson of the affiliate Admission Practices Committee which shall become the presiding committee. The complainant must agree to maintain confidentiality while the complaint is being processed. The chair shall then notify the president of the affiliate of which the noncompliant party is a member.

2. a) Any allegation shall be sent to the presiding affiliate Admission Practices Committee chairperson in writing and shall contain as much specific documentation or evidence as possible. Upon examining the allegation and supporting information, the chairperson shall determine which specific provision(s) of the Mandatory Practices of the SPGP is (are) involved in the alleged noncompliance.

   b) When a party is accused of violating the SPGP, the chairperson shall immediately notify that party of the alleged violation of the SPGP and of the potential noncompliance issue(s). Such notification shall be in writing and shall direct the noncompliant party to respond in writing to each allegation within 30 days. If the noncompliant party does not respond to the initial communication within the specified time, the presiding affiliate chairperson shall refer the complaint to the national Admission Practices Committee.

   c) If the written response by the alleged noncompliant party demonstrates to the satisfaction of the presiding affiliate Admission Practices Committee that there is, in fact, compliance with the Mandatory Practices of the SPGP, then the matter shall be closed.

   d) If the noncompliant party confirms that past practice has not been in compliance with the Mandatory Practices of the SPGP but offers to amend the practice in the future, the presiding affiliate Admission Practices Committee may declare the matter closed.

Statement of Principles of Good Practice: Education, Monitoring Procedures, and Penalties

e) If the presiding affiliate Admission Practices Committee determines noncompliance and the non-compliant party does not offer to amend the practice, the presiding affiliate Admission Practices Committee will take the following action:

- If the practice in question is a Best Practice, the presiding affiliate Admission Practices Committee will educate the noncompliant party as to why the stated practice should be adhered to and will request voluntary compliance.

- If the practice is a Mandatory Practices of the SPGP, the presiding affiliate Admission Practices Committee will refer the case to the national Admission Practices Committee and notify the complainant.

3. The noncompliant party, the original complainant or the affiliate Admission Practices Committee that initiated the complaint may appeal the presiding affiliate Admission Practices Committee's findings to the national Admission Practices Committee within 30 days from the date of the presiding affiliate Admission Practices Committee's findings.

a) The noncompliant party (or other appealing party) shall be entitled to offer new evidence or contest the conclusions of the presiding affiliate Admission Practices Committee to the national Admission Practices Committee via written communications and/or conference calls.

b) The noncompliant party (and other appealing party), and members of the presiding affiliate Admission Practices Committee shall be given at least 30 days prior notice of such deliberations.

c) The affiliate's decision will remain in place, if the decision is not appealed.

d) If an appeal is filed, penalties will not be imposed at that time, pending results of the appeal.

4. In the event an appeal goes to the national Admission Practices Committee after consideration of all the facts relating to the allegations, the committee shall notify the appealing party, the noncompliant party and the presiding affiliate Admission Practices Committee of its decision, including whether a penalty is to be imposed.

5. The national Admission Practices Committee may impose penalties, including a Statement of Non-compliance or exclusion from NACAC-sponsored events. In accordance with NACAC Bylaws, Article V, Discipline, only the NACAC Board of Directors may censure, suspend or expel any NACAC member. Therefore, the national Admission Practices Committee may only recommend such action to the Board of Directors.

6. The Board of Directors will then consider all information, including the recommendation of the national Admission Practices Committee, to suspend or expel a member for non-compliance with the SPGP.

3

Statement of Principles of Good Practice: Education, Monitoring Procedures, and Penalties

7. The decision of the Board of Directors shall be final, unless the noncompliant party files an appeal with the Board of Directors within 30 days after the date of the decision of the board.

8. In this case, neither the affiliate Admission Practices Committee nor the national Admission Practices Committee shall publish the decision, pending results of the appeal. The decisions of the national Board of Directors shall be final and binding on all parties.

B. Penalties

The NACAC leadership, in consultation with the national and/or local Admission Practices Committee(s), may impose on the guilty party one or more of the following penalties:

1. **Statement of Noncompliance:** The guilty party will be formally notified of noncompliance with the SPGP and will be asked to desist engaging in such practices. All members of NACAC and appropriate affiliate leadership may be notified of the practices engaged in by the accused party that have been found to violate the Mandatory Practices of the SPGP.

2. **Exclusion from NACAC-sponsored events, including, but not limited to:** NACAC National College Fairs, professional development opportunities and the national conference. Those out of compliance will not be permitted to register or pay non-member fees for any NACAC-sponsored events. All members of NACAC and appropriate affiliate leadership will be notified of the practices engaged in by the noncompliant party that has been found to violate the Mandatory Practices of the Statement of Principles of Good Practice.

3. **Suspension of Membership and Membership Privileges:** All members of NACAC and appropriate affiliate leadership will be:

   - notified of the practices engaged in by the guilty party that have been found to violate the Mandatory Practices of the SPGP;

   - notified that the NACAC membership privileges of the guilty party have been suspended. Such suspension will last until lifted by the Board of Directors upon the recommendation of the national Admission Practices Committee.

4. **Termination of Membership in NACAC:** All members of NACAC and appropriate affiliate leadership shall be notified in association communication venues of the practices engaged in by the guilty party that have been found to violate the SPGP and that the membership of the guilty party in NACAC has been terminated.

CURSORY REVIEW OF ETHICAL GUIDELINES FOR **AACRAO, ASCA, HECA, IECA,** AND **NAFSA**

Ethical guidelines, in any field, suggest reflective and responsive practices with stakeholders in mind. Considering secondary and higher education professional associations, ethical commitments are communicated in a variety of ways. As suggested earlier in this chapter, the professional setting of counselors determines which other ethical guidelines individuals may need to be fully aware of and operating within. Here, we highlight more information about AACRAO, ASCA, HECA, IECA, and NAFSA. Albeit cursory, it is helpful to close this chapter's discussion of ethical practice by highlighting content and features of ethical standards from the previously mentioned professional associations.

AACRAO. At the time of this text, the American Association of Collegiate Registrars and Admission Officers (AACRAO) (2010) offers three declarations that articulate ethical principles for its members:

> AACRAO members shall: [1] conduct themselves with integrity, fairness, honesty, and respect for others; [2] avoid conflicts between personal interests and professional responsibilities, and resolve perceived conflicts through full disclosure and independent review; [3] dispense complete, accurate, understandable, and truthful information and advice at all times (AACRAO, 2010).

Complimentary to these principles, AACRAO states close to 20 standards of professional practice for its members. These standards incorporate the following themes, along with several others not mentioned: safeguarding institutions' academic integrity; maintenance of privacy and confidentiality of institutional and student records; steward and objectively enforce policies and practices governing institutions; promote postsecondary educational access, broadly and equally; support the development of students, their talents and interests; and disseminate and exercise sound management of institutional records, principles and resources (AACRAO, 2010).

ASCA. The American School Counselor Association (ASCA) (2010) offers five tenets of professional responsibility, which largely center and revolve around the student:

[1] Each person has the right to be respected, be treated with dignity and have access to a comprehensive school counseling program that advocates for and affirms all students from diverse populations including: ethnic/racial identity, age, economic status, abilities/disabilities; language, immigration status, sexual orientation, gender, gender identity/expression, family type, religious/spiritual identity and appearance;

[2] Each person has the right to receive the information and support needed to move toward self-direction and self-development and affirmation within one's group identities, with special care being given to students who have historically not received adequate educational services, e.g. students of color, students living at a low socio-economic status, students with disabilities and students from non-dominant language backgrounds;

[3] Each person has the right to understand the full magnitude and meaning of his/her educational choices and how those choices will affect future opportunities;

[4] Each person has the right to privacy and thereby the right to expect the school-counselor/student relationship to comply with all laws, policies and ethical standards pertaining to confidentiality in the school setting;

[5] Each person has the right to feel safe in school environments that school counselors help create, free from abuse, bullying, neglect, harassment or other forms of violence (ASCA, 2010).

The ASCA (2010) **Ethical Standards for School Counselors** statement uses these five tenets as a foundation of "integrity, leadership and professionalism" as further described in subsections defining their members' work. These subsections include the following areas of responsibility: students; parents and guardians; colleagues and professional associates; school, communities and families; self; profession; and the maintenance of these standards. As this text in its entirety focuses on getting students to college, a particular ASCA standard emerges as instrumental in our discussion: Professional school counselors "are concerned with the educational, academic, career, personal and social needs and encourage the maximum development of every student" (ASCA, A.1.a, 2010).

HECA. Similar to NACAC (as discussed in the previous chapter), the Higher Education Consultants Association (HECA) (2009) suggests a framework of core values that govern the work of its members: sound advice; integrity; respect; and confidentiality. HECA recognizes that any statement of standards or ethical practices cannot assume the responsibility of addressing "all questions or concerns that might arise in the conduct of working with students, families, high schools, colleges and universities…" Therefore, HECA presents "a framework, a guide" that includes three distinct categorizations for standards, as well as an expressed code of conduct for individual consultants. The three categories are: standards for working with students and families; standards with respect to relations with high schools and colleges; and standards of the profession (which has direct alignment to the SPGP).

IECA. Our colleagues at the Independent Educational Consultants Association (IECA) also offer a statement of effective practice set to provide guidance with regard to ethical principles. IECA (2014) categorizes their principles across six content areas: competence; multiple relationships and potential conflicts of interest; relationships with students and families; relationships with colleges, programs and/or schools; relationships with other educational consultants; and advertising and other public statements. A distinguishing note about IECA's statement is the import of individual's training and expertise, as it relates to professional competencies:

> Members practice within the boundaries of their competence, which derives from relevant education, training, acquired knowledge and professional experience. They are straightforward about what they are—and are not—competent to do it. In cases with elements outside their competence, they either consult with or refer clients to appropriate colleagues; and

> Members continually update their knowledge of educational options, both in breadth and in depth, through such activities as site visits, attendance at professional conferences, continuing education and professional reading (IECA, 2014).

These two considerations, in some form, are present across the other associations. However, its statement here speaks to a commitment to continuous development and expertise in practice.

NAFSA. Lastly, the NAFSA: Association of International Educators (NAFSA) offers context for its **Statement of Ethical Principles:**

> Knowledge and awareness of other peoples, countries, cultures and beliefs is of utmost importance. As international educators we recognize that such knowledge is fundamental to the formation of educated persons and informed citizens, and, increasingly, a key to professional, business, and personal success. The acquisition of this knowledge depends, to a great extent, on high-quality programs of international education and exchange. International educators are dedicated to providing such programs and services with the highest level of integrity and responsibility. To accomplish this, we must attend carefully and actively to the ethical obligations that emerge from our relationships with students, scholars, our institutions, international partners, and other legitimate stakeholders (NAFSA, 2009, p. 1).

NAFSA's statement includes descriptions of eight principles: integrity; respect for the law; quality; competence; diversity; transparency; access; and responsiveness. These principles accelerate and define NAFSA's commitment to service, as expressed in the two ideas captured here: "… we will work to extend and improve international education in all its forms and at all levels, including advocating for programs, policies, regulations and laws that reflect these principles"; and "we will work aggressively for the realization of these principles in our personal and professional conduct, throughout our institutions, and in organizations with which we affiliate" (NAFSA, 2009, p. 2).

FURTHER AWARENESS OF **FERPA** AND **NACAC** COMPLIANCE CENTER

FERPA. First and foremost, members of the aforementioned associations, including NACAC, are expected to be well-versed and aware of federal- and state-level laws, statues and policies that inform and/or govern professional activities or expectations. As mentioned earlier in this chapter, the Family Educational Rights and Privacy Act (FERPA) (20 U.S.C. § 1232g; 34 CFR Part 99) is a federal law that impacts college admission professionals. This law applies to all educational institutions receiving funds from the US Department of Education. FERPA stipulates the privacy of student education records; these rights and privileges are held among educational institutions and families until a student reaches the age of 18 or enrolls in postsecondary educational opportunities. For more information about FERPA, you are encouraged to visit the Family Policy Compliance Office Web site, within the US Department of Education, as well as the NACAC Compliance Center, which is described below.

College admission professionals at both secondary and postsecondary institutions must be knowledgeable of FERPA. This awareness is especially imperative as students and families begin to experience the implementation of the law as the student transitions into postsecondary educational institutions. Along with FERPA, federal- and state-level statues that pertain to college enrollment—integrity and honesty of college admission and financial aid applications—are also critical to this conversation regarding ethical practices.

NACAC Compliance Center. The Compliance Center serves as a tremendous online resource for college admission counseling professionals. This resources is ever-evolving, capturing the federal policy considerations for professionals serving at both secondary and postsecondary levels. The contents stand to complement the SPGP, in that they articulate federal statues impacting the transition of students to college. As a means to ensure accuracy and delivery of the most current information, NACAC is a member of the Higher Education Compliance Alliance.

At the time this chapter was written, those who visit the resources on NACAC's Web site will find information regarding FERPA, as well as the following: incentive compensation; gainful employment; the Clery Act; Telephone Consumer Protection Act; veterans; misrepresentation; and verification of high school completion. It is important that professionals view this site as an essential part of continuous learning, training and professional development.

REFERENCES

American Association of Collegiate Registrars and Admission Officers (AACRAO). (2010). *Ethics and practice*. Retrieved from *http://aacrao.org/home/about/ethics-and-practice. Washington, DC: Author.*

American School Counselor Association (ASCA). (2010). *Ethical standards for school counselors*. Retrieved from *http://school-counseling-program.weebly.com/asca-standardsethics.html*. Alexandria, VA: Author.

Higher Education Consultants Association (HECA). (2009). *Higher Education Consultants Association standards and ethics*. Retrieved from *http://hecaonline.org/standards_and_ethics*.

Independent Educational Consultants Association (IECA). (2014). *Principles of good practice*. Retrieved from *http://www.iecaonline.com/pogp.html*. Fairfax, VA: Author.

National Association for College Admission Counseling (NACAC). (2014). *Statement of principles of good practice*. Retrieved from *http://www.nacacnet.org/about/Governance/Policies/Pages/default.aspx*. Arlington, VA: Author.

National Association for College Admission Counseling (NACAC). (2012). *Statement of principles of good practice: Education, monitoring procedures and penalties*. Retrieved from *http://www.nacacnet.org/about/Governance/Policies/Pages/default.aspx*. Arlington, VA: Author.

NAFSA Association of International Educators (NAFSA). (2009). *Statement of ethical principles*. Retrieved from *http://www.nafsa.org/Learn_About_NAFSA/Governance_Documents/Ethics_And_Principles/Statement_Of_Ethics/NAFSA_s_Statement_of_Ethical_Principles/*. Washington, DC: Author.

II. Defining the Work of College Counselors

FROM THEORY TO PRACTICE

Jonathan D. Mathis, PhD

ABOUT "BRIDGING TEXTS"

The editors of this text find great utility in dialogue between the authors and consumers. As such, we have created "Bridging Texts" to offer some reflection and some of our thoughts as the text transitions from one section to another. It is within these short passages that we share some of our take-aways, as well as content that might help frame inquiry while reading. Consider these bridging texts *as a means to continue the conversation, while connecting you to the concepts embedded in the next section.*

. . . .

When scholars write about praxis, they often refer to the manner in which professionals translate theory into action, or practice. The fourth edition of *Fundamentals* begins with chapters that help college admission counseling professionals understand the history, terrain and frameworks governing the work needed for and occurring within the field. It is within these chapters that we are introduced to the foundation of the college counseling professional, as well as how this role is best understood and defined within and outside of secondary school settings. In particular, this discussion includes national organizations and their efforts to support counseling professionals.

Second, this section presents several conceptual and theoretical frameworks suggested to advance the work of counselors, as well as educators who support the college application process. As a cross-section of ideas, the authors helped us to understand the positionality of counselor and student—constantly aware of current development, aspirations and performance, while simultaneously considering the experiences, considerations or opportunities that will cultivate future development.

We then learn about the role and importance of college access and success programming, with attention to program design, structure and student outcomes. Scholars present counselors as conduits who increase access and create opportunities. This idea of counselors as conduits continues in the fourth chapter.

The fourth chapter offers a detailed account highlighting the formation of NACAC, including mission, vision, member convictions, and competencies. It is within this chapter that the authors suggest one of the greatest strengths of NACAC, outside of its premier focus on ethical practice, is the connectivity of its members. The authors use social capital and institutional agents to highlight these points.

Lastly, this section rounds out with an important view of NACAC's Statement of Principles of Good Practice (SPGP) and its influence on practice, ethical and professional performance within the field. The mandates and recommendations highlighted within this chapter set the tone for the remaining sections of the text, especially our move to content that describes what many might describe as the *nuts and bolts of practice*.

As you begin to read section two, think about the manner in which you might see theory, ethical and legal considerations translate into practice. Beginning with the design and operation of the college counseling office and closing with guidance on effective letters of recommendation, the authors offer both conceptual and candid advice for novice and continuing professionals in the field of college admission counseling. Consider how these ideas continue to reinforce theory-to-practice and how these efforts might be best structured to support social capital exchanges, academic and identity development, and ethical practice.

The chapters in the next section include discussions that help us to ground the work in schools. Consider data-driven decision-making across all the enclosed chapters, especially while applying the various suggested conceptual and theoretical frameworks.

Chapter 6:   College Counseling: Making It Work

Lisa Sohmer
@sohmernyc

The world of college counseling and admission is changing to expand beyond high school walls and college campuses. The process is idolized, mythologized and vilified and is the subject of speculation, adulation, gossip, and academic research. As counselors, we are challenged to make the process understandable and manageable so that students and families can make the best college choice with confidence.

In the public, college admission has a reputation for being overly complicated and mysterious, but in reality, the process of selecting and applying to college is pragmatic and student-centered. Everything that students and families, not to mention their counselors, need is available—as long as they know where to look and

CREATING A COMFORT ZONE: THE COLLEGE OFFICE

The thought of applying to college is daunting, and many students don't know where to begin. They may even be reluctant. Even the ones who are eager to get started will have questions and concerns. With so many unknowns, students need a welcoming place where they can find the information and resources that they need.

Engage Students in the Process

"If you build it, they will come" is an oft-quoted line from the 1989 movie, *Field of Dreams,* and the notion holds true for the college counseling process. Counselors

> *In the public, college admission has a reputation for being overly complicated and mysterious, but in reality, the process of selecting and applying to college is pragmatic and student-centered.*

whom to ask. As counselors, we need to take the lead on the research, work together to share what we know, and collaborate with our college colleagues to help increase the number of students who graduate from high school prepared to find the right college and succeed when they get there.

Being a college counselor is an extraordinary opportunity. As the liaison between secondary and postsecondary education, counselors are the bridges that take students from the known high school world to the unknown world of college. Getting students from here to there—the ultimate definition of access—is the primary goal of college counseling. Counselors provide information, remove obstacles and guide students toward their postsecondary experience.

Every student is different, and there is no one-size-fits-all solution to the questions of, "Where should I go to college?" and "How will I get there?" But making the process transparent and enabling students to feel comfortable in their exploration and aspiration will let them find their individual answers.

who create a positive and productive counseling center will involve students—even the hesitant ones—and fully engage them. Students need to understand the steps in the process and to build the confidence they need to take them. The key is communication and making it easy for students to find the information they need.

Changing students' perceptions from thinking the application process happens around them to understanding that it happens because of them is a critically important step. They need to recognize their power in the process and their responsibility to it. To be successful, students must commit to the process and make it their own. This is a critical milestone for students—the steps required to apply to college are themselves excellent training for being college students, because they are unfamiliar. They require the rapid development of new skills in research, the acquisition of information, and the ability to make reasoned decisions and manage their time. By immersing themselves in the application process, students develop these skills naturally over time and then take them along for freshman year in college.

Let Your Office Shout "College"

By the time most students enter the college process in earnest, they are juniors—even seniors—and are used to the usual ups and downs of high school. They know their teachers, their coaches, their peers; they have likely taken the PSAT, SAT and AP exams. Now comes the curve ball, because the college process is new and demanding—and necessary in order to achieve their postsecondary goals. The counselor's message should make it clear that the process is also exciting and attainable.

When students walk into the college office, everything should signal that being there and interacting with a counselor is part of their "college checklist." Set the mood by filling the walls with posters, pennants and other college swag. Check your mailbox and download PDFs that you can distribute to students. Subscribe to magazines like *MyMajors, YourTeen* and *My College Guide,* and make copies available. When representatives schedule their high school visits, ask them to bring something for your collection; they will not disappoint you. Make a stop at the bookstore part of your own campus visit routine; your souvenir may become a student's inspiration. Never forget that while some students have been raised with an expectation that they will attend college and others will need convincing, all benefit when immersed in a college-going atmosphere with the necessary tools for success. However students feel when they enter the college office, they should leave with a better understanding of how to accomplish their short-term and long-term goals.

Fill Your Bookshelf and Share Your Reading List

There is a great and growing selection of college guides and books about the process; some are general and others focus on specific groups of students and colleges. Many are available for download on e-readers. The list changes almost daily, but the tried and true include:

Books for Counselors

- *Colleges That Change Lives* by Loren Pope
- College Board's *Book of Majors*
- College Board's *International Student Handbook*
- *Fiske Guide* (also available as an iPad app)

- *K & W Guide for Students with Learning Disabilities*
- Princeton Review's *How to Pay for College Without Going Broke*
- Princeton Review Regional Guides
- *Rugg's Recs* (also available as PDF)
- The Advocate's *Guide to Colleges for LGBT Students*

Books for Families and Students (and Counselors, too)

- *Admission Matters* by John Reider and Joyce Vining Morgan
- *College Admission* by Robin Mamlet and Christine VanDeVelde
- *David and Goliath* by Malcolm Gladwell
- *Going Geek* by John Carpenter
- *I'm Going to College…And You're Not!* edited by Jennifer Delahunty
- *The Gatekeepers* by Jacques Steinberg

Learn to Think Digitally

Many of the manuals and booklets that are mailed or distributed to counselors and students are now also available in PDF format. Both "green" and space-saving, digital versions are easily emailed to students and families. Searchable archives make it possible to find articles from previous issues, so counselors are not limited to what they have personally received. Including links to articles and Web sites in communications to students and families and adding a distinct "College Counseling" section on your school's Web site creates a digital college counseling library that is available to all.

Another way to maximize access to the information that is available on the Web is creating a list of Web sites that you think are valuable and sharing them with families and students. Supplement your list by asking colleagues, families and students for the Web sites that they have used and found helpful. Your list will be fluid and will reflect your students, your school's mission and your philosophy about counseling, but the following Web sites provide a solid starting point for your research.

General College Resources

- College Board: *www.collegeboard.com*
- College Navigator: *www.nces.ed.gov/collegenavigator*
- College View: *www.collegeview.com*
- College Wiki: *www.collegelists.pbworks.com*
- Common Application: *www.commonapp.org*
- Huffington Post: *www.huffingtonpost.com*
- Naviance: *www.naviance.com*
- National Association for College Admission Counseling: *www.nacacnet.org*
- NextStep U: *nextstepu.com*

Financial Aid Resources

- Affordability and Transparency: *www.collegecost.ed.gov*
- College Answer: *www.CollegeAnswer.com*
- FAFSA: *www.fafsa.ed.gov* and *www.studentaid.ed.gov/completefafsa*
- FAFSA Forecaster: *www.fafsa4caster.gov*
- FastWeb: *www.fastweb.com*
- FinAid: *www.finaid.org*

Standardized Testing Resources

- ACT: *www.act.org*
- College Board: *www.collegeboard.com*
- Fair Test: *www.fairtest.org/university/optional*
- Kaplan: *www.kaplan.com*
- Khan Academy: *www.khanacademy.org*
- Number 2: *www.number2.com*
- Princeton Review: *www.review.com*
- TOEFL: *www.toefl.org*
- Educational Testing Service: *www.ets.org*

Resources for International Students

- EducationUSA: *www.educationusa.info*
- International Student: *www.internationalstudent.com*
- Peterson's: *www.petersons.com*

Resources for Undocumented Students

- *http://www.cuny.edu/about/resources/citizenship/info4noncitizens/info4undocumented.html*
- Repository of Resources for Undocumented Students: *http://media.collegeboard.com/digitalServices/pdf/diversity/Repository-Resources-Undocumented-Students_2012.pdf*

Resources for Students with Learning Differences

- Association on Higher Education and Disability: *www.ahead.org*
- Learning Disabilities Online: *www.ldonline.org*
- National Center for Learning Disabilities: *www.ncld.org*

And, of course, when in doubt, Google it.

Create the Tool to Meet the Need

Books and Web sites can be wonderful sources of information for students, but what if they can't find what they need? In that case, the counselor can create a tool that meets a specific demand. For example, if students are asking questions about interview skills, college visit procedures or how to navigate a college fair, the counselor can create a document with tips for making the most of these experiences. PowerPoint presentations, whether printed or emailed, are especially effective in conveying multi-step electronic processes, like completing the Common Application or registering for standardized tests.

Make Your Place a Safe Place

As you work with students throughout the college process, remember that they are vulnerable. Their confidence wavers. They feel judged. Even the strongest applicants can have a sinking feeling that everything will go wrong. Sometimes they need a place to be alone with their doubts—and then to have their concerns heard and answered. The college office should be a place where questions can be asked without hesitation or recrimination and where there are options, alternatives and choices. Developing handouts that students and families can take home after a meeting is especially helpful, particularly for families where English is not the primary language spoken at home.

There are all kinds of colleges out there—public, private, four-year, two-year, competitive, open enrollment, religious and not, big and small. Before you can encourage students to be open-minded to a variety of college "personalities," you must cultivate that same broad thinking in yourself. The most effective presentations and discussions will include reference to the many options that exist for all students and the understanding that the counselor is there to help facilitate the process and help in finding the right fit for the student.

Remember What It Felt Like to Be 17

At 16 or 17, most students don't know who they are, much less who they will be, but the application process asks them to answer new and difficult questions about their futures. The prospect of declaring a major, planning for a career, and projecting what the future may hold are new concepts for all but the most focused of high school juniors and seniors. As a result, students are especially likely to seek guidance as they search for a topic for their personal statement, the 650 words that are supposed to display their burgeoning writing ability and put their personality, strengths and life experience in the spotlight.

So often, students react to the various applications' essay questions by saying, "But I haven't done anything yet," because they feel the essay needs to contain a revelation, a dramatic moment of self-awareness or a great triumph. In truth, the essay is simply designed as a means for the student to tell a story. Starting with the essay prompt, students can ask themselves a different series of questions, like "What am I good at?" "What do I enjoy?" and "What is important to me?" as a starting place for getting to a story and a way to tell it.

Help Them Stay Connected

For seniors, the college process is all about the next step; the focus is on where they are going, what they will do there and how they will fit in. In all the excitement about the future, it is all too easy for those around them to forget that the beginning of something new means the end of something else; in this case, they are saying good-bye not just to their high schools, but also to their childhoods.

Providing college counseling means understanding the emotions of the high-school-to-college transition and having the ability to assuage the fears and uncertainty that accompany profound change. Sending a mid-August email to new alums, wishing them well and asking them to reply with their college email addresses, can underscore the counselor's support of students as they enter college and remind them that their connection to their high school is ongoing. Inviting graduates back to school before the Thanksgiving holiday extends their connection, makes them feel comfortable returning home and casts them in the role of "experts" in the eyes of current students.

KEEPING EVERYONE IN THE LOOP: SHARING WHAT YOU KNOW

What makes communication in the college process effective? Consistency, clarity and variety. Students and families need the information that the counselor provides and should be encouraged to access it in diverse ways. The college process is complicated, but finding the information that students need to feel comfortable with the process should be straightforward and easy.

There are many ways to communicate with students and families:

- Email
- Web sites
- Facebook
- Twitter
- Instagram
- Bulletin boards
- Handouts
- Questionnaires
- Surveys
- Newsletters
- College nights
- College fairs
- Individual meetings
- Parent coffees

To begin, make your mark in the **digital world** where your students live. Convince them to check their email often by sending them important messages in that format. Create trivia questions (with small prizes) that you ask only by email. Remind students that although colleges may text their enrolled students, most communicate with applicants by email, so it's important that they develop a habit of checking their email on a regular basis. Even with near constant encouragement, students tend to skim their emails, so a clear subject line—like "Important College Info" or "SAT Registration Deadlines"—will help get their attention.

Teach students to avoid the potential pitfalls of **digital etiquette** by encouraging them to review their digital footprints before they enter the application process. Ask them to consider a designated email address for their communication with colleges, and suggest that they delete any posts on Facebook and other social media sites that might be questionable. In recent years, there have been many articles in newspapers and magazines that explore and explain the stumbling blocks that students create with inappropriate use of social media. "What College Admissions Officers Don't Like Seeing on Facebook: Vulgarity, Drinking Photos and 'Illegal Activities'" (Hill, 2012) and "They Loved Your G.P.A. Then They Saw Your Tweets" (Singer, 2013) are two articles that provide clear suggestions and guidelines for counselors and students. The college process includes lessons about judgment and some are taught in the digital space.

That said, counselors, students and families should use the Internet to their best advantage. What's trending now? Facebook? Twitter? Instagram? Think about ways to enhance your own online presence. Many counselors have found that hosting a page on Facebook provides a central place for students to find college information. Others ask students to share photos from campus visits and college fairs to include on Instagram or the school Web site. Some counselors have a professional Twitter feed to share information and to retweet messages from the College Board, ACT, NACAC, and a variety of publications and organizations.

Go old school with bulletin boards, flyers and handouts. Colleges, NACAC, NACAC's affiliate associations, the College Board, and ACT are some of the many organizations and companies that will mail collateral that you can share with students and their families. Having a central bulletin board (either in the college office or a well-trafficked high school hallway) is an efficient way to share everything from your high school's CEEB code to testing dates and deadlines to the schedule of college rep visits.

Having college information visible will create excitement for juniors and seniors and can pique the interest of younger students as well.

The cyclical nature of the college process calendar makes including regular articles in a school-wide newsletter (if one exists) another way to make information available throughout the school community. Letting everyone know that PSATs are being administered, that college representatives are visiting, that students are filing applications, and ultimately, that seniors are receiving decision letters helps students in the process stay on schedule and will also motivate younger students and make the application process less mysterious. If the forum of a newsletter is not available, consider a professional blog, and encourage students and families to subscribe to it.

Families will often need to access college counseling information at night, over the weekend and during vacations. You can help by arranging to place college counseling information on your school's Web site. This is a particularly good way to share forms, calendars, college rep visit announcements, and standardized testing deadlines.

Let everyone—in all grades—understand that college attainment is a school priority and that college counseling is available to all students. Counselors should participate in school-wide events such as Open School Night, Curriculum Night and open houses whenever possible to underscore their expertise and availability to students and families. Once students have begun to progress through high school, more focused college counseling will begin.

To enhance the communication plan, counselors need to find ways to truly interact with students and families, in both small and large groups.

College nights are an important part of the college process and an effective way to help students and families dive into college planning and the application process. Offering an overview of all that will transpire between the start of the junior year and the end of the senior year is more than a chance to provide information; it's also a time to answer questions and establish yourself as an expert within your community. By clarifying the process and making it known that you will provide guidance throughout, you alleviate many concerns and worries and help students begin their research with confidence. College nights are enhanced by PowerPoint presentations and handouts.

Including college representatives can add depth to a college night. As you build your panel, do so with an eye toward being inclusive of a variety of schools so that every student in the audience can envision being admitted to one of the featured colleges. Always offer the reps a few minutes to speak about their own institutions, and then encourage them to address admission issues in general. Take advantage of this opportunity, and ask them to share their insights into effective letters of recommendation, compelling essays, making the most of campus visits, preparing for interviews, and more. If there are topics of particular interest to your school population, such as paying for college or the freshman transition, ask that those be included.

Many schools, districts and communities host college fairs where students and families can interact with college representatives. NACAC hosts 59 national college fairs across the United States each year, as well as an additional 20 fairs concentrating on the visual and performing arts. Counselors can gather and share information about available fairs to encourage students and families to attend. Counselors in areas without easy access to an existing fair can collaborate with their counterparts at other local schools to create a fair for their own students.

While many topics can be presented to a large group, others are better in small ones.

Counseling coffees, hosted in the college office or another suitable school space, provide a more intimate setting and are limited to adults. Parents have their own set of questions and concerns, and there is a benefit to providing them a dedicated forum in which to raise them. Parents and guardians can also be encouraged to reach out to the counseling office by phone or email.

Individual meetings with students—with or without their parents or guardians—will provide insight into their personalities, goals and challenges. These meetings are a chance for students to share their aspirations and also their fears about applying to and enrolling in college. Asking students to complete a self-assessment questionnaire in advance allows you to discover more about them beyond GPAs and standardized test scores and will enhance your ability to guide them. Individual meetings can underscore the idea that applying to college is an individual, rather than a group, experience; students and their friends will likely have different credentials, differ-

ent priorities and, ultimately, different schools on their lists. Further, these meetings can be a reality-check for students and families, a time to put the student's record in perspective and to discuss ways to maximize the student's strengths.

Even though the high school profile is designed to explain the high school composition and culture to the college representatives reading student files, it is a solid tool for sharing your school's history, priorities and offerings and is another way to let students put their experience and record in context. Many counselors share the profile on the school's Web site and make it part of individual and group meetings.

Counselors with large caseloads may not be able to spend time with each student in a one-on-one setting. In this circumstance, group sessions can supplement your communication plan.

For example, if scheduling permits, many high schools offer classes in the college application process, such as College 101. Most often, these classes begin in the spring of the junior year and end with the first semester of the senior year. The classes offer step-by-step instruction in researching colleges, essay writing, financial aid, and completing applications and help students maintain an appropriate timeline for submitting their applications.

As an alternative, consider offering an application completion workshop on a Saturday in December. Arrange to reserve a computer lab or a classroom with laptops, and invite students to spend a few hours with you finishing their applications. Working together as a group will help the students relax even though deadlines are approaching, and having counselors on hand to answer questions provides a safety net for students who need one and assures that the process goes smoothly for all.

However you choose to communicate and what combination of methods and tools you use, it is important to understand your audience and the various constituencies that you serve. English language learners, traditionally underserved students, students with learning differences, first-generation college-bound students, and students with physical and emotional challenges will all need specific direction as they prepare for the highly individual experience of applying to college. Standard communication tools may need to be adjusted in order to meet the needs of a diverse student body.

Communicate with Teachers

High school faculty members are powerful allies in the college application process, and communicating with them is another important step in working with students throughout high school. Faculty members see their students in class on a consistent basis—every student, every day—and have the ability to assess students not only as scholars, but also as members of the school community. Asking teachers to complete a short assessment form or checklist on each student at the end of the sophomore and junior years not only helps them start thinking about students as potential college applicants, but also lets the counselor develop a record of the students' classroom characteristics that are helpful in writing the counselor letter of recommendation.

Like all communication, this, too, is a two-way street. If they are encouraged and made to feel like they are part of the process, teachers can help the counselor communicate the importance of preparing for standardized tests, meeting deadlines, and proofreading and rewriting essays. Finally, teacher letters of recommendation remain a truly important part of the application at many colleges. Teachers should clearly understand how vital their involvement is and should always be thanked for their efforts.

Communicate with Colleges

While colleges are eager to communicate with applicants and their counselors, counselors serve students well by sharing general rules of email etiquette so that students can avoid missteps and mistakes. These communications with colleges may be a student's first "professional" emails and must be different from the emails they send to their friends.

Students need to know that emails to admission representatives should always contain a salutation (with a courtesy title) and show proper spelling and punctuation. Whatever the content of the message, the student should always say "thank you" and close with his or her full name and the name of the high school. Colleges appreciate polite interactions; moreover, including all the information necessary to answer questions and access student files will make the exchange more productive.

When possible, students should communicate with colleges themselves, rather than having a parent or guardian make the contact. If a student is especially anxious about getting in touch with the admission office, the counselor can offer to proofread a draft of an email or to let the student make an initial call from the college office. There will certainly be occasions, however, when a conversation between the counselor and the admission office is the most appropriate communication. Effective student advocacy begins with advisement and continues through the recommendation process, but likely will not end there. Admission counselors will often reach out to the counseling office with questions or the need for clarification during file review; in these instances, the counselor's insight is critical in helping the student be understood.

In the same vein, spending a few minutes with admission representatives as part of their high school visit creates a sense of hospitality, but is also a time to learn about campus admission trends and changes in the undergraduate program and to provide details about the high school program and the particular seniors who will soon be applicants. This conversation supplements the information provided in the high school profile and can highlight specific students in the class, especially those who have demonstrated an interest in attending the visiting college. Finally, many admission offices remain interested in scheduling "counselor calls," which create a time for a conversation about all of the applicants from the high school.

The Importance of Advocacy

College counseling and college admission work best when opportunities are plentiful and accessible to all. As a group, professionals in counseling and admission form a powerful lobby—ever more influential as the number of voices grows. As professionals with a profound understanding of the impact of rigor, access and support as key elements in a K–16 education, our input into the politics of education provides both statistical and anecdotal information to elected officials. Writing letters, sending emails and participating in organized legislative visits are all ways to allow your experience to affect change in a positive way and share what you know.

Get Strong, Be Strong: Students Aren't the Only Ones Who Need to Be Empowered

Because the process of applying to college is ever-changing, counselors spend considerable time and energy working with students to help them feel empowered in the college process. But counselors need support and education, too. Remaining current on the changes in the system is the best way to learn and grow within the field, and the opportunities to learn are everywhere.

First and foremost, the power of personal interaction cannot be overstated—the connections you make and the network of professional colleagues you create will be the most valuable tools during your counseling career. Having the ability to pick up the phone or write an email to get advice, answers, recommendations, encouragement, and support is imperative. Counselors need to be proactive in developing a personal and professional network.

They say the whole is greater than the sum of its parts, and counselors gain strength through their affiliations. Whether joining NACAC, a NACAC affiliate association, a local counseling group, or a social/professional networking site, members receive benefits such as e-newsletters, member directories, informative emails, and members-only events and discounts. Members of these groups also share information and opportunities and can work together toward shared goals.

With more than 13,000 members around the world, the National Association for College Admission Counseling (NACAC) is the preeminent organization in the admission and college counseling field. Uniquely positioned because of its breadth of membership and diverse member categories, NACAC is the primary resource and professional hub for representatives of public and private colleges and secondary schools, as well as community-based organizations (CBOs) and independent counselors.

Joining NACAC is a springboard for counselors seeking professional development opportunities, and the benefits of membership include numerous ways for counselors to expand their knowledge and their reach. The *NACAC Journal of College Admission* combines anecdotal articles about the transition to postsecondary education with statistics-driven analyses of trends and issues within the field. The monthly *NACAC Bulletin* provides member updates, information about the association's internal governance, and articles on association outreach and advocacy. In addition, the *Bulletin* includes listings of NACAC in the press, which is a quick way to find and read current articles about counseling and admission topics.

Each year, the **NACAC National Conference** brings together more than 6,000 global professionals to share ideas, to network and to learn from one another. Many other organizations, including the College Board, American School Counselors Association (ASCA) and the Association of College Counselors in Independent Schools (ACCIS) also hold conferences, summer institute programs and other professional development events. Many presentations from the NACAC National Conference are posted to the NACAC **Knowledge Center,** which also contains a searchable archive of articles, studies, templates, and presentations that have been made available by NACAC and its members for member use.

Beyond NACAC (and closer to home) are the 23 **affiliate associations** that bring together college counselors, admission counselors, CBOs, and independent counselors from a common state or region. Known as ACACs, each association maintains an informational Web site and hosts an annual conference. Many publish online newsletters, provide webinars and offer day-long workshops. The affiliate associations cultivate leadership in their members and provide opportunities for involvement in the kinds of committees and projects that enhance and reinforce the counseling profession and that can be exciting and fulfilling complements to a traditional counseling career.

Ethics and professional integrity are integral parts of the counseling and admission profession, playing a role in every interaction and everything we do. Counselors should understand the expectations of professionalism as detailed in NACAC's **Statement of Principles and Good Practice** (SPGP). This living document, subject to revision each year by a vote of the NACAC Assembly, establishes protocols and expectations and provides guidance and protection to admission counselors and college counselors, alike. The SPGP, in tandem with individual school policies, provides the college counselor with an ethical and operational framework.

Another way to interact and learn from colleagues is the use of the **NACAC Exchange,** the association's listserv, where members can post information and ask questions of their peers. Members are encouraged to share ideas, job opportunities, issues affecting the profession, and other matters related to the field. This free exchange of ideas benefits new counselors as well as more experienced ones as they navigate the ongoing changes in the admission process.

Over the past several years, **LinkedIn** has grown in popularity and is now the most popular of the professional networking sites. For college counselors, LinkedIn provides a multi-level networking tool and a forum for the exchange of ideas. LinkedIn membership is free and can connect counselors with their counterparts at other schools, college admission professionals and providers of services within the counseling field. As an extension of the larger LinkedIn community, there are also LinkedIn Groups, which bring together LinkedIn members with shared professional interests. The selection of groups is searchable, and the site also recommends groups that align with members' experiences and connections.

Many colleges host **breakfasts, receptions and workshops** to introduce themselves to the counseling community, and it is beneficial to attend these events whenever possible. Typically, the admission staff responsible for the area where the event is held will present information about the institution: admission numbers and criteria, new programs and majors, and other news from campus. Following the presentation, there is time for questions and to interact with the reps. This is a chance to speak to the admission team about your school and to suggest a high school visit.

The most elaborate of these events is the **counselor tour.** Colleges will invite groups of counselors to spend time on campus as their guests. The most comprehensive of these visits will include a campus tour, meetings with students, faculty and administrators, an admission presentation, a sample class or participation in an actual one, meals, transportation, and lodging. Colleges make a tremendous investment of both time and money in order to provide the richest possible experience for counselors who visit.

Visiting campus is the best way to fully understand the college and its culture. Beyond this, counselor tours are also an excellent way for counselors to expand their network of peers from other schools. Whether the tour draws from a particular region (Midwest, Northeast, etc.), a specific type of school or is more diverse in terms of participants, counselors should always see tours as an-

other **networking opportunity.** Try to sit with different people during meals, programs and bus rides to maximize your interactions with other counselors, as well as the admission office team. Most counselor tour organizers will share a list of participants with their school/organization affiliation as well as email addresses so that counselors can stay in touch after the tour, but bring a supply of business cards, too.

The demands on counselors' time are understood and appreciated. As a result, many professional development workshops are now offered in the form of webinars. Offering the best of both worlds, **webinars** allow counselors to interact with experts from the larger counseling and admission community without leaving the office. In many cases, webinars are archived and available to watch at a variety of times, and most webinar presenters share the presentations with participants by email so that they can be shared with other counselors, students and families as appropriate.

There's a whole world of opportunities out there, and the counselors who benefit most from them are the ones who recognize the importance of professional development and who are proactive in finding ways to continue to learn and grow. These experiences—and the people you meet through them—will be the foundation of your career.

Conclusion

Over time, each college counselor develops his or her own way of working with students, grounded in best practices and tempered by experience. As long as the counseling is ethically centered and focused on student success, there is no one right way to help students prepare to transition to college. But, in the end, there will be your way.

Discussion Questions

- What are some of the ways to help students feel confident in the college process?

- What can be done to increase parent/guardian engagement with the counselor?

- What are some of the opportunities for professional development?

- What are some of the ways to advocate for students?

- What are the benefits of "affiliating"?

About the Author

Lisa Sohmer has been the director of college counseling at Garden School in New York City (NY) for 18 years. She is a past president of the New York Association for College Admission Counseling (NYSACAC) and was awarded the association's President's Award in 2008. Lisa was elected to the National Association for College Admission Counseling (NACAC) Board of Directors in 2006 and served a three-year term. Lisa is currently the co-chair of the NACAC NYC College Fair.

Lisa has been a member of on advisory panels for The City University of New York (NY) and The College Board, as well as several state and national committees. She is a frequent speaker on topics related to the transition to post-secondary education and has been interviewed by Newsweek, CBS's "Up to the Minute," US News & World Report, The Daily Beast.com, The Wall Street Journal, The Washington Post, The Chicago Tribune, Good Housekeeping, American Airlines' in-flight magazine, Bloomberg.com, education.com, businessweek.com and many other publications.

Lisa graduated from Connecticut College (CT) with a degree in English and government and received a master's degree in journalism from New York University (NY).

References

Hill, K. (2012, October 12). What college admissions officers don't like seeing on Facebook: Vulgarity, drinking photos and 'illegal activities.' *Forbes*. Retrieved from *http://www.forbes.com/sites/kashmirhill/2012/10/12/what-college-admission-officers-dont-like-seeing-on-facebook-profiles-vulgarity-drinking-photos-and-illegal-activities*.

Singer, N. (2013, November 9). They loved your G.P.A. Then they saw your tweets *New York Times*. Retrieved from *http://www.nytimes.com/2013/11/10/business/they-loved-your-gpa-then-they-saw-your-tweets.html?pagewanted=all&_r=0*.

Chapter 7:   Counseling the Crowds: Using Creativity and Accountability to Serve Large Caseloads

Esther B. Hugo, EdD

INTRODUCTION

As the higher education industry has grown, college admission has become big business, equipped with an arsenal of sophisticated sales pitches, computer software programs and targeted marketing techniques. Counselors face the challenge of ensuring that this increasingly complex selection and admission process remains focused on helping students find their best college match. This is a difficult job under any circumstances, but it can prove even more challenging for counselors who work in schools with larger caseloads. Because it is impossible for one person to provide effective services and programs for all students, in these instances, counselors must approach the process strategically. They must create a college-going culture in which the entire school community is focused on students' preparation for a full range of postsecondary options. This model requires that the counselor re-think and expand his or her professional role as a leader and manager whose daily work is aligned with the performance goals for the entire school community.

for *all* public schools, was 470:1 in 2011–12, and the public secondary school ratio was 418:1. These ratios vary substantially by state. In 2011–12, Arizona had the highest number of students per counselor (863), followed closely by California (818). Results of NACAC's annual Counseling Trends Survey indicate that student-to-counselor ratios are significantly lower at private secondary schools than those at public schools. At schools with high caseloads, fewer students enroll in four-year colleges. Counselors at schools with the highest proportion of students eligible for free or reduced price lunch, a proxy for family income, report much lower four-year college enrollment rates and total college enrollment rates for their graduates (Clinedinst, Hawkins, Shanahan, Addington & West, n.d.).

For school counselors who work with larger caseloads, the key question is, "How do I reach students and parents to let them know their options, and which colleges will best meet their needs?" This chapter offers two conceptual frameworks for serving large caseloads of students, as

> *Research clearly shows that counselors, when consistently and frequently available and allowed to provide direct services to students and parents, can be a highly effective group of professionals who positively impact students' college-going rates.*

Within schools, no professional is more important to improving college enrollment than the counselor (McDonough, 2008). Research clearly shows that counselors, when consistently and frequently available and allowed to provide direct services to students and parents, can be a highly effective group of professionals who positively impact students' college-going rates.

However, in many schools, counselors spend too much of their time with what are often referred to as "STDs"—scheduling, testing and discipline. That is, scheduling students for classes, administering standardized tests as part of a broader accountability system and dealing with student behavioral issues (McDonough, 2005). As a result, counselors are not able to spend significant time on college or career readiness counseling.

According to an analysis of U.S. Department of Education data published in NACAC's 2014 *State of College Admission* report, the national student-to-counselor ratio

well as techniques, activities and strategies that counselors can use to help students and families navigate the complex college admission process. Finally, this chapter reviews the use of college-going data in school accountability systems and provides two tools for counselors to use in measuring their interventions and counseling services.

When advising students, counselors impact college preparation by:

1. Providing an understanding of college and its importance

2. Structuring information and organizing activities that foster and support students' self-assessment and college aspirations

3. Educating parents about their role in fostering and supporting college aspirations, setting college expectations and motivating students toward action

4. Focusing the school on its college mission.

Often, counselors who serve large caseloads work in low-income schools where students need greater assistance with the college admission process. A 2008 national survey revealed that 87 percent of all young people want to go to college, and parental aspirations are even higher (Bridgeland et al., 2008). For those underrepresented in higher education, 92 percent of African-American parents and 90 percent of Hispanic parents consider college to be very important to their children. Yet, many underrepresented students do not receive the necessary guidance to navigate the process. Despite the evidence that poor and low-income children benefit enormously when they attain a college education, they are not only less likely to enroll in either two- or four-year colleges, but also less likely to complete a degree once they have enrolled (Isaacs, Sawhill, & Haskins, 2008).

Research on counselor intervention frameworks reveals that academic preparation for college is more important that socioeconomic status in terms of college enrollment (Alexander et al., 1987). More specifically, completion of what are referred to as the "Pipeline Steps" play a key role in the attempt to eliminate the disparity in college participation rates between low socio-economic status (SES) high school graduates and their middle- and upper-SES counterparts. The Pipeline Steps provide a framework for counselors to effectively work with large caseloads, because the information is presented to students and their parents in an easy-to-understand and focused sequence.

The Pipeline Steps

The Pipeline Steps are offered as a research-based framework for organizing and focusing counselor duties, all of which lessen role confusion and ambiguity and result in more efficient and targeted services for students.

The Pipeline Steps, all of which may be facilitated by the school counselor, include:

1. Aspiring to a bachelor's degree

2. Taking the "right courses" (college-prep curriculum)

3. Preparing for and taking entrance exams

4. Applying to and enrolling in a four-year institution

Although the Pipeline Steps play a critical role in closing the socioeconomic college enrollment gap, they are relevant to students and schools from all economic backgrounds. New counselors who wish to organize services for larger populations should consider focusing their counseling programs around these four Pipeline Steps. This focus relieves counselors from ancillary tasks (other duties as assigned) and results in a streamlined and research-based program proven to close achievement gaps between low-income and high-income students. Instead of merely reacting to whatever happens during the school day, the counselor becomes focused on an organized and proactive program of services.

Creating Aspiration to a College Degree

Counselors can encourage aspiration to college by promoting the PSAT or PLAN, and exposing students to college and university representatives through college visits or "college night" activities. Messages about what it takes to get to college should be clear and expressed often, on bulletin boards, school Web sites, and in communications sent home to parents and students. By condensing the college admission process into steps, the counselor consciously removes barriers and increases understanding about the application process.

Taking the "Right Courses"—
a College-Preparatory Curriculum

According to NACAC's 2014 *State of College Admission* report, academic performance in college preparatory courses has been consistently rated as the top factor in admission decisions over the past decade, with about 80 percent of colleges rating it as considerably important. Other top factors include strength of curriculum, standardized admission test scores, and overall GPA. Although admission test scores are among the top factors, they are rated considerably important by about 55 to 60 percent of colleges, substantially lower than grades in college prep courses. (Clinedinst et al., n.d.).

Academic preparation through a rigorous and challenging course load is more important to access and success in college than performance on standardized tests. Counselors can significantly influence students' course-taking patterns by:

• clarifying the courses needed for college

• encouraging faculty members to clearly label their course syllabus descriptions as "college-preparatory"

• encouraging students to attempt honors or Advanced Placement coursework

- providing chances for students to enroll at local community colleges

- providing interventions and support for students who need additional help or who may wish to opt out of these courses.

In 2011, the National Office for School Counselor Advocacy (Bruce, 2012) reported that 59 percent of high school counselors surveyed said they believe it is fair to use "completion of college prep sequence of courses" as a measure to assess their effectiveness.

Preparing for and Taking Standardized Examinations

A counselor's role may include making students aware of the exams, promoting and clarifying fee waiver procedures, securing outside agencies to assist in preparation, and helping students and parents understand test scores and develop testing strategies. An abundance of Web-based programs provides teachers and students with options to familiarize themselves with exam format and content. The PSAT or PLAN may be used as counseling tools—they provide the impetus for college planning and provide concrete feedback as students begin shaping their college identities. Students start to see themselves as college material when institutions initiate communication with them—contact that is often facilitated by exams taken early in high school. Many students will take the PSAT as early as ninth grade. At such an early stage, focusing on the experience of taking the test rather than the score itself is a strategy many counselors use to help students "jump start" the college admission process. Returning score results to students and parents in an evening meeting format offers the opportunity to explain the college process, review the importance of college visits, preview the financial aid process, and discuss next steps in college exploration. This practice also helps to develop the relationship between the school, the counselor, and parents and students.

Completing Applications

While it might be easy to tell a student, "If you don't apply, you can't get in," remember that counselors influence student decisions. Students need assistance and guidance to create a college list, write insightful personal state-

ments or essays, and secure letters of recommendation. Research indicates that receiving assistance with college application essays during the school day increases a student's chance of applying to college by 8 to 11 percent (Cabrera & LaNasa, 2001). For students who may not have access to computers, the counselor might hold application and financial aid workshops in computer centers or school libraries.

The Pipeline Steps provide an operational framework for counselors who serve low-income students and large caseloads by breaking down the college search and application process into a series of manageable steps for students and their families. Research notes that low-income high school seniors who regularly consult with a high school counselor regarding postsecondary plans are more likely to plan to attend college (King, 1996). That is, according to King (1996), low-income students who encounter difficult courses not only rise to the challenge, but also develop greater confidence and higher aspirations as a result. As such, low-income students probably will attend a four-year college if they frequently see a school counselor who recommended they attend a four-year college, took the PSAT, received information on colleges and financial aid directly from postsecondary institutions, or planned to finance their education through need-based grants. King's (1996) research reinforces the pivotal role of the school counselor in the college planning process.

Clearly, schools influence college preparation and choice through expectations and assumptions, the flow of content and information, and via the provision of student assistance services that distill college choices to a feasible few. Another research-based approach for managing large caseloads can be found in the second model framework: Nine Critical Principles for a College-Going Culture.

NINE CRITICAL PRINCIPLES FOR A COLLEGE-GOING CULTURE

Dr. Patricia M. McDonough's model for building a comprehensive college culture specifies that students must have access to information and guidance in a school that fosters college enrollment. The counselor serves as instructional leader in that effort.

In this model, McDonough and McClafferty (2002) offer a template for creating a school environment with a college culture that strives to prepare all students for a full range of postsecondary options through structural, motivational and experiential college-preparatory opportunities. In addition, the school leadership is committed to building a college-going culture, and school personnel provide supportive, consistent messages to students. Counselors, teachers and families are partners in the effort, and all counselors serve as college counselors.

The template's principles for building a college culture in a high school include college talk, clear expectations, information and resources, a comprehensive counseling model, testing and curriculum, faculty and family involvement, college partnerships, and articulation. Examples of the principles and indicators of their presence at school sites are outlined in Table 1.

As is shown in Table 1, all constituents must work together. This is evidenced through clear communication among faculty, administrators and students. Examples of college talk might include an updated Web site, regularly published newsletters and posters displayed throughout the campus.

In my practice as a public school counselor, I compiled all college acceptances in a "Goes to College" list that simply featured student names and their college acceptances. (The waivers that students and parents/guardians had signed in the beginning of the year to receive peer

counseling services—explained later in this chapter—also included permission to publicize students' college acceptance information.) The list was organized with the most selective schools first, followed by state colleges and universities and private schools. The last page of the list featured out-of-state colleges and universities. We also repeated the names of students admitted to more than one college or university. As this list was published, more student acceptances were verified and reported, and the list was continuously revised. While many college counseling offices display college acceptances on an annual map, the list is more portable.

Not only did the "Goes to College" list provide evaluative data on the effectiveness of the school's college program, the list also served several other purposes. The list informed students and parents that we know what we're doing—students from our school are successful in gaining acceptance for college. The list helped seniors become more focused on the process and lessened anxiety for juniors, as they saw where their older friends had been admitted. Ninth and 10th graders saw their friends' names listed and made personal, role-model, real identifications. The message to faculty was, "Look what we accomplished; your outstanding teaching made these students attractive to colleges," while the message to administrators was, "Thanks for your leadership and supporting us in our work. We are a successful school."

Table 1. Nine Critical Principles for a College-Going Culture

College Talk—Clear, ongoing communication among students, teachers, administrators, and families about what it takes to get to college.	Clear Expectations—Explicit, clearly defined goals, communicated in ways that make them part of the culture of the school.	Information and Resources—Comprehensive, up-to-date college information and resources, easily accessible for all students, families and school personnel.
Comprehensive Counseling Model—View of counseling that makes all student interactions with counseling staff opportunities for college counseling.	Testing and Curriculum—Information about and access to "gate-keeping" tests (PSAT, SAT, ACT, etc.) and college-preparatory courses for all students.	Faculty Involvement—Informed, active participation of school faculty in the creation and maintenance of a college culture.
Family Involvement—Meaningful engagement on the part of family members in the process of building a college culture.	College Partnerships—Active links in a variety of forms between the school and local colleges and universities.	Articulation—Ongoing coordination between counselors and teachers among all schools in a feeder group.

Source: McClafferty and McDonough, 2002.

The list was also mailed to all middle schools in the area, so that middle school faculty saw where their perhaps once mischievous students ended up, and to the local realtors and chamber of commerce who partially establish the profile and reputation of the school.

Clear expectations become embedded in college talk communications, as the goals must be articulated as part of the daily business of the school. To understand the importance of expectations, complete the sentence, "Around here, we go to…" or "You can't walk down the hallways without seeing…" Indicators of clear expectations are the explicit statement of postsecondary options in the school's mission statement, development of four-year curricular plans for all students and ongoing opportunities to discuss college preparation.

Students need access to college information and resources, and such information falls within the purview of not only the counselors, but also the faculty. Counselors must have updated resources and create online access for students. This helps reach students in ways in which they are familiar, so creating a Facebook page or a Twitter account might generate awareness and access to programs, services and deadlines.

During the fall, the counselor is often focused on the seniors who are unsure about the process. As such, it is important to regulate services as much as possible during this time. Application workshops on regularly announced days are an effective way to meet the needs of seniors with limited attention spans. For example, I hosted application workshops every day during lunch. Mondays and Wednesdays were reserved for the University of California application, for example, and Tuesdays and Thursdays served as California State University application days. Fridays were reserved for students applying to out-of-state and private colleges and universities. This regular schedule made it easier for students to come to the college center on a specific day. Occasionally, I would conduct application workshop sessions outside on the senior lawn. This encouraged seniors to apply and made them aware of application and testing deadlines. For counselors with large caseloads, it is critical to have organized programs during lunch or the morning break, when students are free to come to the college center.

It is important to note that all resources must be easily accessible for students and their families, as well as school personnel. The counselor's calendar of activities should be posted around the school and distributed at every parent meeting.

Counseling for college must be integrated into the school's comprehensive counseling model. One way to provide more counseling services is to design and implement a college-focused peer counseling program. A peer counseling program enables the counselor to work with larger numbers of students and to disseminate more information and provide more contact and interaction about college admission.

College Peer Counseling

The counselor can use a variety of resources—including students, faculty, administrators, and the community to communicate the college-going message. At the public school in which I worked, I organized a college-focused peer counseling program that used students as counselors. Because I was the only college counselor for the 2,100-member student body, I knew I needed help in reaching such a large caseload. I was also aware of research that indicated that teens are subject to strong peer pressure. Having college peer counselors capitalized on that peer pressure in the best way possible. With peer counselors, the college center continued to serve students—even if I had to be out of the office. As a result, we reached far more students than we would have if I had been working alone.

These college peer counselors were specially trained seniors who assisted their peers in the college admission and financial aid process. Due to confidentiality laws, we had participating students and their parents/guardians sign waivers at the beginning of the year, granting permission to receive college-counseling services from other seniors. These peer helpers agreed to abide by strict ethical standards, including confidentiality. They were also assigned a caseload of approximately 20 students and were responsible for a specific area of expertise, such as maintaining the scholarship board, coordinating field trips, publishing the student bulletin, or taking care of visiting college representatives. They made quick classroom presentations called "college commercials" to remind students about financial aid deadlines, college application workshops or SAT/ACT preparation programs. These counselors sorted mail, kept the computers in the college center running and assisted in organizing College Night.

It was crucial to recruit and select peer counselors carefully. Qualifications included students who were academically strong, independent thinkers and workers, and good writers. Also, I made sure to select a representative group, including those who were tech-savvy, great speakers, leaders, athletes, and cheerleaders. The peer counselor application process involved submission of a brief essay, recommendations from English teachers, interviews, and counseling simulations. These students had first access to the college information center and were highly regarded by the entire school community. Peer counselors were given tests and assigned grades. Several college peer counselors secured jobs in university admission offices after graduation. During our school's regional accreditation program, the peer counseling program earned five commendations.

Training began in the summer and occurred throughout the year, typically before the application or financial aid season. The peer counselors completed their forms early (another form of training) so they could assist other students without worrying about completing their own applications. Peer counselors were trained in counseling skills and technical information. During the fall semester, peer counselors were assigned a caseload of seniors, whom they called into the center, reviewed college plans with, and served as resources to facilitate application completion. During the spring, peer counselors worked with the junior class. Their final examination was to recruit and help train the incoming class of peer counselors.

Standardized tests, such as the PSAT, SAT and ACT, are typically requirements for the college admission process. Therefore, it is vital that schools make the commitment to provide resources to prepare students for these exams. When I worked as a counselor, I would contact test-preparation companies early in the school year and ask them to deliver free test-preparation workshop materials for my students. Sometimes we charged students a nominal fee that was refunded if they attended all workshops. Companies were happy to provide this pro bono service, and my students received excellent test preparation.

The PSAT or PLAN can serve as a counseling tool to educate younger students and their families about the college process. Research shows that having college plans in place by the 10th grade increases the likelihood of enrolling in a four-year college by 21 percent (McDonough, 2008).

Our "Getting Started" meeting, held in January, focused on distributing and interpreting PSAT scores. The principal spoke briefly, and I provided some strategies for students and parents to launch their college search process. Then, a college representative interpreted the PSAT score report. Among our younger students, we always emphasized the experience of taking the test; focusing on the score at this early date is not as important as the experience, because few ninth and 10th graders are accustomed to sitting down and concentrating for a three-hour block of time. Then, a college admission representative provided ideas on how to critically evaluate the communications and mail from various colleges. A financial aid professional previewed the process and offered tips for planning. The other school counselors involved in the program spoke about the upcoming registration process. Frequently, these counselors saw a student only when there was a problem. The "Getting Started" meeting provided them the chance to meet students and families in a positive way. Also, as I worked with the counselors as a team, I felt less isolated in my efforts. Repeating the meeting each year facilitated overall understanding about the college process.

PSAT in the Potty

Another strategy for reaching a mass audience about standardized testing involved the use of a single-colored sheet of paper, which I called "PSAT in the Potty." A college peer counselor perused the SAT and ACT prep books and identified the shorter practice questions, which were typed out in larger print. The questions, both verbal- and mathematics-related, featured a hint to help with the question and the answer. I printed up enough to cover all the bathroom stalls in the school, and college peer counselors would tape the questions on the back of the bathroom stalls each week. One day, one of my students came into the college center and said, "Mrs. Hugo, after I saw your college questions in the bathroom, I thought that you had gone too far. Then I realized that you were just trying to remind us about college."

Creative Communication Strategies

These activities, programs and strategies provide ways to assist students and parents in the school-to-college transition. College preparation and advising must start when students arrive in the ninth grade, if not sooner. Research supports the efficacy of approaches in which the college counselor employs multiple communication methods and involves faculty, parents, external agencies, and institutions.

Research indicates that a high-intensity, college-preparatory curriculum is the single most important factor in college success (Adelman, 2006). In every school-wide mailing, a list of college-preparatory coursework was included (and sometimes translated) so that parents knew which courses counted for college. In addition, we created posters listing college-preparatory courses and displayed them in all classrooms.

The partnership model requires that faculty play an active role in building the college culture by encouraging students, organizing activities in the classroom and engaging in college-related interactions with parents. Teachers can be valuable allies. For example, if I received an invitation for a college tour or field trip that I had already experienced, I would invite faculty members to go, and I covered their classes. With their classes, I would conduct application or essay workshops, while the teachers experienced an enriching and informative day away from school.

It was easy to organize a College Awareness Day, during which faculty members wore their college sweatshirts or hats and talked about their college days during the last five minutes of class.

I also asked teachers for permission to make presentations in their classrooms. I timed the requests to coincide with report card deadlines, so that teachers could sit in the back of the room and grade their papers (while listening to my college-going message). The teachers had a break, and I gained valuable exposure to and interaction with students. I found classroom presentations effective because students felt comfortable asking questions in a smaller group setting. It was important to have a 20- to 30-minute bank of activities that included a study skills, activity-based component. Some sample topics included:

- Calculating your GPA—a discussion about the importance of curriculum and which classes and years count for college

- Getting cash for college—students need to hear the message that college is affordable

- Choosing a college—an introduction to the system of higher education

- Planning your four years—an opportunity for students to understand the connection between curriculum and college requirements

- Managing your time—an explanation of the ways in which college is different from high school and the need for students to adapt to a new schedule and way of thinking and acting. NACAC's *Guiding the Way* series (2010) provides a bank of activities that can be adapted for any school setting or grade level.

Another critical faculty interaction occurred at the beginning of the school year, during the opening faculty meeting. At that time, I conducted a workshop on writing letters of recommendation, explaining the finer points of the faculty letter and what colleges expect from teacher recommendations. Too many teachers were simply summarizing a student's brag sheet, which said little about the student's classroom performance. Once they had concrete examples, the letters of recommendation improved.

Family involvement is key, and parents must be provided with opportunities to learn about the college planning process. Parents can also act as the college center's external voice. I developed a cadre of parent champions who became access and equity models. They conveyed to other parents the importance of meeting deadlines, completing financial aid materials and seeking resources if their students were undocumented. They served as resources and provided bilingual support services to parents who needed additional information and encouragement.

I involved parents in organizing the college center at the beginning of the year, through filing and sorting catalogs and books. They also helped develop a speaker list and media list. Whenever I organized an event, I asked a parent to send press releases to the local media, which helped build community awareness and enhance public relations for our program and school. All upcoming college-focused events were advertised on the local cable television's public service bulletin board. The parents were adept fundraisers, helping purchase supplies and providing funds for scholarships. At information evenings and programs, parents provided decorations and refreshments.

One of my most successful fundraisers was Muffin Mania, a bake sale during which I sold muffins to students. At a local warehouse club (Costco), it was possible to purchase a dozen muffins for about five dollars. A parent picked up the muffins on Tuesday to sell them on Wednesday morning. A parent and teacher supervised the sale of muffins for one dollar each. Sales were promoted on our weekly college-focused broadcast, which was written and delivered over the school public address system by a peer counselor with a flair for humor and drama. We raised about $4,000 annually through muffin sales, which we invested in Advanced Placement materials and student scholarships. Of course, administrators were offered free muffins.

The underlying message of engaging faculty and parents in the counseling programs is that preparing students for college is a team effort. The college counselor orchestrates and manages this effort, ensuring consistency and accuracy of messaging so that all students are hearing the same information and headed toward the goal of securing postsecondary options.

Forming partnerships or interactive links between the school and local colleges and universities facilitates college-related activities, such as field trips and enrichment programs. Some college systems send outreach personnel to high schools. My school benefited from such outreach personnel, and to maximize their weekly or bi-weekly visit to the school, a peer counselor completed summons slips a day in advance or organized classroom presentations for the college representatives. This person became a valued resident expert who was knowledgeable about that particular college system (e.g., community college) and often made presentations in several classrooms during the day. Schools that do not already have such a relationship in place with a local university might consider initiating one through an admission office.

We also enjoyed a steady stream of college interns from local colleges and universities. Each year, I made a presentation in the local university's graduate counseling department, during which I described the wonders of my job. At the end of the presentation, because I knew students were looking for places to do field work, I always offered opportunities at my college center. The program grew so that each semester, two or three interns assisted me. These graduate students ran counseling groups, assisted the other counselors and learned to make classroom presentations. One intern wrote a federal grant for a non-violence program that was funded. After her internship ended, she recruited her friend to work in the center to implement the grant. When she completed her internship, she recruited another grad student to do the program evaluation. This was a tremendous benefit for my school that brought additional resources and did not involve additional work for me. During the financial aid season, staff members from the local university helped with the workshops and presentations. Research indicates that increases in the amount of financial aid information provided by the counselor positively correlates with students' likelihood of applying to college (McDonough, 2005). For those crunch-time dates when applications are due, and because we know that teenagers are professional procrastinators, we organized a "Panic Room" in the computer lab that was staffed by outreach personnel, graduate students, college admission officers, and college peer counselors.

College Representatives

When college representatives wanted to visit our campus, a college peer counselor organized the visits, completed reminder notes to my students a day ahead of time and sent the notes on the day of the visit. Representatives were greeted with a school profile, a "Goes to College" list and a bottle of water. We asked each representative how much time they could spend on our campus, because I had already identified a group of teachers who always appreciated a drop-in guest speaker from a college. If the representative had extra time, presentations would be made in the speech, drama or debate classes. Involving representatives from four-year colleges provides another communication and role model for delivering the college message.

Articulation and communication between schools are essential to continuity of services. In this model, building the college culture is dependent upon clear communication and experiences that occur from kindergarten through 12th grade. Middle school is midway to college; early outreach to middle school parents helps them understand what will be expected when their students reach high school. I served as the guest speaker at the middle school's eighth grade College Night so that parents and students would be aware of the college-preparatory curriculum and college programs in place.

In reviewing these strategies and activities, it is important to note that counselors with large caseloads must achieve a balance between high-quality mass communication and high-quality personal communication (Hugo, 2004). An Action Plan form is available online to assist counselors in leading a team toward full implementation of the Nine Principles. By managing the programs, interventions and services, and involving others in the counseling effort, the counselor frees up time spent on routine or administrative tasks and details so that more time can be spent helping students reach their goals. With a laser-like focus on the Pipeline Steps, and a broad view of building and expanding the school's college-going culture through the Nine Principles, the counselor can successfully implement a school-wide vision and effectively "counsel the crowds."

Using Data to Assess Accountability and Impact

While it may seem overwhelming to both serve a large caseload of students and keep track of their college-readiness data, it is critical to establish benchmarks for the counselor's work to gauge student progress and counselor effectiveness. One way might be to focus on data connected with the Pipeline Steps. The new Common Core State Standards, which feature a college- and career-readiness component, demand that schools demonstrate progress in these areas. The current movement from performance to outcome compels counselors to examine their practice. Serving as leaders to ensure that the school is focused on its mission, school counselors can promote equity and access to rigor and opportunity so that all students can reach their full potential.

When reviewing data, school counselors may realize and discover gaps for groups of students who are underrepresented, underserved or underperforming academically. With the perspective of the counselor's role as an organizer and manager of programs and services, the counselor may be asked to guide, lead, direct, or provide additional school-wide programs and activities to address gaps in achievement (Hatch, 2014). The coun-

selor's role is then to identify the troubling data, and use collaboration, advocacy and leadership skills to lead a team in identifying additional instruction and support. For example, a lack of students of color applying to and enrolling in four-year colleges and universities could lead a team to analyze test-taking and college-prep course-taking. Following the analysis, short- and long-term strategies could be developed to ensure students have access to test preparation for the SAT or ACT, are enrolled in the appropriate courses, and have an understanding and support through the financial aid process.

Counselors who serve large caseloads of low-socioeconomic students might consider research from the College Board which indicates that increasing the number of college applications from one to two can increase the probability of enrolling at a four-year college by 40 percent, and increasing the number of applications from two to three can increase the student's probability of enrollment by 10 percent (Smith, 2011). This suggests that college enrollment among underrepresented students can be impacted by encouraging students to submit more applications and by developing approaches to assist these students in the application process. Adoption of this practice as a school-wide model could lead to standardization of practice and possibly more students being admitted to four-year schools.

The big data question is always, "Who's missing?" and the answer to that question guides the counselor toward action. Hatch (2014) identifies attendance, behavior and achievement as the three most important categories to measure. Data elements should always be disaggregated by ethnicity and gender, and might include such elements as:

- students taking the PSAT, SAT, PLAN or ACT

- students who complete the college-preparatory curriculum

- students enrolled in Advanced Placement courses and passing exams with a score of 3 or higher

- students' college acceptances and destinations.

The Education Trust (2004) recommends analyzing and disaggregating data on the elements outlined in Table 2.

Table 2. Disaggregating and Analyzing Data

Testing	*Enrollment*	*Graduation Rate*
Gender and Ethnicity Achievement Grade Taken ELL/LEP Policy and Practice	Honors, Advanced Placement, College-Prep Coursework Gender and Ethnicity Special Education ELL/LEP Policy and Practice	Gender and Ethnicity Special Education ELL/LEP 8th grade–12th grade
Retention Rates	*GPA/Class Rank*	*Special Education*
Subject Area Grade Level Gender and Ethnicity ELL/LEP Postsecondary Enrollment	Gender and Ethnicity Special Education ELL/LEP	Gender and Ethnicity Disability ELL/LEP
Attendance	*Discipline*	*Dropout Rate*
Time of Day Gender and Ethnicity ELL/LEP Absent and Late Arrival Grade Level	Classroom Time of Day Gender and Ethnicity ELL/LEP Special Education	Transition 8th–9th grade Grade Level Gender and Ethnicity ELL/LEP Reason

Source: Education Trust Conference, 2004.

Table 2 provides categories and examples for disaggregating data and evaluating student achievement, attendance and school policy. This table and the tools that may assist the counselor serving large caseloads are the Action Plan and the Goal-Setting Guide. Each of these tools is available online and assists in developing a data-based plan, assessing resources, assigning responsibilities, and providing multi-level interventions designed to reach larger numbers of students and their families.

Common Core State Standards

The discussion of the use of data is a natural transition to the counselor's role in the Common Core State Standards (CCSS), currently adopted by 45 states. Because of the imbedded college- and career-readiness component, the CCSS provide leadership opportunities for counselors. Coordinating the college- and career-readiness component should be the domain of the counselor. Because counselors are uniquely positioned to view the entire school's achievement and data elements, they can monitor and recommend curriculum, provide formative assessment strategies and galvanize the school toward higher college-going rates. Counselors can work with administrators to ensure equity of school-wide policies, identify performance barriers, and ensure that students are placed

in rigorous classes and have remedial support and tutoring when they need it.

As the Common Core State Standards specify K–12 expectations for college and career readiness, an action brief from Achieve (2013) recommends that counselors:

- Think across grade levels

- Develop comprehensive programs

- Provide academic supports to students

- Create standards-based college and career-focused lessons.

With the Common Core State Standards, counselors can focus on academic preparation without remediation, demonstrate their expertise in transcript evaluation and ensure students are taking a college-prep curriculum to ensure readiness for college. Career technical coursework should be a part of the school's curriculum. As assessment experts, counselors can work with teachers to design and provide intervention programs. The formative nature of the CCSS assessments allow for periodic evaluations and interventions. Finally, as experts in college and career readiness, counselors can help students identify interests linked to major selection, design aspiration-building programs for first-generation students, and provide hands-on application and financial aid workshops. CCSS signal a key shift from high school completion to college graduation for students and for professionals, a shift from performance to outcomes. For example, counselors will be evaluated not on how many financial aid workshops they conducted, but on how many students completed and submitted the Free Application for Federal Student Aid. A tool to aid counselors on strategic planning, goal-setting and multi-level interventions is available online.

With this view, the counselor maintains the position as collaboration expert, but also becomes a leader and architect of the college-going culture, working with faculty and administrators, students and their families. Alignment of college- and career-readiness activities with the school's overall plan makes the counselor's work relevant and pivotal.

Conclusion

It is always a critical time for school counselors because they can make a tremendous difference in the lives of their students. Even for those who serve large numbers of students, creativity attuned to the school's culture is an effective tool. To shape their college plans, students need access to information and guidance in a school culture that intentionally supports the goal of college enrollment. No matter the size of the school or the caseload, the counselor is the architect of that effort.

Closing Questions and Considerations

1. Using the framework of the Nine Critical Principles, conduct an inventory of your school's strengths and weaknesses in each of the nine areas. What is in place? What needs to change? What additional programs and services might be offered?

2. Using the Pipeline Steps as a guideline, maintain a weekly log of your duties as a counselor, and categorize each action as a part of the Pipeline Steps. How much of your time is spent in providing college- and career-readiness services to students? Share the results with your principal or counseling team.

3. In considering your school's culture, what might be the role of social media as an outreach tool for your students?

4. How effective is your financial aid program? Do you maintain records on the numbers of FAFSAs filed? How might you work to increase that number, considering how critical financial considerations are in the college decision?

5. Consider using your voice as a public school counselor to speak with your state legislator about the impact and pressures of your job. With widespread adoption and implementation of the Common Core State Standards, think about how you can represent your role to your policy-makers.

6. Examine the data tools provided. How might you use these tools to focus on a specific population or goal to improve your college-going program?

About the Author

Dr. Esther B. Hugo teaches in the Loyola Marymount University School of Education Master's program and in the UCLA College Counseling Certificate Program. As the academic coordinator of the UCLA program, she expanded the curriculum with courses on community college counseling and international student counseling. She serves as the co-director of NACAC's Directing a Dynamic College Counseling Program and is a past-president of the Western Association for College Admission Counseling. She has twice served on the NACAC Board of Directors. In addition, Esther was elected as the chair of the National College Board Guidance and Admission Assembly Council, and is a former College Board trustee. With the College Board, she worked as the director of the Counselor Training Grant, funded by the James Irvine Foundation. The training program reached over 3,000 public school counselors in 20 school districts. Esther holds a doctorate in educational leadership from UCLA and a master's in counseling from Loyola Marymount University (CA). She continues her 38 years in public education with her service on the school board of the Making Waves Academy Charter School in Richmond, CA. Esther worked as the outreach coordinator for Santa Monica College (CA), the college counselor at Westchester High School (CA), and a secondary school teacher.

REFERENCES

Achieve. (2013). Implementing the common core state standards. The role of the school counselor.

Adelman, C. (2006). The toolbox revisited: Paths to degree completion from high school through college. Washington, DC: US Department of Education. Retrieved from *www.ed.gov/rschstat/research/pubs/toolboxrevisit/index.html*.

Alexander, K.L., Pallas, A.M., & Holupka, Scott . (1987). Consistency and change in educational stratification: Recent trends regarding social background and college access. *Research in Social Stratification and Mobility,* 60, 161–185.

Bruce, M., & Bridgeland, J. (2012) National Survey of School Counselors. True north: Charting the course to college and career readiness. The College Board.

Bridgeland, J.M., et al. (2008). One dream, two realities: Perspectives of parents on America's high schools. Civic Enterprises, citing a poll released by MTV and the National Governors Association.

Cabrera, A.F., & La Nasa, S.M. (2001). On the path to college: Three critical tasks facing America's disadvantaged. *Research in Higher Education,* 42(2), 119–150.

Clinedinst, M.E., Hawkins, D.A., Shanahan, T., Addington, L., & West, E. (forthcoming). *2014 State of College Admission*. Arlington, VA: National Association for College Admission Counseling.

The College Board National Office for School Counselor Advocacy. (2010). School counselor strategic planning tool. Retrieved from *http://advocacy.collegeboard.org/sites/default/files/NOSCA%20Strategic%20planning%20tool.pdf*.

Hatch, Trish (2013). *The use of data in school counseling.* Corwin.

House, R., & Bowers, J. (2004). School counselors: Using data to help all students achieve. Ed Trust Conference.

Hugo, E. (2004). Rethinking counseling for college: Perceptions of school and counselor roles in increasing college enrollment. Unpublished doctoral dissertation, UCLA Graduate School of Education and Information Studies.

Isaacs, J.B., Sawhill, I., & Haskins, R. (2008). Economic mobility in America. The Brookings Institution.

King, J.E. (1996). The decision to go to college: Attitudes and experiences associated with college attendance among low-Income students. The College Board.

McDonough, P. (2008). *Building a college culture: Needs, goals, principles, and a case study.* University of California, Los Angeles.

McDonough, P. (2005). Counseling and college counseling in America's high schools. National Association for College Admission Counseling.

National Association for College Admission Counseling (2010). Guiding the way to higher education: Families, counselors and communities together. Arlington, VA: NACAC.

Smith, J. The College Board Advocacy and Policy Center. (2011). Can applying to more colleges increase enrollment rates? Retrieved from *http://media.collegeboard.com/digitalServices/pdf/nosca/research-brief-applying-colleges-increase-enrollment.pdf*.

Chapter 8: The College Search, the College Choice and Applying to College (Introducing the Taxonomy of Applying to College)

Christopher W. Tremblay, EdD

Disclaimer: Colleges and universities named in this chapter are not intended as endorsements by NACAC or the author. They are merely used as examples from the field of college admission.

COLLEGE SEARCH

Searching for college can be an overwhelming process for students because of the many options in the United States and in the world. The challenge with the college search process is that there is no "one size fits all." That's because there is no one right college for each student. The college search process is designed for students to identify their criteria, research colleges and universities that meet that criteria, and narrow the pool to a reasonable number of schools to which to apply for admission.

The benefit of the college search process is that it can begin at any age—it is never too early to start! Elementary school counselors can begin planting the seed with exposure and conversations about college; middle school counselors can introduce college by connecting them to potential careers; and high school counselors facilitate the formal steps of searching, visiting, applying, and deciding.

Web-based college search engines are the common way for students to begin the search process. Such search engines will use a student's criteria to guide the search. Sample criteria may include geographic location, size, majors offered, and campus setting (urban, suburban or rural).

The most important part of the college search process is gaining knowledge. This knowledge includes facts about the schools, but also includes the features, benefits and opportunities offered at each institution. One can never have too much information about a college. It is also important to obtain that knowledge from multiple sources: online, print, current student perspective, alumni perspectives, admission offices, and social media. A student should never rely on one source of information.

The college search lays the foundation for students' choices about their next steps: where to apply and where to enroll.

COLLEGE CHOICE THEORY

Preparing students for college includes a search, the filing of applications and a decision. The conclusion to engage in that search, to apply to college, to apply for financial aid, and where to enroll involves a series of choices. In order to help students make the best possible choices during the college search and college application processes, among others, one must know and understand the importance of these choices and their theoretical frameworks. According to Bergerson (2009), "the process of choosing whether and where to attend college is frequently viewed as a comprehensive process in which students realize their college-going aspirations through the use of several steps leading to enrollment" (p. 21). Hossler, Braxton and Coopersmith defined student college choice in 1989 as "a complex, multistage process during which an individual develops aspirations to continue formal education beyond high school, followed later by a decision to attend a specific college, university or institution of advanced vocational training" (p. 234). Cochran and Coles (2012) remind us that "the college choice process provides a framework for understanding the journey students take to arrive at their enrollment decisions" (p. 2). They indicate that availability, transparency and quality of information about college are some of the primary factors that impact the college choice process (Cochran & Coles, 2012). Much of that information is provided by high school counselors, college admission professionals, college access professionals, and independent counselors.

College choice theory emerged in the 1970s through the development of models of college choice (Hossler & Palmer, 2008). One of the earliest cited studies was completed in 1975 by Lewis and Morrison and came out of Carnegie Mellon University (Hossler & Gallagher, 1987). The first published model of college choice was by Chapman in 1981 (NACAC, 2008).

Hossler and Gallagher's 1987 sociologically based, three-stage model of college choice is the most well-known version and includes predisposition, search and choice (Bergerson, 2009; Hossler, Schmit, & Vesper, 1999). Predisposition refers to the elements that impact students' postsecondary educational plans (Hossler, Schmit, & Vesper, 1999). These elements typically include a student's academic achievement, peers, family history, and other events in high school (Hossler, Schmit, & Vesper, 1999). The search stage compromises the discovery and evaluation of colleges for future enrollment (Hossler, Schmit, & Vesper, 1999). During the choice stage, students select a college or university from among their options and enroll in that particular school (Hossler, Schmit, & Vesper, 1999). Hossler, Schmit, and Vesper's 1999 research reported that "the best time to influence their [students'] postsecondary plans is during or even before their first year of high school" (p. 128). This emphasizes the importance of developing a college-

A variety of elements, within college, choice exist to facilitate college enrollment. For example, according to Hossler and Gallagher (1987), "at each phase of the student college choice process, individual and organizational factors interact to produce outcomes" (p. 208). Bergerson (2009) notes that providing "students with the skills, knowledge, and information needed to engage in the college choice process…" is a part of preparing students for college (p. 17). Here is where college counseling (providing information, increasing knowledge and building skill sets) intersects with college choice. She also notes, "The

All college-bound students are influenced by a wide range of factors in selecting a specific destination for pursuit of higher education.

going culture in the first year of high school.

In 1989, Hossler, Braxton and Coopersmith cited the federal government's increasing role in financial aid, the decline in the number of high school graduates and the lack of enrollment of African-American students contributed to a major interest in student college choice. According to them, this effort emerged because policymakers and researchers were "interested in understanding the factors that shape the decision to attend a postsecondary educational institution" (Hossler, Braxton, & Coopersmith, 1989, p. 231). Specifically, they noted that "individuals incur costs and benefits not only by deciding to pursue a postsecondary education, but also by deciding what type of postsecondary educational institution they will attend" (Hossler, Braxton, & Coopersmith, 1989, p. 232). They concluded their chapter by indicating that understanding student college choice could impact high school guidance activities (Hossler, Braxton, & Coopersmith, 1989). Furthermore, according to Hossler, Schmit and Vesper (1999), "as students move closer to high school graduation, they (and their parents) learn more about postsecondary educational options" (pp. 132–133). The recommendations from their research call for educational professionals to provide "structured experiences for students to learn about…college options [and to] help form students' consideration sets" (Hossler, Schmit, & Vesper, 1999, pp. 134–135).

increased focus on college preparation in the last twenty years recognizes the complex environment in which students make postsecondary decisions" (Bergerson, 2009, p. 18). For example, the author states that the stages of preparing for college are not linear nor uniform for all students, citing that such processes lead to "anxiety, confusion and extensive planning" (Bergerson, 2009, p. 114).

College choice factors are elements that influence students' college decisions. These include, but are not limited to: academic preparation, interested area of study, parents' education level, socioeconomic considerations, and geography, among others. Typically, more than one factor contributes to a student's college choice.

College choice theory (NACAC, 2008), at its very basic level, assumes that a student is going to college and that the primary decision that exists is in the selection of the particular school. However, some researchers even consider the decision to attend college a part of college choice theory (Long, 2004).

All college-bound students are influenced by a wide range of factors in selecting a specific destination for pursuit of higher education. Most college choice literature focuses on one primary factor or examines the interaction of multiple factors. Borrowing from Paulsen (1990), these factors can be connected to one of these three themes: socioeconomic factors, academic factors and contextual/environmental factors.

Socioeconomic and Racial Factors

Socioeconomic factors derive from societal and economic phenomenon and focus on topics such as race/ethnicity, gender, family income, college costs, perception of the return on investment, and financial aid. All of these factors can play a role in college decision-making. Long's (2004) longitudinal study determined that "college costs alone do not explain who does and does not attend college..." (p. 273). Meanwhile, research by Bers and Galowich (2002) indicate that parental socioeconomic status played a factor for students selecting a community college. Researchers from Howard University specifically considered race-related reasons at historically black colleges and universities (Van Camp, Barden, Sloan, & Clarke, 2009). From a race perspective, these "race-related reasons" looked at the race focus of the school, race self-development of the student and race-related behaviors. And Pitre (2006) compared African-American and Caucasian student aspirations and perceptions about college attendance.

Contextual and Environmental Factors

Contextual and environmental factors include such influencers as aspirations, parental education level, distance of college from home, and first-generation status. Long (2004), in her research, determined that distance was a "less important factor" (p. 294). Meanwhile, the focus group and survey research conducted by Bers and Galowich (2002) identified that planning early for college played a significant role in college choice, with early planners identifying community colleges less than four-year schools. Litten (1982) describes that "parental education has stronger effects on the conduct of the college selection process" (p. 400). In addition, Pitre, Johnson and Pitre (2006) point out in Paulsen's 1990 research that parental encouragement plays a significant role in the process of choosing and attending a college. The majority of the articles reviewed here are about contextual and environmental factors.

Academic Factors

Academic factors are inclusive of intelligence, high school attended, grade point average, standardized test scores, and academic reputation of the college (Wolniak & Engberg, 2007). Academic factors are critical since they play a role in admission to college and ultimately academic

success, which leads to attainment of the bachelor's degree (Wolniak & Engberg, 2007). In the study by Niu and Tienda (2008), the type of high school a student attended did influence the choice of college. Specifically, their research indicated that a more affluent high school translated into students applying to more highly selective colleges and universities.

Altogether, the various factors and perspectives about college choice theory remind us of the variables that impact a student's decisions about pursuing a college education.

APPLYING TO COLLEGE

The college search process naturally informs the process of applying to college. The decision of where to apply should be based on the data collected and knowledge gained based on research and visits to colleges. Frequently, students and professionals will group potential colleges or universities into three "buckets" to help students organize colleges for consideration. Listed below are those categories with an explanation of each.

The Match School

A "match school" is one that is a fit for the student both academically and in his/her heart. From a practical perspective, a student clearly falls in the middle of the admission requirements and is a match for that school.

The Dream or Reach School

While the student may have a slim chance of gaining admission, this represents an aspiration. A dream/reach school is one where the student may fall below in one or more areas, but has the opportunity to be considered.

The Back-Up or Safety School

This type of school is one where a student can pretty much guarantee he/she will be admitted. In this scenario, the student is above the stated minimum or average admission requirements. Students will refer to this type of school as a "safe bet." A back-up/safety school still needs to be one where a student can envision him/herself.

While there is no magical number on how many schools to which a student should apply, recent research by Stamats indicates that the national average as of 2012 was three to four colleges (Sickler, 2012). This number enables a student to apply to a match school, a dream school and a safety school. However, there are many students (20 percent) who apply to six to 11 different colleges and universities (Sickler, 2012).

Taxonomy of Admission Application Venues

Introduction

Since the advent of the first admission office at Columbia University in 1915, applying for admission to college has been a process (Henderson, 2008). This process has many facets, including the exchange of information used in rendering an admission decision. Not only has the type of information collected evolved, so have the ways that students experience the process. This section of the chapter is an overview that demonstrates the evolution of how students have experienced, are experiencing, and may experience the college admissions application process, over the last few decades, currently, and on the horizon.

Applying to college incorporates a variety of steps and a variety of processes. How students apply for admission to college can be categorized into four primary dimensions: traditional, interpersonal, digital, and divergent. Table 1 showcases these dimensions and 16 various ways of applying to college.

The traditional dimension involves the initial ways that emerged with the birth of the college application process. Historically, this is how that process began. The interpersonal dimension refers to the ways that include a human-to-human interaction. The "human presence factor" has enabled the college application process to move beyond facts and figures and incorporate an applicant's personal behaviors and characteristics, among other elements. The digital dimension comprises the use of technology, software and hardware. The digital dimension is the one that has grown the most as technology has been introduced and expanded. The divergent dimension represents a radical change to the application process—pushing the envelope of innovation in the field of college admission. Altogether, 16 types of applying to college have emerged within these four dimensions. This section will introduce and explain all of them.

Traditional Dimension

The basic, fundamental way of applying to college historically was to complete a required admission application form. This paper form is typically filled out using a pen and submitted through the mail (sometimes with transcripts and test scores). This form can be from one page to several pages, depending on the number of questions being asked and data being collected by the particular college or university. Historically, at some schools, these paper forms had been reviewed by high school counselors before they were submitted, especially since counselors had a section to complete as a school official. This was a way of "validating" a student's application. Most recently, the paper application form has taken on a new meaning in a digital world. At Kalamazoo Central High School in Michigan, for example, the counselors created a "Retro Day" in which students could complete a paper application form instead of applying online (see Digital section below).

Table 1. Applying to College: A Process in Four Dimensions

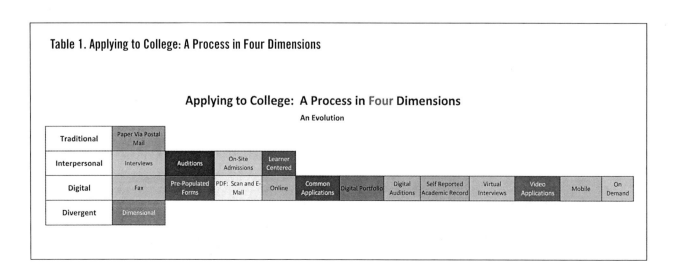

Traditional	Paper Via Postal Mail													
Interpersonal	Interviews	Auditions	On-Site Admissions	Learner Centered										
Digital	Fax	Pre-Populated Forms	PDF: Scan and E-Mail	Online	Common Applications	Digital Portfolio	Digital Auditions	Self Reported Academic Record	Virtual Interviews	Video Applications	Mobile	On Demand		
Divergent	Dimensional													

In some cases, while a paper application may no longer be printed by a college or university, the paper version may be available as a printable PDF on the admission Web site of a college (see the digital dimension for more information). This option is still made available in support of access—catering to a population that may not have full Internet access to apply online. A high school counselor or other adult with access to the Internet could print off the PDF for a student to complete. A paper application may be used by counselors to help a student do a "run through" of completing the application as a pre-application process.

While it is not known which college or university had the first admission application, it is safe to say that information had to have been collected from applicants in the 1600s when Harvard opened.

Application Flashback

In 2014, Wolfman-Arent published an article that chronicled the evolution of Elon College's 1913 paper application. That one-page application featured questions such as, "Is your health good?" and "What county newspaper do you read?" (Wolfman-Arent, 2014). Wolfman-Arent (2014) cited the "lack of standardization" that existed in college applications and the college admission process back then. Elon's 1922 application requested information about a student's "room reservation" in the college dormitory (Wolfman-Arent, 2014). Meanwhile, Elon's 1950s application actually indicated that the $35 deposit was non-refundable "except on doctor's certificate of inability to enter" (Wolfman-Arent, 2014). And by 1977, the Elon admission application began to look standardized, like how most online forms look today (Wolfman-Arent, 2014). Admission questions on applications have come a long way!

Era of Pre-Filled-In Application Forms

Between the advent of the paper application and before the online admission application was born, colleges and universities often sent pre-filled-in applications as a way to save students time in completing the application. For example, all personal and demographic information known about a student (i.e., address, name of high school, gender)—all information pulled from test score reports and inquiry forms—were pre-printed on a student's ap-

plication. This was primarily done as a recruitment tactic by colleges, but it also provided a "convenient factor" for the student, especially for the student applying to five to 10 colleges or universities.

Interpersonal Dimension

Within the interpersonal domain, there are many demonstrations of how the college admission process is more than a data exchange. For example, on-site admission, auditions and alumni interviews are ways in which students become more than a piece of paper and more than demographic data.

On-Site Admission

On-site admission, first used to increase underrepresented minority enrollments by Wayne State University in Detroit, Michigan and then popularized in the early 1990s by Western Michigan University, is the process of reviewing a student's college admission materials in-person, conducting the appropriate admission review/analysis and rendering a decision "on-the-spot" for the student within a matter of minutes (personal communication, Stanley E. Henderson, May 26, 2013). On-site admission enables a student to have insight into the mysterious admission process and an opportunity to present himself/herself. Sometimes students portray on-site admission as a pseudo-interview. While it is not technically an interview, it contains some of the elements of an admission interview. On-site admission ensures that a student receives an instant admission decision. There is some debate about whether on-site admission should be used for students being denied. On-site admission is for everyone. For students not admissible, it becomes a counseling opportunity to educate that student about alternative paths to the same destination, which is often a referral to a community or junior college as a starting point.

Alumni Interviews

Alumni interviews have long been used by private and public colleges as a way to screen applicants, especially applicants who may live quite a distance from the college or university. For many schools, alumni interviews are optional. Some schools, like the University of Richmond (2014), offer non-evaluative interviews. Typically alumni interviews are conducted across the United States in various cities where alumni ambassadors live. Trained alumni ambassadors are graduates of those colleges who volunteer to conduct the interviews and share the results and feedback with the admission office. These alumni interviews are frequently held in a public setting, such as a library or coffee shop. From the student's perspective, these alumni interviews can be very informative and valuable for learning more about the school, especially through the lens of a former student and graduate. Alumni interviews usually take place after a student has applied for admission. Since 100 percent of applicants cannot be interviewed by alumni, students not completing an alumni interview will not be disadvantaged in the admission decision process. Alumni interactions enable students to gain perspective on those colleges and these types of interactions may lead to future networking among those alumni.

Auditions

Auditions frequently are the primary admission evaluation process utilized by performing arts programs and colleges to determine the quality of students' talents and skill set. Auditions are typically held on campus or off-site in person and are usually in addition to the formal application process made with the admission office. Such auditions are conducted by the faculty in the specific discipline. Audition schedules are published well in advance so students can plan accordingly. Universities that recruit nationally may conduct auditions in several regional locations throughout the United States. Not every applicant may be selected or invited to audition since audition policies vary from school to school. Some colleges use auditions to award scholarships in the fine and performing arts. Audition requirements are often published online so a student can appropriately prepare for the audition. Such requirements will describe how to prepare and what to bring.

An emerging approach is the use of the Internet for digital auditions (see the digital dimension for more information).

Learner-Centered

On the horizon would be an admission review called "learner-centered," in which the student makes his/her own admission decision (in consultation with an admis-

sion representative, of course!). Such a process would enable an applicant to self-reflect and engage in the process at the highest level possible. While no known schools are currently doing this, this does reflect a potential upcoming trend, especially as this would align with schools whose missions indicate they are learner-centered. Some individuals would argue that a high school senior does not have the skill set to self-evaluate his/her potential for success in college. This type of admission review may not be favored by the faculty because the screening for success in college has been transferred from the college to the student. This approach is similar to "directed self-placement," which is frequently used within academic departments for placement in specific college courses. It will be interesting to see if this approach ever comes to fruition and with what guidelines.

All interpersonal dimensions are still incorporated into today's admission process, even though technology has begun to trump the protocol. The interpersonal components ensure a "human presence" in a decision that still primarily relies on quantitative data.

Digital Dimension

As the use of technology in higher education has expanded, its application in college admission has also grown. Today's tech-savvy applicants expect this type of technology integration into the process. In a digital context, these have included faxing/scanning applications, applying online, digital portfolios, self-reported information, and applying through mobile platforms.

Faxed Applications and PDFs

As a way to expedite an application and/or bypass the traditional postal service, many school counseling offices would send applications using a fax machine. Now, with enhanced technologies, that practice has made the transition to sometimes sending PDF applications via email. While most colleges have discontinued printing paper applications, they often still make a PDF version available, especially for those students who do not have access to the Internet. A PDF application can be printed, completed by hand and submitted.

Online Applications

In the early 2000s, the first application to college made its online debut as college Web sites evolved, became more sophisticated and were used as a college recruitment tool. In this format, students enter information using a Web form and electronically transmit all of the contents directly to the college/university. The online application was controversial for some because in many cases, it unintentionally excluded the high school counselor's involvement. Online applications have also evolved in look, feel and functionality. Today, students expect a mobile-friendly version of these applications, which means that they feature responsive design, a feature that changes the look and feel of the application based on whether a student is using a desktop computer, laptop, tablet, or smartphone. One feature that arose with the use of online applications was the ability for students to check the status of their application electronically, typically through a college's student information system.

Common Applications

In 1975, the Common Application was born (Common Application, 2014). According to the Common Application (2014) Web site that notes its history: "The Common Application membership association was established in 1975 by 15 private colleges that wished to provide a common, standardized first-year application form for use at any member institution." According to Forbes staff writer Chase Peterson-Withorn (2014), "The launch of the Common Application in 1975…was one of the most expansive attempts schools made toward revolutionizing the college admissions process." In 2013–2014, Common Application (2014) officially retired its paper application, signaling a new era in college admission.

Since then, the Universal College Application (UCA) (2014a) has been established and welcomes applications

Today, students expect a mobile-friendly version of these applications, which means that they feature responsive design, a feature that changes the look and feel of the application based on whether a student is using a desktop computer, laptop, tablet, or smartphone.

Self-Reported Academic Record (SRAR)

A phenomenon that was tested in the early 2000s was the concept of a student self-reporting his/her test scores and grades as part of the admission process. Schools like Rutgers (2014) refers to it as a "Self-Reported Academic Record." Offers of admission made using self-reported data are usually "conditional." Submission of inaccurate or false information typically leads to the revocation of admission as the self-reporting process is built on the honor system, often referred to on college Web sites as "academic integrity." Self-reported data is confirmed typically using the final official high school transcript. Self-reported academic records are not popular, but are growing, especially because it reduces some of the data entry in the admission offices, since the student is inputting his/her own grades. Some schools, like Stony Brook University (2014), tout the environmentally friendly factor of self-reported academic records, especially since it requires only one (instead of two) transcript to be sent, the official one. However, in today's world of electronic transcripts, that is fast becoming a non-issue.

for more than 40 colleges and universities. The Universal College Application uses a technology called "ApplyWithUs" and requires applicants to be at least 13 years old (Universal College Application, 2014b). According to the applicationsonline.com site, "The UCA operates with the goal of connecting colleges and universities to a diverse group of students, allowing applicants to learn about institutions that they may not have considered otherwise. The UCA also reduces the stress of the admissions process by simply and intuitively consolidating complex application requirements into one place" (Applications Online, 2014).

For students using systems like the Common Application, a few clicks can transmit the same data to multiple colleges and universities. Some have criticized the convenience factor of sending one application to multiple schools, as though the process has been too easy. Proponents of access would state that this process increases access to college by making it more efficient. Today, more than 85 percent of college applications are now completed online using Web sites, according to the 2012 NACAC *State of College Admission Report* (Clinedinst, Hurley, & Hawkins, 2012). That percentage has increased from 57 percent in 2004 to 85 percent in 2011 (Clinedinst, Hurley, & Hawkins, 2012). Online functionality enables colleges/universities to automate the data entry transaction of establishing an admission record. Most recently, the ability for prospective students to apply on a mobile device like an iPhone or Android have become available. The evolution to responsive Web design (RWD) has improved this process. Applications filed using digital means are typically signed with a digital signature in lieu of a formal, written signature on paper. A recent report by SlideRoom, based on their Google Analytics, indicated "about 5% of applicants are completing all—or a significant portion—of the application process on their mobile device" (2013, n.p.).

Digital Portfolios

Art and architecture schools have also entered into the digital world by offering applicants the opportunity to present a digital portfolio as part of the application process. In this venue, students upload samples of their works to a Web site for access by faculty making admission decisions. Schools like Illinois State University's College of Fine Arts (2014) expects students to use DropBox to upload digital submissions. Other schools may use SlideRoom, another tool for uploading digital submissions (University of Delaware, 2014). In most cases, a student has to create an account to submit digital items for admission consideration.

Digital Auditions

An emerging approach is the use of the Internet for digital auditions. Using a tool like DecisionDesk, students can upload their vocal or instrumental performances for admission consideration. DecisionDesk™ is a "software-as-a-service company that streamlines media intensive application processes by enabling colleges to accept high volumes of video auditions and video resumes online instead of through the mail" (Knific, 2013, n.p.). Schools like Western Michigan University's School of Music (2014) uses this technology tool for students who live beyond a 300-mile radius.

Virtual Interviews

An emerging trend is the use of video technology to conduct virtual face-to-face interviews. Interviews are not required at very many colleges, but they provide an opportunity to put a face to an application. For example, Bard College (2014) in New York offers applicants an option to interview using Skype. As this technology has been implemented into the application process, sites like happyschools.com now offer tips to students about how to prepare for interviews (Sukumar, 2014). The option of a virtual interview is typically arranged when a student cannot travel to the physical campus for an in-person interview, or when an interview with a local alumnus/alumna is not possible. Some colleges are up-front about the reality of virtual interviews, such as Southwestern University, which states in their FAQs: "It should be noted that alternative interviews are rarely as illuminating as those done in person" (Southwestern University, n.d., p. 1). Coordinating time zone differences can also pose a challenge for virtual interviews. Virtual interviews can be very beneficial for students applying to an international college or university. Skype appears to be the primary tool used to conduct these virtual interviews.

Video Applications

The latest digital alternative in the college application process is the video application. In 2014, Goucher College in Maryland became the first college to announce it was offering a video application (Carlotti, 2014). This two-minute video must answer the question, "How do you see yourself at Goucher?" (Goucher, 2014a). Three criteria are used to evaluate each video: content/thoughtfulness, structure/organization and clarity/effectiveness (Goucher, 2014b). In addition to the video submission, a digital application is still required, along with submission of two writing samples (Goucher, 2014a). Goucher College's president referred to this "video app" as an experiment, one designed to address "undermatching" and relies on the ubiquity of cell phones (Perez-Pena, 2014; Carlotti, 2014).

Admission via Mobile

With the advent of smartphones, the college admission application process has the opportunity to "go mobile." Most colleges these days have developed an "app" (application) on smartphones for students to access information about the admission process. In 2011, John Marshall Law School in Atlanta was touted as one of the first colleges to offer a mobile-friendly admission application (Ezarik, 2011). As colleges and universities have developed responsive-design Web sites, application Web sites are growing in their mobile-friendliness. In a 2013 online article, Sabo discusses trends in mobile admission, concluding that:

> as use of handheld devices for communications continue to rise, colleges can capitalize on this trend by developing more integrated apps that allow students to complete the time-consuming admissions and financial aid process exclusively from their smartphones or other handheld devices (n.p.).

This is a trend worth watching.

Admission "On Demand": A Future Trend?

In the digital realm, the possibilities are endless. However, one concept that is just entering the field is "admission on demand," in which a student can file an application online and then enter a live chatroom for an instant decision. This essentially reflects a digital version of the in-person, on-site admission process. Northern Illinois University (NIU) has offered such a service, and it is referred to as "Virtual Decision Day." According to the NIU Web site, "Virtual Decision Day—like an on-campus, on-the-spot decision day—allows students to experience a virtual check-in, group presentations and private consultations, and to confirm their enrollment and request additional information" (2013, n.p.). As students' expectations for an instant decision grows, admission on demand may become the norm.

Divergent Dimension

The newest dimension, which emerged in 2014, is the divergent dimension. This dimension reflects advanced, radical thinking in the college application process. Currently, there is one such type of divergent component: the dimensional application, created by Bennington College (Hoover, 2014).

"Dimensional Application"

In Fall 2014, Bennington College in Vermont announced that it wanted its applicants for admission to "individually curate" how the college would evaluate them for admission, referring to it as the new "Dimensional Application" (Hoover, 2014, n.p.). This was a radical departure from the traditional admission application process. Bennington's (2014) official news release indicated this dimensional application does not replace the Common Application. According to Bennington (2014), the dimensional application is designed for students to "create a compelling portrait of their academic achievement, and to demonstrate, in their own way, their potential to enrich, and be enriched by, the Bennington community" (n.p.). Bennington (2014) invites students using the dimension application route to be "bold" in the same way that Bennington has been bold in announcing this new component. Bennington (n.d.a) believes this style of application supports a student's "intellectual and creative capacities that lie on a continuum" (n.p.). According to the Bennington (n.d.b) FAQ Web page, the dimensional application is designed for students "who want to do more than respond to a set of given prompts" (n.p.). Applicants using this application format will be evaluated on "the quality of the materials submitted; the caliber of thinking behind them; evidence of a student's readiness to advance a range of work; and markers of a student's capacity to contribute to the Bennington community in multiple dimensions" (Bennington, n.d.b, n.p.).

Evolution of Admission Application Questions

As the application forms have changed and the way to submit them has evolved, new questions emerged over time. For example, asking questions associated with first-generation status has been a growing trend. In an attempt to evaluate any safety concerns, criminal conduct questions have been added over the years, often creating debates (Education from the Inside Out Coalition, n.d.). Elmhurst College (IL) became the first school in the United States in 2011 to ask an LGBT-related question in order to capture information about how to provide support to students identifying with that population (NBC Chicago, 2011). That question is: "Would you consider yourself to be a member of the LGBT (lesbian, gay, bisexual, trans-gendered) community?" (NBC Chicago, 2011). Newest questions may reflect the changing demographics of entering college students and/or an interest by the colleges and universities in collecting information on how to best serve a diverse group of students.

OTHER RECENT APPLICATION TRENDS

Stealth Applications

Another trend is when students bypass the inquiry stage, and their first contact with a college or university is when the application arrives. "A stealth applicant is a prospective undergraduate student whose first recorded contact with an institution is the submission of an application for admission," stated Dupaul and Harris (2012). Ulmer (2008) refers to these applications as "out of the blue applications." This trend emerges when: (a) students did not want to be bombarded with recruitment literature, or (b) a student knew where he/she was planning to enroll and did not need or want to conduct a college search. Some students prefer to remain anonymous during the college search process and becoming a stealth applicant gives them that right and freedom. Many cite the rise in technology as driving an increase in stealth applications. The digital dimension demonstrates how quickly this aspect is evolving. Students now have instant access to college information 24/7.

College Application Creep

A phenomenon that always has potential to exist is "college application creep." This creep is when students become anxious and want to submit their applications to college nearly seconds after they complete their junior year. College application creep has emerged because the technology facilitates this process, and students live in this type of "instant" world. The NACAC Statement of Principles of Good Practice specifically states: "Postsecondary members agree to not notify first-year candidates for fall admission prior to the receipt of a transcript that reflects completion of the final semester of the junior year of high school or the equivalent" (2013, p. 5). Of course, students dual-enrolling in college while still in high school are exempt and would be completing a non-degree admission application, which

can be submitted prior to the final semester of junior year.

CONCLUSION

This chapter introduced various aspects of preparing for college: the search process, the college choice process and the evolution of the college application process. Together, these processes form the comprehensive progression of going from start to finish in planning to enroll in college. The college search process begins with a student researching and gathering a plethora of knowledge. The college choice process involves a variety of decision-making processes throughout the various enrollment steps. The college application has evolved due to a variety of factors. As one can see, the college application process has matured over time. As technologies are developed, we can expect this same process to continue to evolve. What has virtually remained the same is the information that is collected from students in order to establish a college record and make the important admission decisions.

DISCUSSION QUESTIONS

1. How should a college counselor instruct a student on how to conduct his/her college search?

2. What is the most important part of the college search process? Why?

3. In the context of college choice, how should a college counselor approach helping a student create his/her "consideration set"?

4. Why is the college choice process relevant to applying to college?

5. Of the various types of ways to apply to college that were presented, which one should never disappear? Why?

6. Given that the digital dimension of the taxonomy has evolved the most in recent history, where would you anticipate the future of this digital dimension going?

ABOUT THE AUTHOR

Dr. Christopher W. Tremblay is associate provost for enrollment management at Western Michigan University (WMU) (MI). He previously served as assistant vice chancellor for enrollment management, executive director of enrollment management, and director of admissions and orientation at the University of Michigan-Dearborn (MI). He has also previously worked at Gannon University (PA). Tremblay earned his bachelor's and master's degrees from WMU. He has a post-master's certificate in enrollment management from Capella University and a doctorate of education in educational leadership from the University of Michigan. As an enrollment management and admissions professional for 20 years, he has published 12 articles in four different academic journals and has presented at 40 conferences nationally and internationally.

RESOURCES

Resource	Web Site/Link
50 Years of College Choice	*luminafoundation.org/publications/Hossler.pdf*
College Board's College Search	*bigfuture.collegeboard.org/college-search*
Common Application	*commonapp.org*
Decision Desk	*decisiondesk.com*
NACAC's Guide to the College Admission Process	*nacacnet.org/research/PublicationsResources/Marketplace/Documents/GCAP2011_Web.pdf*
NACAC International Resources	*nacacnet.org/studentinfo/InternationalStudentResources/Pages/default.aspx*
NACAC Student and Parent Resources	*nacacnet.org/studentinfo/Pages/Default.aspx*
SlideRoom (digital portfolios)	*slideroom.com*
Universal Application	*universalcollegeapp.com*

REFERENCES

Applications Online. (2014). *Applications online.* Retrieved from *http://applicationsonline.com/clients.*

Bard College. (2014). In *Applying Options.* Retrieved from *http://www.bard.edu/admission/applying/options.*

Bennington College. (2014, September 24). Benning introduces new application option. Retrieved October 2, 2014, from *http://www.bennington.edu/NewsEvents/NewsFullStory/2014/09/24/bennington-introduces-new-application-option.*

Bennington College. (n.d.a). Dimensional application. Retrieved October 2, 2014, from *http://www.bennington.edu/Admissions/apply/dimensional-application.*

Bennington College. (n.d.b). Dimensional application FAQs. Retrieved October 2, 2014, from *http://www.bennington.edu/Admissions/apply/dimensional-application/faqs.*

Bergerson, A.A. (2009). College choice and access to college: Moving policy, research and practice to the 21st Century [Monograph]. *ASHE Higher Education Report, 35*(4), 17–85.

Bers, T.H., & Galowich, P.M. (2002). Using survey and focus group research to learn about parents' roles in the community college choice process. *Community College Review, 29*(4), 68–82. Retrieved from Research Library. (Document ID: 123062951).

Carlotti, P. (2014, September 12). Goucher College aims to level playing field with video application option. *USA Today.* Retrieved October 2, 2014, from *http://college.usatoday.com/2014/09/12/goucher-college-aims-to-level-playing-field-with-video-application-option.*

Clinedinst, M.E., Hurley, S.F., & Hawkins, D.A. (2012). *2012 State of College Admission Report (10th Anniversary).* Arlington, VA: National Association for College Admission Counseling. Retrieved from *nacacnet.org/research/PublicationsResources/Marketplace/Documents/SOCA2012.pdf.*

Cochran, T., & Coles, A. (2012, Winter). Maximizing the college choice process to increase fit & match for underserved students. Washington, D.C.: Institute for Higher Education Policy. Retrieved from *http://knowledgecenter.completionbydesign.org/sites/default/files/321%20Pathways%20to%20College%20Network%202012.pdf.*

Common Application. (2014). *History.* Retrieved from *https://www.commonapp.org/Login#!PublicPages/History.*

Dupaul, S., & Harris, M. (2012). Now you see them, now you don't: Understanding the actions and impact of stealth applicants in college admission. Retrieved from *http://www.google.com/url?sa=t&rct=j&q=&esrc=s&source=web&cd=1&cad=rja&uact=8&ved=0CCIQFjAA&url=http%3A%2F%2Fwww.nacacnet.org%2Fevents%2F2012%2Fsessions%2FDocuments%2FG1.pdf&ei=KBnsU4XUIYiWyATmmIHYBg&.*

Education from the Inside Out Coalition. (n.d.). Policy brief: Criminal history screenings in college admissions. Retrieved from *http://www.google.com/url?sa=t&rct=j&q=&esrc=s&source=web&cd=4&cad=rja&uact=8&ved=0CEQQFjAD&url=http%3A%2F%2Faacrao-web.s3.amazonaws.com%2Fmigrated%2Fadmissions_criminal.pdf_51caedb6afef49.63423909.pd.*

Ezarik, M. (2011, November). Now try this: A mobile (admissions) app. Retrieved from *http://www.universitybusiness.com/article/now-try-mobile-admissions-app.*

Goucher College. (2014a). In The Goucher Video Application. Retrieved October 2, 2014, from *http://www.goucher.edu/admissions/how-to-apply/video-app.*

Goucher College. (2014b). In Goucher Video Application Evaluation. Retrieved October 2, 2014, from *http://www.goucher.edu/admissions/how-to-apply/video-app/evaluation.*

Henderson, S.E. (2008.) Admissions' evolving role: From gatekeeper to strategic partner. In B. Lauren (Ed.) *The college admission officer's guide.* Washington DC: AACRAO.

Hoover, E. (2014, September 24). Applicants to Bennington College may now 'curate' their applications. *The Chronicle of Higher Education.* Retrieved October 2, 2014, from *http://chronicle.com/blogs/headcount/applicants-to-bennington-college-may-now-curate-their-applications/39089.*

Hossler, D., Braxton, J., & Coopersmith, G. (1989). Understanding student college choice. In J.C. Smart (Ed.), *Higher education: Handbook of theory and research* (Vol. V, pp. 231– 288). New York, NY: Agathon Press.

Hossler, D., & Gallagher, K.S. (1987). Studying student college choice: A three-phase model and the implications for policymakers. *College and University,* 207– 221.

Hossler, D., & Palmer, M. (2008). Why understand research on college choice? In *Fundamentals of college admission counseling: A textbook for graduate students and practicing counselors,* (2nd ed., pp. 42– 53). Dubuque, IA: Kendall/Hunt Publishing Company.

Hossler, D., Schmit, J., & Vesper, N. (1999). *Going to college: How social, economic, and educational factors influence the decisions students make.* Baltimore, MD: Johns Hopkins University Press.

Illinois State University College of Fine Arts. (2014). *Admissions & portfolio requirements for the school of art.* Retrieved from *http://finearts.illinoisstate.edu/art/admissions.*

Knific, J. (2013, February 28). *Kent State Streamlines Auditions with DecisionDesk™.* Retrieved from *http://www.decisiondesk.com/kent-state-streamlines-auditions-with-decisiondesk.*

Litten, L.H. (1982). Different strokes in the applicant pool: Some refinements in a model of student college choice. *The Journal of Higher Education,* 53(4), 383– 402.

Long, B.T. (2004). How have college decisions changed over time? An application of the conditional logistic choice model. *Journal of Econometrics,* 121(1,2), 271– 296. Retrieved from ABI/INFORM Global. (Document ID: 653965031).

National Association for College Admission Counseling (NACAC). (2013). Statement of principles of good practice. Retrieved from *http://www.nacacnet.org/about/Governance/Policies/Documents/SPGP_9_2013.pdf.*

National Association for College Admission Counseling (NACAC). (2008). *Fundamentals of college admission counseling: A textbook for graduate students and practicing counselors.* (2nd ed.). Dubuque, IA: Kendall/Hunt Publishing Co.

NBC Chicago. (2011, August 25). *Elmhurst College to ask about sexual orientation.* Retrieved from *http://www.nbcchicago.com/news/local/Elmhurst-College-to-Ask-About-Sexual-Orientation--128378348.html.*

Niu, S.X., & Tienda, M. (2008). Choosing colleges: Identifying and modeling choice sets. *Social Science Research, 37,* 416–433.

Northern Illinois University (NIU). (2013, March 21). NIU sees record number of freshman applicants. Retrieved from *niutoday.info/2013/03/21/niu-sees-record-number-of-freshman-applicants.*

Paulsen, M.B. (1990). *College choice: Understanding student enrollment behavior.* ASHE-ERIC Higher Education Report No. 6. Washington, D.C.: The George Washington University, School of Education and Human Development.

Perez-Pena, R. (2014, September 27). Colleges make it easier for students to show, not tell, in their applications. *The New York Times.* Retrieved October 2, 2014, from *http://www.nytimes.com/2014/09/28/education/college-admissions-goucher-video.html?_r=0?_r=0.*

Peterson-Withorn, C. (2014). Virtual reality and the brave new world of college recruiting. Retrieved from *http://www.forbes.com/sites/chasewithorn/2014/07/07/virtual-reality-and-the-brave-new-world-of-college-recruiting.*

Pitre, P.E. (2006). College choice: A study of African American and white student aspirations and perceptions related to college attendance. *College Student Journal, 40*(3), 562-573.

Pitre, P.E., Johnson, T. E., & Pitre, C. C. (2006). Understanding predisposition in college choice: Toward an integrated model of college choice and theory of reasoned action. *College & University, 81*(2), 35–42.

Rutgers University. (2014). *Self-reported academic record.* Retrieved from *ugadmissions.rutgers.edu/srt/Login.aspx.*

Sabo, R. (2013, August 12). *Mobile apps revamp the college admissions process.* Retrieved from *http://www.onlineschools.com/in-focus/mobile-apps-revamp-college-admissions-process.*

Sickler, E. (2012). 2012 TeensTALK® findings: A comprehensive look at teen trends, attitudes, lifestyles and knowledge with special focus on college search and selection. [PowerPoint presentation]. Retrieved from *www.iowaacac.org/.../2012_stamats_teenstalk_final_comprehensive.pdf.*

Slideshare. (2013, May 31). How many applicants apply to College on a mobile device? Retrieved from *slideroom.com/blog/Apply_to_College_with_mobile_Device.html.*

Southwestern University. (n.d.). Application FAQs. Retrieved from *http://www.southwestern.edu/live/files/2100-fall-2013-application.*

Stony Brook University. (2014). *Self report your academic record.* Retrieved from *http://www.stonybrook.edu/ugadmissions/applying/stars.shtml.*

Sukumar, R. (2014, January 10). *How to prepare for college admissions Skype video interview?* Retrieved from *http://www.happyschools.com/college-admissions-skype-video-interview.*

Ulmer, R. (2008, May 2). Rise of the stealth applicants. *TargetX.* Retrieved from *https://www.targetx.com/rise-of-the-stealth-applicants.*

Universal Common Application. (2014a). *University common application.* Retrieved from *www.universalcollegeapp.com.*

Universal Common Application. (2014b). *University common application.* Retrieved from *https://uca.applywithus.com/users/sign_up.*

University of Richmond. (2014). *Alumni interviews.* Retrieved from *http://admissions.richmond.edu/contact/alumni-interview.html.*

Van Camp, D., Barden, J., Sloan, L., & Clarke, R. (2009). Choosing an HBCU: An opportunity to pursue racial self-development. *The Journal of Negro Education, 78*(4), 457–468. Retrieved from Research Library. (Document ID: 2002175631).

Western Michigan University School of Music. (2014). *Auditions*. Retrieved from *http://wmich.edu/music/auditions*.

Wolfman-Arent, A. (2014, August 12). Elon College's application, 1913: Have you read any Homer? Retrieved from *http://chronicle.com/article/Elon-Colleges-Application/148367*.

Wolniak, G.C., & Engberg, M.E. (2007). The effects of high school feeder networks on college enrollment. *Review of Higher Education: Journal of the Association for the Study of Higher Education*, 31(1), 27–53. doi:*http://dx.doi.org/10.1353/rhe.2007.0054*.

Chapter 9:   The Use of Data in College and Career Readiness

Trish Hatch, PhD
@trishhatch

"By 2020, America will once again have the highest proportion of college graduates in the world … So tonight I ask every American to commit to at least one year or more of higher education or career training … every American will need to get more than a high school diploma."

President Barack Obama
Address to Joint Session of Congress
February 24, 2009

VIGNETTE: WHICH SCHOOL COUNSELOR DO YOU WANT TO BE?

School Counselor #1

Jane, a 20-year veteran in the school counseling department in a large (2,000-student) suburban high school, has always been well-liked by administrators, teachers, parents, and students. She advertises her school counseling program to students and parents in the school newsletter. She provides guidance lessons that review college requirements and promote AP courses to those she thinks are prepared. When she visits classrooms during registration time, she encourages all of her students to schedule appointments if they need any information or assistance with their college applications. She holds college information nights every year in the fall. Most of her students get into "good" colleges, because Jane has an understanding of what it takes to get into which schools, relying on her own experience and phone conversations with college admission counselors. Jane reviews her students' selection of courses. About half of her students take either the SAT or ACT. Jane feels quite accomplished and proud of the fact that each year, some of her students get into Ivy League schools. She creates a "Wall of Fame," posting stars in her office of the schools to which her students was admitted.

School Counselor #2

Shelly is a third-year school counselor. When Shelly first interviewed for the school counselor position, she reviewed the school's achievement data on the state's Web site. She noticed that the school had a graduation rate of 80.1 percent and a 38.6 percent graduation college-eligible rate. She also noticed that both of these statistics had declined over the previous two years and told the administrator that if he hired her, she would work with other educators to reverse this trend. Once hired, Shelly and the newly created data-based decision-making team researched more data and noticed a 12 percent decrease in students taking upper-level math and science courses.

Further analysis indicated a male/female discrepancy, as well as an ethnic achievement gap.

Shelly and the team utilized this data to leverage conversations with other stakeholders and to begin a program service delivery revision to ensure that every student had

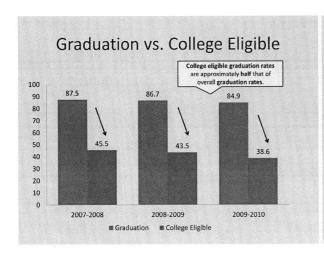

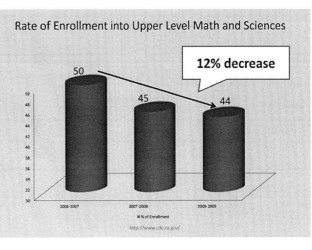

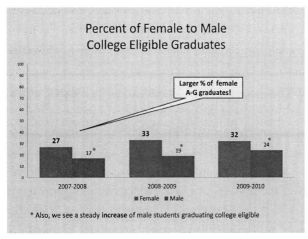

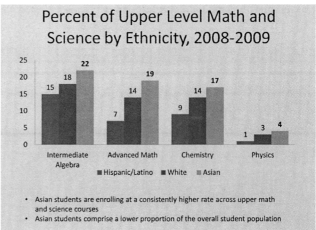

the knowledge, attitudes and skills necessary to achieve their highest potential. She advocated institutionalizing individual student planning meetings each year with every student to promote rigorous courses and graduating college- and career-ready. She evaluated her classroom curriculum to determine what her students needed to know and learn. She utilized AP potential data to advocate for shifting policies regarding who takes AP courses. She recommended reaching out to males and Latinos to take academic risks and inviting parents to college evening programs presented in both English and Spanish. She collaborated with teachers to ensure prerequisites were revised to allow more students to take advanced math and science courses, and she assisted her school counseling team in monitoring students' progress. She and her team began to rely heavily on the data collected via the free, state-sponsored, Internet-based portal that her students utilize to search for and apply to college. The portal contained academic, standardized testing and college application data. Over time, Shelly and her team consistently utilized student performance data (i.e., grades, GPA, test scores, teacher recommendations) to help students with course selection, careers to consider, which standardized test to take, and which colleges to research. Each year, they shared with school administrators and the school board the successes and challenges the data revealed and how they planned on improving the results in order to reach their goals.

Which school counselor do you aspire to be? In which school would you want to be a student or parent? Which school counselor would you want as a colleague?

INTRODUCTION

This scenario above asks the reader to imagine which school counselor they aspire to be or would prefer to have as a colleague. While the second scenario is more in line with current expectations, it might not reflect the reader's current findings in the field. This is due in large part to the significant shift in expectations regarding the use of data for school counselors over the last decade. This chapter is written to provide a brief overview of the use of data in college and career counseling. Focusing on data aligns well with the exciting new initiative by the First Lady called Reach Higher, which calls on secondary school counselors to support college opportunities for first-generation youth. To reach the goal of preparing all students to be college- and career-ready, school counselors in secondary schools must be prepared to use data to plan and evaluate their programs and services. This chapter will provide an overview of the types of data school counselors utilize as they design and measure impact of their activities. Utilizing national organizations, including the American School Counselor Association National Model and the National Office for School Counselor Advocacy (NOSCA) tool documents, this chapter provides samples of district goals and recommendations for implementing the foundation, delivery, management and accountability components of the ASCA National Model. Next, the counselors' use of data as a social justice agent of change is presented, along with recommendations for collecting and evaluating process and perception data. The chapter provides examples of ways to calculate and share results, along with recommendations and cautions on using data profiles. The chapter concludes with a list of ideas for creating a college-going culture. Finally, additional samples and examples are provides in the appendix. Ready to begin? Let's get started.

SCHOOL COUNSELORS AND EDUCATIONAL REFORM

The No Child Left Behind Act (NCLB) of 2001 called for *all educators* to focus on the use of data and accountability. Although school counselors are not specifically mentioned in NCLB or in current federal and state blueprints (United States Department of Education, 2011), as professional educators in schools, counselors are expected to take equal responsibility to ensure their programs and services are data-driven, evidence-based and accountable to the students and stakeholders they serve.

Beginning in 2010, "Building a Grad Nation" called on school counselors to use data to (a) monitor and identify students who are off track and (b) to provide the extra assistance needed to help students graduate college-ready (Balfanz, Bridgeland, Moore, & Fox, 2010). Published yearly, the most recent (2014) version continues to recommend building the capacity to improve graduation and college readiness by using evidence-based strategies, data-driven practices, and developing highly effective and accountable counselors (Balfanz, Bridgeland, Fox, DePoli, Ingram, Maushard, 2014).

For years, the Education Trust Foundation (2009) and the National Office of School Counselor Advocacy (NOSCA, 2011) have promoted the school counselor's role as one of leadership in the use of data as a necessary component in ensuring that every student receives opportunity and access to college and career readiness. Supported by the National Association of Secondary School Principals (NASSP), the school counselor's role in common core implementation includes: recommendations for participation on leadership and data teams, using data to design programs, creating action plans for college and career readiness, identifying gaps and needs, providing interventions, and monitoring progress (Achieve, 2012).

Today's pre-service school counselors now use data as common practice when they learn to design, implement, evaluate, and improve their school counseling programs (American School Counselor Association, 2003; 2005;

2012). Since the release of the American School Counselor Association (ASCA) National Model in 2003, dozens of textbooks and professional articles have emerged to assist school counselors and counselor educators in preparing pre-service and practicing school counselors to incorporate data into their daily work (Young & Kaffenberger, 2009; Stone & Dahir, 2005; Holcomb-McCoy, 2007; Dimmitt, Carey, & Hatch, 2007; Gysbers & Henderson, 2006).

This chapter is written to assist pre-service and current school counselors, counselor educators and college admission counselors in understanding the many ways data can be utilized when promoting a college- and career-readiness culture. Partnering with administrators and other educational leaders, school counselors can ensure that parents and students have access to important and necessary data to make informed college and career decisions. Using data, school counselors can identify areas of need, target interventions, promote equity and access to rigorous educational opportunities for all students, and work within the system to change policies and procedures when needed.

NATIONAL FOCUS ON COLLEGE COMPLETION INITIATIVES AND SCHOOL COUNSELORS

In 2009, President Obama challenged Congress to support his 2020 plan for college completion, meant to address the following educational and economic concerns:

- Only half of all undergraduates complete a college degree in six years.

- Thirty-eight percent of all US students take a remedial course in their first or second year.

- More than 60 percent of jobs will require a postsecondary education.

- Students with a bachelor's degree will earn 40 percent more in their lifetime (29 percent more with a community college degree) than students with only high school diplomas.

- The US is ninth in the world in college attainment for the 25–34-year-old population. (Kanter, Ochoa, Nassif, & Chong, 2011)

President Obama's 2020 College Completion goal called for 10 million more graduates from community colleges, four-year colleges and universities by the year 2020. To accomplish this goal, legislators and educators were asked to create and support opportunities for all students to realize the dream of higher education. To urge participation, President Obama recommended that beginning in 2015, only those states that are implementing assessments aligning with college- and career-ready standards be eligible for formula funds (United States Department of Education, 2011, p. 13).

In 2011, the Secretary of Education Arne Duncan called on school counselors to "own the turf" of college and career readiness. Duncan stated that school counselors play an essential role in preparing all students for college and future years by helping students plan for college, assisting them with creating a path to graduation and by serving as the bridge for students into college. Secretary Duncan implored school counselors to take a leadership role within their schools to become a central part of educational reform in preparing all students to be college- and career-ready (College Board, 2011).

THE COLLEGE OPPORTUNITY AGENDA AND THE REACH HIGHER INITIATIVE

In January 2014, the White House sponsored a summit during which President Barack Obama called for an ambitious agenda aimed at providing new commitments focused on improving college value and removing barriers to competition, with the goal of ensuring college remains affordable. The President called for a renewed effort to reach the North Star goal of once again leading the world in college graduates by 2020. He called for change that results in more students from low-income families being prepared for college, enrolling in quality institutions and graduating ready for the world of work (The White House, 2014).

Following this summit, First Lady Michelle Obama continued the call to action through the Reach Higher initiative, which aims to inspire every student in America to take charge of his or her future by completing education past high school, whether at a professional training program, a community college, or a four-year college or university. The Reach Higher initiative focuses on:

- exposing students to college and career opportunities

- understanding financial aid eligibility that can make college affordability a reality

- encouraging academic planning and summer learning opportunities

- supporting high school counselors who can help more kids get into college (The White House, n.d.).

The First Lady's focus on high school counselors and their role in helping students become college-ready was followed by a listening and learning session on school counseling with senior White House staff and experts from the field, higher education, nonprofit, and professional organizations. This session, held in May 2014, examined the challenges and opportunities facing school counselors as they support students' college aspirations. Among other things, leaders recommended revising school counselor preparation programs to include a renewed focus on data, accountability and college and career readiness, and providing professional development for current school counselors. Not long afterward, the First Lady spoke at the American School Counselor Association (ASCA) Conference about the work of school counselors and their vital role in helping the President reach the North Star goal (American School Counselor Association, 2014).

On July 28, 2014, a special White House convening at Harvard University focused on maximizing school counselors' impact and influence on college enrollment. Discussions included the need for improved professional development and pre-service training, innovative data-driven practices and research, and effective use of college counseling tools and data systems to support school counselors. Attendees were encouraged to inventory existing partnerships and create new commitments that require establishing collaborative relationships with local school districts, higher education institutions, college access groups, and nonprofit organizations with a specific charge to increase college opportunity for all students (The White House, 2014).

As this text goes to press, a similar convening is scheduled for November 17–18, 2014 at San Diego State University (CA). The specific focus of this convening is to bring together *committed leaders and commitment-makers* who are taking the steps necessary to create systemic change in the school counseling profession in several specific areas:

- Designing or revising **school counselor preparation** at **higher educational institutions** to ensure adequate preparation standards for school counselors in college career readiness (CCR)

- Developing, improving and sustaining **partnerships between university training programs and K–12 school districts** to ensure field site placements and activities during fieldwork, and training for site supervisors and administrators to align with new requirements in CCR

- Writing and implementing minimum **credentialing/certificate standards** for all who participate in CCR activities (university training programs, K–12 school districts, college access staff, and not-for-profit noncollege access groups)

- Supporting **professional development in districts** for school counselors and CCR service providers, ensuring a collaborative scaffolding of agreed-upon roles and services

- Creating **policies, practices and procedures** that support hiring, supervision and placement of appropriately trained/certificated/licensed CCR service providers, ensuring responsibilities are tied to training (job descriptions, evaluation tools, etc.)

- Providing opportunities to develop **strategic partnerships with donors, funders and researchers** interested in evaluating or supporting any or all of this work, promoting new systemic change models, and discovering evidence-based practices to support school counselors and the students they serve

Teams from more than 30 states which include members from higher education institutions, pre-K–12 districts, college access partners and not-for-profit organizations, government, state and national leaders, and policymakers, researchers, donors, and funders will gather to formalize and finalize strategic action plans and commitments to improve college- and career-readiness opportunities for all students.

DATA IN SECONDARY SCHOOLS

Before school counselors can begin to utilize data in their college readiness work, they must first understand the many types of data they can access. Since data has multiple purposes and uses, it is categorized differently depending on the focus of the work (Dimmit, Carey, & Hatch, 2007; Hatch, 2014). Categories of data and ways to collect data that are relevant to the work of a school counselor are briefly shared here.

STANDARDS AND COMPETENCY ATTAINMENT DATA

Standards and competency-related data serve as indicators as to whether or not students have mastery (knowledge, attitudes and skills) of specific student competencies. Examples of competencies to be measured may come from the ASCA Student Standards (ASCA, 2005), the National Career Development Association guidelines (National Career Development Association, 2004), accreditation standards and competencies, state school counseling competencies, or the newly drafted ASCA Mindsets & Behaviors for Student Success: K–12 College and Career Readiness for Every Student (ASCA, 2014). Standards and competency data may be collected through pre/post-assessments, activity completion or skill demonstration. Ideally, when students gain the desired content knowledge, acquire or develop positive attitudes or beliefs, and demonstrate skills accurately, behavioral performance or change is not far behind.

ACHIEVEMENT-RELATED DATA (BEHAVIORS)

Achievement-related data measures those fields that the research literature has shown to be correlated to student academic achievement (Dimmitt, Carey, & Hatch, 2007). When data improve in these areas, studies indicate that academic achievement data often improves as well. School counselors and others who are looking to gather achievement-related data to determine measures of success that support student achievement might consider the following data elements:

- discipline referrals
- suspension rates
- attendance rates
- homework completion rates
- course enrollment patterns (college-prep, Honors, AP, IB)
- participation in college-readiness programs such as AVID
- SAT/ACT test taking
- parent participation rates
- participation in extracurricular activities (teams, clubs, organizations).

STUDENT ACHIEVEMENT DATA

Student achievement data are measures for students' academic progress and success (ASCA, 2005; Dimmitt, Carey, & Hatch, 2007). Student achievement data represent outcome goals that school counselors and other educators seek. It is not enough to have enrollment in college-preparatory courses if students do not pass courses and graduate college-eligible. School counselors and others looking to gather data and determine measures of academic achievement might consider the following data elements:

- state standardized test scores (benchmarks and proficiencies)

- changes in achievement levels (math, reading)

- Algebra I passage rates

- ninth-grade promotion rates

- grade point averages

- drop-out rate

- SAT and ACT scores

- passage rates for state high school exit exams

- completion of college-preparation requirements.

School counselors who utilize data can strive to ensure all students obtain the standards and competencies they need to enroll in the appropriate college-preparatory courses leading to an increased likelihood of completing high school college-eligible (see Figure 1).

Figure 1. Competencies for Enrollment in College-Preparatory Courses

Standards & Competency Attainment Data *(Attitude, Knowledge, Skills)*	Student Achievement-Related Data *(Behavior Change)*	Student Achievement Data *(Outcome)*
Attitude (or belief) that college is an attainable goal *Skills* to accurately complete a four-year college-eligible plan *Knowledge* of college requirements	College-prep course enrollment patterns	Completion of college-prep requirements

POSTSECONDARY PLACEMENT AND REMEDIATION DATA

While reporting students' completion of college-preparation requirements is one form of student achievement, monitoring postsecondary placement and remediation data are equally essential. How many students who graduated eligible and who applied and were accepted actually enroll in college and attend? How many enroll and attend but are required to remediate at the freshman level? How many attend and persist to completion on time?

Simply saying students graduate eligible for college and reporting those who state they will enroll is no longer sufficient. Many high schools now collect follow-up data from students one year, two years or even five years after graduation to determine if they accomplished their postsecondary goal. While access to this type of postsecondary data varies, efforts to gain access to this data is recommended as it can be helpful in designing programs or activities for current high school students. For example, if a large number of graduates must take remedial courses in college, then discussion would be necessary as to what interventions or adjustments might be made to the high school's curriculum, and programs (such as early assessment and placement testing) would be warranted.

School counselors and others looking to gather data and determine measures of success beyond high school might consider the following data elements:

Enrollment/participation in:

- Associate degree programs

- Bachelor degree programs

- Career Technical Education (CTE) disciplines beyond high school

- Science, technology, engineering and math (STEM) disciplines

- Advanced training/certificates

- Military

- Employment: related or unrelated to CTE program of study

- Other (not working and not seeking work, deceased, jailed)

- Unemployed (not working but seeking work)

- Status unknown (no contact made after attempts)

- Adult education programs

- Distance learning

- Employment rates of college graduates

- Financial aid awards

- College graduation rates

- Time to degree

- Tuition costs of colleges and universities

TRAINING OF PRE-SERVICE COUNSELORS AND DATA ATTAINMENT

Pre-service training credit hours, certification, credentialing, and licensure for school counselors vary from institution to institution and from state to state, as does the amount of content each pre-service training program provides in school counseling. The Council for Accreditation of Counseling and Related Educational Programs (CACREP) accredits master's and doctoral degree programs in counseling and its specialties offered by colleges and universities in the United States and throughout the world. While the use data, accountability and program evaluation are addressed within the (CACREP) standards, there is no requirement to ensure school counselors learn to use data in relationship to college and career readiness in their school counselor training program (CACREP, 2009).

School Counselors: Poised to Lead?

Poised to Lead: How School Counselors Can Drive College and Career Readiness (Hines & Lemons, 2011) describes school counselors as uniquely positioned to serve as leaders in college and career readiness. Encouraging "proper deployment," the authors identify school counselors as perfectly positioned to lead an agenda of college and career readiness for each and every student. In their unique roles, school counselors:

- have access to college- and career-readiness data

- oversee other student support services

- are responsible for managing student course assignments

- ensure students take the appropriate college- and career-preparatory courses

- are centrally positioned to recognize institutional barriers

- are members of leadership teams

- are equity-focused change agents (Hines & Lemons, 2011).

To ensure school counselors successfully perform their essential role of ensuring all students, particularly those most often underserved, are prepared for a productive future, Hines and Lemon suggest five steps for change in the profession of school counseling. These measures include:

- Revising school counselor job descriptions and evaluation tools at local and state levels to focus on tasks supporting equitable education and preparing all students for college and career

- Revisions to university training programs to focus centrally on educational equity and college and career readiness

- Aligning state credentialing requirements to include college- and career-readiness counseling

- Providing ongoing professional development and support for existing school counselors in equity mindedness in college and career planning

- Aligning counselor evaluations to appropriate measures of college and career readiness (Hines & Lemons, 2011).

The National Office for School Counselor Advocacy (NOSCA)

The National Office for School Counselor Advocacy (NOSCA), formerly in the Advocacy and Public Policy Center of the College Board, was formed to promote the value of school counselors as leaders in school reform, student achievement and college readiness. NOSCA released several important documents in support of the school counselor's leadership role with college and career readiness (College Board, n.d.). Each document is a must-read for school counselors, administrators and other educators working to support a strong equity-focused college- and career-readiness platform.

One of these documents, the 2011 *National Survey of School Counselors: Counseling at the Crossroads,* provides extensive groundbreaking survey data and analysis from more than 5,300 middle and high school counselors nationwide. Virtually all (99 percent) agreed that school counselors should advocate for rigorous academic preparation and college- and career-readiness counseling for students, even if others in the school didn't see this as their role (Bridgeland & Bruce, 2011). Almost all (95 percent) favored more support and leadership empowerment to give students what they need for college. Of specific concern are the reports that in high-poverty schools, 75 percent of high school and 59 percent of middle school counselors wish they could spend more time building a college-going culture.

Although most high school counselors reported supporting accountability measures and incentives to meet 12th-grade college- and career-readiness goals, counselors were not in agreement regarding how they should be held accountable. While most school counselors reported supporting The College Board's *Eight Components of College and Career Readiness* (described below), they revealed a disconnect between the belief in the importance of ideal behaviors and the reality of the work performed by counselors in schools each day. Bridgeland and Bruce (2011) summarized concerns regarding the professional school counselor and provided possible solutions:

> It seems like this profession, which appears to lack a driving mission, a unifying framework and a set of benchmarks to measure success, may already have the resources available to align their mission, role and metrics: NOSCA's Eight Components. (p. 37).

The *College Board Eight Components of College and Career Readiness,* along with the Strategic Planning Tool, serve as a roadmap for creating a college-going culture throughout students' K–12 education. High school is often too late for students to begin important college-going conversations. Research supports beginning postsecondary preparation in elementary and middle school (College Board, 2011). The accompanying level guides for elementary, middle and high school focus on suggested ways that school counselors can: (a) ensure equity for all, (b) use data to inform their practice and (c) promote system-wide work with all stakeholders (College Board, 2011).

- In elementary school, the focus is on building a strong foundation by ensuring students possess the knowledge, skills and early awareness of the importance of rigor in college and career readiness (Components 1–6).

- In middle school, the focus is on deepening the knowledge and skills necessary for academic goal-setting and exploring college and career planning (Components 1–6).

- In high school, the focus is on the full implementation of students' personal and academic goals to ensure the widest range of future options for college opportunity and career pathways (Components 1–8).

Each grade level guide provides a description of the goal, an explanation of why it matters, excellent suggestions, and examples for how school counselors can work system-wide to be equitable and use data to inform their practice. Examples of what to measure, what to look for and what to do are provided in the text (College Board, 2011).

PROFESSIONAL COMPETENCIES, DATA AND COLLEGE-GOING CULTURE

ASCA's School Counselor Competencies (2008) call for school counselors to use data-driven practices to: (a) close the achievement gap; (b) engage in data-driven decision making; (c) review disaggregated school-wide data needs and outcomes with their advisory councils; (d) set goals; and (e) demonstrate a need for systemic change in areas such as course enrollment patterns, equity and access, and the achievement, opportunity and information gaps. For example:

I-C: ATTITUDES

School counselors believe:

- I-C-1. Every student can learn, and every student can succeed.

- I-C-2. Every student should have access to and opportunity for a high-quality education.

- I-C-3. Every student should graduate from high school and be prepared for employment or college and other postsecondary education.

- I-C-7. The effectiveness of school counseling programs should be measurable using process, perception and results data.

- III-B-2e. Every student should learn the importance of college and other postsecondary education and learn to navigate the college admission process. (American School Counselor Association, 2012).

In order to meet these standards, school counselors must not only believe that using data is a necessary component of their role responsibility, but they must also know how to collect, use and analyze data in evaluating the impact of the school counseling program on the students they serve.

ASCA National Model and College-Going Culture

The American School Counseling Association (ASCA) released its third edition of the ASCA National Model in 2012. The ASCA model is a framework for designing, implementing, evaluating, and improving a school counseling program and is one of the most commonly used texts in pre-service training programs. Graduate students and practicing school counselors working within an ASCA Model framework can best use data to address President Obama's 2020 plan for college completion by incorporating the ideas, themes and elements of the *College Board Eight Components of College Readiness* (College Board, 2011) and the Education Trust's *Poised to Lead* (Hines & Lemons, 2011) into their ASCA Model program.

In each of the quadrants of the ASCA Model, today's school counselors will best support a college-going culture when they use data and partner with other educators to:

- Ensure *every* student receives consistent messages of expectation for a college- and career-preparatory K–12 educational experience

- Ensure *every* student receives the knowledge, attitudes and skills necessary to make informed college-going and career-readiness decisions

- Set high expectations for *all* students, particularly those who have been traditionally left out due to opportunity, belief and attainment gaps that may have denied them a chance to pursue their educational goals

- Recognize inequities that may include educational disparities, access inequities, opportunity barriers, and achievements gaps between students of color, low-income and first-generation students

- Advocate for high academic standards and opportunities for the elimination of gate-keeping that denies access to rigorous educational coursework for every student

- Provide interventions necessary for the underserved, underrepresented or underperforming student

- Encourage all students to exert the effort and persistence necessary to achieve their potential.

The next section in this chapter provides support to school counselors seeking to focus their ASCA Model program on using data to create and evaluate a college- and career-readiness program for all students.

Foundation

In the foundation component of the ASCA National Model (2012), a college-going, culture-focused school counseling program ensures components of the program focus (beliefs, vision and mission) include advocating for high expectations for all students with a responsibility to ensure equity and access to college and success. In alignment with the A.3 of the *ASCA Ethical Guidelines* (2010), school counselors:

- Ensure equitable academic, postsecondary and career access and personal/social opportunities for all students through the use of data to help close achievement and opportunity gaps

- Provide and advocate for individual students' career awareness, exploration and postsecondary plans, supporting the students' right to choose from the wide array of options when they leave secondary school (ASCA, 2010).

Whether or not students actively seek it, school counselors ensure through deliberate actions that each and every student receives the benefits of adequate preparation for college and career readiness within the school counseling program.

When school counselors are setting *program goals,* college-readiness data and activities must be reviewed for areas of strength and improvement. The school counselor ensures school-wide program goals—regarding delivering core curriculum on college and career readiness—include how *each and every* student will receive the agreed-upon standards and competencies that align with college and career readiness in their core classroom curriculum. The following provides expectations for goal attainment:

Overarching goal: To increase the number of students who graduate from high school both college- and career-ready and to increase college-going and college-completion rates through the alignment of K–12 and postsecondary curriculum and coordinated student support services.

Figure 2. Sample District College- and Career-Readiness Program Goals

Goal Areas	Elementary School	Middle School	High School
Attendance	__ percent reduction in the number of absences for students identified as truant (6 or more unexcused absences) from Q1–Q3	__ percent reduction in the number of full-day unexcused absences (3 or more) for all students from Q1–Q3	
Behavior	__ percent reduction in school-wide discipline referrals for conflict in grades 3, 4 and 5 from Q1–Q3	__ percent reduction in the number of repeat offenses by students with multiple behavioral referrals	
Behavior	__ percent decrease in discipline referrals for at-risk students (5 or more referrals or 1 or more suspension) who participate in social skills groups		
Study Skills/ Homework	__ percent increase in positive report card marks in areas of homework completion, motivation and study skills from Q1–Q3		
FAFSA			__ percent increase in the percentage of students who apply for FAFSA
Credits		__ percent reduction in the number of students academically at-risk (below 2.0 GPA) from Q1–Q3	__ percent reduction in the number of ninth grade students academically at-risk (below 2.0 GPA) from Q1–Q3
Graduation			Increase high school graduation rates by __ percent __ percent reduction in the number of seniors who are not on target to graduate from Q1–Q4
Graduate-College-Eligible	_ percent increase in college-going and college-completion knowledge for students in grades K–5.	_ percent increase in college-going and college-completion knowledge for students in grades 6–8	__ percent increase in college-going and college-completion knowledge for students in grades 9–12 __ percent increase in the percentage of students who graduate eligible to attend state college or university __ percent increase in the percentage of students who apply for college.
College-Going Rates Postsecondary Success	__ percent increase in students who know what career pathways are and that they lead to postsecondary certificate and/or degree program	__ percent who know pathways that lead to postsecondary certificate and/or degree programs in high-demand, high-wage and family-sustaining careers	Increase number who attend college by __% Reduce need for postsecondary remedial courses by __ percent __percent who graduate and enter postsecondary certificate programs

Program goals:

1. Increase college-going and college-completion knowledge for students grades K–12

2. Increase high school graduation rates

3. Increase college-prep completion rates

4. Increase college-going rates

5. Reduce the need for postsecondary remedial courses

When program goals are created using data-driven interventions, school counselors ensure these include closing the achievement, opportunity and attainment gaps that have historically denied all students access to pursue their educational goals (see Figure 2).

DELIVERY

The delivery system in a college-going, culture-aligned-program ensures each student receives developmentally appropriate comprehensive school counseling core curriculum to obtain the knowledge, attitudes and skills necessary to be college- and career-ready in grades K–12. Best practice occurs when school and district school counseling teams use data and developmental needs to determine which lessons will be delivered and measured for impact at each grade level (K–12).

Following the lesson delivery and pre/post-competency assessment, special consideration may also be given to determine which sub-group may benefit from revisiting the lesson in a small group to ensure equitable opportunity to master the knowledge, attitudes and skills (Hatch, 2012). In addition to core curriculum delivery for students, school counselors provide college-readiness and career-planning information and education nights for students and families. Evaluating the impact of these through survey assessment for knowledge and value can assist with revising and improving the experience for all.

Individual student planning in a college-going culture begins early in the student's career, often in middle school, and includes guaranteed, scheduled one-on-one meetings with a licensed, certified or credentialed school counselor, the student, and his or her parent or guardian for appraisal and advisement. The goal is to support the student's access to rigorous standards-based curriculum,

academic courses, and learning paths for college and career readiness. The meetings should include:

- a full review of attendance data

- behavior and achievement data

- a review of the student's academic profile

- career portfolio developed to-date

- completion of a planning tool document (hard copy or online) [see sample in Appendix] created to assist students and parents in understanding the full magnitude and meaning of the student's educational choices and how those choices will affect future opportunities.

Evaluating the impact of these meetings using post-conference surveys can improve the quality and impact (Hatch, 2014).

When responding to students who are referred for counseling interventions for attendance, behavior or achievement in a college-going, culture-focused program, school counselors react to ensure the activity is focused not only on interventions intended to eliminate the barriers to non-performance. *Capturing the Educational Experience of Young Men of Color* recommends motivational counseling through a lens of high expectations for future educational success that is best obtained by graduating college- and career-ready (NOSCA, 2012). Through consultation, collaboration and teaming, counselors determine the appropriate course of action to support the success of all students.

MANAGEMENT

In the management system, school counselors implement an annual agreement with their administrators for the division and accountability of the school counselor's responsibilities. In a program promoting a college-going culture, the agreement may specify calendar activities, such as parent college planning evening events, participation in college fairs and university field trips, or promoting school-wide college-going culture activities.

Conversations on the advisory council may include school data profile templates or reports on college-going culture program goals and outcomes. Advocating for funding to support access to resources (like technology for students who can't afford computers) or multiple-language, college-readiness documents is another way counselors work to support a college-going culture.

The ASCA national model program calls for school counselors to create core curriculum, small-group and closing-the-gap action plans. School counselors promoting a college-going culture are encouraged to create curriculum action plans that scaffold a developmentally progressive program of study in K–12 for college and career readiness and to collect perception and outcome data to determine the impact of the curriculum.

Small-group action plans are appropriate for students who need an intervention (students with two Fs or more; seniors not on target to graduate; college-eligible students who have not filled out applications or taken college assessment exams; sixth grade students habitually absent; students failing Algebra). Small groups may provide an opportunity to teach attitudes, knowledge and skills to address the barrier to achievement (study skills, college application group, motivation, attendance, behavior, etc.).

The closing-the-gap action plan is appropriate for addressing larger systemic issues. When analyzing schoolwide data, school counselors may uncover equity and access issues leading to discussions about the removal of barriers to opportunities. Implementing social justice strategies in support of a college-going culture, the school counselor can initiate an activity to address a data-driven need or to ensure that underrepresented, underserved and underperforming youth are reached.

Intentional interventions can also be directed toward systemic change and can have a much greater impact on the student body than counseling each student one-on one or in small groups. While groups are important, some of the issues contributing to students' need for group counseling may actually stem from the systems that are contributing to barriers to learning and that the students' anger, frustration and feelings of failure are *systems*, not *student* issues. Examples may include:

- Ethnic and gender gaps in students graduating college-eligible

- Limited AP course availability

- Curriculum guide prerequisite barriers limiting course access

- High failure rates among underrepresented students in certain courses

- Disproportionate discipline rates among certain subgroups

- Lack of college-preparatory materials in the student's native language

- A pervasive belief system by staff that "these kids can't"

- Disproportionate percentages of students failing honors courses

- Inconsistent district policies regarding which students can repeat failed courses

- Disproportionally low numbers of EL students failing the state high school exam

The examples listed above are more likely indicators of systemic issues, not student issues. School counselors are uniquely positioned to analyze data to determine access, opportunity and achievement gaps in schools and to harness the social capital to advocate for change and opportunity in ways others in school are unable to (Ratts, DeKruyf, & Chen-Hayes, 2007; Holcomb-McCoy, 2007; Hatch, 2012; Hatch, 2014). School counselors are often the first educators to notice inequities and lack of access to rigorous course enrollment, skewed failure rates, and disproportionality of achievement rates between underrepresented, underserved and underperforming groups.

ACCOUNTABILITY

Success in creating a college-going culture is seen over time through the school data profile analysis. More immediate results of activities and interventions can be found when students learn the knowledge, attitudes and skills necessary to impact their college-going culture behavior. Closing-the-gap result reports will provide feedback on whether intentional interventions were effective for underserved, underrepresented or underperforming groups. When results reports are analyzed, decisions will be made regarding overall program improvement.

USING DATA AS A SOCIAL JUSTICE AGENT

School counselors serve as social justice advocates when they embody the themes written on the outside of the American School Counselor Association (ASCA) National Model diamond as leaders, advocates, collaborators, and system change agents (ASCA, 2003, 2005, 2012). School counselors promote equity and access to rigor and opportunity so all students can reach their full potential in K–12 schools and beyond. Professional Ethical Standards (ASCA, 2010) call on school counselors to advocate for, lead and create equity-based school counseling programs that will help close achievement, opportunity and attainment gaps—which may deny students the opportunity to pursue future career and college goals (Holcomb-McCoy & Chen-Hayes, 2011).

ASCA's school counselors' ethical guidelines include the following:

> A.3.b. Ensure equitable academic, career, postsecondary access and personal/social opportunities for all students through the use of data to help close achievement gaps and opportunity gaps.

> E.2.g. Work as advocates and leaders in the school to create equity-based school counseling programs that help close any achievement, opportunity and attainment gaps that deny all students the chance to pursue their educational goals. (ASCA, 2010).

Ethical school counselors have high expectations for every student and are social justice advocates who ensure access to rigorous college- and career-readiness curriculums (Education Trust, 2009; Hines & Lemon, 2011; NOSCA, 2011). Utilizing tools for cultural proficiency, school counselors juxtapose barriers against guiding principles, ethics and professional frameworks for effective communication and problem-solving in diverse communities (Stephens & Lindsey, 2011). As agents of change, highly motivated and culturally competent school counselors utilize data to remove institutional and environmental barriers that may deny students rigorous academic, college/career and personal/social opportunities (ASCA, 2010; Hatch, 2012; Holcomb-McCoy & Chen-Hayes, 2011). School counselors are social justice advocates when they:

- disaggregate attendance, behavior, grade, and course-taking patterns with a special focus on diverse populations (ASCA, 2010)
- contribute to school wide systemic change and educational reform, including parent and guardian engagement with school-family-community partnerships (Bryan & Holcomb-McCoy, 2004)
- Promote career and college access and readiness for all students in K–12 schools (NOSCA, 2011)
- Intentionally address inequitable social, political and economic conditions that impede the academic, career,

college-access, and personal/social development of students (Ratts, 2009)

- Develop cultural competence as leaders who acknowledge issues of power, privilege and oppression (Fouad, Gerstein, & Toporek, 2006; Holcomb-McCoy & Chen-Hayes, 2011; Stephens & Lindsey, 2011)
- Research the educational experiences of traditionally marginalized youth (e.g., young men of color) and commit to transforming their opportunities and experiences (Lee & Ransom, 2011; NOSCA, 2012)
- Commit to serving as social justice advocates for underrepresented, underserved and underperforming students (ASCA, 2010; Education Trust, 2009; Holcomb-McCoy & Chen-Hayes, 2011)
- Assess and change school policies, practices and behaviors in culturally proficient ways that serve students, schools, communities, and society (Stephens & Lindsey, 2011).

CATEGORIZATION OF DATA

ACCESS DATA

Another way to categorize data that is important to school counselors is through the systems lens. Access data refers to the right, accessibility or availability a student has to gain entrance or admission to a course, activity or program opportunity. Access data often uncovers inequities by shedding light on the opportunity gaps. Access data can be utilized to advocate for the rights of every student, to promote policy and procedure change, and to advocate for providing more students the opportunity to graduate college-ready (Lee & Goodnough, 2011).

> Jorge, a sophomore, understood all the college-prep requirements he needed to take at his school in order to attend his local university. He had a strong desire to attend college because he knew he would be the first in his family to do so. He reviewed the course catalog and prepared his schedule of courses for junior year. He knew he needed biology and a foreign language (Spanish). Unfortunately for Jorge, his high school had a policy that did not allow students to take certain college-prep courses unless they met the

prerequisite of a 3.0 GPA. At Low-Expectation High School, only 40 percent of the senior English courses offered (four sections out of 10) were approved as college-preparatory courses. For 60 percent of the seniors, graduating college-eligible was not an option—or seemingly a priority.

Access data can be viewed through various policy and resource allocation perspectives that address rights and availability: "Am I allowed to take it? Are there enough sections? Is there enough room for me?" Examples of access data include:

- College-prep courses: Are they open for all? Are there enough courses for all?

- Honors courses: How many are there?

- AP courses: How many are offered?

- Dual-enrollment opportunities: Are these open to all students?

- College assessment (SAT, ACT, PSAT, Aspire): Is there funding so that all can take them? Are they offered locally?

- College-going school counseling curriculum: Do all students receive information? How often? In class? How do we ensure equitable receipt?

  - College-eligibility requirements

  - College-application process

  - Financial-aid literacy

  - Career-exploration and career-assessment knowledge

- College/career exploration programs, inventory assessments, etc.: Who has access? When is the career center open?

- Parent/guardian college/career-readiness evening events: When are these offered? Are they provided in native language?

- Articulation opportunities between middle and high school: Who participates?

- Articulation between high school and college or community college: Who participates?

- College-planning opportunities: Are these guaranteed for all or some students? How often will I receive assistance?

- College visits as an opportunity: Who is invited? What does it cost?

- TRIO, STEM, GEAR UP, Bridge Programs: Who can participate?

- Financial aid/scholarship-planning nights: Who is invited?

- Co-curricular activities such as clubs and sports: Can everyone participate?

- Enrichment activities: Can everyone participate?

- Intervention programs: Will I be invited to participate?

Enrollment or participation data is the next part of the access variable. Enrollment reveals whether students who have access and availability actually do enroll and/or participate in these opportunities. Enrollment data is helpful once disaggregated by gender, ethnicity and other variables to determine patterns of enrollment. Understanding why students who have access don't participate can inform school counselor practice.

SURVEY DATA

Senior exit surveys are administered to provide important feedback regarding the high school experience. For example, Fulton County Schools' 12th grade students took an exit survey during the spring of 2011 as a joint venture between the guidance and counseling and assessment and accountability departments. Topics covered included high school experience, postsecondary plans, college preparation, and career preparation. The response rate for Alpharetta High School was an impressive and helpful 92 percent. When asked to indicate areas in which students would have liked more assistance, 42 percent reported they would have liked more assistance with the college-application process. Utilizing this data, school counselors can advocate for more resources or restructuring of their calendars or responsibilities to meet students' needs (see Figure 3).

Surveys are an efficient and effective way of gathering your own evaluation data. They are relatively easy to develop, complete and, depending upon their length and complexity, easy to analyze. Educators can locate hundreds of survey samples on the Internet; students, parents or faculty can complete the survey online. Current electronic options such as *surveymonkey.com* or those from *google.com* make the process cost-effective and valuable. Both of these Web sites provide survey results in a user-friendly format with automated analysis.

SELECTING DATA

Now that we have discussed the many different types of data that school counselors can utilize to support students, it is important to select which data the school counseling program will prioritize collecting each year. *Building a Grad Nation* recommends that school counselors work with other educators to track early warning indicators, such as attendance, behavior, benchmark tests, and grades in math and reading (Balfanz, Bridgland, Moore, & Fox, 2010). The College Board has created a template with suggestions for each grade level as a starting point (see Figure 4).

Figure 3. Senior Exit Survey Sample

Please indicate areas in which you would have liked more assistance during high school:

Orientation as a new student 16%
Course selection and scheduling 38%
Study skills 31%
Test taking skills 31%
Time management 28%
Career information and options 33%
College application process 42%
Military options 5%

Figure 4. NOSCA Data Elements

Data Elements, By Component	Elementary School	Middle School	High School
College Aspirations			
Attendance, Discipline, Promotion	•	•	•
GPA		•	•
Dropout			•
Academic Planning for College and Career Readiness			
Students reading on grade level in grade 3	•		
Proficiency in state tests for English, math and science	•	•	•
Students enrolled in and completing Algebra I		•	•
Students enrolled in and completing Advanced Placement courses			•
Students enrolled in and completing courses required for in-state university admission			•
Enrichment and Extracurricular Engagement			
Participation in enrichment activities; Participation in extracurricular activities; and Students in leadership positions in enrichment and/or extracurricular programs	•	•	•
College and Career Exploration and Selection Processes			
Participation in college and career exploration programs	•	•	•
College and career/technical school application completion			•
College and career/technical school application submission			•
College and Career Assessments			
Participation in career/interest assessments	•	•	•
Participation in and performance on ReadiStep, PSAT/NMSQT, EXPLORE and PLAN		•	•
Participation in and performance on SAT, SAT Subject Tests and ACT			•
College Affordability Planning			
Participation in early awareness financial literacy and financial aid initiatives	•	•	•
Participation in financial aid planning processes		•	•
Scholarship application completion			•
FAFSA completion			•
College and Career Admission Processes			
Two- and four-year college acceptance			•
Career and technical school acceptance			•
Early Action or Early Decision acceptance			•
Transition from High School Graduation to College Enrollment			
Final transcripts processed			•
Two- and four-year college enrollment			•
Career and technical school enrollment			•

As the school counseling team begins to discuss which data to collect, it is important to also consider data that the administration or leadership team is already collecting, and then decide if the school counseling program will add these to their list as well. Using a Results Report: Impact Over Time-type template like one used by the Michigan School Counseling Association can be helpful in keeping counselors focused on the data they agree to collect each year (see Figure 5).

The Denver Public School Counseling Program has created a public Web page supporting the school counselor's decisions regarding specific data elements for which the profession has taken ownership (see Figure 6). This means that in Denver public schools, counselors have agreed that these particular data elementals will be "owned" by the school counselors because of their agreed importance and value to their program.

Figure 5. Michigan Comprehensive Guidance and Counseling Program: Results Reports: Impact Over Time

School: _____ Date: _____

Academic year		200_–200_	200_–200_	200_–200_	200_–200_
ACADEMIC					
Standard A: acquire knowledge, attitude and skills leading to effective learning	Attendance data				
	Retention rates				
	Average SAT scores				
	% of minorities taking AP classes				
	# of classroom visits per grade level				
	Amount of scholarships awarded				
	# of students accepted to four-year colleges				
	# of students accepted to two-year colleges				
	# of students enlisted in the military				
CAREER DEVELOPMENT					
Standard A: acquire the skills to investigate the world of work in relation to self-knowledge and to make informed career decisions	% of students with interest inventories on file				
	# of students attending career day				
	# of students completing resume and job search				
PERSONAL/SOCIAL					
Standard B: acquire the attitudes, knowledge and interpersonal skills to help them understand and respect self and others	% of students suspended				
	Number of conflict mediations				
	# of students referred for disciplinary reasons				
	# of students in extracurricular activities				
	# of support groups				
NONSTANDARDS-BASED DATA:					
Number of parents attending open house					
Number of volunteer mentors					

Lead School Counselor Signature: _____ Principal Signature: _____

Figure 6. Data Elements Owned by Denver Public Schools

Data Elements We Own		
Academic Success and Graduation	*Student Engagement and Workforce Readiness*	*Postsecondary Readiness*
Graduation, completion and continuation rates	Career exploration and PWR standards	Explore/Plan/ACT
On-track to graduation and retention rates Credits (on-track to graduate) Place Bridge.ppt	Attendance and behavior Attendance.pptx (Hamilton)	Postsecondary goals and exploration
Advance courses (AP, IB, CE, honors, ninth grade algebra, etc.)	Scholar Centric Survey	FAFSA completion rates
GPA and test scores	Extracurricular involvement	College-application rates
Characteristics of a successful learner (homework completion, participation, etc.) Characteristics of a Successful Learner.pptx (CASA)	School climate with regard to student respect, etc. (Student Satisfaction Survey)	Parent perception of student access to college information and support (Parent Satisfaction Survey) Parent Satisfaction Survey.pptx (CASA)

Source: (Denver Public Schools, n.d.)

WHERE IS THE DATA?

Getting access to site and district data is the next necessary step. Sometimes the central office provides the data to the principal, who then shares it with school counselors. Some districts are fortunate enough to have central office personnel who can work directly with school counselors to collect and disaggregate data. As a result of NCLB, many districts now post data on a state Web site. Many state department Web sites have easily accessible databases for several performance measures over time. Using statewide data allows school counselors to analyze their school's performance in relationship to other schools or districts statewide.

In Massachusetts, for example, performance results for the SAT are available online: *http://profiles.doe.mass.edu/state_report/sat_perf.aspx*.

In California, two Web sites provide excellent school data: *http://data1.cde.ca.gov/dataquest* provides a disaggregated database of enrollment patterns, course-taking patterns, staffing, credentialing, and state-wide testing data. *http://www.cpec.ca.gov/OnLineData/OnLineData.asp* provides disaggregated data on high school and college-going rates.

Ed Data Express (*www.eddataexpress.ed.gov/index.cfm*) helps educators find data from their state in achievement categories.

The Data Quality Campaign (*www.dataqualitycampaign.org*) is working to expand the ability of state longitudinal data systems to use data to improve student achievement.

The New York State Education Department's Career Technical Education Office collects post-high-school placement data on students who have been enrolled in New York State Approved Programs: *http://www.p12.nysed.gov/cte/Data/PostHSplacement.html*.

The National Center for Education Statistics' Integrated Post Secondary Education Data System is a primary source for locating college, university, and technical and vocational postsecondary data from institutions in the Unites States (IPEDS) (*http://nces.ed.gov/ipeds/*).

STRATEGIES FOR COLLECTING DATA

Today's state-of-the-art student information database systems (PowerSchool, Learn Sprout and Aeries, for example) provide surprisingly helpful access to student information. Data can be queried and disaggregated into smaller groupings so school counselors can compare changes in students' attendance, behavior or achievement following an intervention or over time. Immediate access to disaggregated data is a powerful and timesaving asset for the school counselor. It allows the professional to proactively query which students in their caseloads are in need (ninth grade students with two Fs; credit-deficient seniors, etc.), instead of waiting for a student to request assistance. Many states are also providing school districts with early warning indicator information based on test, attendance, discipline, and status (i.e., low-income, special education) data.

Commercial packages specifically designed to work with college-planning, readiness and admission data, such as Hobson's newly acquired Naviance (Hobsons, n.d.), allows school counselors to track their students' academic-planning process and college applications. In this way, school counselors can clearly see what still needs to be done to meet deadlines and/or request important documents, like transcripts or teacher recommendations. These sophisticated and comprehensive programs help counselors not only keep track of their student data, but also help students and parents with the college-search and application process, because they are Internet-based and can be accessed at any time with a username and password.

The College Board (SAT) and ACT provide score reports to schools as part of their testing programs. Both the PSAT and the ACT's newest product, Aspire, provide a detailed analysis of each test question for school staff to review and use to determine the strengths and weaknesses that must be addressed in the curriculum. Data for all of these tests can be transmitted electronically or provided in paper format. AP Potential™, a product of the College Board, provides counselors with a free Web-based resource to identify students who have taken the PSAT and who likely will be successful on specific AP exams. This information will aid in both future course selection as well as identify students who should take the AP exam.

ACT provides a report that focuses on the following:

- Performance: student test performance in the context of college readiness

- Access: number of graduates exposed to college-entrance testing and the percent of race/ethnicity participation

- Course selection: percent of students pursuing a core curriculum

- Course rigor: impact of rigorous coursework on achievement

- College readiness: percent of students meeting ACT College Readiness Benchmark Scores in each content area

- Awareness: extent to which student aspirations match performance

- Articulation: colleges and universities to which your students send test results

SCATTERGRAMS

College-going data is commonly reported in a scattergram format (see Figure 7). This visual display of admission-decision information plots GPA, class rank or standardized test scores. It illustrates to students and parents where they are in relation to classmates, other applicants and typically accepted students. This serves to assist the family and the counselor in identifying "safe schools" and "reach schools." In this example, the cumulative grade point average is plotted along the X axis and the combined critical reading and math SAT score is plotted along the Y axis. If you have a program like Naviance, this graphic is available as a report feature. For those who don't have such a program, it can be created in Microsoft Excel using the XY Scatter option in the Chart Wizard. For two reasons, some counseling offices choose not to provide scattergram data for colleges that have only a few applicants. First, it's difficult to maintain the anonymity of a small number of applicants, and second, limited data may not provide an accurate indication of a student's chances of admission. Just because a single applicant from a particular school was admitted in a given year doesn't mean a similar student in a subsequent year will be admitted if the competition from within the school is more intense.

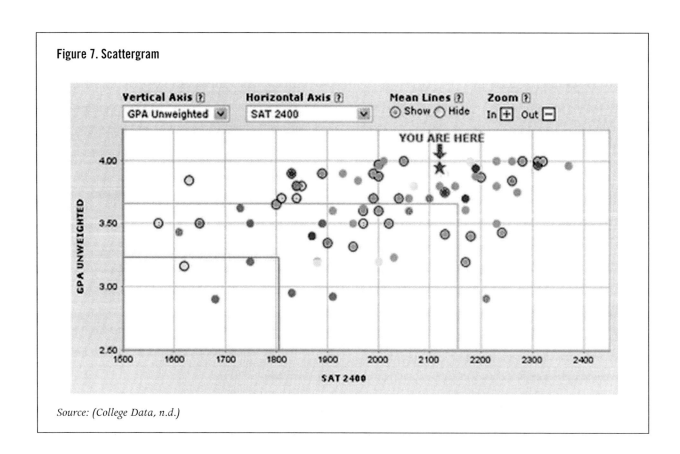

Figure 7. Scattergram

Source: (College Data, n.d.)

STRATEGIES FOR EVALUATING DATA

ANALYZING DATA

Professional school counselors must be adept at analyzing and interpreting the data, as mistakes in data interpretation could lead to the development of new programs or activities that take time, cost money and may not be needed. Knowing how to explain test scores (understanding norms, percentages, stanines, and grade equivalency) is essential when interpreting for students, parents or for program improvement. Understanding how data elements impact one another and how to look for upward and downward trends is essential to designing interventions.

To fully utilize data, it must be interpreted within the context of the larger picture for students, the school system and the community. This involves comparing school data to other schools with similar demographics and looking at ways in which your school may be performing compared to like schools, districts, states, or nations—looking at the data not as a snapshot, but over time, to determine whether the data appear to be improving or not (see Figure 8). A thorough and thoughtful analysis of the data may uncover patterns, trends or discrepancies that may result in a school-wide need, rather than a specific student's need. Analyzing the larger picture may lead to opportunities to recognize and advocate for systems change (Hatch, 2013).

DISAGGREGATING DATA

School counselors disaggregate data by separating the variables to see if there are any groups of students who may not be doing as well as others. These data often bring light to issues of equity and focus the discussion on the needs of specific groups of students (see Figure 9). Although there are many variables by which data may be separated, the common fields include:

- Gender
- Race and ethnicity
- Grade
- Socioeconomic status (income level)
- Home language (English language learners)
- Special education
- Grade level
- Teacher(s)

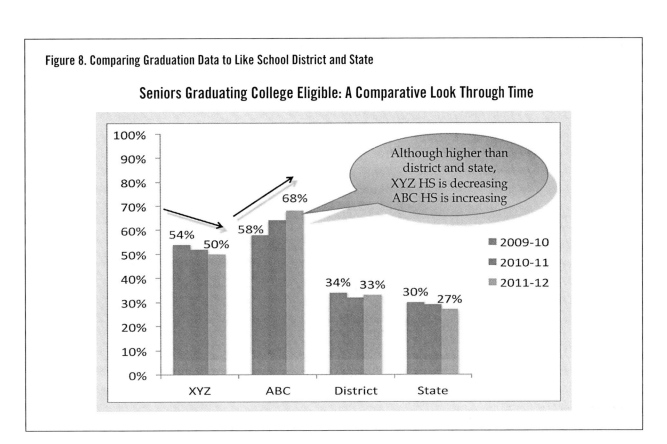

Figure 8. Comparing Graduation Data to Like School District and State

Seniors Graduating College Eligible: A Comparative Look Through Time

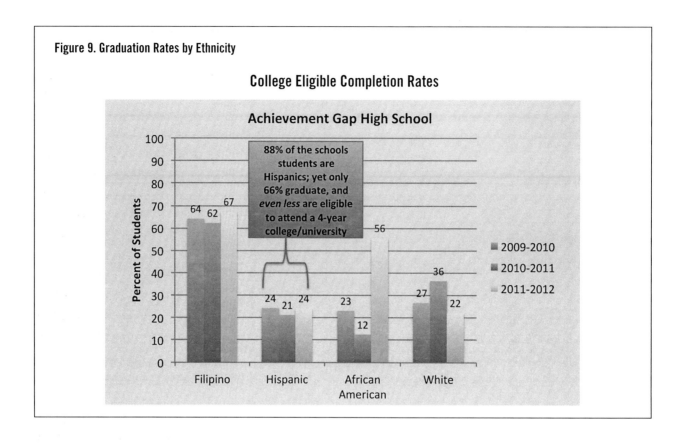

Figure 9. Graduation Rates by Ethnicity

Once data is disaggregated, data teams are encouraged to look for discrepancies between different student groups: How do the graduation rates compare between Filipino, Hispanic, African-American, and white students over a three-year period?

STRATEGIES FOR ANALYZING

DATA TEAMS

Data-based decision making (DBDM) teams provide a group process for defining problems, setting goals, targeting interventions, and evaluating outcomes for students (Dimmitt, Carey, & Hatch, 2007). School-site data teams may include administrators, teachers and representatives from the school counseling department. Data teams analyze school data and discuss ways in which educators can work together to uncover and address student needs. As counselors at your school conduct data conversations, consider including other educators who are equally committed to leadership and data-driven decision making. Reviewing the data could result in conversations to dispel the myth of predetermining the potential of students. It

may be challenging when team members are first learning how to talk with one another about difficult data-driven issues. Johnson (2002) discusses four ways that team members talk about data:

- **Raw debate:** Members hold strong to their position while listening only as a matter of personal strategy.

- **Polite discussion:** Members mask their positions through politeness and never reveal what they are really thinking. This is the most dysfunctional/deceptive form of conversation.

- **Skillful discussion:** A productive way of conversing that incorporates a balance of inquiry and advocacy of own position.

- **Dialogue:** Members suspend their positions and participate in inquiry so that everyone has a thorough understanding of the issue(s); assumptions are probed and new discoveries are made.

Throughout data conversations, counselors are encouraged to maintain a culture of inquiry, exploring perceptions regarding why things are the way they are and engaging in candid conversations about how to improve the academic and college/career-readiness culture of the school (Johnson, 2002). Looking at data over time reveals patterns and identifies student needs and opportunities for advocacy. Disaggregating and cross-tabulating the data allows school counselors to see student trends over time (ASCA, 2012). In this way, school counselors can monitor student progress and look for inequities in access, attainment and achievement (Lee & Goodnough, 2011).

Analyzing the disaggregated data over time can surface equity and access issues and call on school counselors to act on their ethical responsibility to address barriers and gaps; these may be student issues, policy issues, systems issues, or social justice issues. School counselors serve students best when they collaborate with other change agents to identify data-driven and equity-based priorities, determine measures of progress, and seek to implement activities or necessary reforms to support success for every student (Johnson, 2002).

EVALUATING DATA: PROCESS AND PERCEPTION DATA

Today's school counselor collects process, perception and results data to evaluate their programs, activities and interventions (ASCA, 2003, 2005; Dimmitt, Carey, & Hatch, 2007; Hatch, 2014). Process data, much like a lesson plan, records the specific instructions for designing and implementing the activity. It answers the questions: who, what, when, where, and with what?

Perception data (knowledge, attitude and skill) is most often collected through pre- and post-tests to immediately assess the learning that occurred as a result of the activity or intervention. Pre/post-assessments typically contain questions relating to attitude (what do students believe, think or feel?), skill (what skills can they perform?) and knowledge (what knowledge do they possess?). For example, a counselor giving a class presentation about PSAT testing may want to employ a pre- and post-survey. A short survey given at the beginning of the class, followed by the lesson and then a similar post-lesson survey, will provide feedback on the impact data of the lesson (see Figure 10). In-depth instruction on designing pre/post-assessments can be found in *The Use of Data in School Counseling* (Hatch, 2014).

EASY WAYS TO CALCULATE DATA

Many of today's educators often have access to site or district purchased Web-based data and assessment management systems, such as Data Director (Houghton Mifflin Harcourt, 2011), to assist in collecting and calculating benchmark data on common assessment tools. School counselors can utilize these same systems to assess students' knowledge, attitudes and skills on college- and career-readiness assessments. Results are often provided in helpful chart formats. Other forms of data collection and calculation include Clickers, which are hand-held devices that utilize a radio frequency or infrared technology to transmit and record students' responses to questions. Answers are collected, calculated and recorded for viewing.

For those who store data in Microsoft Excel, consider downloading EZAnalyze (n.d.), a free Excel add-on for further data analysis and examination. EZAnalyze (n.d.) provides descriptive statistics, such as mean, median, standard deviation, and range. It also disaggregates data into categories and offers several options for visually representing data with graphs. Advanced features such as correlation, chi square and single factor ANOVA options are available for those interested in doing some basic hypothesis testing. Reports are generated for each analysis. Visit *www.ezanalyze.com* to learn more and download this product.

DEVELOP ACCOUNTABILITY REPORTS

The ways in which we report data vary according to the methods we use to collect it and the audience for which it is intended. For those using commercial programs, basic reports will automatically be generated with options to create additional reports. Those not using a commercial program can create reports in software packages like Microsoft PowerPoint, Word, Excel, or Access.

Perhaps the most basic way that school data is reported is in the school profile. It is critical that whoever is responsible for collecting and analyzing this data have a clear understanding of the kinds of data that should be included in the profile and what should be left out. For instance, AP passage rates and percentages of students admitted to college are good samples of profile data to share with stakeholders. Data that disaggregates passage rates by teacher or acceptance rates by counselor is data

Figure 10. Sample Pre-Test Survey

Junior PSAT Presentation Pre-Test/Post-Test

1. I believe graduating from high school on time is important.

a.) Strongly Agree b.) Agree c.) Unsure d.) Disagree e.) Strongly Disagree

2. What sections are on the PSAT?

    a.) Math, English, Science, Writing
    b.) Math, Critical Reading, Writing
    c.) English, Critical Reading, Math, Writing, History
    d.) English, Math, Critical Reading, Science, Writing (optional)
    e.) English, Math, Critical Reading, Science

3. I have the knowledge I need to register for the PSAT.

a.) Strongly Agree b.) Agree c.) Unsure d.) Disagree e.) Strongly Disagree

4. Why take the PSAT as a junior?

    a.) My teacher told me to
    b.) To prepare myself for the college-entrance exam
    c.) The PSAT can help me earn scholarships if I score well
    d.) Both B and C
    e.) All of the above

6. How many points are deducted if you miss a question on the PSAT?

    a.) none
    b.) ¼
    c.) 1
    d.) 2
    e.) 5

7. The best strategy to earn the maximum points on the PSAT is:

    a.) Answer every question even if I am not sure of the answer before time is called
    b.) Take an educated guess
    c.) Do not guess at all; just stop when time is called
    d.) Pick one letter and fill in all the blank questions before time is called
    e.) None of the above

best utilized internally for purposes of program improvement. The profile is not only a document that is valued by college admission offices, but also by school boards, community members and local realtors, because it contains a snapshot of the school that can be used to see how it compares to others.

In the age of NCLB and overall greater accountability, many counseling programs are using school accountability report cards (SARC) to demonstrate how their counseling program is improving student achievement and success. The most common college admission data found on these report cards show where students are admitted (placement). In addition, evaluative data, standardized testing data or school data may be included. California is considered a leader in the creation of accountability report cards; visit *www.cde.ca.gov/ta/ac/sa/* for more information. Massachusetts has modified the SARC to offer a similar document for school counseling programs, but on a smaller scale; more information is available at *www.masca.org*. While these types of reports tend to focus on more than just college admission, they can be very useful in helping a variety of constituents understand the work of school counselors.

The School Personnel Accountability Report Card (SPARC), originally created to provide a support personnel component to the SARC, is another way school counseling programs can share school profile data and outcomes in college and career readiness. The SPARC is a voluntary, annual, continuous improvement process. Schools create short, easy-to-read report cards to showcase their career- and college-readiness student outcomes. Student support teams collaborate and share contributions to college and career readiness. SPARC reports keep school boards, parents, community partners, and other stakeholders informed about contributions to about student success (California Career Center, 2014).

Here are a few examples:

- Potter Junior High School, found at: *https://www.calcareercenter.org/Uploads/Links/potterjh2014sparcACC.pdf*

- Eleanor Roosevelt High School, found at: *https://www.calcareercenter.org/Uploads/Links/sparc2014eleanorroosevelthsACC.pdf*

OTHER REPORT FORMATS

Producing a report in Access is easily accomplished by using data already recorded in the database for college-going plans (see Figure 11). Although there may be more data contained in the database, only the basic data (name of college, admission decision, student GPA, rank, and SAT critical reading and math score) are used in this report. Figure 12 shows data for the same class, but instead shows all admission decisions for each student sorted by rank.

Figure 11. Microsoft Access Database College-Going Plans Report

Class of 2011 College Going Plans

Destination		Decision	GPA	Rank	Critical Reading	Math
Albright College		Accepted	94.7	11	610	600
Total:	1					
American International College		Accepted	93.36	14	560	540
		Withdrew	85.06	38	460	430
		Accepted	79.75	51		
		Accepted	73.68	63	470	470
		Denied	71.91	71	410	360
Total:	5					
Amherst College		Denied	93.89	12	770	670
Total:	1					
Anna Maria College		Accepted	94.7	11	610	600
		Accepted	92.93	15	570	680
		Accepted	85.06	38	460	430
Total:	3					
Arizona State University		Accepted	93.36	14	560	540
Total:	1					
Assumption College		Accepted	94.7	11	610	600
		Accepted	92.93	15	570	680
		Accepted	92.29	17	570	580
		Accepted	89.36	28	600	580
Total:	4					
Baldwin Wallace College		Accepted	94.7	11	610	600
Total:	1					
Bay Path College		Accepted	94.75	10	540	460
		Accepted	85.06	38	460	430
		Denied	71.91	71	410	360
Total:	3					

Figure 12. Decisions by Rank

Class of 2011
All Decisions by Rank

Rank	Destination	GPA	CR	Math	Decision	Final Decision	Other Plans
1	Colorado School of Mines	98.99	590	610	Accepted		
	Rensselaer Polytechnic Institute				Accepted		
	Saint Michael's College				Accepted		
	Suffolk University				Accepted	Attend	
	Westfield State College				Accepted		
2	College of the Holy Cross	98.61	570	530	Wait List		
	Saint Michael's College				Accepted		
	Stonehill College				Accepted		
	University of Alabama				Accepted		
	University of Massachusetts - Amherst				Accepted	Attend	
	University of New England				Accepted		
	University of Vermont				Accepted		
	Westfield State College				Accepted		
3	Bucknell University	97.17	670	610	Denied		
	Colby College				Denied		
	Drexel University				Accepted		
	Mount Holyoke College				Wait List		
	University of Massachusetts - Amherst				Accepted	Attend	
	University of New Hampshire				Accepted		
4	Hofstra University	96.89	570	570	Accepted	Attend	
	Lasell College				Accepted		
	Saint Michael's College				Accepted		
	University of Massachusetts - Amherst				Accepted		
5	College of Saint Rose	96.73	490	540	Accepted		
	Merrimack College				Accepted		
	Rhode Island College				Accepted		

POSTSECONDARY PLAN DATA

Many school counseling programs collect and publish postsecondary plan data, which consists of senior exit survey information regarding where students go after graduating from high school. Are they headed to college, a job, the military, or some other activity (such as parenting, travel or volunteer work)? For those applying to college, what types of schools did they apply to, where the schools are located, and what was the admission decision? After-high-school plan profile data may also include other useful information, such as the graduating senior grade point average, standardized test scores, class rankings, statistics for which colleges students applied to, and the admission decision of those applications (accept, deny, and wait list). This information is often collected in a database, often a commercial program like Naviance, an application such as Microsoft Access or FileMaker Pro, or a program created specifically for the school or college-counseling program.

Why is this information important to share? The data from the preceding graduating class is most helpful to students and families who may be looking at a particular school. If a student's GPA, class rank and standardized test scores are greater than those of the applicants of the most recent graduating class applying to the same non-highly selective school, the student stands a greater likelihood of being admitted. Conversely, lower scores, GPA and rank may mean admission is less likely. In some schools, this is the most often sought-after information because it allows students to learn from past applicants from their own school and predict with greater accuracy their opportunity for acceptance.

While colleges often will publish the profile of an accepted student, students (and families) want more specific data on which to base their chances of admission. Since secondary schools are vastly different, the colleges accepted student profiles may not accurately reflect decisions from a particular secondary school. For example, in the case of a moderately selective college where dozens of students from the same secondary school apply for admission, the likelihood of all those students being admitted may be negatively impacted, even though they may fit the accepted student profile. The after-high-school plan data will provide some insight into the possibility of admits during the next admission cycle.

However, counselors should take a few precautions when working with this type of data. First, be sure to use data only from the most recent classes. Information that is more than three years old is unreliable, because the profile of an accepted student at a particular institution will likely have changed, especially as more and more colleges admit fewer students. Second, understand that data can be misleading—many students, for a variety of reasons (e.g., intended major or special talent in music or unique skill in athletics), may have been offered admission even though the other data would not necessarily support that decision. Finally, be careful not to release data that could reveal the identity of a student. Some schools will not release data unless a certain number of students have applied to a specific school (often the number is at least 10). This will help to ensure that a student's identity is concealed, which is particularly important in communities where college admission decisions are known to contribute to added pressure and anxiety.

CAUTIONS CONCERNING DATA AND COLLEGE ADMISSION COUNSELING

While data can be very useful, it should not take the place of human interaction. Counseling, whether it be for personal/social reasons, academic or college admission purposes, is most importantly an interaction between the counselor and the student (and/or family). Numbers, figures or statistics cannot replace the conversations and relationships formed by one-to-one counseling. While this may be challenging in schools with limited counselors and large student enrollment, every effort should be made to provide as much face-to-face counseling as possible.

We must also be careful not to let data mislead us. Not all data gives us the information we want, and numbers may tell only part of the story. For example, consider Mandy, a student who may not have the academic profile of an admitted student, but nonetheless has been accepted because of her athletic ability. Consider James, who is not accepted, despite being a superior student with a higher grade point average and standardized test scores. The data might indicate that Mandy was less likely to be accepted, but because of her special talent or unique skill (music or athletics), she is admitted, and James is not. It is important to remember that college admission is not an exact science. Data profiles on accepted students should serve as a guide in this process and not a guarantee, because there is no way to predict what each college or university is looking for when selecting a diverse and talented freshman class.

Celebrate Accomplishments and Seeking Improvement

Sharing individual and program results can be accomplished utilizing a variety of tools. Whether the results are being shared as part of a program evaluation, program improvement plan, student advocacy project, systemic change activity, and/or for purposes of program advocacy, sharing data allows an opportunity to celebrate successes and provide thoughtful recommendations for improvement. Sharing results with the school's stakeholders can effectively communicate the positive impact your counseling program has on students and families going through the college admission process. Delivering a Flashlight PowerPoint presentation to the school board or trustees tells a story and displays the data that has been collected and analyzed (Hatch, 2014). The Center for Excellence in School Counseling and Leadership (*www.cescal.org*) and the Hatching Results (*www.hatchingresults.com*) Web sites host samples and examples of Flashlight PowerPoint presentations that share the results of curriculum and interventions (Hatch, 2014). Another method of sharing includes sending out a local press release about an intervention and the data that supports its effectiveness. Ensure improvements in students' outcomes are part of the school profile and local accountability report card. Regardless of the method used to share results, ensure your stakeholders are informed, as they are key to providing future support to your program.

Final Thoughts

By embracing and utilizing data, school counselors can help students navigate the college admission process more effectively and successfully. As a school counselor who may be just beginning to utilize data, do not be afraid to ask for assistance with collecting, interpreting and reporting it. While a newly hired counselor may possess more advanced technological skills, remember that the more seasoned school counselor holds decades of professional wisdom. Take pride in sharing the volumes of difference you make every day by taking small steps,

and set realistic goals for how data can be used in your program. Small successes can be built upon until data is thoroughly and effectively utilized, and students, families and the greater community will undoubtedly benefit from your efforts.

More Ideas for Using Data to Improve the College-Going Culture

1. Secure a seat on the district and/or school data team to ensure that the school counselor voice is at the table. Bring data to the group that shows whether or not students are successful in their postsecondary educational pursuits. Ensure that each school-level team, including those serving in elementary and middle schools, look at standardized testing, college-going rate and high school course-selection data and focuses on the goal of graduating college-ready. If the data is troubling, have the team look at ways to address the concerns.

2. Examine the data from your school that can be found on the school's accountability report card or the state department of education's accountability Web site. What, if any, opportunity or achievement gaps exist? Are certain populations not equally represented in the college-going, standardized testing or AP data? What can you do to reverse this inequity? Whom else do you need to involve to reduce or eliminate gaps?

3. Work with the person responsible for professional development in your school district to plan a professional development activity for all educators (not just the school counselors) about the college-going data in your school/district. Empower your colleagues to look at ways that, at the school or individual level, they can reverse data trends that have a negative impact on the community's college-going culture.

4. If you find data that is of concern (e.g., few student PSAT test scores, low AP test participation) work with the data team to find ways to reverse the trend. Solicit funding from community partners so all sophomores can take Aspire or all juniors can take the PSAT, or meet with students individually or in small groups to discuss their AP Potential™ score and encourage them to take an AP class. Email reminders to

students or families to ensure that they understand the value of taking such classes.

5. Work with the school administrators and leadership team to analyze the course-selection data and course offerings available to students. Are students graduating with the necessary college core curriculum required for postsecondary success? Look at senior exit data to see if students feel prepared for life after high school. Are students persisting in college? If not, why? Do gaps exist? Propose changes to the curriculum or curriculum guides if the data shows changes are warranted.

ABOUT THE AUTHOR

Trish Hatch, PhD is associate professor, director of the school counseling program at San Diego State University (CA). Dr. Hatch is the author of *The Use of Data in School Counseling: Hatching Results for Students, Programs and the Profession* (2014); and co-author of the *ASCA National Model: A Framework for School Counseling Programs* (ASCA, 2003; 2005) and *Evidence-Based Practice in School Counseling: Making a Difference with Data-Driven Practices* (Dimmit, Carey & Hatch, 2007). Dr. Hatch is the executive director of the Center for Excellence in School Counseling and Leadership (CESCaL), which seeks to improve the profession of school counseling through policy and practice. A former school counselor and administrator, Dr. Hatch served as ASCA's vice president (supervisor/postsecondary) and President of the California School Counseling Association. She has received the ASCA Mary Gehrke Lifetime Achievement Award and ASCA's Administrator of the Year Award. As president and CEO of Hatching Results™ LLC, Dr. Hatch has gathered a team of expert school counselors and counselor educators, who provide grant writing, evaluation, training and consulting on evidenced-based practices, the use of data to improve outcomes for students, programs and the profession. Recently, Dr. Hatch was an invited thought leader to the White House on school counseling and was most recently (July 28, 2014) she was the Featured Speaker at the White House Convening on the Presidents "College Opportunity Agenda" at Harvard University (MA).

REFERENCES

Achieve. (2012, December). *Implementing the common core standards: The role of the school counselor.* Retrieved from *http://www.achieve.org/publications/implementing- common-core-state-standards-role-school-counselor-action-brief*

American School Counselor Association. (2003). *The ASCA National Model: A framework for school counseling programs* (1st ed.). Alexandria, VA: Author.

American School Counselor Association. (2005). *The ASCA National Model: A framework for school counseling programs* (2nd ed.). Alexandria, VA: Author.

American School Counselor Association. (2008). School counselor competencies. Alexandria, VA: Author.

American School Counselor Association.(2010). Ethical standards for school counselors. Alexandria, VA: Author.

American School Counselor Association. (2012). ASCA school counselor competencies. Retrieved from *http://www.schoolcounselor.org/asca/media/asca/home/SCCompetencies.pdf*

American School Counselor Association. (2012). *The ASCA National Model: A framework for school counseling programs* (3rd ed.). Alexandria, VA: Author.

American School Counselor Association. (2014). Mindsets and Behaviors for Student Success: K–12 College- and Career-Readiness Standards for Every Student. Alexandria, VA: Author.

American School Counselor Association. (2014, July). First Lady Michelle Obama addresses the ASCA Conference on July 1, 2014 [Video file]. Retrieved from *http://www.schoolcounselor.org/school-counselors-members/professional-development/annual-conference/2014-conference-webstream/first-lady-s-address.*

Balfanz, R., Bridgeland, J.M., Fox, J.H., DePoli, J.L., Ingram, E.S., Maushard, M. (2014, April). Building a grad nation: Progress and challenge in ending the high school dropout epidemic. *GradNation.* Retrieved from *http://gradnation.org/sites/default/files/17548_BGN_Report_FinalFULL_5.2.14.pdf.*

Balfanz, R., Bridgeland, J.M., Moore, L.A., & Fox, J.H. (2010). Building a grad nation. Retrieved from *http://pearsonfoundation.org/downloads/BuildingAGradNation_FullReport.pdf.*

Bridgeland, J., & Bruce, M. (2011). 2011 National survey of school counselors: Counseling at a crossroads. Washington, DC: Hart Research Associates. Retrieved from *http://www.civicenterprises.net/MediaLibrary/Docs/counseling_at_a_crossroads.pdf.*

Bryan, J., & Holcomb-McCoy, C. (2004). School counselors' perceptions of their involvement in school-family-community partnerships. *Professional School Counseling, 7*(3), 162–171.

CACREP. (2009). *http://www.cacrep.org/wp-content/uploads/2013/12/2009-Standards.pdf.*

California Career Center. (2014). 2013–2014 Support personnel accountability report cards. SPARC. Retrieved from *https://www.calcareercenter.org/Home/Content?contentID=418.*

California Department of Education. (2013). School accountability report card (SARC). Retrieved from *www.cde.ca.gov/ta/ac/sa/.*

California Postsecondary Education Commission. (2011). Useful links. Retrieved from *http://www.cpec.ca.gov/Links/UsefulLinks.asp.*

College Board. (2011, November 14). Own the turf: A message from secretary of education, Arne Duncan [Video file]. Retrieved from *http://www.youtube.com/watch?v=1pIkbo7pjTg.*

College Board. (n.d.). NOSCA: National office for school advocacy. Retrieved from *http://nosca.collegeboard.org/resources.*

College Data. (n.d.). Admissions profile. Retrieved from *http://www.collegedata.com/cs/about_admissions_profile.jhtml.*

Denver Public Schools. (n.d.). Data elements we own. Retrieved from *http://dps-counseling.wikispaces.dpsk12.org/Data+Elements+We+Own.*

Dimmitt, C., Carey, J., & Hatch, T. (2007). *Evidence-based school counseling.* Thousand Oaks, CA: Corwin Press.

Education Trust. (2009). *National center for transforming school counseling at the education trust.*

Fouad, N.A., Gerstein, L.H., & Toporek, R.L. (2006). Social justice and counseling psychology in context. In R.L. Toporek, L. Gerstein, N. Fouad, G. Roysircar, & T. Israel (Eds.), *Handbook for social justice in counseling psychology: Leadership, vision, and action* (pp. 1–16). Thousand Oaks, CA: Sage.

Gysbers, N.C. & Henderson, P. (2006). *Developing and managing your school guidance and counseling program.* Alexandria, VA: American Counseling Association.

Hatch, T. (2012). The ASCA National Model themes: Advocacy and social justice. In American School Counselor Association (Ed.), *The ASCA national model: A framework for school counseling programs* (3rd ed.)(pp. 14–16). Alexandria, VA: Author.

Hatch, T. (2014). *The use of data in school counseling: Hatching Results for students, programs   and the professions.* Thousand Oaks, CA: Corwin Press.

Hines, P., & Lemons, R. (2011). Poised to lead: How school counselors can drive college and career readiness (p. 7). Retrieved from: *http://www.edtrust.org/sites/edtrust.org/files/publications/files/Poised_To_Lead_0.pdf.*

Hobsons. (n.d.). Naviance. Retrieved from *http://www.hobsons.com/education-solutions/solutions/plan-learn/naviance.*

Holcomb-McCoy, C. (2007). *School counseling to close the achievement gap: A social justice framework for success.* Thousand Oaks, CA: Corwin Press.

Holcomb-McCoy, C., & Chen-Hayes, S.F. (2011). Culturally competent school counselors: Affirming diversity by challenging oppression. In B.T. Erford (Ed.), *Transforming the school counseling profession* (3rd ed.) (pp. 90–109). Boston, MA: Pearson.

Johnson, R.S. (2002). *Using data to close the achievement gap: How to measure equity in our schools.* Thousand Oaks, CA: Corwin Press.

Kanter, M., Ochoa, E., Nassif, R., & Chong, F. (2011). Meeting President Obama's 2010 college completion goal (slide 9). [PowerPoint slides]. Retrieved from *http://www.ed.gov/sites/default/files/winning-the-future.ppt*.

Lee, V.V., & Goodnough, G.E. (2011). Systemic data-driven school counseling practice and programming for equity. In B.T. Erford (Ed.) *Transforming the school counseling profession* (3rd.ed). Columbus, OH: Pearson Merrill Prentice-Hall.

Lee, J., & Ransom, T. (2011). *The educational experience of young men of color: A review of research, pathways, and progress.* New York, NY: The College Board.

Massachusetts School Counselors Association. (2010). MA MODEL resources. Retrieved from *www.masca.org/index.php?option=com_content&view=article&id=116:ma-model&catid=53:ma-model&Itemid=117*.

National Career Development Association. (2004). National career development guidelines (NCDG) framework. Retrieved from *http://associationdatabase.com/aws/NCDA/asset_manager/get_file/3384?ver=16587*.

National Center for Education Statistics. (n.d.). Integrated postsecondary education data system. Retrieved from *http://nces.ed.gov/ipeds/*.

National Office for School Counselor Advocacy. (2011). Eight components of college and career readiness counseling (p. 37). Retrieved from *http://media.collegeboard.com/digitalServices/pdf/nosca/10b_2217_EightComponents_WEB_100625.pdf*.

National Office for School Counselor Advocacy. (NOSCA). (2011). *High school counselor's guide: NOSCA's eight components of college and career readiness counseling.* New York, NY: The College Board.

National Office for School Counselor Advocacy. (2012). *Transforming the Educational Experience of Young Men of Color*, 1.

No Child Left Behind Act of 2001, 20 U.S.C. § 6319 (2008).

Ratts, M., DeKruyf, L., & Chen-Hayes, S.F. (2007). The ACA advocacy competencies: A social justice advocacy framework for professional school counselors. *Professional School Counseling*, 11(2), 90–97.

Stephens, D.L., & Lindsey, R.B. (2011). *Culturally proficient collaboration: Use and misuse of school counselors.* Thousand Oaks, CA: Corwin.

Stone, C., & Dahir, C. (2005). *The transformed school counselor.* Belmont, CA: Wadsworth Publishing.

The White House. (n.d.). The First Lady's reach higher initiative. The White House. Retrieved from *http://www.whitehouse.gov/reach-higher*.

The White House. (2014, Aug.). Fact sheet: Improving college opportunity. *The White House.* Retrieved from *http://www.whitehouse.gov/the-press-office/2014/08/13/fact-sheet-improving-college-opportunity*.

The White House. (2014, Jan.). Fact sheet: The President and First Lady's call to action on college opportunity. *The White House.* Retrieved from *http://www.whitehouse.gov/the-press-office/2014/01/16/fact-sheet-president-and-first-lady-s-call-action-college-opportunity*

United States Department of Education. (2011). College- and career-ready standards and assessments (p. 13). Retrieved from *http://www2.ed.gov/policy/elsec/leg/blueprint/faq/college-career.pdf*.

Young, A., & Kaffenberger, C. (2009). *Making data work.* Alexandria, VA: American School Counselor Association.

Chapter 10: Practical Information Regarding Standardized Assessment: Articles from The College Board and ACT, Inc.

David Hawkins
@HawkinsNACAC

INTRODUCTION

Standardized admission tests are a ubiquitous component of the college application process for millions of American high school students each year. While not all colleges do so, more than 70 percent of colleges require that students submit scores from either the SAT or ACT exam as a condition for admission. In 2013, approximately 1.66 million students took the SAT exam, and 1.79 million took the ACT exam (NACAC, 2013). According to NACAC's annual State of College Admission report, college admission officers at all types of institutions—including the most highly selective—consistently view

whether to invest time or money in strategies d. affect admission test participation.

Finally, counseling professionals serve a growing as brokers of information between students/families, schools/districts and colleges/universities. Counselors are often asked to oversee the administration of admission tests, assist students and families when difficulties arise, and communicate with colleges and universities about their students' admission test scores. Maintaining a firm and independent knowledge base about the theory and practice of standardized admission tests is therefore an essential part of the counselor's skill set.

Maintaining a firm and independent knowledge base about the theory and practice of standardized admission tests is therefore an essential part of the counselor's skill set.

admission test scores as the second most important factor in college admission decisions after high school grades in college preparatory courses/strength of high school curriculum (NACAC, 2013). As this chapter reflects, institutions that conduct research into the predictive power of admission test scores generally have found that high school grades provide a better predictor of success in first-year college courses than the admission exams, though the combination of the two tend to provide slightly stronger predictions.

Counseling professionals are therefore understandably immersed in the multi-faceted consequences of widespread test use for high school students and their families. Most visibly, advising students and families involves a knowledge of the principles of standardized testing, the practical use of admission tests by colleges and universities, registration and score reporting procedures, test preparation and, in general, the extent to which students and families should spend time and energy on admission tests during the application process.

Counseling professionals must also be able to interpret admission test scores, both individually and in the aggregate, as part of their role in crafting and evaluating school or district policies related to standardized testing. As such, counselor fluency in data analysis constitutes a critical component as schools and districts consider

In response to growing and, in some cases, unwarranted emphasis on test scores in college admission and other contexts, NACAC convened a Commission on the Use of Standardized Tests in Undergraduate Admission in 2008 to examine ways in which counseling and admission professionals, as well as NACAC, could counter the undue influence afforded to the tests. For counseling professionals, the Commission's report noted:

> While admission tests are useful to many college
> and university admission offices, they are second to
> a student's performance in challenging coursework.
> Therefore, efforts to ensure that schools are
> preparing their students for college should not
> look to a single admission exam for an assessment
> of their progress, but to the strength of the school's
> curriculum and students' performance in those
> courses as their primary indicator. (NACAC, 2009)

In addition to encouraging an appropriate perspective on the role of standardized admission tests, the Commission report emphasized the importance of equipping college admission counseling professionals with an independent knowledge base from which to advise students and families.

Accordingly, NACAC instituted new best practice recommendations in 2009 for college admission counseling professionals, noting that professionals should:

- familiarize themselves with published inter-association standards for educational and psychological testing, particularly with respect to test score use and interpretation, test bias and score differences between subgroups;[1] and

- educate staff in understanding the concepts of test measurement, test interpretation, and test use so they may consider standardized tests in their appropriate context. Such education may be obtained from NACAC, institutions of higher education, or other associations independent of companies that sponsor the test or test preparation activities or have stated positions for or against test usage. *In addition, all members that make use of admission tests should acquire education and/or training in the appropriate use of specific tests from the sponsoring agencies.* (emphasis added) (NACAC, Statement of Principles of Good Practice)

With the latter (emphasized) guidance in mind, the following chapter will provide counseling professionals with an overview of the SAT and ACT, as well as information about the use of the assessments when working with students and families.

It is important to appreciate the roles of The College Board, which is the sponsoring agency of the SAT, and the ACT as providers of commercial resources that are used by schools and colleges. As such, stakeholders and consumers of these services benefit from maintaining an independent knowledge base from which to evaluate the function and utility of each service. The first section in this chapter provides an overview of the SAT for counseling professionals.

. . . .

STANDARDIZED TESTING FROM THE COLLEGE BOARD
The College Board
@CollegeBoard

Tests Associated with the College Admission Process

Founded in 1900, the College Board was created to expand access to higher education. Today, the membership association is made up of more than 6,000 of the world's leading educational institutions and is dedicated to promoting excellence and equity in education. One key part of the College Board's portfolio is its suite of college admission assessments. First administered in 1926, the SAT was created to democratize access to higher education for all students and to ensure that students who did not attend the most exclusive high schools had a chance to go to college. Today, the SAT serves as both a measure of students' college readiness and as a valid and reliable predictor of college outcomes.

Admission test scores provide colleges and universities with useful information that supplements student academic records and other relevant information in the selection process. Admission tests provide uniform measures across students, as opposed to school records for which standards are known to vary across institutions (College Board, 2011). The College Board offers a variety of assessments that may prove useful to the higher education professional in assessing the capabilities of applicants.

SAT® and PSAT/NMSQT®

The SAT is designed to test the subject matter learned by students in high school and how well they apply that knowledge—the critical thinking skills necessary to succeed in college. The current test is offered seven times a year in the United States, with an additional three administrations offered during the school day for districts and states that choose to have all students take the SAT, and six times a year internationally. It consists of 10 separately timed sections measuring critical reading (SAT-CR), mathematics (SAT-M) and writing (SAT-W). The test includes multiple-choice questions, student-produced responses (mathematics only) and a 25-minute essay (writing). The test takes three hours and 45 minutes. Most students take the test during junior or senior year of high school, and most colleges and universities use the SAT to help in making admission decisions.

The PSAT/NMSQT may be the first national standardized test many students take in preparation for college. It is offered in October of each year. The test is cosponsored by the College Board and National Merit Scholarship Corporation. Roughly equal numbers of sophomores and ju-

---

[1] *Further reading:* Standards for Education and Psychological Testing. *(2014). American Educational Research Association (AERA), American Psychological Association (APA), and National Council on Measurement in Education (NCME). Information available at:* http://www.apa.org/science/programs/testing/standards.aspx.

niors take the PSAT/NMSQT each year, although about 10 percent of students take it prior to their sophomore year. The test measures critical reading, mathematics and writing skills. In addition to providing students with insight into current college readiness and practice for the SAT, PSAT/NMSQT scores are used by a number of scholarship and recognition programs, most notably the National Merit Scholarship Program, the National Hispanic Recognition Program and the National Scholarship Service.

As will be discussed later in this section, The College Board has committed to a redesign suite of assessments. For more information on the Fall 2015 launch, go to: *deliveringopportunity.org*.

SAT Subject Tests™

SAT Subject Tests are the only national admission tests that are designed to measure students' knowledge and skills in particular subject areas and their ability to apply that knowledge. They are closely linked to the high school curriculum and give students an additional opportunity to distinguish themselves and showcase their skills in a particular subject area. Each test contains multiple-choice items administered in one hour. There are six Subject Test administrations per year, although not all tests are offered in every administration.

CLEP®

The College Board also offers the College-Level Examination Program (CLEP), a credit-by-exam program testing mastery of college-level material acquired in a variety of ways—through general academic instructions, significant independent study or extracurricular work. CLEP exam-takers include adults just entering or returning to school, military service members, and traditional college students. This rigorous program allows students of a wide range of ages and backgrounds to demonstrate their mastery of college-level material in introductory subjects and to earn college credit. Students can earn credit for what they already know by getting qualifying scores on any of the 33 examinations in five subject areas.

Advanced Placement®

The Advanced Placement (AP®) Program currently offers more than 30 courses across multiple subject areas. Each course is developed by a committee composed of college faculty and AP teachers, and covers the breadth of information, skills and assignments found in the corresponding college course. The Advanced Placement Program allows students to take college-level courses in a high school setting. The AP Examinations are administered each year in May and represent the culmination of college-level work in a given discipline in a secondary school setting. Rigorously developed by committees of college and AP high school faculty, the AP Exams test students' ability to perform at a college level. Research has demonstrated that students who pass AP Exams perform in subsequent courses as well as or better than students who take the corresponding introductory course in college (Patterson & Ewing, 2013); and that higher performance on AP Exams is associated with higher college performance in the subject area and fewer credit hours taken to obtain a bachelor's degree (Godfrey, Matos-Elefonte, Ewing, & Patel, 2014).

Redesigned Assessments

Throughout its 100-year history, the SAT has undergone multiple changes to maintain its successful use in combination with factors such as high school grade point average (HSGPA) to assess student preparedness for and to predict student success in postsecondary education (Lawrence, Rigol, Van Essen, & Jackson, 2002). Over the past two years, drawing on extensive input and advice from College Board members, partner organizations (such as the National Merit Scholarship Corporation, which cosponsors the PSAT/NMSQT), and postsecondary and K–12 experts, the College Board has undertaken an extensive redesign of the SAT and the related PSAT-suite of assessments. These assessments—which are part of the College Board Readiness and Success System—will be focused on the few skills that evidence shows matter most for college and career success, and will provide more actionable results for students and educators beginning in middle school. The redesigned exams will be introduced in the 2015–16 school year.

- For **eighth** and **ninth** graders, the PSAT 8/9 will be offered in either the fall or spring; this test will replace the College Board's current eighth and ninth grade assessments.

- **Tenth** graders will have the option to take the PSAT/NMSQT during the fall of their sophomore year or the PSAT 10 during the spring of their sophomore year (the PSAT 10 is a parallel form of the PSAT/NMSQT that will be made available to sophomores only).

- **Eleventh** graders will continue to have the option to take the PSAT/NMSQT in the fall, when students are typically eligible to enter the National Merit Scholarship competition.

- The SAT will continue to be offered in both the spring and the fall for **11th** and **12th** graders during national and school day administrations.

The redesigned exams will provide the higher education community with a more comprehensive and informative understanding of students' readiness for college-level work, will more clearly and transparently focus on the knowledge, skills and understandings that students need to be successful in college and careers, and will improve the links and connections between assessment and instruction by better reflecting the meaningful, engaging and rigorous work that students must undertake in the best high school courses being taught today (College Board, 2014). The College Board will maintain and improve the SAT's high level of technical quality, as well as its rigorous SAT validity research agenda.

Notably, the redesigned SAT Evidence-Based Reading and Writing and (optional) Essay portions of the exam will incorporate key design elements supported by evidence, including:

- The use of a range of text complexity aligned to college- and career-ready reading levels

- An emphasis on the use of evidence and source analysis

- The incorporation of data and informational graphics that students will analyze along with text

- A focus on relevant words in context and on word choice for rhetorical effect

- Attention to a core set of important English language conventions and to effective written expression

- The requirement that students interact with texts across a broad range of disciplines.

The key evidence-based design elements that will be incorporated into the redesigned SAT Math Test include:

- A focus on the content that matters most for college and career readiness (rather than a vast array of concepts)

- An emphasis on problem solving and data analysis

- The inclusion of a calculator as well as no-calculator section and attention to the use of the calculator as a tool.

The College Board is committed to ensuring that the content and format of the redesigned SAT are clear and transparent and that the exam reflects the best of classroom work and work outside the classroom.

The complete test specifications and related material, including implementation support for K–12 and higher education, can be found at *www.deliveringopportunity.org*.

PREPARING FOR THE SAT

Generally, students do well on the SAT because they are exposed to and apply rigorous course material in high school, and take rigorous core courses. Specifically, research has shown that taking rigorous courses in math is positively associated with SAT scores (St. John, Musoba, & Chung, 2004). The best preparation, then, is to apply oneself to a challenging high school curriculum.

Coaching schools offer courses where SAT preparation is structured by an official instructor who educates students in "test-taking strategies or 'tricks' [that] enable test takers to 'beat the test'…to take advantage of flaws in the test or in the testing system" (Powers, 2012, p. 2).

The College Board has long maintained that test preparation is largely ineffective, and the SAT is not "coachable" (Buckman, Condon, & Roscigno, 2010). In addition to coaching schools, students may also hire a private tutor designed to help them prepare for the SAT (Aurini & Davies, 2004). However, research suggests that, on average, coaching results in a small, positive effect on SAT score.

While studies have provided slightly different estimates, on average, the effect of coaching on the math section is between 10–20 points, and between 5–10 points for the verbal section, or 15–30 points in total (Briggs, 2001, 2002; Briggs & Domingue, 2009; Buckman, Condron, & Roscigno, 2010; Powers & Rock, 1999). These findings correspond with a meta-analysis conducted by Becker (1990) who found that, from 1953 to 1988, the expected gain from coaching was nine points on verbal and 16 points on math.

Despite this research, the College Board has recognized that the culture and practice of high-priced test preparation can drive inequality. As part of the redesign of its college-readiness assessments, the College Board is partnering with Khan Academy to develop free, world-class test practice available on-demand, to everyone, everywhere. This content is designed to help students review and develop key academic concepts from their high school curricula and familiarize themselves with the SAT item formats, not deliver "insider" tips or tricks. The practice materials developed by and with Khan Academy will include personalized lessons on test content, official SAT practice questions and full-length tests.

Validity Evidence

Test Content

The SAT tests the critical reading, mathematical, and writing skills that students have developed over time and that they need to be successful in college. The College Board regularly studies state standards, district curriculum frameworks, and the course content of first-year college courses to ensure that the SAT does indeed measure and reflect the content knowledge and cognitive processes that students need to be ready for—and successful in—college.

Evidence for the relationship between the SAT critical reading and writing sections and school curriculum and instruction is derived from the strong link found between the skills assessed on the SAT, with the curricula reflected in results from a large-scale national survey (Milewski, Johnsen, Glazer, & Kubota, 2005). Evidence for the connection between the SAT mathematics section and school curriculum and instruction was derived from a common set of standards in the field of mathematics education. More recently, the College Board surveyed more than 5,000 high school and college instructors in English Language Arts (ELA) and mathematics to assess the knowledge, skills and topics taught in high school classrooms and the value placed on these topics in higher education (Kim, Wiley, & Packman, 2011). The survey results dem-

onstrated strong support for the ELA and mathematics topics assessed on the SAT, with instructors rating the vast majority of topics on the SAT as both important and covered in their classrooms.

In addition, the development of each of the three SAT sections (critical reading, writing and mathematics) is guided by the work of a test development committee composed of both high school and college teachers in that subject area. These educators review and discuss each new form of the test. These reviews are done both by mail and at the site of the committee meeting. The pre-meeting reviews allow for deep consideration and reflection on each question and the test as a whole, plus an opportunity for a reviewer to check a reference or to make sure that no wrong answer on a multiple-choice question can be successfully defended as correct. The concerns identified during the reviews by committee members are discussed in the committee meeting with College Board staff and test developers. Each concern must be resolved before the test moves into production and printing for its scheduled administration.

College Outcomes

The fundamental test of validity for an assessment like the SAT is that it is predictive of college success. Over the last seven years, the College Board has collected higher education outcome data from four-year institutions to document evidence of the validity of the SAT for use in college admission. Research has examined the relationship between SAT scores with outcomes such as first-year grade point average (FYGPA), cumulative GPA through college, English course grades, mathematics course grades, retention at different points in time, and college completion in four and six years.

Much of the validity evidence documenting the relationship between SAT scores and outcomes such as FYGPA, for example, is represented as correlation coefficients. A correlation coefficient is one way of describing the linear relationship between two measures (Anastasi & Urbina, 1997). Correlations range from -1 to +1, with a perfect positive correlation (+1.00) indicating that a top-scoring person on test #1 would also be the top-scoring person on test #2, and the second-best scorer on test #1 would also be the second-best scorer on test #2, and so on through the poorest performing person on both tests. A correlation of zero would indicate no relationship at all between test #1 and test #2. An often-cited rule of thumb for interpreting correlation coefficients (Cohen, 1988) is that a small correlation has an absolute value of approximately .1; a medium correlation has an absolute value of approximately .3; and a large correlation has an absolute value of approximately .5 or higher.

Validity coefficients in educational and psychological testing are rarely above .3 (Meyer et al., 2001). While this value may sound low to people without a detailed understanding of correlation coefficients, it is sometimes helpful to consider the correlation coefficients representing other more familiar relationships in our lives. For example, the association between a major league baseball player's batting average and his success in getting a hit in a particular instance at bat is .06, the correlation between antihistamines and reduced sneezing and runny nose is .11, and the correlation between prominent movie critics' reviews and box office success is .17 (Meyer et al., 2001). The uncorrected, observed or raw[2] correlation coefficient representing the relationship between the SAT and FYGPA tends to be in the mid .3s. When corrected for restriction of range, the correlation coefficient tends to be in the mid .5s, representing a strong relationship.

It is a commonly heard misunderstanding that the SAT does not predict anything more than grade point average at the end of the freshman year of college (FYGPA). Perhaps many people would be surprised to learn that the SAT remains similarly, if not slightly more, predictive of cumulative GPA through four years of college. Other large-scale studies and meta-analyses (aggregating multiple studies on the topic) provide strong support for the notion that the predictive validity of test scores, such as the SAT, are not limited to near-term outcomes such as FYGPA, but predict longer term academic and career outcomes, as well (Sackett, Borneman, & Connely, 2008). For example, research showed SAT scores of gifted adolescents to be predictive of earning a PhD, gaining tenure in academia and receiving patents (Lubinski, Benbow, Webb, & Bleske-Rechek, 2006).

The SAT and HSGPA are each a strong predictor of FYGPA. The combination of both together provides an even stronger prediction relationship (Patterson & Mattern, 2013), with the multiple correlation typically in the mid .6s (Mattern & Patterson, 2014). The results are consistent across multiple entering classes of first-year, first-time students (from 2006 to 2010), providing further validity evidence for the SAT in terms of the generalizability of the results. In addition, the SAT provides incremental validity above and beyond HSGPA in the prediction of FYGPA.

One way to think about the added utility of the SAT over and above HSGPA to predict FYGPA is by examining the amount of error in the prediction of FYGPA by HSGPA alone, by SAT scores alone, or with HSGPA and SAT scores together, particularly for students with highly discrepant HSGPAs and SAT scores (much stronger HSGPA than SAT scores or vice versa, after the measures have been standardized). Previous research (Kobrin, Camara, & Milewski, 2002; Mattern, Shaw, & Kobrin, 2010) has found that about 16–18 percent of students would be considered highly discrepant favoring their HSGPA, 16–18 percent would be considered highly discrepant favoring their SAT scores, and about 65–68 percent would be considered non-discrepant. A recent study (Mattern, Shaw, & Kobrin, 2011) of more than 150,000 first-year students attending 110 four-year institutions found that using students' HSGPAs without their SAT scores to predict their FYGPA for admission would likely result in those students with much higher SAT scores than HSGPAs (discrepant favoring SAT) not being admitted, though they would have performed just as well in college as the admitted students with much higher HSGPAs than SAT scores. In other words, without SAT score information, there is a sizeable percentage of students that would be overlooked for admission to an institution when they could have been quite successful there. Consistent with essentially all differential prediction research conducted on the SAT and HSGPA with FYGPA, using the students' HSGPAs in

---

[2]   *Raw, as opposed to corrected for restriction of range, which factors in the reduced variance in the predictor and criterion resulting from only analyzing the higher SAT scores and FYGPAs available for the admitted/enrolled students instead of all applicants. Note that it is a widely accepted practice to statistically correct correlation coefficients for restriction of range since only a sample (admitted/enrolled students) is available for analysis as opposed to the population (all applicants) for which the measure (SAT) was used to make decisions.*

conjunction with their SAT scores results in the smallest amount of error in the prediction of FYGPA across all students (Mattern & Patterson, 2014).

A variety of factors are thought to contribute to this greater error in prediction, such as different grading standards, rigorous coursework and access to resources across high schools. For example, while high schools tend to have similar grade distributions, they vary in achievement levels of students. Thus, including standardized test scores in the prediction of college performance helps to mitigate this prediction error by offering a standard for comparing students across different schools (Zwick, 2013).

Ultimately, each postsecondary institution is unique, with its own specific admission needs. This situation often requires tailored guidelines on the most effective use of test scores and other information in the evaluation of candidates for admission. To aid in this process, the College Board offers the Admitted Class Evaluation Service, a free online service that predicts how admitted students will perform at a college or university generally, and how successful students will be in specific courses. ACES studies provide the information needed to confirm or improve current admission and placement policies and can identify the optimum combination of measures to predict a student's future performance at a given institution.

DEMOGRAPHIC GROUP DIFFERENCES

Often, SAT score consumers notice average score differences among demographic groups and conclude that the test must be flawed. Presumably, it is reasoned, if the SAT were a fair test, no student demographic characteristics would matter, as average scores would be similar across groups. Therefore, some people assume that any difference in SAT performance by demographics must indicate test bias for/against a demographic group.

Socioeconomic (SES) Status

According to Peter Sacks (1997), author of Standardized Minds, "one can make a good guess about a child's standardized test scores simply by looking at how many degrees her parents have and what kind of car they drive" (p. 27). This comment is illustrative of frequent criticism that the SAT is merely a wealth test, because there is a correlation between student scores and socioeconomic status (i.e., parental income and educational attainment).

Proponents of this claim often support their arguments by stating that the SAT only covers content that is learned by wealthy students, rather than material covered in high school (Goldfarb, 2014).

It is true that there is a relationship between SES and most educational measures (Camara & Schmidt, 1999). However, direct tests of the claim that the relationship between admission test scores and college grades was an artefact of SES revealed quite the opposite: Even when SES was statistically controlled, the relationship between test scores and grades remained high. Further, researchers found evidence supporting the notion that SES is related to characteristics measured by the test, which also affect grades (Sackett, Kuncel, Arneson, Cooper, & Waters, 2009; Sackett, Kuncel, Beatty, Rigdon, Shen, & Kiger, 2012). For example, students from affluent families may have more access to the kinds of rigorous course material associated with high performance on admission tests, as well as in college.

Race/Ethnicity and Gender

Over the years, there have been concerns expressed about potential racial/ethnic and/or gender bias in the tests. The testing agencies have attempted to eliminate any bias in the tests. On the SAT, for example, all items are pretested and reviewed. Pretesting can serve to ensure that items are not ambiguous or confusing, to examine the item responses to determine the difficulty level or the degree to which the item differentiates between more or less able students, and to understand whether students from different racial/ethnic groups or gender groups respond to the item differently (also called "differential item functioning"). Differential item functioning (DIF) analyses compare the item performance of two groups of test-takers (e.g., males versus females) who have been matched on ability. Items displaying DIF indicate that the item is functioning differently for one subgroup than the way it functions for another. Items with sizeable DIF, favoring one group over another, will then undergo further review to determine whether the item should be revised and re-pretested, or eliminated altogether. Items also undergo a sensitivity review to ensure the items avoid stereotyping and language or symbols that are sexist, racist, or otherwise potentially offensive, inappropriate, or negative toward any group.

Many critics of tests and testing presume that the existence of mean score differences by subgroups indicates that the test or measure is biased. While consistent group mean differences are important to pay attention to, these differences do not necessarily signal bias. Groups may have different experiences, opportunities or interests in particular areas that can impact performance on the skills or abilities being measured. Many studies have found that the mean subgroup differences found on the SAT (e.g., by gender, race/ethnicity, socioeconomic status) are unfortunately also found in virtually all measures of educational outcomes, including other large-scale standardized tests, high school performance and graduation, and college attendance.

SAT Optional

Organizations such as the National Center for Fair and Open Testing (FairTest) argue that standardized admission tests, such as the SAT, create a significant barrier to entry for academically qualified minority, first-generation and low-income applicants. In an attempt to address these concerns, some colleges and universities, such as Mount Holyoke College (MA) and Bates College (ME), and more recently, Temple University (PA), have adopted test-optional policies (Peligri, 2014). However, out of more than 1,800 four-year, nonprofit colleges and universities across the United States, 78 percent still require or recommend a college entrance exam as part of their admission policy. Approximately 90 percent of students send scores to these institutions for consideration in the admission process.

Generally, the most common test-optional approach that colleges have used to attempt to increase diversity on their campuses is class rank (or percent plans). Recent research has shown that as a whole, institutions that have shifted to test-optional policies have "done little to meet their manifest goals of expanding educational opportunity for low-income and minority students" (Belasco, Rosinger, & Hearn, 2014, p. 13).

Some critics of the SAT have argued that scores should be replaced with class rank as an admission criterion because it is more equitable than SAT scores and grades; and some university systems (California, Texas, Florida) have adopted these policies. Through this approach, a fixed percent of students (usually the top 4–20 percent) are admitted from each high school, regardless of test scores, school quality or rigor of coursework. However, percent plans do not ultimately increase diversity on campus (Carnevale & Rose, 2003). For example, a recent study of 193 selective colleges and universities by Carnevale, Rose and Strohl (2014) found that using a 10-percent plan would have resulted in a qualified applicant pool that was, on average, 6 percent black and 11 percent Hispanic, which did not significantly differ from the existing racial/ethnic composition of schools, which was 4 percent black and 7 percent Hispanic. In addition, the percent plan approach may also create other problems, such as admitting top-ranked students from lower quality high schools, which can lead to higher dropout rates and lower retention rates (Zwick, 2002).

Test optional policies have predictable results. In particular, students who choose not to submit SAT scores (but who have taken the SAT) score more than 100 points lower on average than students who submit scores. Additionally, research on test-optional institutions has consistently demonstrated that students with higher SAT scores have higher college outcomes on average (e.g., FYGPA and graduation rates), regardless of whether the students submitted SAT scores (Robinson & Monks, 2005; Wainer, 2011).

. . . .

INTERLUDE

David Hawkins

At present, the ACT and SAT are generally interpreted on equal footing by colleges and universities. In addition, many states have begun introducing the ACT as a requirement for high school students, either as an accountability measure or a college-preparation activity. Given the emphasis on college readiness as a national priority, the profile of these tests as school-wide measures seems likely to grow. Despite similarities in their predictive ability, as well as a growing consistency in the tendency of colleges to accept either test for application purposes, there are structural differences between the two tests. The second section in this chapter provides an overview of the ACT for counseling professionals.

Using ACT's Assessments in College Counseling

Wes Habley, EdD
ACT, Inc.
@ACT

The information provided through ACT's assessment programs provides college counselors with a set of integrated resources that assist them as students explore and make choices regarding colleges to attend and academic programs that will most likely lead to success. Unfortunately, many parents and students focus almost entirely on the test results, believing that scores alone are the determinant of admission to and success in college. While test scores are important in the decision-making process, the best decisions are the product of multiple, timely and accurate information sources. Additional information collected through ACT's assessment programs can promote discussion with students who are making important decisions about college. In addition to scores on ACT's test of educational development, there is a wealth of information that provides insights, as well as stimuli, for discussion as counselors work with students.

The purpose of this overview is to introduce the broad categories of information available to college counselors through ACT's family of assessment programs. It should be noted that there will be significant and continuous enhancements to ACT's family of assessments in the years ahead. These enhancements will maintain the core functions, while expanding the utility not only of the cognitive assessments, but also of the additional sources of information available to counselors. During this time period, enhancements in the scope, the format and the reporting of information to students, parents and counselors will be ongoing. While several of these enhancements are included in this chapter, others are currently in the planning stage, and still others are in exploratory mode. Readers are encouraged to visit *www.act.org* on a regular basis to monitor these enhancements.

Cognitive Assessment

Cognitive Components

ACT's core cognitive components are derived from periodic national curriculum surveys conducted every three to five years. These surveys collect data about what entering college students should know and be able to do to be ready for college-level coursework in English, mathematics, reading, and science. The most recent version of the curriculum survey can be found at: *www.act.org/research-policy/national-curriculum-survey*. The scale for the ACT tests provides for scores ranging from 1–36 in four subject areas: English, Mathematics, Reading, and Science. The composite score is the arithmetic mean of the four subject area tests, also reported in a range of 1–36. The subject area tests are described below.

Test	Content
English	75 questions, 45 minutes: Measures standard written English and rhetorical skills
Mathematics	60 questions, 60 minutes: Measures mathematical skills students have typically acquired in courses taken up to the beginning of grade 13
Reading	40 questions, 35 minutes: Measures reading comprehension
Science	40 questions, 35 minutes: Measures the interpretation, analysis, evaluation, reasoning, and problem-solving skills require in the natural sciences

In addition, normative information is provided for the composite and individual subject scores, which allows for comparison of individual scores with those of students at the state and national levels.

Benchmark Scores

Subject area benchmarks are reported in ACT's assessment programs. The benchmarks are derived from ongoing research on the relationship between ACT scores and student performance in college classes. Benchmark scores represent the level of achievement (score point) on the ACT subject-area tests required for students to have a 50 percent chance of obtaining a B or higher or about a 75 percent chance of obtaining a C or higher in corresponding credit-bearing, first-year college courses. These college courses include English composition, college algebra, introductory social sciences, and biology. From time to time, the benchmark scores are adjusted based on continuing research. The current benchmarks are:

College Course	ACT Subject Test	Benchmark Score
English Composition	English	18
College Algebra	Mathematics	22
Social Sciences	Reading	22
Biology	Science	23

The most recent information on the benchmarks can be found at: *www.act.org/solutions/college-career-readiness/college-readiness-benchmarks*.

As mentioned earlier, significant incremental and value-driven changes in the ACT will be introduced during the next several years. For upcoming changes in the subject tests and in the scoring and reporting of the tests, readers should refer to: *www.act.org/actnext*. The familiar 1-to-36 scores used on the ACT will not change. However, starting in 2015, students who take the ACT test also will receive new readiness scores and indicators designed to show performance and preparedness in areas important to success after high school. The sections below provide descriptions of those scores and indicators.

STEM Score

The STEM score represents the student's overall performance on the science and math portions of the exam. This new score can help students connect their strengths to career and study paths in science, technology, engineering, and mathematics that they might not otherwise have considered, particularly when used with their results from the ACT Interest Inventory (described later in this chapter).

Progress Toward Career Readiness Indicator

This indicator helps students understand their progress toward career readiness and helps educators prepare their students for success in a variety of career pathways. It will provide an indication of future performance on the ACT National Career Readiness Certificate™ (ACT NCRC®), an assessment-based credential that certifies foundational work skills important for job success across industries and occupations. The most recent information on the National Career Readiness Certificate can be found

at: *www.act.org/solutions/college-career-readiness/college-readiness-benchmarks*.

English Language Arts Score

This score combines achievement on the English, reading and writing portions of the ACT for those who take all three test sections, enabling students to see how their performance compares with others who have been identified as college-ready.

Text Complexity Progress Indicator

This measure tells students if they are making sufficient progress toward comprehending the complex texts they will encounter in college and during their careers. The information will help students plan future study to improve their reading comprehension.

While information provided through the ACT is useful in college choice and admission, most educators believe that discussions about the skills necessary to succeed in college must take place sooner than the eleventh and twelfth grades. Early identification of academic concerns can lead to guidance on interventions that can mediate those concerns. In 2014, ACT's EXPLORE and PLAN programs were discontinued as ACT Aspire™ was introduced. ACT Aspire™ is a computer-based, longitudinal assessment system that connects growth and progress from elementary grades through high school in the context of college and career readiness. ACT Aspire subject areas are the same as those for the ACT: English, math, reading, science, and writing for Grades 3–8 and early high school (Grades 9–10). ACT Aspire predicts performance on the ACT. Additional information on ACT Aspire can be found at: *www.discoveractaspire.org*.

NON-COGNITIVE COMPONENTS

While cognitive assessment is critical to assisting students in college planning, additional information on student demographics, characteristics, plans, and needs broaden the perspective and enhance decision-making. Simply stated, the success of college planning is directly related to the breadth and depth of information that guides student decisions. The following non-cognitive information sources are collected and reported through ACT's assessment programs.

High School Grade Information

A common finding in educational research is that that high school grades are predictive of college grades and that test scores and high school grades combined are a better predictor of college than either is alone. Although selected high school/course grade information is collected through ACT's assessment programs, college counselor access to high school transcripts provides a more complete and up-to-date record of student academic performance.

Student Reported Information

As one component of ACT's assessment programs, students are asked to share information about several areas that are important to the college counseling process. Among these are:

- Educational and vocational plans—this includes student preference (or lack thereof) for choice of academic program, as well as certainty in that choice.

- Academic/planning needs—includes need for assistance in writing, reading, study skills, mathematics, and educational/vocational planning.

- Interests—includes interest in honors programs, independent student and ROTC.

- Plans for financial aid and employment while in college.

- Ranking of college choice factors and preferences—includes institutional type, student body composition, location, size, cost, and availability of academic program.

Students should opt to participate in the ACT Educational Opportunity Service (EOS) when they register to take the ACT. Registration in the EOS provides students with information about educational and financial aid opportunities by making their contact information available to colleges and scholarship agencies that meet EOS eligibility guidelines. About 88 percent of the ACT-tested high school graduating class of 2012 opted into EOS during high school. The most recent information on EOS can be found at: *www.act.org/eos*.

Educational and Career Plans

The **ACT Interest Inventory** provides a focus on career exploration, not by identifying the one "right" occupation or educational program, but rather by providing information on student interest patterns and connecting those patterns to careers and educational programs. The Interest Inventory points students to career areas they may wish to explore. The Inventory is based on the well-documented construct that students will be most satisfied and will be most likely to succeed if they enroll in academic programs that lead to careers consistent with their interests.

The ACT World-of-Work Map (*www.act.org/world/world.html*) summarizes the results of the Interest Inventory and displays basic similarities and differences among various occupational clusters. The Map is designed to engage users in the process of career exploration. Like any map, it needs compass points. All occupations can be organized according to their involvement with four types of basic work tasks, working with data, ideas, people, and things. Usually one or two of these basic work tasks capture the primary nature of an occupation; for example, editors work mostly with people and ideas. These basic work tasks are the Map's compass points. Individual ACT Interest Inventory results are provided through several levels of ACT assessment programs. Results are reported as regions of the World-of-Work (WOW) Map, and each region contains one or more career areas. Users can follow up with career exploration using the World-of-Work Map found on all of ACT's student Web sites (e.g., *www.planstudent.org*). The interactive map permits users to drill down to descriptions of specific occupations. An interactive version of the WOW Map can be found at: *www.act.org/world/world.html*.

Associated with the World-of-Work Map is the Map of College Majors (*http://www.act.org/majorsmap/*). The Map of College Majors is a searchable graphic that shows the locations of 80 popular majors. It is based on the interests of thousands of college students. Each point on the map corresponds to the interests of actual students in that major.

INFORMATION ABOUT COLLEGES FROM THE ACT

Every year, ACT surveys colleges to obtain data on areas critical to college choice and admission. College information is shared with college counselors through ACT's reporting systems. These reports provide college information based on the most recently completed academic year.

Although data are reported by the college and are generally accurate, counselors should consult with college web pages and catalogs for possible changes. College information provided to counselors and students includes, but is not limited to the following:

A. Enrollment figures include both undergraduate and graduate students during the previous academic year.

B. Size of the community in which the college is located.

C. Admission selectivity as described by the college. The chart below serves only as a general guideline. There is considerable overlap among the selectivity categories and colleges often make exceptions to the stated policy.

Admission Policy and Typical Class Rank of Admitted Students	Typical ACT Composite Score of Admitted Students
Highly Selective: the majority of accepted first-year students are in the top 10 percent of their high school graduating class	25–30
Selective: the majority of accepted first-year students are in the top 25 percent of their high school graduating class	21–26
Traditional: the majority of accepted first-year students are in the 50 percent of their high school graduating class	18–24
Liberal: some of the accepted first-years students are from the lower half of the high school graduating class	17–22

D. Costs associated with attendance, including tuition, fees, room and board, as well as travel and incidental expenses.

E. High school average GPA for first-year students.

F. Student's chances in 10 of attaining a first-year GPA of C or higher at colleges in the choice set. This element is based on research that includes ACT scores, high school grades and performance of students enrolled at colleges in the choice set.

G. Relative rank of student test scores as compared to the scores of students in the college's previous first-year class.

INTEGRATION OF INFORMATION

Success in college and career planning rests on the counselor's ability to integrate multiple sources of information and to raise questions where incongruities occur between or among data elements. The sections below provide examples of questions that may arise through a more in-depth exploration of cognitive and non-cognitive data.

College Planning

• Has the student identified colleges appropriate for his or her level of educational development, as indicated by high school performance and subject area, STEM and Language Arts scores?

• Is there congruence among test scores, high school grades, field of study, self-reported need for assistance, and interest inventory results?

• Do the chosen colleges offer the student's preferred program of study? What percentage of each college's students are enrolled in that area? If the program is not available, how does the student plan to resolve this discrepancy?

• Is the student aware of any inconsistencies between the stated preferences for type of college and the characteristics of the schools considered, such as location, type, cost, and size?

• Is the level of admission selectivity consistent with grades and test scores? Are there colleges in the choice set that are a better academic fit for the student?

• What cost limitation does the student indicate? Is the student aware of hidden costs, such as the cost of travel to a college distant from home? If a selected school costs more than the student and family can pay, does the student plan to seek financial aid? If so, does time remain to do so, and are application materials needed?

Career Planning

Has the student made tentative educational and career plans? If so:

• Are the plans based on realistic factors, such as educational development and interests, or are they influenced by factors such as parental expectations and sex-role stereotypes?

- Is the career plan consistent with the Career Readiness Indicator?

- Are the student's degree objective, educational major and career plans consistent?

- Do the student's differential levels of educational development (as indicated by high school grades and ACT scores) support the educational and career plans?

- Do the student's interests support the educational and career plans?

- Are more possibilities for educational and career plans suggested by:

  o Differential levels of educational development, as indicated by grades, and test scores?

  o Interest Inventory scores?

  o Actual or planned extracurricular activities?

If there is reason to believe that plans or interests have changed, students should be encouraged to update their information through their student Web account: (*https://services.actstudent.org/OA_HTML/actibeCAcdLogin.jsp*) and incorporate these changes into the decision-making process.

Successful college counseling relies on access to timely and accurate cognitive and non-cognitive information available that supports student college choice and admission decision-making. Significant enhancements in ACT's assessment programs should improve the quality of and counselor access to data. These enhancements will maintain and expand the core functions not only of the cognitive assessments, but also of the additional sources of information available to counselors. During this time period, enhancements in the delivery, scope, format, and reporting of information to students, parents and counselors will be ongoing. Because these changes will be ongoing, readers are encouraged to visit *www.act.org* on a regular basis to monitor these enhancements.

REFLECTION QUESTIONS

1. How do you answer questions from students or parents about the difference between the tests, and whether taking one test or the other provides an advantage in the admission process?

2. Where can counselors post registration and test dates for the year so that students can readily access the information?

3. When should students start thinking about taking the various tests mentioned in this chapter?

4. How can counselors make sure that students and their families have all the information necessary regarding taking the appropriate tests for college admission?

5. How can counselors help students find out about accommodations available to them based on their financial or disability needs?

6. How would you advise a student or family who are concerned about the influence of testing in college admission? What is the appropriate way of describing the role of standardized admission tests in college admission decisions?

7. How would you describe the test-optional admission process to a student or family?

8. What resources can college counselors provide students that will help them become more familiar with the standardized tests listed in this chapter (e.g., practice tests, FAQ sheet, etc.)

9. How would you speak to a school or district administrator about the use of admission test scores as an indicator of academic achievement in your school or district?

10. What would you consider valid or invalid uses of admission tests results by your school or district?

About the Authors

David Hawkins has served as the director of public policy and research for NACAC since 2000. David is the creator and editor of NACAC's State of College Admission report, conducts government relations advocacy, and serves as a media liaison for NACAC. David's prior work experience includes service as Research Director for the Democratic Congressional Campaign Committee and as a Congressional Affairs specialist for the Department of Housing and Urban Development in the Clinton Administration. David received both a bachelor's and master's degree in government from the College of William and Mary in Williamsburg, VA.

Wes Habley, EdD currently serves as senior associate with Thomas Brown Associates after retiring as assistant vice president for strategic partnerships at ACT, Inc. On his retirement, Habley was awarded ACT's first Lifetime Achievement Award. He earned his bachelor's degree in music education and his master's degree in student development from the University of Illinois-Urbana/Champaign (IL). His doctorate in higher education administration was earned at Illinois State University (IL) where he was recently inducted into the College of Education Hall of Fame. Habley has more than 50 published works on academic advising and student retention. His most recent publications include *Increasing Persistence: Research-based Strategies for College Student Success* (2012), *Academic Advising: a comprehensive handbook* (2000, 2008), *Status of Academic Advising* (2004) and *What Works in Student Retention* in (2004, 2010). He has delivered more than 200 presentations at professional meetings and has served as a consultant or workshop leader at more than 125 colleges in the US, Canada, and the Middle East. Habley is a founding Board member of NACADA and served as President and Treasurer. He served for 22 years as the director of the Summer Institute on Academic Advising and is the recipient of NACADA's awards for service and for outstanding contributions to the field of advising.

The College Board, founded in 1900, was created to expand access to higher education. Today, the membership association is made up of over 6,000 of the world's leading educational institutions and is dedicated to promoting excellence and equity in education. Each year, the College Board helps more than seven million students prepare for a successful transition to college through programs and services in college readiness and college success—including the SAT and the Advanced Placement Program. The organization also serves the education community through research and advocacy on behalf of students, educators and schools.

References from Essays

Anastasi, A., & Urbina, S. (1997). *Psychological testing (7th ed.).* Upper Saddle River, NJ: Prentice Hall.

Aurini, J., & Davies, S. (2004). The transformation of private tutoring: Education in a franchise form. *The Canadian Journal of Sociology, 29*(3), 419–438.

Belasco, A., Rosinger, K., & Hearn, J. (2014). The test-optional movement at America's selective liberal arts colleges: A boon for equity or something else? *Education Evaluation and Policy Analysis,* 1–18. Prepublished June 12, 2014, DOI: 10.3102/0162373714537350.

Briggs, D. (2001). The effect of admissions test preparation: Evidence from NELS: 88. Chance, 14, 10–18.

Briggs, D. C. (2002). SAT coaching, bias and causal inference. (Unpublished doctoral dissertation). University of California, Berkeley: Berkeley, CA.

Briggs, D.C., & Domingue, B.W. (2009). The effect of admissions test preparation: new evidence from ELS:02. Unpublished Working Paper. Retrieved from *www.colorado.edu/education/faculty/derekbriggs/publications.html.*

Buckman, C., Condron, D., & Roscigno, V. (2010). Shadow education, American style: Test preparation, the SAT and college enrollment. *Social Forces, 89,* 435–461.

Camara, W.J., & Schmidt, A.E. (1999). *Group differences in standardized testing and social stratification* (College Board Research Report No. 1999-5.) New York: The College Board.

Carnevale, A.P., & Rose, S.J. (2003, March). Socioeconomic status, race/ethnicity, and selective college admissions. New York: Century Foundation.

Carnevale, A.P., Rose, S.J., & Strohl, J. (2014). Achieving racial and economic diversity with race-blind admissions policy. In R. Kahlenberg (Eds.) *The future of affirmative action: New paths to higher education diversity after Fisher v. University of Texas* (pp. 187–202). New York: Century Foundation.

Clinedinst, M.E., Hurley, S.F., & Hawkins, D.A. (2013). 2013 State of College Admission Report. Arlington, VA: National Association for College Admission Counseling.

Cohen, J. (1988). *Statistical power analysis for the behavioral sciences* (2nd ed.). Hillsdale, NJ: Erlbaum

College Board (2011). *Guidelines on the uses of college board test scores and related data.* New York, NY: Author.

College Board. (2014). *Test specifications for the redesigned SAT®.* New York: Author. Retrieved from: *https://www.collegeboard.org/sites/default/files/test_specifications_for_the_redesigned_sat_na3.pdf.*

Godfrey, K., Matos-Elefonte, H., Ewing, M., & Patel, P. (2014). College completion: Comparing AP, dual-enrolled, and nonadvanced students. (College Board Research Report No. 2014-3). New York, NY: The College Board.

Goldfarb, Z. (2014, March 5). These four charts show how the SAT favors, rich, educated families. *The Washington Post.* Retrieved from *http://www.washingtonpost.com/blogs/wonkblog/wp/2014/03/05/these-four-charts-show-how-the-sat-favors-the-rich-educated-families/*

Kim, Y., Wiley, A., & Packman, S. (2011). National curriculum survey on English and Mathematics (College Board Research Report 2011-13). New York: The College Board.

Kobrin, J., Camara, W. J., &Milewski, G. (2002). Students with discrepant high school GPA and SAT I scores (College Board Research Note RN-15). New York: The College Board.

Lawrence, I., Rigol, G. W., Van Essen, T., & Jackson, C. A. (2002). A historical perspective on the SAT 1926-2001. (College Board Research Report 2002-7). New York: The College Board.

Lubinski, D., Benbow, C.P., Webb, R.M., & Bleske-Rechek, A. (2006). Tracking exceptional human capital over two decades. *Psychological Science,* 17(3), 194–199.

Mattern, K.D., & Patterson, B.F. (2014). Synthesis of recent SAT validity findings: Trend data over time and cohorts (College Board Research in Review 2014-1). New York: The College Board.

Mattern, K.D., Shaw, E.J., & Kobrin, J.L. (2010, April) A case for not going SAT-Optional: Students with discrepant SAT and HSGPA performance. Paper presented at the meeting of the American Educational Research Association, Denver, Colorado.

Mattern, K.D., Shaw, E.J., & Kobrin, J.L. (2011). An alternative presentation of incremental validity: Discrepant SAT and HSGPA performance. *Educational and Psychological Measurement,* 71(4), 638-662.

Meyer, G. J., Finn, S. E., Eyde, L., Kay, G. G., Moreland, K. L., Dies, R. R., Eisman, E. J., Kubiszyn, T. W., & Reed, G. M. (2001). Psychological testing and psychological assessment: A review of evidence and issues. *American Psychologist,* 56, 128-165.

Milewski, G., Johnsen, D., Glazer, N., & Kubota, M. (2005). A survey to evaluate the alignment of the new SAT writing and critical reading sections to curricula and instructional practices (College Board Research Report 2005-1). New York: The College Board.

National Association for College Admission Counseling. (n.d.) Statement of principles of good practice. Retrieved from *http://www.nacacnet.org/about/Governance/Policies/Pages/default.aspx.*

National Association for College Admission Counseling. (2009). Report of the commission on the use of standardized tests in undergraduate admission. Arlington, VA: Author.

Patterson, B. F., & Ewing, M. (2013). Validating the use of AP exam scores for college course placement. (College Board Research Report No. 2013-2.) New York, NY: The College Board.

Patterson, B. F., & Mattern, K. (2013). Validity of the SAT for predicting first-year grades: 2010 SAT validity sample. (College Board Statistical Report No. 2013-2.) New York, NY: The College Board.

Peligri, J. (2014, July 7). No, the SAT is not required. More colleges join test-optional train. USA Today. Received from *http://college.usatoday.com/2014/07/07/no-the-sat-is-not-required-more-colleges-join-test-optional-train.*

Powers, D.E. (2012). Understanding the impact of special preparation for admissions tests. (ETS Research Report No. RR-12-05). Princeton, NJ: ETS.

Powers, D.E., & D.A. Rock. (1999). Effects of coaching on SAT I: Reasoning test scores. *Journal of Educational Measurement,* 36(2), 93–118.

Robinson, M., & Monks, J. (2005). Making SAT scores optional in selective college admissions: A case study. *Economics of Education Review,* 24(4), 393–405.

Sackett, P.R., Borneman, M.J., & Connelly, B.S. (2008). High-stakes testing in higher education and employment: Appraising the evidence for validity and fairness. *American Psychologist,* 63, 215–227.

Sackett, P.R., Kuncel, N.R., Arneson, J.J., Cooper, S.R., & Waters, S.D. (2009). Socioeconomic status and the relationship between the SAT® and freshman GPA: An analysis of data from 41 colleges and universities (College Board Research Report No. 2009-1). New York, NY: The College Board.

Sackett, P.R., Kuncel, N.R., Beatty, A.S., Rigdon, J.L., Shen, W., & Kiger, T.B. (2012). The role of socioeconomic status in SAT-grade relationships and in college admission decisions. *Psychological Science,* 23(9), 1000–1007.

Sacks, P. (1997). Standardized testing: Meritocracy's crooked yardstick. *Change,* 29 (2), 24–31.

St. John, E., Musoba, G., & Chung, C.H. (2004). Academic preparation and college success: Analyses of Indiana's 200 high school class. (IPAS Research Report 04-03). Bloomington, IN: Indiana Commission for Higher Education.

Wainer, H. (2011). Uneducated guesses: Using evidence to uncover misguided education policies. Princeton, NJ: Princeton University Press.

Zwick, R. (2002). Fair game? The use of standardized admissions tests in higher education. New York, NY: RoutledgeFalmer.

Zwick, R. (2013). Disentangling the role of high school grades, SAT scores, and SES in predicting college achievement. (ETS Research Report No. RR-13-09). Princeton, NJ: ETS.

Chapter 11: Academic Planning for High School Students: Careful Choices Cultivate Postsecondary Opportunity and Success

Grant H. Blume
@grantblume

INTRODUCTION

Students face numerous choices as they navigate four years of high school. An inevitable juggling act involves balancing choices about social life, leadership activities, part-time employment, family, sports, and other extracurricular activities, all of which place demands on a limited amount of time. Yet, in addition to all of these choices, which may be a source of fulfillment, growth, angst, or stress, a student must also make choices each year about the academic courses she will take to maximize her educational experience in high school and prepare her for success in college.

This chapter focuses on the choices students make about their academic coursework in high school. These critical choices are sometimes overlooked by students and their parents who instead may focus on adding more extracurricular or leadership activities to a résumé in hopes of gaining an edge in the college admission process. Stu-

little attention to or ignore the importance of supporting students in their pursuit of rigorous high school coursework, this chapter provides important information that can fill that void.

The chapter begins with a broad overview of trends, at both the high school and postsecondary levels, pertaining to the important role rigorous high school academics play in US education. Next, relevant research on the connection between high school coursework and postsecondary outcomes is discussed with a focus on how this evidence can support counselors when they recommend rigorous coursework to students. Following this, the chapter then segues from research to practice and presents counselors with strategies for supporting and advising students as they face choices about academic courses in high school. The chapter ends with a summary of main points, plus discussion questions intended to stimulate further reflection on the material.

High school counselors can help their students succeed in the postsecondary academic environment by encouraging students to take rigorous academic courses in high school.

dents may also neglect to think carefully about curricular choices if they are unsure of their postsecondary plans. This chapter makes the case, however, that taking rigorous academic courses in high school is the most effective means by which a student can prepare for college, while simultaneously maximizing her odds of successful admission outcomes.

High school counselors can help their students succeed in the postsecondary academic environment by encouraging students to take rigorous academic courses in high school. This chapter provides counselors with relevant knowledge pertaining to the important connection between high school students' academic coursework choices and their success in college. The chapter also equips counselors with suggestions for advising their students on how to make careful choices about high school academics that align with the students' postsecondary goals. Given that recently published guides on high school counseling (e.g., Chen-Hayes, Ockerman, & Mason, 2013; Nelson, 2011; Shelton & James, 2005) pay

A few caveats are warranted prior to proceeding to the chapter's material. First and foremost, this chapter offers suggestions and advice to counselors with an acknowledgement that resources vary dramatically across US high schools (Attewell & Domina, 2008). One high school may offer both Advanced Placement and International Baccalaureate curricula, along with ample courses in lab science, while another high school in the same state or even in the same city has no advanced coursework options and limits students to one year of lab science due to capacity constraints. The counselor at the latter school understandably faces daunting challenges in advocating for students to take a full college-prep curriculum, given the high school's circumstances. The point here, and throughout the chapter, is not that a student needs access to a dazzling Advanced Placement high school curriculum to succeed; rather, the point this chapter makes is that a student maximizes her chances for postsecondary success when she takes advantage of whatever rigorous academic opportunities are available to her at her high school.

Related to this first caveat is the topic of tracking. Tracking is a mechanism by which students are sorted into curricular pathways often referred to as "tracks" based on others' (teachers, principals, administrators) judgment of the students' ability. Tracks may be explicit, in that a student is outright enrolled in one track and takes courses only within that track during high school, or implicit, meaning a formal track does not exist, but students are dissuaded from taking courses outside what is judged to be their level of ability. The two most common tracks in US high schools are a standard track (which may have a technical/vocational element in the later years of the curriculum) and a college-preparatory track (Conley, 2013). The research on tracking and its perpetuation of inequity within the US education system is extensive (see, for example, Oakes [2005] and Darling-Hammond [2010]) and ultimately lies beyond the scope of this chapter. Nonetheless, the topic of tracking is relevant to setting the stage for this chapter's content, because the chapter assumes that students have at least a modest level of self-determination in choosing the academic courses they want to take during high school. Put another way, this chapter presumes the absence of tracking to the extent that an explicit or implicit track would limit a student's opportunity to fully develop her intellectual potential and aspirations.

The second caveat is that this chapter's focus on the connection between high school coursework and postsecondary success is not intended to disparage the important role of technical, vocational and career-readiness curricula in high schools. High school counselors in the United States undoubtedly advise students on workforce readiness as much as college readiness. Like others (e.g., ACT, 2006; Conley, 2013; Gaertner, DesJardins, & McClarty, 2014), this chapter takes the opinion that academically rigorous coursework in high school benefits students, regardless of their post-graduation plans. As such, the chapter focuses on how counselors can support students' postsecondary plans by encouraging careful choices about academic course-taking, assuming the student has at least some interest in continuing her education after high school. This chapter's material ties careful academic planning in high school to college readiness and postsecondary success. Taking academically rigorous courses in high school pays dividends, regardless of college attendance (Koedel & Tyhurst, 2012; Rose & Betts, 2004).

Related to the caveat that this chapter is not intended to disparage the important role of technical/vocational education, neither is this chapter meant to downplay the critical role that the arts—both visual and performing—ought to play in a student's high school experience. Theater, choir, band, and orchestra, along with the wide range of visual arts offered in high schools, are essential to cultivating a student's intellectual development and cultural understanding. The emphasis of this chapter—encouraging students to pursue to the greatest extent possible a rigorous academic curriculum—can undoubtedly exist in concert with a student's active engagement in the arts.

The final caveat is that while the chapter's material draws heavily from existing research, some empirical debates about cause and effect are placed aside in the spirit of focusing on relevant, practical advice for counselors. For instance, the question of AP coursework and college success is a classic example of differentiating between correlation and causality; the College Board (e.g., Hargrove, Godin, & Dodd, 2008) suggests enrollment in AP courses increases postsecondary success. Researchers, on the other hand, are skeptical of such claims (e.g., Geiser & Santelices, 2004; Klopfenstein & Thomas, 2009). Likewise, tenets of Common Core adoption include increased high school academic rigor and college readiness (Conley, 2013), although critics question if such outcomes are realistic (e.g., Ravitch, 2013). This chapter puts aside such controversies and instead focuses on the knowledge and skills that will best equip counselors to support high school students and the myriad choices they face about academic coursework.

Background

College readiness, broad access to postsecondary education, and increases in college degree attainment (both associate and baccalaureate degrees) continue to be on the forefront of the nation's education policy agenda. The Obama administration has made college attendance and degree attainment a public priority, as did preceding presidential administrations; governors and state legislatures also increasingly focus on the important relationships among college attendance, degree attainment, and a state's economic prosperity and stability (Blume & Zumeta, 2013). Policymakers' focus on the need for postsecondary education will thus likely continue to increase as more jobs require at least some college coursework, if not a bachelor's degree (Carnevale, Smith, & Strohl, 2013). Conley (2013) puts this labor market trend bluntly, noting that "the era of succeeding with little formal education and lots of hard work is pretty much over" (p. 23).

The growing attention on college attendance coincides with national and state efforts to improve college readiness. Stakeholders across the education spectrum increasingly realize that simply getting more students into college is nonsensical if those students are not prepared for college-level work. Accordingly, increasing college readiness is closely related to decreasing the need for remediation at the nation's colleges and universities (Conley, 2007). High schools, and community colleges to a lesser extent, have been identified as key players in potential efforts to decrease postsecondary remediation rates (Attewell, Lavin, Domina, & Levey, 2006; Kirst & Venezia, 2004). This drive to decrease the need for remediation manifests in high schools as efforts to shore up student achievement in English and math, two core areas of academic study critical to postsecondary success.

The emergence and rapid adoption of the Common Core State Standards (CCSS) across the US is an additional trend that directly affects the academic climate of American high schools. The CCSS movement is closely tied to a related movement in education reform that seeks to make all students "college or career ready" by graduation (Conley, 2014). The essence of the Common Core is to "transform current [K–12] instruction by focusing teacher attention on fewer, higher and deeper standards" in math and language arts (NGA/CCSSO, 2010, as cited in Kirst, 2013, p. 2). Although a discussion of Common Core policy and politics is beyond the scope of this chapter (see Conley [2014] for a thorough, well-

balanced discussion) it is worthwhile for counselors to recall that these reforms will likely reshape curriculum in US high schools for the next decade.

The widespread adoption of the Common Core curriculum, while likely strengthening and standardizing, to some extent, the rigor of high school academics, has not addressed a significant barrier for college-bound students in the United States: the misalignment between high school graduation requirements and minimum academic requirements for admission to college. States' high school graduation requirements have historically been and remain today misaligned with the minimum requirements for college admission (Dounay, 2006). This misalignment, in turn, creates significant confusion for students and counselors alike who must navigate multiple sets of standards (Kirst & Bracco, 2004). For example, a high school graduation requirement of two years of science does not fulfill the admission requirement of two years of lab science at most colleges and universities. Since most states have adopted a Common Core curriculum, but not yet required Common Core classes for graduation, a high school diploma remains a weak signal of academic content mastery and college readiness (Change the Equation, 2013).

The importance that admission offices place on academic rigor is perhaps not surprising given the weak value of a high school diploma and the increasing prevalence of remediation on college campuses. Table 1 contains the five factors of greatest importance to admission offices when considering applicants. Note that three of the top five factors are related to academics, and the top two factors—grades in college-prep courses and strength of curriculum—pertain directly to the rigor of the applicant's high school coursework.

Table 1: Percentage of Colleges Attributing Different Levels of Importance to Factors in the Admission Decision (2012)

Factor	Considerable importance	Moderate importance	Limited importance	No importance
1. Grades in college-prep courses	82.3%	11.6%	4.4%	1.7%
2. Strength of curriculum	65.0	25.2	6.6	3.1
3. Admission test scores (ACT, SAT)	56.1	31.3	9.2	3.4
4. Grades in all courses	49.8	37.5	11.6	1.0
5. Essay or writing sample	19.7	38.1	25.2	17.0

Adopted from Clinedinst, Hurley, & Hawkins, 2013, p. 12

In fact, in the context of grades in college-preparatory courses and the strength of the student's curriculum, more than 90 percent of surveyed admission officers place considerable or moderate importance on these two factors. Whereas much has changed in the past two decades in terms of the high school landscape and the college admission environment, this "considerable importance" placed on grades in college-preparatory courses and strength of curriculum has remained consistently high since the National Association for College Admission Counseling began collecting these data in the early 1990s (Clinedinst, Hurley, & Hawkins, 2013).

High School Rigor and College Outcomes: A Brief Review of the Literature

Research goes back at least three decades on the important connection between rigorous academic coursework in high school and postsecondary success. This section of the chapter briefly surveys more recent research on high school rigor and academic outcomes, with a focus on knowledge that is of potential value to counselors who advise and interact with students and parents. Perna

(2005) provides a detailed background on this literature that extends beyond the material discussed here.

Academic rigor in high school matters for a range of outcomes related to high school completion, college access and postsecondary degree attainment (Long, Conger, & Iatarola, 2012). Although this has been a longstanding and widely accepted fact among researchers who explore the relationship between high school achievement and postsecondary outcomes (e.g., Adleman, 1999, 2006), increasingly sophisticated research provides empirical evidence to reinforce the idea that students who pursue rigorous coursework in high school increase their likelihood of success in college.

The methods for empirically evaluating the effects of high school rigor on postsecondary outcomes typically take one of three approaches (Table 2).

Descriptive analyses that identify corollary relationships are the most conventional approaches across the literature. These descriptive analyses, however, do not account for selection bias, which undoubtedly confounds the relationships of interest.[1]

Isolating the effect of one type of course, such as a math course, on a particular postsecondary/workforce

Table 2: Typology of Research Linking Academic Rigor in High School to Postsecondary Outcomes

	Benefits	Drawbacks	Examples	Prevalence
Descriptive Analysis	Intuitive and easy to understand; makes use of wide range of available data	No controls for selection bias make causal inference dubious	Adelman (1999, 2006)	Widespread
Single Type of Course	Often able to make plausible claims of causal relationships	May have limited relevance for practitioners in the field; statistical methodology can be complex	Gaertner et al. (2014); Schwartz et al. (2009)	Modest but increasing
College-Preparatory Curriculum	Captures the importance of rigor across multiple academic areas; provides flexibility in measuring a range of outcomes	Requires extensive transcript data for analysis; depends on researchers' varying definitions of what defines a "college-prep" curriculum	Jackson (2014); Long, Conger, & Iatarola (2012)	Rare but increasing

[1]   *"Selection bias" means the empirical relationship of interest—in this case, between high school course rigor and college outcomes— that is likely driven by an unobservable characteristic, such as a student's intrinsic level of motivation. That is, a student who selects into rigorous high school coursework is also more likely to exert a significant amount of effort once in college. In this way, the rigorous high school coursework is not the causal driver behind the student's achievement in college, but rather, the rigorous high school coursework and the high level of college achievement both reflect the student's underlying level of motivation.*

outcome is the second type of method found across this body of literature. These studies generally provide more robust findings than descriptive analysis and allow for plausible claims of causality. On the other hand, making those causal claims often depends on complex statistical methods that may not be accessible to the average reader.

The third method, one that also relies on advanced statistical techniques, is the case where researchers use a collection of courses in aggregate to represent a college-preparatory curriculum to evaluate the curriculum's causal relationship to postsecondary outcomes. While most relevant to counselors who help students design their high school schedules across four years, this third type of method is the rarest across the literature. This type of study also depends on how the researchers design what constitutes a "college-preparatory curriculum," a definition that may vary across studies and in local high school contexts.

Two of the most widely cited studies on the relationship between high school coursework and postsecondary outcomes are US Department of Education reports published by Adelman (1999, 2006). Adelman (1999) was one of the first comprehensive studies to explore, with nationally presentive data, the characteristics of high school course-taking, plus how those characteristics predicted postsecondary outcomes, such as academic achievement and degree completion. The author is careful to point out that the methodology in these reports (ordinary least squares [OLS] regression models) do not lead to causal claims (Adelman, 2006). Nonetheless, these studies have framed a generation of scholarship that has posed much-needed research questions about the interconnectedness of high school choices and college outcomes.

Across the multitude of research topics that encompass high school course-taking and postsecondary outcomes, researchers have long been interested in causal connec-tions between enrollment in high school math courses and postsecondary outcomes (Adelman, 2006; Gaertner, DesJardins, & McClarty, 2014). Past scholarship has concluded, largely based on descriptive analysis, a strong correlation between a student taking rigorous math courses in high school and her increased odds of graduating from high school, enrolling in college and doing well in college as measured by grade point average (Adelman, 2006). Recent studies using quasi-experimental methods confirm this supposition.[2] Gaertner, DesJardins and McClarty (2014) find that Algebra II is a strong predictor of college success when such success is measured by the student's collegiate grade point average. Long, Conger and Iatarola (2012) identify positive associations between a student taking rigorous math courses in high school and her likelihood of enrolling at a four-year university, noting that across the five core academic areas that comprise a college-preparatory curriculum, completing an advanced math course causes the largest increase (9.4 percentage points) in the probability of the student enrolling at a four-year college (p. 313).

Enrollment in rigorous high school math courses is positively associated with college major choice in addition to the increased probability of attending a four-year college and higher grade point average. Trusty (2002), for example, found that women taking rigorous math classes in high school are more likely to choose math- or science-related majors in college. This association for female students between high school math and pursuing math/science majors in college has significant workforce implications, given the dramatic levels at which women are underrepresented in science, technology, engineering, and math (STEM) fields (Beede et al., 2011).

Moving beyond the topic of math in particular, scholars have recently sought to look more broadly at the effects of rigorous high school coursework. Two prominent

---

[2] *An important distinction should be made here regarding the difference between encouraging students to pursue advanced math courses and the requirement of a particular math class for all students in a high school or district school. The latter, known most recently as "Algebra for All," has been a movement to eliminate remediation and require all students in a particular year, usually the ninth grade, to enroll in Algebra I. The "Algebra for All" movement, along with more states requiring Algebra II for graduation as a response to No Child Left Behind standards (Gaertner, DesJardins, & McClarty, 2014), has led to significant increases in the years of algebra completed by the nation's high school students. On the other hand, "Algebra for All" has its critics, due to the policy's association with negative effects on the achievement outcomes of high-skill students in schools that expanded algebra coursework (Nomi, 2012).*

studies in this area of research are Long, Conger and Iatarola (2012) and Jackson (2014). Using longitudinal administrative from Florida, Long, Conger and Iatarola (2012) examined a broad range of outcomes, such as high school academic achievement, high school graduation, enrollment at a two-year college, and enrollment a four-year college. The authors found the "difference in [secondary and postsecondary] outcomes associated with moving from zero to one rigorous course is larger than moving from one to more than one rigorous courses" (Long, Conger, & Iatarola, 2012, p. 287). Jackson (2014) identified additional positive outcomes associated with a rigorous high school curriculum; a rigorous high school curriculum increased the probability of earning a four-year degree, plus higher wages were tied to increased rigor in one's high school coursework (p. 92).

What Is Academic Rigor?

The meaning of the term "academic rigor" is twofold; academic rigor pertains to the *content* of the course, plus the *intensity* of the material within the course.[3] Academically rigorous courses, considered the bedrock of a college-preparatory curriculum for much of the 20th century, comprise five areas: English and language arts, math, science, social studies, and foreign/world languages (Adelman, 2006; Conley, 2010, 2014). Determining what is rigorous in terms of intensity is more subjective, but courses are often considered more rigorous than a typical high school course if the course is part of the Advanced Placement (AP) or International Baccalaureate (IB) curricula. Likewise, courses that provide students college credit (e.g., dual-enrollment programs) through a partnership with a local college or university are considered more rigorous than courses awarding high school credit alone.

Many high schools also offer "honors" courses that are designed to be more intensive compared to conventional courses offered at the high school. The challenge with courses labeled "honors" is that in their admission

processes, colleges and universities often have limited means to gauge the intensity of an honors course at one high school compared to an honors course at another high school.[4] This variation in honors coursework across high schools can grow even more complex when one considers that high schools vary how they weight honors courses in a student's cumulative grade point average. For the sake of parsimony, this chapter will use the terms "advanced" and "rigorous" as synonymous adjectives to capture honors, AP, IB, and dual-enrollment courses.

This multidimensional characteristic of rigor, in terms of content and intensity, means there are few clear-cut answers for students when they ask a counselor if a particular course is sufficiently rigorous. Rather, rigor is best considered in a spectrum of "less rigorous" to "more rigorous." For example, a high school junior may face a choice in which she can choose one of three courses to take her junior year: physics, AP Spanish or graphic design. Is either physics or AP Spanish more rigorous than graphic design? Yes, given that graphic design is not in one of the five academic categories that constitute a core college-preparatory curriculum. Is AP Spanish more rigorous than physics? In this case, the answer is unclear without more information from the student. Additionally, the question of rigor should always be one factor among multiple considerations. Does she plan to take the AP exam in Spanish? Is she interested in taking an AP science course in her senior year? Does she hope to pursue a STEM major in college? Questions like these provide context to help a student make a choice that is both adequately rigorous and aligned with her postsecondary plans.

The nuances of each of the five academic areas comprising a college-preparatory curriculum warrant a brief discussion. These nuances are not universal characteristics of a rigorous curriculum by which every counselor must advise students and by which every admission office makes admission decisions. Rather, this variation

---

[3]   *The term "intensity," used in this case to describe a dimension of rigorous coursework, is borrowed from Attewell and Domina (2008).*

[4]   *This is, accordingly, one benefit of AP and IB coursework in the context of admission committee decisions; an admission officer can be relatively certain that an AP or IB course at one high school provides students with a level of rigor similar to those students enrolled in the same AP or IB course at a high school in another state.*

simply illustrates that academic choices for a high school student abound, given the intersection between a high school's resources and curricular offerings, plus a student's preferences and college plans.

English

Four years of English coursework is the most universal high school graduation requirement in the United States. This requirement has been common in US high schools, but was vociferously recommended in the 1980s publication, Nation at Risk (National Commission of Excellence in Education, 1983) and became universal by the early 1990s (Murnane, 2013). The type of English coursework offered by high schools varies widely and ranges from general language arts to British literature. Since four years of English is the standard for US high school students, a more rigorous English curriculum may be one that contains greater intensity within courses (i.e., advanced coursework, such as AP or IB courses).

Mathematics

As discussed previously, enrollment in high school math courses can reap significant benefits for college-bound students. High school math course offerings typically include pre-algebra, algebra, geometry, algebra II and/or trigonometry, pre-calculus, and calculus. A number of states and school districts incorporate strands from more than one of these areas of mathematics into an integrated curriculum, which thus bears the name "Integrated Math I, II, III" and so on (Reys, Dingman, Nevels, & Teuscher, 2007). Since high school math graduation requirements vary widely across the United States, counselors must advise students carefully to ensure a student's high school math courses meet the expectations of the colleges and universities to which the student aspires to attend. For example, colleges and universities typically view a more rigorous curriculum to be four years of math with the student reaching at least Algebra II, but preferably pre-calculus or calculus by her senior year. Compare this expectation of colleges with the fact that in 2006, only 10 states required four years of math for high school graduation, and six states required a mere two years of math for a student to earn a high school diploma (Reys, Dingman, Nevels, & Teuscher, 2007).

Science

Science, in the context of a college-preparatory curriculum, is synonymous with lab science. That is, the three central branches of physical science—biology, chemistry and physics—comprise a core high school science curriculum. States and school districts may blend branches of science into single-year courses, much like an integrated math approach. These integrated science courses typically draw from the three central branches of science, plus earth science (geology, meteorology, etc.). Choosing to take lab science courses in high school can be difficult for a student who also faces a range of options in environmental, engineering and other applied science fields. Historically, admission officers would advise students to focus on lab science if a student aspired to maximize the rigor of her high school curriculum and thus maximize her competitiveness for admission to selective colleges and universities. This recommendation has eased in recent years with the advent of AP and IB courses in such fields as computer science and environmental science. Nonetheless, a high school student's science coursework is most rigorous when she takes three years of lab science, plus an additional advanced lab science course (IB Biology, AP Chemistry, etc.) in her junior and senior years. The benefit of this recommendation for a student to complete three years of lab science, plus one additional year of advanced lab science is substantiated by research. Schwartz, Sadler, Sonnert, and Tai (2009) find that "deep coverage" of an area of science in high school is attributed with higher grades in introductory college science courses compared to a high school student whose curriculum emphasized "breadth," which is not associated with higher grades (p. 818).

Social Studies

Social studies courses tackle "content knowledge, intellectual skills and civic values necessary for fulfilling the duties of citizenship in a participatory democracy" (National Council for the Social Studies, 2014). Typical social studies courses include such social science areas as government and civics, economics, geography, and history. A student may have a range of social studies courses from which to choose, depending on a high school's resources. Since most students in the United States complete either three or four years of social studies coursework in high school, rigor in the context of social studies depends more on the intensity of the course rather than the number of courses a student completes. Advanced social studies coursework (i.e., AP/IB, dual-enrollment or honors classes) may be particularly accessible to students, since this area of coursework does not carry the strict sequential prerequisites of advanced coursework in other areas of a college-preparatory curriculum. Put another way, whereas a student may need to take Physics I before taking AP/IB Physics or Spanish III before AP/IB Spanish, enrollment in an advanced history or economics course may depend on an instructor's sense of the student's ability or cumulative GPA and not on the completion of an introductory course in that field.

Foreign Language

Foreign language coursework is a requirement for the vast majority of four-year colleges and universities (National Association for College Admission Counseling, 2014). Even though the percent of high school students who have enrolled in any type of foreign language has increased in past decades, more than half of American students (56.4 percent) in 2000 did not take any foreign language courses during high school (National Center for Education Statistics, 2013). Two years of foreign language is a typical minimum requirement of colleges and universities, so students have an opportunity to demonstrate added rigor in their coursework choices by completing more than two years of a foreign language. Since many universities require foreign language as a requirement for earning a bachelor of arts degree, strategic college-bound students may wish to pre-emptively earn college credit to fulfill this requirement by either taking an AP/IB exam in foreign language or earning foreign language college credits while in high school through dual-enrollment opportunities.

A question arises in this discussion of the five core academic areas of a college-preparatory curriculum and the possibility of taking advanced coursework in such areas; similar to the research questions posed by Schwartz, Sadler, Sonnert, and Tai (2009) in their analysis of science coursework, is a high school student who aspires to attend college better served by *breadth* across academic areas or *depth* within a few? This question, like questions about the rigor of individual courses, is difficult to answer without the context of an individual student. In general, however, keep in mind that a student who pursues a "depth" strategy is likely able to access the most challenging courses at her high school by her junior and senior years. A student who pursues a "breadth" strategy, on the other hand, will undoubtedly benefit from surveying a wide range of academic topics but will not advance toward the most rigorous courses in any of those given fields.

Consider two hypothetical students. Student A embraces a *breadth* approach and completes two years of Spanish and two years of French in high school. Student B takes a depth strategy and completes four years of French. Student A will only reach Spanish 2 and French 2 by her senior year, while Student B could ostensibly enroll in AP French by her senior year if such a course was offered by her high school. The intellectual challenge Student B faces in AP French presents a more demanding course of study, compared to Student A who will only reach a second-year level of proficiency in Spanish and French.

A similar case could arise with science coursework; a student who has completed biology, chemistry and physics could perhaps face a choice in her senior year between taking an elective science course, perhaps in earth science, or an AP course in a lab science. While the earth science course would no doubt be rewarding, the AP lab science course would likely present greater intellectual challenge as the student immerses herself in that material. The completion of an AP lab science course would also demonstrate intellectual tenacity to an admission officer considering this student as an applicant.

An additional question arises related to grades in advanced courses and the college admission process; is a student better served by taking a conventional high school course and earning an "A" (hypothetically speaking) or by taking an advanced course, such as an AP or IB course on the same topic, and risk earning a lower grade? This is a question frequently posed to high school counselors with no clear-cut answer. There are, however, contextual factors for counselors to consider while advising students. Since grades in college-preparatory courses are of considerable importance to a significant proportion of college admission offices (recall the figures in Table 1) a counselor must encourage a student to think carefully about how the added curricular intensity of an advanced course will affect her grade. Is the tradeoff between a conventional course and an advanced course the difference between earning an "A" and a "B+", respectively, or the difference between earning an "A" and a "C"? Furthermore, even though high school students may fixate on grades, a counselor can ask other questions to extend the student's thinking in weighing the tradeoffs of taking advanced courses. For example, is the student worried about a lower grade in an AP class, but is motivated to take an AP exam and receive a score that awards college credit? Is the student concerned about the grade she may receive in a college-level dual-enrollment course, but are her family circumstances such that earning college credit while in high school would ease the financial burden of working toward a bachelor's degree after graduating high school? The benefits of advanced coursework are multifaceted. A counselor can be a valuable source of perspective to students otherwise preoccupied by grades and grade point averages.

who encourage their students to pursue rigorous academic coursework are helping these students improve their odds of success in and beyond high school.

TRANSLATING RESEARCH TO PRACTICE: FIVE SUGGESTIONS FOR COUNSELING STUDENTS ON CHOICES ABOUT ACADEMIC COURSEWORK

The five suggestions offered at this point translate the chapter's material discussed thus far into strategies that counselors can keep in mind when advising students and their parents. Considering that among their high school colleagues, counselors often serve as advocates for college-bound students (Chen-Hayes, Ockerman, & Mason, 2013), these suggestions are also relevant to counselors who participate in school-wide strategy and planning related to academic offerings and policies. Returning to a point made at the introduction of this chapter, these suggestions assume that a high school does not have a rigid track that separates students into distinct pathways where a student must choose all "college-prep" or all

The exposure to and immersion in a rigorous curriculum made up of English, math, science, social studies, and foreign language coursework prepare a college-bound student to excel in whatever major she chooses in college.

There are ultimately two arguments—a philosophical one and a pragmatic one—for high school students to pursue rigorous coursework built around the five academic areas that comprise a college-preparatory curriculum. Philosophically, the five core academic areas that comprise a college-preparatory curriculum represent the foundation of a liberal arts education. The liberal arts, in turn, are the cornerstone—albeit an evolving one—of American higher education. The exposure to and immersion in a rigorous curriculum made up of English, math, science, social studies, and foreign language coursework prepare a college-bound student to excel in whatever major she chooses in college.

Pragmatically, academic rigor in high school appears to be a causal driver behind higher academic achievement in high school and an increased probability of college enrollment (Long, Conger, & Iatarola, 2012). Counselors

"vocational/technical" courses. Rather, the presumption with these recommendations is that students have some independence to choose their academic coursework.

1. Communicate to students and parents that taking rigorous academic courses in high school (especially beyond those required for graduation) benefits the student in many meaningful ways.

A counselor can promote rigorous academic courses depending on what motivates a student and her parents. The three most compelling reasons to enroll in academically rigorous coursework that are likely to resonate with students and parents are:

- Increased competiveness in the college admission process;

- College readiness, i.e., an increased likelihood of academic success once in college; and

- The potential for postsecondary cost-savings, either through dual-enrollment or achieving scores on AP/IB tests that award college credit.

Students also stand to gain beyond these practical benefits. Even though counselors may work with high school students who are quite certain they are destined to become doctors, for example, the fact remains that nearly 80 percent of American college students change majors at least once (Leonard, 2010)—taking a robust set of college-preparatory courses in high school prepares students for success across a wide range of college majors. Regardless of their post-graduation plans, career-minded students (and parents) may find value in reminders that taking rigorous coursework in high school is associated with high wages (Rose & Betts, 2001, 2004) and labor market mobility (Koedel & Tyhurst, 2012).

2. Recall that what constitutes a rigorous choice for the student may not always be intuitive.

This chapter provides an overview for what constitutes a rigorous, college-preparatory curriculum in high school. The factors and nuances of what makes up rigorous coursework will vary at each high school and for each student. Within these varying contexts is where counselors can help students navigate the important choices they face about academic coursework.

Navigating these choices requires that a counselor keep in mind that the factors that make a particular choice more or less rigorous may not always be intuitive to the student or her parents. In other words, a student may assume a particular high school course increases her competitiveness for admission to college or better prepares her for the major she intends to pursue in college when, in fact, this is not the case from the perspective of the college admission officer (or existing research on the topic).

For instance, a student hoping to study business at a four-year college is better off in high school taking pre-calculus or calculus instead of an applied business math course. Calculus pays a twofold dividend; calculus makes a student more competitive for admission at the universities to which she applies, plus calculus is nearly always required for any undergraduate degree in business. By taking pre-calculus or calculus, the student thus increases her odds of admission and increases her odds of excelling in courses required for her major. A similar hypothetical

scenario could arise for a student who aspires to study medicine in graduate school. This high school student might expect that taking applied science classes or vocational courses in healthcare will demonstrate to prospective undergraduate institutions her resolve to major in pre-med. In reality, however, this student will maximize her chances for admission (and subsequent success in college-level science courses, e.g., Schwartz, Sadler, Sonnert, and Tai, 2009) by focusing on lab science—biology, chemistry and physics—and any advanced lab science coursework she is able to complete.

3. Remind students (and parents) that taking on academically challenging coursework provides cognitive benefits, too.

The prospect of taking advanced academic coursework in one's junior and senior years no doubt elicits groans from students (and the parents who will do their best to keep these students academically focused). For the high school freshman or sophomore who dislikes a particular academic area, such as foreign language or science, the outlook might feel particularly bleak considering multiple years of this material is in the student's future.

Although students may have a difficult time appreciating the challenges they face while experiencing such challenges firsthand, emerging research increasingly suggests that the ability to overcome obstacles, persist and persevere are key skills that are highly predictive of academic achievement among many other broad indicators of success (Duckworth, Peterson, Matthews, & Kelly, 2007). In short, learning how to overcome the challenges of a rigorous academic course and ultimately succeed in such an environment helps a student to develop "grit" (Hoerr, 2013) and the cognitive skills required for academic success in college (Conley, 2010).

With this point, it is worthwhile to remember the value in striking a balance among the student's academic ability, taking rigorous academic coursework and the student's quality of life. Kretchmar and Farmer (2013) find that an "extreme" high school program, in which a student takes more than 10 advanced academic courses, is not associated with higher academic achievement in college when compared to a moderate level of high school course-taking in which a student takes at least five advanced courses. In other words, there is likely a ceiling associated with a student challenging herself and a subsequent "tipping point," when too much challenge stretches the student beyond her capacity and pushes her toward burnout and despair. Insofar as a counselor can be an advocate for rigorous coursework, a counselor may sometimes need to stand in as an advocate for the student in advising one fewer rigorous advanced courses, if that ultimately improves the student's wellbeing.

4. Think about the senior year not as the conclusion to high school, but rather, as a springboard to prepare for college coursework.

The widespread but altogether false notion that senior year "doesn't matter" has negative consequences for students upon entry into the workforce or once they arrive at college (Conley, 2001; Kirst & Bracco, 2004; National Commission on the High School Senior Year, 2001). Efforts to broadly remedy the decline in students' academic effort in their senior year—colloquially referred to as "senioritis"—would likely require a concerted school-wide initiative at any given school to change an attitude engrained in most American high schools (Conley, 2001). This pervasive attitude among high school seniors leads many students to ask, "What good is a senior year?" (Roderick, Coca, Moeller, & Kelley-Kemple, 2013). A counselor can confidently answer this question with a number of potential benefits that flow from putting effort into one's senior year.

Students are sometimes unaware that the colleges and universities to which they gained admission and committed to attend will require a final, year-end transcript upon the student's graduation from high school. A student's offer of admission, in fact, is often conditioned on successful completion of senior-year courses. A counselor can remind students that a precipitous drop in effort in the senior year, and the poor grades that result from such a drop in effort, threaten whatever offers of admission the student has received.

Students who face financial barriers to attending college may benefit from taking dual-enrollment courses that concurrently award college credit for completed high school courses. These credits, earned in high school but applied to an associate or bachelor's degree, can decrease the cost and shorten the time required to earn such a degree. In this way, the student may benefit from thinking of senior year coursework not as her last year of high school, but rather, as a "jump start" to her first year in college.

5. Start with the end in mind; encourage students as early as the eighth and ninth grades to plan carefully when it comes to enrolling in rigorous academic courses.

The sequential nature of high school coursework requires forethought from students who intend to take advanced courses in their junior and senior years. As mentioned earlier in this chapter's discussion of social science coursework, a benefit of advanced social science coursework (e.g., AP Psychology, IB Economics) is that these courses typically have minimal prerequisites for enrollment. At the other end of the prerequisite spectrum are advanced courses in foreign language, math and science. In each of these areas, the sequential coursework that leads to the advanced course itself requires careful and deliberate planning.

Consider a student who aspires to take calculus. Calculus is among the most demanding high school courses. A high school student must successfully move through three prior years of math (and perhaps even a specific math class in the eighth grade) to enroll in calculus her senior year. A similar pathway typically exists for AP/IB courses in lab science and foreign language. Juggling course sequences, or the sequences required for a number of advanced courses, requires planning on the part of the student that can be encouraged and supported by the counselor.

The importance of early planning has spurred researchers to recommend that efforts to increase college access and readiness begin before high school (Bonous-Hammarth & Allen, 2005; Gándara, 2002; Perna, 2005). Scholars note that middle and junior high school outreach that stresses the importance of taking rigorous academic courses increases the odds that students will be prepared for and take those courses upon arriving at high school. In particular, students appear to reap benefits in high school math courses from taking algebra in the eighth grade (Perna, 2005).

A counselor who seeks to inspire high school students to plan with forethought as they make coursework choices may wish to invoke the help of colleagues from college admission offices. Inviting admission officers to present to eighth or ninth graders and their parents about the importance of taking rigorous academic courses in high school bucks the convention of having college admission officers talk only to juniors and seniors about the college application process. The message from the admission officer may motivate students early on to take the sequential courses necessary to reach advanced courses in the latter years of high school.

CONCLUSION

Counselors play a critical role in helping students increase their postsecondary options and their odds for postsecondary success by educating students and parents about the benefits of taking academically rigorous courses in high school. Research increasingly demonstrates that taking rigorous coursework in high school yields benefits during and after high school. The courses that constitute a "rigorous curriculum" are not set in stone, but rather, vary across high schools, given the school's resources and students' abilities. These contextual factors and the many nuances of what constitutes a college-preparatory curriculum reinforce the critical need for the information, advice and careful guidance that counselors provide to students.

In their discussion of how academic rigor positively affects high school and college outcomes, Long, Conger and Iatarola (2012) make a policy recommendation that also serves as salient advice for high school counselors who advise students on course-taking. "An appropriate policy," the authors note, "may be to shift students from taking no rigorous courses into taking some rigorous courses, while avoiding going overboard in advocating for additional rigor for students with already demanding curriculum" (p. 316–317). This advice is fitting given counselors' role in creating opportunity for their students. A student already taking eight advanced courses may not need a counselor's encouragement to enroll in the ninth advanced course. A student who is enrolled in no advanced coursework, but is fortunate to have a counselor that nudges her to take one or two advanced courses, on the other hand, extends the trajectory of her high school academic coursework and opens doors to opportunity and success in college and beyond.

DISCUSSION QUESTIONS

1. This chapter assumes a high school environment where students are not tracked. If you encountered curricular tracks at your high school—that is, a defined college-preparatory track and a separate technical/vocation track—what material presented in the chapter would you be able to incorporate into how you counsel students?

2. A teacher at your high school who teaches band and orchestra confronts you to express frustration that "you have told students that band and orchestra won't help them get into college." This teacher notes, as a case in point, that his "star" oboe player dropped orchestra because it conflicted with AP French this year. How would you respond to your colleague?

3. To what extent would this chapter's material be useful if you were asked to present to a local school board on the topics of college readiness and redesigning your high school's curriculum?

4. What are the tradeoffs and nuances associated with assuming that "more is always better" when it comes to rigorous academic coursework in high school?

5. What elements of this chapter would be useful in planning "parent night" programs at your high school for ninth, 10th, 11th, and 12th graders' parents? How would your message about rigorous coursework vary across those parent groups?

ABOUT THE AUTHOR

Grant Blume's work focuses on analyzing and evaluating state and institutional policies that shape postsecondary access for college-bound students. His research uses national data sets, statewide longitudinal data, and institutional data to analyze the role of policy in students' educational choice making. Blume, a former admissions counselor at the University of Oregon and the University of Washington, has served on the National Association for College Admission Counseling's (NACAC) government relations committee and as chairperson of the Pacific Northwest Association for College Admission Counseling (PNACAC) government relations committee. He is currently completing a PhD in public policy and management at the University of Washington's Evans School of Public Affairs. Blume is a pre-doctoral fellow of the US Department of Education's Institute of Education Sciences and an affiliated scholar of Harvard University's Scholars Strategy Network.

REFERENCES

Adelman, C. (1999). *Answers in the toolbox: Academic intensity, attendance patterns, and bachelor's degree attainment.* Washington, DC: US Department of Education.

Adelman, C. (2006). *The toolbox revisited: Paths to degree completion from high school through college.* Washington, DC: US Department of Education.

Attewell, P., & Domina, T. (2008). Raising the bar: Curricular intensity and academic performance. *Educational Evaluation and Policy Analysis, 30*(1), 51–71.

Beede, D., Julian, T., Langdon, D., McKittrick, G., Khan, B., & Doms, M. (2011). *Women in STEM: A gender gap to innovation.* Economics and Statistics Administration, Issue Brief# 04-11. Washington, DC: US Department of Commerce.

Blume, G. & Zumeta, W. (2013). The state of state college readiness policies. *American Behavioral Scientist, 58*(8), 1071–1092.

Bonous-Hammarth, M. & Allen, W. (2005). A dream deferred: The critical factor of timing in college preparation and outreach. In W. Tierney, Z., Corwin, Z. & J. Colyar, (Eds.). *Preparing for college: Nine elements of effective outreach* (pp. 155–172).

Byun, S.Y., Irvin, M.J., & Bell, B.A. (2014). Advanced math course taking: Effects on math achievement and college enrollment. *The Journal of Experimental Education,* (ahead-of-print), 1–30.

Carnevale, A., Smith, N., & Strohl, J. (2013). *Recovery: Job growth and education requirements through 2020.* Center on Education and the Workforce, Georgetown Public Policy Institute. Washington, DC: Georgetown University.

Change the Equation. (2014). *Out of sync: Many Common Core states have yet to define a Common Core-worthy diploma.* Washington, DC: Author.

Chen-Hayes, S., Ockerman, M., & Mason, E. (2013). *101 solutions for school counselors and leaders in challenging times.* Thousand Oaks, CA: Corwin Press.

Clinedinst, M., Hurley, S., & Hawkins, D. (2013). *State of College Admissions, 2013.* Washington, DC: National Association for College Admission Counseling.

Conley, D. (2013). *Getting ready for college, careers and the Common Core: What every educator needs to know.* San Francisco, CA: Jossey-Bass.

Conley, D. (2010). *College and career ready: Helping all students succeed beyond high school.* San Francisco, CA: Jossey-Bass.

Conley, D. (2007). *Redefining college readiness.* Eugene, OR: Education Policy and Improvement Center.

Conley, D. (2001). *Rethinking the senior year.* NASSP Bulletin, 85(625), 26–41.

Darling-Hammond, L. (2010). *The flat world and education: How America's commitment to equity will determine our future.* New York: Teachers College Press.

Dounay, J. (2006). *Alignment of high school graduation requirements and state-set college admissions requirements.* Denver, CO: Education Commission of the States (ECS).

Duckworth, A., Peterson, C., Matthews, M., & Kelly, D. (2007). Grit: Perseverance and passion for long-term goals. *Journal of Personality and Social Psychology, 92*(6), 1087–1101.

Fitzpatrick, C., & Costantini, K. (2012). *Counseling 21st century students for optimal college and career readiness: A 9th-12th grade curriculum.* Hoboken, NJ: Taylor & Francis.

Gaertner, M., Kim, J., DesJardins, S., & McClarty, K. (2014). Preparing students for college and careers: The causal role of Algebra II. *Research in Higher Education, 55*(2), 143–165.

Gándara, P. (2002). *Meeting common goals: Linking K–12 and college interventions.* In W. Tierney & L. Hagedorn (Eds.), Increasing access to college: Extending possibilities for all students (pp. 81–103). Albany, NY: State University of New York Press.

Hargrove, L., Godin, D., & Dodd, B. *College outcomes comparisons by AP and non-AP high school experiences.* Research Report No. 2008-3. New York: The College Board.

Hoerr, T. (2013). *Fostering grit: How do I prepare my students for the real world?* Alexandria, VA: ASCD.

Jackson, C. (2014). Do college preparatory programs improve long-term outcomes? *Economic Inquiry,* 52(1), 72–99.

Kirst, M. (2013). *The Common Core meets state policy: This changes almost everything.* Policy Analysis for California Education (PACE); Policy Memorandum, March 2013. Stanford, CA: Stanford University.

Kirst, M. & Bracco, K. (2004). Bridging the great divide: How the K–12 and post-secondary split hurts students, and what can be done about it. In M. Kirst & A. Venezia, (Eds.). *From high school to college: Improving opportunities for success in postsecondary education* (pp. 1–30). San Francisco, CA: Jossey-Bass.

Klopfenstein, K. & Thomas, M. (2009). The link between Advanced Placement experience and early college success. *Southern Economic Journal,* 75(3), 873–891.

Koedel, C., & Tyhurst, E. (2012). Math skills and labor-market outcomes: Evidence from a resume-based field experiment. *Economics of Education Review,* 31(1), 131–140.

Kretchmar, J. & Farmer, S. (2013). How much is enough? Rethinking the role of high school courses in college admission. *Journal of College Admission Policy,* 220, 28–33.

Long, M., Conger, D., & Iatarola, P. (2012). Effects of high school course-taking on secondary and postsecondary success. *American Educational Research Journal,* 49(2), 285–322.

Murnane, R.J. (2013). U.S. high school graduation rates: Patterns and explanations. *Journal of Economic Literature,* 51(2), 370–422.

National Association for College Admission Counseling. (2014). Your high school classes will open the doors to college. Retrieved from *http://www.nacacnet.org/studentinfo/articles/Pages/Your-High-School-Classes.aspx*

National Center for Education Statistics. (2013). *Digest of Education Statistics, 2012.* Chapter 2, Elementary and Secondary Education, Table 56. Washington, DC: US Department of Education.

National Commission of Excellence in Education. (1983). *A nation at risk: The imperative for educational reform.* Washington, DC: US Government Printing Office.

National Commission on the High School Senior Year. (2001) *The lost opportunity of a senior year: Finding a better way.* A preliminary report. Princeton, NJ: Woodrow Wilson Foundation.

National Council for the Social Studies. (2014). National Council for the Social Studies: About NCSS. Retrieved from *http://www.socialstudies.org/about.*

National Governors' Association and Council of Chief State School Officers (NGA/CCSSO). (2010). *Common Core State Standards.* Washington, DC: NGA/CCSSO.

Nelson, M. (2011). *The school counselor's guide: High school guidance curriculum activities.* New York: Routledge.

Nomi, T. (2012). The unintended consequences of an algebra-for-all policy on high-skill students: Effects on instructional organization and students' academic outcomes. *Educational Evaluation and Policy Analysis,* 34(4), 489–505.

Oakes, J. (2005/1985). *Keeping track.* New Haven, CT: Yale University Press.

Perna, L. (2005). The key to college access: Rigorous academic preparation. In W. Tierney, Z., Corwin, Z. & J. Colyar, (Eds.). *Preparing for college: Nine elements of effective outreach* (pp. 113–134).

Ravitch, D. (2013). *Reign of error: The hoax of the privatization movement and the danger to America's public schools.* New York: Alfred A. Knopf.

Reys, B., Dingman, S., Nevels, N., & Teuscher, D. (2007). *High school mathematics: State-level curriculum standards and graduation requirements.* Columbia, MO: Center for the Study of Mathematics Curriculum.

Roderick, M., Coca, V., Moeller, E., & Kelley-Kemple, T. (2013). *From high school to the future: The challenge of senior year in Chicago Public Schools.* Chicago: The University of Chicago Consortium on Chicago School Research.

Rose, H., & Betts, J.R. (2001). *Math matters: The links between high school curriculum, college graduation, and earnings.* San Francisco, CA: Public Policy Institute of California.

Rose, H., & Betts, J.R. (2004). The effect of high school courses on earnings. *Review of Economics and Statistics,* 86(2), 497–513.

Sadler, P. & Tai, R. (2007). The two high school pillars supporting college science. *Science,* 317(27), 457–458.

Schwartz, M., Sadler, P., Sonnert, G., & Tai, R. (2009). Depth versus breadth: How content coverage in high school science courses relates to later success in college science coursework. *Science Education,* 93(5), 798–826.

Shelton, C. & James, E. (2005). *Best practices for effective secondary school counselors.* Thousand Oaks, CA: Corwin Press

Trusty, J. (2002). Effects of high school course-taking and other variables on choice of science and mathematics college majors. *Journal of Counseling & Development,* 80(4), 464–474.

Chapter 12:   Writing an Effective College Recommendation Letter

Rod Skinner

As we read about college applicant pools growing larger and deeper and hear about under-resourced and under-staffed admission offices trying to manage those numbers, it is natural to wonder if our counselor reports ultimately even matter. If an admission officer is moving through applications at a 20-minute-clip, how much air time will our thoughts about an applicant really receive?

The answer, as is the case with most complex enterprises like college admission, is, "It depends." Some colleges and universities do not require recommendations at all; others make recommendations optional and use them only to determine the fates of the most marginal of applicants; but a considerable number of colleges and universities still view the recommendation as an integral and vital part of the application. This chapter provides guidance for writing counselor letters for this last group of colleges.

From Dean Whitla's groundbreaking studies in the 1960s to the research of William Fitzsimmons and Warren Reed in the early 1980s to NACAC's own 2011 *State of College Admission* report, evidence clearly demonstrates the importance of counselor and teacher recommendations.

curricular strengths "were more likely to be admitted if they had strong counselor reports" (p. 24). In the most selective applicant pools, colleges are looking for ways to distinguish one highly accomplished applicant from another; they are, as more than one admission director has said, "looking for tiebreakers." So, in selective admission environments, counselor and teacher recommendations do matter.

STORY CORE

Now that we have established the value of the letter, let's explore what makes an effective letter—the kind that will enable each student to emerge in as full and as distinctive a light as possible.

The late Fred Hargadon, former dean of admission at Swarthmore College (PA), Stanford University (CA) and Princeton University (NJ), was fond of saying that stories are "the coin of the realm" in college admission. Grades and test scores are, of course, essential parts of an evaluation, but, at some point, strong numbers become commonplace, and colleges look elsewhere to make distinc-

Some colleges and universities do not require recommendations at all; others make recommendations optional and use them only to determine the fates of the most marginal of applicants; but a considerable number of colleges and universities still view the recommendation as an integral and vital part of the application.

In the 2011 NACAC study, nearly two-thirds of the colleges and universities indicated that counselor and teacher recommendations played considerable (19.4 percent for counselors; 19 percent for teachers) to moderate (45 percent for counselors; 44.2 percent for teachers) importance in determining which academically qualified students to admit. As a rule of thumb, the more selective a school, the more likely a counselor or teacher recommendation will carry significant weight in an admission decision. (Of those colleges and universities accepting less than 50 percent, over half gave considerable importance to the counselor letter [52 percent] and teacher recommendations [51 percent].) As the Fitzsimmons/Reed report (1992) puts it, students with the same level of academic and extra-

tions between candidates. Not only that, but colleges and universities also want to create the most dynamic community possible; they know that big numbers are not necessarily indicative of personal charisma, character, original thought, humor, courage, and all of the other qualities that bring energy, depth, kindness, and cohesion to a community. Or, at the very least, they know that those numbers do not tell the whole story. More often than not, for instance, the sharpest intellect or the deepest and most original thinker at a given high school is not always the top-ranked student. The single most important thing in undergraduate education is the education students receive from one another. So, which students are the best educators? Who will make those around them better now and 50 years from now? The ability, then, of a student and the student's school counselor and teachers to tell the stories of that student can be the difference-maker.

THE POWER OF STORIES

The power of stories, of course, holds across cultures and across time, from the street corners of ancient Greece where Homer told tales of Ulysses to the medieval mystery plays, created to make Christian doctrine accessible to the masses, to the TED talks of today. Think also of the propagandistic spinnings of just about any political campaign you can name or the micro-vignettes of commercial advertising or the passing down of family lore from generation to generation or the vital news embedded in the spirituals sung by the slaves in the antebellum South. Tellingly, "story-telling" has become a hot item in the business world. Most business schools now offer courses on how to tell the story of a corporation to potential investors or customers (with titles like "Use Stories to Deliver Business Value," "Every Leader Tells a Story" or "Whoever Tells the Best Story Wins") and on how to acculturate new or young employees with company-specific, internal narratives. In the realm of institutional advancement, i.e., development or fundraising, schools about to undergo capital campaigns can now hire teams who coach institutions in the art of telling their story. The bottom line: persuasion, assimilation, affiliation, and connection in any facet of human endeavor depend on the telling of a good, compelling story. College admission is no exception.

What Makes a Good Story/Letter

Seen essentially as a story, the college recommendation letter becomes less mysterious and much more familiar. We all trade in stories daily. As a result, we are all experts on stories: We recognize a good story when it comes our way, and we are acutely aware when a story bombs. Armed with this expertise, let's, as English teachers say, "unpack" the various elements of a good story and, by extension, a good letter of recommendation.

RECOMMENDATION OR REFERENCE?

There is an ongoing debate about whether "recommendation" is really the right term for what counselors and teachers write. "Recommendation" can carry with it the unfortunate and unhelpful connotation of selling or pushing a case. Terms like "reference" or "report" seem more consistent with the story analogy and more consistent with what we are really trying to accomplish: present as true and full and thoughtful a picture of the student as possible. Just as a story can fall flat if the teller tries too hard, so, too, a school letter can be a turn-off if it shifts into marketing mode and strays from who the student really is.

Timing and Length

The best stories use time masterfully. They tend to be lean, direct and respectful of the listeners' time; they never overstay their welcome. Nothing can kill an interesting story more effectively than taking too long to tell it.

Appropriate length is also crucial to the effectiveness of the counselor letter. Unless there are unusual circumstances that need significant additional clarification, the letter should be no more than 500 to 800 words. Letters that run longer than that often suffer from what colleges call "prep prose," writing that is more about the writer's wonderful eloquence than about the student.

At the same time, there are many examples of highly effective letters that are much shorter than 500 words. For counselors with heavy caseloads and many other responsibilities besides college counseling, it may not be humanly possible to crank out 500-word letters. Remember that the best counselor letters capture the essence of the student. In many cases, a well-constructed paragraph can describe a student quite effectively. Sometimes even a sentence or two can do the job. ("From the way she zeroes in on the most important details in a history reading or a biology experiment to the uncanny way she has of knowing when a classmate or a teacher needs a kind or a firm word, Thyra reads the world and responds to it with a maturity way beyond her years; she is a true presence" or "It took some time and more than a little hand-holding, but Ryan has finally figured out how to be an effective student. He is ready for whatever college requires of him.") Whatever the length, all the principles outlined below hold true.

Details

John Carlos Williams, an important American poet of the early 20th century, once stated that his fundamental principle of writing was, "no ideas/But in things." That is, the best writing begins with details from the concrete world; generalities and abstractions by themselves won't cut it.

Again, think of your favorite stories. Why do you like them so much? Why do they stay with you over the years? Most likely because the storyteller gave you details that made the story come alive for you; as the story unfolded, it became more and more palpable in your own imagination; it awakened most, if not all, of your senses. Those are the same sorts of vivid details you want to provide in your letters. If you are successful, the student will, as college admission officers say, "step off the page" (i.e., become a living, breathing person in the mind of the college reader).

Of course, you don't want to overload your letter with details. Every detail must contribute in some way to the main point you are trying to make about the student. Remember that the admission reader will be moving quickly and efficiently through each letter; any detail, no matter how intriguing or fun, that distracts from the central message is ultimately not serving the student well. In talking about those painful moments when a writer needs to cut good stuff in order to preserve the unity of the story, William Faulkner, the great American writer, observed that sometimes a writer has to kill his own children. It is a difficult, sometimes painful process, but the best writing often demands these sorts of sacrifices.

We also need to be wary of inappropriate details. Avoid descriptions of physical appearance ("George never let being overweight limit his extracurricular activities" or "June is one of the prettiest, best-dressed girls in the school") unless that detail is essential to understanding the character and personality of the student (for instance, the brave and resolute student who overcame some sort of physical disability to thrive in school). You would be dismayed by how often commentary about a student's looks crops up in counselor and teacher letters and not surprised by how poorly that commentary reflects upon the writer's judgment.

DETAILS MATTER

Edgar Allan Poe set ground rules for short story writing that still hold true. He believed that a compelling short story strives for "a single effect" and that every sentence in the story should advance the cause of that single effect. To that end, the writer should have the beginning and end of the story in mind at all times; in fact, the first and last lines of the story should be the strongest of the entire composition. Counselor and teacher letters should follow the same rules. Every detail must count.

A good test of a letter would be to use just the first and last sentences (or first and last paragraphs) of your letter to describe a student. Would an outsider reading those two sentences (or paragraphs) get a clear sense of who that student is?

Structure

At its most fundamental, every letter must have a beginning, middle and an end. So, at minimum, a letter will most likely need three paragraphs: an introduction to establish the central theme or guiding image of the student's story; a body to develop and explain that theme with evidence from the student's life; and a conclusion to restate that theme and perhaps to speculate about the student's promise for the future.

You would be dismayed by how often commentary about a student's looks crops up in counselor and teacher letters and not surprised by how poorly that commentary reflects upon the writer's judgment.

KEYHOLE DESIGN

There is a lot to be said for the old tried-and-true keyhole design for letter structure. Start broadly, anecdotally ("Just the other day, I was reminded of why we admire Allison so much when she spoke to the whole school about the difficult topic of affirmative action"), and then narrow your thoughts to the "thesis statement" or main point ("Few students can match the personal magnetism, grace and courage Allison brings to this community"). Then, in the body, expand on these three qualities ("Allison's magnetism and courage are not reserved for large public settings. We see them every day in and out of the classroom"). In the opening line of the concluding paragraph, restate the theme in a different, deeper way ("Allison, then, is as fully formed as a teenager can be: comfortable in her own skin and ready to take on the world"), and close with a look to the future ("We don't know what direction Allison's life will take during and after college, but we do know that, wherever it leads, she will have many followers walking with her").

However, you should not feel locked into a three-paragraph structure. Let the facts and the important moments of a student's life dictate the structure. Perhaps you need a full paragraph to describe the student's gift for leadership or to explain difficult family circumstances or a sudden dip in academic performance. Perhaps the student's high school life breaks into pronounced phases so a more chronological approach makes sense. Perhaps a particularly powerful and lengthy quote from a parent or another person close to the student demands its own paragraph. Perhaps the student leads such a balanced life that a letter with an introductory paragraph, a paragraph for academics, a paragraph for extracurricular activities, and a concluding paragraph is the only way to go. Assemble your details, see how they connect with one another and then structure your letter accordingly. Where a prompt asks you to comment on a particular attribute or set of attributes in the student, the same advice applies, with the attribute now dictating content and structure.

Voice and Diction

Vocabulary and voice—that is, the words you choose and how you use them—also contribute to the intensity, coherence and effectiveness of a letter. Every word, just like every detail, must count. As a result, you want to use words with both specificity and power or, even more to the point, you want to use nouns and verbs with specificity and power. Adjectives and adverbs are nice, but, ultimately, they are window dressing, cosmetics. Sentences can exist without adjectives and adverbs; they cannot exist without nouns and verbs. If you find yourself using a lot of high energy modifiers, really laying on the descriptors, step back and be a hard-nosed editor; you may be trying too hard to make chicken soup out of chicken poop. A savvy reader can cut through all that gaudy description and figure out pretty quickly that, as Gertrude Stein once said of a fellow author, "there is no there there."

At the same time, you don't want to get too highbrow. This is not the time to haul out the thesaurus and cram your letter with big words. Apply the same advice you are giving your students about the essay to yourself: be direct, be clear, be compelling, be yourself. Letters full of words you wouldn't normally use won't be inspiring; they will be stiff, unnatural and potentially boring. Every admission cycle, a story will circulate about a favorite letter of recommendation from an unexpected source: the school janitor, the hospice patient, the stranger a student met on a train. One such letter came from the manager of the convenience store where a student studied every night because he had no electricity at home. These letters move the reader, not because they use fancy language, but because they have something real and heartfelt to say. Again, it's about the central story, "the single effect"; the language and the voice you use should always serve that purpose.

Again, it's about the central story, "the single effect"; the language and the voice you use should always serve that purpose.

WORDS, WORDS, WORDS

Sample of dynamic verbs: absorb, animate, brighten, build, convey, create, dazzle, develop, devour, drive, earn, embrace, endure, establish, explore, flex, focus, galvanize, hesitate, initiate, inspire, observe, penetrate, persevere, recover, see, solve, surprise, tolerate, transform, understand, unearth, yearn.

Sample of dynamic nouns: charisma, compassion, courage, decency, durability, edge, force, generosity, gentleness, grace, grit, humility, impact, indifference, influence, intellect, inventiveness, maturity, originality, pluck, poise, power, resilience, self-reliance, serenity, wit.

Sample of words/phrases to avoid because they might be inappropriate, nondescript, clichéd, or misunderstood: as (when used as a conjunction), buxom, cute, fairness, goes his/her own way, good, interesting, nice, manly, marches to her/his own drummer, one-of-a-kind, pleasant, pretty, satisfactory, solid, unique, verbal, well-mannered.

CONTENT

Earlier in this chapter, we noted that a well-constructed letter will usually include a section about the student's academic life, a section about his/her extracurricular activities, and most likely some ruminations about the student's character or personal qualities. Let's examine those three sections in greater detail.

Academics

A standard letter will highlight a student's academic successes, citing particular projects and performances, quoting teachers where possible and providing some overview of that student's history in your classrooms.

If the student has encountered difficulties in the classroom, the counselor letter is the perfect place to explain those difficulties. One of the crucial responsibilities of the counselor letter is to provide a **context for performance**. Yes, a teacher letter might also give some back story for a particular grade in a particular course, but the school letter should address the sorts of larger external factors, like chronic illness, learning differences, concussions, family disruptions or tragedies, psycho-social struggles, etc., that might have prevented the student from performing as well as she or he could have. (More on the presentation of those issues later.) Without that context for performance, colleges might assume that the student was simply lazy or unmotivated.

Similarly, an effective letter will show how a student has triumphed over adversity or touched the sun with his or her brilliance. The letter should not only describe extraordinary circumstances, but it should also bring to life extraordinary achievement. When asked how admission officers make distinctions between so many qualified candidates, an admission officer from a most selective university replied, "We look for students who go beyond the obvious, beyond the ordinary." School letters will clearly and substantially show when a student meets that standard.

Extracurriculars

Context for performance also applies to what you write about a student's extracurricular life. Your task is not to glorify or sensationalize your student's activities so that they grab a reader's attention; rather, your responsibility is to present those activities in a meaningful, clear and accurate light. As much affection and enthusiasm as you might have for a student, don't let those feelings move you to make statements or assessments that are out of proportion with reality. Resist the temptation to present the actress who has played several leads in school plays but has had no success outside of school as the next Oscar winner. If an ambitious student has landed a big-time summer internship because Mom and Dad have big-time connections, keep that achievement in perspective. Distinguish between local heroes and those students who have that magical "It" factor that will make them a star in any setting, no matter how heady.

At the same time, if there are extraordinary achievements or circumstances, be sure to present them fully. If a student has had to work 20 hours a week to help her family make ends meet, report that. If a long commute or bus ride to school has really hampered the student's ability to engage in the extracurricular life of the school, let the college know. If the student committed some courageous, instinctive act of leadership (speaking out in a school-wide assembly against hateful graffiti; openly be-friending a less-than-popular student), make clear and pointed note of it. If a student did well in a competition where you know he matched his abilities with the best and brightest the country or the world has to offer (an international linguistics competition or a world catch-and-release tournament) and did well, explain the significance of that competition and celebrate it.

Colleges are eager to hear about the "real deals" on your campus. But if, in your telling, all students are the real deal, then colleges will begin to question your judgment and doubt your powers of discrimination. They might begin to wonder whether you can recognize true excellence when you see it. And, as a result, they might discount what you say even when, like the boy who cried wolf, what you are saying is absolutely true. Your mantra should be, "Everything in perspective; everything in proportion."

GATHERING MATERIAL

One of the challenges we face, particularly if we have a large caseload, is how to capture the essence of a student, how to get his or her story right, so that colleges will see him or her as enthusiastically and fully as we do. The task of collecting meaningful information about each student becomes paramount. If you have the luxury of meeting with the student several times over the course of the process, some of that information comes your way naturally. However, for those who can only meet with a student once or twice at the most, other forms of information become crucial.

One approach is to have students and parents do some of the work for you. Asking students to fill out a mock application in the spring or summer of junior year (some schools use a version of the Common Application) serves two purposes: students get a practice run at the application, and you gain access to quality self-reporting.

You might also develop a questionnaire for parents to fill out. While you will not get 100-percent return, most parents are eager to tell you about their child. Completing this form helps reduce parental anxiety because it gives them something to do. Parent responses can also give you a heads-up about any misunderstandings or biases parents might have about the process. And, of course, you can learn things about the student that you might not

know otherwise. Sometimes the anecdote or image a parent provides can be exactly what you need to pull all the parts of a student's story together.

Some schools ask each student to pick a classmate to write a peer review. This approach has multiple benefits: In addition to the information it provides you, the peer review gives the student a first taste of how he/she is seen by others, and it gives the peer reviewer an appreciation for the difficulties and complexities of writing a recommendation.

Finally, you might want to develop a student evaluation form for teachers to fill out. Rather than burden every teacher, each junior can pick the two teachers most likely to write his/her teacher recommendation. If structured properly, this evaluation can serve two purposes: first, as a full-blown outline for an eventual teacher letter of recommendation, and, second, as source of good classroom insights for the counselor letter. A less extensive form could be used to get information from adults who have worked with students outside the classroom (coaches, club advisors, job supervisors, youth group leaders, etc.).

KEEPING THE TASK MANAGEABLE

- **Expect proper requests.** A student should approach you in person with a request and give you three to four weeks' notice.

- **Discuss the question of waiving rights.** If a student does not waive his/her rights, the student will be allowed to read your recommendation at the college at which s/he matriculates (if the college keeps the letter on file). Students who do not waive their rights run the risk of having colleges think they are trying to hide something. If you have the option, encourage students to waive their rights; confidentiality will make the letter more believable.

- **Keep copies.** Keep copies of everything you send out. Often a student will reappear with additional requests for other applications or scholarships.

- **Don't send the wrong letter to the wrong school.** Colleges have fun with our mistakes when we write, "I think Julia is well-suited to the academic program at Whitman" and then send the letter off to Whittier! Be careful. To avoid the problem, don't name the college in your letter.

- **Be aware that you are developing a reputation.** Believe it or not, colleges begin to identify individual counselors (and teachers) who write recommendations year after year. Some they trust, and others they don't. You must be honest and present students as they are, not as perfect creatures. You must also make sure that you write as thoughtfully and as clearly as possible. The credibility you have as an advocate for a student is directly related to the care you take with the letters you write. Also, because you are a voice and often the face of your school to the colleges, they will form opinions about the quality of your school based on the quality of your work. Never forget that you are an agent for your school.

Questions to Consider

If you have a hard time getting started on a letter, you might want to think through the answers to the following questions:

- How would you describe the student's intellectual abilities? Can she work independently? Write persuasively? Read with depth and wisdom? Synthesize challenging material into concepts? Present a line of reasoning persuasively? Assimilate new ideas or counter-arguments? React well to setbacks? Get work done in a thorough and timely fashion? Is she curious about the subject material or more focused on the grade?

- How would you describe the student's personal qualities and extracurricular life? Has he engaged with his school community or with communities outside the school? Does he have leadership abilities? Is he mature? Motivated? Reliable? Resilient? Does he have a sense of humor? Does he see himself and the world realistically and accurately? Is he humane? Kind? Does he have the courage to stand up for what he thinks is right even if it might make him unpopular? Does he have a calming or steadying effect on others? Has he pursued any activities energetically and achieved a level of success and expertise in those areas?

Once you have answers to the questions above (or any other questions you might have devised), look for patterns or themes. What seem to be the student's strengths, the student's weaknesses? How has that student grown during his/her high school years? Has the student been a late bloomer? A dogged plugger? Has the student found joy in the work? What are the most memorable and admirable aspects of the student?

Stories That Are Difficult to Tell

What you have learned so far applies to any recommendation you might write. But there is a much smaller group of letters that require special attention, because they must tell the stories of disciplinary infractions, learning issues, medical issues, or other difficult circumstances. These are the letters that keep us up at night. In many ways, how we handle these letters and the conversations around these letters establishes our reputation with colleges and students and families.

There is a wide range of opinions about what should or can be disclosed. Some school policies dictate full disclosure on disciplinary cases, reasoning that reporting the infraction and requiring the student to do the same is part of the teachable moment. Some schools do not disclose any cases, reasoning that the teachable moment has already occurred within the school and that then reporting the infraction to the colleges could result in additional punishment and therefore constitutes double jeopardy for the student. Still other schools and school districts forbid any form of disclosure for legal reasons.

Before you begin a letter that involves any sort of disclosure, make sure that you know your school's and/or district's disclosure policies. What do those policies permit? What do they forbid? Does your school, for instance, have established, published procedures for reporting disciplinary cases? How does your school handle the reporting of medical leaves? Does your school have an Acceptable Use Policy for computer and other electronic media? Does your school have a conduct and/or confidentiality statement of any kind?

If such procedures and policies do not exist, you should not disclose; without the support of institutional policy, you might very well expose your school and yourself personally to legal action.

Shaping School Policy

In recent years, hacking, misbehavior on social media, and sexual assault have become the new and uncomfortable frontier of student discipline on college and high school campuses. As you and your school attempt to develop school policy around these thorny issues, you might consider consulting two sources. In the world of social media, particularly around issues of privacy and transgression, no group is more cutting-edge than the Berkman Center for Internet and Society (cyber.law.harvard.edu). You would do well to visit that site on a regular basis. In terms of sexual assault, several colleges have issued statements outlining community standards in very direct terms. High school administrators could find helpful models of language and policy as they seek to craft their own school and district policies.

Disclosure Statements

Examples of disclosure statements include:

- District policy does not permit the reporting of any disciplinary infractions.

- Under school policy, any disciplinary infraction that results in a suspension or dismissal shall be reported to the colleges.

- Only those disciplinary infractions that involve malicious conduct, dishonesty or other forms of integrity violations will be reported to the colleges.

Questions to Consider as You Write the Difficult Letter

- Can I tell a student's story honestly without jeopardizing that student's college chances?

- What will serve the student best? What parts of his or her life are appropriately private and need to be protected? Which of his or her mistakes, tragedies, etc. belong in the public arena?

- At the same time, what is fair to the colleges with whom we have a trusting relationship? Trust, truth and integrity are currency in this profession. Without them we have no credibility, and no power.

- Can we talk about a student's vulnerability in a compelling way? Can a student's mistakes actually have a positive impact on the letter?

- Are the following issues fair game for a school letter?

  - Bi-polar disorder

  - Depression/anxiety/obsessive compulsive disorder

  - Abuse, psychological or physical

  - Eating disorders

  - Family divorce

  - Plagiarism

  - Learning disabilities (ADD/ADHD)

  - Hospitalization

  - Extensive absence

  - Suicidality

  - Suspected drug use or sales

  - Criminal conviction

  - Harassment/bullying

  - Sexual identity

Summary of Pointers for Managing Difficult Letters

- Establish clear guidelines around discipline and extended leaves, and publish them.

- Consult with administrators and school or district lawyers about school or district policies.

- Ask a supervisor to read and approve difficult letters.

- Ask students and parents to help you with explanations of difficult events.

- Establish a clear relationship between your office and the office(s) that handles disciplinary matters so that you know the full record of each student.

- Call colleagues in other schools who can give you feedback and advice about how best to handle difficult circumstances.

- Be absolutely sure to obtain family permission (student and parents) before reporting any learning issues or health (psychological or physical) issues. You cannot disclose those issues without family permission.

- Remember that you speak for your faculty and your school. You cannot report hearsay. Only report observable, verifiable fact. Avoid subjective or judgmental language or phrasing.

- If punishable behavior is strongly suspected but not verified (that is, if the student is breaking rules or behaving maliciously but has not yet been caught in the act), use the approach of "commission by omission," writing a thinner, flatter letter than you usually do in which you only say what you absolutely have to say (courses, grades, activities) and no more. "Commission by omission" can also be helpful when you have to write a letter about a student about whom you feel less than enthusiastic.

A Few Don'ts

- Don't make half-baked, poorly phrased or exaggerated statements that could undermine your long-term credibility with the colleges.

- Don't, as a general rule, make reference to race, sex, religion, appearance, or politics in the letter. As stated earlier, it is only permissible to do so if such a reference is crucial to the student's story.

- Don't use judgmental language unless you have specific evidence, hard facts to back up those judgments. (Also, if you're feeling a strong need to make potentially damaging judgmental statements, ask yourself, "Why?" How do these statements serve the main story, the single effect, of your student?)

- Don't write a separate letter for each college. Outside of those rare cases where you might have special, specific connections to a college, "customized" letters will add little if any extra value to a student's file. In fact, you run the risk of putting the wrong college name in the letter, thereby undoing any good work you might have done.

Additional Notes for Teachers

Most of the above advice is applicable to teachers. At its core, a teacher letter also wants to tell the academic story of the student: Is she a worker? How was he as a citizen of the classroom? How energized is his intellectual life? How does his/her mind work when tackling complex issues? What habits/anecdotes come to mind that capture the essence of the student?

Still, there are a few additional pieces of advice, specific to teachers, that should be noted:

- Write primarily about academic matters. Describing a student's academic qualities is your primary responsibility. You are the expert here, the only one who can convey this information. Subtopics could include: creativity, intellectual curiosity, initiative, commitment, writing skills, speaking skills, analytical ability, work habits, growth, independence of mind, resilience, ability to collaborate, willingness to take risks, ability to assimilate new, challenging information. You should also provide a context for the grade the student received in your class. Adjectives alone are meaningless and easily forgotten. Provide examples and anecdotes to support your descriptions. If you say, "Joe likes to grapple with ideas," provide an example of that behavior from your own experience.

- Wherever possible, make evaluative and comparative statements. Colleges need help in assessing where a student falls in your class and a description of the level or quality of that class. Helpful statements include: "One of the two As I gave in that section," "a strong tester, but quieter in the class than others," "my go-to person when the class was stumped by a question," etc.

- Comment on academic difficulties without damning the student. Colleges know that students have weaknesses. You should acknowledge problems that a student has encountered in your class and your assessment of their causes. Is the student struggling with material because it is difficult or because s/he is struggling with poor or inconsistent work habits? Be specific. For example, if a student works in spurts, describe his/her best work and then describe the work that is less effective. If a student has improved, give concrete examples of that improvement.

- Provide a sentence about your own years of teaching so that the admission office will have some sense of your experience evaluating students.

- In fairness to the student, if you feel that you cannot write a positive letter of recommendation, decline the request as gently as possible, and direct the student elsewhere for possible letter-writers.

- Include any comments you have on the personal qualities of a student, supporting those comments with your own observations and experiences. Colleges are interested in such qualities as character and leadership, so provide examples *as they have occurred in your experience of working with the student*. Avoid speculation or arm-chair psychology; use observable behavior and performance.

- Limit your letter to 500 to 800 words; write a long letter only when there are special circumstances to explain.

- Don't write at length about the content of your curriculum. Anything more than one or two sentences slows the overall narrative of the letter and suggests that you are validating yourself rather than talking about a student's qualifications. (Exceptions may be necessary for unusual courses out of the mainstream or for independent study courses. In that case, you may wish to create a one-paragraph description and attach it as an addendum.) The focus of the letter itself must be the student, not your course.

- Avoid revealing sensitive, personal information without checking with your guidance office. Topics that fall into this category include difficult divorces, extended illnesses, diagnoses of learning differences, and sibling or family issues. In general, you should not focus on the family or anything personal; what the colleges want to know from you is how the student functions academically.

- Don't send up "red flags" without providing examples and explanations. For example, if you say, "Ashley questions authority," you may be signaling to a college that this student is difficult to live with, when your intention was to describe her intellectual independence. Be clear by providing examples.

- Write about your direct experience with the student; don't try to write your own version of the counselor letter. Don't ask the student, already burdened with her/his own work, for a resume and then use that to make a laundry list of the student's activities. This is filler. The student will provide his/her own list of activities, and the school letter will comment on his/her level of involvement. This is not your domain. However, if you have coached a student, worked with her on a community project, lived with him in a dormitory, or advised her in some capacity outside the classroom, then write freely about your observations. At the same time, don't lose sight of your primary task: to describe the student as an intellectual being.

- Avoid clichés or general, empty phrases like, "shows great potential," "will be an asset," "respected by peers and teachers alike," "is a unique person," etc. Keep your language fresh, specific and precise.

- Don't overstate or understate a student's case in accordance to what you think should happen to the student or in anticipation of how you think the college will respond to the student. By doing so, you could unknowingly damage or inflate the student's chances of admission. Simply tell the student's story fully and truthfully and let the college take it from there.

- Do use spell check and at least one proofreader. You don't want to lose credibility because of a careless or inadvertent error.

- Do use the active voice and, wherever possible, the present tense. Remember that you are telling a story. The best, most compelling stories feel immediate; they grab the reader and pull him/her directly into what is being said. The passive voice and the past tense can have a distancing effect, as though the writer does not really want to let the reader in, but would rather keep the reader at arm's length. You want to write in such a natural way that you are, in effect, having a conversation with the reader.

FINAL THOUGHTS

Writing letters of recommendation is one of the most daunting and burdensome tasks we do as counselors (and teachers), but it can also be one of the most important, soul-satisfying things we do. The best letters connect us with that student in ways that only the deep, reflective process of writing can do. There is purity and power in that process. Writing the letter forces us to pause in this crazy admission schedule and carefully consider the whole student: What is the true story of this student? What do the colleges need to know in order to understand and appreciate this student? What do I need to know and be thinking about in order to get the story right? It is an intense process, one that requires our most alert, generous, wise, and dynamic selves. When we bring that level of attention and commitment to the letter, we do the student a great service; we become the best sort of advocate. The most compelling letters transport the student into the room where the admission reader toils through applications; the more vividly the student is rendered, the more the student's application breathes much-appreciated life into that reader's work, and the more likely the student is to emerge distinctively in the admission process. Can there be a more welcome responsibility in the work we do?

So, in answer to the question posed at the beginning of this chapter, yes, all the effort we put into letters of recommendation is worth it. It is a responsibility that we, as committed and caring advocates for our students, must embrace fully and gladly.

ABOUT THE AUTHOR

Rod Skinner is currently director of college counseling at Milton Academy in Milton, Massachusetts. In his 30+ years in secondary education, he has worked at schools in Boston, Connecticut, California, and Florida. Rod has also chaired the Admission Practices Committee for the National Association for College Admission Counseling, and served five years on the board of the Common Application. While in Florida, he directed the SACAC Summer Institute for Secondary School Counselors for ten years. Presently, Rod teaches on the faculty of the Harvard Summer Institute on College Admissions, presents at a number of conferences annually, chairs the Oversight and Advisory Committees at The Mountain School in Vershire, Vermont, and serves on the board of trustees for Boston Collegiate Charter School.

REFERENCES

Fitzsimmons, W., & Reed, W. (1982). Counselor recommendations. *The College Board Review,* 124(24).

III. Identifying Pathways and Options

FROM KNOWING TO GOING

Raquel M. Rall, PhD • Jonathan D. Mathis, PhD

This next content transition moves us from an articulation of the work of counselors to even further described strategies and access points for students' transition to college. In other words, here is a necessary shift from common requisites to a dialogue of individualized factors—those that make the general dream of college, for the multitudes, a reality, even if for one student at a time. Authors composing the content of the third section of this text sought to provide information and guidance for practitioners who are working with students to facilitate the transition to college. One might define this transition as shifting a student's attitude from knowing to going.

The authors acknowledge the rich potential of creating a readily accessible, relevant and current college-going learning environment. This environment would need to be wide-spread and structured enough to accommodate the needs of a large number of students, while also displaying possible institutions and the means by which students might apply. The learning environment, too, includes the import of academic planning, as well as appropriate standardized assessments, while also accumulating support, via letters of recommendation, for the application. We see these letters as a prologue to college matriculation, while embodying a spirit of advocacy and support for students' dreams.

It is also in this learning environment where attention to individual needs is a non-negotiable. The authors point to counselors and students possibly using more personalized postsecondary planning tools, which might include a renewed approach and focus on college fit. These efforts might also be inclusive of appropriate colleges for individual students, based not only on an academic profile, but also attention to skills, talents or available financial assistance.

Arguably, many students state they want to go to college. That espoused goal, however, needs to be more than just a thought; it needs to lead to action on the part of both counselors and students. Counseling professionals are encouraged to first identify and pursue foundational elements needed by an individual student, to ensure college as a future possibility. Second, these professionals must consider those opportunities that foster students' postsecondary choice. A student's choice might be linked to special skills and talents, academic achievements or possibilities for merit-based institutional aid. These considerations, again, move us from a focus of knowing the work and helping students become aware of processes to getting students to enroll and begin their journey at a postsecondary institution appropriately aligned with their goals.

Chapter 13:   Postsecondary Options

Patrick O'Connor, PhD
@collegeisyours

A key part in helping students build a life after high school includes an introduction to choices they could make to continue their education—and that isn't always as easy as it sounds.

Many students begin their postsecondary exploration with all kinds of impressions that can limit their search. This includes:

- Students who are sure they can't go to college, because they can't afford it, weren't successful in high school or think college "isn't for them"

- Student who aren't sure if college is worth the cost of attendance

- Students whose only postsecondary interest is the college(s) from which both parents graduated

- Parents who come in with a copy of the latest mass-produced "best college" rankings and insist their child only focus on these "good" colleges

- Students whose perception of college is shaped largely by the success of a college's athletic programs

- Students who see no need for college, since their parents have had successful careers without ever attending college.

Because this pre-existing knowledge can prevent a comprehensive review of postsecondary possibilities, it's important to create an approach to the exploration of these possibilities that allows students to engage in what Lee (2002) refers to as "unlearning," or going beyond what they think they know, in order to have a greater understanding of the myriad options that exist.

A vital first step in this unlearning involves introducing the student to available postsecondary options, including an understanding of the different kinds of four-year colleges; two-year colleges; vocational and technical training programs; training available through the military; post-graduate study before entry into college, and taking time off before entering college, also known as a "gap" year.

FOUR-YEAR COLLEGES

With more than 2,200 options (College Board, 2014), four-year colleges represent the largest group of postsecondary institutions in the United States. While each four-year college creates its own degree requirements, most gener-

ally, degrees and programs are designed with two components:

1. *General education requirements.* In order to have a strong understanding of all parts of the world around them, students have to take a prescribed number of introductory courses in English, math, science, social sciences, and the humanities and arts.

2. *Major requirements.* Students are then required to complete courses in the field of study they want to focus on at a more in-depth level. This study can include courses designed to prepare students for specific careers (such as accounting or education); courses that build on general education knowledge to give the student a greater understanding of a particular academic area (like history or biology), or courses that provide more information on a number of subjects (like general studies).

With so many choices, students often wonder how to find the colleges that will best meet their interests and needs. A number of online tools help students structure their college search; they ask students to define their college interests by categories that can include the size of the college, the majors offered, the athletic options at each college, and more.

In order to make sure the student's preconceived notions about college don't put artificial limits on these search engines, a good first step is to make sure students have challenged their assumptions involving each of the major parameters of a search for four-year colleges before heading to the computer. These major parameters include:

Cost

Many students and parents begin the college selection process convinced some colleges are simply out of reach because they cost too much, or because the student will not qualify for financial aid. Too often, this prevents a student from applying to a college that offers significant financial aid based solely on the student's high school grades and test scores, factors that can lead to scholarships that will make a more expensive college more affordable—and, in some cases, free.

Students and parents are wise to consider cost—and the issue of student debt after college—as one factor in choosing a college, but writing a college off in the early part of the process as "too expensive" can artificially limit the student's options. Students should develop a list of colleges that include several choices where significant financial aid would not be needed to attend, but that should by no means be the only factor in developing the list.

Major

Students often feel they can't begin the college search process without knowing what they will study in college. This can be particularly relevant when the student is feeling pressure to go to college to "get a good job," even though the student's interests or talents may not align with the careers that are in high demand, according to current employment projections.

If a student's career or academic interests are well-defined in high school, major can be an important factor in exploring four-year colleges. Concurrently, if the student is certain he/she has no idea what he/she wants to major in, this information is just as useful in the college exploration process, since many colleges encourage students to spend up to two years exploring different areas of study before declaring a major.

Counselors can help students complete a wide array of career exploration activities in high school and use those results in the college search—even, and especially, if the answer to, "What do you want to study?" is "I don't know." Students should also consider how committed they are to their major; a student who is convinced engineering (or music) is his/her field of study will probably want to include technical colleges (or music conservatories) in his/her college search, while a student torn between engineering and music (or wanting to study both) will have a very different list of schools.

Location

Unlike these other categories, many students begin the college search with strong assumptions about what they don't want. More than one student has started the exploration process with statements like, "I'm certainly not going to a college in the middle of a cornfield," and "Of course I won't be living at home when I go to college. I want this experience to be mine!"

Students often assume that colleges located in or near big cities offer more to do than colleges in rural areas, when the opposite is often true. Many students return from visiting an urban college having discovered the city and the college are combined in a way that there isn't enough of a sense of campus for the student. On the other hand, a college that is hours away from a major city may have more student events on any given weekend than one student could possibly attend, since the college knows that if the campus doesn't meet the extracurricular needs of the students, students won't enroll.

Distance from home is another factor that needs to be broached with both care and clarity. Some students may have so strong a desire to strike out on their own that they overlook a college five miles away that has everything the student is looking for. At the same time, the student may have economic or personal needs that require him/her to begin college by staying at home. Maximizing personal autonomy is an important goal in the college selection process, but that goal can be achieved in many ways for the same student.

Size of College

Many students begin their college search convinced that the only place they can get individualized attention is at a small college. On the other hand, some students are unwilling to look at any college with fewer than tens of thousands of students because they want a college with lots of "school spirit."

In both cases, students are talking about the qualities they are looking for in a college, and this quality-based approach to the college search usually helps students look past many preconceived notions about colleges—except when it comes to the size of the college. Students often need help considering the many limited-enrollment programs at big colleges that offer personalized attention, as well as the smaller college campuses with rich traditions that create a strong sense of community surpassing that of much larger schools. Getting past the assumptions about colleges based on size can be challenging, but it is in the student's best interest to make the effort.

Research Universities and Liberal Arts Colleges

This same quality-based approach to choosing a college is important in understanding the wide array of options at research and liberal arts institutions. There are several definitions of what constitutes a research university (see, for example, Carnegie Foundation, 2014), but most of them suggest that one of the top priorities of these institutions is a commitment to graduate education and research led by professors. There are just as many definitions for a liberal arts college (see, for example, My College Guide, 2014), and these definitions suggest students attending a liberal arts college will receive a broad exposure to the humanities, arts, sciences, social sciences, and mathematics fields while also majoring in one or more areas of interest.

Students will want to look past these labels and look at the qualities and offerings of each individual college associated with either group. Research universities have the reputation of being large schools where professors are focused more on research or graduate students, but many of these schools require full professors to teach undergraduates, and many are able to use the strength of their research programs to offer research opportunities to undergraduates. In addition, many research universities have programs or majors that offer undergraduate students the same breadth and depth of study as liberal arts colleges.

Liberal arts colleges are often considered schools that offer a wide array of majors with fewer opportunities for research, but students will want to look past this generalization as well. Many liberal arts colleges require students to engage in some kind of research (often in the form of a senior project) under the supervision of one or more full professors, where the research can span more than one area of interest.

Research universities and liberal arts colleges work from their strengths to offer learning opportunities tailored to meet the needs of a wide array of students. College-bound students should investigate these opportunities and evaluate them on how well they meet the student's goals for going to college, not on the historic labels attached to the school.

Length of Program

Finally, students and parents will want to make sure they understand that many students are staying at four-year colleges for more than four years. The National Center for Education Statistics (2014) reports that 59 percent of the students who enrolled at a four-year college in 2006 had a bachelor's degree by 2012—that's six years later.

While there are a number of personal factors involved in the time it takes for a student to complete a degree (the economy, family circumstances), some colleges have expanded the requirements in some programs that virtually guarantee students will need more than four years to earn a bachelor's degree. Parents and students should be advised to look closely at requirements for specific programs when exploring college options, so they can make fair comparisons of cost, time for completion and career preparation when looking at all of their options.

Two-Year Colleges

Slightly more than 1,600 two-year college options are offered in the United States (College Board, 2014). While the purpose of two-year colleges has changed since their introduction in the early 1900s (Geller, 2001), two-year colleges generally serve three specific purposes:

Career Preparation

Many of the certificates and associate degrees offered by two-year colleges prepare students for a specific career. While some of these degrees may include completion of general education classes, many require students to complete more than half of their coursework in a major or concentration tailored to meet the needs of a specific career in technology (auto technician, applied engineering), healthcare (x-ray technician, medical transcription specialist) or small business (accounting assistant, business administration).

Transfer Preparation

Both junior colleges and community colleges offer students the opportunity to complete general education classes that will meet degree requirements at many four-year colleges. The transfer option is often used by students who want to begin their college career close to home; save money on tuition by completing general education classes at a lower-priced college, or earn higher grades than they received in high school in order to transfer to a more selective four-year college.

Remediation

A growing number of two-year college students enroll in junior or community colleges in order to improve reading and math skills, as well as the basic study skills needed to be a successful college student. These classes are sometimes taken so students can transfer to another college, and they are often taken so students can attain basic levels of literacy needed to apply for a job.

As is the case with a search for four-year colleges, students and parents often begin the two-year college search with assumptions that can prevent them from realizing all of the opportunities two-year colleges have to offer. For two-year colleges, these assumptions include:

Prestige

Because many two-year colleges are *open admission* colleges (they do not require a high school diploma or strong grades in high school for admission), many students assume all classes at two-year colleges are remedial, or reruns of what students learned in high school. This perception can make it difficult for a student to look forward to college if economics or personal circumstances require them to begin their college career at a two-year college, especially when they would rather be at a different institution, and are academically eligible to do so.

While many two-year colleges have an open admission policy, most require students to take placement tests before registering for classes. The results of these tests help students enroll in classes that will challenge them without overwhelming them; for students with strong academic skills, this means they will be able to take a wide array of demanding classes with other students who have similar abilities.

Students needing additional assurance about the quality of two-year college classes should be directed to online *transfer guides* that show how much credit these classes are given by more selective colleges. While policies vary from college to college, most four-year institutions will grant transfer credit of up to two years of full-time study at a two-year college, an indication that these transfer classes are just as demanding as similar classes offered at four-year colleges.

Transferability

The transfer guide is also an important tool to use when students and parents assume *all* classes from two-year colleges will transfer to all four-year colleges. Each four-year college has its own standards, but most will not give

credit to any two-year class that focuses on remedial academic skills; many will not give credit to classes with a curriculum that is more career-oriented than academically oriented, and some will not give credit to academic electives with a curriculum that is narrowly focused.

Students planning to transfer to a four-year college also need to know the difference between *elective* credit and *course* credit. A history major who takes five history classes at a two-year college may find out his/her four-year college will accept all of the classes for transfer credit, but will only accept one of them as course credit toward the college's degree requirements in history. The credits for the other four classes would count as elective credit, meaning the college will give the student credit for having taken the classes, but those classes won't count toward the number of history classes the student has to take to earn a history degree.

Since many transfer students start at a two-year college to save time and money, they'll want to work closely with the counselors at both the two-year college and the four-year college to make sure the classes they are transferring will help them reach their goal.

Location and Cost

Students considering two-year colleges often assume they have no choice but to go to the college closest to home, since most two-year colleges do not offer student housing. In addition, students looking to save money by attending a two-year college assume the cost of a two-year college goes up significantly if the student isn't a resident of the city or state where the college is located.

The College Board (2014) reports that about 70 two-year colleges give housing to all first-year students who ask for it—and this housing is guaranteed. In addition, many two-year colleges are located in cities and college towns where affordable student housing is available to all students, no matter what college they attend. Combined with the possibility of living with other relatives or family friends, going to a two-year college has the same array of geographic possibilities as choosing a four-year college.

In terms of cost, many *public* two-year colleges are supported by the taxes of residents, so attendance can be more expensive if a student is from a different city, county or state. On the other hand, *private* two-year colleges charge the same tuition for all students, and some public two-year colleges offer in-district tuition for residents of neighboring towns. Some restrictions may apply, but students should be encouraged to explore these options if they want to look beyond local college options. Many two-year colleges also offer degrees that can be earned completely online.

Career Preparation

Students often select a two-year college because it offers a shorter path to a better-paying job than four-year colleges. This is also why two-year colleges are appealing to students returning to college after some time away from school; the two-year college offers the opportunity to try a career out, and see where it may take the students.

Community colleges were designed for students to explore career options, but students need to be aware of the limited connection between some two-year programs and their four-year counterparts. For example, a student considering engineering will come across many of the key career concepts by taking two-year college courses in applied engineering, but this coursework will have far less math and theoretical science than an engineering degree will require.

Students also need to consider if the requirements of a two-year degree are more than those required for a specific career. Many two-year colleges offer programs in culinary arts that thoroughly prepare a student for a career as a chef, but students many not have to complete a degree of any kind if their desire is to be a cook at the local restaurant. Having a credential or degree usually opens more career opportunities for students, but not always; if the primary goal of attending college is to find a better job, students should understand all of their training possibilities—and how they relate to one another—before choosing a specific path.

Certificate Programs at Community Colleges

Knowing that some careers require less than two years of training, many community colleges offer certificate programs that expose students to the key terminology and skills needed to be successful in a specific field. Since many of these certificates require only a year of study, students can quickly earn the certificate and gain an entry-level position in the field to see if they truly like the work they are doing. Students happy with their work can

often return to the community college to take the additional coursework needed to earn a two-year degree in the field. This can be especially helpful if the field requires some kind of degree for advancement.

Students looking at a certificate option should understand the limits of transferability of many of the courses. While many of these courses will apply toward the requirements of an associate degree, the vocational focus of many of these courses limits their transferability to four-year colleges, or even to other two-year institutions. Students will want to work closely with an academic advisor or counselor at the two-year institution to understand the possibilities of earning transfer credit for these classes.

VOCATIONAL AND TECHNICAL TRAINING PROGRAMS

The Association for Career and Technical Education (2014) estimates that there are 9,400 postsecondary technical and career education programs in the United States. Because this number includes the career programs offered at two- and four-year colleges, it is difficult to determine how many independent vocational programs exist, but a quick online search reveals hundreds of vocational programs open to students in most major cities.

These vocational programs vary greatly from two- and four-year colleges, and two of these differences play a large role in comparing postsecondary options for students seeking an experience after high school that leads to job opportunities. As a whole, independent vocational programs tend to focus their entire curriculum on career-related skills, requiring few general education classes in order to complete a certificate or diploma. This focus means some of these programs can be completed in less than two years, and many in less than one year, far less time than is necessary to complete a degree from a two- or four-year college.

While these differences are significant, students should ask many of the same questions about the curriculum and services of a vocational school they ask when investigating two- or four-year colleges. Students should compare the courses offered by different programs that prepare students for the same career, and closely investigate the job placement services each program offers. These investigations should reveal the names of companies that hire graduates of these programs, giving students the opportunity to contact the employers to see if graduates of one program are better prepared in the field than those of other programs.

Students also need to look closely at financial aid offers presented by different programs, just as they would for any other postsecondary institution. This is particularly important because students may be completing a vocational program in a matter of months, and many educational loans require students to begin paying loans back six months after leaving school. This short timetable is something students should consider in careers where jobs may take time to find.

Just like students considering two-year colleges, students need to understand whether the diploma or certificate from a vocational program is necessary for a particular field, if it is part of a career ladder that creates other opportunities and if any of the coursework completed in the program is transferable to two- or four-year colleges, if the student wishes to pursue further study. It is best to work with counselors at both the vocational program and the school the student plans on transferring to in order to get a clear understanding of their options.

Finally, students should consider if they are prepared for the rigorous schedule many vocational training programs require of their students. A vocational program may not include traditional academic courses, but students will still need to study, read, review, and complete homework in vocational programs, tasks that require time and focus. Students considering a vocational school may want to talk with a career counselor in order to get a better understanding of the demands of vocational school and to determine if work or other family obligations may prevent them from getting the most out of their experience.

Military Training

One of the best examples of on-the-job training involves enlistment in a branch of the United States Armed Forces. By working closely with military recruiters, students can get a better understanding of the training options available through the United States Air Force, Army, Coast Guard, Marines, and Navy that can guide students into a variety of career options, including some options that can transfer for college credit. As is the case with any postsecondary option, students are strongly encouraged to get a clear understanding of the obligations that come with enlisting in the armed forces and if the training they seek in a specific career is guaranteed by the branch they select.

Additional military options await students in hundreds of two- and four-year colleges that house programs in the Reserved Officers Training Corps (ROTC), or other officer-training programs with similar benefits. Students committing to these programs receive financial assistance to attend college; in exchange, students make a commitment to serve in a branch of the armed forces for a period of active duty that usually lasts four years, followed by reserve duty that is usually an additional four years.

Finally, students with strong academic records and good physical abilities can apply to any of the United States Military Academies, where they can earn a four-year degree in a number of academic, vocational and military fields, with all expenses paid. Successful applicants typically have superior grades and extracurricular accomplishments, can pass a rigorous physical exam and must receive an appointment to an academy, typically offered by a member of Congress.

Post-Graduate Years

Some students get to the end of their high school careers and simply need another year to be ready for college. Perhaps their time management skills need some honing, or they're just beginning to get a feel for what it means to explore literature, do a real research paper or really get the most out of school. They're in the 12th grade, and they've passed all their classes, so they can't really stay at your school, but college isn't quite for them just yet.

Enter the idea of a post-graduate, or PG year. PG years are designed to give students the opportunities they need to make sure they'll get the most out of college, and they've been around for years. PG years are usually offered by private high schools, but students enrolled in PG programs aren't really in grade 13—the PG curriculum at most high schools has classes that aren't available to the other students in the high school, so it's really more like a school within a school. It's also important to note that most PG programs have a strong athletic component, since many PG students are athletes who need an additional year to bring up either their academic or athletic skills.

Gap Years

While some students may need another year of school to prepare for college, other students know they want to go to college, but not right away. For many of these students, a "gap" year between high school and college can give them the breather they need to make the most out of the college experience. Perhaps they want to teach English as a second language in another country, or join their family on a long visit to explore their heritage or do volunteer work they never had time for in high school. If that's the case, these students are very likely to take the year off and return to college with a new perspective on themselves and on the world, a view colleges value in their students.

Most students who have successful gap years usually plan them out before they apply to colleges as high school seniors. That means that if a student comes to you in April of their junior year to explore gap options, there's a good possibility it's a good idea; however, if they come to you in April of their senior year, you'll need to use your best counselor skills to determine if this request is based on a legitimate interest, or if there is a concern about being "ready" for college that needs to be addressed. The less specific their plan is, the less likely the student will get anything out of the year off, and the less likely they are to actually head on to college. If you ask for their plans, and they begin with, "Well, I'm not sure," it's time for a deeper discussion.

Many counselors are surprised to find that most colleges are more than happy to let admitted students have a gap year. The student usually gives the college an enrollment deposit and signs a commitment to attend the college the following fall; many colleges also require the student to pledge not to take other college classes during the gap year.

The gap year option is offered by many private colleges and some public colleges, but it is always better to ask than assume a college's policy on gap years.

FACTORS TO CONSIDER WHEN EXPLORING THESE OPTIONS

As students and families review the wide array of programs and colleges that offer learning opportunities after high school, it's important to keep the following factors in mind:

Cost

The wide range of tuition and fees makes cost an important consideration. New efforts are underway to help students determine if the cost of a particular program is "worth it," but answering that question is harder than it may seem. Is the value of college only measured by the career options a degree offers? Are the life experiences of living on campus and away from home worth the extra expense? Are there programs other than the student's "first choice" that would offer a similar experience that cost significantly less? This is where much of the counseling comes into the college counseling experience, where the counselor helps the student look past the data and logistics of applying to determine the best path for the student to pursue.

Early College

A number of school districts are offering the opportunity for students to take classes at a local college while also attending high school. These early college programs vary greatly, but many will allow 11th- and 12th-grade students to earn enough college credit to earn an associate degree either in high school or after an additional year of study at the local community college.

Students pursuing early college will want to make sure they understand the transferability of the college credits they are earning in high school. Many early college programs focus on career readiness and will include courses specific to a particular career. These courses may not be accepted for course credit at four-year institutions; in addition, students may have to take these courses in lieu of high school academic electives that can help students gain admission to four-year institutions right after high school.

For-Profit Institutions

For-profit colleges and postsecondary programs have the distinct goal of educating students while making money at the same time. In recent years, some for-profit colleges have been investigated for the large percentage of their revenues that come from students receiving federal assistance to go to college and the high dropout rates at some for-profit colleges.

Just as students need to get past the labels of "big" colleges and "liberal arts" schools, they will want to look closely at the same key elements of a for-profit college. After considering cost, curriculum, campus atmosphere, reputation, and comparative strengths of other available programs, the student will want to work closely with the counselor to make sure they fully understand the financial obligations they are taking on when enrolling at a for-profit institution.

International Options

US students looking for an international experience will want to evaluate the study abroad options available at each college. Many colleges will offer a semester or year of coursework taught by their own instructors at international locations, while others will partner with colleges abroad where students can take courses taught by professors working at that school. Students taking classes where these agreements are in place are generally assured that these classes will transfer for credit.

Other students who want to look beyond the study abroad options at their own school may want to enroll as a guest student at another US college that offers the international experience the student is interested in. In this case, the student will need to get the consent of his/her home institution to apply as a guest student, and make sure the study abroad program at the other institution is available to him/her as a guest student. Students pursuing this option will also want to make sure the courses will transfer back to their home school.

Another option open to US students is studying at the international campus of a US college. More and more colleges are opening campuses abroad, both to meet the study abroad needs of US students and to serve the growing college needs of students overseas. Since many of these programs also allow overseas students to study at the college's campus in the US, many students are attracted to the strong international presence of these programs.

Some US students want to maximize their overseas learning experience by applying as an international student to a college based outside the country. Because the admission requirements and deadlines vary greatly from college to college and from country to country, students are strongly advised to speak with their college counselor about these plans as early as the start of the junior year. This discussion should include awareness of the value of an overseas degree in the US job market, the value of the degree when applying to US graduate schools, and the transferability of credits to US colleges, should the student wish to return to the US to study before completing a degree overseas. Counselors will want to become familiar with cross-national partnerships or multi-institutional agreements. For example, familiarity with the Bologna Process of the European University Association (2014) that governs European universities, as well as the transfer agreements and articulation agreements governing the offerings of each overseas college that is of interest to the student, becomes imperative.

Online Options

A growing number of institutions are offering online classes, certificates and degrees, either as part of, or instead of, traditional face-to-face instruction. Depending on their design, online classes can allow students to complete the work at their own pace, or give them flexibility to learn in ways that meet the demands of their personal or professional lives. This is especially true with the advent of Massive Online Open Classes, or MOOCs, where colleges offer a course, certificate or degree online to the general public at little or no cost.

The flexible nature of online education is viewed to be its best attribute, but it can also be its greatest hindrance. Students excited by the idea of "class on my time" need to make sure they have the discipline to develop a personal schedule that will allow them to meet the demands of an online course, as well as the self-advocacy skills to reach out for help through the Internet—a skill that is very different from talking to an instructor after a face-to-face class. This is especially important if the student is studying a subject that is new to him/her or challenging for him/her. Many students will find the techniques needed to secure additional help online as an additional barrier to learning subject matter that is hard for them to begin with.

Students considering an online class as part of their college experience will want to work closely with their academic advisor to evaluate the student's schedule and readiness to meet the unique demands of this approach to learning. Students considering a completely online certificate or degree will want to work closely with their college counselor to evaluate these same attributes, as well as the value of the online degree in the workplace, graduate schools and when transferring to another institution.

TRANSFERRING AND REVERSE TRANSFERRING

Economic conditions are leading more students who are academically eligible to enter a four-year college right after graduation to consider transferring to a four-year college after a year or two of study at a local community college. This is requiring students and college counselors to be more aware of transfer policies at four-year institutions *before* starting college in order to get the most out of the community college experience. A similar trend is occurring with students who complete four-year degrees, then return to a community college to pick up a handful of classes to prepare them for graduate school. Known as *reverse transferring,* many college graduates will return to ask their college counselor for help in selecting a local college that would be the best choice to take required science courses for medical school, required history classes for law school or accounting classes for an MBA degree.

CASE STUDIES

All of these postsecondary options create multiple pathways for students to consider. While the following case studies present a cursory overview of some of each student's interests, they are intended to put the information presented in the chapter into practice.

Paul will be the first in his family to go to college, and is the only child in his family. A good student, Paul has already been contacted by several colleges out of state to let him know about merit scholarship opportunities, including some colleges with strong neuroscience programs Paul is interested in. Paul is excited at the idea of going away to college, but he is also concerned he will miss his family too much. This same sentiment has been expressed by Paul's father, who says he thinks it will be hard for him to "let him go."

Possibilities for Paul Include:

- Researching four-year colleges (both close to home and farther away) that offer neuroscience programs

- Researching four-year colleges (both close to home and farther away) that offer strong science programs that would prepare Paul for admission to a strong graduate school in neuroscience

- Investigating two-year colleges close to home that would allow Paul a gradual demonstration of autono-

my; this research would include investigation of two-year colleges that have articulation agreements or automatic acceptance policies with colleges with strong neuroscience programs, where all of Paul's credits would be accepted for transfer, or he would automatically be admitted to the neuroscience program

- Looking into gap year programs where Paul would defer college for a year, while engaging in neuroscience research to see if this is something he really wants to pursue

- Reviewing four-year colleges farther from home, where Paul could enroll as a full-time online student for a semester.

Pursuing these options (and others) maximizes Paul's options and gives the counselor time to help Paul and his family explore any separation anxiety that is natural during the senior year.

Julie is a natural-born computer programmer. At 16, she's already skipped one grade and sold three smartphone apps that are doing very well. Julie has never been a great student, but has drawn the attention of a few four-year colleges. Her current interest lies in learning more about current trends in computer programming; after that, her path is unclear.

Possibilities for Julie Include:

- Looking at vocational and technical training programs that offer computer programming

- Reviewing the certificate and two-year options available at community colleges

- Considering a gap year to work as an intern or independently writing code

- Developing a list of four-year colleges with strong computer science programs, and determining if it would be best for Julie to apply as a freshman or transfer student at those institutions

- Investigating the computer training and programming options in the military.

With Julie's advanced computer skills, it would be more challenging to find a technical training or military program that would meet her interests, but these could still be viable options.

Brandon is a very bright student whose family has limited means. His parents didn't complete high school and are certain they can't afford any college, which is why they are insisting Brandon start at a local community college.

Possibilities for Brandon Include:

- Completing a college search based on Brandon's interests

- Reviewing the results of this search with Brandon and his parents, making sure to discuss the financial aid opportunities at each school, as well as the honors college options available at larger colleges, especially research institutions

- Looking into the options available at the local community colleges, including scholarships for high-achieving students, transfer agreements and articulations with four-year colleges

- Reviewing the financial aid options available to Brandon at highly selective colleges, making sure Brandon's parents realize how affordable some of these options can be

- Discussing the option of enrolling in ROTC at a four-year college.

USE OF DATA

Because the college selection process is a blending of head and heart, counselors and students can use data sources to develop a postsecondary plan that includes student visits to colleges and programs, where additional data can be gathered. Intangible factors of the college selection process (the "feel" of the campus, the "fit" with other students on campus) can be ascertained via the following:

- Results of career interest inventories (Discover, ACT World of Work, state-developed tools)

- Results of career aptitude batteries (ASVAB, state-developed tests)

- Online college search engines that compare student interests to the qualities of two- and four-year colleges (College Board, Zinch, College Navigator)

- High school grades

- Where applicable, results of standardized test scores (SAT, ACT)

COLLEGE-GOING CULTURE

Effective college counselors prepare students to make the most of postsecondary options by building a series of experiences familiarizing students and their families with these options long before students have to select which options to pursue and which programs to apply to. These activities include:

- Familiarizing students with different college options by taking class field trips to museums, cultural events and middle-school-focused admission activities held at nearby college campuses (grades 6–11)

- Bringing in speakers from different colleges to address the qualities of their institution (grades 6–11)

- Creating a robust career counseling program for students to explore possible job options, with an emphasis on the education and training tracks required for specific careers and the use of career interest and aptitude measures (grades 6–11)

- Holding grade-specific college night programs for students and their families that introduce the idea of college (grade 6), the academic requirements for all postsecondary options (grade 7), and exploration of various college and vocational training programs through individual tours and visits of these programs and their facilities (grades 8–11).

CONCLUSION

With tens of thousands of postsecondary options available, students can see the college selection process as an exciting opportunity to explore a host of possibilities, or look at the menu of choices and be overwhelmed by a sense of not knowing where to begin.

This is where a college counselor can make a world of difference. Using a multitude of strategies, including individual counseling sessions, small- and large- group discovery activities, evening programs for parents, and guided online searches in the school's computer lab, students can develop a strong sense of the opportunities that best meet their goals, abilities, needs, and interests, while developing a good sense of what doesn't work for them as well.

A well-developed relationship with the student that includes activities in self-awareness and career awareness, combined with the well-honed expertise of a college counseling professional to help the student compare and contrast different options, can create an atmosphere of opportunity that will inspire the student to embrace college selection and create a number of strong options for his/her life beyond high school.

DISCUSSION QUESTIONS

1. The wide array of postsecondary options suggests students need ample time to be introduced to these choices and to consider which options will best meet the student's academic, career and personal goals without taking away the focus on success in school. What demands (time, resources, access to students, caseload) most challenge reaching this introduction, and how can those demands be overcome?

2. Students in the same school or the same neighborhood may have common assumptions about postsecondary options that need to be overcome. What assumptions are common among the students and families you work with, and what strategies can be used to overcome those assumptions?

3. Students also may have individual assumptions about postsecondary options they are unwilling to share, for fear of being judged as naïve, ignorant or unusual. What strategies are most effective in working with your students and families to bring these individual assumptions out in a non-judgmental way?

ABOUT THE AUTHOR

Patrick O'Connor is associate dean of college counseling at Cranbrook Kingswood School in metropolitan Detroit (MI). A past president of NACAC and Michigan ACAC, Patrick also teaches Counseling in the College Selection Process as both a graduate class and professional development program. Patrick is the author of *College is Yours 2.0*, and writes regularly for *Huffington Post, HS Counselor Week,* and his own website, collegeisyours.com. His work has also appeared in *The Washington Post, The Christian Science Monitor,* and *Diverse: Issues in Higher Education.*

Patrick is on the Common Application Outreach Advisory Board, the board of directors of the Michigan College Access Network, and the credentialing commission for the American Institute of Certified Educational Planners.

A member of the Political Science Faculty at Oakland Community College, he is a recipient of the Outstanding Faculty Award from Oakland Community College (MI), the Margaret Addis Service to NACAC Award, NACAC's Government Relations Award, and the William Gramenz Award (for outstanding contributions to college counseling in Michigan.) He holds five college degrees, including a PhD in education administration.

REFERENCES

Big Future. Retrieved from *https://bigfuture.collegeboard.org/college-search.*

Bogart, Julie. (2011) What are liberal arts? *My College Guide.* Retrieved from *http://mycollegeguide.org/articles/8/145/what-are-liberal-arts.*

Bologna—an overview of the main elements. Retrieved from *http://www.eua.be/eua-work-and-policy-area/building-the-european-higher-education-area/bologna-basics/Bologna-an-overview-of-the-main-elements.aspx.*

Brown, Adam. (2010, October 5). Liberal arts college vs. university. The Admission Centre. Retrieved from *http://www.theadmissioncentre.com/2010/liberal-arts-college-vs-university/#axzz1qzBWKCGL.*

Classification description. Carnegie Foundation for the Advancement of Teaching. Retrieved from *http://classifications.carnegiefoundation.org/descriptions/basic.php.*

Colleges that offer any ROTC program ROTC. CollegeToolkit.com. Retrieved from *http://colleges.collegetoolkit.com/colleges/browse/rotc/results/any_rotc_program/1.aspx.*

Fast facts—degree completion. (2014). National Center for Education Statistics. Retrieved from *http://nces.ed.gov/fastfacts/display.asp?id=40.*

Geller, Harold A. (2001). A brief history of community colleges and a personal view of some issues (open admissions, occupational training and leadership). Resources Information Center Document ED 495881. Fairfax, VA: George Mason.

How many career and technical programs are there in the United States? Association for Career & Technical Education. Retrieved from *https://www.acteonline.org/general.aspx?id=2733#many_cte*.

Lee, S.S. (2002–2003). Unlearning: a critical element in the learning process. *Essays on Teaching Excellence,* 14(2). Retrieved from *http://ucat.osu.edu/OSU_users/essays/v14n2.html*.

Should parents be concerned when their student decides to change majors. Retrieved from *http://www.universityparent.com/tennessee-state-university/articles/newsletter-only/should-parents-be-concerned-when-their-student-decides-to-change-majors-6/*

What is the difference between a college and a university? Retrieved from *http://wiki.answers.com/Q/What_is_the_difference_between_a_college_and_a_university*.

What is the military obligation following college graduation? Retrieved from *http://www.uml.edu/Army-ROTC/about-Us/FAQ.aspx*.

WEB SITES TO EXPLORE

For College Searches

- Big Future (two- and four-year colleges): *www.bigfuture.collegeboard.org*

- College Navigator (two- and four-year colleges and certificate search): *http://nces.ed.gov/collegenavigator*

- Community College Finder (community colleges only): *www.aacc.nche.edu/Pages/CCFinder.aspx*

- Fiske Guide to the Colleges (four-year colleges): *www.fiskeguide.com*

- Petersons: *www.petersons.com*

- Rugg's Recommendations on the Colleges (four-year colleges): *www.ruggsrecommendations.com*

- Technical Schools Directory: *www.techschooldirectory.com*

- Zinch: *www.zinch.com*

For Military Training

US Air Force: *www.airforce.com*

US Air Force Academy: *www.usafa.af.mil*

US Army: *www.army.mil*

US Coast Guard: *www.uscg.mil*

US Coast Guard Academy: *www.cga.edu*

US Military Academy (West Point): *www.usma.edu*

US Marine Corps: *www.marines.com*

US Navy: *www.navy.com*

US Naval Academy: *www.usna.edu*

For Post Graduate (PG) Years

Post Graduate Boarding Schools: *www.boardingschoolreview.com/pg_boarding_schools.php*

The Postgraduate Year: *http://privateschool.about.com/od/students/qt/pgyear.htm*

For Gap Years

Gap Year: *www.nacacnet.org/studentinfo/articles/pages/gap-year-.aspx*

USA Gap Year Fair: *www.usagapyearfairs.org/programs*

Chapter 14: Working with Diverse Student Populations

Chrystal A. George Mwangi, PhD
@DrChrystalGM

College counseling is growing increasingly complex as students with diverse backgrounds, talents and goals seek access to postsecondary opportunities (Bridgeland & Bruce, 2011; Kinzie, Palmer, Hayek, Hossler, Jacob, & Cummings, 2004).

In order to effectively provide support and advocacy for students and families, it is critical that practitioners are prepared to address the needs of multiple demographics (Bryan, Holcomb-McCoy, Moore-Thomas, & Day-Vines, 2009; McDonough, 2005). This chapter provides a review of relevant data, research and recommendations to equip practitioners with foundational knowledge and resources for working with today's students. Three questions are explored: (1) What student demographic trends are having a major impact on college counseling practice and what are these students' college preparation needs? (2) What are key practices for effectively engaging and meeting the needs of diverse student populations? (3) What resources can practitioners reference when working with diverse student populations?

This chapter examines the characteristics, college preparation needs and factors related to finding a college "fit" for four broad student demographics, which are broken down into sub-populations. These include: (1) underserved students (homeless/foster care students; undocumented immigrant students; LGBT students); (2) students with special talents (performing/visual arts students; student athletes; students seeking a gap year); (3) students with distinctive social connections (military-connected students; student legacies); (4) students considering community college (students with academic readiness challenges; students seeking a low-cost college option). While these groups do not provide an exhaustive account of existing diverse student populations, they provide a useful starting point for discussing this critical topic and reflect some of the major demographic groups seeking access to college that have not been previously emphasized in other chapters. Each section includes a description of the student demographic; an overview of questions students might ask in determining a college "fit"; recommendations for working with the student demographic; and additional references and resources.

WORKING WITH STUDENTS WHO ARE UNDERSERVED

The national college access and completion agenda acknowledges that the US economy cannot thrive without a commitment to ensuring postsecondary opportunities and success for populations traditionally underserved. While other chapters in this text focus on traditionally underrepresented groups including low-income students, first-generation to college students and students of color, this chapter focuses on three populations that are not discussed elsewhere: homeless/foster students, undocumented immigrant students and LGBT students. While each of these three student demographics have distinct needs and characteristics, all share the challenge of (in)visibility. Factors such as fear, previous negative experiences, and lack of trust or personal readiness can prevent students from disclosing aspects of their identity, immigration status or home environment to school staff. Therefore, practitioners must emphasize an inclusive and safe space for all students—one in which resources are available to meet a wide range of college preparation needs and emphasizes the importance of considering campus climate for diversity when engaging in college selection. In addition to building trusting relationships, working with each of these student populations requires being knowledgeable of the policies and programs that impact them.

Homeless and Foster Care Students

There are approximately 1.3 million homeless youth in US public schools, and according to the National Center for Homeless Education (NCHE), this number has increased 85 percent since the economic downturn. The term "homeless" refers to lacking a fixed, consistent and adequate nighttime residence; however, homeless students' circumstances can vary from living in a friend's home or hotel/motel, residing in a homeless shelter, sleeping in cars, public parks, or abandoned buildings (Tierney, Gupton, & Hallet, 2008).

There is a pipeline that exists between homeless youth and the foster care system. The National Center for Family Homelessness reports that homeless children are more than 10 times as likely to be placed in foster care than non-homeless youth. The Administration for Children, Youth and Families (ACYF) calculates that there are approximately 400,000 children in foster care and the average length of time in the system is 22.4 months. Studies examining college access for foster youth highlight that these students often have high college aspirations, but are challenged by a number of barriers and inequities. For example, annually, 30,000 foster youth "age out" of the foster care system at age 18, but only half complete high school, and approximately 20 percent go to college (Unrau, Font, & Rawls, 2012). Similarly, 40 percent of homeless adults lack a high school diploma, and fewer than two percent have a college degree (Tierney et al., 2008).

Homeless youth and foster care youth are often low-income, first-generation students. Research shows that a college degree can lead to a number of positive outcomes for these students and is one of the few ways that they can significantly improve their economic circumstances, earning potential and social/cultural capital within their families and communities (Engle & Tinto, 2008). When students in the bottom income quintile earn a college degree, their chances of moving out of this income bracket increase by 50 percent (Office of the President, 2014). Thus, access to college, and particularly finding the right college fit to improve the probability of academic success and degree completion, are critical.

While these students share similar needs to first-generation and low-income students (see chapters 17 and 18 on these populations), the lack of a stable residence for homeless and foster youth creates unique needs as well. For example, homelessness can often affect academic progress in college (e.g., high absence rates, inadequate homework space, lack of consistent access to the Internet or other resources to complete assignments). For homeless students and foster care students, finding a college fit may require consideration of additional questions, such as:

- Are there funding opportunities or fee waivers available to homeless/foster youth in my state or specifically at this institution?

- If I live on campus, what is the availability of housing options during campus breaks?

- What employment and transportation options are available to me at this institution?

- What types of healthcare services are available at this institution, and what are the associated costs?

- What academic support and counseling programs are offered at this campus, and are they free of charge?

- Does this campus offer targeted support programs, counseling, and/or mentoring for homeless students and/or for students aged out of the foster care system?

Recommendations and resources. Because homelessness is often perceived as a stigma, students experiencing this or who are in foster care may wish to remain invisible and not openly discuss this aspect of their lives. Therefore, identifying these students can be a challenge, and yet, gaining their trust is critical. Research also highlights that many homeless and foster youth have lower levels of self-esteem and academic confidence (Tierney et al., 2008). Thus, in addition to building a trusting relationship, it is important to consider how your work with these students can foster efficacy, as well as build upon students' resilience, persistence and ambition.

There are important policies that you should be aware of that directly impact homeless students or foster care youth. For example, the **McKinney-Vento Homeless Assistance Act** is an important federal policy for addressing the education of homeless youth. This act has helped to increase the number of homeless youth enrolled in K–12 education by more than 30 percent over the past 20 years (Tierney et al., 2008). It seeks to remove barriers to school attendance for homeless students, promote the success of these students through interagency collaboration, and prohibit school segregation between homeless and non-homeless students. You can learn more about the McKinney-Vento Act on the NCHE Web site: *http://center. serve.org/nche/legis/mv.php.*

Cost is often a primary factor for obtaining access to college among homeless and foster care youth. Yet, there are a number of programs and policies that can help to make college preparation and college-going more affordable for students. These students may qualify for fee waivers or fee reductions for SAT/ACT tests, AP exams and college applications. The FAFSA process can also work differently for homeless and foster care youth. For example, the **College Access and Opportunity Act** allows unaccompanied homeless students to declare an independent status on the FAFSA (Dukes, 2013). However, it is important that students know that this will require their living situation to be verified by a McKinney-Vento school district liaison, a homeless or transitional shelter director or an independent living program.

Another policy addressing cost is the **Promoting Safe and Stable Families Amendment** (part of the Foster Care Independence Act). This amendment provides state governments with funding to pay for the Educational Training Voucher (ETV) program. ETV gives up to $5,000 per year to foster care youth enrolled in postsecondary education (up to age 23). Students have to enroll in ETV prior to turning 21 (see the Foster Care to Success Web site for information about ETV: *www.fc2success.org/programs/education-training-vouchers*). Some states have specific college-related programs targeting foster care youth, ranging from scholarships to college tuition waivers. Additionally, there are a number of private scholarship programs, including the Casey Family Programs, which provides up to $10,000 per year to foster youth. However, these students must be under age 25 and have spent at least 12 months in foster care without being adopted.

Lastly, it is important to recognize and be prepared to act as a resource for the personal needs students may have that are less directly related to college preparation, such as information on local homeless shelters. State coordinators for homeless education, social services staff and homeless shelter staff can serve as resources and as partners in working with homeless and foster care youth, as well as in building your knowledge about local resources available to students.

Additional resources to assist you in working with homeless students and foster care students:

- Foster Care to Success—*www.fc2success.org*
- Legal Center for Foster Care and Education—*www.fostercareandeducation.org*
- National Association for the Education of Homeless Children and Youth—*www.naehcy.org*
- *Providing effective financial aid assistance to students from foster care and unaccompanied homeless youth: A key to higher education access and success. Version 2.0.* Retrieved from the California Court Appointed Special Advocates for Children Web site: *http://www.californiacasa.org/Downloads/Providing_Effective_Financial_Aid.pdf*

Undocumented Immigrant Students

Twenty percent of young people growing up in the United States are immigrants or have parents who emigrated from other countries, and it is projected that by 2040, one in

every three children in the United States will grow up in an immigrant household (Suarez-Orozco, Suarez-Orozco, & Todorova, 2008). While the majority of today's immigrant families enter and remain in the United States legally, there are a number of families with an undocumented status. The National Immigration Law Center defines an undocumented immigrant as a foreign national who either entered the United States without legal authorization or who entered legally, but experienced a lapse in legal status. There are nearly 3.2 million undocumented immigrants under age 24 in the United States (Perez, 2010), and approximately 65,000 undocumented students graduate from US high schools annually (Gonzales, 2009). While the exact number is unknown, Educators for Fair Consideration (E4FC) cite research estimating that 7,000 to 13,000 undocumented students are enrolled in US colleges and universities.

Many undocumented students were brought to the United States at a young age and have attended school in this country for the majority of their lives. Some students do not learn of their undocumented status until the college preparation process or a job search, when they are asked to produce a social security number. While research highlights that many undocumented students often have above-average academic achievement and college aspirations in comparison to US-citizen peers, only 10 percent of these high school graduates will enroll in college (Perez, 2010). This is due to a number of factors, including the lack of a pathway to US citizenship and the high cost of college. The average income of undocumented immigrant families is 40 percent less than US-native families and legal immigrant families (Gonzales, 2009), which makes financing college unaffordable, particularly due to limited or no access to government financial aid.

For undocumented students, the combination of a pathway to US citizenship and a college degree can create major gains in upward economic mobility, such as opportunities for better-paying and benefited jobs. Because these individuals would likely pay more in taxes and have more funds to invest in the economy, these outcomes can also positively impact US society (Gonzales, 2009). Yet, currently there is not an overarching federal policy that provides undocumented students with access to US citizenship or a college degree. Due to these limitations, undocumented students must consider the answers to a number of questions when determining college fit:

- What funding opportunities exist for me if I attend this institution?

- What private scholarships or grants exist nationally or within my state, local community or at the college that I'm interested in that I qualify for as an undocumented immigrant?

- Does my state offer in-state tuition policies, and, if so, what is the process for obtaining in-state tuition?

- Does my state have a policy targeting college access for undocumented immigrants? If so, what does this policy entail?

- What are the formal and informal college admission policies regarding undocumented immigrants at the institution(s) I am interested in attending?

- Are there support networks or programs for undocumented students at this campus?

Recommendations and resources. Undocumented students may not openly disclose their immigration status to you for a number of reasons, including fear of deportation or their own lack of knowledge about their status. Legally, you are not permitted to ask students of their immigration status, and therefore, it is important that you ensure all students are aware of the resources available to undocumented students and that you communicate your ability to serve as a resource, particularly if you reside in a state with a large population of this demographic.

Serving as a resource requires you to remain current regarding federal- and state-level policies related to undocumented immigrants and particularly to undocumented youth seeking access to college. At the federal level, the **Development, Relief and Education for Alien Minors (DREAM) Act** was introduced to Congress in 2001, but has yet to be enacted into law. The DREAM Act would create a pathway to US citizenship by allowing qualified undocumented students the ability to obtain permanent resident status and then, with successful college enrollment or military enlistment, eventually become eligible to apply for US citizenship (Gonzales, 2009). This policy would also allow students to be eligible for some forms of federal financial aid.

Although the DREAM Act has not passed at the national level, recently the Obama administration enacted the **Deferred Action for Childhood Arrivals (DACA) pro-**

gram, which allows undocumented students to request temporary relief of deportation while in school and allows them to apply for work authorization. The deferred action is valid for two years and can be renewed for an additional two years, but requires an application and is granted on a case-by-case basis. While national policy regarding undocumented immigrant students continues to be debated, a number of states have developed policies that expand or restrict access to college for these students. For example, the National Conference of State Legislatures reports that 18 states currently have provisions allowing undocumented students eligibility for in-state tuition, five states allow eligibility for state financial aid, two states prohibit admission to undocumented immigrants at public postsecondary institutions, and three states specifically prohibit in-state tuition for this population (see the NCSL Web site for additional details: *www.ncsl.org/research/education/undocumented-student-tuition-state-action.aspx*).

Because undocumented students cannot qualify for federal financial aid, they should be made aware of alternative college funding opportunities as well as low-cost college options. Some states offer in-state tuition rates to these students, but these policies can require a number of forms and processes that students may need assistance with to complete. Typically, students need to have attended school in the United States for at least three years and graduate from high school in the state of residence. There also are a number of privately funded national-, state- and local-level scholarships that exist for undocumented students. Additionally, some private colleges offer reduced tuition prices or scholarships for undocumented immigrants. Due to cost, many college-bound undocumented students initially enroll in community college as a more affordable option; however, this can create under-matching (selecting an institution below one's academic qualifications), which can lead to negative academic outcomes. Therefore, providing students with an understanding of the transfer process is important if the student's ultimate goal is a bachelor's degree (see section on "Working with Students Interested in Community College" in this chapter for additional information).

Additional resources to assist you in working with undocumented immigrant students:

- Educators for Fair Consideration—*www.e4fc.org*

- MALDEF Scholarship Resources—*www.maldef.org/leadership/scholarships/index.html*

- NASFAA Student Aid Tips Sheet for Undocumented Students—*www.nasfaa.org/WorkArea/linkit.aspx?LinkIdentifier=id&ItemID=6528*

- National Immigration Law Center—*www.nilc.org*

- Perez, W. (2009). *We ARE Americans: Undocumented students pursuing the American dream.* Sterling, VA: Stylus.

- Rebecchi, M. (2013-2014). *Advising undocumented and deferred action students.* Retrieved from the National College Access Network Web site: *www.collegeaccess.org/images/documents/Advisor_Toolbox_doc/Advising_Undocumented_Students_Rev_4_.pdf*

LGBT Students

LGBT stands for individuals who identify as lesbian, gay, bisexual, or transgender. While the term "LGBT" is used in this chapter, it can also be expanded to include individuals who identify as queer, intersex, asexual, or ally. There are additional identities, including genderqueer and other identities within the asexuality spectrum that may have similar needs and experiences in the college preparation process as well.

A study of 10,000 LGBT teenagers conducted by the Human Rights Campaign found that 56 percent were out to their immediate family, and 91 percent were out to close friends. However, the survey showed that only 28 percent were out to teachers, and 11 percent were out to school coaches. Therefore, as with the other student populations discussed in this section, the needs of LGBT youth may go unrecognized by school staff, including counselors working with them in the college preparation process. Yet, LGBT students can face a number of challenges during their secondary and postsecondary experiences, including increased rates of mental health issues, sexual health risks, substance abuse, and family issues leading to negative health outcomes (Angeli, 2009). These challenges are not due to students' sexual identity, but are often a result of a negative environment (e.g., a hetero-normative school climate, bullying, lack of same-identity role models, safe spaces or support). Therefore, selecting an inclusive and supportive campus climate for LGBT students is important. Questions that these students might ask as they search for colleges or make an ultimate decision include:

- What is the campus climate like regarding LGBT students? Is there an institutional commitment to LGBT issues? Is this reflected in action, such as programming, safe spaces, safe space training programs, gender-neutral housing/bathrooms, trans healthcare options, etc.?

- Am I interested in academic resources or opportunities around LGBT issues? If so, does the campus offer LGBT-focused academic centers, LGBT studies programs or LGBT courses?

- What social organizations, support services or counseling services are available related to my identity/identities? How important might these services and support be to my college experience?

- What are the campus nondiscrimination policies?

- Is data collected on out LGBT faculty/staff and students? If so, what does the data say?

- Is the surrounding community outside of the institution a safe and inclusive space for LGBT individuals?

Recommendations and resources. As with the other populations discussed in this section, there may be a number of risk factors impacting the academic achievement and college preparation of LGBT youth. For example, the differences in priorities and experiences between LGBT and non-LGBT students is reflected in research highlighting that while many non-LGBT youth report their top three challenges as academics, career/college aspirations, and financial pressures related to college or job; for LGBT youth, the top three reported challenges were non-accepting families, school problems/bullying, and fear of being out or open (Human Rights Campaign, 2012). Unlike their heterosexual peers, the stressors that LGBT students find most salient may not be college- or academic-related, but may impact their overall academic success. Therefore, addressing the whole student is important to the college preparation process, and it is important that you are educated on working with this population of students so that you can be prepared to be a resource and source of support.

Because many LGBT youth do not disclose their sexual identity to school staff, it is important that your office be communicated as a safe and inclusive environment for all students. Additionally, information and resources targeting LGBT students (e.g., scholarships) should be accessible to all students. You should assume that there are LGBT youth who attend your school, even if students have not come out to you.

Students who are out to you may seek guidance in considering whether/how they want to identify and disclose information about themselves during the college application and enrollment process (e.g., disclosing sexual identity in a college application essay, college admission interview or to one's college roommate). While there is not a correct answer to this question, it is important that you are able to help students process their decision, as well as possible outcomes regarding this decision. Furthermore, research suggests that while campus climate for LGBT students is not the number-one criteria for selecting a college or university among this population, it is often one of the top five factors (Burleson, 2010). Therefore, encouraging students to consider how inclusive and welcoming a campus may be to LGBT students and to issues of diversity more generally can also be critical to finding a positive college fit.

Additional resources to assist you in working with LGBT students:

- Baez, J. et al. (2007). *The gay and lesbian guide to college life*. New York: The Princeton Review.

- Consortium of Higher Education Lesbian Gay Bisexual Transgender Resource Professionals—*www.lgbtcampus.org*

- Gay, Lesbian, & Straight Education Network—*www.glsen.org*

- LGBT-Friendly Campus Pride Index—*www.campusprideindex.org*

- It Gets Better project—*www.itgetsbetter.org*

- Point Foundation (scholarships and scholars program)—*www.pointfoundation.org*

WORKING WITH STUDENTS WITH SPECIAL TALENTS

For some students, a special talent plays a major role in the college preparation process and search for the best college fit. This section discusses two types of talents that can both create complexities and open up a wealth of opportunities in college choice: the performing/visual arts and athletics. Students interested in formally pursuing the arts or athletics often have a number of additional factors to prepare for and consider, such as portfolios, auditions and special recruiters. Many students engage in

years of preparation and commitment to their talent and view college as a means of continuing to hone their skills and potentially build them into a career.

Additionally, this section includes students interested in a "gap year." While students pursuing a gap year have differing needs than those in the arts or athletics, they often share a similar desire to sharpen a skill or interest, which can provide future direction in the consideration of postsecondary options.

Students in the Arts

The forms of art that students pursue in college is wide-ranging and can include dance, drama/theater, instrumental music, vocal music, music education, visual arts, and film. Research illustrates a number of positive associations between arts participation and academic achievement and college aspirations. For example, students participating in school music or performing arts are more likely to report college aspirations than their peers (Child Trends, 2012). Additionally, Ruppert (2006) found that students with high arts involvement perform better on standardized tests, watch less television and have higher levels of civic engagement than peers.

Questions that a student with a desire to pursue visual or performing arts in college should consider include:
- How significant is the pursuit of this talent to my overall college selection? Where does it rank in comparison to other aspects of the institution(s) I am considering?

- Am I intending for this talent to be my academic major, or is it something that I am willing to engage in more informally while in college (e.g., student organization)?

- Is the arts program a good fit for my skills and needs? Is the campus a good overall match for my needs as a student?

- How large is the program, and how often will I have the opportunity to perform?

- Do professors in the major work directly with undergraduate students? What resources are available to undergraduate students (e.g., studio space)?

- What is the reputation of the program in the field? Where are graduates placed professionally?

- What types of funding or professional opportunities are available (e.g., scholarships, internships)?

- What is the acceptance rate for students in the program/with my special talent?

Recommendations and resources. It is important to work with students to help determine how much of a role their talent will ultimately have on their college choice. Students who hope to pursue a professional career in the arts will have differing needs from students who want to continue involvement in the arts more recreationally. Working with students' performing/visual arts teachers or other professionals can help to determine students' skill level and fit with particular institutions. There may also be differing expectations between students and their parents regarding the role the arts will play in the students' college and career goals. Yet, regardless of the level of influence the arts has when selecting a postsecondary option, it is important that students consider the institution as a whole, not solely one program, because interests may change while in college, an injury can occur that prevents performance or admission may be gained to the institution, but not to the arts-related major/program.

You should also educate yourself on the different options available to students and the impact that these options can have on their ability to pursue their special talent. For example, there are a number of degree options in the arts that each has differing academic requirements and meaning to future employers. These include a bachelor's of arts (BA), bachelor's of music (BM), bachelor's of music education (BME), and a bachelor's of fFine arts (BFA). Additionally, while many students select a program within a traditional four-year college or university, there are other institutional options, such as conservatories or schools of art and design that may be of interest to students.

The college application timeline and materials are often different for students seriously pursuing the arts as part of their postsecondary experience. Students with this talent should start the process early and begin preparing samples of their work and learning the requirements of the program(s) they are interested in pursuing. It is important that students are aware of auditions, portfolio requirements or resumes specifically targeting their talent that may be expected in addition to the traditional application materials. Students may also be eligible for talent-based scholarships that have extra requirements.

Students interested in pursuing their talent in college may benefit from attending summer programs in the arts on a college campus to get a sense of the experience. During the college search, suggest that students inquire to colleges about any special events, opportunities or contacts for prospective students interested in the arts. There are often targeted college fairs and other events for students in the arts such National Portfolio Days (*www.portfolioday.net*) to help students assess their talents and prepare for the college search process.

Additional resources to assist you in working with students in the arts:
- Association of Independent Colleges of Art and Design (AICAD)—*www.aicad.org*
- Educational Theatre Association—*www.scholtheatre.org*
- NACAC's list of performing arts and visual arts college fairs—*www.nacacnet.org/college-fairs/PVA-College-Fairs/Pages/default.aspx*
- NACAC's tips for performing and visual arts students—*www.nacacnet.org/studentinfo/articles/Pages/Prospective-Performing-and-Visual-Arts-Students.aspx*
- National Association for Music Education—*http://musiced.nafme.org*

Student Athletes

Nearly 7.8 million students participate in high school athletics (National Federation of State High School Associations, 2014). However, only three percent to 11 percent of high school athletes go on to play at the National Collegiate Athletic Association (NCAA) level in college (percentage varies based on gender and sport) (NCAA, 2013). Approximately two percent of high school athletes receive sports scholarships to play in the NCAA (NCAA, 2013). The NCAA regulates more than 460,000 student athletes at over 1,200 colleges, universities and affiliate organizations (NCAA, 2013).

The NCAA defines student athletes as college students who are listed on the varsity team, practice with the team/receive coaching from the varsity coach or receive student aid based on athletic talent (Irick, 2013). Yet, there are thousands of students who play sports in college outside of the NCAA, either through other associations or non-association related teams (e.g., club sports).

Students considering playing sports in college may want to consider the following questions:

- How significant is the pursuit of this talent to my overall college choice? Where does it rank in comparison to other aspects of the institution?

- Am I intending to play sports at the varsity level, or am I am willing to engage in athletics more informally (e.g., club sport)?

- Is the athletic program a good fit for my skills and needs? Is the campus a good overall match for my needs as a student?

- How large is the athletics program, and how often will I have the opportunity to play?

- What types of sports-related funding opportunities are available?

- What is my level of athletic talent, and how does that fit within the team? What is the likelihood of me making the team?

- What are expectations of players (e.g., practicing, academics)?

- What type of academic support is available for student athletes at the institution?

- What is the environment like within the athletic program (relationship among team members, relationship with coach(es))?

Recommendations and resources. Similar to student artists, it is important for students interested in college athletics to begin the process early, often beginning to communicate with colleges of interest early in sophomore or junior year. Yet, understanding the athletic eligibility requirements of an association is important as early as the 9th grade. Work with students and their families to determine how important athletics are to the overall college selection for a student and for students to understand that, ultimately, they are selecting a college, not solely an athletic team. Additionally, you should have knowledge of the different athletic associations and divisions to help students understand the choices they have and the impact of those choices on their ultimate goals.

Student athletes, particularly those planning to play NCAA sports, will experience a different application timeline and process than their peers. Therefore, it is important that you are knowledgeable of the recruitment process and are prepared to provide guidance to students. For example, factors such as preparing a video showcasing talent or having an official visit are often part of recruitment. Some students may need to wait an additional year after high school to improve their athletic skills (see the previous chapter for information on the postgraduate [PG] year). The NCAA also has a number of requirements and regulations for student athletes and the recruitment process. Yet, it is critical that students understand that although they may meet academic eligibility requirements to play a collegiate sport, this does not mean that they have met the college's admission requirements.

There are a number of individuals who may be involved in the college preparation process of student athletes, including school coaches, private coaches, college recruiters, and external recruiting agencies/scouts. Building relationships with high school coaches is critical for you to remain a part of the process and to work collaboratively with athletics staff. One suggestion is to work with your school's coaches to have a college night information session for student athletes. Invite local college athletics staff that can give general advice. Information can be provided to students about eligibility requirements and factors to expect during their college search. Additionally, this provides an opportunity to inform students and families of the recruitment process and rules regarding athletic recruitment.

Additional resources to assist you in working with student athletes:

- 2014–15 NCAA Guide for the College Bound Student Athlete—Retrieved from the NCAA Web site: *www.ncaapublications.com/productdownloads/CBSA15.pdf*

- Graduation and college success rates for college athletics programs—*http://fs.ncaa.org/Docs/newmedia/public/rates/index.html*

- National Association of Intercollegiate Athletics—*www.naia.org*

- National Collegiate Athletic Association (NCAA)—*www.ncaa.org*

- National Junior College Athletic Association—*www.njcaa.org*

- NCAA Eligibility Center—*www.eligibilitycenter.org*

Students Interested in a Gap Year

The American Gap Association Web site states that a gap year is, "A structured period of time when students take a break from formal education to increase self-awareness, learn from different cultures and experiment with possible careers." Although it is called a gap "year," the experience may be longer or shorter, occur in the United States or abroad, and typically involves activities such as teaching, engaging in research, studying/learning a language, working (job/internship), or volunteering. There are no formal estimates on student participation in gap years, although a number of organizations have recently formed to meet what appears to be a growing demand for this experience.

Research suggests that students often engage in a gap year for personal development or due to academic burnout (Haigler & Nelson, 2013). While parents may worry that a gap year will lead to a student not returning to school, Haigler & Nelson's (2013) study of 280 students taking a gap year illustrated that 90 percent enrolled in college within a year of the experience. Many students did find that the experience either confirmed original ideas about a career path/academic major or that it opened up a path they had not previously considered. Additionally, students who participated in a gap year found that they gained a stronger understanding of self, other cultures or professional goals as a result of the experience (Haigler & Nelson, 2013). For additional information, see the previous chapter, which provides a brief overview of the gap year option.

Before pursuing a gap year, students should ask themselves the following questions to determine if that decision is the best fit:

- Why am I interested in doing a gap year?

- What type of experience would I like to have? Individual or with a group? Formal program or informal experience? In the US or abroad? Work experience, academic experience, volunteer experience, a combination? Length of experience?

- What financial factors must I consider? What types of costs will I incur? Will my experience be paid or unpaid? Are there fees associated with the experience? Is there financial support available?

- What do I hope to achieve as a result of this experience? How can this experience help me personally, academically or professionally?

- Will colleges and universities view my gap year positively or negatively? Do I want to apply to college now or wait until after my gap year?

Recommendations and references. A number of resources are emerging to facilitate this experience, including the option to receive college credit and gap-year scholarships. Some colleges offer their own type of gap-year experience for first-year students. Yet, pursuing a gap year instead of going directly from high school to college can be an emotional decision for students and families. Therefore, communicating with students and parents, as well as facilitating communication between them, can be critical. To have a successful experience, students should have a developed plan for the gap year.

It is also important to help gap-year students navigate the college preparation process. As discussed in the previous chapter, students should begin planning early if they are considering this option. Students should also consider whether they will apply to college and request a deferment or wait to pursue the application process after the gap year is complete. Both options have pros and cons. For example, by deferring for a year, students have a guaranteed college or university that they will be able to attend after the experience. However, the gap year may lead the student to desire a different college option afterwards, and therefore, the student may lose the deferment deposit if he/she ultimately chooses not to attend the institution.

Additional resources to assist you in working with students considering a gap year:

- American Gap Year Association—*www.americangap.org*

- AmeriCorps—*www.nationalservice.gov/programs/americorps*

- CityYear—*www.cityyear.org*

- NACAC's Gap Year Tips—*www.nacacnet.org/studentinfo/articles/pages/gap-year-.aspx*

- USA Gap Year Fairs—*www.usagapyearfairs.org/programs*

- Year Out Group—*www.yearoutgroup.org*

WORKING WITH STUDENTS WITH SOCIAL CONNECTIONS

Students' social networks can be major assets during college preparation. Family and community members can provide much-needed encouragement, support and guidance as students prepare for college and make the decision of where to enroll. However, there are distinct social connections that may have a unique impact on postsecondary planning. Two of these types of connections are described: military and college legacy.

Military-Connected Students

The Department of Defense (DOD) reports there are more than 3.5 million US military personnel, and many students have a connection to this sector, whether through their own service or as the child or other relative of a military service member. While these categories (student veterans and students from military families) are discussed together in this section, the needs of each group are also distinct and unique.

The United States is seeing the largest college enrollment of student veterans since World War II (DiRamio & Jarvis, 2011). From 2000–2010, approximately two million student veterans enrolled in a postsecondary institution, with much of this influx a result of the Post-9/11 GI Bill (DiRamio & Jarvis, 2011). Only 15 percent of these students are traditional-aged collegians, and nearly two-thirds are first generation to college (National Center for PTSD, 2014). Almost half are married and/or have children (National Center for PTSD, 2014). This population comprises approximately four percent of the total US undergraduate population (Radford, 2011). Last year, more than one million student veterans and their dependents (e.g., spouses, children) received benefits for postsecondary education (National Center for PTSD, 2014).

There are currently more than 1.2 million children between the ages of five and 18 years of age that have one or two parents in the military, and more than 90 percent of these children attend US public or private schools (Office of the President, 2011). These children are increasingly entering high school and preparing for college. However, their needs and experiences can often differ from their peers. For example, the DOD reports that children from military families often attend seven to nine schools before high school graduation and, on average, move every two to three years.

Students with military connections may want to consider the following questions as they prepare for college:

- What are my needs regarding program flexibility (part-time vs. full-time enrollment; online/distance education options)?

- Does the institution have a liaison or office targeting military-connected students (e.g., veteran student services)?

- What types of academic support and counseling services are available at this institution?

- What are my military-related education benefits? How do these benefits compare across different institutions?

- Does this institution offer academic credit for military experience?

- What are my needs related to geographic location (e.g., military parents relocate often, but I may be interested in an institution in close proximity to other relatives)?

Recommendations and resources. Two key issues impacting the college preparation of military-connected students are education benefits and the personal needs and challenges that impact the process. Both student veterans and the spouses/children of military service members can qualify for education benefits that help fund a college degree. It is important to remain knowledgeable about these options and provide students with the resources they need to take advantage of these benefits. For most veterans, the **Post-9/11 GI Bill** is the most comprehensive benefit for funding college, but there are other government programs that may provide greater benefits. Service members' dependents may also be eligible for benefits, which include transfer of Post-9/11 GI Bill benefits and the **Dependents' Educational Assistance (DEA)** program. The Veterans Benefits Administration (*www.benefits.va.gov*) provides a number of tools and fact sheets to describe and compare benefits, as well as explain eligibility.

Military service members and their families often experience a number of challenges, including frequent moves, emotional stress and other risk factors due to deployments and trauma, and difficulty adjusting to one's environment. While these issues may not directly impact college preparation, they can negatively impact academic progress and success. Therefore, practitioners should consider and acknowledge students' military experiences in the college selection process. Yet, you should not assume all experiences create negative outcomes. Children of military parents may find transitioning to college less challenging than their peers due to frequent moving throughout their lives. Similarly, veterans' service experience can bring a wealth of knowledge and skills to college.

Because most veterans are married and/or have children, program flexibility may be a major concern. Helping students assess their personal and professional commitments, as well as providing information for a number of postsecondary options (e.g., full-time, part-time, online/distance education) can assist in determining the best fit. Additionally, many veterans experienced an interruption in their college enrollment due to military service or did not go directly to college after high school and so have had significant time away from formal classrooms. In both of these instances, connecting students with college bridge programs specifically targeting veterans (e.g., Veterans Upward Bound), can help these students engage in the college selection process and transition successfully to a postsecondary institution. Greater numbers of colleges and universities are also offering specific programs and services targeting veterans, so it is important that students are aware of the resource offerings at the campuses they are considering.

Additional resources to assist you in working with students who are military-connected:

- Astor, R.A., et al. (2012). *A pupil personnel guide to creating supportive schools for military students.* New York: Teachers College Press.

- GI Bill Tools and Resources—*www.benefits.va.gov/gibill*

- Military Child Education Coalition—*www.military-child.org*

- National Association of Veterans Upward Bound—*www.navub.org*

- Student Veterans of America—*www.studentveterans.org*

Student Legacies

Student legacies comprise one of two categories: (1) primary legacies—students whose parent(s) attended the institution as undergraduate(s) and (2) secondary legacies—

students with looser affiliations to an institution; this can include a parent who attended as a graduate student or a sibling or extended family member who attended as an undergraduate. Flagship public universities, selective private universities and liberal arts colleges are institutions most likely to consider legacies in the admission process (Kalenberg, 2010). How much of an impact legacy preference makes in admission decisions vary widely, potentially ranging from two to five times higher than the acceptance rate of the general applicant pool (Kalenberg, 2010). Student legacies should ask themselves a number of questions when determining college fit:

- Is the decision to apply my decision or my parent's/family's decision?

- How might attending an institution that someone in my family attended impact my college experience or make me feel?

- How does the institution that I am applying to perceive legacies? Does the institution consider legacies as part of the admission process, and, if so, how?

- Are there non-admission-related programming, scholarships or services targeting legacies at the institution (e.g., via alumni services)?

Recommendations and resources. Working with legacy students and their families can create an additional level of emotion and attachment to the desire to be admitted into an institution. However, colleges and universities vary widely in their treatment of legacies. Some institutions directly state they do not consider legacies in admission, whereas at other institutions, being a legacy can be a major tipping factor in an admission decision. It is important that students and their parents not make assumptions and are aware of the practices and perspectives of the institution. Students and their families must also understand that being a legacy does not guarantee admission. Therefore, it is important to assess whether the student's academic qualifications align with the academic profile of admitted students.

Although the student may have been on the campus numerous times for alumni events, he or she should show interest in the institution through formal channels as well (e.g., contacting the admission office, doing a formal campus tour). This can ensure that the admission office is aware of the student's interest in the university. Additionally, it creates some level of separation between the college experience of his or her family member and the experience that he or she might have as a student at the institution, which allows the student to make a more rounded assessment of whether the institution is a fit. Similarly, it is important that the decision to attend the institution goes beyond pleasing a family member.

There are not recent research or reports available for working with legacy students. However, the following resource discusses legacy admission preferences:

- Kahlenberg, R.D. (2010). *Affirmative action for the rich: Legacy preferences in college admissions.* New York: The Century Foundation Press.

WORKING WITH STUDENTS INTERESTED IN COMMUNITY COLLEGE

As outlined in the previous chapter, community colleges serve a wide range of needs for students after high school. Some students may select a community college to pursue career training or an associate degree in a specific field. Others see community colleges as a step toward a bachelor's degree and already have the goal of transferring in mind when selecting this option. Students who attend community colleges also range widely in level of college-readiness due to the open access mission of these institutions. Some students may lack the academic credentials necessary to be a competitive applicant for a four-year institution. Yet, particularly since the economic downturn, greater numbers of high-achieving students are pursuing community college as a low-cost option on the pathway to a four-year degree. Working with students who are seeking community college as their postsecondary option requires understanding these different needs and long-term goals.

The American Association of Community Colleges approximates 7.7 million students (45 percent of all undergraduates) are enrolled in public two-year colleges. Two types of students considering community college will be described in this section. One reflects students who seek a college degree, but do not have a strong high school academic profile. The second group of students reflects the savvy consumers who may be competitive four-year college applicants, but are seeking a way to minimize college costs by beginning at a community college and eventually transferring to a four-year institution.

Students with College-Readiness Challenges

Each year, thousands of students enroll in college lacking basic mathematics, reading and/or writing skills. A 2012 ACT report found that only 25 percent of students who took the ACT met college-level readiness benchmarks across science, math, reading, and English. High school performance can be misleading in predicting academic preparation for college, as many high school honors students take remedial classes in college, and four out of five students in college development courses have a 3.0 or above GPA in high school (Strong American Schools, 2008). Lack of academic preparation can lead to a number of negative college outcomes, including poor performance in classes, high enrollment in developmental/remedial coursework, and attrition or lengthened time to degree. Therefore, while college is certainly an option for students who are academically underprepared, it is critical that these students are careful in selecting a college to meet their needs and goals.

As discussed in the previous chapter, community colleges provide a viable option for students who may currently lack the academic skills to be a successful applicant to a four-year institution. Additionally, there are a number of students who choose to enroll in a community college to pursue career training in a profession that does not require a four-year college degree. Students considering community college for these reasons might ask some of the following questions:

- What is my ultimate goal if I attend a community college? An associate degree? A career-training certificate? Transferring to a four-year college or university?

- What are my academic strengths and challenge areas? Will I need to take developmental coursework in college?

- What are my levels of time management and study skills? Do I need additional help in building these skills while in college?

- What types of academic support services are offered at the community college (e.g., learning communities, academic advising, tutoring, learning support services)?

- What types of practical experiences are available (e.g., internships, apprenticeships)?

- Are there alternatives to community college that may still meet my academic needs (e.g., a summer bridge program)?

Recommendations and resources. While some students facing academic preparedness challenges may come to you with an intent to apply to community college, others may not view it as an immediate option due to negative perceptions of this institutional type or because the student may not be considering college as an option at all. Discussing students' short-term and long-term academic and career goals can help to determine whether community college will provide the best fit. Students who did not perform well in high school academically, but who ultimately would like a four-year degree should know that their performance in community college will often provide more weight in the transfer admission process than their high school performance. However, it is important that these students take courses that will transfer to a four-year college or university. Because of the wide range of student needs that community colleges serve, students considering this option should understand concepts like remediation/developmental coursework, the types of degrees and/or certificates offered, and the transfer process.

It is also important to consider how your school encourages college-readiness and promotes a college-going culture. Successful enrollment in college is a process that starts as early as middle school, and therefore, encouraging students to start early in considering and preparing for college is key to college access. Engaging in practices that promote a college-going culture in one's school and ensuring that all students have the tools and knowledge to have postsecondary options and make an informed decision about those options is critical.

For more information to assist in working with students with college-readiness challenges:

- American Association of Community Colleges—*www.aacc.nche.edu*

- Long, B.T., & Boatman, A. (2013). The role of remedial and developmental courses in access and persistence. In A. Jones & L. Perna (Eds.) The state of college access and completion: Improving success for students from underrepresented groups (pp. 77–98). New York: Routledge.

- NACAC's Step-by-Step: College Awareness and Planning for Families, Counselors and Communities—*www.nacacnet.org/steps*

- Research and Resources on Developmental Summer Bridge Programs from the National Center for Postsecondary Research—*www.postsecondaryresearch.org/index.html?Id=Research&Info=Developmental+Summer+Bridges*

Students Seeking a Low-Cost College Option

Community colleges are increasingly an option for high-achieving students who are seeking a low-cost pathway to a bachelor's degree. While the cost of college continues to rise, the number of school-age children coming from low-income households has also risen for the past decade (Engle & Tinto, 2008). College affordability will continue to play a large role in enrollment decisions for many students and families. Yet, it is estimated that over the past nine years, students who started at community college and then transferred to a public or private nonprofit four-year institution saved more than $20 billion (Mullin, 2012).

Attending community college at some point during the college experience is becoming the norm for bachelor's degree earners, with nearly 30 percent having started at a community college and almost half taking one or more courses at a community college (Mullin, 2012). Research shows that there is no significant difference between the success of students who start at a four-year institution than their peers who start at a community college and transfer (Mullin, 2012).

Yet, there are still a number of challenges that exist with the transfer function between two- and four-year institutions that may create barriers to students seeking to transfer. This is reflected in data showing that while 80 percent of entering community college students cite a bachelor's degree aspiration, only 20 percent of these students transfer to a four-year institution (Altstadt, Schmidt, & Couturier, 2014). Students considering community college as the first step toward a bachelor's degree might consider the following questions to determine if this option is the best fit:

- What is the net price comparison of my attending a community college versus a four-year institution? Does this price differential make community college a more accessible college option?

- What do I want my college experience to be? Does it matter whether I commute from home or live on campus? Will I need to have a job to finance college or other expenses?

- Does the community college(s) I am in interested in offer any programs targeting advanced students or students with specific major interests (e.g., honors program, learning community)?

- What is the success rate of students who desire to transfer to a four-year institution? Is my community college of interest a "feeder school" for a specific four-year institution? What kind of support or guidance is provided in the transfer process?

- On average, how long do students remain at this community college before transferring to a four-year university? Do students tend to complete an associate degree before transferring?

- Is it possible for me to obtain college credits as a high school student (e.g., dual enrollment)?

Recommendations and references. When working with students who are considering community college with the goal of transfer, it is important to help them understand the transfer process. Students and their families should be aware of terms such as "articulation agreements" and "guaranteed admission programs," as well as how these terms apply to their community college of interest.

Community colleges are increasingly developing programs that target advanced students who are seeking a two-year institution as a means to eventually secure a four-year degree. These include merit scholarships, honors programs and major-related learning communities. Yet, it is important that students are made aware that these special programs often have earlier and specific (rather than rolling) admission deadlines.

Discuss with students their long-term transfer plans during the college preparation process. For example, some four-year colleges and universities offer transfer students academic scholarships, while others only provide academic scholarships to first-time, first-year students. Additionally, some institutions offer special support or advising to transfer students in the transition to a four-year university. Students should also consider how the specific transfer process works between the community college and the four-year institution(s) they may be

interested in transferring to in the future (e.g., process for credit transfer).

Lastly, it is important that you encourage students and families to consider a wide range of college options and college funding opportunities. While community college may be the best fit financially, there are also other factors that impact a student's satisfaction and success in college. Students should be aware that the net price of a four-year degree may be affordable without first attending community college. Financial aid information and assistance with completing the FAFSA will be critical for students to compare their options. Students may also benefit from taking dual-enrollment courses at the local community college (if available) to earn college credits while still in high school, which may reduce the overall cost of college.

For additional resources to assist you in working with students seeking community college as a low-cost option:

- American Association of Community Colleges—*www. aacc.nche.edu*

- College Board's Net Price Calculator—*http://netprice-calculator.collegeboard.org*

- NACAC Special Report on the Transfer Admission Process (2010)—*www.nacacnet.org/research/research-data/Documents/TransferFactSheet.pdf*

- National Collegiate Honors Council's information on honors programs at two-year colleges—*http://nchchonors.org/hs-students-counselors-parents/honors-programs-at-2-year-colleges*

CONCLUSION

There are three primary limitations of this chapter. First, it is not an exhaustive review of diverse student demographics. There are a number of other populations who also face unique needs and challenges in college preparation. Second, the student populations described in this chapter are not mutually exclusive. For example, a student can be both an athlete that is first-generation to college or an undocumented student seeking a low-cost college option through community college. It is important for counselors to be able to address these intersections and not make assumptions about what a student may need based on one aspect of identity or context. Third, this chapter focused on the unique college preparation needs and characteristics of each student demographic, not more general college preparation practices, which can be found in other chapters within this textbook.

There are more than 28 million students enrolled in middle and high schools across the United States (Bauman & Davis, 2013), and these students are bringing an increasingly diverse range of knowledge, resources, experiences, and needs to the college preparation process. It is important for you, as a practitioner, to remain aware of shifts in student demographics that are impacting college enrollment trends. Even more important is being prepared to work with increasingly diverse students entering the education pipeline. NACAC provides a wide range of resources on its Web site to help you stay current on this issue. Additionally, there are reflective questions that you should ask yourself that may lead to greater success in working with diverse student populations and in providing assistance as they seek a positive college fit:

- What are my own perspectives, assumptions and biases about diverse students?

- Would students assess my office space as a safe and inclusive environment?

- Do the resources and information that I provide to students reflect a diverse set of needs and contexts? Are these resources available to all students?

- What sense do I have of the diversity at my school? How do we define diversity at our school? Does our school environment and leadership promote a welcoming and inclusive climate to all students?

- How can I build or strengthen a network of individuals or organizations that can provide me with tools for working with diverse students?

- How can I work with school staff, student organizations, parents, students, the local community, and colleges to ensure that the diverse needs of students are being met in the college preparation process?

- How can I remain committed to my own professional development around student diversity and shifting student demographics?

About the Author

Chrystal A. George Mwangi is an assistant professor in higher education. Her scholarship broadly centers on 1) structures of opportunity and educational attainment for underrepresented populations along the P-20 education pipeline; 2) impacts of globalization and migration on US higher education at the student, institution, and policy levels; and 3) African and African Diaspora populations in higher education. Dr. George Mwangi worked for a number of years as a college administrator including positions in undergraduate admissions, multicultural affairs, student conduct, and academic advising. She has also engaged in education research and policy work for organizations including the Council for Opportunity in Education, the Pell Institute for the Study of Opportunity in Higher Education, and Higher Education for Development. Her work has been published in journals including *Diversity in Higher Education* and the *Journal of Student Affairs Research & Practice*.

References

Altstadt, D., Schmidt, G., & Couturier, L.K. (2014). *Driving the direction of transfer pathways reform*. Boston: Jobs for the Future.

Angeli, M. (2009) *Access and equity for all students: Meeting the needs of LGBT students.* (Report 09-14). Sacramento: California Postsecondary Education Commission.

Bridgeland, J., & Bruce, M. (2011). *2011 national survey of school counselors: Counseling at a crossroads.* New York: The College Board.

Bauman, K., & Davis, J. (2013). *Climates of school enrollment by grade in the American Community Survey, the Current Population Survey, and the Common Core of data.* (SEHSD Working Paper 2014-7). Washington, DC: U.S. Census.

Bryan, J., Holcomb-McCoy, C., Moore-Thomas, C., & Day-Vines, N.L. (2009). Who sees the school counselor for college information? A national study. *Professional School Counseling, 12*(4), 280–291.

Burleson, D.A. (2010). Sexual orientation and college choice: Considering campus climate. *About Campus, 14*(6), 9–14.

Child Trends. (2012). *Participation in school music or other performing arts.* Retrieved from *http://www.childtrends.org/?indicators=participation-in-school-music-or-other-performing-arts.*

DiRamio, D., & Jarvis, K. (Eds.). (2011). When Johnny and Jane come marching to campus. *ASHE Higher Education Report, 37*(3). San Francisco: Wiley/Jossey-Bass.

Dukes, C. (2013). *College access and success for students experiencing homelessness: A toolkit for educators and service providers*. Greensboro, NC: National Center for Homeless Education.

Engle, J., & Tinto, V. (2008) *Moving beyond access. College success for low-income, first-generation students*. Washington, DC: Pell Institute.

Gonzales, R.G. (2009). Young lives on hold: The college dreams of undocumented students. Washington, DC: The College Board.

Haigler, K., & Nelson, R. (2013). *Gap year, American style: Journeys toward learning, serving and self-discovery*. Advance, NC: HEII.

Human Rights Campaign. (2012). *Growing up LGBT in America: HRC youth survey report*. Retrieved from *http:// hrc-assets.s3-website-us-east-1.amazonaws.com//files/ assets/resources/Growing-Up-LGBT-in-America_Report.pdf*.

Irick, E. (2013). 1981–82 – 2012–13 *NCAA sports sponsorship and participation rates report*. Indianapolis: NCAA.

Kahlenberg, R.D. (2010). *Affirmative action for the rich: Legacy preferences in college admissions*. New York: The Century Foundation Press.

Kinzie, J., Palmer, M., Hayek, J., Hossler, D., Jacob, S., & Cummings, H. (2004). *Fifty years of college choice: Social, political, and institutional influences on the decision-making process*. Indianapolis: Lumina Foundation.

McDonough, P. (2005). *Counseling and college counseling in America's high schools*. Alexandria, VA: NACAC.

Mullin, C.M. (2012). *Transfer: An indispensible part of the community college mission*. (Policy Brief 2012-03PBL). Washington, DC: AACC.

National Center for PTSD. (2014). *Characteristics of student veterans: VA campus toolkit handout*. Retrieved from *http://www.mentalhealth.va.gov/studentveteran/docs/ ed_todaysStudentVets.html*.

National Collegiate Athletic Association. (2013). *Probability of competing beyond high school*. Retrieved from: *http:// www.ncaa.org/about/resources/research/probability-competing-beyond-high-school*.

National Federation of State High School Associations. (2014). *2013–2014 High school athletics participation survey*. Retrieved from: *http://www.nfhs.org/ ParticipationStatics/PDF/2013-14_Participation_Survey_ PDF.pdf*.

Office of the President. (2014). *Increasing college opportunity for low-income students: Promising models and a call to action*. Retrieved from *http://www.whitehouse.gov/sites/ default/files/docs/white_house_report_on_increasing_ college_opportunity_for_low-income_students_1-16-2014_ final.pdf*.

Office of the President. (2011). *Strengthening our military families*. Retrieved from *http://www.defense.gov/home/ features/2011/0111_initiative/Strengthening_our_ Military_January_2011.pdf*.

Perez, W. (2010). Higher education access for undocumented students: Recommendations for counseling professionals. *Journal of College Admission, 206(1)*, 34–37.

Radford, A.W. (2011). *Military service members and veterans: A profile of those enrolled in undergraduate and graduate education in 2007-2008*. (Report 2011–163). Washington, DC: NCES.

Ruppert, S.S. (2006). *Critical evidence: How the arts benefit student achievement*. National Assembly of State Arts Agencies.

Strong American Schools (2008). *Diploma to nowhere*. Washington, DC: Strong American Schools.

Suarez-Orozco, C., Suarez-Orozco M., & Todorova, I. (2008). *Learning a new land: Immigrant students in American society*. Cambridge, MA: The Belknap Press.

Tierney, W.G., Gupton, J.T., & Hallett, R.E. (2008). *Transition to adulthood for homeless adolescents*. Los Angeles, CA: Center for Higher Education Policy Analysis.

Unrau, Y., Font, S., & Rawls, G. (2012). Readiness for college engagement among students who have aged out of foster care. *Children and Youth Services Review, 34(1)*, 76–83.

Chapter 15:   Financial Aid Partnerships and Possibilities

Kristan Venegas, PhD
@kristanvenegas

Introduction: Financial Aid in College Admissions

College students are expected to assume an increasing portion of the costs linked to their postsecondary education (Jones-White, Radcliffe, Lorenz, & Soria, 2013). Our current financial aid system is a mix of federal, state, institutional, regional, and private resources. In this chapter, we consider these different financial aid resources and offer practical advice on how to access these resources. We begin with a brief overview of the historical origins of our modern federal and state aid systems. This context is important because it can help practitioners understand the underpinnings of aid policy as it relates to the students they serve.

This chapter focuses on options for undergraduate students; it was designed with three key questions in mind: (1) What do college access, admission and outreach practitioners need to know to help their students access financial aid? (2) What are possible practices for working with students and families? and (3) What are key concerns for special populations, and what do practitioners need to know regarding working with these populations? Throughout the chapter, we refer to terms that are unique to financial aid. If you encounter a term that you are not familiar with, please refer to the Glossary of Terms section that leads off the section entitled, "A Few Basics: A Short Review of the Financial Aid Application Process."

Understanding Federal Financial Aid

Our modern federal system of financial aid includes grant and loan aid. Federal financial aid is only available to US citizens and those who qualify based on immigrant status. The Free Application for Federal Student Aid, or FAFSA, is most commonly associated with federal financial aid. The FAFSA has been identified as a financial aid gatekeeper (Bettinger, Long, Oreopoulos, & Sanbonmatsu, 2009); this form must be completed by the submission deadline in order to be considered for either of the aid options noted below.

Grant Aid

Grant aid is money that does not have to be paid back; it is based on a combined legacy of the Educational Amendments of 1972, the established of Pell Grants and student

activism. The result of these efforts was grant assistance for low-income students pursuing college in the US that is (1) based on a combination of merit and income status and (2) portable. Portability was and continues to be an important factor, because students are able to use these funds at an approved institution of their choice.

More than 80 percent of students who attend four-year institutions in the United States receive some form of financial aid; this number is just under 80 percent at two-year institutions (US Department of Education, 2014). The most common grant from the federal government is known as the Pell Grant. From 2012–2013, the average Pell Grant aid distributed to students was $3,477. In 2014, the maximum amount that college students can be awarded under the Pell Grant increased to $5,730. There are a few additional federal grant programs, but they typically do not offer the same amount of funding and are more likely to change based on federal priorities.

Loan Aid

In the early 1980s, the federal government began a system of student loan borrowing. Student and family loans are sources of funding that are required to be paid back based on the specific terms and interest rates agreed upon at the time of borrowing. The decision to make these loans available was influenced by the push of middle-class families who also wanted some form of assistance to send their students to postsecondary education. There are two types of federal loans available to finance postsecondary education—student loans and parent loans. Though the names of these programs have changed over time, these two categories of lending have remained the same. Recent shifts have placed limits on the amount of lending, caps on interest rates, and changes in eligibility for subsidized and unsubsidized loans. The federal government currently manages all student loan programs, which helps students and families manage their loan debt through one resource.

Understanding State Financial Aid

States awarded about $11.2 billion in total state-funded student financial aid in the 2012–2013 academic year (NASSGAP, n.d.). State-level financial aid has a legacy that reaches back to the development of land grant institutions in the mid to late 1800s. States would incentivize their top talent to stay in state to study as a means of preventing "brain drain" from one state to another. Most state-level programs require evidence of a GPA of 3.0 or above, state residency and good citizenship. Some states also require a particular score on a college entrance exam like the ACT or SAT. Other states expect students to place within a certain level of ranking within their graduating high school class. State-level funding can be a mix of income- and merit-based awards. In some cases, students and families are required to submit financial information to access an income-based scholarship. The FAFSA tends to be the gateway form to access aid in this case, but again, individual states may have additional forms to complete.

According to the National Association of State Student Grant and Aid Programs (NASSGAP), all 50 states (and Puerto Rico and Washington, DC) have state need-based financial aid programs, and 30 states have state merit-based programs (NASSGAP, 2009–2010, Table 8). The awarding of financial aid is usually done through a state-level higher education agency, but in some cases, students and high school staff are responsible for making this information available to prospective colleges and universities. For example, Nevada identifies which students are eligible for its Millennial Scholars Grant and creates a database that Nevada institutions can use when developing individual financial aid packages. It's important that counselors know what options are available in their state and identify those resources applicable for the students they serve.

UNDERSTANDING INSTITUTIONAL, REGIONAL AND PRIVATE RESOURCES

Federal and state financial aid resources tend to be some of the most widely known avenues by which to access financial aid, but there are also institutional, regional and private resources to consider. In addition to state and federal governments, private foundations, individual donors, and specific colleges and universities all offer financial aid for postsecondary education (Tierney, Venegas, & Mari Luna De, 2006).

Private and Regional Resources

The ebb and flow of these resources is not always predictable, because funding priorities for the various organizations can change, but it's important for college access professionals to understand the options that are available to students. There are national scholarship lists available on the Web sites of national organizations, like the Mexican American Legal Defense Fund (MALDEF) list and American Association of University Women (AAUW). It's worth taking time to understand which scholarship opportunities might be available to your student population. Some businesses also offer matching scholarship dollars for employees and children of employees. Businesses may also be involved in offering scholarships to support the local community. Like grants, scholarships do not have to be repaid.

Institutional Resources

Depending on the type of institution, colleges and universities will be able to offer students a number of scholarship, loan, work-study, or other financial aid options. It's vitally important that students work with institutions to understand what options are available. For more information about institutional financial aid allocation decisions, see chapter 16. Not all financial aid opportunities are listed on the financial aid Web sites of colleges and universities. It's really up to the student and those supporting that student to make sure that all resources are exhausted, including alumni- and academic major- specific departments.

One of the key takeaways from this section of the chapter should be that counselors and students understand the proactive and individualistic nature of seeking financial aid. There are forms to complete, processes to monitor and decisions to make. Students have to report specific background information about their family, their socioeconomic status and other issues when applying for financial aid (Venegas & Hallett, 2008). Incomes and access to other financial options can be quite different and require a sometimes more challenging conversation about a student's ability to pay.

In the next section of the chapter, we expand on the information provided by centering our discussion on the "basics" of the financial aid application process. This chapter is by no means exhaustive; but it offers a foundation on financial aid and addresses main steps that you will need to take in applying for financial aid.

A Few Basics: A Short Review of the Financial Aid Application Process

In this part of the chapter, we define key terms in financial aid, offer a process graph of the financial aid process and provide a checklist of what you can do to prepare for the financial aid application. We begin with the following glossary of terms.

Glossary of Terms

Cost of Attendance (COA)

The cost of attendance or budget is determined by the college or university that the student is attending. This figure is based on reasonable costs to attend the student's program of study (subject to federal guidelines). The COA usually includes tuition, fees, books, housing, travel, childcare, and other expenses that can be directly related to the cost of attending school. Non-school-related costs cannot be included in the COA. This value typically sets the maximum amount that can be borrowed in student loans (federal or private).

Direct PLUS Loan (PLUS)

This loan program was initially created for parents of undergraduate students who needed to borrow money to pay for their child's college expenses. The original name of the program was the Parent Loan for Undergraduate Students (PLUS). Like the Direct Unsubsidized Loan, the PLUS loan accrues interest while the student is in school. The maximum amount that a student can borrow in this loan program is capped by their Cost of Attendance. No payments are required on this loan until after the student leaves school (however, interest does accrue, as noted above). This loan has a 10-year repayment period (although that can be extended under certain repayment programs).

Direct Subsidized Loan (Subsidized Loan)

This is a type of direct loan that is made to students who demonstrate financial need. Under this program, the interest accrued on the loan while the student is in school is paid by the federal government. Since July 1, 2012, these loans have only been available to undergraduate students. Graduate students who borrowed after July 1, 2012 are no longer eligible for this loan program.

Direct Unsubsidized Loan (Unsubsidized Loan)

This is a type of direct loan that is made to any eligible student; financial need is not required to be eligible for this loan. Interest accrues on this loan while the student is in school, and that interest is then added to the principle that the student borrowed. When out of school, the student is required to repay the loan. After leaving school, the student is charged interest on both the principle and the interest that accrued during school. Graduate students are eligible to borrow up to $20,500 in this loan program each year. No payments are required on this loan until after the student leaves school (however, interest does accrue, as noted above). This loan has a 10-year repayment period (although that can be extended under certain repayment programs).

Expected Family Contribution (EFC)

This figure is calculated using a formula set by the federal government. The EFC is based on the student's family's income and some assets as reported by the student on their FAFSA. The EFC is the amount that the student is expected to contribute to their education.

Federal Perkins Loan (Perkins Loan)

This is a federal student loan program that is only available to students with demonstrated financial need. Funds for this program are distributed to the awarding colleges or universities who then determine which students at their institution are eligible for the loan (within certain federal guidelines). The amount awarded to each student is dependent upon what the institution has available, but can never exceed more than $8,000 per year per student. Perkins loans have a five-percent interest rate, they are subsidized (no interest is accrued while the student is in school), and the school is considered the lender so payments are made to the school directly after the student graduates (or drops below half-time enrollment). This loan has a 10-year repayment period, and is subject to cancellation for teachers who serve in certain school districts or teach certain subjects.

Federal Student Loans

These are student loans funded by the federal government. There are two types of federal student loans: the William D. Ford Federal Direct Loan (direct loan) and

Federal Perkins Loans (Perkins loan). Federal student loans do not have to be repaid until the student leaves school (graduates or drops to less than half-time enrollment). The interest rate is fixed each year. Interest paid on federal student loans may be tax deductible. There are many repayment plans, including an option to tie the monthly payment to the student's income, and students can request temporary postponements on their payments if they suffer economic hardship or return to school. Federal student loans also have forgiveness programs depending on the student's occupation.

Federal Work-Study (FWS)

The work-study program provides funds for a student to earn in part-time employment while they are in school. Work-study employment is typically on-campus, with some exceptions. Funds for this program are distributed to the awarding colleges or universities who then determine which students at their institution are eligible (within certain federal guidelines). Students are awarded an amount of work-study, which they then earn by working and receiving a regular paycheck. Once they have earned all of the funds awarded to them, the work-study is exhausted. This is considered a need-based aid program, so students must demonstrate high need to be eligible for the award.

Free Application for Federal Student Aid (FAFSA)

All students must complete this application to receive federal aid. Students submit demographic information, information about their enrollment plans for the year, and information on their income and assets from their proceeding year's federal income tax returns. The Department of Education uses this information to calculate the student's EFC and their eligibility for federal aid. This information is then passed to the college or university, which is then responsible for calculating which aid programs the student qualifies for and notifying the student of their available funding for the year.

Merit-Based Aid

Merit aid is the broad term that includes all the scholarships, grants and discounts that a college offers an admitted student without consideration of financial need. Merit aid is based on student skills or abilities, such as academic or athletic achievements, student talent, or student demographic information. This aid is also referred to as "non-need-based aid."

Need

A student's "need" is a set value derived by a formula: the Cost of Attendance (COA) minus the Expected Family Contribution (EFC) equals the student's calculated need. If this figure is high (i.e., close to the cost of attendance, because the EFC is zero or very low), then the student is considered to be "high-need." If this figure is low (because the student's EFC is higher than their COA), then the student is considered to be "low-need."

Need-Based Aid

This is any form of aid that is awarded to students based on their need. For graduate students, need-based aid programs are typically only the Perkins Loan or Federal Work-Study. Students with a high need can expect to receive need-based aid. Students with a low need will not qualify for need-based aid.

Pell Grants

These are need-based federal grants awarded to first-time undergraduate students. The award does not need to be repaid and depends on a student's financial need, the costs to attend school, full-time versus part-time student status, and plans to attend college for a full academic year or less. The maximum Pell Grant award for 2014 is $5,730.

Student Loans

These are loans offered to students to pay for educational costs. Student loans are funds that are borrowed and must be paid back with interest. Student loans can come from two sources: the federal government (see Federal Student Loans) and private student loans (see Private Student Loans). These definitions represent the basics of financial-aid-related terms and are adapted from the Federal Student Aid Web site, *studentaid.ed.gov*. You can visit this site for additional information and definitions of other terms as well. Figure 1 offers the five main steps of completing financial aid forms. It is written so that it can be shared with the student audience as they prepare to apply for financial aid. Additional details and considerations are noted under each step.

FIGURE 1. GETTING READY TO COMPLETE FINANCIAL AID FORMS: FIVE EASY STEPS

1. Engage in the costs of college conversation with those who will be helping to support your education, including yourself. Consider these key questions:

   a. Who will support you in paying for college? How much and when will they be able to contribute?

   b. What are the limits and expectations based on this support?

   c. Will you attend full-time or part-time?

   d. Are there employment expectations for you, and how might that impact your financial aid eligibility?

   e. If you plan to take out loans:

      i. Who will be responsible for repayment?

      ii. Will you need a co-signer? If so, who might co-sign for you?

      iii. What are the interest rates, and what are the terms of repayment?

2. If eligible, go to *fafsa.ed.gov* and set up your FSA ID information.

   a. Beginning Fall 2015, students and their families will be expected to select a login and password. These credentials will be used for FAFSA, as well as loan repayment tracking and access to other information related to federal financial aid.

   b. If you are not a US citizen or resident, do not complete and submit the FAFSA. Contact the college you hope to attend for more information about their admission processes.

3. Gather together your previous year and current year tax information for you and your parents.

   a. You'll need this information to complete FAFSA and possibly college or university related forms.

   b. If you are considered an independent student, you do not have to include your parents' information. You can check with the federal government Web site, as well as your college or university Web site, to determine how independent students are currently defined.

   c. If you do you have current year information, don't delay in applying for FAFSA; include your past year information to get a file started—you can always update to the new year once you have that information.

4. Identify the college that you are interested in attending.

   a. You will need to list your top five to six on the FAFSA.

   b. You should go to their individual Web sites and identify what forms are needed. As noted in the previous sections, many colleges have their own processes.

5. Determine eligibility for state-level financial aid programs.

   a. Check state aid programs' Web sites, as applicable, and determine your eligibility.

   b. Identify any required documentation.

Completing the five steps mentioned above will help students and families to be better prepared for the financial aid process. Encouraging students and families to do this prep work will help to save time for practitioners as well. Many of these steps can be or must be completed at home. The list serves as appropriate "homework" for individuals in college access and admission programs. Now that this list of preparation steps has been identified, we turn to a timeline of the financial aid process. The following timeline highlights major points from high school to college.

Figure 2. Timeline of the Financial Aid Process

Senior year of high school and/or year before transferring from a community college to a four-year institution:

Fall: Investigate the financial aid options at the colleges/universities you plan to attend.

- Get your financial aid login and password (beginning Fall 2015).

Spring: Submit FAFSA application no later than March 2.

- Complete any required state-level forms.
- Complete all of your college/university aid applications.
- Once you receive your financial aid offer(s), compare them to make sure that they cover the cost of attendance.
- Discuss your options with trusted advisors.
- Use financial aid calculators to help you understand your options. They are available at every college Web site and at the *fafsa.ed.gov* page.
- Contact the school with any questions or concerns.
- Finalize your financial aid offer.

Summer: Finalize your financial aid offer, and hurry!

- If you haven't finalized youxr financial aid offer by the end of July and you plan to attend school in August, it's time to make sure that this gets done ASAP. Follow the steps that are noted in the Spring.
- All students should be verifying the terms of any student loans that they have or plan to take out.
- Complete loan entrance counseling as required by your school.

Freshman, Sophomore and Junior Year Basics

Fall: Pull together your materials to apply for financial aid.

Spring: Submit FAFSA application no later than March 2.

- Complete all of your required college forms.
- Complete any state-level forms.
- Check your student loan debt by logging into your federal student loan portal. You should do this every year.

Community College Transfer/Senior Year Basics

Fall: If you plan to transfer to a four-year college or go on to graduate school, pull together your materials to apply for financial aid.

- Check your student loan debt by logging into your federal student loan portal. It's especially important that you do this during the fall of your final year of college. If you think that any of your loan information is incorrect, you need to begin looking into it now.

Spring: If you plan to go onto graduate school, submit FAFSA application no later than March 2.

- Complete all of your required college forms.
- If you are graduating or not returnixng to school in the fall and have taken out student loans, prepare to do your loan exit counseling and make plans for your repayment options.

The timeline (see Figure 2) gives an overview of the steps for applying for financial aid. Keep in mind that it does not include specific information on applying for private scholarships. Those timelines can vary throughout the academic year. This section of the chapter focused on specific tasks associates with the financial aid process. For those who are interested in understanding more about the research on financial aid awareness and applications, the next section presents previous research in this area.

Practices in Financial Aid Awareness and Applications

There are two important reasons for including a discussion of financial aid research in this chapter. First, practitioners can benefit from a stronger understanding of research that seeks to explain financial aid decision-making behaviors. Second, most of the research on financial aid awareness and applications tells us that: (1) students do not fully understand the financial aid process, (2) the financial aid application process is challenging, and (3) the financial-aid-related forms are confusing. These findings tend to hold particularly true.

The Perna (2006) model informing student college choice provides a framework for understanding how the availability of resources, including the family's income, as well as the student's expected financial aid package, influences college choice (see chapter 2 for a more detailed discussion of the Perna model). Students and their families weigh the expected monetary and non-monetary benefits of attending an institution against the expected costs, considering both the direct costs and foregone earnings (Perna, 2006). An understanding of financial aid options and opportunities might help students and their families make educated decisions about the affordability of institutions to which they apply. Other relevant reading and ideas can be found in:

- The Cultural Ecology Model, by William G. Tierney and Kristan M. Venegas (see figure 3)

- "Challenges and Opportunities for Improving Community College Student Success," by Sara Goldrick-Rab (This article can be found in the *Review of Educational Research*.)

- *Innovations in Financial Aid,* by A. Kelly and Sara Goldrick-Rab.

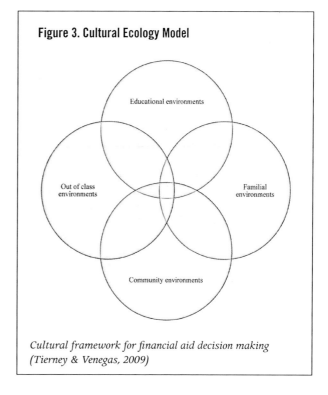

Figure 3. Cultural Ecology Model

Educational environments

Out of class environments

Familial environments

Community environments

Cultural framework for financial aid decision making (Tierney & Venegas, 2009)

Current Resources for Financial Aid Awareness and Applications

There are various places that college admission and access counselors can use to assist student and families through this pathway. Of course, a natural place to request assistance will be the college or university where a student plans to attend. Fortunately, there are also a number of additional resources to assist with financial aid information. These resources are organized into two categories. The organizations listed here are likely to be considering key financial aid policies and analysis of how they might impact students and families. They may also offer cutting-edge financial aid interventions.

Policy and advocacy centers related to financial aid:

- Excelencia in Education

- IHEP

- Lumina

- National Association for Student Financial Aid

- The Institute for College Access and Success

- The Pell Institute (Council for Opportunity in Education)

Like the policy and advocacy centers noted above, the practice and information clearinghouses noted in the

Undocumented students in Texas, New Mexico and California are able to attend any postsecondary institution, pay in-state tuition rates, and receive state-level financial aid at public colleges and universities.

next list offer specific programs and techniques related to college access and financial aid. These resources are also national in scope; they will allow the user to gain a broader understanding of how other student-focused programs help their students access financial aid and make decisions about choosing financial aid. It is important to note that with the exception of the federal government site, most of these Web sites focus on financial aid access, not management over time.

Practice and information clearinghouses:

- Federal Government Financial Aid Web site
- National Association for College Admission Counseling (NACAC)
- National College Access Network (NCAN)
- College Board
- Mexican American Legal Defense Fund
- Pulias Center for Higher Education

A Note on Working with Special Populations

Access to necessary information about paying for college is not equivalent across student groups (Perna, 2006). As mentioned earlier in this chapter, the financial aid process is quite individual, and most of this differentiation is based on financial status. However, in some cases there are additional circumstances that impact student aid eligibility. Three categories of special populations are noted here.

International students. Students who are not US citizens or meet criteria for state-level funding or participation in the federal DACA program are typically not eligible for state or federal financial aid in the US. Some students may have additional provisions, but these are rare cases and should be understood in collaboration with a financial aid professional. If an international student is pre-admission, it is still advisable for the student to connect with his or her intended institution to follow up on

financial aid pathways and resources. There may be scholarship resources for international students, but they are not considered within the scope of this chapter.

Foster youth. Students who are foster youth and/or wards of the court are often eligible to be considered as independent students. They are typically given an estimated family contribution of zero and treated as adults. There is often additional state-level aid for this student population, and colleges and universities may also have additional funds or policies that change the cost of attendance and housing options for these students. It's important that foster youth work closely with the financial aid offices at their chosen institution(s) to identify particular options that may be open to them.

Undocumented students. In recognition of the size and the scope of undocumented students in the US, it is worth taking a few moments to clarify a few points based on current law and policy. Students who are undocumented and have not completed the DACA process are not able to apply for federal student aid. Students who have completed the DACA process are able to apply for federal student aid. At the state level, there are wide differences in the access to resources for undocumented students. Many states are starting to allow undocumented students to attend colleges and universities with eligibility to pay in-state tuition; others follow more restrictive or expansive policies. For example, at the time of this writing, undocumented students in South Carolina are not able to attend a postsecondary institution. Undocumented students in Texas, New Mexico and California are able to attend any postsecondary institution, pay in-state tuition rates, and receive state-level financial aid at public colleges and universities.

Conclusion

College counselors serve as one of the most vital forms of financial aid information for certain underserved populations (McDonough & Calderone, 2006). The purpose of this chapter was to address this essential question: What do college access, admission and outreach practitioners need to know to help their students access financial aid? College access professionals must make sure that financial information is available, accessible and relevant to people of different groups (Perna, 2006).

Possible practices for working with students and families were reviewed, including five steps to consider before formally engaging in the financial aid process, as well as a timeline for activities and key definitions. Special populations, including undocumented students, international students and foster care youth were also considered. A list of key policy, advocacy and practitioner resources in the US were also included. Finally, trends in current and emerging research were addressed to help readers frame their understanding of research-driven practice. It's important to note that because financial aid is policy-driven, elements of this information are subject to change. For example, state-level policy for undocumented students and homeless youth is shifting rapidly. Federal student loan policies have also varied in terms of interest rates and subsidies. An informed college admission and access professional should check on current policies at the beginning of each academic year and check again at various times throughout the year using the resources noted in this chapter.

DISCUSSION QUESTIONS:

1. What types of resources can you provide your student that have the key components and checklists necessary to apply for financial aid (e.g., page in the counseling office, flyer to go home, etc.)?

2. Who are the financial aid experts that you can call on to help you with questions your students may have?

3. When should you encourage your students to begin to gather the necessary information for college aid?

4. Where might you post a compiled list of financial aid resources (loan information, scholarship information, etc.) that is readily accessible by students?

5. When and how can you engage families of students in the financial aid process so that they feel involved in the process and comfortable to share information necessary to direct them to the appropriate resources?

ABOUT THE AUTHOR

Kristan M. Venegas is an associate professor of clinical education and research associate in the Pullias Center for Higher Education at the University of Southern California (CA), and the faculty lead for the educational counseling master's degree program. Her research focuses on college access and financial aid for low-income students and students of color. Her work has been published in multiple research and practitioner venues. She was named an education expert by the National Hispanic Media Coalition and was selected emerging leader by the National Association of Academic Advisors in 2012. She was an American Council in Education Fellow in 2013–14.

REFERENCES

Bettinger, E., Long, B.T., Oreopoulos, P., & Sanbonmatsu, L. (2009, September). The role of simplification and information in college decisions: Results from the H&R Block FAFSA experiment (NBER Working Paper No. 15361). Retrieved from *http://www.nber.org. libproxy.usc.edu/ papers/w 15361.*

Deil-Amen, R., & Rios-Aguilar, C. (2000). From FAFSA to Facebook: The role of technology in navigating the financial aid process. In Kelly, A., & Goldrick-Rab, S. (Eds.), *Innovations in Financial Aid.* Harvard Education Press (in press).

Goldrick-Rab, S. (2010). Challenges and opportunities for improving community college student success. *Review of Educational Research,* 80, 437–469. Retrieved from doi: 10.3102/0034654310370163.

Jones-White, D.R., Radcliffe, P.M., Lorenz, L.M., & Soria, K.M. (2013). Priced out? The influence of financial aid on the educational trajectories of first-year students starting college at a large research university. *Research in Higher Education,* 55(4), 329–350.

NASSGAP. 44th Annual survey report on state-sponsored student financial aid 2012–2013. Retrieved from *www.nassgap.org/survey/NASSGAP_Survey_ Instrument_2013-14.pdf.*

NASSGAP. State data quick check. Retrieved from *http://www.nassgap.org/survey/state_data_check.asp.*

Perna, L.W. (2006). Understanding the relationship between information about college prices and financial aid and students' college-related behaviors. *The American Behavioral Scientist,* 49(12), 1620–1635.

Tierney, W.G., & Venegas, K.M. (2009). Finding money on the table: Information, financial aid, and access to college. *The Journal of Higher Education,* 80(4), 363–388.

Tierney, W.G., Venegas, K.M., & Mari Luna De, L.R. (2006). Introduction: Financial aid and access to college: The public policy challenges. *The American Behavioral Scientist,* 49(12), 1601–1603.

US Department of Education, National Center for Education Statistics. (2014). *The Condition of Education 2014* (NCES 2014-083). Grants and Loan Aid to Undergraduate Students.

Venegas, K.M., & Hallett, R.E. (2008). When a group presentation isn't enough: Financial aid advising for low-income urban college-bound students. *College and University,* 83(4), 16.

Chapter 16: Demystifying Enrollment Management: How Finances Impact Access

Angel B. Pérez
@Angelbperez

Author's Caveat:

This chapter is intended to give counselors a behind-the-scenes look at how colleges and universities in the United States balance meeting their institutional goals while managing budget constraints. The reality is, institutions of higher education are businesses that need to engage business practices in order to survive. It is the job of the enrollment manager to grapple with the need to bring in a class, raise enough tuition dollars to meet budget guidelines and still grapple with what makes higher education a unique kind of business—its intention to serve the public good and create access for students. How a college decides to manage its financial side of the house can have a significant impact on who gains access to the education at that institution. While the fiscal management of a college or university is extraordinarily complex and varies from institution to institution, there are practical tools counselors can use to best advise their students. This chapter will introduce counselors to enrollment management while equipping them with advice to share with prospective students and parents applying to college.

Today, colleges and universities increasingly find themselves struggling to balance the needs of the institution while cultivating their mission. At the same time, colleges are supposed to serve the public good and create access and opportunity for young people. Institutions of higher education are unique enterprises. They need to engage in business practices in order to thrive, but they have responsibilities to society that serve the greater good (Chambers, 1981). Institutions of higher education need to be fiscally sound to survive and simultaneously provide access for students from all socioeconomic backgrounds. In an era of decreasing state and federal appropriations, skyrocketing costs of running institutions and a fragile global economic climate, how do institutions balance mission and money? Admission and financial aid professionals find themselves in the seemingly contradictory undertaking of working with students to create ac-

cess and opportunity while enrolling a class that meets the fiduciary obligations of the institution. As Andrew Roth states in his *Journal of College Admission Ethic Series* article, "Admission officers must serve two masters whose interests are not always the same." (1998)

In today's economic climate, finding the balance between students that fulfill the philosophical and mission-driven goals of the university and those who can bring financial resources to the institution to help the institution stay afloat is a challenge. As Kalsbeek and Hossler state in their 2008 article, "At most institutions the enrollment goals are the revenue goals; successful enrollment management requires the management of financial aid in such a way that the number, mix and profile of enrolled students produces the desired net revenue after aid." (2008)

Only a handful of colleges and universities in the United States can afford to admit students without regard to their ability to pay. Most people in the counseling profession label this practice "need-blind admission." The contrasting (and most common practice) is "need-aware admission" (some institutions may also refer to this practice as need-sensitive). Need-aware admission is when an institution takes into account a student's finances before it can make a final admission decision.

If you ask any chief enrollment officer, he or she will immediately tell you they wish they didn't have to take a student's ability to pay into account when building a class. Need-aware admission is a practice directly related to fiscal resources and is not a representation of a school's ethics or values. All institutions have a financial bottom line, and they need to engage in practices that ensure their survival. The job of modern-day enrollment officers is two-fold: They need to provide access while making sure the institution brings in enough revenue to thrive.

Unfortunately, there are many who make value judgments about schools that can't afford to admit students without taking their ability to pay into account. The assumption is made: Need-aware is bad, and need-blind is good. This perspective comes from deeply rooted beliefs about what higher education in the US represents. Since the 1965 Higher Education Act, Americans affirm that higher education is the path toward upward social mobility. We believe a college education should be available to all, regardless of their socioeconomic status, and that colleges and universities, with some help from the government, should provide the resources for students who can't afford an education to obtain one (Roth, 1998).

The financial challenges facing higher education are steep—and these challenges directly affect who gets into college today and how much an education will cost. Tuition costs have increased dramatically and far exceed the average rate of inflation. At the same time, the costs related to running an institution of higher education have also increased exponentially. The growth in the number of students attending college is wonderful, but it has tremendous implications on costs and competition.

Additionally, significant changes in demographics are impacting the resources colleges are having to put into their financial aid budgets to meet student demand. For example, a majority of the students in the southern and western United States (two areas of major student growth) are low-income (Layon, 2013). Meanwhile, family income is not rising at a rate fast enough to keep up with tuition increases. All of this is happening during a time when receiving a bachelor's degree is considered compulsory to be competitive in today's economy.

Colleges are dealing with all of this while balancing many other pressures. Institutions want to increase academic quality and programming, shape diversity, comply with federal regulations, uphold the mission, ensure they meet enrollment targets in all majors, build athletic teams, orchestras, theater programs, and beyond. It's quite the juggling act, and if they don't strategically meet all of these priorities while balancing financial needs, they can begin to go down a slippery slope. So how does all of this play itself out in an admission committee?

BEHIND THE SCENES

Given all the media attention college admission has received in the past decade, most people are aware of a few aspects of what happens in a college admission office. There is the process of recruiting students, reading their applications, advocating for them in some form of committee process, and then class-shaping or crafting. It's the "shaping" the public knows little about. This is where the final decisions are made and colleges and universities try to balance the needs of a student with the needs of the institution. Up to this point, admission officers are reading files and making suggestions about who should be admitted, but the final round, called "shaping," is where the

chief enrollment officer looks at the numbers and figures out what the class looks like (statistically) in its entirety. The first state of the admission process looks at individuals. The final stage looks at groups of students, or the class as a whole.

Institutions input the data of all the individual applicants and potential "admits" into an enrollment model to see if the numbers make sense and meet all institutional goals. The enrollment model is a formula that tends to be complex, multi-layered, data-driven, and statistical in nature. The way institutions build a model is by figuring out how much money the institution needs in the coming year to survive financially. They then explore how many students they need to enroll in order to meet those goals. Institutions take into account the amount of financial aid they can award, the number of continuing students they have on campus and how much predicted total revenue admitting certain students would bring to the institution. Institutions also take into account that students with different levels of financial need enroll at different rates, so they pay very careful attention to the amount of funding each applicant needs. This formula will also include student demographics to help the enrollment manager understand what the class looks like not only from a financial perspective, but also from a demographic one.

As Kalsbeek and Hossler point out in their 2008 article, enrollment managers use sophisticated formulas and technology to help them figure out what their ideal class is going to look like.

> Today's practice of enrollment and net revenue management typically uses a precise segmentation of student populations based upon multiple characteristics that are known to affect the likelihood for enrollment; these include financial resources, academic profile, geographic origin, academic program, and any number of demographic and so-called non-cognitive factors. Any combination of these variables can be used to profile and segment a group of applicants, calculating the statistical likelihood of enrolling at a given institution, all things being equal. (Kalsbeek & Hosseler, 2008).

This entire practice is called "predictive modeling." Enrollment officers take years of data from admitted and enrolled students (this includes financial aid applicants, full-spay students, etc.) and predicts how many students are likely to enroll and how much revenue will be produced based on historical data (Berg, 2012).

The chief enrollment officer usually does this modeling in partnership with the treasurer, the head of financial aid and, at some institutions, an institutional research officer. Yet, the job of the chief enrollment officer is to balance the fiscal needs of the institution with other institutional priorities—all while trying to do what's best for students and their families. A chief enrollment officer needs to make sure that he or she brings in the revenue needed for the institution to survive, but is probably balancing all the other needs of the institution: geographic and ethnic diversity, academic rigor and quality, selectivity, diversity of student talent, etc. For large universities with several colleges, all of this is balanced while meeting specific enrollment targets for particular schools and majors.

While this all seems extraordinarily complex, it is done with the utmost care. Admission officers are advocates for each of the students whose files they read, and they care deeply about the students they wish to accept. Most admission officers do not know how much money a student needs to be able to attend college, and most do not engage in conversations about predictive modeling or financial need. The job of the admission officer is to evaluate the student and make a recommendation regarding admissibility. Most colleges and universities engage in an application reading process in which counselors are asked to "read their conscience." Counselors are asked to consider: Has the student done the work required to be successful at the institution? What would the student add to the campus community? Is this student a good fit? Does the student deserve a spot in the class? It isn't until the end of the process that finances may come into play.

While each institution practices different enrollment modeling, there are a few that are quite common. Some institutions will put the data of all the students the admission officers want to admit into the enrollment model after all the files are read and admission counselors have made decisions about their ideal candidates. They run the model and see how close they are to meeting targets. In this scenario, the chief enrollment officer usually has to return to the admission team and let them know that

they either have to bring in or remove a certain number of students based on what the model has revealed. Perhaps they spent too much financial aid, perhaps they have too many students of one particular gender or they have not admitted enough people to meet their revenue goals. All of this has to be rectified by the counseling staff before the model is run again.

In a different scenario, some colleges will go into admission committee for a week or two, discuss all of the students they want to admit and build the model as they go along. Every time they admit a student, they plug him or her into the model, knowing that in certain financial categories, they can only admit a certain number of students. This way, they know how many spots they have in each category and ensure they meet those targets along the way. Even in this process of predictive modeling, there are tradeoffs. At some point, you have to take people out of the model and put others in to meet the institution's goals.

The greatest myth about need-aware admission is that students who have the highest need are the ones who are usually pulled out of the equation. This simply isn't the case. Besides fiscal pressures, admission officers are balancing seemingly never-ending institutional priorities. If an admission committee needs to remove students from the "admit pile" because they have offered too much financial aid, they don't automatically take out students who have the highest financial need. They may look at students with lower academic profiles, or students in demographic areas where the institution has already met their goals. A student who needs $20,000 in financial aid is just as susceptible to further discussion as is a student who needs $60,000.

Admittedly, this is the most challenging time of the year in university enrollment offices. Admission counselors are told they have to remove students they have already recommended for admission. The committee then has to begin making even more complex decisions. If we are over budget, which students do we remove? If we need more students of a particular gender, whom do we remove to make room for others? What sacrifices do we make to meet this particular goal? Admission officers do this carefully, thoughtfully and with a lot of passion. Each student is discussed several times before a final decision is made about his or her admission. There have been instances when admission officers have shed tears over the fact that a particular student they were advocating for is no longer admissible because they do not meet an institutional priority.

A great example of this was featured in a 2009 *Time Magazine* article, which revealed how Skidmore College in New York struggles with these issues. After the counselors read all of the files, the director of financial aid ran the budget projections and figured out how many students they could afford to admit.

> Starting about March 1, the admission committee does "triage," Bates says, (Skidmore's admission dean) scrapping some applications stamped FA-Y for financial aid—yes, which are occasionally scrawled with a dollar amount. (Students who apply but don't qualify for aid are not penalized for trying; they get lumped in with the rest of the "full pays"). Needy applicants with weaker academic records, spotty senior-year grades or little interest in Skidmore are booted to the wait list. (Fitzpatrick, 2009)

Like Skidmore, all colleges have some process at the end of their application cycle in which they fine-tune their incoming classes by removing some students and including others to meet institutional goals. A chief enrollment officer is also balancing all the other needs of the institution: geographic and ethnic diversity, academic rigor and quality, selectivity, diversity of talent, legacy admits, athletic team demands, etc.

The most important thing for college counseling professionals to have is a clear understanding of the complexity of how college and universities struggle with balancing mission and money. As we have seen in the examples demonstrated earlier, "every college and university is some combination of a socially conscious provider of educational services and a business searching for revenues and cost cutting methods" (Weisbrod et. al., 2008).

PRACTICAL TOOLS FOR COUNSELING PRACTITIONERS

Let's face it, counselors like statistics. They want to know what the average GPA and test scores were for an admitted class so they know how to advise students looking to apply

to a particular university. They seek information about the average financial aid award for students attending a school, or what characteristics seem most attractive to admission officers reading the files. Some of this information is very much attainable through college Web sites and meetings with admission officers. However, counselors will never know how the fiscal needs of an institution change from year to year or how their students will fair in the enrollment modeling process. The job of the counselor is to understand the process and its challenges, partner with admission officers to understand how the process works at different institutions, and then help counsel families accordingly.

While the practices of financial-aid-awarding and predictive modeling at colleges and universities are complex and individual to each campus, there are practical tools that counselors can use to help families engage in best practices when applying to schools. Below are practical tips for counselors and families that will help demystify some of the financial aid process for families.

APPLYING FOR AID

While the media likes to perpetuate the myth that applying for financial aid hurts students, it's simply not true. While need-aware institutions have limited funding, these resources are made available to students that need them. Simply put, if a student needs financial aid to afford an institution, he or she should apply. Some students are told that if they apply for aid the office of admission will discriminate against them, so they wait until after they get admitted and then ask for financial aid. This is often a dangerous route to take because need-aware institutions tend to spend all of their funds on admitted students who applied for aid. If a student is admitted and then asks for financial aid, the answer will often be no. If a family thinks they may need financial aid in order to afford the education, they should apply. If they qualify for aid and are admitted, this will ensure they get the resources they need. If they don't qualify for aid, they are put in the same category as students who did not apply for financial aid, so either way, applying does not hurt them in the process.

DEADLINES

While most institutions have strict deadlines for financial aid, need-aware institutions have the least amount of flexibility. If students do not fill out their forms by a stated

While not all institutions engage in these practices, it does not hurt when a student demonstrates sincere interest in the institution he or she would like to attend.

deadline, they risk eligibility for any aid. While the safest route for students to take is to always fill forms out on time, they must understand that there is often very little flexibility at institutions that are highly tuition-dependent. Each institution is allotted a certain dollar amount that the enrollment office can use to help students fund their education. Once that aid is distributed, it is rare that institutions have any funding left over. One of the most difficult conversations enrollment offices have is with students who are admitted to the college and then inform the institution they are seeking aid. It's often too late.

OUTSIDE SCHOLARSHIPS

It is important that students become familiar with the policies of the institution they are enrolling in regarding outside scholarships. A few colleges and universities in the United States will take outside scholarships and reduce the student's loan component and/or make the funds available directly to the student. Other institutions will take those funds and reduce the amount of institutional grant aid that the student will receive. In this scenario, the student's total financial award remains the same, but the outside scholarship replaces the funding that the institution awards the student. Another key factor for students to keep in mind is that it is their responsibility to inform the financial aid office of any outside scholarships. If outside scholarships are to be applied to their accounts, the student often serves as the liaison between the scholarship organization and the college or university.

DEMONSTRATED INTEREST

In today's higher education landscape, it is often difficult for enrollment officers to predict if a student is actually interested in enrolling at their institution. Many institutions are tracking how much contact a student has had with them. This contact could be in the form of a visit to campus, an interview, a phone call, email, high school

visit, etc. Some institutions take this demonstrated interest into account and use it to enhance a student's financial aid award. If they know that a student is really interested, awarding some extra funding to the award may entice the student to enroll. Some institutions call this "preferential packaging." It is a practice in higher education where students who are highly sought-after are offered a more generous financial aid award (McPherson & Schapiro, 2010). While not all institutions engage in these practices, it does not hurt when a student demonstrates sincere interest in the institution he or she would like to attend.

ACADEMICS MATTER

When colleges and universities need to remove students who require financial aid from their enrollment model, they are probably going to first consider students whose grades have fallen. It is difficult to justify awarding limited financial resources to a student who has not kept up his or her grades. Students should strive to do their best and keep their grades strong all throughout their high school career. It could have a significant impact on both admission and financial aid outcomes.

FINANCIAL SAFETIES

Helping families understand the complexities of financing a college education can be a difficult challenge. One of the most important conversations counselors can help families engage in is defining the difference between what they can afford to pay and what they are willing to pay. While some families can afford an expensive private school, some have a bottom line on what they are willing to pay. Open and honest conversations early in the college search process will ensure the entire family understands the different sacrifices willing to be made. In today's economic climate, it is also important that counselors help families choose financial safety schools. These are institutions whose tuition pricing families are willing to pay. While financial aid is an option at all colleges, and students should apply to the schools they desire to attend the most, it is important for students to apply to schools whose price the families are willing to finance. When it comes to creating a list of schools to apply to, including all kinds of diversity is important—and pricing diversity is a must. A great way to get a sense of what a family may have to pay is by having the parent fill out the college's net price calculator. Each school is federally mandated to have one of these on their Web site. While the calculation will not be 100-percent accurate (because it usually does not take into account any merit aid or complicated family circumstances), it will give families a ballpark figure that will help them determine whether or not they should pursue admission to a particular institution.

VALUE JUDGMENTS

As stated earlier, there are many counselors who believe need-aware institutions are "bad" and need-blind institutions are "good." Avoiding these value judgments and helping families understand what these terms actually mean is important. If students choose not to apply to a college because it is need-aware, they could be missing out on an extraordinary opportunity. The majority of institutions of higher education in the United States are need-aware institutions doing the best they can with the resources they have. They want to make sure they use the resources they have to serve the public good, while being fiscally responsible and securing the institution's fiscal health for the future. "The handful of schools that practice a 'need blind,' full-need approach to financial aid are distinguished mainly by their exceptional resources, both of endowment and of affluent high-quality applicants, that allow them to sustain the practice." (McPherson and Schapiro, 1998)

ENCOURAGE HONEST CONVERSATIONS

Most admission officers are afraid to tell a counselor that a student was not admitted because they had to be pulled out at the end of the process for issues of funding. Yet, the more counselors encourage admission officers to have honest, trusting and confidential conversations with one another, the more each party will understand the work of the other. Often, admission officers fear that the counselor will react negatively, or that they are addressing a taboo issue. Yet, if a counselor exhibits a clear understanding of the complexity of the process and tells an admission officer that he/she understands if a student was not admitted for reasons of finance, both parties may walk away with a greater understanding of the process and significant growth in their collegial relationship.

ETHICS

The stress of the college admission and financial aid process can lead many families to engage in unethical behavior. It is the job of the counselor to help guide families in making ethical decisions throughout the process. When families engage in unethical behavior, they risk becoming ineligible for any aid, and students risk being expelled from an institution. Some families try to hide income and assets in order to qualify for more aid. According to section 490(a) of the Higher Education Act, penalties for providing false information on the FAFSA can include a fine of up to $20,000 and/or up to five years in prison. Hiding assets isn't worth the risk.

CONTINUED PROFESSIONAL DEVELOPMENT

It is important that counseling professionals seek continuous training and professional development in financial aid. Every school is unique and sets differential policies around financial aid. In addition, the federal government changes policies almost every year. Colleges and universities have

The stress of the college admission and financial aid process can lead many families to engage in unethical behavior. It is the job of the counselor to help guide families in making ethical decisions throughout the process.

a difficult time keeping up with all of the federal changes each year, but in order to be effective, counselors and financial aid officers need to seek continuous training on the landscape. The national organization for financial aid officers is the National Association of Student Financial Aid Administrators (NASFAA). Becoming a member or attending its workshops will ensure counselors receive the most up-to-date information and are engaging in best practices.

Conclusion

Understanding how colleges balance mission and money helps contextualize many issues the public tends to debate: Why are more public universities recruiting out of state and admitting more non-residents? Non-residents pay more and, in turn, supplement budgets. Why are colleges giving merit aid dollars to students who have no financial need? If a college costs $60,000 and gives a student with no financial need $20,000 in merit aid, they still make a $40,000 profit. Why is it that a student who had everything the college required and more didn't get in? While the answer to that can be extraordinarily complex, the one answer most counselors don't address is that the institution perhaps could not afford the student.

As this chapter highlights, institutional economics are individualized and highly complex. In reality, only key administrators at an institution really understand the inner workings of how financial aid budgets, revenue goals and tuition revenue modeling really affect who gets in and how much each student will pay. The goal of the counselor advising students seeking admission to college is not to understand the intricacy of each institution's financial modeling and practices. The key is to understand the general categories that colleges fall into and have a clearer understanding as to why decisions are made. This can only help counselors become better advisors and help guide families in understanding how the inner workings of an institution impacts access. Counselors play an integral role in helping students and families navigate not only where they should apply to college, but also how they are going to finance it. The kind of information they provide could help a student to make decisions that are pivotal to their journey to higher education. For example,

if a counselor is working with a student who is afraid of applying to a college because it has a need-aware admission policy, the counselor can help explain this practice to the student and highlight its realities, but also encourage the student to proceed if it in fact is the best-fit school for the student. Simply put, an understanding of enrollment management can strengthen the efforts of college counselors.

The great news is, all colleges and universities, including those with very limited resources, are intent on helping students and families finance their dreams of an education. Enrollment officers work tirelessly to achieve the extraordinarily complex work of institutional management while serving the public good. The best enrollment professionals partner with counselors globally and create trusting collegial relationships that serve both students and institutions well. While fiscal challenges impede the majority of institutions from admitting all the students they would like, enrollment officers are adamant about using ethical practices to serve their institutions and meet the needs of the public. The key to their success is balancing the fiscal health of their institution while creating the most access and opportunity possible for young people. Counselors serve as key partners in creating these opportunities. By providing the most up-to-date and transparent financial aid information to the students and families they serve, they can guide students to opportunities they could have never imagined.

About the Author

Angel B. Pérez has served in secondary and higher education leadership positions on both coasts of the US and travels globally to speak on issues of American higher education. The author of numerous articles, his writing is featured in US and global publications. Angel teaches in the college counseling certification program of UCLA where he received the appointment of Master Teacher. A frequent keynote speaker at conferences, Angel is a Fulbright Scholar alumnus and recipient of NACAC's 2009 John B. Muir Editor's Award. He currently serves as vice president and dean of admission and financial aid at Pitzer College (CA).

REFERENCES

Berg, B. (2012, July/August). Predictive modeling: A tool, not the answer. *University Business*.

Chambers, C.M. (1981). Foundations of ethical responsibility in higher education administration. *New directions for higher education*, 1981: 1-13.

Fitzpatrick, L. (2009, April 6). The financial aid game. *Time Magazine*.

Kalsbeek, D.H., & Hossler, D. (2008). Enrollment management and financial aid: Seeking a strategic integration. *College and University*, 84(1).

Layton, Lyndsey. (2013, October 16). Study: poor children are now the majority in American public schools in south, west. *The Washington Post*. Retrieved from *http://www.washingtonpost.com/loca/ education/2013/10/16/34eb4984-35bb-11e3-8a0e-4e2cf80831fc_story.html*.

McPherson, M., & Schapiro, M. (1998). *The student aid game: Meeting need and rewarding talent in American higher education*. Princeton, NJ: Princeton University Press.

McPherson, M., & Schapiro, M. (2010, March 25). The blurring line between merit and need in financial aid. *Change: The Magazine of Higher Learning*, March, 25, 39.

Roth, A. (1998). Admission, ethics and financial aid: Formulating and applying an ethical framework to the need-blind debate. *Journal of College Admission*, Summer.

Weisbrod, B., Ballou, J., & Asch, E. (2008). *Mission and money: Understanding the university*. New York, NY: Cambridge University Press.

IV.   Serving Our Students and Families

FROM AWARENESS TO ACTION

Raquel M. Rall, PhD

Identifying the resources useful in supporting aspiring and/or college-bound students is just but one step in helping them prepare for college. The shift from section three to section four represents an even more direct move and use of the concepts discussed. It is not enough for counselors to be aware of the requisites for college and the options available to students; counselors must strategically and intentionally engage in actions that will help students realize their postsecondary potential.

College counseling is truly an exception to the "one size fits all" mentality. To maximize effectiveness, college counselors must know more than the requirements; they need to be familiar with whom they serve. The juxtaposition of more students in general (and more diverse students in particular) in K–12 education with the recognition that the nation is becoming increasingly dependent upon technology use creates a college-going environment necessarily influenced by external factors. So what are the unique aspects to college counseling in the 21st century?

In the next section, the authors discuss the role of the college counselor in recognizing, understanding and meeting the needs of diverse student populations. Working with traditionally marginalized students, including those students who are first in their families to go to college or students who have disabilities, may require college counselors to expand their knowledge-base and professional affiliations in order to best serve constituents.

No amount of reading and research can prepare a college counselor for all of the intricacies that inform a student's academic history and future plans. In chapter 17, the author discusses the role of college counselors in creating opportunities for marginalized students. In chapter 18, counselors can read about working with first-generation students. In chapter 19, the author shares resources about working with students with learning disabilities. In chapter 20, the author discusses the role of social media in the college application process, and in chapter 21, the author offers advice on how to help students write a strong and meaningful college admission essay.

Knowing as much as possible about intersectionalities that inform students' paths to college is vital. In order to best elevate efforts producing college access and success, college admission counseling professionals might work directly with students and their families. These efforts demonstrate commitment to identities and challenges, while alleviating fears and misconceptions.

Chapter 17: The Role of Counselors in Facilitating College Opportunities for Marginalized Student Populations

Adrian H. Huerta
@UCLadrian

INTRODUCTION

In 2014, researchers, policymakers and educators debated the purpose and value of higher education, frequently in *The New York Times,* with captions that commonly read, "Is college worth it?" or "Best return on investment for a [X] major." The debate focused on what students and families should do with their postsecondary goals and the type of institutions to avoid. Voices commonly absent from these national discussions include high school college counselors and admission representatives, who traditionally serve as facilitators of the college-going process for students across the country and who are on the pulse of the needs of different student populations. The purpose of this chapter is to discuss the role of college counselors in facilitating college opportunities for traditionally marginalized student populations and their families.

For the purpose of this chapter, marginalized student populations include first-generation, low-income, and traditionally underrepresented racial and ethnic groups. High school contexts, coupled with students' race and ethnicity, gender, and socioeconomic status, influence the types of positive or negative engagement between college counselors and their students (Corwin, Venegas, Oliverez, & Colyar, 2004; Engberg & Wolniak, 2010; McDonough & Calderone, 2006; Moore, Henfield, & Owens, 2008; Perna, Rowan-Kenyon, Thomas, Bell, Anderson, & Li, 2008; Tierney & Venegas, 2009). These combined characteristics add another level of perplexity to the increased competition to gain access to four-year colleges and universities for low-income, first-generation, and racial and ethnic minority student populations (Espinoza, 2011; McDonough, Antonio, Walpole, & Perez, 1998). The competition for access to selective, public four-year colleges has shifted from in-state students to a concerted effort to recruit out-of-state and international students, who are able to shoulder the larger tuition cost differences. Where does this new predicament leave marginalized students and their families when they discuss college options with school counselors? The purpose of this chapter is to share the current research and practice strategies used to engage different high school student populations to reach higher education; and to explain how college counselors are a linchpin in facilitating college opportunities for traditionally marginalized students.

COLLEGE COUNSELORS AND MARGINALIZED STUDENT POPULATIONS

Who enrolls in college based on race and ethnicity, gender, and income status?

Facilitating college access and enrollment remains a contentious issue for college counselors because of the backgrounds of some students within high school contexts (Espinoza, 2011; McDonough, 1997; Engberg & Gilbert, 2014; Stephan & Rosenbaum, 2013). This is not to say students' racial or ethnic backgrounds are an impediment, but historically, these groups' relationships with postsecondary education has been riddled with various hurdles. College counselors are burdened with performing various administrative tasks to support the basic functions of high schools, including lunch supervision, course scheduling, test monitoring, discipline, and other administrative support (Hill, 2012; McDonough, 1997, 2005), which reduces the amount of time dedicated to sharing college knowledge with students and their families (Engberg & Gilbert, 2014).

In all communities, the intersections of students' race, ethnicity, gender, and socioeconomic status influence how opportunities are presented by educators; college counselors may shape how perceptions, high school context and local community are constructed and internalized (Bryan, Holcomb-McCoy, Moore-Thomas, & Day-Vines, 2009; Deli-Amen & Tevis, 2010; McDonough & Calderone, 2006; Stephan & Rosenbaum, 2013). The intersectionality of students' background is especially salient in low-income and underresourced schools, where college readiness is not typically cultivated by high schools until students reach their junior or senior year, whereas high-income communities discuss college-planning from nearly birth (Deli-Amen & Tevis, 2010; Klugman, 2012; Mullen, 2010). All of these multiple realities interact and impact the college-going aspirations for students, the types of four-year institutions they pursue, and the level of academic and emotional readiness these students possess (Deli-Amen & Tevis, 2010; Hallett & Venegas, 2011; Mullen, 2010). For example, Klasik (2012) studied the experience of almost 9,000 students attending 750 high schools across the United States, using longitudinal data to determine the necessary steps to become prepared for and matriculate into college (see Table 1).

Table 1. Percent of Students who Completed Steps to Four-Year College Enrollment, by Group

	Asian/Pacific Islander	Latino[1]	African American[2]	White
10th grade bachelor degree aspirations	95.6%	89.8%	92.8%	92.9%
Enrolled in a four-year college	59.4	28.9	39.8	53.4
% decline	-36.2	-60.9	-53	-39.5

(Adapted from Klasik, 2012)

[1] *The terms "Latino" and "Hispanic" are used interchangeably throughout the chapter.*
[2] *The terms "black" and "African American" are used interchangeably throughout the chapter.*

The findings, across Asian/Pacific Islander, Latino, African American and White student groups, display a decrease in aspirations for bachelor degree attainment, in comparison to actual enrollment. This decline, ranging from 36 percent to nearly 61 percent might stem from a number of realities.

It is possible that the confidence of the students in this study wavered about feeling (un)prepared for college, or that the students received mixed information about college, contributing to the decline of college hopes among those students. While determining the exact source for the decline in students' college-going aspirations is near impossible, in part because the students are still adolescents and are still developing physically and cognitively and are influenced by various factors (Nakkula & Toshalis, 2006; Savitz-Romer & Bouffard, 2012), but as the focus of this chapter is on marginalized student populations, the larger percentage of decline for black and Latino populations is noteworthy. How do college counselors step in and recognize those challenges and remain privy to the impact and social and cultural significance of race and ethnicity, gender, and low-income status on students' college-going dreams? The next section attempts to unpack the often complicated relationship between racial and ethnic groups' interactions with college counselors.

RACIAL AND ETHNIC GROUPS

The social and academic experiences of students from different racial and ethnic backgrounds in K–12 education vary widely (Carter, 2005; Ferguson, 2001; Kozol, 2005; Lareau, 2011; Moore, Henfield, & Owens, 2008; Oakes, 2005; Suárez-Orozco, Suárez-Orozco, & Todorova, 2008; Valenzuela, 1999). While some racial and ethnic groups are welcomed into a high school environment and provided a superior education based on the schools' perceptions of the students' abilities and the culture of the high school, (Auerbach, 2004; Teranishi, 2010; Valenzuela, 1999), other groups are not afforded the same educational equity to achieve and be college-ready by 12th grade (Contreras, 2011; Howard, 2003; Lareau, 2011). Some teachers and counselors believe Asian Americans and Pacific Islanders (AAPI) serve as the "model minority," possessing all the valued social and intellectual traits to excel in high school and later on in college. Scholars have challenged educators to recognize not all AAPI students and their families have the same social and economic resources, English language acquisitions or college-going rates to navigate the higher education system (Kim & Gasman, 2011; Teranishi, 2010; Teranishi, Ceja, Antonio, Allen, & McDonough, 2004). The combined work of these authors has pushed educators and policymakers to recognize the educational gaps for Cambodians, Hmong, Laotian, Vietnamese, Native Hawaiians, and other Pacific Islanders, who often need to receive additional outreach in order to complete high school and pursue a college education (Terniashi, 2010, Teranishi & Pazich, 2014). Counselors cannot assume AAPI students—or any student groups—have the available resources to navigate the postsecondary system by themselves. Specifically, educators must acknowledge certain groups are often omitted from serious discussions about educational inequities and limited college-going efforts (Fann, 2005). Fann's work has documented how counselors often suggest community colleges for their high-achieving Native-American students who live in rural environments. The rationale for the counselors was to promote a less expensive postsecondary institution and a college option in close proximity to the students' homes.

As counselors, we must work toward providing students and their families with all the necessary information about financial aid and the support systems available in postsecondary institutions, such as Student Support Services through TRiO and the McNair Scholars Program. These types of programs often help students become better integrated into their college or university, which helps with retention and student persistence (Rendon, Jalomo, & Nora, 2000; Tierney, 1992). Too often, we stress the short-term goals of technical, vocational or other two-year focused programs, instead of promoting long-term social mobility (Dowd, 2003; Howard, 2003). This perception is disappointing, but not surprising. Some counselors believe they're looking out for the best interests of black, Latino and Native-American students and their families when they encourage them to attend more affordable two-year options, instead of enduring the additional strain on the families' limited economic resources if the students were to attend four-year postsecondary institutions (McDonough & Calderone, 2006).

Community colleges can provide the illusion of opportunity for students to be transfer-ready in two years, but these schools are unable to properly support their students (Deli-Amen, Rosenbaum, & Person, 2005; Dowd, 2003). For some low-income, racial and ethnic minority communities, college-going is a process that requires family support and encouragement. Simultaneously, college includes the stress of leaving home and a disconnect from the daily activities to which the student has become accustomed (Fann, 2005; Perez & McDonough, 2008). Although, various scholars have stressed the need for students to disengage from their families in order to immerse themselves in the new college environment (Tinto, 1993), the separation does not work for all first-time college-goers who are exploring the new college-student identity (Savitz-Romer & Bouffard, 2012; Tierney, 1992).

College Enrollment of Latino Students

Although not purely a racial group, Latino students' experiences in the educational pipeline are met with mixed results by college counselors (McDonough & Calderone, 2006; Solórzano, Villalpando, & Oseguera, 2005). The educational results for Latinos in high school and college completion are influenced by families' country of origin, English language acquisition, socioeconomic status, and parents' education level (Kasinitz, Mollenkopf, Waters,

Holdaway, 2008; Stanton-Salazar, 2001; Suárez-Orozco, Suárez-Orozco, & Todorova, 2008; Valenzuela, 1999). Mexican Americans and Central Americans experience various hurdles to successfully reach and complete higher education. Racism, poverty and attendance at under-resourced public schools are all examples of these barriers (Crosnoe & Turley, 2011; Solórzano et al., 2005).

Almost 10 years ago, Solórzano and colleagues (2005) captured the limited educational mobility for Latinos involved in the education system—for the 100 students who begin elementary school, only two will graduate from college (See Figure 1). The educational attainment numbers remain almost completely stagnant and require critical discussions on how to improve the situation (see National Center for Education Statistics, 2013 for current information). It should be noted that Latino families who are college educated are better equipped to communicate with counselors and request appropriate courses for their children to prepare for college admission. When low-income Latino families place blind faith in educators to show genuine concern and best intentions aimed at preparing their children for college admission, often Latino students do not receive the needed guidance or support to achieve it (Crosnoe & Turley, 2011; Rodriguez & Cruz, 2009; Stanton-Salazar, 2001; Suárez-Orozco et al., 2008; Perna, 2000; Valenzuela, 1999). Although pivotal moments occur when counselors provide much-needed and critical information to students in order to facilitate students' college-going goals (Espinoza, 2011), most of the counseling interactions do not result in Latino students being prepared

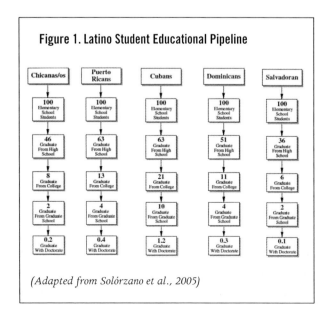

Figure 1. Latino Student Educational Pipeline

(Adapted from Solórzano et al., 2005)

for four-year colleges (Contreras, 2011; Corwin et al., 2004; Espinoza, 2011; McDonough & Calderone, 2006).

Gender

The gender gap in college access and readiness is an emerging area of concern for educators, policymakers and parents. Over the last 25 years, scholars have worked toward understanding how males and females gain access to college information, feel different forms of pressure and expectations from peers and parents, and navigate the higher education system to complete the college process (Buchmann, Diprete, & McDaniel, 2008; DiPrete & Buchmann, 2013). Female students' success can often lead educators and counselors to compare both groups and ask men, "Where are you with college-going plans?" Various studies stress that men are not putting forth the same effort in homework completion or enrollment in rigorous high school courses as their female peers (Buchmann, 2009; DiPrete & Buchmann, 2013), while others contend that young men are being treated differently and unfairly by educators (Saenz & Ponjuan, 2009).

From kindergarten to college completion, females earn better grades in all subjects, including math and science (DiPrete & Buchmann, 2013). Most notably, females have outpaced males in high school completion, college enrollment and bachelor's degree attainment (Buchmann, 2009; DiPrete & Buchmann, 2013; Williams, Bitsóï, Gordon, Harper, Saenz, & Teranishi, 2014). (See Figure 2.)

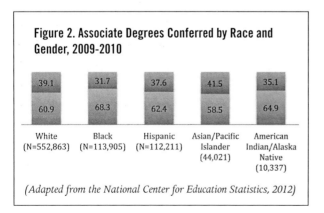

Figure 2. Associate Degrees Conferred by Race and Gender, 2009-2010

White (N=552,863)	Black (N=113,905)	Hispanic (N=112,211)	Asian/Pacific Islander (44,021)	American Indian/Alaska Native (10,337)
39.1	31.7	37.6	41.5	35.1
60.9	68.3	62.4	58.5	64.9

(Adapted from the National Center for Education Statistics, 2012)

The disparities between males and females discussed here indicate that college counselors need to reexamine the college-going needs of young men. Young men of color are experiencing challenging schooling environments, which may contribute to the low national high school

graduation rate, around 50 percent, and in some communities, even lower (Howard & Huerta, 2014; Williams et al., 2014). The final section provides new factors and perspectives for college counselors to consider when engaging young men of color in the college-going process; the crucial role college counselors play in shaping college-going goals for students; and how school- and district-wide efforts could help change the condition for male students. At this moment in society, when young men are placed on the non-college track, their access to accurate and timely college information is limited (Huerta, McDonough, & Allen, 2014; Vigil, 1999).

Recently, the need to support men of color has reached national attention from the federal government. The impetus for this concern is the 50-percent high school graduation rate (on average), the overrepresentation of males of color in school suspension and expulsion, and the low number of young men of color enrolling in and completing higher education (Fergus, Noguera, & Martin, 2014; Noguera, Hurtado, & Fergus, 2012; Williams et al., 2014). President Obama has addressed the current dire status of males of color with his My Brother's Keeper initiative, which is aimed at bringing public and private partnerships together to support the social and academic needs of young men of color to reach their potential. Why is this important for college counselors? Counselors must provide the appropriate social and academic support for young men of color to develop college-going behaviors and goals. High school males are less likely to seek college information from their high school counselor (Bryan et al., 2009) and often search for college information from their peers or family, which is usually inaccurate if those individuals do not have college experience (Bonous-Hammarth & Allen, 2005; Robinson, 2011; Perez & McDonough, 2008).

As mentioned earlier, the high academic achievement and college degree completion of females is not a new phenomenon, but only has recently captured society's attention due to the fact that females now represent more than 50 percent of college matriculates and completers (DiPrete & Buchmann, 2013). Different studies have stressed that high school males and females receive conflicting messages about college-going (Fann, 2005; Howard, 2003; Perez & McDonough, 2008). Male students of color are more likely to begin their postsecondary education at community college, but do not achieve similar levels of academic completion as their female peers (Harris & Wood, 2013; See Figure 2;) Some Latinas are encouraged to attend colleges in close proximity to their family in order to maintain relationships with younger siblings (Perez & McDonough, 2008), while some Latino males often enter college feeling unsupported and marginalized (Huerta & Fishman, 2014). An additional point to stress is that female high school students more actively seek advice and guidance from their college counselor, whereas males do not search for counselor support (Bryan et al., 2009). In addition to gender, a student's socioeconomic status influences the types of social, cultural and intellectual capital necessary to interact with educators (Bourdieu, 1986; Carter, 2005; Swartz, 1998).

Socioeconomic Status

Past research has stressed that college counselors often encourage low-income students to attend two-year colleges or local, less-selective universities because of the potential financial strain on students and their families (Fann, 2005; McDonough and Calderone, 2006; Perez & McDonough, 2008). Whether low-income students were high-achieving or not, it did not impact the type of college counseling provided to the student. What resulted were college counselors who guided low-income students to a less-selective college than their wealthier peers (Radford, 2013). The types and methods of college counseling provided for low-income students vary based on caseload, administrative duties and the culture of the counseling department in high schools (Espinoza, 2011; McDonough, 1997). Unfortunately, the majority of low-income students receive little support and encouragement to apply to selective four-year colleges, which typically leads them to under-matched schools that do not meet the students' social and academic needs or challenges (Radford, 2013). The question for college counselors is, "How do we advocate and support all students' needs, without additional resources, when we are aware of the economic stresses low-income families experience?"

We must be sure to provide students with access to the various services and programs offered by the school district and by local nonprofits, such as fee waivers for college applications, college entrance exams and advanced placement exams in a timely manner. But, remember that while financial aid is available for students, we still need to match our students with caring professionals at a local or distant college who will be sensitive to our students' financial situations. Though the purchasing power of federal aid does not cover all of the anticipated and unanticipated expenses of tuition, books, materials, and other items required to attend a two- or four-year college (Heller, 2005), college counselors should not allow college costs to overpower students' goals to pursue higher education.

Ultimately, low-income status plays a large role in the lives of students and their families and influences the types of high schools students attend (Contreras, 2011; Frankenberg & Orfield, 2012; McDonough, 1997). How we examine and understand how opportunities and resources are distributed to different high schools is important in figuring out how to provide low-income and underrepresented minority students with relevant and rigorous curriculum, including multiple advanced placement courses, international baccalaureate courses and electives that mirror undergraduate seminars that will adequately prepare students for the academic demands of college (Hallett & Venegas, 2011; Radford, 2013; Mullen, 2010). How do counselors meet the college-going needs and goals of their students with sometimes limited resources? Counselors must piece together opportunities and constantly negotiate college resources to support students even when they do not have the support of the school administration (Hill, 2012).

Pushing K–12 school districts to forge stronger bonds with public and private higher education is crucial for students to succeed. There appears to be a mountain of challenges for underrepresented students to reach higher education and a large burden that rests on the abilities and commitment of college counselors to work and develop strategies to support an effective college-going culture. The following section highlights the different models used by college counselors across the US to serve underrepresented students and their families.

Developing a strong college-going culture at a high school requires the support and investment not only of the college counselor, but also of the students, families, teachers, school administration, and district offices (Hill, 2012; McDonough, 1997; Tierney, Corwin, & Colyar, 2005). Students must believe in themselves and their abilities to be prepared for and succeed in college (Fergus, Noguera, & Martin, 2014; McDonough, 1997; Savitz-Romer & Bouffard, 2012). Counselors must engage in and share timely and accurate information with parents about how to prepare and support their children for postsecondary education (Bonous-Hammarth & Allen, 2005), and other educators and administrators should make a concerted effort to graduate college-ready students (Hill, 2012). However, these relationships between all of the stakeholders are not always in harmony, for a variety of reasons. Counselors must try a multitude of strategies to equip students and parents with college knowledge in order to prepare them for their next steps. McDonough (1997) lays the foundation for other researchers to examine the role of college counselors in different types of high schools and the importance of college-going cultures. The organizational culture of those schools signals to students the acceptable and expected pathways to higher education; the culture dictates how college counselors engage families, students and their colleagues in the pursuit of higher education.

One of the many implications suggested here is the importance of building stronger relationships between school districts and local colleges and universities. The need for increased access to and success in college requires closer bonds between the education systems to ensure students are not displaced in the process (McDonough & Gildersleeve, 2006; Venezia & Kirst, 2001, 2005). These efforts, in action, are discussed in chapter 23 of the textbook.

STRATEGIES FOR FACILITATING COLLEGE OPPORTUNITIES FOR MARGINALIZED STUDENT POPULATIONS

College counselors have increasingly used digital technologies as one method to distribute information about higher education to students and families. This means of disseminating information has caused concern for some because of the digital divide (Goode, 2010; Mathis, 2010; Robinson, 2009, 2011; Venegas, 2006, 2007). In 2006, Venegas was one of the first higher education scholars to highlight the gap between low-income students' limited knowledge about how to use college Web sites and portals, owning core computer and printer equipment, and infrequent access to fast and reliable Internet. The most

startling revelation was that college counselors at that time also had limited knowledge about how to navigate college portals and complete required online financial aid forms, which further impacted the students' college access (Robinson, 2009, 2011; Venegas, 2006, 2007). So, there is an issue of access to the digital information, as well as an issue of knowing how to use the technology. Educators in high school and college innately believe the current generations of college students are prepared to use technology seamlessly, which is not true (Goode, 2010; Robinson, 2011). This may serve as a potential lesson for college counselors to not assume high school students are able to navigate and locate accurate information about financial aid and college requirements from various Web sites. Robinson (2009) stresses low-income students will favor their peers over questionable information they retrieve online, which may undermine the accuracy of college knowledge being shared.

One method to alleviate the stresses of overburdened counselors' caseloads, as described in chapter seven, is to incorporate the use of video games that teach college-knowledge strategies. Mathis (2010) provides a clear rationale as to how and why video games can help college counselors better prepare students to gain access to a four-year institution. His suggestions require investments in professional development seminars for teachers and counselors to be versed in the programs, which will better prepare educators to engage high school students. Recently, Castleman and Page (2013) developed a text-messaging-based initiative to increase college matriculation for low-income and first-generation college students. The text-based application sends reminder texts with information about individual college deadlines, financial aid form reminders, and opportunities to meet with a student peer and/or college counselor. The initiative has increased college matriculation for students in their pilot areas in Georgia, Texas and Massachusetts, but, ultimately, the college-bound students received significant support from meeting individually with college counselors when attempting to navigate the complicated forms and potential roadblocks in matriculating into college.

Some researchers acknowledge the constant strain of time and resources on college counseling and have proposed new college counseling methods, which include the use of college coaches, outside college-access organizations or peer college counselors. (Espinoza, 2012; Stephen & Rosenbaum, 2013; Tierney & Venegas, 2006). Stephen and Rosenbaum (2013) detailed the role of college coaches who worked with low-income students attending Chicago public schools on developing college-going goals. What is unique about college coaches is that they do not report to individual school administrators, but rather, to district offices, allowing them additional flexibility to work on the larger goals of information sharing and scaffolding to boost students' aspirations and motivation to attend four-year college. Although there are shortcomings related to the type of institutions students selected, there was an overall increase in four-year college enrollment because of the increased information about financial aid, application deadlines and postsecondary institutional differences. Additionally, the low-income and racial ethnic minority students avoided two-year colleges because of the increased information about the low transfer and student support resources provided by Chicago community colleges. What the article did not discuss was the overall cost associated with college coaches, who are supporting dozens of urban high schools, which may cause district administrators to be cautious of implementing similar programs.

INFORMING PRACTICE

As previously mentioned, developing a college-going culture requires a concerted effort by teachers and administrators. For example, Jaffe-Walter and Lee (2011) highlighted the efforts of building a college-going culture for low-income, recently arrived immigrant students who are English-language learners. The teachers constantly stressed the importance of students attending college after high school and being future-oriented with their studies and life plans because it leads to social mobility. Teachers, college counselors and school leadership worked in partnership to promote college access and the school-wide goals that emphasized the college-going process.

Most recently, Engberg and Gilbert (2014) used national longitudinal data about 21,000 high school students to advance the discussion of college counseling and describe the following models: divergent, emergent and convergent. These typologies describe the counselors' average caseload, hours devoted to the college-choice process and the goals of the counseling center. The re-

sources measured in each of the 940 high schools across the country focused on the number of offerings of college fairs, college course offerings and financial aid seminars, because of the strong influence as predictors of enrollment at four-year institutions. The schools are considered divergent when counseling departments are not centered on building a college-going culture and offer limited resources to facilitate the college-choice process for their students. The schools in the emergent model offer a high abundance of resources and behaviors to emphasize college preparation for their students, and four-year matriculation is the primary goal. Lastly, the convergent schools offer the most resources and college-going norms that suggest a near perfect alignment of environment for facilitating college-going behaviors.

Various social science scholars have examined individual student and family interactions with college counselors, moments of success and challenges for student and counselor relationships, and different counseling models based on school types, that impact the college-going outcomes of students based on race and ethnicity, gender, and socioeconomic status (Espinoza, 2011; Howard, 2003; McDonough, 1997; Moore, Henfield, & Owens, 2008). All of these various studies ultimately reveal that college counseling is difficult, and different student populations require various forms of attention and support to get prepared to attend four-year institutions. Espinoza (2011) captured the essence of this type of caring for students and coined the term, "pivotal moments," which is used by educators invested in students and can alter students' life trajectories. However, simultaneously, some educators did not provide the same attention and support that students required. This one example highlights the delicate balance of time, personality and relationships between students and college counselors.

To facilitate college opportunities for marginalized communities based on gender, income status, and race and ethnicity, college counselors must work with school administration and others to create social spaces for these students to discuss their stresses about being underrepresented in higher education and provide methods to support their college-going goals. Taking stock of the resources and opportunities available to these students can help counselors figure out the best methods for presenting them with information regarding college. Facilitating college-going for marginalized students requires college counselors to learn how student backgrounds inform college preparation and aspirations, identify colleagues with which to collaborate, and determine potential strategies for intervention. College counselors play a pivotal role in helping to shape the postsecondary future of these students who have traditionally been marginalized.

ABOUT THE AUTHOR

Adrian H. Huerta is a PhD Student in the Higher Education & Organizational Change program at the University of California, Los Angeles, where he is also a research assistant in the Choices Project that focuses on access, equity and diversity in higher education. His research focuses on college access, gang knowledge versus college knowledge, and leadership development for young men of color with an emphasis in Latino males. Previously, he worked with first-generation and low-income college students in the McNair Scholars Program at the University of Southern California (CA) and has over ten years of experience in college access and outreach programs.

ADDITIONAL RESOURCES

Application Crunch (college-knowledge game)

- *www.futureboundgames.com/application-crunch-faq*

College Board Counselor Workshops

- *counselorworkshops.collegeboard.org*

College Summit

- *www.collegesummit.org*

Mellon Mays Undergraduate Fellowship

- *www.mellon.org/grant_programs/programs/higher-education-and-scholarship/mellon-mays-fellowship*

McNair Scholars Program

- *mcnairscholars.com*

National College Access Network

- *www.collegeaccess.org/accessprogramdirectory*

Principles of Building a College-Going Culture

- *collegetools.berkeley.edu/resources.php?cat_id=9*

The College Board Young Men of Color Initiatives

- *youngmenofcolor.collegeboard.org*

US Department of Education, TRIO Programs

- *www2.ed.gov/about/offices/list/ope/trio/index.html*

REFERENCES

Auerbach, S. (2004). Why do they give the good classes to some and not to others? Latino parent narratives of struggle in a college access program. *Teachers College Record*, 104(7), 1369–1392.

Bryan, J., Holcomb-McCoy, C., Moore-Thomas, C., & Day-Vines, N.L. (2009). Who sees the school counselor for college information? A national study. *Professional School Counseling*, 12(4), 280–291.

Bonous-Hammarth, M., & Allen, W.R. (2005). A dream-deferred: The critical factor of timing in college preparation and outreach. In W.G. Tierney, Z.B. Corwin, & J.E. Colyar (Eds.). (2005). *Preparing for college: Nine elements of effective outreach* (pp. 155–172). Albany, NY: State University of New York.

Bourdeiu, P. (1986). Forms of capital. In J.E. Richardson (Ed.), *Handbook of theory and research for the sociology of education* (pp. 241–258). New York: Greenword Press.

Buchmann, C. (2009). Gender inequalities in the transition to college. *Teachers College Record*, 111(10), 2320–2346.

Buchmann, C., DiPrete, T.A., & McDaniel, A. (2008). Gender inequalities in education. *Annual Review of Sociology*, 34, 319–37.

Castleman, B.L., & Page, L.C. (2013). The not-so-lazy days of summer: Experimental interventions to increase college entry among low-income high school graduates. *New Directions for Youth Development*, 140, 77–97.

Carter, P.L. (2005). *Keeping' it real: school success beyond the black and white.* New York, NY: Oxford University Press.

Crosnoe, R., & Turley, R.N.L. (2011). K–12 educational outcomes of immigrant youth. *The Future of Children,* 21(1), 129–152.

Contreras, F. (2011). *Achieving equity for Latino students: Expanding the pathway to higher education through public policy.* New York: Teachers College Press.

Corwin, Z.B., Venegas, K.M., Oliverez, P.M., & Colyar, J.E. (2004). School counsel: How appropriate guidance affects educational equity. *Urban Education,* 39(4), 442–457.

Deli-Amen, R., & Tevis, T.L. (2010). Circumscribed agency: The relevance of standardized college entrance exams for low ses high school students. *The Review of Higher Education,* 33(2), 141–175.

DiPrete, T.A., & Buchmann, C. (2013). *The rise of women: The growing gender gap in education and what it means for American schools.* New York: Russell Sage Foundation.

Dowd, A. (2003). From access to outcome equity: Revitalizing the democratic mission of the community college. *The ANNALS of the American Academy of Political and Social Science,* 586, 92–119.

Engberg, M.E., & Wolniak, G.C. (2010). Examining the effects of high school contexts on postsecondary enrollment. *Research in Higher Education,* 51, 132–153.

Engberg, M.E., & Gilbert, A.J. (2014). The counseling opportunity structure: Examining correlates of four-year college-going rates. *Research in Higher Education,* 55(3), 219–244.

Espinoza, R. (2011). *Pivotal moments: How educators can put all students on the path to college.* Cambridge, MA: Harvard Education Press.

Fann, A. (2005). *Forgotten students: Native American high school students' narratives on college-going.* Paper presented at the Association for the Study of Higher Education annual meeting, Sacramento, CA.

Ferguson, A.A. (2001). *Bad boys: Public schools in the making of black masculinity* (law, meaning, and violence). Ann Arbor, MI: University of Michigan Press.

Flores-Gonzales, N. (2005). Popularity versus respect: School structure, peer groups and Latino academic achievement. *International Journal of Qualitative Studies in Education,* 18(5), 625–642.

Frankenberg, E., & Orfield, G. (Eds.). (2012). *The resegregation of suburban schools: A hidden crisis in American education.* Cambridge, MA: Harvard Education Press.

Goode, J. (2010). Mind the gap: The digital dimension of college access. *Journal of Higher Education,* 81(5), 583–618.

Hallett, R.E., & Venegas, K.M. (2011). Is increased access enough? Advanced Placement courses, quality, and success in low-income urban schools. *Journal for the Education of the Gifted,* 34(3), 468–487.

Hill, L.D. (2008). School strategies and the "college-linking" process: Reconsidering the effects of high schools on college environment. *Sociology of Education,* 81, 53–76.

Hill, L.D. (2012). Environmental threats to college counseling strategies in urban high schools: Implications for student preparation for college transition. *Urban Review,* 44, 36–59.

Heller, D.E. (2005). Can minority students afford college in an era of skyrocketing tuition? In G. Orfield, P. Marin, & C.L. Horn (Eds.), *Higher education and the color line: College access, racial equity, and social change* (pp. 83–106). Cambridge, MA: Harvard Education Press.

Hossler, D., Braxton, J., & Coopersmith, G. (1989). Understanding student college choice. In J.C. Smart (Ed.), *Higher education: Handbook of theory and research* (Vol. V, pp. 231–288). New York: Agathon Press.

Howard, T.C. (2003). A tug of war for our minds: African American high school students' perceptions of their academic identities and college aspirations. *The High School Journal,* 87(1), 4–17.

Howard, T.C., & Huerta, A.H. (2014, September 25). Why we should care about boys and young men of color? *Huffington Post.* Retrieved from *http://huff. to/1rkxgSl.*

Huerta, A.H., & Fishman, S.M. (2014). Marginality and mattering: Urban Latino male undergraduates in higher education. *Journal of the First-Year Experience & Students in Transition,* 26(1), 85–100.

Huerta, A.H., McDonough, P.M., & Allen, W.R. (2014). College can change my life: Comparing gang knowledge versus college knowledge for marginalized Latino male high school student. *Unpublished paper.*

Kim, J.K., & Gasman, M. (2011). In search of a "good college": decisions and determinations behind Asian American students college choice. *Journal of College Student Development,* 52(6), 706–728.

Lareau, A. (2011). *Unequal childhoods: Class, race, and family life* (2nd ed.). Berkeley, CA: University of California Press.

Jaffe-Walter, R., & Lee. S.J. (2011). "To trust in my root and to take that to go forward": Supporting college access for immigrant youth in the global city. *Anthropology and Education Quarterly,* 42(3), 281–296.

Kasinitz, P., Mollenkopf, J.H., Waters, M.C., & Holdaway, J. (2008). *Inheriting the city: The children of immigrants come of age.* New York: Russell Sage Foundation.

Klasik, D. (2012). The college application gauntlet: A systematic analysis of the steps to four-year college enrollment. *Research in Higher Education,* 53, 506–549.

Klugman, J. (2012). How resources inequalities among high schools reproduce class advantages in college destination. *Research in Higher Education,* 53, 803–830.

Kozol, J. (2005). *The shame of the nation: The restoration of apartheid schooling in America.* New York, NY: Three River Press.

Mathis, J.D. (2010). Increasing the capacity of college counseling: Through video game design. *Journal of College Admission,* 14–23.

McDonough, P.M. (2005). Counseling and college counseling in America's high schools. In D. Hawkins (Ed.), *The 2004–05 state of college admission.* Washington, DC: National Association for College Admission Counseling.

McDonough, P.M., & Calderone, S. (2006). The meaning of money: Perceptual differences between college counselors and low-income families about college costs and financial aid. *American Behavioral Scientist,* 49(12), 1703–1718.

McDonough, P.M., Antonio, A., Walpole, M., & Perez, L.X. (1998). College rankings: Democratized college knowledge for whom? *Research in Higher Education,* 39, 513–537.

McDonough, P.M., & Gildersleeve, R.E. (2006). All else is never equal: Opportunity lost and found on the P-16 path to college access. In C. Conrad & R. Serlin (Eds.), *The SAGE handbook for research in education engaging ideas and enriching inquiry* (pp. 59-79). Thousand Oaks, CA: SAGE Press.

Moore, J.L., III, Henfield, M.S., & Owens, D. (2008). African American males special education: Their attitudes and perceptions toward high school counselors and school counseling services. *American Behavioral Scientist,* 51(7), 907–927.

Mullen, A.L. (2010). *Degrees of inequality: Culture, class, and gender in American higher education.* Baltimore, MD: John Hopkins University Press.

National Center for Education Statistics (2012). *The Condition of Education 2012.* Retrieved from: *http:// nces.ed.gov/fastfacts/display.asp?id=72.*

National Center for Education Statistics (2013). *Digest of Education Statistics.* Retrieved from: *http://nces. ed.gov/programs/digest/2013menu_tables.asp.*

Noguera, P., Hurtado, A., & Fergus, E. (Eds.). (2012). *Invisible no more: Understanding the disenfranchisement of Latino men and boys.* New York: Routledge.

Oakes, J. (2005). *Keeping Track: How schools structure inequality* (2nd ed.). New Haven, CT: Yale University Press.

Perez, P.A., & McDonough, P.M. (2008). Understanding Latina and Latino college choice: A social capital and chain migration analysis. *Journal of Hispanic Higher Education,* 7(3), 249–265.

Perna, L.W. (2000). Differences in the decision to attend college among African Americans, Hispanics, and whites. *Journal of Higher Education,* 71(2), 117–141.

Perna, L.W., Rowan-Kenyon, H.T., Thomas, S.L., Bell, A., Anderson, R., & Li, C. (2008). The role of college counseling in shaping college opportunity: Variations across high schools. *The Review of Higher Education,* 31, 131–159.

Radford, A.W. (2013). *Top student, top school? How social class shapes where valedictorians go to college.* Chicago, IL: University of Chicago Press.

Rendon, L.I., Jalomo, R.E., & Nora, A. (2000). Theoretical considerations in the study of minority student retention in higher education. In J.M. Braxton (Ed.), *Reworking the student departing puzzle.* Nashville, TN: Vanderbilt University Press

Robinson, L. (2009). A taste for the necessary: A Bourdieuian approach to digital inequality. *Information, Communication & Society,* 12(4), 488–507.

Robinson, L. (2011). *Information-channel preferences and information opportunity structures.* Information, Communication, and Society, 14(4), 472–494.

Rodriguez, G.M., & Cruz, L. (2009). The transition to college of English learners and undocumented immigrant students: Resource and policy implications. *Teachers College Record,* 111(10), 2385–2418.

Saenz, V.B., & Ponjuan, L. (2009). The vanishing Latino male in higher education. *Journal of Hispanic Higher Education,* 8(1), 54–89.

Savitz-Romer, M., & Bouffard, S.M. (2012). *Reading, willing, and able: A developmental approach to college access and success.* Cambridge, MA: Harvard Education Press.

Solórzano, D.G., Villalpando, O., & Oseguera, L. (2005). Educational inequalities and Latina/o undergraduate students in the United States. *Journal of Hispanic Higher Education,* 4(3), 272–294.

Stanton-Salazar, R. D. (2001). *Manufacturing hope and despair: The school and kin support networks of U.S.-Mexican youth.* New York: Teachers College Press.

Stephan, J.L., & Rosenbaum, J.E. (2013). Can high schools reduce college enrollment gaps with a new counseling model? *Educational Evaluation & Policy Analysis,* 35(2), 200–219.

Suárez-Orozco, C. Suárez-Orozco, M.M., & Todorova, I. (2008). *Learning a new land: Immigrant students in American society.* Cambridge, MA: Harvard University Press.

Swartz, D. (1998). *Culture and power: The sociology of Pierre Bourdieu.* Chicago, IL: University of Chicago Press.

Teranishi, R.T. (2010). *Asians in the Ivory Tower: Dilemmas of Racial Inequality in American Higher Education.* New York: Teachers College Press.

Teranishi, R., & Pazich, L.B. (2014). Intersectionality. In R.A. Williams, L.E. Bitsói, E.T. Gordon, S.R. Harper, V.B. Sáenz, & R. Teranishi (Eds.), *Men of color in higher education: New Foundations for developing models for success* (pp. 35–54). Sterling, VA: Stylus Publishing.

Teranishi, R., Ceja, M., Antonio, A., Allen, W.R., & McDonough, P.M. (2004). The college choice process for Asian Americans: Ethnicity and socioeconomic class in context. *The Review of Higher Education,* 27(4), 527–551.

Tierney, W.G., & Venegas, K.M. (2006). Fictive kin and social capital: The role of peer groups in applying and paying for college. *American Behavioral Scientist,* 49(12), 1687–1702.

Tierney, W.G., & Venegas, K.M. (2009). Finding money on the table: Information, financial aid, and access to college. *Journal of Higher Education,* 80(4), 363–388.

Tierney, W.G., Corwin, Z.B., & Colyar, J.E. (Eds.). (2005). *Preparing for college: Nine elements of effective outreach.* Albany, NY: State University of New York.

Tinto, V. (1993). *Leaving college: Rethinking the causes and cures of student attrition* (2nd ed.). Chicago, IL: University of Chicago Press.

Venegas, K.M. (2006). Internet inequalities: Financial aid, the Internet, and low-income students. *American Behavioral Scientist,* 49(12), 1652–1669.

Venegas, K.M. (2007). The Internet and college access: Challenges for low-income students. *American Academic,* 3(1), 141–154.

Venezia, A., & Kirst, M.W. (2001). Bridging the great divide between secondary schools and postsecondary education. The Phi Delta Kappa, 83(1), 92–97.

Venezia, A., & Kirst, M.W. (2005). Inequitable opportunities: How current education systems and policies undermine the chances for students persistence and success in college. *Educational Policy,* 19(2), 283–307.

Williams, R.A., Bitsói, L. E., Gordon, E.T., Harper, S.R., Sáenz, V.B., & Teranishi, R.T. (2014). *Men of color in higher education: New Foundations for developing models for success.* Sterling, VA: Stylus Publishing.

Chapter 18: If Not Us, Then Who? Working with First-Generation Students

Kya Dixon
@kya_csf_dc

Phyllis Jeffers-Coly
@MadamePJC

Nicole E. Smith

First-generation college students are those students whose parents did not earn a college degree. They are the first in their immediate family to pursue a college degree. According to a 2010 study by the National Center for Education Statistics (NCES), 50 percent of the college population is made up of first-generation students. Students of color made up the largest demographics of first-generation students—48 percent of all Latino and Hispanic college students, 45 percent of black or African-American college students, 32 percent of Asian college students, and 35 percent of Native-American students are all first-generation students. Of students who identified themselves as Caucasian, only 28 percent were first-generation college students. Though higher in minority groups, these numbers show the overarching trend of first-generation college attendance in all American demographics (Lynch, 2013).

While they may come from high- or middle-income families, according to the Higher Education Research Institute 2007 profile of First-Generation College Students (*First in My Family . . .*), a significant number of first-generation students come from low-income backgrounds. Given their low income status, most cite making more money as an important reason for pursuing a college degree. As noted in the 2013 CIRP Survey, financial factors play a major role in their college choices as they are twice as likely to report financing college as a major concern in the college selection process. Their concerns are a result of having to not only contribute to paying for their own education but also of being responsible for contributing to their household income. They often express a desire to not create a financial burden for their families as a reason for not wanting to attend college or the basis for why they think they cannot afford to attend college.

First-generation students tend to have lower educational aspirations, which is confirmed by the fact that first-generation students are underrepresented among college-going students (HERI, *First in My Family*). In 2003–04, among first-time college students with family incomes of $32,000 or lower, 57 percent of students started at a two-year or less-than-two-year college, rather than at a four-year institution (Balemian & Feng, 2013). Many first-generation students often opt to attend community college rather than matriculate directly to a four-year institution as a result of anxieties surrounding the cost of school, or convey a lack of information about degrees and

the college process, availability of resources, and poor academic preparation. According to a 2001 NCES study, only 54 percent of students whose parents had completed high school and only 36 percent of students whose parents had less than a high school diploma enrolled in college immediately after finishing high school, in contrast to 82 percent of non-first-generation or continuing-generation students (Balemian & Feng, 2013).

Beyond socioeconomic characteristics, first-generation college students' perspectives and feelings about being first in their immediate family to pursue a college degree are also important to take into account. These feelings can range from excitement all the way to guilt and shame. It is important to recognize and acknowledge common feelings your students may experience as they consider college. Here are some examples of the feelings first-generation students may have surrounding college:

Confusion and anxiety—Being a teenager is already a stressful process. Combine this with the college process and you have an anxious student on your hands. First-generation students have to learn about the college process while maintaining a focus on all the other responsibilities they have within their school and personal life. They may also not be aware of all of the resources available to them or know where to seek out help when needed. The prospect of eventually being away from home for the first time and being concerned about their ability to fit in can also be sources of anxiety.

Excitement—Going to school is an exciting time! Many students are looking forward to being on their own and being the first person in their family to attend college. For many, college is their gateway to a better life, new experiences, growth opportunities, and a way to secure resources to assist their family and community.

Guilt—Many first-generation students experience feelings of guilt about having an opportunity to attend college, unlike their other family members or peers. They may also feel torn about leaving their family, particularly if they play a key role in sustaining their household. Many may feel the need to put off going to school or return home versus going away to college for fear of being an outcast in their families and/or communities. Many first-generation students also feel guilty about building new support systems and making new friends who are different from their family and community, but whom they need on campus in order to be successful in college and take full advantage of the experience. Families do not always understand and may feel replaced or threatened by the students' new experiences, exposure and opportunities. The guilt they feel is similar to that of a survivor who feels like he/she is leaving those he/she loves behind. Students express how difficult it is to return home after being away at school to friends and family who are not supportive of their academic journey.

Responsibility—First-generation students often feel a level of responsibility to their school, community and/or families to be successful in college while still offering support at home. Many may be pressured by family members to return home frequently, contribute financially to their household, or feel an obligation to maintain friendships and relationships that they may outgrow while in college.

Pride—First-generation students often feel a level of pride when it comes to being the first in their family to attend college, especially if they did not originally plan to attend. They may also be one of a small percentage of students within their community who are attending college. Pride can also prove to be a double-edged sword when students feel like they should know everything or have it all figured out and do not ask for help or seek out services when they need it most.

It is important, as a counselor, to recognize the above feelings and to keep the lines of communication open in order to provide as much support as possible so students know they are not alone. It is critical for first-generation students to have access to school- and community-based programs to counsel and advise them so that they can successfully navigate the college choice and financial aid processes. It is important to encourage and counsel first-generation students in a way that results in positive outcomes for them, their families and the larger society. Doing so, in light of a myriad studies on first-generation students often coming from a negative and deficit standpoint, requires counselors to start by first engaging first-generation students from a positive and asset-based approach.

STRENGTH-BASED APPROACH: POSITIVE PSYCHOLOGY AND NON-COGNITIVE SKILLS

Currently, common college counseling practice often involves a deficits-based approach, where college counselors direct students toward a limited range of choices based on the weakness of their application profile, rather than emphasizing assets not typically evaluated in the college admission process. Strengths-based counseling practices can provide a great framework for supporting first-generation college students through the college application and enrollment process. Although there is no substitute for academic preparedness, standardized test scores and GPA only predict success in the first year of college. However, non-cognitive skills may predict a student's longevity and true success in college and thereafter. For students whose profiles typically turn the National Association for College Admission Counseling's (NACAC) factors in the admission process table on its head, in terms of having the greatest strengths in the least important areas, the assessment of non-cognitive skills may present an opportunity to more holistically evaluate a student's potential for college success and beyond (NACAC, 2014).

First-generation students, many of whom attend high schools without a rigorous college-preparatory curriculum and have standardized test scores that are not competitive, are often directed toward lower tier, less-challenging colleges although they are capable of excelling at a more competitive colleges. These students may also be presented with other challenges as first-generation college students. First-generation college students often have a high level of responsibility at home that may include caring for siblings, managing household finances or working full-time to help support their families. As a result, these students may develop useful skills that standardized tests cannot measure. Even the personal statement may not accurately portray their high level of responsibility, as students are often hesitant to share their experience or view their situation as a hindrance rather than as an asset that has helped them develop skills that can propel them forward. Counselors can help students re-frame their stories so that students recognize the assets rather than the deficits.

POSITIVE PSYCHOLOGY

Positive psychology, defined as the study of how human beings prosper in the face of adversity, shifted the psychology profession's paradigm by redirecting focuses away from the disorder (Seligman & Csikszentmihalyi, 2000). One might argue that a similar shift is necessary in college counseling in order to effectively advise first-generation college students. Positive psychology, according to the Positive Psychology Center at the University of Pennsylvania, "is the study of the strengths and virtues that enable individuals, communities and organizations to thrive." Thus, positive psychology focuses on "how things go right" instead of "how things go wrong" (Positive Psychology Institute, 2014).

The underpinning beliefs of positive psychology may offer great value as counselors seek new and more effective counseling approaches that may help close the college access and achievement gaps for first-generation college students. In fact, the strengths-based approach is currently used by many college access organizations and colleges. Additionally, positive psychology serves as the foundation for current research supporting alternative measurements of potential for success in college and beyond. However, strengths-based approaches are rarely part of a continuum of services backed by the same assets-based philosophy. A student might be serviced by a community-based organization that subscribes to a strengths-based approach through positive youth development practices, but the colleges to which she applies may not practice similar approaches to student development. Thus, the student finds herself in an environment that may not value her strengths in the same way. In order to meet our national goal of increasing the number of Americans earning a college degree, we must adopt philosophies and practices that will aid in improving the number of first-generation students that complete college. College counseling practices that highlight and build upon students' strengths can help our nation achieve its higher education degree attainment goals by increasing the enrollment, persistence and graduation of first-generation college students.

Non-Cognitive Skills

There is growing interest in assessing non-cognitive skills, especially as it relates to the issues surrounding college access and success for first-generation college students. For the purposes of this chapter, non-cognitive skills refer to non-academic skills unrelated to IQ that can predict success. Therefore, this discussion includes an introduction to multiple works using other terminology under the umbrella of non-cognitive skills. Whether referred to as non-cognitive skills, non-cognitive factors, grit, charac-

ter, social and emotional learning, soft skills, or maybe even 21st-century skills, these factors are part of a growing body of literature that promotes the consideration, measurement and development of these non-academic skills as predictors of success in life.

For example, Robert Sternberg's Triarchic Theory of Human Intelligence explains three types of intelligence: practical, creative and analytical (Sternberg, 1985). Practical intelligence or "street smarts" is how one reacts to one's environment and one's ability to adapt to it or change it to suit his or her needs (Sternberg, 1985). Creative intelligence is how one approaches new information or a new task or how one can apply existing knowledge to a new problem (Sternberg, 1985). Analytical intelligence is how one processes and analyzes information or "book smarts" (Sternberg, 1985). Standardized tests can measure neither practical nor creative intelligence, as they are both non-cognitive skills, yet all three types of intelligence are important and portray a more complete picture of potential for success.

Non-Cognitive Factors

William Sedlacek, author of the *Beyond the Big Test: Non-cognitive Assessment in Higher Education*, is a strong proponent of evaluating non-cognitive factors, especially for what he calls "nontraditional students," which include both first-generation students and students of color. Sedlacek asserts that non-cognitive factors are important for all students, but especially important for nontraditional students, because their standardized test scores may provide a limited view of these students' actual potential. According to Sedlacek, non-cognitive factors include "adjustment, motivation and student perceptions, rather than the traditional verbal and quantitative (often called "cognitive") areas typically measured by standardized tests" and high school grades, which only predict success in the first year of college (Sedlacek, 2004). Thus, Sedlacek suggests eight non-cognitive factors to consider in college admission because of their positive relationship to various indicators of college success.

Upon review of the non-cognitive factors, one might conclude that development of these skills can lead to success that exceeds the confines of a collegiate career. Indeed, success beyond college is the goal for anyone who embarks on the college journey. Sedlacek provides a framework for accessing non-cognitive factors called the Non-cognitive Questionnaire (see appendix). Counselors can use this tool to assess students in a nontraditional way that highlights assets proven to predict success in college and beyond.

Sedlacek's research has been used as a basis for scholarship recipient selections by the Bill & Melinda Gates Foundation's funded scholarships, including the Gates Millennium Scholarship, the United Negro College Fund, Hispanic Scholarship Fund, Asian & Pacific Islanders American Scholarship Fund, and American Indian Graduate Center, as well as College Success Foundation for Washington State Achievers and District of Columbia Achievers.

GRIT

Angela Duckworth's research around grit and her Grit Scale have gained increasing attention in education circles. The Duckworth Lab, within the Positive Psychology Center at the University of Pennsylvania, focuses on two areas that predict success in life: grit and self-control. Grit has gained the most national attention and is the focus of this discussion. Grit, derived from Big Five personality trait, conscientiousness, is defined by Duckworth as "a tendency to sustain interest in and effort toward very-long-term goals" (Duckworth, Peterson, Mathews, & Kelly, 2007). Grit is finishing what one starts and not straying off the path because of failure, distractions or other interests. The "hypothesis that grit is essential to high achievement evolved during interviews with professionals in investment banking, painting, journalism, medicine, and law" (Duckworth et al., 2007). Interviewees remarked that star performers were distinguished by grit with many in awe of peers who did not seem as gifted but became very accomplished as a result of their sustained commitment (Duckworth et al., 2007). Conversely, many who were very gifted were not as accomplished. (Duckworth et al., 2007). Although IQ may be the most well-researched predictor of success, the aforementioned researchers suggest that grit may be as essential as IQ to high achievement (Duckworth et al., 2007).

A counselor familiar with the concept of grit has the ability to approach a first-generation student with average academic credentials with new eyes and counsel that student from an asset-based perspective. Counselors can

use the Grit Scale (see appendix), a very simple 12-item questionnaire, to assess the grittiness of students. Recognizing grit in a first-generation student, as demonstrated through exceptional commitment, allows counselors to see potential they may not have otherwise recognized and thus provide the students with the same support and resources they might provide to a student considered "gifted and talented." Additionally, counselors need to encourage first-generation students to pursue passions with not just intensity, but also stamina (Duckworth et al., 2007). Parents, educators and counselors need to teach first-generation students to anticipate failure and understand that excellence in any discipline or area of one's life requires years of "time on task" (Duckworth et al., 2007).

THE HIDDEN POWER OF CHARACTER

In *How Children Succeed: Grit, Curiosity and the Hidden Power of Character*, Paul Tough challenges the cognitive hypothesis and champions the non-cognitive traits of perseverance, conscientiousness, curiosity, optimism, and self-discipline, all under the category of character and provides examples of studies to prove his assertion (Tough, 2012). Tough is careful to make clear that non-cognitive skills are not perceived as a replacement for cognitive skills. Tough's book shares common threads with Sedlacek's eight non-cognitive factors. Sedlacek refers to preferring long-time goals over short-term needs, which Tough calls "perseverance." What Tough describes as curiosity, Sedlacek calls either knowledge in an acquired field or intellectual curiosity. Clearly, Tough subscribes to Duckworth's definition of grit and Big Five personality traits, conscientiousness. Tough's work, particularly the stories he shares of individuals, provides a moving, if not compelling, argument that non-cognitive skills may be just as important as cognitive skills.

DAVID AND GOLIATH

In *David and Goliath*, Malcom Gladwell shares his theory of "desirable difficulty," or sometimes what one may perceive as a disadvantage may actually be an advantage (Gladwell, 2013). Therefore, a student who might seem to be an underdog is not as outmatched as he or she may initially appear. The intent is not to minimize any challenges or barriers first-generation students face but to think again of the skills students develop in overcoming obstacles and see them as assets. As radical and possibly inflammatory as this idea may seem in the context of first-generation college students, consider Gladwell's assertion that individual merit is more important than the quality of a college one attends. It may not always be true, but the best students from mid-tier schools are often more successful than good students who attended an elite school. Being a big fish in a small pond may have significant advantages, such as providing opportunity and support while encouraging individuality and innovation (Gladwell, 2013). Existing research supports the idea that students attending Ivy League colleges may be small fish in a big pond with fewer opportunities to be published than students who do not attend an Ivy League college.

know how to advise or counsel their child(ren). It is important for us to educate as well as empower parents/guardians through this process and be as supportive and transparent as possible. The earlier we identify students who may be considered first-generation, the earlier we can begin to work with their families. Early identification will give counselors, and the family, more time to prepare for and understand exactly what the college process will look like and how the family can work to ensure that their first-generation student is ready for college financially, emotionally and academically.

Supporting first-generation students and their families does not begin and end with an application or survey. In order to be effective, counselors need context; they really have to try to know the students and families they

As counselors, we must address not only a student's college, academic and emotional needs, but also their family's basic needs as well.

Even if one does not agree with Gladwell or thinks that he makes quite a leap to support some of his theories, one should appreciate Gladwell's point that we see David as an underdog only because we do not see David's strengths. David can defeat Goliath not by playing by Goliath's rules, but by using his own strengths. David cannot overpower Goliath physically, but David can use his agility and his talent to defeat Goliath. As a counselor, consider applying this same logic to your first-generation students. What are their strengths? How can you help them win?

WORKING WITH PARENTS/GUARDIANS OF FIRST-GENERATION STUDENTS

Parents are a vital part of the college application process, particularly with first-generation students. Research shows that parental involvement is associated with a greater likelihood of aspiring to attend college and actually enrolling. When working with first-generation students, we must counsel the student as well as the family through the process. This can often be quite challenging, since parents are used to being in a situation where they are in control and usually know all the answers. Our first-generation students do not have parents who have gone through the college application process, so they may not

serve. In order to obtain parental buy-in, it is important to cultivate relationships with the families you serve by maintaining open and consistent communication, as well as offering wrap-around services and supports. As counselors, we must address not only a student's college, academic and emotional needs, but also their family's basic needs as well. The student's family is crucial to their college experience and must be treated as such throughout the college counseling process.

When addressing first-generation parents, it is important to make the process as simple and as transparent as possible. For many, it is an exciting but also stressful time. Families and students are trying to make sense of a process that they have never experienced. It is easy to forget that not everyone understands things that we often take for granted or that they will understand it the first time we explain it. Transparency means keeping families abreast of where their student is in the college search, application and enrollment process as consistently as possible. Being transparent means communicating with families throughout the process in language and terms they understand. This must include using a variety of communication methods, including phone calls, emails, written notices, flyers, social media, and face-to-face conferences.

CULTURAL SENSITIVITY

Understanding and fostering diversity in higher education is paramount for practitioners who are dedicated to ensuring that students from disadvantaged and traditionally underrepresented groups have access to postsecondary education. Being culturally sensitive and culturally competent allows us to service our first-generation students and families in a way that honors who they are, their background and, more importantly, how they identify themselves. As previously stated, looking past applications that gather information about a family's background is vital to servicing students correctly. This includes personally asking a student and their family how they identify themselves racially, socially, religiously, and culturally. For example, the relationship between elders and children within the family, thoughts and beliefs surrounding education, religious/spiritual beliefs, and gender roles all vary by family and culture. Once you begin to develop a sense of how a student and their family identify themselves, you can then begin to become familiar with their cultural beliefs, attitudes and values associated with their cultural background. Unfortunately, one size does not fit all, and even families who have similar backgrounds must be counseled differently. It is important to view a student and their family as unique before making the assumption that their values, beliefs and attitudes are consistent with that of their ethnic or racial group.

Understanding a family culturally also means understanding that language and cultural identity are not necessarily one and the same. Language may or may not be a barrier in the educational process. For some populations, their native tongue may be their second, not first language, if they speak it at all. Counselors must be mindful that even if a student may not be fluent in their home language, it does not mean they do not strongly identify with the cultural values and identity of their language community. For others, English is their second language, and they may come from a household where only their first language is spoken. This does not necessarily mean they have not assimilated into the mainstream culture. You may also find students and families who reject their background and may not openly admit to, or may even reject, their cultural heritage.

When it comes to the value of college, assisting families in seeing college as a long-term investment may be one of the biggest barriers a counselor may face. Being financially stable often, for low-income, first-generation students and their families, takes priority. Often, the family puts primary emphasis on having everyone in a household contributing financially. This stance often means that a student attending college is not a family priority, especially when it not only costs money to attend, but also takes away, at least initially, from the number of working hours and income a student can bring into the household. As a result, families, including the student, may not be available to meet during traditional hours. Parents may not be able to take off during the day or may start their day extremely early. Students may have to work immediately following the school day or may have to take care of younger siblings or family responsibilities and may not be able to stay after school to attend meetings and/or sessions. Keeping all of the above in mind, it is important to keep high expectations, remain culturally sensitive and adjust one's hours to match those of the availability of your students' families. Having extended office hours or meeting times that reflect your family's schedules is vital to their success.

FIRST-GENERATION STUDENTS WHO DO NOT LIVE WITH BIOLOGICAL PARENTS

Many of our first-generation students may not live with biological parents, and unfortunately, the first time we may find this out is during the college counseling process. It is important to find out as early as possible who a student lives with, and if it is not their biological parent(s), exactly what the situation is. Many students may be living with extended family members, family friends, other families, etc. for a variety of reasons. While some students may be in foster care or wards of the court, they may have other reasons for living with individuals other than their biological parents. These reasons can range from simply claiming a different address so the student can attend a particular school, to their parents living in another country, all the way to their parents being deceased. Each situation will call for a different protocol and will need to be handled differently, especially when it comes to the financial aid process

THE COLLEGE CHOICE AND APPLICATION PROCESS

First-generation students often have not had enough exposure to have a schema to tap into concerning college. They experience information constraints about the college-going process and are influenced most by their counselors and teachers when it comes to selecting a college. African-American and Latino students are significantly more likely than other students to be influenced in their college plans by their high school counselors. However, these students are the most likely not to have counselors, to have unprepared counselors or to be assigned to counselors who are pulled away from college counseling to work on other counseling tasks (College Board, 2005). Yet, our students need to be exposed to as much college information as possible. It is extremely important for access providers and counselors to expose and guide students so they can continue to research colleges on their own and ultimately be an "educated consumer." Exposing students to college search Web sites, taking them on college tours, inviting in college admission reps to speak about a college, attending college fairs, and hosting a panel comprised of current students in college and who have graduated college are all ways to get your students exposed to and excited about college.

No matter where a student stands academically, college is a choice they can make. For many of our students, as well as their families, it is important for counselors and advisors to remain positive and reassure them that if they want to go to college, they absolutely can. Our students need us to help them identify their passions, assets and strengths.

ASSESSMENTS

Assessments assist in laying the foundation to have objective conversations with first-generation students about their likes, what would make good fit and to allow them to learn about themselves. This information lays the groundwork for students to make educated decisions based on what they know about themselves and helps empower students to make decisions from a position of strength and self-confidence, verses being influenced by peers or others who may have a student's best interests at heart, but may not necessarily have the best information to assist students.

There are a variety of assessments, paid and free, that counselors can utilize for students. Depending on the size of the student caseload, school's level of technology and resources, counselors can pick and choose which assessments they feel will allow them to best identify a student's assets. Some common assessments that counselors use include NAVIANCE (career and personality assessments), the College Board (career assessments), GRIT Survey, and Myers-Briggs Type Indicator. Counseling experts, such as Dr. Steven Antonoff, also offer free resources via their Web sites that can easily be downloaded and utilized with your students.

Depending on the size of the student caseload, school's level of technology and resources, counselors can pick and choose which assessments they feel will allow them to best identify a student's assets.

These assessments can also be combined with Web sites that allow students to research colleges and compare themselves to their peers and admission requirements. Some Web sites, such as CollegeResults.org, Big Futures (via the College Board) and College Prowler allow students to gather data, see schools in a two-dimensional fashion, and compare themselves to the school's criteria and last incoming class.

COST OF COLLEGE: APPLYING AND DEMYSTIFYING THE FINANCIAL AID PROCESS

According to the 2013 CIRP Freshman Survey results, college costs and financial aid are among the top concerns of incoming college freshmen nationwide. Specifically, more than half (53.9 percent) of first-generation college students indicated that college costs were a major factor in their enrollment choice, in comparison to 43.8 percent for continuing generation students. This anxiety, while well-founded when considering the significant inflation of college costs over the last few decades, is exacerbated by the lack of adequate and accurate information about paying for and the payoffs of college. Research has found that students and their families, particularly first-generation

A high percentage of students across academic ability levels expected to receive financial aid based on their "academic, athletic or other achievements."

college-bound students, are not well-versed in how much college costs and how to pay for it (Wyer, 2014). As noted by Judith Scott-Clayton of the National Bureau Of Economic Research, young people—particularly those from disadvantaged backgrounds—often have incomplete and inaccurate information that lead them to underestimate the benefits of higher education and to persistently overestimate costs and are uninformed about sources of potential aid.

The information constraints or misconceptions first-generation students and their families face include overestimating costs. Subsequently, students who are the most uninformed about the costs of college are the most likely to believe they could not afford to attend. Specifically, as the College Board and Art & Science Group, LLC, a higher-education research firm, jointly reported, students from lower- and middle-income families—those most likely to receive some form of need-based financial aid—are more likely to rule out colleges on the basis of sticker price alone, 58 percent and 62 percent respectively, compared to more affluent students at 48 percent (2012).

Additionally, information constraints or misconceptions about college costs include students' perceptions about merit aid. A high percentage of students across academic ability levels expected to receive financial aid based on their "academic, athletic or other achievements." For example, when asked if they thought they would more likely receive financial aid from colleges based on family income, need, or their academic, athletic or other achievements (accepting multiple responses), almost three-quarters of respondents (72 percent) indicated that they would receive aid based on their "academic achievements." Around 22 percent indicated they would receive aid for other achievements (not based on academics), and about 9 percent indicated they would receive aid based on their athletic abilities. Sixty-four percent of students with the lowest combined math and verbal SAT scores (less than 1110), compared to 83 percent of those in the mid-range (1110 to 1290) and 90 percent of high-

ability students (above 1300) indicated they would likely receive merit aid based on their academic achievements. By income, 80 percent of students with a family income of $60,000 to $100,000, and 84 percent of students with a family income over $100,000 were more likely to say they will receive aid based on their "academic achievements," compared to 63 percent of students from families with incomes under $60,000. This sense of entitlement to merit scholarship dollars is complicated by a lack of understanding of the forms of financial aid, including grants and loans, and how they impact a student's ability to pay for college. This data suggests that the "merit scholarship arms race" may very well have created a very strong and pervasive sense of entitlement on the part of the current generation of students, even among those with lesser academic ability, as well as those with greater need. In fact, on average, students expect their financial aid award (excluding loans) to cover 50 percent of their college costs with students from lower income families expecting aid to cover an average of 64 percent of college costs, compared to 52 percent of costs for middle income and 35 percent of college costs for students from the most affluent families (College Board & Arts and Science Group, 2012).

Academically talented low-income and first-generation students may not be fully aware that they actually may be able to secure lower net costs, including aid packages without loans, at highly selective private and public institutions than at less selective ones. A recent study using administrative data from North Carolina finds that nearly 60 percent of highly qualified students in the bottom quartile of family income failed to attend the most selective institution for which they were eligible, as did 64 percent of those whose parents had no college education. Similarly, a 2009 study of Chicago Public School students found that fewer than half of students in academically advanced high school programs attended the most selective institution they could attend—and 20 percent of these students never even applied to a four-year college. Both qualitative and quantitative evidence suggests that this apparent under-matching is due to inadequate information and support throughout the college decision and financial aid application process. Students who severely over-predict net costs (or report not knowing net costs at all) are significantly less likely to apply to or enroll in selective colleges and universities (Scott-Clayton, 2012).

RISING COSTS INFLUENCE PERCEPTIONS OF COLLEGE AFFORDABILITY

Price over-predicting is certainly understandable in light of the fact that tuition rates have risen continuously since the early 1970s. After adjusting in-state, undergraduate tuition rates for inflation, the national average tuition costs increased from $2,695 in 1973 to $7,963 in 2010, an increase of 195 percent. In fact, tuition at public four-year universities (Hiltonsmith & Draut, 2014) has increased by an average of 20 percent or $1,282 and by 18.5 percent at public two-year schools or $414 since 2008 (2007–2008 academic year). And the total cost, including room and board, at four-year public institutions has increased by an average of $2,292 during the same period.

The misperceptions held by students, their families and the general public about the actual cost of college are adversely affecting application and enrollment decisions. Clearly, the role of financial aid in reducing the cost of college is not well understood or not having a sufficient impact. And a pattern in nearly all of the findings documents the extent to which more needy students and families are adversely affected by a wide range of factors relating to price, aid and affordability. For those concerned about and committed to college access and success, it is imperative to tackle the information constraints regarding the cost of college and how to cover those costs, as well as the value or benefits of completing a college degree head on. At the end of the day, many of us in the college access arena understand that access to financing guarantees is especially important to low-income students. In general, students and their parents tend not to believe that college is affordable and to believe financial aid is uncertain at best. Thus, college counselors in all contexts must be prepared to assist students in understanding college costs and how to cover them. This includes introducing students to financial aid options, making a case for the value of investing in higher education, helping families

fill out the FAFSA and other financial aid forms, explaining financial aid packages to families, and ultimately, assisting families in selecting the best package. Counselors also have the ability to advocate on a student's behalf to receive more money, particularly when a student has received additional funding from other schools.

Thus, it is important to provide first-generation college students with a clear message about the long-term benefits of their college education when discussing costs. In February 2014, the Pew Research Center reported a number of findings about the increasing value of a college degree and, in contrast, the cost of not going to college. According to Pew, college-educated young adults are outperforming their less-educated peers. They earn higher wages and face lower rates of poverty and unemployment. Another way to speak to the benefits of a college degree is to compare it to other forms of investment and their respective returns. According to the Brookings Institution's Hamilton Project:

> [O]n average, the benefits of a four-year college degree are equivalent to an investment that returns 15.2 percent per year. This is more than double the average return to stock market investments since 1950, and more than five times the returns to corporate bonds, gold, long-term government bonds, or home ownership. From any investment perspective, college is a great deal. (College Board, 2013)

APPLYING FOR FINANCIAL AID

In addition to counseling students on the value of a college degree and how it benefits them, their families, communities and the broader society, it is imperative to guide them through the oft times confusing and unfamiliar process of securing financial aid and helping to identify other strategies for covering and/or reducing college costs. As a counselor, it's important to understand all of the various avenues that favor our first-generation students and share that with parents so they can see that college can be affordable regardless of their income level or status.

At the outset, students need to understand that they have access to federal funds, which, depending on income, may include the Pell Grant, Federal Supplemental Educational Opportunity Grant or subsidized student loans. Securing financial aid typically begins with the Free Application for Federal Student Aid (FAFSA). With this one application, students can apply for financial aid at multiple colleges and from multiple funding sources (federal, state, institutional, and private providers of assistance). However, financial aid forms, including the FAFSA, can be confusing even for professionals who are familiar with the forms, let alone for families who have never filled out a FAFSA before. It makes it even more difficult when FAFSA changes year to year and each school has its own policies and paperwork surrounding the financial aid process. Preliminary research at Ohio State University shows that not filing the FAFSA on time and not completing verification, yet enrolling are among the early warning signs for dropping out. Additionally, a recent experimental study by Bettinger, Long, Oreopoulos, and Sanbonmatsu (2009) confirms what many college access providers and counselors know: the complexity of financial aid applications can itself become a significant barrier to college access. In the study, low-income families who received information and application assistance increased immediate college entry rates by 8 percent, and after three years, they accumulated significantly more time in college than the control group.

Thus, developing the financial and financial aid literacy of students and their families is critical to their college success. It is important, then, to assist families in filling out and completing financial aid forms, to hold workshops, bring in volunteers to assist families, have local tax providers come in and provide free tax assistance, and ensure that families understand the financial aid process.

Training programs and materials are available for counselors and access providers from a number of sources. One such resource is National Training for Counselors and Mentors (NT4CM), which provides **free** training and support for counselors and mentors who assist students and their families in preparing financially for college. NT4CM is a comprehensive training program that delivers up-to-date information regarding federal and state student aid programs, scholarship searches and financial aid fraud. Participants also learn how to access free resources, such as fact sheets, brochures and PowerPoint presentations that can be used in counseling and outreach to students. A number of states participate in the in-person training,

and there are occasionally webinars so that anyone can get training online.

Additionally, the office of Federal Student Aid of the US Department of Education provides publications, fact sheets, online tools, and other resources to help students prepare and pay for college. Resources include the Free Application for Federal Student Aid (FAFSA) Loan Information and Consumer Protection information. Counselors and students can obtain hard copies of many of the publications from the US Department of Education's Publication Center (*www.edpubs.gov*) or by calling 1-877-4-ED-PUBS (1-877-433-7827). TTY/TDD callers can use 1-877-576-7734.

The US Department of Education's new College Affordability and Transparency Center provides a user-friendly and comprehensive look at college costs, but the data are limited and could be misinterpreted without the proper context. To ensure the information is useful and not misinterpreted, users should be aware of the following: the new center highlights cost, but doesn't necessarily provide consumers with any context to assess the value of an institution. For example, an institution may cost more because it provides a higher teacher-to-student ratio or access to expensive, cutting-edge equipment. It is important for students and parents to keep in mind that these data are only one factor to consider when judging if an institution is a good value. Additionally, because the data are from previous academic years, recent changes to tuition and fees and financial aid are not necessarily reflected.

A side-by-side comparison can inform a student's college choice, which can be done by using College Navigator, a free consumer information tool from the US Department of Education. It has information about nearly 7,000 postsecondary institutions in the United States, including accreditation status, programs offered, retention and graduation rates, prices, aid available, degrees awarded, campus safety, and more.

The National Association of Student Financial Administrators (NAFSAA) also provides a range of resources for assisting students with FAFSA completion and securing resources for covering and/or reducing college costs. NAFSAA resources include user-friendly, reproducible tip sheets for students who face unique challenges when applying for financial aid. These tip sheets are designed to help unique student populations, including adult learners, veterans, undocumented, and formerly incarcerated students, as well as students who are foster care alums or wards of the court, overcome these challenges to successfully navigate the financial aid process and access higher education. Foster Care to Success (FC2S) is a national non-profit organization that works with college-bound foster youth. FC2S provides support they cannot get from a parent or guardian—like financial backing for college in the form of scholarships and grants, care packages and family-like encouragement, academic and personal mentoring, and help with internships and employment-readiness skills.

STATE GRANTS

Many states have need- and merit-based programs to assist students with covering college costs. For example, Pell-eligible residents in DC can participate in the Tuition Assistance Program (DCTAG), which assists students by off-setting the cost of tuition at public four-year state institutions up to $10,000, as well as awarding $2,500 for private HBCUs or for a DC student to attend a college located within DC. According to the National Association of State Student Grant and Aid Program's (NASSGAP) most recent survey data, in the 2011–12 academic year, the states awarded about $11.1 billion in total state-funded student financial aid. The majority of state aid remains in the form of grants. In 2011–12, almost 4.2 million grant awards were made, representing about $9.4 billion in need- and non-need-based grant aid. Of the grant money awarded in 2011–12, 74 percent was need-based, and 26 percent was non-need-based, a notable increase in the percentage of need-based aid from previous years. Funding for undergraduate need-based grant aid increased nationwide, from about $6.4 billion in 2010–11 to about $6.8 billion in 2011–12, an increase of 6 percent. Need-based state grant aid uses a range of eligibility criteria to provide funding support to students. They vary by state, but many programs combine one or more elements, including:

- requiring students to be degree-seekers
- determining by need, as determined by FAFSA, in some cases, a set specific estimated family contribution
- income limit (state or federal)

The National Association of State Student Grant & Aid Programs (NASSGAP) has a searchable database that provides summary data on state need-based funding amounts and types. More specific information on current-year funding, award formulas and amounts per student can be found by visiting your respective state higher education agency; a linkable list by state can be found via the State Higher Education Executive Officers Association. Additionally, the National Association of Financial Aid Administrators provides an interactive map to obtain information on state grant programs (*www.nasfaa.org/students/State_Financial_Aid_Programs.aspx*).

SECURING MERIT AID SCHOLARSHIPS

Unfortunately, access to federal aid is not enough to put a dent in the cost of a student's education. Students should pursue merit-based aid, which is awarded to students who do something exceptionally well (like music, athletics or academics) or to students who plan to have a career in an area that will benefit the community or the country (like teaching, science, math, and engineering). Some state grant programs use a combination of need and merit to determine eligibility. And, while students tend to overestimate their eligibility for institutional merit scholarships, there are scholarships for everything nowadays. Thus, it is important that, as a counselor, you familiarize yourself with as many scholarships as possible and track those scholarships that reflect your student population. Sharing scholarships, in a way that students can easily learn about and apply to them, is also another system that needs to be considered and ironed out based on your school's dynamics. First-generation students often understand the concept of scholarships equating with "free money," but often do not understand how to complete scholarship applications. It's important to familiarize yourself with scholarships that target first-generation students and know your students well enough that you can personalize the scholarship application process. For students who may not be strong academically, there still are a variety of scholarships they can still apply for. Becoming familiar with local and national scholarships that allow students to leverage their other strengths or highlight their talents can assist with the cost of college. Matching students with scholarships that match their strengths will increase their ability to obtain money for college. It is also helpful to be transparent and explain to students why they may or may not be a good candidate for a particular scholarship. It's important for students to not waste their time on scholarships that may not be a good match. This may be due to GPA, background, interests, etc. Aid can be secured in many cases from institutions that value and invest in diversity. Many, including highly selective institutions, offer programs that offer a substantial amount of money and/or are willing to meet any unmet need for students who fall into certain categories. Many schools offer fly-in programs where they will fly in students, for free, to experience the college and to see if it would be a good fit.

Students research non-institutional scholarships via a range of college search engines, including The Big Future by the College Board and Fastweb (two searchable scholarship databases). Organizations such as the Hispanic Scholarship Fund and the United Negro College Fund list scholarships for specific student populations. Many institutions also post non-institutional scholarship opportunities via social media and on their respective Web sites. Additionally, there are a variety of scholarships that target first-generation as well as low-income students. This list is by no means exhaustive in nature. It simply highlights the most popular scholarships for this population:

- Gates Millennium
- Coca-Cola Scholars
- Ron Brown Scholarship
- Jackie Robinson Scholarship
- Shawn Carter Scholarship
- Hispanic Scholarship Fund
- NAACP
- UNCF
- Dell Scholarship
- Horatio Alger
- Wendy's Heisman
- AXA Foundation
- POSSE Foundation
- Questbridge
- Congressional Black Caucus
- Congressional Hispanic Caucus
- Hispanic Heritage

- Educators for Fair Consideration
- My Turn
- Sam Walton/Walmart
- Bonner Scholars
- I'm First

DOING THE MATH: COVERING COLLEGE COSTS

According to *Trends in College 2013*, while $8,893 is the average tuition and fee price at public four-year institutions, the average net price, the price actually paid by individual students, is $3,120. The net price is the amount paid by full-time undergraduate students after subtracting federal tax credits and deductions as well as grant aid (College Board, 2013).

At the end of October 2011, the federal government required all postsecondary institutions receiving federal funding and enrolling first-time, full-time, degree-seeking students—including public, private non-profit and for-profit schools—to post a net price calculator (NPC) on their Web sites. A net price calculator enables students and families to provide financial and personal information in order to determine what their expected annual net cost or financial aid award is likely to be from any given college. These online tools can make it much easier for prospective students and their families to look past often scary "sticker prices" and start figuring out which colleges they might be able to afford. In theory, net price calculators were required in order to provide early, individualized estimates of what a specific college will cost *after* grants and scholarships. The net price is what students and their families would have to earn, save or borrow to go to that school. This early information about college costs and financial aid can help students discover that their dream school may be more (or less) affordable than they thought—*before* they have to decide where to apply. However, NPCs, as reflected in initial research completed by Student Poll and The Institute for College Access and Success and other higher education organizations, are not always easy to find, easy to use or accurate.

A tip sheet on NPC titled, "Making Cents of College Costs, Financial Aid, and Net Price" and it's corresponding presentation slides are available online from the 2013 NACAC conference in which The Institute for College Access and Success presented its research and recommendations on net price calculators and financial aid award letters, while counseling professionals from uAspire and Stuyvesant High School discussed their experiences using those tools with students and families and shared best practices for counselors.

Because of the limitations of net cost calculators, it is important to help students to see indirect college costs. Indirect costs include any expenses that students incur that are not paid directly to the institution. They include transportation, books, computer equipment, supplies, childcare, and housing. Whether students live on campus or off campus, they must pay for housing and food, buy books and supplies, and cover transportation and other basic living costs. Room and board and other living costs are not reflected in NPCs. These are expenses people face whether or not they are in school. Because students tend to think of living expenses as part of the cost of going to college, they may not fully realize that they must come up with the funds to cover these costs. Students from more affluent families can often safely assume that their families will cover such costs. Yet, for low-income and many middle-income students, the cost of living poses a significant hurdle. Even those who receive grant and/or scholarship aid sufficient to cover tuition and fee charges may struggle to cover living expenses. These are very real costs students incur for which many students do not have disposable income to cover. Thus, they use financial aid refunds to cover their basic needs. This is one factor that influences student borrowing behavior; students often take out loans that exceed their cost of attendance. Therefore, students should be counseled to determine these costs and to set a corresponding budget so they can manage their resources. They should also be advised that wages from summer and part-time jobs, including work study, can assist them with covering these costs throughout the academic year.

And, while there is an ongoing effort to improve transparency in higher education that includes standardizing award letters—because institutions have historically not issued awards in ways that allow students and their families to compare them with one another easily—it is important to work closely with students as they review financial aid awards in relationship to costs.

Research shows that "in-state residents at public institutions who were eligible for Pell Grants enrolled at dramatically higher rates when there was a gap of less than $1,000 between their level of need and the amount of their award package" (Noel Levitz, 2007). Therefore, it is important to help students calculate, on their own, what their out-of-pocket or gap in aid might amount to and help them identify ways to cover their gap in aid, as well as indirect college costs that are not paid directly to the institution they are attending.

For example, in Ohio, a student who is Pell-eligible who is attending any of the public four-year institutions will face a significant gap in aid, even if he or she decides to commute or live off campus. At one of the state's most affordable four-year institutions, a student's tuition and fee totals $6,246 for the 2014–2015 academic year, which is not fully covered by a maximum Pell award of $5,730. Certainly, a student in this situation can anticipate being awarded the Ohio College Opportunity Grant that amounts to approximately $516, which is the difference between the institution's tuition and fees and the student's Pell award. Additionally, in a standard financial aid package for a student with a full Pell estimated family contribution (EFC), federal need-based aid, which includes subsidized federal loans and SEOG grant funds (Student Educational Opportunity Grant), will be awarded. He or she may also qualify for last-dollar grant aid from access organizations. However, if the student lives on campus, he or she will need $15,564 to cover his/her direct costs, which consists of tuition, fees, and room and board. A standard package for a Pell-EFC student who does not have any merit aid from the institution will total $11,230 before he or she pursues self-help aid beyond the initial $5,500 offered in loans, which is a combination of a $3,500 subsidized direct loan and a $2,000 unsubsidized loan. From this point, he or she will be expected to have his/her parent apply for the Parent Plus Loan to cover direct costs, with a difference being available for any anticipated indirect costs. If the parent is denied, the student will be offered an additional $4,000 in unsubsidized student loan funds. This still leaves the student with $9,500 in student loans as an entering freshman, a $434 gap in aid for direct costs, and without enough awarded aid to cover books and other indirect costs or incidentals.

Knowing this math and being able to teach students how to do these calculations is a critical part of the college choice and enrollment process. While students will qualify for scholarships both from their prospective institutions and private sources, it is important to understand what bare-bones, need-based grant aid gets in today's higher education marketplace. From there, students and those who support them can anticipate the need to persistently identify other ways to cut and/or cover their college costs each year.

It is important for families to realize that there are schools that are willing to pay for a variety of areas: grades, diversity, talents, etc. Many of our first-generation students and families often limit themselves to local schools or HBCUs. Encouraging students to open up their options and apply to schools they may not initially think they would like to attend may work out in their favor. Students may be able to access institutions that may be considered out of their range simply because the school is looking for certain areas of diversity.

Lastly, encouraging students to be as creative and resourceful as possible also helps with the cost of funding their own education. Providing students and families with a college supply list and having students advocate on their own behalf with organizations they are involved in as well as with adults in their lives who want to help can add up over time. Also, encouraging students to save as much money as they can and kindly suggest money and/or actual items from their college supply list to people who would like to help and when it comes to holidays, birthdays, etc. can add up over time.

ADDITIONAL CONSIDERATIONS: GETTING THERE AND RESERVING A SPACE

And, even when our students get great financial aid packages, find schools that are a great fit and are willing to attend, there are expenses that will incur prior to matriculating to campus. One such expense that can sometimes be an issue is transportation. We need to think outside the box and assist our families in coming up with ways that will allow students to minimally travel home on an as-needed basis. This may come in the form of emergency funds from the student's school or religious group, vouchers from transportation companies, booking tickets well in advance to guarantee the cheapest price possible, and also encouraging students to speak with their college to see if there are alternative housing options so that if they cannot come home over breaks, they have the option to stay at the university, if needed.

Concerning deposits, it's important to become familiar with university policies surrounding deposits and down payments. Certain schools will waive certain fees while others will not allow a student to register for classes or move in if their deposits and/or down payments are not paid in full. The more familiar you are, the easier it will be to prepare a family, as well as assist them in navigating the process and making a decision about a school. Deposits are normally non-refundable. It's important that a family is fully committed and confident that they can afford a school before paying any kind of deposit that they will not be able to get back if they decide it is not the right fit.

OTHER WAYS TO REDUCE COLLEGE COSTS

In addition to securing financial aid, there are a number of other ways to lower the costs of pursuing and obtaining a college degree.

Students and their families may consider special college savings programs. NAFSAA provides a side-by-side comparison chart of savings options to help families.

Students, particularly adult learners, can explore getting college credit for on-the-job training and life experience. The American Council on Education's (ACE) College Credit Recommendation Service helps students gain access to academic credit for courses or exams, such as job-related training taken outside of a degree program. Veterans and non-traditional students with substantial life experience in one or more areas should explore prior-learning assessment opportunities that allow them to earn college credit for work-based training, as well as by completing a portfolio course.

Students should know that they can earn college credits by examination and test out of subjects they already know. Earning the required score on The College-Level Examination Program® (CLEP) test allows students to earn credit and save the cost of taking the course. For example, students who are fluent in Spanish or French can take the associated CLEP exam, which can allow them to cover the language requirements in most curricula at a significant savings. Students who have not scored the required AP test score may take a comparable CLEP exam. Additionally, students further along in their college careers may use CLEP to cover general education requirements they need to complete in order to graduate. Plus, many colleges and universities offer their own tests that let students skip certain classes or earn credits if you pass. Admission representative or academic advisors are best to discuss this option with students. Many school districts allow students to earn high school and college credit simultaneously, and they are often free or very low-cost. These programs vary by state, but they include dual-enrollment, tech-prep and career pathways opportunities, as well as Advanced Placement and International Baccalaureate programs.

at a four-year public or private institution. However, it is important to advise students comprehensively on how to maximize attending a community college so that they actually do obtain a college degree in the long-run.

In some cases, this means identifying community colleges that confer baccalaureate degrees. But, in most cases, it means understanding the transfer agreements between community colleges and the local and regional four-year institutions. Students who want to save money that way need a clear road map; they have to see a comprehensive pathway toward degree completion, which certainly may include some of the aforementioned options, including

In some cases, this means identifying community colleges that confer baccalaureate degrees. But, in most cases, it means understanding the transfer agreements between community colleges and the local and regional four-year institutions.

Accelerated degree programs are another way for students to save money as they pursue a degree. Many states have mandated that their public institutions identify specific programs that students complete in three years rather than four. Students can also attend summer school, even the summer just after graduation, to reduce the time and cost of their degree.

Students and their families should become familiar with federal tax benefits for higher education that will reduce their college costs. The federal government provides a number of tax incentives that can help defray the cost of higher education. These incentives come in a couple of forms: *tax credits*, which directly reduce tax liability, and *deductions*, which reduce the amount of income paid on taxes. NASFAA provides a multi-page, user-friendly resource guide on educational tax benefits.

And, while concerns continue to be raised about student success and completion at community colleges, articulated by education thought leaders ranging from the Gates Foundation to the Lumina Foundation to the American Association of Community Colleges (AACC), community colleges continue to be important options that allow students to complete a significant portion of their college education at a far more affordable price than what they might pay

dual enrollment in high school. Most states have a clear and delineated system for identifying course articulations between institutions. However, recruiters from four-year institutions may not be well-versed in these options, so it is critical for counselors to be familiar with these opportunities. To obtain more information on transfer articulation agreements and state transfer policies, you can consult the NACAC Transfer Knowledge Hub, which provides a link to the Education Commission of the States' (ECS) Transfer and Articulation Database, offering information on articulation agreements searchable by state. You may also consider contacting your Tech Prep councils or entities, as well as attending your respective state-wide college counseling association trainings and conferences to obtain institutional updates from your community colleges and other higher education institutions.

TUITION WAIVERS/DISCOUNTS/RECIPROCITY

Many states have programs that allow residents to attend a university in another state without having to pay out-of-state tuition. Check with states or with specific universities about available tuition exchange or reciprocity programs, and ask about how to sign up. Some programs include:

- The Southern Regional Education Board Academic Common Market—provides tuition discounts for more than 1,900 academic programs in Alabama, Arkansas, Delaware, Florida, Georgia, Kentucky, Louisiana, Maryland, Mississippi, North Carolina, Oklahoma, South Carolina, Tennessee, Texas, Virginia, and West Virginia. The Regional Contract Program enables students to pursue a professional health degree at out-of-state institutions, but pay in-state tuition at public institutions or reduced tuition at private institutions.

- The Midwest Student Exchange—students from Indiana, Kansas, Michigan, Minnesota, Missouri, Nebraska, North Dakota, and Wisconsin may be eligible for tuition reductions at certain Midwest public and private schools.

- The Western Interstate Commission for Higher Education—for students in Alaska, Arizona, California, Colorado, Hawaii, Idaho, Montana, Nevada, New Mexico, North Dakota, Oregon, South Dakota, Utah, Washington, and Wyoming. The Western Regional Graduate Program enables residents to enroll in available graduate programs outside of their home state at resident tuition rates. The Professional Student Exchange Program enables students majoring in the healthcare professions to enroll in selected out-of-state professional programs.

- The New England Regional Student Program—enables New England residents to enroll at out-of-state New England public colleges and universities at a discount. Students are eligible when they enroll in an approved major that is not offered by the public colleges and universities in their home state. More than 700 undergraduate and graduate degree programs are offered. Participating states are Connecticut, Maine, Massachusetts, New Hampshire, Rhode Island, and Vermont.

Additionally, the Center for College Affordability provides a comprehensive guide that outlines a range of options for reducing college costs overall, as well as specific recommendations for individual students and families.

BEING A BRIDGE BUILDER: WORKING WITH OTHERS TO MAXIMIZE THE IMPACT

The only way to truly be able to assist our students in being successful is to serve as bridge builders to institutes of higher education, as well as community groups in your area that service your students and families. Sometimes, we also have to extend our scope of services beyond the senior year of high school and assist students in getting settled in the first few months of their freshman year and also be available as a resource throughout their college experience.

COLLEGE AND UNIVERSITY CONNECTIONS

It's important to find schools that value your students and are willing to not only invest money but time as well into ensuring their success. Sometimes this comes in the form of specialized programs that are set up specifically for first-generation students. Other times, it comes in the form of individualized relationships you develop as a counselor with staff at a particular school. While these relationships do not guarantee admission or student success, they do leverage your ability to have a student gain an opportunity at a university or within a program they may not normally have. Over time, as your relationship deepens and you experience a level of student success at those institutions, you can begin developing a cohort approach to sending students to those institutions. We want schools to care and invest in our students the same way we do as counselors. Students also gain confidence and are more willing to attend a school where they personally know students who come from their same community and have a similar background, and who are experiencing success. In turn, students can mentor one another and provide an additional layer of support for one another.

COMMUNITY GROUPS/CBOS

Community groups and organizations play a huge role in our families' lives. They provide a myriad of services, support and outlets that often complement the services that schools offer students. Sometimes, community-based organizations have the ability to provide more services, including more one-on-one time. When schools and CBO partners share a common vision and utilize a holistic approach to servicing students, it allows one to leverage combined resources to maximize services, funding and impact on students. Many schools have begun meeting with their community partners on a regular basis and developing a shared vision that targets specific goals and outcomes for both parties. If you do not have one in your school, you can easily begin to start one by researching the various community partners that service your school and the students in your area and invite them to an initial meeting to discuss collaborating with one another.

Programs Specifically for First-Generation Students

There are several programs that are in existence that support first-generation students and can be found within your own school, community and on the college campuses that service your students. Many campuses have their own programs for first-generation students, as well as federally funded government programs to support students. Listed below are a few of the national programs that target first-generation students:

- AVID—Advancement Via Individual Determination
- CollegeEd
- College Summit
- Talent Search (part of TRIO)
- Dual-enrollment programs
- Upward Bound (part of TRIO)
- Student Support Services (part of TRIO)
- Urban League
- Summer Bridge Programs

Conclusion

Working with first-generation students presents both exceptional challenges and rewards. This is because students frequently lack the appropriate support, as well as parents who have experience-based knowledge to guide them through the college process. This requires a significant amount of patience, guidance and expertise on the part of the counselor. Taking into account a family's financial needs, ethnic background and individual situation is crucial. Counseling often involves a deficits-based

Working with first-generation students presents both exceptional challenges and rewards. This is because students frequently lack the appropriate support, as well as parents who have experience-based knowledge to guide them through the college process.

approach, where the focus tends to be on things students lack rather than on their assets. What was presented in this chapter facilitates the reframing of student stories as an area of strength. The personal statement is a way for students to highlight their assets that often go unnoticed. In addition, first-generation college students and their families often overestimate the cost of college, which may, in turn, cause them to rule out viable options or college completely. Lastly, connecting first-generation students to supportive programs and systems allows them to receive the encouragement, support and guidance they so desperately need to successfully complete college. A counselor must enhance their knowledge-base in the area of programs, community partners and colleges that believe in and favor first-generation students and equally want to support their admission, persistence and success in college. It is our responsibility to serve as bridge builders, since we know that our students need a tremendous amount of encouragement, support and guidance not only to get in, but also to get through and successfully graduate from college.

About the Authors

Kya Dixon is senior program officer, college programs at the College Success Foundation (DC), a college access and scholarship provider that selects low-income students using non-cognitive factors. Kya leads a team who supports the recipients of the DC Achievers Scholarship to ensure that scholars are successfully navigating college by accessing resources proven to increase college completion rates for under-represented students. Kya also has ten years of experience in higher education institutions, specifically in financial aid. She earned her master's in higher education from Drexel University (PA) and bachelor's degree in American studies from Trinity College (CT).

Phyllis Jeffers-Coly's twenty years in higher education includes teaching composition, leadership, literature and women's studies at Montgomery Community College (MD), the University of Maryland, College Park (UMCP) and the College Access and Transition Program (CAT) at the University of Cincinnati (OH) as well as seven years of enrollment management and student affairs experience at Central State University (OH) where she served as the dean of enrollment services. Her experience in higher education policy and advocacy also includes working for the White House Initiative on HBCUs, American Association of University Women, Maryland (AAUW) and the office of Congressman Robert C Scott. She holds a bachelor's in English from North Carolina Central University (NC) and a master's in English language and literature from UMCP.

Nicole E. Smith is currently the senior program officer, school programs and the co-director of the Summer Academic Enrichment Program for the College Success Foundation DC. She is the former principal of Philadelphia YouthBuild PCS (PA), the acting principal and Director of Education at LAYC YouthBuild PCS in DC, co-founder of the Teaching Excellence Center, and the former Head Start assistant director at the Columbia North YMCA in Philadelphia, PA. Additionally, she served as the Director of Education at Women Organized Against Rape, and worked for the PA Department of Probation and Parole. She received her bachelor's in education from Indiana University of Pennsylvania (PA) and her master's in urban education from Temple University (PA).

REFERENCES

Balemian, K., & Feng, J. (2013). First generation students: College aspirations, preparedness and challenges. [PowerPoint]. College Board AP Annual Conference. Retrieved from *https://research.collegeboard.org/sites/ default/files/publications/2013/8/presentation-apac-2013-first-generation-college-aspirations-preparedness-challenges.pdf.*

Bloom, J., Hutson, B., & He, Y. (2008). *The appreciative advising revolution.* Champaign, IL: Stipes Pub.

Brooks, S., & Little, K. (2013). Partnerships to promote college affordability, enrollment and success [PowerPoint]. College Board Dream Deferred Conference 2013. Retrieved from *http://media. collegeboard.com/digitalServices/pdf/diversity/2014/ partnerships-promote-college-affordability-enrollment-success.pdf.*

Caumont, A. Pew Research Center. (2014, February). 6 key findings about going to college. Retrieved from *http://www.pewresearch.org/fact-tank/2014/02/11/6-key-findings-about-going-to-college.*

College Board. Education pays 2013: The benefits of higher education for individuals and society. Retrieved from *http://trends.collegeboard.org/sites/ default/files/education-pays-2013-full-report.pdf.*

College Board. (2013). Trends in student aid 2013. Retrieved from *http://trends.collegeboard.org/sites/ default/files/student-aid-2013-full-report.pdf.*

College Board. (2013). Trends in college pricing. Retrieved from *http://trends.collegeboard.org/sites/ default/files/college-pricing-2013-full-report.pdf.*

College Board and Art & Science Group, LLC (2012). A majority of students rule out colleges based on sticker price. *Student Poll, 9*(1). Retrieved from *http://www. artsci.com/studentpoll/v9n1/index.html.*

Department of Education. (2014). Expansive survey of America's public schools reveals troubling racial disparities. Retrieved from *http://www.ed.gov/news/press-releases/expansive-survey-americas-public-schools-reveals-troubling-racial-disparities).*

Duckworth, A.L., Peterson, C., Matthews, M.D., & Kelly, D.R. (2007). Grit: Perseverance and passion for long-term goals. *Journal of Personality and Social Psychology, 92*(6), 1087–1101.

Factors in the admission decision. (2014). Retrieved from *http://www.nacacnet.org/studentinfo/articles/Pages/Factors-in-the-Admission-Decision.aspx.*

Gladwell, M. (2013). *David and Goliath: Underdogs, misfits, and the art of battling giants.* New York: Little, Brown and Company.

Higher Education Research Institute. (2007). First in my family: A profile of first generation college students at four year institutions since 1971. Retrieved From *http://www.heri.ucla.edu/pdfs/pubs/briefs/firstgenresearchbrief.pdf.*

Hiltonsmith, R., & Draut, T. (2014, March). The great cost shift continues: State higher education funding after the recession. Retrieved from *http://www.demos.org/publication/great-cost-shift-continues-state-higher-education-funding-after-recession.*

Institute for College Access and Success. (2013). Making cents of college costs, financial aid and net price:A student-centered perspective. Retrieved from *http://www.ticas.org/pub_view.php?idx=915.*

Institute for Higher Education Policy (2012, September). Supporting first-generation college students through classroom-based practices. Retrieved from *http://www.ihep.org/assets/files/publications/s-z/%28Issue_Brief%29_Walmart_MSI_Supporting_FGS_September_2012.pdf*

Lynch, Matthew. (2013) "It's Tough to Trailblaze: Challenges of first-generation college students" Diverse. Retrieved from *http://diverseeducation.com/article/50898/.*

NACAC. (2014). Transfer Knowledge Hub [Web site]. Retrieved from *http://www.nacacnet.org/research/transfer/Pages/State-Policies-on-Transfer.aspx.*

Noel Levitz. (2007) Access Alert: How the neediest students can gain access and succeed through strategic financial aid awarding. Retrieved from *noellevitz.com/papers-research-higher-education/2007/neediest-students-access-financial-aid-awarding.*

Scott-Clayton, J. (2012, February). Information constraints and financial aid policy. National Bureau of Economic Research (NBER) Working Paper Series. Retrieved from *nber.org/papers/w17811.*

Sedlacek, W. (n.d.). Non-cognitive admissions variable. Retrieved from *http://williamsedlacek.info/publications/surveys/noncognitiveadmissions.html.*

Sedlacek, W. (n.d.). Non-cognitive minority admissions variables questionnaire items for supplementary admissions questionnaire ii. Retrieved from *http://williamsedlacek.info/publications/surveys/noncognitiveminority.html.*

Sedlacek, W. (n.d.). Scoring key for supplementary admissions questionnaire ii. Retrieved from *http://williamsedlacek.info/publications/surveys/ncqskey.html.*

Sedlacek, W. (n.d.). Supplementary admissions questions ii. Retrieved from *http://williamsedlacek.info/publications/surveys/universityofmaryland.html.*

Sedlacek, W. (1993). Employing noncognitive variables in the admission and retention of nontraditional students. Retrieved from *http://williamsedlacek.info/publications/articles/employing1.html.*

Sedlacek, W. (2004). Beyond the big test: Noncognitive assessment in higher education. San Francisco: Jossey-Bass.

Sedlacek, W. (2005). The case for Noncognitive measures. In W.J. Camara & E.W. Kimmel (Eds.) Choosing students higher education admissions tools for the 21st century (pp. 177–193). Mahwah, NJ: Lawrence Erlbaum.

Seligman, M., & Csikszentmihalyi, M. (2000). Positive psychology: An introduction. American Psychologist, 55(1), 5–14. Retrieved from *http://www.ppc.sas.upenn.edu/ppintroarticle.pdf.*

Sternberg, R.J. (1985). Beyond IQ: A Triarchic Theory of Intelligence. Cambridge: Cambridge University Press.

What is positive psychology? (2012, January 1). Retrieved from *http://www.positivepsychologyinstitute.com.au/what_is_positive_psychology.html.*

Wyer, K. (2014) The American Freshman: National norms 2013. Higher Education Research Institute. Retrieved from *http://heri.ucla.edu/briefs/TheAmericanFreshman2013-Brief.pdf.*

FURTHER DISCUSSION QUESTIONS CONCERNING FIRST-GENERATION STUDENTS

Classroom

1. Assist students in developing their own personal goals as a practitioner and what their plan looks like over the course of the next five years.

2. Have students assess their network and see what areas are strong and what areas they need to work on in order to build the largest support network for their students.

3. Have students assess their personal work space. Is it set up in a manner that shows they are a professional? Is it welcoming for students and families? Do you have resources available?

4. Have students assess the college-going culture in their school and find ways to improve it.

5. Have students assess things they may want to add or incorporate into their college culture to increase parental involvement and comfort.

6. Have students research local, regional, state, federal, and other programs that specifically target first-generation students. Have them compile a manual or resource guide that includes these programs.

Personal Reflection Questions

Personal Experience

1. What is your earliest memory concerning when you decided to attend college? Who helped you in that process? Who were your biggest advocates? How did they support you?

2. What messages did you receive, positive and negative, about your ability and potential to go to college?

3. What high school preparation did you receive?

4. What supports were lacking from your college application experience?

5. What generation, in your family, are you? How does that affect your outlook professionally?

6. Who paid for college?

7. How did you decide what college to attend? Was it your first choice? Why did you attend that college?

8. What was your experience in college? What advice would you give your younger self?

Personal Beliefs

1. What are your personal attitudes and beliefs surrounding first-generation students?

2. Are there certain populations that you are not comfortable working with? How do you plan to address this so you can fully support this population of students? What information do you feel would be most helpful to obtain? What supports, within your school and community, can you pull from?

3. What populations do you feel most comfortable working with?

4. What are your strengths as a counselor?

5. What are your weaknesses? How do you plan to strengthen them?

6. What do you want for your students? List 4–5 outcomes, and work on a detailed action plan to meet them.

(continues)

FURTHER DISCUSSION QUESTIONS CONCERNING FIRST-GENERATION STUDENTS *(continued)*

7. How strong are your connections with other colleagues? Community partners? What systems can be put in place to strengthen/build these relationships?

8. How often do you attend professional development opportunities specifically for college access and success?

9. What listservs, blogs, pages, organizations, etc. do you belong to that help strengthen your practice?

College Center/Office

1. Is your office set up in a manner that is student-centered and friendly?

2. Can students easily access the counseling/college suite?

3. Are there up-to-date resources and handouts that students can access?

4. What trainings can be offered to school faculty, parents and students concerning the college process?

5. Identify all cultures/languages located within your school. Ensure your school has literature, handouts and posters that reflect these cultures/languages.

6. What are steps you can take to assist your school in building a college-going culture?

7. How can you create a culture and environment that focuses on institutional systems and change verses the inadequacies of students and families?

8. What systems are working in your school? What systems are not? How you do plan to change the systems that are not working?

College Center Support

1. How frequently do you meet with your students? What goal can you set to ensure you are meeting with students as frequently as possible?

2. How often does the college counseling department meet and share information with the rest of the school faculty? Is the information being shared helpful? Do the meetings allow you to gain information to assist students with their future goals and passions? Is there a place where you can collaborate with faculty to ensure student success?

3. Are there clear transition plans that allow students to move as easily as possible to college?

4. Is there time built in to allow the college team time to connect with colleagues to plan, discuss students, share ideas, improve systems, etc. in order to fully support students?

5. Does the college counseling team value other opinions and diverse backgrounds of staff and students? Is the team culturally sensitive and aware of the various communities in your school? If not, how can you work toward that goal?

(continues)

FURTHER DISCUSSION QUESTIONS CONCERNING FIRST-GENERATION STUDENTS *(continued)*

Academic Support

1. How are students selected for classes? How can you ensure students are taking the highest level courses that make them attractive for college (AP, honors, IB, dual-enrollment)?

2. Are there additional opportunities for students who are high-performing, such as dual-enrollment programs to earn college credits or internships that allow students to explore their interests?

3. Does your school taught the skills necessary to be successful in college, such as study skills, note taking, organization, time management, etc.? If not, how can you incorporate it into the curriculum?

4. Does your school offer support services for students who need them? Can students who do not have an IEP or 504 plan also easily access support services when needed?

Family and Community Support

1. How and when are parents included in the postsecondary planning process?

2. How rich are your school-based supports? How flexible are these supports in meeting the family's needs at your school?

3. How rich are your community-based supports? How can you strengthen your relationships with local businesses, community partners and colleges to increase career and postsecondary information and opportunities for students and families?

4. How well does your school engage families? What types of activities, socials, trainings, etc. are held to provide information, as well as relationship-building opportunities for your families?

5. Is there a forum set up where parents and students can offer feedback about support you currently offer, as well as support they feel they would like?

6. Are there multiple resources provided to families in a variety of languages? Are resources current and easily accessible?

7. Are their multiple avenues for parents to receive information? Does your school have a user-friendly Web site? Newsletter? Email? Can parents easily access the college counseling team when they have questions?

8. What opportunities lie within your school for community partners to get involved?

9. Are there certain programs community partners can offer, for free or minimal charge, to students during the school day or after school?

Take-Aways, Resources or Tools for Serving First-Generation Students

Early College Planning/First Generation Sites

- Center for Student Opportunity
- Dream to Reality (ACT Guide)
- First in the Family
- Public Education Foundation/Map2College

Financial Aid/Covering College Costs

- Dollars for College Toolkit
- Free Application for Federal Student Aid (FAFSA)
- FAFSA Forecaster

College Research/Selection

- Big Future
- College Prowler
- CollegeResults.org

Books

- *Admission Matters: What Students and Parents Need to Know about Getting into College*, by Sally P. Springer, Jon Reider and Joyce Vining Morgan
- *The College Application Essay*, by Sarah M. McGinty
- *College Finder*, by Steven Antonoff
- *College Match: A Blueprint for Choosing the Best School for You*, by Steven Antonoff
- *'I'm First' Guide to College*, by the Center for Student Opportunity
- *Letting Go: A Parent's Guide to Understanding the College Years*, by Karen L. Coburn and Madge L. Treeger
- *Write Out Loud*, by Carol Barash
- *StrengthsQuest*, by Donald O. Clifton and Edward Anderson

- *Now, Discover your Strengths*, by Marcus Buckingham and Donald O. Clifton
- *Read, Willing, and Able*, by Mandy Savitz-Romer and Suzanne M. Bouffard
- *The EQ Edge: Emotional Intelligence and Your Success*, by Steven J. Stein and Howard E. Book
- *Beyond the Big Test*, by William Sedlacek
- *How Children Succeed*, by Paul Tough
- *The Tipping Point*, by Malcolm Gladwell
- *Outliers*, by Malcolm Gladwell
- *The First-Generation Student Experience: Implications for Campus Practice, and Strategies for Improving Persistence and Success*, by Jeff Davis

Surveys/Instruments

- Appreciative Advising Inquiry
- College Match Survey
- MBTI Personality Assessment
- Career Cluster Assessment
- Search Institute: 40 Developmental Assets
- Grit Scale (Duckworth)
- EQ-i (Emotional Intelligence Quotient)
- Strengths Finder Assessment

Tools

- OnCourse
- WhyTry:Resilience
- Education

Chapter 19:   Students with Learning Disabilities and the College Application Process

Terence J. Houlihan
@SurviveUrTeens

INTRODUCTION/BACKGROUND

No resource regarding the college application process would be complete without the inclusion of material specifically dedicated to students with learning disabilities. Between the years of 2001 and 2010, the number of college applicants indicating that they had a learning disability had grown to almost 400,000—an increase of 50 percent (Henderson, 2001; Vickers, 2010; United States Government Accountability Office, 2009). The US Department of Education (2011) revealed that 88 percent of colleges currently enroll students with learning disabilities. Of particular interest is that in 2011, almost all (99 percent) of two-year and four-year public institutions enrolled students with learning disabilities. Of the general "disability" categories reported, "specific learning disabilities" was the highest, with 31 percent, followed by ADD and ADHD at 18 percent, "psychological or psychiatric conditions" at 15 percent, and 11 percent of disabilities were a "health impairment/condition." The remaining categories included "visual/auditory impairments," "speech disorders," "traumatic brain injury," and others.

In looking at those percentages, it is reasonable to conclude that most high school counselors helping students with the college application process will be working with students who have a learning disability. However, even though the nation's postsecondary institutions are reporting higher numbers of students with disabilities, not all of them offer programs to assist students with those specific disabilities. Just as there are very few private K–12 schools exclusively for students with disabilities, there are only a handful of colleges that are specifically geared toward students with learning disabilities. Surprising to many applicants and parents is the reality that if a student will require the use of supportive services in college, many institutions charge additional fees. But before addressing those particular concerns, it is important to look at the landscape of services for students with disabilities and best practices for school counselors.

KEY TERMS ASSOCIATED WITH SPECIAL EDUCATION

It is incumbent upon school counselors to be versed in the verbiage associated with special education. Given that many school counselors are often asked to be part of committees and, by law, are mandated service-providers (if counseling services are outlined on a student's IEP), knowing terms such as IEP, 504, LD, etc. is invaluable.

IDEA

The Individuals with Disabilities Education Act (IDEA) is the nation's federal special education law that guarantees public schools serve the educational needs of students with disabilities. IDEA requires that schools offer special education services to eligible students as outlined in a student's Individualized Education Program (IEP), and it specifies requirements to guarantee a Free Appropriate Public Education (FAPE) for these students in the least restrictive environment (LRE). IDEA was first passed in 1975, but is reauthorized every few years, the most recent being 2006.

Disabilities under IDEA

IDEA lists 13 different disability categories under which three- through 21-year-olds may be eligible for services. Although school counselors are not special education teachers, it is important to become familiar with the different categories.

The disability categories listed in IDEA are:
- autism
- deaf-blindness
- deafness
- emotional disturbance
- hearing impairment
- intellectual disability
- multiple disabilities
- orthopedic impairment
- other health impairment (ADD/ADHD, asthma, diabetes, etc.)
- specific learning disability (areas of oral expression, listening comprehension, written expression, basic reading skills, reading fluency skills, reading comprehension, mathematics calculation and mathematics problem solving)
- speech or language impairment
- traumatic brain injury
- visual impairment (including blindness).

IEP

Once a student has been formally evaluated by a team of psychologists and educators and found eligible for special education services, the parents work with a school team to develop an Individualized Education Program (IEP). It is important to note that this evaluation will be crucial when it comes to applying for accommodations on standardized tests such as the SAT and ACT. Sometimes, this school team is referred to as a committee on special education (CSE), when it convenes to discuss the findings and develop an IEP. Typical attendees of CSEs are the student's parents/guardians, the CSE chairperson, a special education teacher, a general education teacher, other service providers, and the student (when appropriate). School counselors are not required to attend these meetings, but may do so at the parent's request. In fact, ASCA (2104) outlines inappropriate responsibilities for school counselors in relation to the IEP such as "serving in any supervisory capacity related to the implementation of the IDEA, serving as the school district representative for the team writing the IEP, or coordinating, writing or supervising the implementation of the IEP."

The IEP is a legal document outlining the services and support the school will provide for the student with the disability. An IEP needs to be written and agreed upon before a student can begin receiving services, and it must be reviewed and updated each year.

While each state differs in how it develops an IEP, the Individuals with Disabilities Education Act requires that every IEP include the following:

- the student's current performance

- annual goals and objectives to meet those goals

- strategies needed to allow the student to participate in the general education curriculum.

Non-Public Schools

Given that slightly more than 5 million US K–12 students (10 percent) attend private schools, it is important to address special education services in non-public schools. IDEA regulations are very clear about the rights of "parentally placed private school children with disabilities" (US Department of Education, 2006). In fact, the law requires the local educational agency (LEA) to "locate, identify, evaluate, and provide services to all children in the school district served by the LEA." Because many private schools do not offer special education services, the responsibility of identifying students with special needs often falls on school counselors. Therefore, school counselors working in non-public schools should become familiar with the policies and procedures of their LEA.

Section 504

Commonly misconstrued with an IEP is the 504. A 504 refers to Section 504 of the Rehabilitation Act of 1973. Section 504 is a national law that protects qualified individuals from discrimination based on their disability (US Department of Health and Human Services, 2006). Schools that receive federal funding are obligated to serve students under Section 504. Kaloi (2014) sees a 504 plan as a viable option for a K–12 student if the child has an identified learning disability (LD) or attention-deficit/hyperactivity disorder (ADHD) but does not meet the requirements of IDEA for special education services and the supports the child is currently receiving are informal accommodations or ongoing support at school (National Center for Learning Disabilities).

LD

According to IDEA (2004), a learning disability is:

> a disorder in one or more of the basic psychological processes involved in understanding or in using language, spoken or written, that may manifest itself in an imperfect ability to listen, think, speak, read, write, spell, or to do mathematical calculations, including conditions such as perceptual disabilities, brain injury, minimal brain dysfunction, dyslexia, and developmental aphasia.

School counselors may read or hear about a student's dyslexia-related difficulties in reading, dysgraphia-related difficulties in writing or dyscalculia-related difficulties in mathematics. Each of these disorders is considered a learning disability.

ADD/ADHD

As previously mentioned, of the students with disabilities who are attending college, ADD/ADHD is the second most common disability reported. Of particular interest is the fact that in the late 18th century (Crichton, 1798), some school-age children were being identified with disorders whose symptoms seem to be in line with the symptoms of ADHD. Since that time, it has been a widely accepted belief that ADHD is a disorder of childhood, and parents and teachers could expect children to simply grow out of ADHD after their adolescence (Barkley, 2006). Contemporary research (Lange et al., 2010) into ADHD has shown that half of children diagnosed with ADHD retain the symptoms of ADHD well into their adult years. Thus, school counselors working with high school students will certainly have students with ADD/ADHD assigned to their caseloads. Since the publication of the *Diagnostic and Statistical Manual of Mental Disorders, 5th Edition,* (American Psychiatric Association, 2013), the disorder identified as ADHD has been placed under the category of neurodevelopmental disorders and is grouped into inattentiveness and/or hyperactivity/impulsivity.

What Are the Expectations for School Counselors?

Different school systems have different expectations for the level and depth at which school counselors are expected to be involved in the special education services of students, and because of this, it is best to look at the American School Counselor Association's position statement (2014):

> Professional school counselors work with students individually, in group settings, in special education class settings, and in the regular classroom. Professional school counselor responsibilities may include but are not limited to:

- providing school counseling curriculum lessons, individual and/or group counseling to students with special needs within the scope of the comprehensive school counseling program

- providing short-term, goal-focused counseling in instances where it is appropriate to include these strategies in the individual educational program (IEP)

- encouraging family involvement in the educational process

- consulting and collaborating with staff and families to understand the special needs of a student and understanding the adaptations and modifications needed to assist the student

- advocating for students with special needs in the school and in the community

- contributing to the school's multidisciplinary team within the scope and practice of the comprehensive school counseling program to identify students who may need to be assessed to determine special education eligibility

- collaborating with related student support professionals (e.g., school psychologists, physical therapists, occupational therapists, special education staff, speech and language pathologists, teachers of deaf and hearing impaired) in the delivery of services

- providing assistance with developing academic and transition plans for students in the IEP as appropriate.

The ASCA position statement is an appropriate model for school counselors to look to when considering which services are within their scope for students with disabilities.

School Counselor Services

In the last decade, school counselors have been more widely considered an integral part of the team that delivers services to students with social, behavioral or emotional needs that impact their learning (Rock & Leff, 2014). Students with a 504 plan or an IEP may receive specific school counseling services under *related services.* The IDEA (2004) definition of related services is "developmental, corrective and other supportive services... as may be required to assist a child with a disability to benefit from special education." Some of these services include counseling, early identification and assessment, parent counseling, and training, among others. Related services can be provided directly through individual or group counseling, or they can be delivered indirectly by consulting with a teacher or parent/guardian.

IDEA (2004) specifically includes transition services as part of related services for students with disabilities that are often performed by professional school counselors. For the purposes of this chapter, the term "transition services" specifically references all activities associated with postsecondary education. IDEA (2004) does require that students with disabilities be invited to the "IEP Team meeting when purpose includes consideration of postsecondary goals."

According to Rock and Leff (2014), some other support services that:

> may involve the school counselor are assessments, interpretation of assessments, positive behavioral support services, case management, advocacy, collaboration with other pupil support specialists, social skills training, activities to improve self-esteem, support for high school completion, dropout prevention, self-determination training, vocational programming, career development, evaluation of college options, and referral to outside agencies (p. 364).

Accommodations vs. Modifications

In order for school counselors to excel in their delivery services to students with disabilities, it is important to distinguish between accommodations and modifications. School counselors may sometimes assist with the administrative task of applying for extended time on SAT/ACT exams on behalf of students, and as such, it is crucial that school counselors become familiar with the accommodations/modifications listed on a student's IEP or 504 plan.

Hamilton and Kessler (2014) define an accommodation as "a change that helps a student overcome or work around the disability," while "a modification…is a change in what is being taught to or expected from the student." Both types of interventions are set up to support students with disabilities, and some students may, in fact, need both. Essentially, accommodations are changes in the environment that allow students with disabilities to engage in a mainstream course of study, while modifications have more to do with changes in what is being taught to students with disabilities.

Examples of accommodations include:

- Teacher provide notes/outlines
- Preferential seating
- Daily planner checks
- Extended time on tests, including standardized tests

Some examples of modifications include:

- Reduction of homework and/or class work
- Changes to the curricula, including alternative reading assignments
- Copies of tests to use as a study guide
- A change in grading scales to simply pass/fail

Applying for Accommodations on Standardized tests

Perhaps one of the most time-consuming and visible advocacy roles a school counselor engages in while working with students with disabilities is applying for accommodations on standardized tests. As mentioned previously, school counselors are often responsible for applying to the College Board and the ACT so that students with specific accommodations for extended time on tests may be afforded that accommodation. It is important to note that the final decision rests with the either the ACT or the College Board, but school counselors who are applying for testing accommodations on behalf of students are required to follow proper protocol throughout the process.

Both the ACT and the College Board require specific documentation that identifies the accommodation requested; this supports the need for the accommodation on standardized tests and provides a history of the accommodations the student received while in school. Both organizations are very clear that accommodations are not automatically guaranteed. The ACT's statement in the print version of its 2013–2014 ACT Extended Time National Testing reads:

ACT provides test accommodations in accordance with Title III of the Americans with Disabilities Act (ADA). Schools provide accommodations under different regulations. Thus, having a diagnosis and receiving accommodations in school do not guarantee approval of those accommodations for the ACT (p. 1).

The College Board's *College Counseling Sourcebook* (2013) points out, "…students … should be aware of the differences between school and test environments, and understand that not all accommodations that are used in school will necessarily be needed for a standardized test" (p. 11:20).

The *College Counseling Sourcebook* is an excellent resource for school counselors and is very detailed about the accommodation application process for the PSAT/NMSQT, SAT, SAT Subject Tests, and AP Exams:

1. State the specific disability, as diagnosed; diagnosis should be made by a person with appropriate professional credentials, should be specific and, when appropriate, should relate the disability to the applicable professional standards;

2. Be current (in most cases, the evaluation and diagnostic testing should have taken place within five years of the request for accommodations);

3. Provide relevant educational, developmental and medical history;

4. Describe the comprehensive testing and techniques used in arriving at the diagnosis (including results with subtest scores [standard or scaled scores] for all tests);

5. Describe the functional limitations (for example, limitations to learning that result from the diagnosed disability);

6. Describe the specific accommodations being requested on College Board tests;

7. Establish the professional credentials of the evaluator (for example, licensure, certification, area of specialization).

Examples of accommodations include:

* presentation (e.g., larger print, Braille)

* responding (dictating to scribe, use of a computer)

* scheduling (frequent breaks, extended time)

* setting (small-group environment, adaptive furniture) (pp. 11:20-21)

Even though school counselors make the official request, the College Board points out that parents can request accommodations on their own. In this case, school counselors can best serve families by collaborating with them during the process.

What is often overlooked is the time required for the College Board to process the application. Seven weeks is the standard timeframe identified by the College Board, and its website now has an SSD (Services for Students with Disabilities) Calendar that outlines deadlines for each of its tests. School counselors need to be mindful that if additional documentation is requested to substantiate the accommodation request, the College Board asks for an additional seven weeks. Therefore, it is incumbent upon school counselors to plan well in advance for accommodation requests.

The ACT has risen in popularity among high school students. By 2012, the numbers of ACT test takers surpassed the number of SAT test takers by about 2,000 (Strauss, 2012). Just like the College Board, the ACT has a process for accommodation requests, although it is slightly different.

While school counselors or families can apply for accommodations on the College Board tests well in advance of registering for the actual exam, the ACT requires that students sign up for the exam first and then file for an accommodation request, only if they are requesting 50 percent additional time. This type of application can be completed online. The ACT identifies a separate type of application for students who are requesting accommodations other than 50 percent additional time, called "Special Testing." This type of application must be done in print, and the application also serves as registration for the actual ACT test.

The ACT's *2013–2014 Request for ACT Special Testing* states that it "is designed for students whose documented disabilities require accommodations that cannot be provided at a test center. Examples include:

* More than time-and-a-half testing time

* Testing over multiple days

* Alternate test formats (Braille, DVDs or a reader)

* Use of a scribe or computer for the Writing Test (typically for disabilities that prevent students from writing independently)

* Extended time on the Writing Test only (students with developmental writing disorder, written expression disorder or dysgraphia) (p. 1)

Another difference between the College Board and the ACT is the amount of time a plan or diagnosis has been in place. The ACT's requirement is limited to a diagnosis having been made within the last three school years, while the College Board generally accepts diagnostic testing made within the last five years.

The perception among school counselors, students and parents is that it is more difficult to be granted accommodations by the ACT (Moore, 2010). However, according to both organizations, the ACT grants accommodations to just over 90 percent of applicants, while the SAT offers 85 percent of their applicants' accommodations. This perception is most likely based in the differences between the application procedures for the two organizations: because the ACT has two separate categories and processes while the College Board has just one process, applicants perceive this as more difficult.

Given the detailed process for requesting accommodations, it is sensible for school counselors to become familiar with specific areas of a student's IEP, 504 plan or private psychoeducational evaluation, particularly the assessments/diagnostic tools. Some of the most common cognitive assessments include:

- Wechsler Adult Intelligence Scale (for students 18 or over) or Wechsler Intelligence Scale for Children
- Woodcock-Johnson Tests of Cognitive Abilities
- Stanford Binet Intelligence Scales (when individually administered)
- Kaufman Assessment Battery for Children
- Differential Ability Scales
- Reynolds Intellectual Assessment Scales

When it comes to learning disabilities or ADHD, both the ACT and the College Board will ask for information about tests of academic achievement, in addition to the cognitive assessments. Some of the most common academic achievement assessments include:

- Woodcock-Johnson Tests of Achievement (general and extended batteries that include fluency measures)
- Scholastic Abilities Test for Adults
- Wechsler Individual Achievement Test, with reading rate measure
- Kaufman Test of Educational Achievement

Advocacy

Although never stated in an IEP, 504 plan or a private psychoeducational evaluation, advocating on behalf of the students is one of the most important services the school counselor delivers. According to the ASCA Model (2012),

"Advocating for the academic achievement of every student is a key role of school counselors and places them at the forefront of efforts to promote school reform" (p. 4). Whether it is in the form of reminding classroom teachers about the contents of a student's accommodations, speaking directly to teachers about a student's concerns, or addressing issues surrounding school policy and students with disabilities, school counselors do allocate a good portion of their time advocating for students with disabilities. As stated, these advocacy efforts are not outlined in a student's documentation, because they are intrinsic to the role of a school counselor. It goes without saying that in order to best advocate for students with learning disabilities, school counselors must be well-versed in the areas that impact a student's learning and techniques that assist him or her in achieving academic success. However, advocating for students with learning disabilities brings with it a few challenges, because of the different attitudes and beliefs some educators have regarding special education services.

Research points to the reality that some educators possess negative attitudes toward students with disabilities and that the cause of this is a lack of adequate training (Praisner, 2003). Therefore, these educators often feel unprepared and unmotivated to provide services to students with disabilities effectively. Other studies (Milsom, 2002) indicate that graduate school programs for school counselors require minimal training related to students with disabilities, leaving school counselors with a type of on-the-job training. Finally, Milsom (2006) suggests that one of the most effective ways school counselors can advocate for students with disabilities is to "conduct needs assessments to identify potential systematic, programmatic and attitudinal areas for change in order to create positive environments for students with disabilities" (p. 72). Just creating an awareness level among teachers about the needs that students with learning disabilities have, school counselors can make the environment for these students more positive.

DIFFERENCES IN SERVICES OFFERED IN HIGH SCHOOL AND COLLEGE

The public school system identifies age 18 and/or high school graduation as the point at which special education services end, due to a Free and Appropriate Public Education (FAPE) under IDEA. Because of this provision, postsecondary institutions are under no legal obligation to offer services to students with learning disabilities. However, under Section 504 of the Americans with Disabilities Act (1990), colleges are required to provide appropriate adjustments as necessary to ensure that it does not discriminate on the basis of disability. These differences are often the biggest stumbling block to college applicants and their families, and school counselors can help to alleviate some of the confusion and point students in the right direction. Even though the requirements for receiving services in high schools and colleges may differ, many colleges do offer specific services for students with learning disabilities. Unlike the services offered in high school, these services often require additional fees, a separate application, limited space, and/or schedule requirements.

Disclosure

One of the biggest steps a student with disabilities has to take when he or she is deciding to apply to college is whether or not to disclose the disability to a college. College applicants are required to disclose a disability to their school if they are seeking accommodations. When looking at recent research, it is clear that a minority of high school students with disabilities opt to disclose their disabilities to colleges.

The National Longitudinal Transition Study-2 (NLST2) found that 63 percent of postsecondary students who had documentation in high school with a disability diagnosis did not consider themselves to have that disability by the time they entered college (Newman et al., 2011). In that same study, just fewer than 30 percent of college students with disabilities identified themselves as having a disability and informed their postsecondary schools of their disability. That number drops to 20 percent when it comes to those students who go on to receive accommodations or supports while in college. Just because a student discloses his or her disability on an application does not mean that he or she will go on to obtain accommodations.

The most common type of accommodation afforded to college students with disabilities is additional time to complete tests, with almost 80 percent of all postsecondary students with disabilities receiving accommodations.

There are a variety of reasons why students choose not to disclose their disability to colleges. Because of the developmental process, some students believe that entering college is stepping into the world of adulthood, and they may view the support services they received in high school as preventing them from becoming independent. Another reason could be that some students are embarrassed. Still, if a student wants to apply to a college without disclosing his or her disability, he or she has that option; but students can disclose it at any time. Almost all postsecondary institutions allow for disability disclosure to take place at any time during a student's course of study. In fact, the majority of postsecondary institutions are encouraging these students to disclose their disability. Raue and Lewis (2011) found that 79 percent of postsecondary institutions distribute materials designed to encourage students with disabilities to identify themselves. Of interest is that the larger, four-year public institutions were more likely to distribute these materials.

Ultimately, it is up to the student to make the choice about disclosure, but school counselors can assist students in arriving at that decision through a thoughtful process that involves listening to a student's (and parents') concerns, educating students about the types of services colleges offer, and encouraging students to learn more about their own disabilities and the types of supports necessary to best help them succeed in college.

Encouraging Self-Advocacy

While advocacy is a key component of the school counselor's role, encouraging students with disabilities to become self-advocates is crucial to their success as students. During the transition into postsecondary institutions, students with disabilities need to recognize that they are moving from a system where parents, school counselors, teachers, and other school staff usually advocated on their behalf to a system where they will be expected to advocate for themselves. Expecting students with disabilities to automatically learn self-advocacy skills is setting them up for failure. Therefore, this task is one that is highlighted by numerous sources as essential to a learning-disabled student's success in college (Rock & Leff, 2014; Uretsky & Andrews, 2013; College Board, 2012; Milsom, 2006).

Offering traditional self-advocacy skills, such as effective communication and self-awareness, is part of

ASCA's National Standards for Students (2004) and can be delivered to students in a classroom setting, group or in individual sessions. In the interest of time, delivery of self-advocacy skills to students with disabilities in a group setting would be ideal, and it would allow group members to role-play with one another to practice these skills. For confidentiality reasons, however, meeting individually with students to review their documentation (IEP, 504 plan, private evaluation) in an effort to inform them about their disability and how it impacts their learning would work best.

The *College Counseling Sourcebook* (2012) encourages students with disabilities to be self-advocates:

> A "self-advocate" communicates his or her needs with logical and positive language. To be an effective self-advocate, you must understand your disability, know how it impacts your learning, and become comfortable with describing your disability and your academic-related needs to others. At the college level, you are responsible for identifying and requesting support services. Parents aren't normally involved with your education at the college level, and most colleges prefer working directly with you, the student (11A: 1).

Communicating this to students with disabilities and their parents is not just a vital part of the transition process; it is also valuable for the student's high school experience. Early on in high school, most of these students are not fully aware of the details of their documentation; some might be able to communicate the name of the disability, but they are most likely unaware of the way in which the disability impacts their ability to retain and/or process information. Hamblet (2009) found that most high school students are not involved in the writing of the accommodation plans and may not even be aware of the exact accommodations to which they are entitled. Furthermore, many could not identify the reason for their accommodations. Too often, students are left out of the IEP process in high school. Understanding the full scope of their disability and/or documentation is a key component for a student's overall success both in high school and postsecondary institutions.

In addition to students becoming familiar with their documentation, these students can begin to attend their IEP meetings in high school, as a way to prepare them to be self-advocates (Varrassi, 2014; Uretsky & Andrews, 2013; College Board, 2012). Unfortunately, because special education committees are used to having just parents present at the IEP meeting, the student is often not invited, so school counselors may have to offer the suggestion to the student, parents or committee.

The reason for all of this emphasis on self-advocacy is that, according to Hamblet (2009), "colleges expect students to be in charge of their own learning and to find ways to get information they need on their own" (p. 11).

Researching Programs

If students are interested in receiving additional accommodations during their postsecondary studies, it is important to invest a significant amount of time in researching programs. At this point in the journey, it is expected that the college-bound student is willing to disclose his or her disability and has the appropriate documentation in place to offer a college when he or she discloses. Most postsecondary institutions will accept an IEP, 504 plan or private evaluation from a student's high school, as long as it is within the last three years and offers sufficient evidence of the need for additional learning supports. However, postsecondary institutions are allowed to set their own limits on how old that testing can be, and, if a student's documentation does not fit a college's requirements (because it is outdated or missing a diagnostic tool), it is incumbent upon the student to seek out and provide the missing information. High schools will not simply retest a student with an IEP to provide additional documentation to a postsecondary institution, as they are not required by law to do so. Therefore, the financial burden falls on students and families to seek out private psychoeducational testing.

That being said, numerous colleges and universities have comprehensive support programs specially designed for learning-disabled students. These programs do more than just ensure students are granted accommodations; they are typically staffed by individuals trained in the area of learning disabilities. According to the *College Counseling Sourcebook* (2012), the most common types of services offered to students through these support programs include:

- Study skills training

- Tutoring services

- Provisions for alternate testing

- Availability of taped textbooks

- Course load modifications

- Preregistration for courses

- Taping of lectures

- Specialized study aids (11F: 2)

In additional to these academic services, personal and vocational counseling services may also be provided.

As these services go above and beyond those that postsecondary institutions are required to provide under Section 504, many colleges and universities will charge a significant fee for them, on top of the regular tuition costs. Listed below are just a sampling of different programs and fees from a variety of colleges across the nation:

- University of Arizona, Tucson (SALT): $5,200 annually

- Curry College, Milton, MA (PAL): $3,000–7,000 annually, depending on scope of desired services

- University of Iowa, Iowa City (REACH): $6,000 annually

- St. Thomas Aquinas College, Sparkill, NY (Pathways): $3,700 annually

- American University, Washington, DC (Learning Services Program in the Academic Support and Access Center): $3,000 annually

To offer a brief example of the types of services offered by these institutions, the SALT (Strategic Alternative Learning Techniques) Web site at the University of Arizona offers the following to students who qualify:

- Flexible tutoring schedule

- Group study sessions

- Meetings with a strategic learning specialist, the point person for SALT Center and campus resources, who will design an individualized learning plan

- Workshops for reading and writing strategies, time management, organization, and study skills

It is worth mentioning that while tutoring services are offered at almost any college, this type of tutoring is quite different from a resource room, where students receive one-to-one support from a special education teacher.

- Psychological services

- Open access to the SALT Center Computer Resource Lab, where students can use dictation software, audio textbooks and the latest learning apps

From this information, it is fair to assume that learning support programs offered at postsecondary institutions can range from $3,000–$10,000 annually. If students are looking for a college experience that is open only to students with learning disabilities, there are only two options within the US. Both Landmark College (VT) and Beacon College (FL) identify themselves as institutions exclusively for students with learning disabilities, and their tuition costs are $49,000 and $32,000 per year, respectively.

Accommodations in College

Again, postsecondary institutions are not required to offer accommodations and services just because they were written on a student's IEP, 504 plan or private evaluation that their high school followed. Unless specifically identified in the supporting documentation provided, colleges typically will not offer accommodations. Given all of this, students may find that accommodations they became used to in high school are no longer available to them.

But, once students are approved for accommodations, the most widely used types are extended time testing, access to audio textbooks and permission to record classroom lectures (Hamblet, 2009). Other than that, most colleges will not offer additional accommodations, because they expect students to become independent learners, and they cost money, and according to the law, colleges are not required to pay for such services.

It is worth mentioning that while tutoring services are offered at almost any college, this type of tutoring is quite different from a resource room, where students receive one-to-one support from a special education teacher. Tutoring services at colleges are typically offered by other students, or they might come from a business that is strictly profit-driven.

What to Ask

Doing research online is an appropriate place to begin the process, but it is recommended that students also speak directly with a representative from a college's office for disability services to learn more information. School counselors, college admission officers and representatives from campus disability service offices encourage students to have this conversation (Varrassi, 2014; Uretsky & Andrews, 2013; The Connor, 2012; College Board, 2012; Hamblet, 2009). This conversation can either be over the telephone or while a student is visiting the campus. When a prospective student is visiting campus, it is highly recommended that he or she speak with other students who are receiving accommodations.

This conversation requires planning. Prior to contacting a college's office for disability services, school counselors should meet with students to discuss topics and/or specific questions that ought to be addressed. Some school counselors prefer to have this conversation with parents present as well. This is an opportunity for these students to begin to practice their self-advocacy skills. It might even require some role-playing to give students who are wary that extra confidence.

> *Prior to contacting a college's office for disability services, school counselors should meet with students to discuss topics and/or specific questions that ought to be addressed.*

School counselors need not look far for lists of sample questions that should be asked in this conversation. The *College Counseling Sourcebook* (2012) and the National Association for College Admission Counseling both offer a list with suggested questions (Uretsky & Andrews, 2012). The following questions have been compiled from both resources and are meant to be a guide for the conversation.

Preliminary Questions

1. Do full-time professionals staff the program? Do these staff members have previous experience working with students with disabilities?

2. What documentation do you require in order to support my disability? How current should it be? Are there any specific diagnostic tools that you are specifically looking for in the documentation?

3. If I am approved for accommodations, how will I be notified, and are others notified as well? What are my responsibilities for making sure I receive the services I need?

4. Who is responsible for arranging accommodations? Is there a contact person in your office who serves as an advisor, or would the advisor be from a separate office?

5. What is the advisement system for students with special needs? Will advisors help with course selection and course load options?

6. Is there an active support group on campus for students with disabilities? Is this group part of the learning support program (if there is one at the college), or does it exist on its own?

7. How well-informed are professors and instructors regarding students with disabilities? Are they willing to work with these students? What procedures are in place in case there is an issue with receiving accommodations?

8. How many students at the college receive accommodations? Is it possible for me to speak with them to get a sense of the atmosphere?

9. Are the classrooms/buildings physically accessible? How many accessible dorm rooms are available?

Detailed Questions

1. What accommodations are available—for example, tape recorders, taped texts, note takers? What is the procedure for accessing textbooks on audio?

2. Are waivers or substitutions granted to students who, because of a disability, cannot pass certain courses, such as foreign language or statistics?

3. Does the college provide adaptive equipment for student use? Is adaptive software, such as voice recognition software or writing support software, available on campus? Is training for the use of the software provided?

4. Where do students go to take tests with modifications? How is this service arranged?

5. How is the need for class notes met for qualifying students? Are note takers trained?

6. Does the college provide printed materials in alternative format?

7. What kind of tutoring is available? Are the tutors peers or trained, experienced staff? Is tutoring available in all subjects? Is there a limit to the amount of tutoring I may receive? Is there an additional fee?

8. Does the college offer courses or workshops in study skills or writing skills?

9. Are there counseling/psychological services provided to assist freshmen students with the transition from high school to college?

10. Are there any considerations that students with disabilities should know about regarding the admission process at the college?

11. Do you provide information about the graduation rate and/or the retention rate for students who are served by your office?

12. Are there provisions made for having to miss classes based on the nature of a particular disability or a medical condition?

13. What services are offered at an additional cost?

The Emotional Component

The college search process can feel overwhelming to students and their families and, as with any life transition, produce anxiety for all involved. In particular, students with disabilities tend to feel this anxiety to a greater degree (Connor, 2012; Uretsy & Andrews, 2012). This affective state does not seem to diminish once students with disabilities have been accepted to college; in fact, researchers found that undergraduate students who reported having a learning disability experienced low self-esteem, sadness and anxiety as compared to their peers (Davis et al., 2009).

During the search process, it is normative for students who've been receiving accommodations through their high school years to experience uncertainty about the prospect of entering college with an entirely different system of accommodations. Hamblet (2009) identifies that parents are often shocked at how different the services for students with disabilities are at the postsecondary level. This is where it is important for school counselors to step in as both the empathic, supportive listener and the professional educator who is ready to walk college applicants and their parents through the process.

CONCLUSION

It is clear that school counselors need to plan early interventions when working with students with disabilities. The educative process is multi-layered and not as simple as, "What college do you want to go to?" and then sending students on their way. In addition to classroom lessons, school counselors can begin to work with these students in groups and individually early on in high school to help them and their families achieve academic, personal and postsecondary success. Advocating for these students and helping them to develop academic and interpersonal strategies, along with educating them about their specific documentation, offer them the skills for self-advocacy, which they will need to employ when they begin their college search and venture off to college.

The skillsets that school counselors are required to have for these tasks include knowledge of the special education landscape, the administrative tasks associated with applying for accommodations on standardized tests, best advocacy practices, and directing students and families to resources on colleges that provide support services for students with learning disabilities.

By advocating for students with learning disabilities, school counselors essentially model for them the advocacy skills that will be required for them to be successful in their postsecondary studies.

REFLECTION QUESTIONS

1. What are some examples of disabilities under IDEA?

2. What are some similarities and differences between an IEP and a 504 plan?

3. How would you explain the differences between accommodations and modifications for a teacher in your building?

4. What are some of the specific cognitive and academic assessments that the College Board and ACT would accept when applying for accommodations?

5. Identify the differences between high school and college when it comes to services for students with learning disabilities.

6. Why might high school students be reluctant to disclose their learning disability to colleges?

7. Identify the most common types of accommodations and supportive services that colleges provide for students with learning disabilities.

8. How are tutoring services at colleges different than the services students with specific accommodation plans received while in high school?

9. What are some ways that school counselors can advocate for students with learning disabilities?

10. In discussing a college visit with one of your students, the conversation turns to the student's concerns about what questions they should ask the office of student services. What are some preliminary questions you might suggest?

ABOUT THE AUTHOR

Terence J. Houlihan has been an educator and school counselor for almost 20 years. He has appeared in training videos for educators and is a sought-after conference presenter, with addresses to local, state, regional, and national conferences. Terence also facilitates training seminars for high school and middle school educators at the national and international level on the developmental changes associated with adolescence and speaks to parent groups about raising teenagers. In addition to being a high school counselor, he is an adjunct lecturer for the graduate program in counselor education at the City University of New York, Lehman College (NY) and the College of New Rochelle (NY). Terence has written for the National Association of School Superintendents and the American School Counselor Association.

REFERENCES

ACT. (2013). 2013–2014 ACT extended time national testing. Retrieved from *http://www.act.org/aap/pdf/ExtendedTimeNational.pdf*.

ACT. (2013). 2013–2014 request for ACT special testing. Retrieved from *http://www.act.org/aap/pdf/SpecialTestingRequestForm.pdf*.

American School Counselor Association. (2012). *The ASCA national model: A framework for school counseling program, third edition.* Alexandria, VA: Author.

American School Counselor Association. (2014). *The professional school counselor and students with special needs.* Retrieved from *http://www.schoolcounselor.org/files/PS_SpecialNeeds.pdf*.

Barkley, R.A. (2006). *Attention-deficit hyperactivity disorder: A handbook for diagnosis and treatment.* Guilford: New York, NY.

Barr, V.M., Harttnan, R.C., & Spillane, S.A. (1995). Getting ready for college: advising high school students with learning disabilities. *LD OnLine: The world's leading website on learning disabilities and ADHD.* Retrieved from *http://www.ldonline.org/article/6132.*

CAPE (Council for American Private Education). (n.d.). *CAPE*. Retrieved August 1, 2014, from *http://www.capenet.org/facts.html*.

Center for Parent Information and Resources. (2010). *Key terms to know in special education*. Retrieved from *http://www.parentcenterhub.org/repository/keyterms-specialed*.

Connor, D. J. (2012). Helping students with disabilities transition to college: 21 tips for students with LD and/or ADD/ADHD. *Teaching Exceptional Children, 44*(5), 16–25.

Crichton, A. (1798). An inquiry into the nature and origin of mental derangement: comprehending a concise system of the physiology and pathology of the human mind and a history of the passions and their effects. Cadell Jr., T., Davies W., London [Reprint: Crichton A (2008) An inquiry into the nature and origin of mental derangement. On attention and its diseases. J Atten Disord, 12,200–204].

Davis III, T.E., Nida, R.E., Ziomke, K.R., & Nebel-Schwalm, M.S. (2009). Health-related quality of life in college undergraduates with learning disabilities: The mediational roles of anxiety and sadness. *Journal of Psychotherapy and Behavioral Assessment, 31*(3),228–234.

Hamblet, E.C. (2009). Helping your students with disabilities during their college search. *Journal of College Admission,* Fall, 6–15.

Hamilton, K. & Kessler, E. (n.d.). Accommodations and modifications: Wait, they're not the same? Retrieved from *http://nichcy.org/accommodations-and-modifications*.

Henderson, C. (2001). College freshmen with disabilities: A biennial statistical profile. *American Council on Education, Health Resource Center,* 1–45.

Lange, K.W., Reichl, S., Lange, K.M., Tucha, L., Tucha, O. (2010). The history of attention deficit hyperactivity disorder. *Atten Defic Hyperact Disord, 2,* 241–255.

Milsom, A.S. (2002). Students with disabilities: School counselor involvement and preparation. Professional School Counseling, 5, 331–338. Reprinted in T.P. Remley, M.A. Hermann, & W.C. Huey, (Eds.). (2003). *Ethical and legal issues in school counseling* (2nd ed., pp. 381–393). Alexandria, VA: American School Counselor Association.

Milsom, A.S. (2006). Creating positive school experiences for students with disabilities. *Professional School Counseling Journal,* 10(1), 66–72.

Moore, A. (2010, November 4). Accommodations angst. *The New York Times.*

Newman, L., Wagner, M., Knokey, A.M., Marder, C., Nagle, K., Shaver, D., Wei, X., with Cameto, R., Contreras, E., Ferguson, K., Greene, S., & Schwarting, M. (2011). *The post-high school outcomes of young adults with disabilities up to 8 years after high school. A report from the national longitudinal transition study-2* (NLTS2) (NCSER 2011-3005). Menlo Park, CA: SRI International.

Praisner, C.L. (2003). Attitudes of elementary school principals toward the inclusion of students with disabilities. *Exceptional Children,* 69(2), 135–145.

Raue, K., & Lewis, L. (2011). *Students with disabilities at degree-granting postsecondary institutions* (NCES 2011–018). US Department of Education, National Center for Education Statistics. Washington, DC.

Rock, E., & Leff, E. (2014). The professional school counselor and students with disabilities. In B.T. Erford, *Transforming the school counseling profession* (4th ed.) (pp. 350–391).

Strauss, V. (2012, September 4). How ACT overtook SAT as the top college entrance exam. *The Washington Post.*

The College Board. (2012). *The college counseling sourcebook: Advice and strategies from experienced school counselors* (7th ed.). The College Board, NY.

US Department of Education: Office for Civil Rights. (2007). *Keys to success: attitude, self-advocacy and preparation*. Excerpted from *Transition of students with disabilities to postsecondary education: A guide for high school educators*. Retrieved from *http://www.ship.edu/ODS/pdfs/Self-advacacy_for_Higher_Education*.

US Department of Education: Office of Special Education Programs. (2006). *Children enrolled by their parents in private schools*. Retrieved from *http://idea.ed.gov/explore/view/p/,root,dynamic,TopicalBrief,5*.

US Department of Health and Human Services: Office for Civil Rights. (2006). *Your rights under section 504 of the rehabilitation act*. Retrieved from *http://www.hhs.gov/ocr/civilrights/resources/factsheets/504.pdf*.

United States Government Accountability Office. (2009). *Higher education and disability education needs a coordinated approach to improve its assistance to schools in supporting students*. United States Government Accountability Office: 1–45.

Uretsky, M., & Andrews, D. (2013). Finding the right fit: using the college search process to reduce anxiety for students with learning disabilities and ADHD. *Journal of College Admission,* Fall, 47–52.

Varrassi, V. (2014). Planning for college success for students with learning disabilities. Retrieved from *http://www.ncld.org/parents-child-disabilities/teens/planning-college-success-for-students-with-learning-disabilities*.

Vickers, M.Z. (2010). Accommodating college students with learning disabilities: ADD, ADHD, and dyslexia. The John William Pope Center for Higher Education Policy, Pope Center Series on Higher Education.

What Is IDEA? (Individuals with Disabilities Education Act). (n.d.). National Center for Learning Disabilities. Retrieved from *http://www.ncld.org/disability-advocacy/learn-ld-laws/idea/what-is-idea*.

APPENDIX

Colleges with Learning Support Programs (Additional Fees) for Students with Learning Disabilities*

1. Adelphi University, Garden City, NY (Learning Resource Program)

2. American International College, Springfield, MA (Supportive Learning Services)

3. American University, Washington, DC (Academic Support & Access Center)

4. Appalachian State University, Boone, NC (Learning Assistance Program)

5. Augsburg College, Minneapolis, MN (CLASS)

6. Barry University, Miami, FL (Center for Advanced Learning)

7. Beacon College, Leesburg, FL (exclusively for LD students)

8. Bethany College, Bethany, WV (Program for Academic and Social Success)

9. Brenau University, The Women's College, Gainesville, GA (The Learning Center)

10. California State University, Northridge (Thriving & Achieving Program)

11. Centenary College, Hackettstown, NJ (Project ABLE)

12. Central Lakes College, Brainerd, MN (Occupational Skills Program)

13. Clark University, Worcester, MA (no program title)

14. Concordia College, Bronxville, NY (Connections)

15. Curry College, Milton, MA (Program for Advancement of Learning)

16. Daemen College, Amherst, NY (Gersch Experience)

17. Davis and Elkins College, Elkins, WV (Supported Learning Program)

18. Dean College, Franklin, MA (Arch Learning Community)

19. DePaul University, Chicago, IL (Productive Learning Strategies)

20. East Stroudsburg University of Pennsylvania, East Stroudsburg, PA (Students in Transition to Academic Realization)

21. Edinboro University of Pennsylvania, Edinboro, PA (no program title)

22. Fairleigh Dickinson University, Teaneck, NJ (Center for College Students with Learning Disabilities)

23. Frostburg State University, Frostburg, MD (no program title)

24. Gannon University, Erie, PA (Program for Students with Learning Disabilities)

25. George Mason University, Fairfax, VA (C.R.E.S.T.)

26. Georgian Court University, Lakewood, NJ (The Learning Center Program)

27. Graceland University, Lamoni, IA (Chance)

28. Hofstra University, Hempstead, NY (Program for Academic Learning Skills)

29. Iona College, New Rochelle, NY (College Assistance Program)

30. Kean University, Union, NJ (Project Excel)

31. King's College, Wilkes-Barre, PA (no program title)

32. Landmark College, Putney, VT (exclusively for LD students)

33. Limestone College, Gaffney, SC (Program for Alternative Learning Styles)

*This list is not exhaustive.

(continues)

APPENDIX *(continued)*

34. Lincoln College of New England, Southington, CT (ACCESS)

35. Long Island University, C.W. Post Campus, Brookville, NY (Academic Resource Program)

36. Loras College, Dubuque, IA (Lynch Learning Center)

37. Louisiana College, Pineville, LA (Program to Assist Student Success)

38. Lynn University, Boca Raton, FL (Institute for Achievement and Learning)

39. Manhattanville College, Purchase, NY (Higher Education Learning Program)

40. Marist College, Poughkeepsie, NY (no program title)

41. Marshall University, Huntington, WV (Higher Education for Learning Problems Center)

42. Marymount Manhattan College, New York, NY (Academic Access Program)

43. McDaniel College, Westminster, MD (Academic Skills Program)

44. Mercyhurst College, Erie, PA (Learning Differences Program)

45. Misericordia University, Dallas, PA (Alternative Learners Project)

46. Missouri State University, Springfield, MO (Learning Diagnostic Center)

47. Mitchell College, New London, CT (Bentsen Learning Center)

48. Mount Ida College, Newton, MA (Learning Opportunities Program)

49. Mount St. Joseph University, Cincinnati, OH (EXCEL)

50. Muskingum College, New Concord, OH (The PLUS Program)

51. New Jersey City University, Jersey City, NJ (Office of Specialized Services and Supplemental Instruction)

52. Nicholls State University, Thibodaux, LA (The Louisiana Center for Dyslexia and Related Learning Disorders)

53. Northeastern University, Boston, MA (Learning Disabilities Program)

54. Notre Dame College, South Euclid, OH (Academic Support Center)

55. Oak Hills Christian College, Bemidji, MN (Assisted Learning Program)

56. Reinhardt University, Waleska, GA (Academic Support Office)

57. Roosevelt University, Chicago and Schaumburg, IL (Learning & Support Services Program)

58. Sacred Heart University, Fairfield, CT (Special Learning Services)

59. St. Gregory's University, Shawnee, OK (Partners in Learning)

60. St. Thomas Aquinas College, Sparkill, NY (Pathways)

61. Schreiner University, Kerrville, TX (Learning Support Services Program)

62. Southern Illinois University, Carbondale, IL (ACHIEVE)

63. Union College, Lincoln, NE (Teaching Learning Center)

64. University of Arizona, Tucson, AZ (SALT)

65. University of Connecticut, Storrs, CT (Beyond Access)

66. University of Dayton, Dayton, OH (FIRST)

67. University of Denver, Denver, CO (Learning Effectiveness Program)

This list is not exhaustive.

(continues)

APPENDIX *(continued)*

68. University of Hartford, West Hartford, CT (Learning Plus)

69. University of Indianapolis, Indianapolis, IN (Build)

70. University of North Texas, Denton, TX (Office of Disability Accommodation)

71. University of the Ozarks, Clarksville, AK (Jones Learning Center)

72. University of Wisconsin, Oshkosh, WI (Project Success)

73. Ursuline College, Pepper Pike, OH (FOCUS)

74. West Virginia Wesleyan College, Buckhannon, WV (The Learning Center)

75. Westminster College, Fulton, MO (Learning Disabilities Program)

*Print Resources**

Grossberg, B. (2012). *Applying to college for students with ADD or LD: A guide to keep you (and your parents) sane, satisfied, and organized through the admission process.* Magination Press: Washington, DC.

Kravets, M., & Wax, I. (2014) *The K&W guide to colleges for students with learning differences, 12th edition: 350 schools with programs or services for students with ADHD or learning disabilities.* The Princeton Review: Framingham, MA.

Mangrum, C.T. II, & Strichart, S.S. (2007). *Peterson's colleges for students with learning disabilities or ADHD.* University of Michigan.

Nadeau, K. (2006). *Survival guide for college students with ADHD or LD, 2nd edition.* Magination Press: Washington, DC.

Quinn, P.O., & Maitland, T.L. (2011). *On your own: A college readiness guide for teens with ADHD/LD.* Magination Press: Washington, DC.

*Online Resources for Counselors, Students and Parents**

ADDitude: Strategies and Support for LD and ADHD

The leading destination for families and adults living with ADHD and learning disabilities.

additudemag.com

Affordable Colleges for Students with Disabilities

A complete guide to college financing for students with disabilities. Find expert advice on loans, grants and scholarships specifically for students with disabilities, as well as resources to help with the job search after graduation.

http://www.affordablecollegesonline.org/spotlight/affordable-colleges-for-students-with-disabilities/#three

College Academic Support

This Web site is designed to be a resource for high school students and college students with learning disabilities, ADHD and other learning challenges. It is also intended to provide resources to help students prepare for the transition from high school to college.

collegeacademicsupport.com

LD Online

The world's leading Web site on learning disabilities and ADHD.

http://www.ldonline.org/indepth/college

The National Center for Learning Disabilities

The National Center for Learning Disabilities improves the lives of all people with learning difficulties and disabilities by empowering parents, enabling young adults, transforming schools, and creating policy and advocacy impact.

ncld.org

---

*This list is not exhaustive.

(continues)

APPENDIX *(continued)*

*Scholarships**

Buckfire and Buckfire Disability Scholarship Program

The disability scholarship will be awarded to a student who is currently attending an accredited college or university and is open to students with any type of disability, including but not limited to physical disabilities, medical conditions, mental and psychiatric conditions, speech and language, learning disabilities, behavioral conditions, and all other conditions.

http://www.buckfirelaw.com/library/disability-scholarship.cfm

Michael Yasnick ADHD Scholarship Program through Shire.

Undergraduate students diagnosed with attention-deficit/hyperactivity disorder (ADHD) were each awarded $2,000 and one year of ADHD coaching to support the transition to higher education in colleges, universities, vocational schools, and technical schools. Recipients were selected from 2,380 applicants across the United States. Shire recognizes these individuals for their involvement in school, work and communities, as well as their experiences in meeting the challenges of living with ADHD.

http://www.shireadhdscholarship.com/US/defaultwinners.aspx

The Ralph G. Norman Scholarship

This fund was established to provide assistance to young adults with learning disabilities so they may pursue higher education. This scholarship is available to current residents of Arkansas only. This scholarship is for students who are ineligible for SSI or SSD funding.

http://ldarkansas.org/norman.cfm

The Learning Disabilities Association of Iowa

Awards three $1,000 scholarships to Iowa high school seniors with learning disabilities.

http://www.lda-ia.org/Scholarships.htm

Anne Ford and Allegra Ford Scholarship

The Anne Ford and Allegra Ford Thomas Scholarships offer financial assistance to two graduating seniors with documented learning disabilities (LD) who are pursuing postsecondary education.

www.ncld.org/about-us/scholarships-aamp-awards/the-anne-ford-and-allegra-ford-scholarship-award

Anne & Matt Harbison Scholarship P. Buckley Moss Society

Nominations for the Anne and Matt Harbison Scholarship (students with learning disabilities) can be made only by members of the P. Buckley Moss Society.

www.mosssociety.org/page.php?id=30

Marion Huber Learning Through Listening Awards

Each year, Learning Ally offers two endowed scholarship awards for outstanding students with print and learning disabilities.

www.learningally.org/about-learning-ally/awards

RiSE Scholarship Foundation, Inc

The RiSE Scholarship Foundation, Inc. is a non-profit resource and scholarship opportunity for high school students who learn differently.

risescholarshipfoundation.org

*This list is not exhaustive.

Chapter 20:   Resources and Social Media for College Counseling

Patty Montague
@patty_montague

Graduation requirements for high school students change. Entrance requirements for colleges change. Admission tests change. Financial aid rules change. Digital communication options change. Whether you are or will be a counselor in a public school, private school, community-based organization, or in private practice, one of the most important things you can have is a set of resources and community networks that you are able to reference. If you join a department of counselors, then the first place you should always go is to your supervisor to see if the information you need is already available. However, as many counselors discover quickly when a student is the first to apply to a college not usually on the general radar of that particular department, or you are the first to deal with a student presenting challenges that others have not faced, you will need a variety of resources to which you can refer to find the answers to your questions. This chapter provides an overview of various resources counselors can utilize to acquire and disseminate useful college admission information.

PROFESSIONAL ORGANIZATIONS

As a counselor who works with students at this very critical juncture of their lives, professional organizations provide a community of members who are able to answer questions, a ready bank of electronic resources, opportunities for professional development, and ethical and professional standards to which members ascribe. Another benefit of belonging to professional organizations is that there are often email listservs that members can use to post queries, as well as respond to others' queries.

The **National Association for College Admission Counseling** (NACAC—publisher of this book) is the premiere membership organization for information and research specific to college admission counseling. The members of this organization include both professionals who work with students from the middle and high school side of the desk and those in admission offices on the college side of the desk. This organization provides opportunities for unique networking and communication among members and a foundational code of ethics and standards for professionals. In addition to providing print and electronic resources and professional development opportunities, NACAC is committed to advocacy and public policy for students and the professionals who work with them dur-

ing the college admission process. Grants are available for programs and counselors to attend professional development opportunities. There are also resources for students and parents in the process, and NACAC sponsors National College Fairs and National Performing and Visual Arts Fairs throughout the United States. The Web site for more information is *www.nacacnet.org*.

Under NACAC are 23 affiliates that cover the entire globe. These affiliates also offer resources, networking, professional development, and advocacy. Many also have grant opportunities for counseling programs and counselors to attend professional development events. A full listing of affiliates and the states/regions covered may be found on the NACAC Web site.

Additional membership organizations for counselors working with students in middle/high school include:

- The **American School Counselor Association (ASCA)** is an organization for school counselors in any workplace environment. State and District of Columbia associations are also available. Information about ASCA and links to the associations can be found on ASCA's Web site: *www.schoolcounselor.org*

- The **Association for College Counseling in Independent Schools (ACCIS)** is an organization specifically for college counselors in independent schools: *http://accisnet.org*

- The **American Counseling Association (ACA)** is an organization for professional counselors in a variety of settings: *http://www.counseling.org*

The following professional organizations are specifically for independent counselors:

- **Higher Education Consultants Association (HECA)**: *http://hecaonline.org*

- **Independent Education Consultants Association (IECA)**: *www.iecaonline.com*

SOCIAL MEDIA AND TECHNOLOGY AS COUNSELING TOOLS

Whether it is Facebook, Instagram, Vine, Snapchat, Twitter, Flickr, Tumblr, Pinterest, or the latest social media site that I have not even heard of yet, students are finding social media sites and using them. Many colleges have strong social media presences and are trying to connect with prospective students by getting them to like them on Facebook, follow them on Twitter, subscribe to their blogs, etc. YouTube channels specific to particular colleges and apps that can be downloaded to devices are yet another way that students and counselors can connect and learn more about schools.

In the same way that these tools are being used to the colleges' advantage, counselors can use them to become informed about the most recent news, communicate and network with other professionals, and disseminate information to students and families. There is a College Admissions Counselors Facebook page where members are able to pose questions and post articles. It doesn't matter if this is your first year in the field or your 30th, someone will likely have experience and can offer advice or alternate resources for answers. The listservs of the various professional organizations can also provide a link to others who may be able to help for particular situations.

To get information to students, a school counseling Web site is beneficial. The main information and links don't need to change year to year, and creating a culture where students know where to look first for information can reduce the time needed to repeat general information. There should be contact information for the counselors, any forms necessary for students to complete, information about the college application process, and links to Web sites that will benefit your students in the college search, application and enrollment process. Setting up a counseling Facebook page or Twitter account can also be helpful to communicate with students and parents. One public school counselor uploads pictures of colleges visited to the guidance Facebook page in folders so that students can see different campuses. She also lists counseling events being held at school and college visits at the school or in town. She followed her school protocol for social media and turned on privacy settings that would not allow other posts to the account.

Another counselor follows many Web sites covering financial aid information, testing, local college admission offices, and, in turn, is able to simply retweet deadline reminders, tips for completing the financial aid process and information the colleges are sharing. However the communication is delivered, it is important to ensure that all students and parents are able to access the content, and that counselors find alternate means of delivery to those

who may not be able to access it themselves. A counseling center with computer stations or available technology in other areas of the school would be advised to ensure all students have access to digital communication.

Social Media Trends in College Admission

From hashtags to tweets, the use of social media has changed the way people communicate. One such venue where this is increasingly noticeable is college admission. This generation of high school students has been exposed to the Internet and various social media technology outlets since early adolescence. In order to keep up with the changing times, college admission offices have to implement social media marketing strategies to not only disseminate information to students about their respective institutions, but to also maintain a competitive advantage. One such way to communicate with perspective students is through blogging. Colleges and universities will typically employ current students to share their campus experiences as a way to connect with perspective students. This recruitment strategy is appealing to this generation because it allows for personal and real-time engagement (Davis, Deil-Amer, Rios-Aguilar, & Canche, 2012).

The University of Massachusetts Dartmouth Center for Market Research conducted longitudinal studies in 2007 and 2008 that highlighted the implementation of social media technology in college admission offices at four-year accredited colleges and universities (Barnes & Mattson, 2009). The studies showed that colleges and universities "were outpacing the more traditional Fortune 500 companies as well as the Innovative Inc. 500 companies in their use of social media to communicate with their customers (i.e., students)." For example, in 2008, 13 percent of Fortune 500 and 39 percent of Inc. 500 companies had a public blog, compared to 41 percent of college admission offices. Additionally, the studies showed that admission offices primarily use social networking (e.g., Facebook and Twitter) and 55 percent think social media is "very important" to their future recruitment strategies (Barnes & Mattson, 2009).

Social Media Benefits and Warnings

Students need to understand the dangers of social media usage in their everyday lives. Recently, Juan Enriquez (2014) did a Ted Talk on digital tattoos. Many times the message to students is about a "digital footprint," but the idea that digital information has permanence, like a tattoo, is a lesson that many students need to hear and understand. It does not just disappear as a footprint might. Whether it is the negative or inappropriate use of a social media site without recognizing the impact and far reach of that usage, or the use of an email address that would make a counselor blush, students need to be educated to always think before posting, joining, texting, etc. Students should have a professional email address to use for all communication. They need to look not only at the photos they have posted, but also at ones they may be tagged in by others. Talk to students about changing privacy settings if they have not already done so, and reiterate that everything they do online, texting, Snapchatting,

for Schools. By 2000, there were 800 schools who participated in the program. An independent research company evaluated the program and found that students who had access to laptops in schools spent more time engaging in collaborative work, as well as problem solving and critical thinking. Additionally, these students reported greater reliance on active learning strategies and spent more time doing homework on computers (Gulek & Demirtas, 2005). Protheroe (2005) also indicates that computer-based teaching had a particularly positive effect on at-risk students.

Venegas (2007) conducted case studies that highlighted the disparities of computer and Internet access between students at public schools and students at private schools in Southern California. One of the first things noted is

As technology continues to advance at a rapid pace, it's inevitable that its impact will continue to be felt in the classroom and impact student learning.

etc. is public and permanent! What a student does online can have an impact on someone's perception of his or her character. If a college or university does an online search of a student, what they might find could potentially portray the student in a negative light.

Access to and Use of Technology

As technology continues to advance at a rapid pace, it's inevitable that its impact will continue to be felt in the classroom and impact student learning. Research indicates that the use of technology enhances educational outcomes particularly for those students whose schools provide all students with laptops (Gulek & Demirtas, 2005). Protheroe (2005) notes that "in addition to positive effects on achievement in major subject areas, effective use of technology fostered development of more positive student attitudes towards themselves and towards learning" (p. 47).

In 1997, Microsoft Corporation fully implemented the Anytime Anywhere Learning Project in collaboration with Toshiba America Information Systems' Notebooks

that the majority of the students from the public schools were low-income students of color, and the students from the private schools were middle- to upper-class Caucasian and Asian students. At one public school in particular, there were only three computers in the college counseling office for a population of 1,500 students. Those computers were outdated, rarely functional and even blocked students from accessing their free email accounts. Venegas (2007) also found that most times the college counseling staff at the public school was poorly trained on how to use the computers themselves and were unable to assist the students who needed it. At one of the private schools, though, there were an abundance of functioning computers throughout the school that provided reliable Internet access, as well as college counselors who were properly trained to assist the students. Mathis (2010), however, notes "that educators should not look at increasing technology as a solution to meet all needs of learners. Instead, technology might be seen as a resource that changes the culture of schools to be able to meet the needs of and sustain outcomes for learners." Colleges' and universities' use of technology as a resource is highly prevalent, particularly throughout the college application process. For example, most institutions now have online applications, and, for some, it's the only way for students to apply. Additionally, colleges and universities use the Internet for students to access their online portals, which affects how students navigate their financial aid packages, campus housing and the registration process (Venegas, 2007). Unfortunately, some students do not have consistent and reliable access to a computer and the Internet to view this information. Without this access, students can potentially miss important information and deadlines, which can affect their admission and matriculation.

Games as a Means to Support College Counseling

As mentioned previously in this chapter, this generation of students is accustomed to immediate access to information and instant gratification, given their use of the Internet and other technological outlets. Video and web-based games provide the same instant access to information. "Games almost always give verbal information either 'just in time'—that is, right when players need and can use it—or 'on-demand'—that is, when the player feels a need for it, wants it, is ready for it, and can make good use of it" (Gee, 2007, p. 8). Gee also notes that games allow for system thinking, where players think about how their current actions might impact future actions. Amory (2006) notes that video and computer-based games have the ability to change the educational landscape.

For example, the University of Southern California founded FutureBound through a partnership between the Pullias Center for Higher Education and the Game Innovation Lab. FutureBound is a series of educational games used to prepare middle school and high school students for the transition to postsecondary education (FutureBound Web site, 2014). One particular game, Mission: Admission, was launched in 2012 and can be played via Facebook. It is specifically for high school students to help them understand the skills and strategies that are necessary during the college search process. Mathis (2010) suggests, "A structured play experience, such as an online college access game, not only supports inquiry, but students may walk away with invaluable support and content for next steps in navigating the admission process" (p. 16).

RESOURCES FOR CURRENT RESEARCH AND NEWS

As advocates for student success, counselors can best promote change and/or improvements within their counseling practice by referencing research to administrators or policy-makers. The following Web resources all provide research that will be helpful to counselors working with students as discussed in chapter 9.

NACAC Research Center conducts research that is of value to professionals working in college admission. *The State of College Admission,* based on surveys of professionals in high school and colleges, is released annually and is free to members or available for a fee for nonmembers. Other research reports, briefs and discussion papers are also available to members.

www.nacacnet.org/research

National Survey of Student Engagement (NSSE®) annually releases results of surveys of students from four-year colleges and universities about engagement in student activities and learning.

nsse.iub.edu

Integrated Postsecondary Education Data System (IPEDS) collects data from every institution that participates in the federal student financial aid programs. The reports and data that are part of the College Affordability and Transparency Center come from this common data set, but users can search variables themselves to get personalized data reports.

http://nces.ed.gov/ipeds

Higher Education Research Institute annually releases a report on the American freshman from data collected through surveys. The report includes data from questions about the admission and enrollment process, attitudes toward issues and demographics.

www.heri.ucla.edu

Education Commission of the States (ECS) provides access to research articles, including articles on factors to improve school persistence and impacts of interventions.

www.ecs.org/html/researchstudies/index.asp

Staying Abreast of the Latest News

In addition to research, counselors benefit from being current on topics that are happening in the news. *The Journal of College Admission, Inside Higher Ed* and *The Chronicle of Higher Education* can all provide timely news and articles relevant to college counseling. Counselors can also receive personalized news by setting up an RSS feed or setting up a Google Alert to have news specific to content desired delivered directly to their email inboxes.

The College Search

For some students, the college search process starts with consulting the Internet, for others it starts via books. Additionally, some students start the college search by attending a college fair or by visiting a campus.

Demonstrated Interest

Simply submitting an application to a college or university should adequately show a student's interest, right? Not necessarily. In addition to the traditional application requirements, such as grade point average, rigor of curriculum and standardized test scores, colleges and universities might also take into consideration the personal statement, essay, letters of recommendation, and demonstrated interest (NACAC, 2009). The idea of demonstrated interest isn't new, and institutions are at times wary of those students who might not be serious about their school (Rivard, 2014). Deardan, Li, Meyerhoefer, and Yang (2011) note that students who contact the institutions in which they are interested are more likely to be admitted. NACAC (2009) found that private and smaller institutions placed greater emphasis on factors outside of the traditional admission requirements, including demonstrated interest.

Demonstrated interest can be shown in a multitude of ways. Visiting a college campus, submitting an application early, communicating with an admission representative, or attending an information session are all ways for institutions to gauge a student's interest. Some institutions that use demonstrated interest to make an admission decision say it helps them to determine where to focus their recruitment efforts (Rivard, 2014). "Furthermore, colleges and universities believe that applicants who signal their interest are more likely to contribute to campus activities, have more meaningful college experiences and give back to their alma maters as alumni" (Deardan et al., 2011, p. 2).

Aside from the traditional ways of gauging student interest, colleges and universities also use technology to obtain this information. For example, institutions are able to calculate student interest by tracking the open rates of mass emails they send, as well as tracking the click rates of links within those emails. Typically, colleges and universities will use third-party vendors to assist them with

Figure 1. Factors Institutions Consider in the Admission Decision by Importance

	Grades in college prep courses	Strength of curriculum	Standardized test scores	Grades in all courses	Essay/ writing sample	Teacher rec.	Demonstrated interest	Counselor rec.
Total	74.9%	61.5%	54.3%	52.1%	26.6%	21.1%	20.9%	20.4%
Control								
Public	73.6	62.6	64.1	46.2	14.3	9.9	5.6	13.2
Private	75.2	61.0	50.8	54.5	31.3	25.3	26.5	23.1
Enrollment								
Fewer than 3,000 students	70.3	55.3	47.5	53.2	27.3	24.7	29.2	22.3
3,000–9,999	84.4	72.7	63.6	46.1	26.3	18.4	4.1	17.1
10,000 or more	81.0	73.8	72.1	57.1	23.3	7.1	7.1	16.3

Adapted from NACAC (2009).

print and Web-based campaigns that will allow them to track this information.

There are school counselors, though, who argue that going above and beyond to show extra interest in an institution seems more like a business venture as opposed to a college search process. The concern is that institutions that use demonstrated interest as a part of their application process might miss out on a stellar student. For example, some students might not have the means to visit a college campus, because the expense is far too great for their families, or they missed an admission representative's visit to their school, because they were studying for a test (Rivard, 2014). Both of these missed opportunities could potentially hinder a student's admission into an institution.

Books

Over the years, collections of books on counselor shelves have diminished with the availability of digital content, but having a few good books to reference or have available in a counseling center for students and families to peruse can be useful. This collection should cover the entire spectrum of college admission, including general college information, financial aid, admission testing, special populations, and major and career exploration. In addition, having information about gap-year options, international options and military service can be good resources depending on your population. Of course, if funding is not there to buy resources, many online sites deliver similar content. Those are covered later in this chapter.

The Big Books

These books contain comprehensive listings of two-year and/or four-year colleges in the United States and may include Canadian and select international colleges. In addition, each may have other resources in the front or back that may cover which schools offer specific majors, testing policies for schools, and additional Web resources. These are updated annually. The listings are basic facts, and those reading need to be aware that if they are reading a prior year's book, the information about admission and scholarship deadlines may have changed, and costs probably have changed. These books can be especially helpful for those early in the process who just want to

know what is available in a certain state. The names now include the year of graduation for the current class, but searching an online bookstore or asking at a local bookstore should provide the most recent editions for each of the following:

- *The College Handbook* by the College Board
- *Four Year Colleges* by Peterson's
- *Two Year Colleges* by Peterson's
- *Profile of American Colleges* by Barron's

The "Best of" Books

While the writers and publishers of these books are making a value judgment that excludes the vast majority of colleges, and any of a number of those excluded could be "the best" fit for the student being advised. The following books provide greater information about the schools that are highlighted, and for the new counselor or for a counselor who has a student looking at school that is not as familiar, having one or more of these books can provide a greater understanding of the school and its culture.

- *Fiske Guide to Colleges* by Edward Fiske
- *The Best 379 Colleges* by Princeton Review
- *Insider's Guide to Colleges* by Yale Daily News
- *The Ultimate Guide to America's Best Colleges* by Gen Tanabe and Kelly Tanabe

Another book that limits the schools highlighted, but can be especially good for those students and families who are questioning why and how to go about the college search process is *Colleges that Change Lives* by Loren Pope. This book highlights just 40 liberal arts colleges from regions throughout the US, and while not the most well-known, the schools come alive through the writing. Students and families who have read the book find that they have a greater appreciation for the search and are better prepared with questions to ask when visiting colleges or speaking to representatives from different schools.

General Information about College Admission

These books provide insight into the nuances of the admission process and are particularly written for students and parents.

- *Admission Matters: What Students and Parents Need to Know About Getting into College* by Sally P. Springer, Jon Reider and Joyce Vining Morgan

- *College Admission: From Application to Admission Step by Step* by Robin Mamlet and Christine VanDeVelde

- *College is Yours 2.0* by Patrick O'Connor (especially to recommend to students)

- *Fiske Guide to Getting into the Right College* by Edward Fiske

Web Sites

Besides the specific Web sites below, many of the Web sites for professional organizations have enhanced resources for their members. Also, many colleges have a presence on YouTube with virtual tours, information about admission and sometimes advice on the admission process at their schools.

Two good starting points for the college search are below. Both contain a variety of content, including videos.

KnowHow2Go is a site dedicated to helping students from low socio-economic backgrounds and from families in which they will be the first to attend college to maintain those aspirations. It is a campaign developed collaboratively between The American Council on Education, Lumina Foundation and the Ad Council.

http://knowhow2go.acenet.edu

The College Navigator Web site, with the direct link below, is also available through the College Affordability and Transparency Center Web site listed below. The site allows students to search for colleges through many different variables, including location, size, type, major, activities, etc. Students can compare up to four colleges side by side, and students can export an excel file with "favorite" colleges to save.

http://nces.ed.gov/collegenavigator

Big Future is a comprehensive site from the College Board that includes information on preparing for college, a college search tool, a major and career search, and information about paying for college. The site offers numerous videos from students and others for a more personal approach to the process.

https://bigfuture.collegeboard.org

Electronic Transcripts and Career and College Readiness Database Systems

Parchment, Naviance©, Electronic Transcript Exchange, Scrip-Safe International©, SENDedu—these are some of the names of electronic delivery systems available to students and schools to transmit transcripts or supporting documents to colleges. Some states have career and college guidance database systems that allow students in those states to have personal accounts that counselors can use to track career and college readiness activities throughout middle and high school (many using XAP© as the supporting service). Examples of these are GaCollege411 and CaliforniaColleges.edu. In addition, Naviance is a college and career guidance software tool that many private schools and some public schools are using to manage student progress in these areas through the college application process. Regardless of how transcripts and other supporting documents are submitted, all FERPA guidelines should be followed in regards to releasing any student records.

Database systems like these can greatly streamline the work that is needed to support all college-bound students and can make it easy to readily identify students who may need additional support with the process through reports on progress with applications. While no service is perfect, and oversight is needed, submitting documents electronically allows counselors and students to be able to see the status of submitted documents from the high school side. Students should also be told to check the status of submitted documents on the college side—often easily available through electronic systems through the college's Web site once an application is submitted.

APPLICATION HELP

Helping students with applications can be daunting, because the students themselves sometimes find applying to college overwhelming. Application workshops held in computer labs can be beneficial, allowing you to work with many students at one time and take them step by step through the process. For counselors lucky to be in a state that has a robust college and career Web site that is used as a guidance tool throughout high school, then working on the same site to complete applications may not seem as intimidating for students.

Working with a college guidance curriculum to go through the steps is another way to help students complete applications. In the NACAC publication, *Step by Step: College Awareness and Planning for Families, Counselors and Communities* by Mary Lee Hoganson, Phyllis Gill and Joan Mudge, the late high school curriculum has a sample copy of a Common Application that students can use to create a draft before entering information online and advice about essay writing, listing activities, and requesting teacher and counselor recommendations.

Below are application Web sites that allow students to create a central application that can be sent to many schools. Individual schools may require students to complete additional information, questions and essays specific to that school.

Common Application—This site provides an application that students can use to apply to any of the over 500 member colleges.

www.commonapp.org

EDU, Inc. Common Black College Application—Students can apply to all member institutions for a single fee.

www.connecttocollege.net/application.asp

Universal Application—This application option allows students to apply to more than 40 different institutions.

www.universalcollegeapp.com/

CAREER COUNSELING

Helping students to identify personal strengths and preferences in order to determine possible future careers and then identify the necessary postsecondary education is an important aspect of school counseling programs. Understanding whether a certain career will require that the student take courses in lock-step from freshman year through graduation, or if the career training allows for more variability in courses taken and order taken is information that can be found through online research. For instance, nurses and engineers have a more defined coursework path, and deciding after a year or two of college to transfer into either major may mean longer time to graduate, whereas transferring into other majors may not require additional time in college.

There are several good Web sites that offer free career search tools and informations. Two of those are listed below.

My Next Move is a Web site of the Department of Labor. Students can browse careers by industry or outlook, or they can complete the interest profile and then can explore careers based on the amount of preparation (education) needed for the job that fit their profile. The list of results also indicates if a particular career has a bright outlook, is a green job or if there are apprenticeships in the career area. Clicking on a career reveals a user-friendly page of facts about it, including knowledge, skills, abilities, personalities, technology, and education needed, as well as average national wages and links for wages in every state.

www.mynextmove.org

Big Future, the site listed under College Search as well and created by the College Board, also has a section on Exploring Careers. The site allows students to explore and watch videos about different careers and explore majors.

https://bigfuture.collegeboard.org

RESOURCES FOR WORKING WITH SPECIAL POPULATIONS

Lynne Shallcrosse, in an article for *Counseling Today,* wrote:

> The essence of being an effective counselor with any person is to truly understand this person and the many aspects of who they are and their life. It's so much like a jigsaw puzzle. The more pieces of the puzzle you have in place, then the closer and closer you are to fully understanding that person, and the more effective you can be with your helping. (2013)

For the person working as a college counselor, this means trying to meet each student where they are by understanding cultural, religious and social influences, gender identity and sexual orientation, and family dynamics, in addition to having general competency in general adolescent developmental. This can be one of the more tricky areas to feel proficient, as we all enter the profession with biases based on our own backgrounds. Chapters 17, 18 and 19 all discuss college counseling for special populations in greater detail.

First Generation and Underserved Populations

The fears and concerns of a student and his/her parents about applying and going to college when there is no family history of college attendance can be difficult to understand for the counselor who comes from a tradition of college attendance. The same can be said for students coming from low-income families or those from communities where there is no college-going culture. Whether it is explaining the difference between high school graduation requirements and college entrance requirements, applying to college, for financial aid or for on-campus housing, these students often require more time advising.

In addition to traditional counseling, finding outreach programs or developing special programs within the school community can be beneficial. Also, working with colleagues on college campuses to understand available bridge programs to help these students enroll and persist is also important. Federal programs may be operated in communities, on school campuses or on college campuses under Gear Up or Trio funding and have names like Gear Up, Upward Bound, Educational Talent Search, and Educational Opportunity Centers. Community-Based Organizations (CBOs) are often grassroots and are specific to a geographic location, but some have offerings in many locations or have expanded into other areas. Some of these larger programs include A Better Chance, Posse Foundation, the 100 Black Men, and College Possible.

Counselors can search for programs through the following websites:

The **NACAC Directory of College Access and Success Programs** has a search feature that allows NACAC members to search for programs by name, city or state.

www.nacacnet.org/learning/communities/casp/Pages/default.aspx

The **National College Access Network** Web site has a complete listing of members by state.

www.collegeaccess.org/Member_Directory

The following Web sites are designed particularly for first generation and underserved populations and the people who help them.

I'm First is a Web site developed by the Center for Student Opportunity. There is a college search feature that has information on retention and graduation, scholarships and programs for underrepresented students, student and faculty diversity statistics, and admission information. There are also videos of first-generation students speaking about their college experiences, as well as of successful business people who were first-generation college students, and blogs written by current students.

www.imfirst.org

KnowHow2Go was previously mentioned in the College Search section, but deserves repeating here, since this site is dedicated to helping students from low socio-economic backgrounds and from families in which they will be the first to attend college to maintain those aspirations.

http://knowhow2go.acenet.edu

National Center for Homeless Education provides resources and information for those who work with students experiencing homelessness. The resources links cover a variety of topics pertaining to education for this population, including information for those working with foster children and children with incarcerated parents.

http://center.serve.org/nche/about.php

Undocumented and Deferred Action for Childhood Arrivals

The first time a counselor realizes that he/she is working with a student who is undocumented or who has DACA status may come as a surprise. Often the perception of the availability of options for these students may be different than the reality, especially depending on the state in which the student resides. The big takeaway from this section should be **while it may not be an easy process, there are postsecondary options for these students!**

College Advising Guide for Undocumented Students is provided by the Illinois Association for College Admission Counseling. This Web site provides resources for counselors, a listing of colleges throughout the United States that have completed questionnaires about the admission practice and financial aid process, and options at those schools for this population, relevant federal and state legislation, and career planning for undocumented and DACA students.

www.iacac.org/undocumented

Undocumented Student Tuition: Overview is on the Web site of the National Council for State Legislatures. This site provides the listing of the states that allow these students to attend college for in-state tuition, those that allow students to receive state financial aid (undocumented and DACA students are not allowed to receive any federal student aid), as well as the states that limit or ban access to postsecondary education.

www.ncsl.org/research/education/undocumented-student-tuition-overview.aspx

For Undocumented Students is a section on the College Board's Big Future Web site that provides videos, personal stories, and information for students and counselors on college admission and financial aid for this population.

https://bigfuture.collegeboard.org/get-started/for-undocumented-students

Veterans

For those who would like resources to help veterans with the process of searching for, applying to and enrolling in college, below are several sites that can help with advising this special population. With the recent signing of the Veterans Access, Choice and Accountability Act of 2014, public colleges that want to be able to continue to receive GI Bill payments will need to offer in-state tuition beginning in the fall of 2015 to veterans, regardless of residency or to dependents who use transferred Post-9/11 benefits.

Student Veterans of America provides support to veterans to succeed in higher education. Campus chapters provide peer support to help veterans persist to graduation.

www.studentveterans.org

US Department of Veteran Affairs education and training Web site has the full listing of military education benefits by service and a GI Bill comparison tool.

www.benefits.va.gov/gibill

American Council on Education has a special section on military students and veterans, including information on veteran-friendly postsecondary institutions and college credit for military service.

www.acenet.edu/higher-education/Pages/Military-Students-and-Veterans.aspx

FINANCIAL AID AND SCHOLARSHIPS

With the ever-rising cost of college, financial aid resources are a must for any counselor helping students and families with the college process. In addition to the resources below, many colleges and universities have financial aid officers that are willing to present at school financial aid evenings. Contact the financial aid office directly to see if that is a service they can provide.

Books

The books below are updated annually. Students may find being able to do a manual search for scholarships more pleasant than receiving the daily emails that may come from an online search. Many scholarships may be open to students in grades nine through 12, so this is one area where younger students can start working on applications. For the students who are in the throes of completing applications, they will often find that their best source for information about financial aid and scholarships is from the colleges or universities themselves.

- *Financial Aid Handbook* by the College Board
- *Scholarships, Grants, and Prizes* by Peterson's
- *Scholarship Handbook* by The College Board
- *The Ultimate Scholarship Book* by Gen Tanabe and Kelly Tanabe

WEBSITES

College Affordability and Transparency Center— Within this Web site are actually six different links that allow users to search for institutions by different criteria, including: the College Scorecard, which looks at college affordability; the Net Price Calculator Center, which either lets the user enter data to determine the net price of the particular college or links to the institution's net price calculator; the College Navigator, which allows students to conduct an online college search; the College Affordability and Transparency List, which allows users to view various institutions by high and low tuition and net price, as well as viewing the institutions with the greatest increase in price over the time indicated; 90/10 information, which lists the institutions not meeting the requirement of receiving at least 10 percent of income from non-Title-IV sources; and State Spending Charts, which report the per-student spending level of the state, as well as giving a narrative about the economic climate.

http://collegecost.ed.gov

Free Application for Federal Student Aid—This site is where students apply for any federal student aid programs, including Pell grants, federal work-study and federal student loans.

https://fafsa.ed.gov

Financial Aid Toolkit—This site *for counselors* provides information to those interested in learning more about types of aid, in particular federal financial aid.

www.financialaidtoolkit.ed.gov/tk

Federal Student Aid—This is a comprehensive site *for students* that explains financial aid, where it comes from and how to apply.

https://studentaid.ed.gov

CSS/Financial Aid Profile is a financial aid tool of the College Board used in addition to the FAFSA by more than 400 colleges to determine financial need.

http://student.collegeboard.org/css-financial-aid-profile

The resources provided are just a starting point for the counselor working with students who aspire to attend college. As with any profession, counselors need continuing education and professional development to stay current on information, issues and tools relating to supporting student success. The continual changes that occur in college admission necessitates that counselors are particularly attuned to new information and best practices. Creating a team atmosphere of support with other counselors, teachers and administrators will help students and families know that your school is dedicated to helping each student reach his/her full potential.

DISCUSSION QUESTIONS

1. How can membership in at least one professional organization benefit the counselor who is advising students in the college admission process? Research at least one professional organization mentioned and provide a listing of the resources that the organization provides that could benefit all populations with which you work.

2. Is the use of digital content or social media necessary for counselors to effectively communicate with their students and families? Support your response with specifics.

3. In which ways can you use the books and Web sites provided in this chapter to better educate students who do not have a family member who has attended college or students from low socioeconomic backgrounds to prepare for, apply to and enroll in college.

4. What additional resources are there in your community, state or region that would benefit your work helping students with the college search and enrollment process?

ABOUT THE AUTHOR

Patty Montague is a college counselor at the Marist School (GA). She has a bachelor's degree in secondary math education from Clemson University (SC) and a M.Ed. in school counseling from Valdosta State University (GA). She is the former chair of NACAC's Inclusion, Access and Success Committee, and formerly served on the Southern Association for College Admission Counseling (SACAC) Board of Directors.

REFERENCES

Amory, A. (2007). Game object model version II: A theoretical framework for educational game development. [Abstract]. *Educational Technology Research & Development*, 55(1), 51–77.

Barnes, N.G. (2009). Reaching the wired generation: How social media is changing college admission. NACAC Discussion Paper. Retrieved from *www.nacacnet.org*.

Barnes, N.G., & Mattson, E. (2009). *Social media and college admissions: The first longitudinal study.* Retrieved from the Society for New Communications Research Web site: *http://sncr.org/sites/default/files/mediaandadmissions_0.pdf.*

Davis III, C.H.F., Deil-Amen, R., Rios-Aguilar, C., & González Canché, M.S. (2012). *Social media and higher education: A literature review and research directions.* Report printed by the University of Arizona and Claremont Graduate University.

Dearden, J., Li, S., Meyerhoefer, C., & Yang, M. (2011), Demonstrated interest: signaling behaviorin college admissions, working paper. *FutureBound.* Retrieved from *http://www.futureboundgames.com.*

Enriquez, J. *Your online life*, permanent as a tattoo. Retrieved from *http://www.ted.com/talks/juan_enriquez_how_to_think_about_digital_tattoos.*

Gee, J.P. (2007). *Good video games and good learning: Collected essays on video games, learning and literacy.* New York: Peter Lang.

Gulek, J.C., & Demirtas, H. (2005). Learning with technology: The impact of laptop use on student achievement. *The Journal of Technology, Learning, and Assessment,* 3(2). Retrieved from *www.jtla.org.*

Mathis, J.D. (2010). Increasing the capacity of college counseling through video game design. *Journal of College Admission.* Retrieved from *www.nacacnet.org.*

National Association for College Admission Counseling. (2009). *Factors in the Admission Decision* (6th issue).

Protheroe, N. (2005). Technology and student achievement. *Principal-Effective Intervention,* 85(2). Retrieved from *www.naesp.org.*

Rivard, R. (2014) *Students are asked to demonstrate more interest in colleges than just applying.* Retrieved from *www.insidehighered.com.*

Shallcrosse, L. (2013). Multicultural competence: A continual pursuit. *Counseling Today.* Retrieved from *http://ct.counseling.org/2013/09/multicultural-competence-a-continual-pursuit.*

Venegas, K.M. (2007). The Internet and college access: Challenges for low-income students. *American Academic,* 3(1), 141–154.

Chapter 21:   The College Essay: Helping Students Find Their Voice

Rod Skinner

First Thoughts

For many students, writing the college essay is the great challenge of the college application process. Fraught with questions of identity (Who am I? What really matters to me? Will they like me?) and voice (How do colleges want me to speak? Who is my audience? Do I sound smart enough?), the college essay can often seem more of a barrier than an opportunity, stalling a student's application process. Because of these questions, it is helpful for college admission counseling professionals to view the college essay as a chance for both reflection and discovery.

In a piece written a number of years ago, the psychologist Michael Thompson described the college process as a failed rite of passage, arguing pointedly and rightly that,

and divided into two components: knowledge of cognition, including one's knowledge of his/her own cognition or about cognition in general; and regulation of cognition, or the activities that students use to control their learning (Schraw, 1998). The ability to monitor and self-assess cognitive processes involves actively thinking about why and how decisions are made. Although the process is highly individualized, college counselors can help facilitate metacognitive development by providing opportunities for self-reflection and self-assessment throughout the college application process, especially as it pertains to writing the essay.

There may be agreement established with this point: the college essay, or personal statement, encourages stu-

The transition from high school to higher education occurs during an overwhelming period of change for adolescents. Counselors witness the social, emotional and cognitive development phases occurring throughout secondary school.

by focusing on college results and not on the moral and social growth of the student, we have robbed students of a crucial developmental moment. But, perhaps, if we can turn the energy of students to the self-discovery inherent in the creation of a college essay, we can restore some developmental luster to the college process. This effort first requires a conversation about self-discovery, aligned with the concept of metacognition.

Thoughts About Metacognition

The transition from high school to higher education occurs during an overwhelming period of change for adolescents. Counselors witness the social, emotional and cognitive development phases occurring throughout secondary school. These experiences can easily influence students during the college search and application processes. College counselors can utilize this critical period, when students are at times overly self-aware, but often still new to deep, meaningful self-reflection, to promote metacognitive development. Metacognition, according to John H. Flavell (1979), is comprised of an individual's "knowledge and cognition about cognitive phenomena" (p. 906). This concept is often described as "thinking about thinking"

dents to engage in this metacognitive process of self-knowing; however, students need to be equipped with the proper tools to accomplish the task. The process will take time, so it is vital that students begin reflecting on their own cognition well before the application deadline. To help students prepare for the task of writing, college counselors can encourage metacognitive growth, explain the purpose of the college application essay, and provide guidance regarding the structure, voice and content of students' writing.

With metacognitive processes in mind, this chapter describes what makes a compelling college essay by exploring the key elements of the essay, such as content, voice, tone, and length. This chapter also provides various methods for helping students identify and develop essay topics, including self-discovery exercises that encourage students to contemplate and connect the dots—the important moments and people—in their lives.

Purpose of the College Essay

One need only glance at a few college applications to see that the college essay is no longer the stand-alone exercise it used to be. Many colleges ask for supplemental essays, and those essays can range from the expected—"Why do you want to come to [name of college]?—to the singular—"What do you do for fun?" Even the old standby short-answer question asking the student to describe an extracurricular activity has been re-categorized as supplemental. For the overall purposes of this chapter, "essay," or occasionally, "personal statement," will serve as short-hand for the full range of writings requested by colleges. A later section of this chapter will cover supplemental essays and other writings in more detail, noting the particular roles each plays in the student's application.

WHAT THE ESSAY IS (AND WHAT IT IS NOT)

As much as the student may have strong feelings to the contrary, the college essay is one part of the application that is truly in her/his control. No matter the topic, the student gets to choose what to write about; the extent to which that choice frees the student to speak fully and naturally as a developing and engaged human being often determines the extent to which the essay has value or impact in the college process. Cynics have often wondered whether the colleges "even read those things," given how many applications they now receive, but NACAC studies and others show that, the more selective a college and the more qualified and high-powered its applicant pool, the more likely the college is to look at qualitative factors like the essay to distinguish a qualified applicant from the rest of the pool.

Students and families can often make the mistake of thinking that the essay is some kind of marketing piece. They reduce its function to a delivery system for all the impressive things the student has done in his/her high school career. But, of course, those activities are already listed in the extracurricular section. The essay-as-activities-delivery system wastes an opportunity to tell a compelling, distinctive story.

A wonderfully wise parent once observed that "families think the essay is about presenting oneself but, really, it's about *revealing* [my italics] oneself." A successfully revelatory personal statement can have a powerful, cohering effect on an application. After reading such an essay, college admission readers use comments like, "Things really came together"; the student who wrote her/his essay with genuine voice has been known to "step off the

page," the writing being so authentic, so present. Conversely, for the student who has worked too hard to impress with a sophisticated vocabulary (beware the thesaurus, the most deadening of verbal dinosaurs!) or who has allowed the essay to be co-opted by well-meaning adults (the only "massaging" known to increase rather than relieve stress), "things can begin to go clank," as an admission officer once put it; the essay and its voice just do not ring true.

A PERSONAL ESSAY MANIFESTO

"The personal essay demands that we jump in with both feet, yelling for all we're worth … (T)he real possibility of the personal essay…is to catch oneself in the act of being human. That means the willingness to surrender for a time our pose of unshakable rectitude, and to admit that we are, despite our best intentions, subject to all manner of doubt and weakness and foolish wanting. It requires self-awareness without self-importance, moral rigor without priggishness, and the courage to hang it all on the line. It's a hard thing to do."

–Tobias Wolff

Bottom line: Hold on to that notion of revealing. Colleges want to gain insight into what makes a student tick. They want insight into, as one admission dean has put it, "the student's developing sense of identity, self and purpose." Or, even more colloquially, what's the kid's story?

GETTING THE STORY STARTED

As discussed in greater length in the recommendations chapter (see chapter 12), the power of story is universal. From classroom to boardroom to dorm room to locker room, story is, to quote the venerable Fred Hargadon, "the coin of the realm." Stories do all that we would want an essay to do: They bring specificity and heart to the reader; they show instead of tell; and, because of these qualities, they meet the "stickiness quotient"—that is, they attach to the reader's memory and stay there.

Our task as counselors is to help students identify their various life stories and to help students choose the story that would most fully capture their lives for a reader who has never met them before. If we take hold of the metacognitive process here, we are asking students to truly engage in storytelling as a form of self-assessment. As students consider what to write, they begin to demonstrate increased autonomy in thinking and learning about themselves, and these efforts, in turn, make the reader aware of their true potential (Andrade & Valtcheva, 2009). As James Miller, dean of admission at Brown University (RI) puts it, "We want to read a real story, a piece of good nonfiction." Before pen touches paper or finger touches keyboard, it is important for the student to heed that ancient Delphic maxim, first ascribed to Socrates and later modified by Descartes: Know thyself.

The art and science of knowing oneself has become an increasingly important concern in the world of education. Paul Tough, Carol Dweck, William Damon, Richard Weissbourd, Angela Duckworth, and Martin Seligman are but a few of the many researchers exploring the affective domain of children and teens. David Brooks, *The New York Times* op-ed writer, has written extensively on the moral and psychological character of this generation of students. Grit, resilience, happiness, joy, and self-regulation have become such persistent buzzwords, such a part of popular culture, that they have teetered on the edge of cliché and inspired any number of humorous riffs about parents hiring "joy coaches" or sending their children to "grit camps." Joking aside, it is important to note that self-regulation, the core element of grit, resonates powerfully with metacognition's "regulation of cognition."

In a January 2013 article in *Education Week*, David Conley, lamenting the second-class status of the non-cognitive realm, makes the case for "metacognition" as the new way of thinking about the non-cognitive. He argues that cognition, the acquisition of knowledge in isolation, only tells half the story of knowing. Metacognition, he writes, "is a more complex form of cognition," because it involves seeing the connections, the deeper, cohering substructures of knowledge, and because it requires the learner to know how he or she learns and how knowledge connects to one's inner self.

In a very real sense, a student applying to college must call upon metacognitive sensibilities in order to understand her/his own life. It is not enough to say what happened. The student must discover what the event might mean and be able to recognize how that meaning might bear on other events in the student's life.

Seen in this light, the essay is not a 650-word inconvenience that one must slog through in order to go to college; it can be an important developmental exercise, one that, in the best ways, challenges, stretches and reaffirms one's sense of self. Or, put another way, writing the college essay can be a profoundly grown-up (or at least growing-up) act. When a student writes a thoughtful, successful essay, things come together not just for the admission officer, but for the student as well. The impact can be revelatory on all sides.

SELF-DISCOVERY EXERCISES TO FACILITATE THE WRITING PROCESS

Enough theory; let's move to practice. What follows are several exercises that can help students begin to mine the narrative gold of their lives. It is important to reiterate that these ideas are suggestions, not prescriptions. Also, a number of these exercises work well as complements to one another, so try more than one. Ultimately, of course, use what makes sense for your students.

Life Mapping

This idea borrows heavily from the career-mapping exercise described in *You Majored in What? Mapping Your Path from Chaos to Career* by Katharine Brooks, EdD, executive director of the Office of Personal and Career Development at Wake Forest University (NC). Students can do it by themselves, or counselors can use it as a group exercise.

Ask each student to jot down all the important people, events, accomplishments, keepsakes, experiences, etc. in their lives on a large piece of paper. Students will be tempted to list these items in some sort of linear fashion—outline, columns, etc.—but encourage them to write randomly, using as much of the paper as possible.

Next, ask the students to spend some time contemplating the whole page and to then begin thinking about which items connect to one another. After taking that time to think (five to 10 minutes usually does the trick), students should draw lines between the items they feel are connected. Since there will usually be more than one set of lines, students might want to use different colored pens or markers to distinguish each set.

Once the students have finished their "maps" of experience, they should then take some time mulling over the significance of those maps. What themes do they see? What sorts of stories, big-picture messages about their lives begin to emerge? This is the most challenging and the most important part of the exercise. Patterns won't necessarily emerge quickly, so students need to be patient. Our experience has been that, if students hang in there, it is worth their while. More than a few of them have told us that the maps gave them the direction they needed for their essays and, in some cases, for their college lists as well.

Keirsey Personality Test or Temperament Sorter

Closely associated with the Meyers-Briggs Type Indicator, the Keirsey Temperament Sorter (KTS) is a free, easily accessible online tool to help students assess their personalities and know themselves better. While the KTS by itself will most likely not lead directly to a good essay, it might well trigger thoughts and memories that could help students think through the stories they want to tell, and, if done before the mapping exercise, it could help students see the connective tissue between various events in their lives.

Self-Portraits

Ask students to draw a picture that captures or symbolizes an important aspect in their lives. It can be literal, whimsical, abstract, grand, or miniscule. Then ask each student to describe the picture (in a private meeting or in a group discussion, depending on what works best for you) and, most importantly, to explain why she/he chose that particular image. The seeds of a story or of a crucial theme in the student's life could emerge from that discussion.

Family and Friends

The student can ask people who really know him/her to share their favorite stories about the student. Hearing how she/he is seen by others can sometimes spark new insights about oneself. And sometimes that story from a grandparent is just the story the student needs to start building an essay.

Dreams, Memories, Reflections

Carl Jung built his formidable career on the idea that the true meaning of our lives resides in our dreams and memories. Ask students to consider what past events, what experiences tend to run through their minds regularly, what dreams tend to recur. Then ask them to do a little digging and suss out why it is that those dreams or memories still tug at them. Maybe there are important understandings that the subconscious is still trying to process; maybe there is good meat for an essay there.

Adjectives

Sometimes, as part of the beginning of the college process, students fill out forms or mock applications provided by the college office. If so, it is not uncommon for those forms to include a section where the student has to choose six or so adjectives that describe him/her best. As a follow-up to that particular exercise, ask the student to tell the story behind one of those adjectives: Why that adjective? What story/incident/experience would help explain/give proof of the relevance of that adjective to the student?

Six-Word Memoir

A recent phenomenon has been the rise of the six-word memoir. Essentially, the writer attempts to tell her/his life story in six words. It doesn't have to be a life story, however. A recent public radio series, on the anniversary of Martin Luther King's "I Have a Dream" speech, asked each guest to compose a six-word response to a question about the current state of race in America. If you are meeting with students in groups, you could give them a prompt ("How does it feel to be a senior right now?"; "What is the most meaningful thing you have ever done?"; "Describe your life"; or devise the prompt that works for your counselees. For inspiration, google the six-word memoir site; there are lots of ideas there). Ask them to write a six-word response to that prompt, then collect the responses and hand them back out so that no one has her/his own response. Next, ask each student to read the response she/he has and then guess who the author is. It is a fun game, it can have great community-building value because students often learn more about their classmates, and, finally, in the discussion that can ensue from the response, the author sometimes ends up expanding on the theme and fleshing out the idea introduced in the response. Good potential fodder for an essay.

If six-word memoir as group activity will not work, the exercise could still be helpful when trying to coax an idea out of a stumped senior. Ask the senior to compose a six-word reflection on whatever the two of you might have been discussing and see where that leads.

Free Writing

Free writing is a technique pioneered by Natalie Goldberg to break through inhibitions and bring flow to a person's writing. The basic rule is that the writer needs to write continuously for a specified period of time (usually 10 to 15 minutes at a time) without regard to grammar, structure or coherence. The writer cannot lift his/her pen from the paper and cannot stop to edit, correct or rethink. The writing does not have to be rushed, but it should be quick and uninterrupted. If the writer cannot think of anything to write, then she/he writes about that; if the writer is bored or ill-at-ease with the exercise, then she/he should write about those feelings. The writer may well stray off-topic or jump suddenly from point to point. All of this randomness is okay. The point of the free-write process is to limber up the writer's thinking. Much of what the writer produces in the free write will be of little use, but the writer should review what she/he produced and look for ideas that could be developed into a larger, more coherent and formal piece of writing.

A Writing Mantra

Over time, after decades of guiding and inspiring students to find their voice as writers, Natalie Goldberg has refined her approach to a simple four-word mantra: "Shut up and write."

SOME FINAL THOUGHTS ON GETTING STARTED

One thought that seems to stymie students regularly is the assumption that the essay will not work unless it describes something spectacular, heart-wrenching, cataclysmic, or a life event global in its impact. In fact, nothing could be further from the truth. What counts is the meaning an event has for the author. The danger of the spectacular essay is that it can actually be harder to say something personal and distinctive. Students who have

lived through experiences like Hurricane Katrina, 9/11, the collapse of family finances in 2008, death of a loved one, or divorce and disintegration of family often feel an intense need to write about it, and, for their own health and well-being, they should; they need to get those thoughts and feelings on paper. Whether what they write then constitutes an effective college essay is a different matter.

Once they have written such an essay, they need to step away from it, away from the immediate emotion of it. Later, when they can look at the essay with a more dispassionate set of eyes, they need to ask the hard questions: Is the telling of this story distinctive to me, or does it sound as though anybody living through the same experience could have written it? Do I as an individual emerge from this essay? If the answers to these questions are "yes," then the student may have the makings of a good essay. If not, then discuss the details of the experience to make sure that there are not any submerged distinctive elements; if none surface, then gently begin to guide the student to a different topic. If the student insists on sending the essay anyway, then make sure that it is as well-written as possible so that at least the essay will not hurt the application.

An old saying in theater muses that there are no small parts, just small actors. Remind students that some of the most effective essays are the ones that find real depth and complexity in the smallest, seemingly most inconsequential events. Such essays demonstrate a student's capacity for nuance, inventiveness, wonder, and resourcefulness. A veteran admission officer once mused in a meeting with counselors that one should never underestimate the ability of the adolescent to reduce the interesting to the ordinary. Imagine, then, how delighted and refreshed that admission officer would have felt when he saw a student transform the ordinary into the interesting! W.H. Auden once declared that poetry makes the ordinary extraordinary; in that regard, the best college essay writers are poets of the admission world.

Another stumbling-block to writing the essay: committing those first words to paper. Students will talk of spending whole weekends or even entire weeks on their essay. Anyone who has faced a daunting writing assignment is familiar with the avoidance two-step. The would-be writer sits down at the computer. Human and computer exchange blank stares. Nothing really happens. Suddenly, the writer feels an overpowering desire for a glass of water or experiences a keen interest in cleaning his or her room. The writer leaves the computer for minutes, even hours, before returning to try again. And then the cycle repeats until eventually the writer glances at the time at the bottom of her/his computer screen and realizes that almost a whole day has gone by. Now the task that seemed more than formidable enough in the morning is even larger and more daunting in the evening.

So, how can our beleaguered student break this cycle? First, the student can treat the essay like an in-class assignment, set the clock for one hour and get to work. Once the hour is up, the student is done for the day; whatever she/he has written now functions as a rough draft. One caveat: If the student finds himself/herself in a real groove at the end of the hour, the student can ride that momentum and continue writing for as long as she/he can.

A second, related technique is for the student to set an appointment with himself/herself: "From 9:00 a.m.–11:00 a.m. Saturday morning, I will work on my college essay." Again, once the time is up, the student steps away from the computer unless inspiration has struck.

Surgical Strikes

The college application does not need to devour gobs of time and take over a student's senior year experience. By and large, the actual doing of the application requires only 12 to 20 hours of actual work. The more strategic the student can be about completing the application, the less time the whole process will consume. Making clear appointments with oneself and holding fast to those appointments is a good place to start. Surgical strikes are much more effective and liberating that weeks of well-meaning wandering.

The Writing Itself

Now that we have dispensed with a number of impediments and anxieties and the student is ready and eager to tell his/her story, it is time to consider some pointers about the actual writing.

Structure

Students long-schooled in the five-paragraph essay might find it initially hard to resist the gravitational pull of that tried-and-true structure. Remind students that they are trying to tell an important story from their life in as natural and fluid a way as possible. Few stories conform to five-paragraph exposition. At the same time, students should also resist seeing the essay as a creative writing assignment. The beautifully wrought opening description of the forest setting where the student's story will eventually take place can leave the reader looking in vain for the student; in a 650-word essay, where every word is at a premium, that opening is potentially wasteful.

So, what structure is effective? The student's story must determine that. Form follows content, not the other way around. For a lucky few students, the story will emerge Athena-like immediately, and there will be little need for editing or rethinking. For most, however, more work is involved, and the student needs to be patient with the process as story and, with it, structure unfold. Students should not worry about length in the first draft. The important thing is to get all of the possible ideas down, follow all leads, explore all trails, no matter how far off-track they may seem. Often the real story lies at the end of that unexpected trail; where the student starts is not necessarily where the student needs to end. The first hundred words or so end up being what Roger Rosenblatt calls "a clearing of the throat."

Depending, then, on what the student wants to say, almost any structure could potentially work. For the student trying to show the steady accumulation of awareness and growth over time, a chronological arrangement might make perfect sense. For the student trying to show a disruptive episode in her/his life that she/he eventually resolved, a more random structure with quick cuts and fragments that, by the end, become more ordered might be effective. In short, a good structure will reinforce content.

Every essay, regardless of structure, will need to have a beginning, a middle and an end. In an ideal world, the beginning should be a "grabber," a beginning statement with enough intrigue, energy and heart to pull the reader in. The best openings usually raise questions to which the reader is then eager to find answers, and, of course, the answers can only be found in the rest of the essay: "It was only last year that I began to appreciate being left-handed"; "Apologizing is not as hard as people think it is"; "I am not by nature a patient person, but, since I started going to a school that is not in my neighborhood, I have learned to be."

Another effective approach is *in medias res,* the technique of starting in the middle of the story: "Until that moment, I hadn't really thought of myself as a leader…" There are several benefits to this approach. First, it forces the writer to get down to the business of the story immediately: no clearing of the throat here. And, with that immediacy comes the specificity and the energy of being in the core of the story. Finally, the reader is initially disoriented and, as a result, completely engaged because there are so many questions to figure out (Where have I landed? What's going on?).

Another structural aspect the writer should always keep in mind is the use of key words from the topic or the essay prompt. The smart and strategic use of key words ensures that even the most far-flung narrative never loses touch with the main idea of the essay. So, if the student decides to write his/her Common Application in response to the "Describe a place or environment where you are perfectly content" prompt, his/her essay will need to provide an ongoing rumination on what it means for the writer to be *content* and what it means to be *perfectly* content. The words *content, perfect, environment,* and *place* (and other variations on those words) will need to run through the rumination—the more nuanced and subtle the placement of those key words the better. That way, the structure is almost a subconscious map for the reader; the reader always feels at home in the essay. Beginning the essay with, "The place or environment where I feel perfectly content is…" does not constitute a particularly effective or sophisticated use of key words. That sort of heavy-handed, unimaginative technique reeks of early high school and calls into question the writer's maturity as a thinker and a writer.

As a test of structure, the student might want to read the opening paragraph, then the opening lines of the body paragraphs and finally, the closing paragraph. Do all of those elements connect to one another? Is there a sense of forward motion from one paragraph to the next? Does the closing paragraph advance understanding of the ideas

and questions raised in the first paragraph? If the answer is "yes," then the student most likely has a tight essay.

VOICE

Voice is both the simplest and most difficult part of writing the personal statement. College admission officers relish those essays in which the student is writing in such a natural, unforced voice that it feels as though the student is sitting in the room having a conversation with them. So, we counselors say helpful things like, "Just write like yourself." True advice, but anxiety-producing for more than a few students. The best way to reduce this anxiety would be to infuse your school's curriculum with autobiographical writing and personal narrative assignments from the earliest age possible so that, by the time the student sits down to write the college essay, personal writing feels familiar and doable.

However, since the mandate of this chapter does not involve curriculum reform, let's look at some other in-the-moment advice that might help students find their voice.

A Comfortable Audience

Students should write the essay as though they are telling the story to an adult with whom they feel comfortable: a parent, a grandparent, a favorite aunt or uncle, a mentor. That mindset will keep the language animated, personal and somewhat elevated (but not overly elevated).

Levels of Language

Some people think of voice as being high-brow, middle-brow or low-brow. Students should employ high-brow only if they are truly at home with big words and sophisticated syntax. Low-brow in small doses can provide effective elements of surprise and accent in writing, but only if the writer knows how to use it wisely. Otherwise, low-brow should stay in locker rooms and in private conversations with friends. Middle-brow is really the level that works best. It allows students to stay relaxed, but with enough formality to be persuasive with the adult reader.

Diction

Students should be precise in their language, always looking for the most accurate and vivid ways to convey their story. (Students eager to build their vocabulary so that they have more dynamic language at their fingertips might want to try freerice.com, a challenging, fun on-line word game that also provides rice to the developing world.) But, as noted earlier, they do not want to over-reach and use big, unfamiliar words that will make their prose awkward or forced. Relatedly, they do not want to assume an "adult" way of talking that feels lifted from a Victorian novel. It is remarkable, for instance, how often stiff, almost anachronistic wording like amongst, amidst, whilst creeps into the work of the teenaged writer, a sure indication of the anxiety surrounding the essay: "If I use words that sound important, maybe what I have to say will sound important, too." The adventurous student who wants to experiment with some language should definite-ly do so, but she/he might want to run it by a counselor or English teacher before sending it off to a college.

Tone and Confidence

Tone really has to do with the confidence of the writ-er's voice. Does the student sound assured, relaxed and at home in his/her story? Or do small red flags of anxi-ety—the self-conscious word, the unintentional moment of self-praise, the overwrought description, the hint of rigid thinking—emerge? A favorite high school English teacher once counseled me to have "the proper arrogance of a writer"— that is, to feel so secure and comfortable in my ideas that there would be no need to overwrite or push a point too hard.

Even when a student finds a good story, there can be that limbo moment of lingering insecurity when the stu-dent still worries whether the admission powers-that-be will deem his/her story good enough, that moment when external pressures can cause them to doubt the story. We counselors need to sense that moment and, in effect, grant the student permission to tell the story she/he needs to tell. We need to imbue them with a healthy dose of that proper arrogance.

CONTENT AND ESSAY TYPE

We covered the general notions about content in the "Fi-nal Thoughts About Getting Started" section, so we will not belabor those points here. Instead, we offer some bul-let points for students to help guide their thinking about content, possible pitfalls and power points.

"IT FEELS LIKE I'M BRAGGING"

Another common stumbling-block for students is the fear that writing about themselves will come across as bragging. Here we return to the idea of the essay as revelation, not presentation. If the student is sharing a story about something truly meaningful in his/her life, there is nothing to fear; all the energy will go to making sure the reader understands how important that some-thing is, not to telling the reader how great the student is. The facts of the story are the facts of the story, so the student simply needs to relate them as clearly and as compellingly as possible. At the same time, the student should take care to avoid adjectives and adverbs that can come across as self-congratulatory. It is fine to write, "Last spring I helped organized a community clean-up event that eventually involved all the students and teachers in my school." It is not so fine to write, "Last spring, despite incred-ible odds, I managed to pull together the most successful community event my school has ever seen." Cagier students should also beware the "humble-brag," the not-so-subtle craft of aggran-dizing oneself through seemingly modest, self-effacing statements: "It wasn't the award, but rather the look on that young child's face that was important"; "You have to wonder about the judgment of all those people who say I am great at what I do."

- First and most importantly (that's why we're repeating this point), there is nothing wrong with writing about a common experience; it is what you do with it that matters. Some of the most powerful essays come from the most humble of topics: weekly Wednesday after-noon chats over homemade lasagna with a grandmoth-er; fishing with buddies off a pier in Boston Harbor; lessons learned over a summer of working with the buildings and grounds crew at one's high school; car-ing for a younger sibling or cousin; the Fourth of July parade in one's hometown. In one memorable essay, a student wrote about getting together with a group of friends to conduct an experiment he had read about in *Omni* magazine: making a pickle. Nothing spectacular, just some buddies having a bit of nerdy fun on a Friday night. What clinched the success of the essay was the author's closing rumination on friendship and the passage of time, very understated, but moving. The bottom line: If it means something to the student, and if the student can convey that meaning to the reader, then the essay will work.

- Second, a common, simple topic can work; a simplistic, superficial treatment of that topic will not. When thinking about the topic, the student must be, as the poet Theodore Roethke put it, "fascinated with the difficult." The student must dig deeply into the complexity of the topic, poking into all the possible corners, mulling over all the possible ramifications and implications. That full engagement with the topic will reveal the student's level of curiosity and capacity for nuanced, mature thought. If, in considering a potential topic, the student discovers there are not that many corners to poke around in after all, then she/he needs to find another topic.

- Be specific; be concrete. Generalizations and abstractions may often be true, but they are not distinctive; anybody can say them. Anecdotes, incidents and vivid details—in short, the personal specifics of a student's life—are distinctive. The student needs to populate his/her essay with those specifics.

- Avoid topics like the community service trip to Costa Rica, the family trip to Europe, the favorite horse. These are purchased experiences, revealing more about the student's socioeconomic privilege than about the student him- or herself. Such topics show that the student has, to borrow from a recent documentary, won the lottery of birth, but, unless she/he can show her/his own initiative, character, understandings, insights gained from this experience, little else. An essay about a month in London that talks about the historical sites and the cultural mix of the city in broad terms may be doomed from the start. An essay about the riveting but upsetting rant the student heard at Speaker's Corner that traces the student's thinking as she/he tries to

make sense of that rant can be very effective, because there the reader would see the student's mind and sensibilities at work.

- Do not try to be funny if you aren't. Humor can be very effective, but it is one of the hardest things to do well. And there is little if any middle ground; humor either scores a laugh or it bombs. A student who misses the mark may end up eliciting laughter she/he did not intend. If you think you have something funny to say, run the essay by your counselor or English teacher to make sure the humor works.

- Another difficult topic to write about is the performing arts. You can say many true and beautiful things about the joy of singing in close harmony with your a cappella group or about the transcendent moment when you really became a character onstage, but all of that will sound an awful lot like what other performers might say. So the challenge will be how to make this very important, but ephemeral, hard-to-pin-down experience distinctive to you. Think about how performing speaks to and develops your larger sense of yourself: Why is performing important to you? How did you come to performing in the first place? Who were your mentors? What particular personal challenges did a piece of choreography, a solo, a dramatic role present? What did you learn about yourself and others from the group dynamics of your ensemble? In other words, be as specific, anecdotal and personal as you can.

- One's spiritual beliefs, one's faith, can also present a challenging essay topic. For some students, faith will be a core element of their lives and, therefore, a part of themselves they might want to share with the colleges. As with the essays on performing, students will need to move beyond the general truths and benefits of a strong faith and explore the particular reasons why faith is so important to them as individuals. Students will also need to show that, as strong as their faith might be, they are open, broad-minded thinkers, ready to encounter a full range of worldviews. As institutions of spirited and groundbreaking intellectual inquiry and as communities of extraordinary diversity, colleges are not eager to admit dogmatic, doctrinaire thinkers of any stripe.

SUPPLEMENTAL ESSAYS

With applicant pools getting larger and stronger every year, colleges must face the not-always-happy task of distinguishing one highly qualified applicant from another. Supplemental essays are a primary way of making such distinctions. Beyond the generalized "love" of the Common Application and other universal instruments, colleges want to feel the particular love demanded by college-specific supplemental essays. The more selective the college and the more competitive its pool, the more often the supplemental essay is likely to be the difference-maker in admission decisions; in fact, a number of highly selective institutions have found that the supplemental essay served as the tip factor in the majority of their decisions. For colleges that are test-optional and colleges that do not offer interviews, the supplemental essay can take on added significance, since it provides the sorts of information and insights that can help the colleges know the student better and gauge more precisely where the student sits in relation to the rest of the applicant pool.

Supplemental essay topics run the gamut from the common ("Why [name of college]?"; "Tell us something about your background and about the ways that background has shaped who you are today") to the more individualized and quirky ("Celebrate your nerdy side"—Tufts University [MA]; "What's odd about odd numbers?"—University of Chicago [IL]). This section will unpack the meaning of these supplemental questions and suggest ways students might want to approach them.

THE COMMON TYPE

The Why [College] essay would seem straight-forward (and, for the most part, it is), but that does not mean it does not have its own perils. At its core, the Why essay wants to know whether the student has done her/his homework: How well does the student really know us? The earnest student can provide an essay chockfull of knowledge about the college and still miss the mark if that knowledge echoes what many other students might be citing in their supplement. A Why Columbia essay, for instance, can dutifully enumerate the excitements of learning in New York City and declaim the rigorous satisfactions of the core curriculum but lack distinctiveness. As noted before, this is a matter of digging into the

complexity of the topic and, consistent with the notion of revealing, elucidating the ways in which strengths and interests of the particular student match up with the community and the resources of the particular college.

Faced with the Why [College] essay the student would do well to imagine himself/herself at that college. Where will the energies of that student go? How will she/he engage with the community of that college? What activities? What courses? What professors? The witty remark about dorm living from the tour guide, the special light in the eyes of the alumni interviewer when talking about the college, the recent curricular innovation that speaks directly to the student's own talents, the specific insights and observations of a former schoolmate now attending that college are all potentially energizing and distinctive elements to add to the supplement. As dorky as it might make the student feel in the moment, she/he should take extensive notes during campus tours so that, when it comes time to writing the supplement, the student has a store of good info at his/her disposal. (See the appendix for a sample campus tour information sheet.) Students who are not able to visit colleges should make especially vigorous use of the other resources: college Web sites; guidebooks with more narrative descriptions of the colleges, like *The Fiske Guide to Colleges*; high school visits by college admission officers; feedback from alumni from their high school; among others.

Some colleges present a variation on the Why [College] prompt. A college, for instance, might ask the applicant to pick a course she/he would like to take at the college and then explain why. On some levels, this variation might seem less daunting: It is not dependent on a student's visiting campus and it gives the applicant a narrower and therefore clearer direction. At the same time, it does require the student to investigate the college's course offerings fully and to really have some sense of what she/he might want to learn. The student will want to find the course that really sparks excitement; in that excitement lie energy and distinctiveness.

The extent to which the student has engaged in the sort of metacognitive work described earlier, the extent to which she/he really knows himself/herself, will determine, in no small part, the power of his/her response to the Background essay prompt. What place, what community does the student call home? Has the student grown up under any unusual circumstances? What have been the seminal events in that student's life? Who have been the guiding hands? What does the student really care about? What are the student's non-negotiable principles? What does the student like about himself/herself? Where does she/he see a need for growth? The life-mapping exercise can really help the student write the Background essay, for it is asking the student, in essence, to tell her/his life story, or at least some salient, vital parts of it.

QUIRKY ESSAYS

The first thing to keep in mind when responding to the quirky essay prompt is that the supplement is inviting the student to play. As much as possible, the student wants to have fun with this essay, the serious fun of deep contemplation and adventurous thinking, granted, but fun nonetheless. The prompt is really saying, "This is the way we like to do things around here; are you game?" The student who enters fully into the spirit of this invitation will invariably write a strong essay.

So, how should the appropriately playful student approach this essay? Where is the "work" of this essay? The work is figuring out exactly which parts of herself/ himself she/he wants to bring to this play date: What do I want the college to know about me? And what does the college seem to want to know about me?

Let's deconstruct a supplemental essay prompt from a few years ago. The prompt asked, "If you saw a $50 bill lying on the sidewalk, what would you do?" The good-hearted student might respond with the plan of first trying to find the owner but, if unsuccessful, then donating the money to a worthy cause. This is a heartfelt, noble response, but does the student get the full bang for his/ her buck, so to speak, with this response? Has the student really dug into the complexity of the question? Has the student put her/his individual stamp on the question? Has the college really learned anything that might help that student emerge from that college's pool of highly qualified applicants? Exploring the question a bit further we discover that the college really wanted the student to engage in some vigorous moral reasoning. That reasoning could lead to considerations of property, responsibility to others, the greater good, individual lib-

erty, etc. Operating under the principle that the most difficult-to-prove or -justify approaches often make for the most interesting discussions, the student might have embraced the challenge (and here playfulness kicks in) of proving that it would have been perfectly acceptable to just keep the money. That approach would automatically carry with it the distinction of being the road less taken. The best responses, in short, are those that go beyond the obvious.

Another supplemental essay prompt, one that perhaps requires its own category, is "Write on a topic of your own choice." Beware the submerged hazards of this question. At first blush, it can seem like the easiest and most attractive option. But, like an open-book test where there is no excuse for the lack of fact or evidence nor of a fully developed thesis, it carries with it expectations that might actually demand the most of the student. The success of the topic-of-your-choice essay hinges, not surprisingly, on the topic's degree of difficulty. A softball question that does not demand the student's keenest, most inventive thinking is doomed to mediocrity at best. The student should employ reverse engineering, determining first what she/he wants to reveal about herself/himself and then devising the topic that will force her/him to use her/his full powers of conceptualization to arrive at that revelation.

A FINAL THOUGHT ON TOPIC-OF-YOUR CHOICE

Students should be aware that colleges that offer the topic-of-your-choice option among its prompts may give special scrutiny to that option. In fact, it may even be a test of the student's judgment and ambition. Did the student pick that option because she/he was trying to duck the other prompts, or did she/he have some legitimately important things to say that could only have been expressed through the topic-of-your-choice option? In any event, the bar will be set high for this option; students should choose it only after some careful thought.

General Advice for the Student: Dos and Don'ts

- Keep the number of advisors on your essay to a minimum, ideally just your counselor and another teacher whose judgment and writing ability you trust. Too many advisory voices will lead to confusion, not clarity; since each reader will bring a personal perspective, every time you add an advisor, you also add another opinion that needs to be assimilated with everything else you have heard.

- Do not put the name of the college in your essay, thinking that doing so will be the cherry on top of your demonstrated interest in the college. (A notable exception would, of course, be the Why [name of college]? supplemental essay.) Colleges will not be impressed; in fact, they might consider it pandering, obsequious behavior, in which case you have hurt, not helped your application. You also run the risk of putting the wrong name with the college, a surefire way to kill the legitimacy of your application. Besides all that, if you are putting that kind of energy into marketing yourself to the college, then you are diverting attention from the primary task of the application: sharing *your* story.

- Remember that spell check is useful but not infallible. It will miss spelling errors. So make sure that you proofread your essay after you spell-check. If you are not a good proofreader, then find someone who is to help you.

- Don't wait until the last minute to write your essay. Give yourself time to put the draft aside and then come back to it with a more objective, discerning set of eyes. That's how the most effective editing happens.

- Wherever possible, use the present tense; it will give your writing immediacy, direction, and will therefore help engage the reader more quickly and more fully. By the same token, avoid the passive voice at all costs; the passive voice is the most indirect way of speaking and can put distance between you and the reader and between you and your own story.

- Loading up your essay with adjectives and adverbs does not make the essay better. Nouns and verbs are the real engines of good writing. If you are using a lot of adjectives and adverbs, it could mean that you are losing track of what you want to say or, worse, that you did not have enough to say in the first place. The role of adjectives and adverbs is to accent the meaning of nouns and verbs, to give them added depth or edge.

- As a final step in revising an essay, read it aloud. Your ear is a very reliable judge of the fluency of your prose. It will tell you when the phrasing is awkward; it will pick up on run-on sentences, wordy constructions and forced word choice. Your ear will lead you to a more natural, conversational voice.

General Advice for the Counselor

One of the magical moments in a counselor's work with a student is that day when the student brings in a draft of the essay and, in it, reveals a deeper, more complicated side of himself/herself. We should be honored that the student has placed such trust in us, and we, in turn, should honor that trust by treating the essay with great care and sensitivity. While the importance of this revealing essay to the student is indisputable, the essay may not be college-essay ready; in fact, it may not even be college-essay appropriate. The counselor will need to validate the essay as a personal and necessary statement, but also must help the student disengage enough from the emotion of the essay to determine whether the essay is ultimately what the student wants to send to the college. If the student does want to send the essay to the college, then the counselor needs to help the student become the clear-eyed editor willing to make the tweaks, cuts and editions necessary for transforming the emotional powerful first draft into an equally powerful piece of finished writing.

Handled well, the brave essay in which the student makes himself/herself vulnerable to the counselor can lead to very meaningful discussions between counselor and student, discussions where counselor and student grow to know the student better. The essay, in effect, triggers a metacognitive partnership between counselor and student, and it reminds us counselors why we chose this career in the first place.

There is a wide divergence of opinion about the level of help the counselor should provide the student in the actual writing of the essay. Some counselors hold themselves to a strict policy of never putting pen to paper and instead providing oral feedback: "It is interesting that you chose to focus on your community service work after all that you have said and written about the importance of family. How do these two ideas connect?" Others will only frame their feedback as questions or general comments: "What are you really trying to say here?"; "Isn't this point inconsistent with what you said earlier?"; "Watch out for fragments and run-on sentences"; "The main point of this essay is not clear." Still others, eager to help the student tell his/her story as compellingly as possible, will suggest rephrasings and restructurings.

As you and your community talk through your own position on appropriate help, keep in mind the central importance of the student speaking in her/his own voice. No matter what the level of help, it should never result in the student speaking in a voice other than his/her own: first, because the student is verifying that all the work on the application is his/hers and, second, because inappropriate help short-circuits the very important developmental work that can take place through thoughtful and authentic creation of the essay. If we help too much, we have failed the students as teachers and as counselors.

RULES OF CONFIDENTIALITY

Occasionally, the student will reveal personal information in the essay that will compel the counselor to step out of the college counseling role and act decisively to safeguard a student's health and well-being. In keeping with the ground rules of confidentiality, if the essay indicates that the student or someone else is in danger of being injured, the counselor should consult the appropriate authorities in the school or school district. Indeed, counselors should verse themselves completely in school policies regarding student conduct and safety so that, should a student essay contain alarming information, there will be no doubts about how to proceed.

QUESTIONS FOR REFLECTION: FINAL ADVICE TO THE STUDENTS THEMSELVES

Since we have spent the lion's share of this chapter arguing that the college essay needs to be a student-centered

and student-driven enterprise, it seems only right that we direct some thoughts to the students themselves.

What follows are some questions and advice that students might want to consider as they give their essays a final review and then an exhortation for the students to stay true to themselves.

- Does this essay sound like me? What will the reader know about me by the end of the essay? What, ultimately, do I want the reader to know?

- Above all else, initial jitters aside, you really do want to write for yourself. Counselors, teachers, parents, and other well-meaning adults may have strong opinions about what you should or should not write, and there is nothing wrong with weighing the relevance of some of these opinions. But, remember, this is your story, no one else's. You want colleges to accept you as you are, not as someone else thinks you should be. There is integrity and a grounding comfort in staying true to yourself. Long after this process is over, you will draw strength from having managed important tasks like the essay on your own terms. And that strength will give you the resilience and the confidence to meet the challenges and difficulties in later life. Barbara Hofer, a professor at Middlebury College (VT), found that the degree of ownership students took in the college process correlated directly with their success in college. In other words, if you make the essay and the rest of the application yours, you stand a much better chance of flourishing in college and beyond.

When asked why he wrote, John Updike, the great American novelist, essayist and poet, replied that he had stories that only he could tell and that, if he didn't tell them, they would never be told; no one would know them. Students would do well to embrace that same sense of responsibility and urgency when writing the college essay. Each student has within him/her stories that only she/he can tell. Colleges are eager to hear those stories. To students who say, "I don't have any stories" or "I can't think of anything," we say, "Strap on that metacognitive work gear and start digging. The stories are there; you just need to spend more time getting to know yourself."

The college essay cannot be dismissed as a one-off event for the college process. As suggested before, the complementary abilities to know oneself and to tell one's story are *life skills*. They are the abilities that, properly and vigorously exercised, lead to maturity and wisdom. This work is not easy work; it will require industry, ingenuity, humility, resilience, stamina, and patience. There will be dead-ends, false starts, days when the student might despair of ever getting anything worthwhile written. But, thinking back to Michael Thompson's rite of passage, isn't that the way it's supposed to be? The most satisfying journeys are often the most challenging ones. The meaningfulness of a rite of passage depends in no small measure on the difficulty of the trials it asks the young quester to endure. In so many ways, the college essay can be one of those meaningful trials. How often have we, as counselors, seen a student wrestle and wrestle with an essay topic, refusing to give it up but never quite bringing it to any kind of compelling expression, only to witness the light in that student's eyes when all of a sudden she/he recognizes the true story she/he wants to tell? That moment of recognition would not have happened without the student enduring those earlier frustrations. And in that moment, that exciting time of coming-to-self, we see Thompson's failed rite of passage being set right.

About the Author

Rod Skinner is currently director of college counseling at Milton Academy in Milton, Massachusetts. In his 30+ years in secondary education, he has worked at schools in Boston, Connecticut, California, and Florida. Rod has also chaired the Admission Practices Committee for the National Association for College Admission Counseling, and served five years on the board of the Common Application. While in Florida, he directed the SACAC Summer Institute for Secondary School Counselors for ten years. Presently, Rod teaches on the faculty of the Harvard Summer Institute on College Admissions, presents at a number of conferences annually, chairs the Oversight and Advisory Committees at The Mountain School in Vershire, Vermont, and serves on the board of trustees for Boston Collegiate Charter School.

References

Andrade, H., & Valtcheva, A. (2009). Promoting learning and achievement through self assessment. *Theory into Practice, 48*(1), 12–19. Retrieved from *http://www.jstor.org/stable/40071571*.

Brooks, K. (2010). *You majored in what?: Mapping your path from chaos to career.* New York: Viking.

Buhner, S.H. (2010). *Ensouling language: On the art of nonfiction and the writer's life.* Rochester, VT: Inner Traditions.

Conley, D. (2013, January 22). Rethinking the notion of 'non-cognitive.' *Education Week.*

Damon, W. (2009). *Path to purpose: How young people find their calling in life.* New York: Free Press.

Dweck, C. (2007). *Mindset: The new psychology of success.* New York: Ballantine Books.

Duckworth, A. (2009). Self-discipline is empowering. *Phi Delta Kappan, 90*(7), 536. doi: 10.1177/003172170909000720

Flavell, J.H. (1979). Metacognition and cognitive monitoring: A new area of cognitive-developmental inquiry. *American Psychologist, 34*(10), 906–911. Retrieved from *http://jwilson.coe.uga.edu/EMAT7050/Students/Wilson/Flavell%20(1979).pdf*.

Goldberg, N. (2014). *The true secret of writing: Connecting life with language.* New York: Simon & Schuster.

Goldberg, N. (1990). *Wild mind: Living the writer's life.* New York: Bantam Books.

Goldberg, N. (2005). *Writing down the bones: Freeing the writer within.* Boston and London: Shambhala.

Jen, G. (2013). *Tiger writing: Art, culture, and the interdisciplinary self.* Cambridge, MA: Harvard University Press.

Hofer, B, & Moore, A. (2011). *The iConnected parent: Staying close to your kids in college (and beyond) while letting them grow up.* New York: Simon & Schuster.

Lamott, A. (1995). *Bird by bird: Some instructions on writing and life.* New York: Anchor Books.

Rosenblatt, R. (2011). *Unless it moves the human heart: The craft and art of writing.* New York: HarperCollins Publishing.

Schraw, G. (1998). Promoting general metacognitive awareness. *Instructional Science, 26,* 113–125. Retrieved from *http://wiki.biologyscholars.org/@api/deki/files/87/=schraw1998-meta.pdf.*

Seligman, M. (2006). *Learned optimism: How to change your mind and your life.* New York: Vintage Books.

Tough, P. (2013). *How children succeed: Grit, resilience, and the hidden power of character.* New York: Houghton Mifflin Harcourt.

Weissbourd, R. (2010). *The parents we mean to be: How well-intentioned parents undermine children's moral and emotional development.* Boston and New York: Houghton Mifflin Harcourt.

Zinsser, W. (1976). *On writing well: The classic guide to writing nonfiction.* New York: HarperCollins Publishing.

Zinsser, W. (2005). *Writing about your life: A journey into the past.* New York: Marlowe and Company.

APPENDIX: EVALUATING A COLLEGE VISIT

Name of college _____ Date visited _____

Special circumstances affecting the visit ("There was a blizzard," "I had a stomach bug," "I was visiting a family friend," etc.) _____

Names of people to remember (tour guide, interviewer, admission officer, professor, etc.) _____
_____

Distinctive features of the school (What is it promoting about itself? What is it most proud of?) _____
_____

Academic programs (strong majors, popular classes, classes I would love), including any special programs (engineering, architecture, dance, etc.) _____
_____

Core or General Education requirements (foreign language, math, science); possibility of double major or minor, pre-professional advising (pre-med, pre-law, pre-business) _____
_____

Career counseling (Does the school help students find internships, jobs? Where do graduates go?) _____
_____

Appeal of the physical campus (buildings, grounds, neighborhood, dorms, facilities for art, athletics, etc.) _
_____
_____

Off-campus opportunities (Does the surrounding town/city offer additional social outlets, internship opportunities or cultural opportunities that students take advantage of?) _____
_____

Extracurricular programs in my areas of interest _____
_____

Quality of life (food, housing, social activities, community spirit, etc.) _____
_____

Students (Are they happy? Energized? Are they academically motivated? Are there students like me here? Would I fit in?) _____
_____

Relationships among students, and between students, faculty and administrators? (What are "hot topics" on campus? Do people talk about tension, recent changes, problems?) _____
_____

Admission profile (important criteria, testing requirements, essay topics, etc.) _____
_____

My general impressions (both positive and negative) _____
_____

❑ Definitely on my college list   ❑ Maybe on my list   ❑ Off my list

V. Advancing Our Work

FROM OPERATION TO COOPERATION

Todd M. Laudino

Previous content sections in *Fundamentals* have provided an overview of the college counseling landscape, described and analyzed the role of the college counselor, and illuminated the various pathways to higher education. The fourth section was composed of chapters describing how the college counselor works with diverse student populations, including strategies for serving students and their families.

Authors challenged traditional methods of working with marginalized student populations, first-generation students and students with learning disabilities by presenting the latest research on college opportunities for each of these populations. Each chapter also included practical strategies for assisting students in the college preparation and application process. The second half of section four also emphasized the importance of student-centered college counseling. Authors described modes of counseling delivery, including outside resources and social media, as well as strategies for assisting students in writing the college essay. The chapters in section four, intended to empower both the counselor and the students that he/she serves, provided a glimpse into the work of college counselors.

The final section of *Fundamentals* includes those chapters that discuss furthering the work of college counselors in and outside of the classroom, while also anticipating the future needs of students and their families. To ensure continued access to and success in higher education for our students, college counselors must remain cognizant of the emerging educational needs of our society, while keeping both feet firmly planted in the present.

Authors in section five discuss additional opportunities to engage students and their families, including a discussion of early college awareness programs that promote exploration without the immediate pressure of the application process in chapter 22. Chapter 23 focuses on creating partnerships outside of school by identifying allies in the community, including colleges or universities, parents and community-based organizations. Empowering local stakeholders to take on roles in college access and success affords students additional support throughout the transition into higher education. Another method of support, discussed in chapter 24, is to continue working with students after graduation, specifically during the summer before attending college or university. *Fundamentals* closes with an engaging discussion about the future of higher education, and how continuing to provide our students with postsecondary opportunities requires partnerships with stakeholders in our children's education, coming from every facet of society.

The final section of *Fundamentals* emphasizes the importance of establishing partnerships and planning to address the future needs of students considering higher education options. In a postsecondary landscape increasingly shrouded by conversations about looming student debt and unemployment, it is helpful for students and their families to be equipped with timely and relevant knowledge to prepare them for the future. College counselors, utilizing deliberate communication and thoughtful collaboration, will continue to increase the higher education opportunities available to their students, both current and future.

Chapter 22:   The Early Years: Exploring Postsecondary Options in Middle and Elementary Schools

Robert Bardwell
@Bardwellr

Never before in the history of K–12 education has there been as much focus on postsecondary education from our leaders in Washington, DC as there has been recently.

We have heard from President Obama during his State of the Union Address in February 2009:

> And so tonight, I ask every American to commit to at least one year or more of higher education or career training. This can be community college or a four-year school; vocational training or an apprenticeship. But whatever the training may be, every American will need to get more than a high school diploma. And dropping out of high school is no longer an option. It's not just quitting on yourself, it's quitting on your country, and this country needs and values the talents of every American. That is why we will provide the support necessary for you to complete college and meet a new goal: by 2020, America will once again have the highest proportion of college graduates in the world. (Obama, B., 2009)

We have heard from First Lady Michelle Obama:

> Reach Higher is my new initiative, and it's about inspiring every student in America to take charge of their future by completing their education past high school—whether at a professional training program, or a community college, or a four-year university or college. Because while it's good news that high school graduation rates have climbed to their highest levels ever in this country, we also know that in today's world, a high school degree simply isn't enough. To get a good job, to compete, you have got to reach higher. (Obama, M., 2014)

And we have heard from Secretary of Education Arne Duncan:

> The release of the Common Core State Standards is an important step toward the improvement of quality education nationwide… As the nation seeks to maintain our international competitiveness, ensure all students, regardless of background, have access to a high-quality education, and prepare all students for college, work and citizenship, these standards are an important foundation for our collective work. (Duncan, 2010)

If we are ever to reach these goals, we have to start the postsecondary planning process much earlier than previously considered to be the right time. In the early days of developmental guidance programs, only high-school-level counselors were concerned with the postsecondary plans of our students—were they going to college, work or the military?

Research (Foster & Reeves, 1989; Fuchsen, 1989; Bialystok & Hakuta, 1994; Gilzow & Branaman, 2000) has shown that learning a second language is now best begun in the first few years of life, as it gives students enormous benefits in their cognitive development as well as in other aspects of their academic achievement. Thus, it is no longer acceptable to begin to learn a second language starting in high school. Using the same logic, then, we also must begin postsecondary career and college planning, goal setting and, perhaps most importantly, aspiration-building long before the high school years.

While the ASCA National Model (ASCA, 2012) calls for counselors at all levels to provide counseling and program support around three broad domains—academic, social/emotional and career—some middle and elementary school counselors historically were not interested, not trained and not involved with the career (or future planning) aspects of their work. Until now.

Current literature (Beyond the Rhetoric, 2010; Coming to Our Senses, 2008) is quite clear that our elementary and middle school students must be exposed to college-going ideas, information and awareness activities in order to aspire to attend college or postsecondary training opportunities. In many cases, the idea of higher education comes from the family and/or the community in which a student lives, but we can no longer only rely on those who live with or around our high school students to motivate the next generation to continue its education beyond high school.

The idea that new generations of high school graduates will surpass their parents' level of education has hit a plateau (Chen Delos, 2008). The recent downturn in the economy and widespread fears that college graduates complete their postsecondary training with huge debt and high unemployment has caused some families and communities to no longer encourage the next generation to reach higher than the previous one. While it is certainly true that college debt has surpassed the $1 trillion mark (Leonhardt, 2014), the average individual student loan debt hovers at $29,400 (Project on Student Debt, 2013) and some college graduates do face challenges in finding meaningful work, the average four-year college graduate will earn $21,000 more per year due to their postsecondary training. Additionally, the unemployment rate for college graduates in 2012 was 4.1 percent, compared to 11.2 percent for workers with only a high school diploma. College graduates are more likely to receive health insurance, volunteer in their communities, vote, and are less likely to smoke or be obese (Baum, Ma & Payea, 2013). The evidence is quite clear—higher education matters.

Therefore, it is critical that school counselors at all grade levels (Pre-K–12) possess knowledge of postsecondary educational opportunities—college, vocational training programs, employment, and military. This is no longer optional, and if elementary and middle school counselors choose not to provide this much-needed information to students and families, it borders on negligence. As the African proverb so aptly states, "It takes a village to raise a child," and to help more students reach their post-high-school goals, counselors at all levels are essential parts of that village.

A note of caution is required when we talk about beginning the college process earlier. A great number of educators, school counselors and policy makers become weary whenever we engage students in college planning activities earlier in their lives, as this can undoubtedly create additional stress and angst for both the student and their family. Let's be clear that there is a difference between awareness and aspirational activities and actually researching and apply to college. Elementary- and middle-school-level students need to know what their postsecondary options are, why getting a degree or certificate after high school is important for their future and that postsecondary options do exist for all students, regardless of their current financial situation or life circumstances. The key here is awareness and exploration. Elementary and middle school students do not need to have a college list nor finalize what they want to study that early. The post-high-school planning process is very much develop-

mental, and, for most students, time and additional life experiences help them to formulate the specifics of their actual plan. However, if these students never aspire to graduate and go beyond high school, then they may be relegated to low-paying, low-skill jobs that will inevitably impact their future lives, and most likely in a negative way.

It is absolutely necessary for educators or individuals involved in early college awareness activities to help explain to both students and family members that talking about college at an earlier age is perfectly fine, as it helps students begin to investigate options and explore ideas. But we are not going to thrust applications or financial aid applications in their faces at an early age and expect them to be completed. Instead, the focus should be on implementing developmentally appropriate activities along the way that help raise awareness and knowledge, yet without creating a hysteria that certain tasks and decisions must be made earlier.

THE ROLE OF SCHOOL COUNSELORS IN ELEMENTARY AND MIDDLE SCHOOLS IN PREPARING ALL STUDENTS FOR POSTSECONDARY SUCCESS

Creating a college-going culture early in a student's educational career is essential to ensuring he or she actually enrolls and persists later on. While there are numerous other factors that will ultimately determine success once there, one thing is clear: early awareness and exposure is critical in their postsecondary planning process.

Elementary and middle school counselors are well trained to specifically address several factors that lead to success later in school and ultimately prepare for success in postsecondary pursuits. In this section, we will deal specifically with topics that should be part of every middle school comprehensive developmental school counseling program. As a result, each topic should be integrated into large group, classroom, small group, or individual school counselor-led activities. Families and the community at-large should also be included in programs when appropriate. If possible, and to whatever degree appropriate, some can also be included in an elementary school program, but would obviously have to be adapted to the age and skill level of the students.

ACADEMIC STUDY SKILLS AND BELIEFS THAT PROMOTE ACADEMIC EXCELLENCE

The focus on academics is perhaps the most time-consuming issue for most middle school counselors as pre-adolescents enter into a world of several changes. They begin to exert their independence both in and outside of school and perhaps no longer wish to follow the rules or lose their motivation. For some, they begin to encounter material that may be more challenging and do not have the strategies or coping mechanisms to adequately deal with the changes. Middle school students also typically have to deal with multiple teachers rather than a single classroom teacher, which is the model found in most elementary schools. This can create more opportunity for personality conflicts and difficulty balancing the rules with their desire to chart their own course. As a result, all of these factors can lead students to a point where support is needed.

Traditional middle school counseling programs that consist of classroom-based lessons about study skills, organizational skills, note-taking, and test preparation will be most helpful to students at this level. Counselors may want to consider using evidenced-based curricula like Student Success Skills (*http://www.studentsuccesssskills.com*) which have been thoroughly researched and are proven to have a positive impact on student achievement. Home-grown curricula can also be effective, but counselors should ensure that proper pre- and post-testing occurs to determine if students are benefiting from the time and material being taught.

With the adoption of the Common Core State Standards (CCSS) by the vast majority of states, it becomes even more critical for school counselors to take the lead in promoting academic excellence (Hatch, 2014; Achieve, 2012). Specific recommendations that align with the CCSS will be discussed later in the curriculum section, but suffice it to say that counselors should be leading the charge when it comes to Common Core integration and alignment. Putting politics aside, as not all will agree with the Common Core vision, the tagline of the Common Core states "Preparing America's Students for College and Career," which is certainly school counselor turf.

It should also be noted that there is a growing body of evidence (Sedlacek, 2005; Kamentz & Keane, 2012) that focuses on the non-cognitive traits that help students aspire to, attend and find success in college. Things like motivation, perseverance, social capital, and goals often can play a huge role in whether students can find success in their postsecondary pursuits. Counselors at all levels should certainly be aware of the role these factors play in student success and postsecondary education attainment, especially since some of the factors should be topics included in the school counseling curriculum and instruction. The work of Angela Duckworth relating to grit— "the combination of perseverance and passion that leads to a relentless pursuit of goals" (Duckworth)—is another hot topic generating lots of interest in the world of higher education as more focus is placed on a student's internal goals and motivation for success rather than his or her academic credentials.

VALUES, ATTITUDES AND INTERESTS AS PART OF CAREER AWARENESS, EXPLORATION AND LIFE PLANNING PREPARATION

Middle school is an ideal time to begin the process of exploring careers and postsecondary options in a more formal and intentional way. There are dozens of age-appropriate counselor/teacher-led lessons that allow students the opportunity to learn critical information about the world of work, set future goals and determine how to achieve those goals (see Resources section for links to sample lessons).

Currently, 23 states have mandated career or student learning plans (SLP) or portfolios for all students starting in middle school (Rennie Center, 2011). Creating a portfolio provides the opportunity for students to discuss with a counselor or staff person what their interests are, set future-oriented goals and create methods to accomplish their goals, all of which are then written into the plan. In schools where mandated plans are not in place, counselors can create a school-based portfolio system. It can be as simple as a folder where a student's career planning assessments or documents are stored and then follows a student into high school. More sophisticated plans consist of preprinted folders or worksheets that require initial completion, followed by regular (at least annually) updates. Digital or online portfolios are also becoming more popular. Electronic portfolios allow a student, staff person and even a family member to access the information electronically and require no physical storage or maintenance, but do require a student to have computer access to update and utilize the information contained within it. The key to any successful portfolio system, hard copy or online, is that it must be regularly updated and utilized or else it becomes a wasted opportunity.

In many states, one-stop online portals also exist to assist middle (and high) school students with their career and college exploration. North Carolina (*cfnc.org*), Massachusetts (*www.yourplanforthefuture.org*) and Missouri (*missouriconnections.org*) are examples of state portals where students (and others) can create accounts to assist with their career and college search activities at no cost. Similar to the portfolios outlined above, these Web sites have numerous resources and activities for students, all of which provide critical information to move the student closer to making decisions about his or her future work and postsecondary training needs.

Ideally, any of these portfolio-based systems should be incorporated into developmentally appropriate, comprehensive school counseling programs and integrated fittingly into grade-level curriculum. A well-developed plan to integrate such activities into existing school counseling curriculum or subject matter (e.g., English) curriculum is necessary. Such educational activities should not be haphazardly provided to students or, worse yet, given to some but not to others. As students get older, the activities should build upon the work they did previously.

CURRICULUM PLANNING, COURSE SELECTION AND FUTURE COURSE OF STUDY

The idea that students can choose classes they want in high schools and in some middle schools is perhaps a foreign concept for most since their early education has been prescribed for them. While there are certainly required courses and credits to earn a diploma, high school students have a great deal of latitude in most cases to pick courses they want or in what year they will take them. Knowing which courses to take and in what year to take them is critical for college admission and success after high school. While modifications can be made to an academic plan along the way, the best bet is to get it right the first time to avoid problems later on.

Take, for example, a student who wishes to become an engineer. Taking Algebra I in eighth grade (if available) is critical so he can complete the appropriate math sequence in early high school (e.g., Geometry, Algebra II, Pre-Calculus, and Calculus or some similar pathway). Not taking the right course in the right year could prove problematic when trying to reach that goal directly out of high school. Planning ahead is absolutely critical in such cases.

Most middle school students are simply unable to plan so far ahead, especially if they do not know what career they want later in life. The best a counselor can hope for is to provide awareness and resources so when they are ready to make such decisions, they know where to go for help. Middle school counselors also know that once in high school, students may be further along in their decision-making process, so choices in high school regarding course selection should be easier. In many cases, students also need to be exposed to material several times, so starting in middle school and continuing into high school will hopefully provide the consistency necessary to remember the information and act accordingly when the time comes.

EXPLORING ALL POSTSECONDARY OPTIONS

While the majority of this chapter is about college options, it is critical for middle school students to be exposed to all options after high school. It is important for students who are not interested in traditional college options, at least not right away, to hear about the other options upon high school graduation—vocational training, apprenticeships, employment options, or military service.

As discussed elsewhere in this chapter, counselors and providers should make an effort to be inclusive in their language around postsecondary options. While it is acceptable to provide classroom lessons and activities solely focused on college, it is critical to explain to students that there will be other activities/lessons about the other options after high school. It would also then be appropriate to plan activities that focus on military, work or vocational training. Such activities will certainly expose all students to ideas and things they may not know, which can only help them.

PAYING FOR COLLEGE

This is perhaps the biggest challenge for middle school counselors for several reasons. One is that counselors typically feel the least confident in topics related to paying for college (College Board, 2011). Beyond that, most middle school students and families are not interested in talking about this subject, thinking that this is something they will deal with later and is not urgent. Some are so overwhelmed by the anticipated cost of college that they simply cannot handle the subject. Unfortunately, ignoring the subject does not make it go away, but instead just transforms what could be a manageable task into an overwhelming burden as the students get closer to graduation.

Counselors should provide very basic information for students and families. They do not have to be experts on the subject, but can educate and refer to specially trained college financing experts. Helping families understand the need to begin planning early is perhaps the most important lesson here. So is helping students understand how the financial aid process works and that some students are able to pay little to nothing for college depending upon the family financial situation and institution at which they enroll. Learning about scholarships and the impact that one's grades have on securing merit and need-based aid is an important lesson to teach to students prior to enrolling in high school. Like early career exploration and awareness, learning the basics of college financing early in the process is equally important.

OTHER CONSIDERATIONS

Of course school counselors provide services to all students, but it must be noted that some students need more support from school staff. This is particularly the case with some traditionally underrepresented groups—low-income, students of color, first-generation, and students with disabilities. In some cases, the school counselor is the only adult in a child's life to provide these underrepresented students with college-going information (Cabrera & LaNasa, 2000). A recent report (2013) by ACT found that while 95 percent of low-income family students aspired to attend postsecondary education, only 59 percent actually enrolled, compared to 87 percent and 71 percent of all test takers. Furthermore, only 69 percent of low-income ACT-tested students took the recommended core curriculum (as compared to 84 percent of high-income students), and only 20 percent of the students met at least three of the four ACT College Readiness Benchmarks,

compared to 62 percent of all test takers. Clearly, a disconnect exists.

While providing additional support for these students requires more work on top of a myriad of endless paperwork, duties and other mandated tasks, our students deserve the opportunity to be advantaged. The problem lays in that the national average public school student-to-counselor ratio in 2010–11 was 471:1, and public school counselors spend an average of only 23 percent of their time on postsecondary education counseling. Private school counselors had a student ratio of 278:1 and spent 53 percent of their time on postsecondary counseling activities. Counselors at higher income schools had both lower caseloads and were able to spend more time delivering postsecondary counseling services (NACAC, 2014). Another study (Radford & Ifill, 2013) found that only 18 percent of freshmen had spoken to their counselor about college, as compared to teachers (21 percent), friends (53 percent) and parents (63 percent for fathers and 77 percent for mothers). It is clearly problematic if the person in the school who should have the most knowledge about college is the least likely person students talk to about college knowledge and options.

While we talk of high student-counselor caseloads, expectations to complete non-counselor duties and the inability to make meaning of their work, school counselors should hold out hope that things are changing. In June 2014, Secretary of Education Arne Duncan sent a letter to the chief education officer in each state. In part it read:

> As educators across the country work to empower all students to meet the academic and career preparation demands of the 21st century, the role of school counselors has never been more important. School counselors are often the vital link between students' aspirations for the future and tangible opportunities for postsecondary success. They are also particularly important for our neediest students, who require expert and accessible guidance as they navigate a challenging and complicated college admissions and career preparation landscape. (Duncan, 2014)

This letter was followed by a speech by First Lady Michelle Obama at the American School Counselor Association's annual conference and a historic gathering of school counseling leaders, practitioners, counselor educators, policy makers, researchers, community-based organizations, and funders, all of whom were interested to learn more about the White House Reach Higher initiative. More high-level meetings and work remains to position school counselors in their rightful place to help all students reach postsecondary goals, but at least the conversations are beginning.

However, until change occurs at the national level regarding the role of school counselors, those at the local level must continue to provide the services and opportunities we know will help students achieve their postsecondary goal—regardless of the barriers that exist.

THE ROLE OF ALL ELEMENTARY AND MIDDLE SCHOOL STAFF IN CREATING EARLY AWARENESS AND EXPLORATION OPPORTUNITIES

While school counselors should be the key staff members in a school to coordinate and encourage early college activities, they are just one piece of the puzzle. After all, some elementary and middle schools have no counselors whatsoever, and, if they do, they often are solely focused on the social/emotional needs of the students. The last thing they have time to do is take on preventative or forward-thinking work. All staff, from administrators to teachers to support staff (clerical, custodial, cafeteria), should be engaged in efforts to raise awareness and deliver opportunities that expose students to the college-going agenda.

Let's break early awareness activities into the following categories (loosely constructed around McClafferty & McDonough's [2002] nine critical principles of a college culture). Each will warrant further discussion and conversation.

- College talk and aspirations

- Curriculum (both for school counselors and classroom teachers)

- Faculty and student activities

- Family engagement

- College partnerships

COLLEGE TALK AND ASPIRATIONS

The human species has an incredible gift—to be able to communicate with a rich vocabulary that we use extensively to share information and ideas. Early goal-setting is an incredibly important task (Savitz-Romer, 2012; Gilkey, Seburn & Conley, 2011; Hossler et al., 1999; Savitz-Romer & Bouffard, 2012; Choy, 2001), one that gives all individuals, both young and old, the opportunity to plan. While some believe that this is a personality trait that comes easier to some than to others, everyone should be able to set goals, even if only for the short-term. In order to plan ahead, there has to be conversation and discussion to plant the seeds of what opportunities lay ahead. If a child is never exposed to what a nurse does, for example, how can he aspire to be one? Of course, motivation plays a huge role in one's ability to follow through on goal achievement, but no good goal happens without pre-thought and planning.

Creating a college-going culture is more than just implementing a curriculum or implementing activities to get students to think about postsecondary training. There must be a belief that the students can, should and will go on to college or other training. Education does not stop at high school graduation. When the adults in a child's world do not believe that postsecondary training is or should be an option, then a belief gap exists that is hard, if impossible, to overcome. School-based employees must believe that all students are capable and will continue their education. Some believe that school employees are the single most important factor impacting student achievement. Believing in a child's future educational aspiration does not mean that he or she will go—the child may not be ready for some time—but helping to create a vision, setting a goal and formulating a plan to achieve the goal are essential for all students to believe that college is an option for them.

School staff must be careful not to let their own beliefs or biases influence their belief that a student is or is not college material or capable of postsecondary success. No judgments or assumptions should be made. For example, if a child is on free/reduced lunch or is homeless, that child should be given the same opportunities as a more privileged child. While he may face additional barriers to postsecondary education, there are no limits to his options.

- Use local college/university names for grade level team names, small breakout curriculum groups, advisory groups, or physical education team names.

- Invite alumni of the elementary or middle school to return to speak to students about their experiences during and after college. This could be very similar to a career day program, but speakers would be sure to highlight the fact that he/she attended that very school and is now successful in their current career in part due to their college degree.

- Be a role model by sharing your life story when appropriate. Talk about one's challenges, barriers, successes, and opportunities in both higher education and employment experiences.

- Use inclusive language in the school environment. Don't make assumptions that students will or will not go to college. Talk about all postsecondary options—work, further training (college or vocational) or military. Treat all the same so as not to be viewed as biased.

CURRICULUM

It could be argued that, every day, teachers and counselors are helping students reach higher education, simply because of the curriculum being taught. But we should take this idea one step further by encouraging faculty or others who impact what is being taught in the classroom to consider other ways to make connections. Such ideas can be simple and matter-of-fact or can involve major discussion and debate among stakeholders as to what should be taught.

- The recent national debate about the Common Core State Standards (CCSS) is by far the most heated debate in public education in some time. Regardless of one's view, it is imperative that students be exposed to a rigorous and challenging curriculum that adequately prepares all students for career and college success. Suffice it to say, educators who assist in developing and who are responsible for delivering a curriculum must ensure that the curriculum will give the students the necessary skills for future success. If barriers exist to either delivering or understanding the curriculum, discussion among peers and district leaders must occur

in order to seek solutions. Simply ignoring or passing the problem to the next year's staff is not an option.

- The adoption of the CCSS now requires earlier exposure to Algebra (among other things) to all middle school students. It is therefore essential for elementary and middle school leaders, counselors and faculty to align the curriculum appropriately to allow students early exposure and mastery of algebra, as that has often been a benchmark barrier. Trusty & Niles (2003) and Adelman (2006) found that taking courses in high school beyond Algebra 2 increased the likelihood of completing a college degree. Another study (Choy, 2001) found that students whose parent had a college degree were more likely (55 vs. 34 percent) to take Algebra prior to ninth grade. Additionally, students who took advanced math classes in high school were 32 percent more likely to enroll in college four years later if their parents had a bachelor's degree. With all of the resources, information and knowledge about the importance of math, we have to ensure that our middle school students are given the proper math instruction and sequence.

- Incorporate literature, information or fun facts into the curriculum that ties to colleges/universities, especially ones that are in close proximity or that have an established partnership. When teaching geography, use college campus maps to learn basic geography skills (e.g., directions, streets, scale, and distance). In math class, use college names and vocabulary in word problems.

- When discussing entertainers, sporting icons, business leaders, artists, authors, politicians, or other important individuals being studied, teachers can easily integrate where the individual went to school into the conversation.

- Have a discussion with the class about the difference between a name-brand school and lesser known schools. This can also lead into stereotypes and values of certain types of schools (e.g., four-year college vs. vocational school). Challenge their assumptions and beliefs, especially if they are biased or uninformed.

- Incorporate college ideas and information into journal writing or other assignments, particularly when they can be tied to current events or other activities within the current content. Say, for example, when students are being taught to write a business letter, the letter can be addressed and sent to a college admission office, requesting to be added to the mailing list or to have information sent to the student.

- Create online scavenger hunts with incentives or prizes where students have to seek information about a variety of colleges and postsecondary training options. Produce crossword puzzles, word search or other game-like activities containing college-related names or information. Use them as assignments for downtime or when there is a substitute or make them part of a career unit or school counselor lessons.

- Counselors who have regular access to students through their classroom counseling curriculum should hold students to the same standards of reading and writing that other staff in the school maintain. This not only gives students practice in the desired skill, but also puts the counseling staff on a level playing field (as much as possible) when it comes to academic expectations of the students. If there are generally acceptable lesson formats used by the teaching faculty, then counselors should be doing the same. Do now, bell work, activators, ticket to leave or think, pair, share type activities should replicate other classrooms throughout the school.

FACULTY AND STUDENT ACTIVITIES

The faculty at any school do more than just deliver curriculum. They are the heart and soul of the educational institution. In addition to the day-to-day teaching and learning responsibilities, faculty can do much to support the counselor-led or whole school initiatives to help children aspire to college or postsecondary training. And in many cases, such activities require little to no effort on their part.

- On designated days, faculty and staff can wear their college gear—a T-shirt, sweatshirt or hat with the name of their alma mater. This can be done, say, on a monthly basis (e.g., fourth Friday of the month) or can be done in conjunction with special events or activities (e.g., college signing day or as part of College Application Week).

- Have a class adopt a college, and then wear the appropriate school colors for school assemblies or other activities.

- Faculty members regularly share information with their students about the college that they attended, their experience at college and how that experience impacted their life.

- Have faculty members create, along with their students, handmade pennants with the name of the college/university that they attended. Give students the opportunity to look down the road and create a pennant of their own. Have faculty then hang their pennant outside their door in the hallway so all who enter can see what school they attended.

- Create a college-of-the-day or college-of-the-week program in which one institution (either locally or regionally) gets highlighted through announcements, window or bulletin board displays, and contests. Start with colleges that school staff attended so that information builds a connection and awareness off that institution.

- Ask staff members to bring in a picture of themselves wearing their cap and gown from their alma mater and display it with inspirational captions and messages.

- Create bulletin board or hallway displays that celebrate college and post-high-school educational opportunities. Students could bring in their own pictures from pre-school or elementary school programs or from sporting or other camp type events. Encourage students to bring in pictures of their family members or friends who have completed some sort of training program. Ensure all students have at least one picture to contribute to the display and help those who do not draw or create one on a computer.

- Create a cardboard life-size drawing of a student in a cap and gown with space cut out for a face. Then write the words "Future Graduate of _____." Then have each student write out where they want to graduate from, whether it be middle or high school or a college. Take a picture of each student in the class, and then make an appropriate display to celebrate their future graduation plans.

- Organize a door decorating contest among classrooms, grades or groups. Have each group/class decorate a door with critical information about a school of their choice, which encourages creativity and team building. Create a rubric for judging, and award prizes for top scorers.

- Play games. Numerous well-known games exist that focus on postsecondary educational options. Bingo, trivia, Jeopardy, Who Wants to Be a College Student? and the GPA game are some that can easily be adapted to any grade level. In addition to being fun, such games provide an opportunity to learn new college lingo and vocabulary. (Samples can be found on the NACAC Web site. See Resource section for Web link.)

Family Engagement

As will be discussed later in this chapter, families are certainly critical to ensuring that students aspire to go to, enroll in and successfully complete college. However, there are still specific activities that can be planned for our elementary and middle school students and their families.

- Coordinate developmentally appropriate educational programs for parents and other family members. However, this can be rather tricky, because some family members do not believe they need this information so early in their child's education. For example, planning a program about financing a college education, while very important for families to hear early in the elementary years, may not be well-attended because people do not believe they need that help. Instead, plan a fun event, say, a student-led curriculum night, and find an opportunity to briefly talk to the group about planning for life after high school and the financing options that families have. Provide them with information and local providers who can help navigate the early financial planning process. Be sure to offer such programs at times convenient to most families. Repeat the program multiple times if necessary.

- Host a family potluck dinner program highlighting speakers (faculty, staff and students) or activities relating to college. Make it fun and entertaining, and combine this with other initiatives to maximize attendance and participation.

- Invite family members to tour the local college campus. If there are students whose family members either attend or work on campus, have them help with the tour and activity in whatever way is possible.

- Lead focus groups with parents, extended family members and community representatives to discuss ways to involve the college in the school, whether that is through curriculum activities, programs or outreach. Personally invite parents who work at local college(s), encouraging them to bridge communication efforts and assist with planned activities.

College Partnerships

In addition to K–12 educators now getting on board, realizing that early awareness activities do matter and are critical to the success of enrolling potential students upon graduation from high school, college admission officers and college administrators also realize that they must be engaging students and families (appropriately) at a younger age. Therefore, colleges will often provide funding and support in an effort to be more involved with elementary and middle school students, raising awareness and opening doors.

Here are some ways to enter into partnerships with colleges/universities that will benefit both parties:

- Take students on a tour of a local college where they can visit classrooms, dining halls, sports arenas, and dormitories. Engage students in hands-on activities within classrooms, and talk to faculty about what they teach and how they help students reach their career goals. Have the college create a scavenger hunt game that encourages students to pay attention to details along the way. Award prizes (college T-shirts, pencils, notebooks) for the individuals or groups that get the most correct answers.

- Create a speakers bureau or career-day-type program where professors and other staff from the local college visit the school to share information and their expertise on a specific topic.

- Adopt a local college sports team(s). Write letters/emails to the coaches and players. Use the newspaper/Internet to do research about their wins/losses and incorporate that into math lessons. Invite the coaches and players to come to speak to the students. Take a field trip to watch the team play a home game. Limited funding? Ask families to assist with transportation or a local business or the college itself to fund transportation. On a national level, create activities related to the NCAA March Madness Basketball tournament, football playoffs or College World Series.

- Look into what research local college professors are doing, perhaps in your city or town. Make connections to the curriculum and invite the professor, researchers or college students to speak to the class about the project. For example, say the local college is examining why a regional lake is polluted. Have the science teacher integrate this into the curriculum, and then have your students participate directly in the project. Invite college representatives involved to talk about specifics.

- Invite college faculty to speak to middle and high school faculty about curriculum, specifically math and English, areas where students may find themselves challenged with placement tests and college-level work. Discuss ways that K–12 educators can ensure that high school graduates are better prepared to enter college.

- Investigate if articulation agreements exist with local colleges for high school students who complete specific courses. While certain Advanced Placement (AP) scores will often earn high school graduates college credit or exemptions from certain classes, colleges can do the same thing for numerous other classes in which high school students demonstrate mastery of material (and thus can earn college credit or have introductory level classes exempted). The possibilities are endless, but require much discussion and effort to articulate the two curricula. Students benefit as a result of this collaboration, because the communication ensures both K–12 and college faculty are on the same page about what is being taught at both levels.

Engaging Families and Community in the Early Years

In addition to school counselors, teachers, administrators, and other school-based staff members sharing college-going ideas, information and awareness activities, families and communities at large also must maintain high standards and expectations that postsecondary education is critical to future success. While school counselors should be the point person inside a school to unlocking doors and discussing postsecondary educational opportunities for all students, the out-of-school influences on postsecondary education attainment can be even stronger. There are numerous cultural, socioeconomic, societal, and geographical factors that often determine whether a child has college aspirations and if they are able to pursue training beyond high school.

Let's talk first about the term "families" versus "parents." While all children have two biological parents, the fact is that today's families look very different from families a few generations ago. Today, we have a wide variety of family constellations, ranging from single-parent, same-sex, grandparents, or other extended family members, foster and adoptive. Using the term "parents" or "guardians" may be an inaccurate description, so the term "family" or "families," while more broad, is much more accurate.

Families and the individuals within the family are still the single most influential factor in determining whether a student goes on to further education (Bordua, 1960; Conklin & Ricks Dailey, 1981; Hossler, Schmit & Vesper, 1999; MacAllum et al. 2007; McDill & Coleman, J. 1965). This makes total sense, as the family teaches children things such as values, goals and aspirations and models behavior, expectations and lifestyles. A child whose primary caregiver never went to college and has a decent lifestyle may feel very differently about college than a child who lives at home with both parents who earned advanced degrees. A child in an immigrant family might have different expectations or pressures from the family compared to a child whose family is well established in the community.

From an early age, children pick up on expectations of them. Therefore, it is necessary for all family members to create expectations that some sort of education beyond high school is essential to success later in life. Some families will do better with this than others. Families who see a college degree as a way to a better life will have the expectation that the child(ren) will go to college. Those who believe that a college education is no longer the path to economic and personal prosperity and that the cost and sacrifice to the family is not worth it anymore will

Culture often plays a huge role in the level of familial support and extent of one's aspirations for higher education, so it is important for school personnel to understand the context from which a student comes (Chen-Hayes, 2012).

most likely not encourage their children to attend training right away. This does not mean that a child whose family is not supportive of higher education cannot attend college. It means that the child will have to find the motivation from within or from external sources and may find himself without emotional or financial support from the family.

Culture often plays a huge role in the level of familial support and extent of one's aspirations for higher education, so it is important for school personnel to understand the context from which a student comes (Chen-Hayes, 2012). Counselors at all levels must be culturally competent in order to ensure that students and families from all backgrounds and cultures are treated equitably. Holcomb-McCoy & Chen-Hayes (2011) discuss numerous ways for counselors to demonstrate cultural competence, including a self-assessment checklist of 91 items.

While some families will wholeheartedly support (and, in some cases, require) a child to go to college, others do not subscribe to the opinion that high school graduates should go on to postsecondary training. They will likely then withhold their emotional support and/or financial assistance for the child seeking higher education because they do not approve of the plan. Counselors should thus be attuned to the following issues as they relate to postsecondary opportunities:

- **Cultural norms**—Cultural beliefs and expectations often trump dominant mainstream beliefs about following postsecondary educational opportunities. For example, some families believe that girls should not go to college, but instead should get married and have a family. Other families have expectations that after graduation, the children will stay home and help care for the younger family members. To leave home to go to school, or even to commute, is considered selfish and disrespectful.

- **Work**—Some families expect students to get a job to help support the family financially. In some cases, this may happen before the student even graduates from high school.

- **Cost**—College is seen as a waste of money and time, despite evidence to the contrary that it can actually provide advantages to a student and his family. The end result is students who may not have the financial resources to attend college, and the financial aid system may be unable to assist, especially if the student is a dependent child.

- **Documentation status**—Some students who are not legal citizens or have family members who are undocumented may have challenges completing the admission and financial aid application process. Due to the fear of being discovered and deported, the student is not allowed to consider postsecondary options.

- **Religion**—Some religious faiths expect that high school graduates complete mandatory service obligations before enrolling in college.

EARLY AWARENESS RESOURCES FOR SCHOOL COUNSELORS AND STAFF

The good news for counselors and others interested in providing early college awareness is that now there are numerous resources available to assist in the effort. A sampling of resources include:

NACAC has developed numerous online resources for both members and nonmembers. Most appropriate for early awareness work is its *Step by Step: College Awareness and Planning for Families, Counselors and Communities*. Available at *www.nacacnet.org/research/PublicationsResources/Marketplace/student/Pages/GuidingEducation.aspx*, the *Step by Step* curricula includes middle school and early and late high school versions, as well

Educators and service providers who come into contact with elementary and middle school students must understand this critical role. This will ensure that our young people today will have the information and tools they need to reach whatever postsecondary degree or certificate they desire.

as resources for parents/guardians, including financial aid information. The NACAC Web site has many other free resources, including PowerPoint presentations, lesson plan materials and other helpful documents, some of which are available in Spanish. NACAC members have the added benefit of searching the Knowledge Center for hundreds of other sample documents, links and policy briefs, all with the sole purpose of providing material at one's fingertips to help students in the college search and application process.

NACAC also maintains a listserv for members and nonmembers to share ideas, resources and information. Called the Exchange, the electronic email-based system allows registered users to post a question seeking assistance or to share information. Posts can be received individually or in batches, either on a daily basis or in weekly digest version. Go to *www.nacacnet.org/learning/communities/ Exchange/Pages/default.aspx* for information about the Exchange and to sign up.

American School Counseling Association (ASCA) (*schoolcounselor.org*)—ASCA provides resources for school counselors across the grade span both in its online Resource Center, via webinars, and in person, via workshops and conferences. Most recently it has developed a College Admissions Specialist Certificate through its online ASCA U academy. Membership is required to access most resources, and fees apply for professional development programs.

Federal Department of Education—The federal government has numerous resources to help students and families navigate the college search and application process, as well as the financial aid process. Specifically for middle school students is a workbook entitled, *My Future, My Way: First Steps Toward College: A workbook for Middle and High School Students,* which includes information about types of colleges, careers, checklists, and

activities. *https://studentaid.ed.gov/resources and https:// studentaid.ed.gov/prepare-for-college*

KnowHow2Go.org—A Web site complete with many resources and a whole section dedicated to middle school students, including quizzes, virtual tours and financial aid information.

ECMC Foundation (*ecmcfoundation.org/details/believing.html*)—The ECMC Foundation's mission is to inspire and to facilitate improvements that affect educational outcomes—especially among underserved populations—through evidence-based innovation. Resources include several free, downloadable curricula and training guides, as well as scholarships and one-stop assistance centers in selected locations.

ACT (*act.org*)—ACT has extensive research on College and Career Readiness initiatives, the Common Core State Standards and college readiness benchmarks. Visitors have access to issue briefs, policy reports and case studies, as well as in-depth curriculum analysis and recommendations for K–12 personnel.

College Board (*collegeboard.org*)—The College Board has numerous resources for counselors to provide support for postsecondary education, including the Eight Components of College and Career Readiness (*nosca.collegeboard. org/eight-components*). Included for each component are specific action steps for students, for schools and districts, for parents/families, and within the community. Additionally available to download for free are level-specific (elementary, middle and high school) toolkits to assist school personnel to create a college-going culture across the K–12 span and close gaps that exist between underperforming/underrepresented students and those who traditionally have had easy access to postsecondary educational opportunities.

The *Pathways to College Online Library* (*pathwaysto-college.net*)—This free resource allows users to search a database of numerous publications, research reports and Web sites for resources to ensure college and career readiness for students at all grade levels.

CONCLUSION

It should be clearly evident that early exposure and awareness activities are essential to raising aspirations and ensuring that students who wish to pursue an education beyond high school have the knowledge and skills to do so. K–12 educators, including school counselors, the family and greater community, continue to be the factors that have the greatest influence on postsecondary attainment and success. Therefore, it is necessary for there to be intentional, thoughtful and age-appropriate preparation activities to engage and expose our children to the benefits of postsecondary education. Educators and service providers who come into contact with elementary and middle school students must understand this critical role. This will ensure that our young people today will have the information and tools they need to reach whatever postsecondary degree or certificate they desire.

DISCUSSION QUESTIONS

1. As a school counselor or service provider working with elementary or middle school students, what will you do differently now that you have this information about the importance of early exploration and awareness activities?

2. You are discussing goal setting and future planning with a seventh grade class. Yet, Joe is uninterested in what you are doing and tells you he is not going to college. What can you do to get him on task with the rest of the class?

3. As a middle school counselor, you have 482 students in your caseload. You struggle to meet the needs of all of them and do preventative work, especially around the career and college piece. What are three things that you can do relatively easily that you are not currently doing to engage students and teachers in conversation about making future plans?

4. You are a school counselor at Lucky You Elementary School. The principal calls you into her office and tells you that an anonymous donor has given $500 for an early college awareness program. You can have three school-wide assemblies that week and spend the $500 as you see fit. What are you going to do?

5. You are given permission to do only one program this year at your middle school on the topic of early awareness. What will it be, and why?

6. The PTA is interested in sponsoring a career and college awareness week program at your elementary school. You have spoken to the principal, Mr. I'm Notinterested in the past and he is opposed. The PTA president asks you to talk with Mr. I'm Notinterested. What do you do?

7. You are a counselor at Harmony High School. Despite your ongoing efforts to encourage early awareness activities in your feeder elementary and middle schools, you know the counselors organize little to no early college awareness activities. How could you get your middle and elementary school counterparts on board with early awareness activities?

ABOUT THE AUTHOR

Robert Bardwell is a school counselor and the director of school counseling at Monson Innovation High School (MA). He is a member of the Board of Directors of the American School Counselor Association (ASCA) and a past president of the Massachusetts School Counselors Association. He is a member of the Professional Development Committee of the National Association for College Admission Counseling (NACAC) and a past president of the New England Association for College Admission Counseling (NEACAC). He has served NACAC as both an assembly delegate and chair of its Ad Hoc Committee on Graduate Coursework.

He received his bachelor's degree from Springfield College (MA), his MEd from University of Massachusetts Amherst (MA) and his CAGS from American International College. He is an adjunct professor at Westfield State University (MA) and has published numerous articles and presented at more than 25 national conferences around the country and in 10 states.

References

Achieve. (2012). Implementing the common core standards: The role of the school counselor. Retrieved from *http://www.achieve.org/publications/implementing-common-core-state-standards-role-school-counselor-action-brief.*

ACT. (2013). The condition of college & career readiness 2013. Retrieved from *http://www.act.org/research/policymakers/cccr13.*

American School Counselor Association. (2012). *The ASCA national model: A framework for school counseling programs* (3rd ed.). Alexandria, VA: Author.

Bialystok, E., & Hakuta, K. (1994). *In other words: The science and psychology of second-language acquisition.* New York, NY: Basic Books.

Baum, S., Ma, J., & Payea, K. (2013). *Education pays 2013: The benefits of higher education for individuals and society.* Retrieved from *http://trends.collegeboard.org/sites/default/files/education-pays-2013-full-report-022714.pdf.*

Bordua, D. (1960). Educational aspirations and parental stress on college. *Social Forces, 38*(3), 262–269.

Cabrera, A., & LaNasa, S. (2000). *Understanding the college choice of disadvantaged students.* San Francisco, CA: Jossey-Bass.

Chen-Delos, R. (2008). Students Are No Longer Surpassing Parents' Educational Achievement. Retrieved from *http://diverseeducation.com/article/11803.*

Chen-Hayes, S.F. (2012). Empowering multiple identities in college readiness and admission. In National Association for College Admission Counseling (Ed.), *Fundamentals of college admission counseling* (pp. 150–170). Arlington, VA: National Association for College Admission Counseling.

Choy, S. (2001). *Students whose parents did not go to college: Post-secondary access, persistence, and attainment.* Retrieved from *http://nces.ed.gov/pubs2001/2001126.pdf.*

Clinedinst, M.E., Hurley, S.F., & Hawkins, D.A. (2013). *2013 State of College Admission Report.* Arlington, VA: National Association for College Admission Counseling.

College Board. (2008). *Coming to our senses: Education and the American future.* New York: Author.

College Board. (2011). *School counselors literature and landscape review: The state of school counseling in America.* New York: Author.

Conklin, M., & Ricks-Dailey, A. (1981). Does consistency of parental educational encouragement matter for secondary school students? *Sociology of Education, 54*(4), 254–262.

Duckworth, Angela L. (2009, November). True grit: Can perseverance be taught? Ted Talks.

Duncan, A. (2010, June 2). Statement on national governors association and state education chiefs common core standards. Retrieved from *http://www.ed.gov/news/press-releases/statement-national-governors-association-and-state-education-chiefs-common-core-.*

Duncan, A. (2014, June 30). Key policy letters from the Education Secretary and Deputy Secretary. Retrieved from *http://www2.ed.gov/policy/elsec/guid/secletter/140630.html.*

Foster, K. M., & Reeves, C. K. (1989). Foreign language in the elementary school (FLES) improves cognitive skills. *FLES News, 2*(3), 4.

Fuchsen, M. (1989). Starting language early: A rationale. *FLESNEWS, 2*(3):1, 6–7.

Gilkey, E., Seburn, M, & Conley, D.T. (2011). Student aspirations, background characteristics, and a four-part model of college and career readiness. Paper presented at American Research Association, New Orleans, LA. Retrieved from *https://www.epiconline.org/publications/student-aspirations-background-characteristics-and-a-four-part-model-of-college-readiness.*

Gilzow, D.F., & Branaman, L.E. (2000). *Lessons learned: Model early foreign language programs.* McHenry, IL: Delta.

Hatch, T. (2014). *The use of data in school counseling.* Thousand Oaks, CA: Corwin.

Holcomb-McCoy, C., & Chen-Hayes, S.F. (2011). Culturally competent school counselors: Affirming diversity by challenging oppression. In B.T. Erford (Ed.), *Transforming the school counseling profession* (3rd ed.) (pp. 90–109). Boston: Pearson.

Hossler, D., Schmit, J., & Vesper, N. (1999). *Going to college: How social, economic and educational factors influence the decisions students make.* Baltimore, MD: The Johns Hopkins University Press.

Kamentz, D., & Keane, L. (2012). Make them thirsty: Using non-cognitives to get students to and through college. In National Association for College Admission Counseling (NACAC) (Ed.), *Fundamentals of college admission counseling* (pp 122–133). Arlington, VA: National Association for College Admission Counseling.

Leonhardt, D. (2014, May 27). Is college worth it? Clearly, new data say. *The New York Times.*

MacAllum, K. et al. (2007). *Deciding on postsecondary education: Final report* (NPEC 2008-850). Washington, DC: National Postsecondary Education Cooperative, US Department of Education.

McClafferty, K., & McDonough, P. (2002). *Creating a college culture.* Los Angeles: University of California, Los Angeles.

McDill, E., & Coleman, J. (1965). Family and peer influences in college plans of high school students. *Sociology of Education,* 38(2), 112–126.

McDonough, P.M. (1997). *Choosing colleges: How social class and schools structure opportunity.* Albany, NY: SUNY Press.

Obama, B. (2009, February 24). Remarks of President Barack Obama, address to joint session of Congress. Retrieved from *http://www.whitehouse.gov/the_press_office/Remarks-of-President-Barack-Obama-Address-to-Joint-Session-of-Congress.*

Obama, M. (2014, May 7). Remarks by the First Lady at San Antonio signing day Reach Higher event. Retrieved from *http://beforeitsnews.com/obama/2014/05/remarks-by-the-first-lady-at-san-antonio-signing-day-reach-higher-event-2-2463146.html.*

Progress of Education Reform. (2012). Teacher expectations of students: A self-fulfilling prophecy? Retrieved from *http://www.ecs.org/clearinghouse/01/05/51/10551.pdf.*

Project on Student Debt. (2013). Student debt and the class of 2012. Retrieved from *http://projectonstudentdebt.org/files/pub/classof2012.pdf.*

Rennie Center (2011). Student learning plans: Supporting every student's transition to college and career. Retrieved from *http://www.renniecenter.org/topics/student_learning_plans.html.*

Savitz-Romer, M. (2012). *Professional college knowledge: Re-envisioning how we prepare our college readiness workforce.* Arlington, VA: National Association for College Admission Counseling.

Savitz-Romer, M., & Bouffard, S. (2012). *Ready, willing, and able: A developmental approach to college access and success.* Cambridge, MA: Harvard Education Press.

Sedlacek, W.E. (2012). Using non-cognitive variables in assessing readiness for higher education. In Bowman, P.J., St. John, E.P., & Stillman, P.K. (Eds.), *Diversity, merit and higher education: Toward a comprehensive agenda for the 21st century.* Brooklyn, NY: AMS Press.

Southern Regional Education Board. (2010). *Beyond the rhetoric: Improving college readiness through coherent state policy.* Atlanta, GA: Author.

Trusty, J., & Niles, S.G. (2003). High-school math courses and completion of the bachelor's degree. *Professional School Counseling, 7*, 99–107.

Walton Radford, A., & Ifill, N. (2013). Preparing students for college: What high schools are doing and how their actions influence ninth graders' college attitudes, aspirations and plans. Arlington, VA: National Association for College Admission Counseling.

Chapter 23: School-Family-Community Partnership Strategies for Promoting College Readiness and Access*

Julia Bryan, PhD

Dana Griffin, PhD

Lynette Henry

* This chapter was originally printed in *Fundamentals of College Admission Counseling (Third Edition)*.

School counselors and college counselors in high schools and community settings can play critical roles in promoting college readiness and college access, but they cannot do it alone. Partnerships with school administrators, teachers, parents, community members, colleges, businesses, and other stakeholders in students' education are vital in the college-choice and readiness process. Essentially, partnerships provide the support, resources, helping hands, and finances that counselors need to meet the academic, personal-social and college-career needs of large caseloads of students. Counselors are leaders in building partnerships with school stakeholders to promote college readiness and access for students (American School Counselor Association, 2010; Bryan, 2005).

reer schools. According to President Barack Obama (US Department of Education, 2010), some postsecondary education is necessary for everyone, and all students should leave school college- and career-ready.

Further, "college readiness" means that students are engaged with rigorous curricula that build the academic skills necessary for entering college, without the need for remediation. However, while academic preparation is critical to preparing for college, it is not the only criteria for college readiness. In addition to adequate academic preparation, college readiness means that students have the college aspirations, college knowledge and planning, and financial preparation required to successfully enroll and succeed in postsecondary education.

When school counselors implement partnerships that result in a spider web of resource-rich relationships or networks of trust that provide college-related information, resources, and support for students and families, they help build social capital for students and families that enhances their college readiness and access.

This chapter describes comprehensive and culturally relevant strategies that school and college counselors in K–12 schools and community settings can use to establish school-family-community partnerships that enhance students' academic preparation, build students' college aspirations, and provide students and their families with college planning and financial aid information conducive to successful enrollment in postsecondary institutions. We highlight the critical components of a comprehensive multi-system college-readiness partnership program, offer some parent involvement and outreach strategies for collaborating with African-American and Latino families, describe how to locate and leverage resources through community asset mapping, and describe a partnership process model for building school-family-community partnerships focused on college readiness.

In this chapter, "college" refers to a wide range of postsecondary institutions, including two-year and four-year colleges, technical and vocational colleges, and ca-

Therefore, partnerships to enhance college readiness must be focused on addressing all key aspects of college readiness, including college-career outcomes for students (Bryan, 2005; Epstein, 1995; Henderson & Mapp, 2002). Strong partnerships should exist among school staff, family members, community members, and community-based organizations, such as colleges, faith-based, and non-profit programs that support college readiness and greater access to college among students who are traditionally underrepresented in colleges (e.g., low-income students, students from racially or ethnically diverse backgrounds, etc.).

Research has documented the effects of partnerships on academic achievement, attendance, behavior, and other academic-related outcomes (Epstein & Van Woorhis, 2010; Henderson & Mapp, 2002). Recently, research in the realm of college counseling and higher education has highlighted the importance of school-college/university partnerships, school-business partnerships and other school-family-community partnerships in creating a college-going culture in schools, increasing parental involvement in the college-choice and preparation/readiness process, and promoting college access for underrepresented students (Auderbach, 2004; Fan, Jarsky, & McDonough, 2009; Gandara & Moreno, 2002; Jarsky, McDonough, & Nunez, 2009; Rowan-Kenyon, Bell, & Perna, 2008). Indeed, in a national study, Militello, Schweid, and Carey (2011) found that team work, collaboration partnerships, college-focused interventions, parental outreach, and multilevel systemic interventions are integral components of high-poverty, high-minority schools that are successful in promoting college readiness and access. Counselors and staff in these schools recognize that partnerships with families and community members are an integral component of building a college-going culture (McDonough, 2005).

To make college-readiness programs effective, especially for low-income students and students of color, school and college counselors must include and collaborate with families, colleges and universities, and community members and organizations (Tierney, 2002). In fact, parent support and encouragement are chief predictors of college application and enrollment (Bryan, Moore-Thomas, Day-Vines, & Holcomb-McCoy, 2011; Cabrera & La Nasa, 2001; Perna & Titus, 2005). Parents of color, in particular, tend to have high expectations that their children will attend college and a desire to support them in college-going (Auerbach, 2007). However, they often lack the college knowledge necessary to help their children navigate the college-choice, college-application and financial-aid processes. For low-income parents and parents of color, school counselors can be important sources of social capital (social ties or networks that provide information, resources and support) in the college process (Bryan, Moore-Thomas, Day-Vines, & Holcomb-McCoy, 2011). When school counselors implement partnerships that result in a spider web of resource-rich relationships or networks of trust that provide college-related information, resources, and support for students and families, they help build social capital for students and families that enhances their college readiness and access. Research has indicated that partnerships with parents and outreach programs are successful in increasing students' college knowledge and building networks and capacity

for college applications and enrollment (Auerbach, 2004; Gandara, 2002). These network relationships can also encourage (consciously or unconsciously) the development of norms, attitudes and beliefs necessary for applying to and enrolling in college (i.e., cultural capital).

Educational aspirations can be defined as the educational and vocational dreams students have about their future, or a combination of an individual's ambitions (the ability to look ahead and invest in the future and their inspirations; the ability to invest the required time, energy and effort) (Quaglia & Perry, 1995; Sirin, Diemer, Jackson, Gonsalves, & Howell, 2004). Youths' education aspirations are influenced by a variety of factors, including race and the educational level of parents (Sirin et al., 2004). Additionally, the postsecondary educational aspirations of students are influenced by the aspirations that school counselors, parents, close relatives, teachers, and peers have for them (McDonough, 2005; Trusty, 2002). Furthermore, high school counselors' postsecondary aspirations or expectations for students may influence whether or not students talk to the school counselor about college, which may be particularly detrimental in the college plans of low-income students and students of color (Bryan, Holcomb-McCoy, Moore-Thomas, & Day-Vines, 2009).

Partnerships can result in a plethora of college-readiness-focused programs and activities that encompass early-intervention programs, pre-college outreach programs and K–16 partnerships. These programs include college centers for students and families; parent educations workshops on college applications and financial aid nights; teacher-student mentoring, adult-student mentoring (e.g., business mentors) and cross-age peer mentoring programs; college visits and tours; after-school and out-of-school academic enrichment programs; summer bridge programs, summer camps and school-college partnerships programs on college-related issues; pre-college outreach programs staffed by parent/family and community volunteers; school-college readiness curricula in schools; and involving college counselors, recruiters and community volunteers in the school at the classroom-, grade- and school-wide levels (Auerbach, 2004; Gandara, 2002; Gandara & Moreno, 2002; Militello, Schweid, & Carey, 2011; Perna, Walsh, Rorison, & Fester, 2010). However, rather than implement these programs and activities haphazardly, it is important that school counselors implement a comprehensive and multi-system program of partnerships designed to support a college-going culture and meet the multiple college-readiness needs of students.

A COMPREHENSIVE PROGRAM OF COLLEGE-READINESS PARTNERSHIPS

Developing a comprehensive, multi-system, coordinated program of college-readiness partnerships requires intentional planning to address the critical goals of college readiness and provide the key supports that students and families need in the college-choice process (Weinstein & Savitz-Romer, 2009). Comprehensive, multi-system partnership programs provide a network of services aimed at important college-readiness goals that intervene at various levels or systems (i.e., at student, family, classroom, grade, school, and community levels). Augmented by ongoing, systematic and culturally competent college counseling, a comprehensive college-readiness partnership program targeted at multiple levels allows counselors and their partners to intervene in ways that change the structure, culture and environment of schools (McDonough, 2005). These partnerships allow counselors, other school staff, families, and communities to leverage relationships, resources and strengths in ways that can help improve schools' capacity to enhance college-going outcomes (e.g., college aspirations, college knowledge, college application rates, college enrollment, and graduation rates) (Cabrera et al., 2006; Cabrera & LaNasa, 2001; Gandara, 2002; McDonough, 1997).

As counselors work to involve partners in delivering college-readiness services and programs to students, they must target the students who need help the most. In high schools, counselors can use data to examine college application and enrollment data by gender, race and income status. Disaggregating the data will allow them to determine which students are going to college and which ones are not. In middle schools, counselors can survey students about their college aspirations and college knowledge to determine the accuracy and extent of students' knowledge and exposure to college. As research indicates, low-income students and students of color are typically the ones who need the most help in the college process. Therefore, given the inability of programs to serve everyone, partnership programs should especially target the students who need it most.

Counselors must also focus on intervening early in order to increase access for these students. Focusing on intervention activities as early as sixth grade and through twelfth grade will enhance counselors' effectiveness in removing students' and families' academic and financial barriers to college enrollment. Becoming college-ready is a complex process that begins in middle school and even earlier (Cabrera et al., 2006). Early and continuous intervention is critical in ensuring that students are college-ready. Starting early, preferably before eighth grade and as early as elementary school, means that counselors can partner with teachers and other school staff, parents, and other stakeholders to help students who are struggling academically (Swail & Perna, 2002). The numerous barriers that families face in the college-going process make it important for counselors to intervene early. Indeed, students, parents, teachers, and counselors make decisions early that affect whether or not students go to college.

School counselors can provide a wide range of college-readiness services and programs by engaging partners in there critical ways: (1) involve families in the college-readiness process to build families' college and financial aid knowledge and social and cultural capital in culturally sensitive ways; (2) involve mentors and volunteers to extend students' social networks and exposure to college; (3) involve postsecondary educational institutions and community organizations in creating college-related experiences and rigorous academic enrichment programs, both in school and out of school, to improve students' academic achievement and college-readiness skills.

Involve families in the college readiness process to build families' college and financial aid knowledge and social and cultural capital in culturally sensitive ways. Consistently, research shows that parent involvement is a predictor of whether or not students apply to and enroll in college (Bryan, Moore-Thomas, Day-Vines, & Holcomb-McCoy, 2011; Cabrera & LaNasa, 2001; Perna & Titus, 2005). Parent involvement serves as a predictor of college aspirations and expectations for students from low-income backgrounds (Hossler & Stage, 1992; Hossler, Schmit, & Vesper, 1999). Parents are extremely valuable in the college choice and preparation/readiness process because they are the individuals students most often turn to, other than teachers and counselors (Auerbach, 2004). Yet, families who are not college-educated typically lack the college knowledge and information to help their children navigate the pathway to college. Consequently, parents may have inaccurate beliefs about the possibility of their children attending college or about the steps to college. Therefore, ongoing, systematic parent involvement and parent education are key elements of college-readiness partnerships (e.g., the Puente Project) (Gandara, 2002). Sporadic parent involvement is not enough to provide families with the information and support they need to help their children in the college-choice process.

School counselors should work with school staff, parents and community members to ensure that parent involvement activities are consistent through the academic calendar and that activities focus on enriching parents' college knowledge—that is, knowledge of what they need to do to help their children prepare for college, knowledge about financial aid and applying for and enrolling in college, and knowledge of the advantages and disadvantages of various college and career options. In particular, school counselors should help parents learn strategies for helping their children move successfully through elementary school to college. They should also help them build confidence to become involved in their children's education and help them find support from other families and community organizations to build their children's college-going behaviors (Tierney & Auerbach, 2005).

As school counselors plan their college-readiness program, they must include a range of parent activities throughout the academic year. For instance, throughout the middle and high school grades, parents should be invited to and involved in college-readiness workshops that help them build their knowledge about the college-choice and readiness process. Certainly, eleventh and twelfth grade parents and their children should be involved in hands-on college application and financial-aid workshops. Parents should also be involved in planning and joining their children on college visits.

An urgent need exists for culturally specific, family-centered activities geared toward college-readiness goals (Tierney, 2002). It is important that counselors be culturally sensitive in planning and interacting with families by recognizing and affirming their cultural strengths and identities. Too often, schools are unwelcoming to parents, excluding those who do not fit the middle-class mainstream norms. Counselors must create a welcoming and culturally supportive climate for low-income parents and racially and ethnically diverse parents. Later in this chapter, we offer some culturally specific strategies for engaging African-American and Latino parents.

Involve mentors and volunteers to create interest and aspirations, leverage resources, and extend students' social networks and exposure to college. Resources are frequently limited in pre-college, early intervention, and other college-readiness programs. While these programs provide critical support for low-income students and students of color, they are understaffed and underfunded (Perna, Walsh, Rorison, & Fester, 2010; Tierney, 2002). Many of these programs rely on parent and community volunteers to serve many roles, including assisting with program activities and mentoring students (Perna, Walsh, Rorison, & Fester, 2010). Parents, teachers and mentors can provide valuable assistance, support and resources for college-readiness partnership programs.

Mentors can be important role models for students in the college process, often providing critical information about the college-preparation and application process that students may not be able to obtain from family or community members (Center for Higher Education Policy Analysis [CHEPA], 2005; Swail & Perna, 2002). When mentors are familiar with the often hidden or unspoken norms and rules related to preparing for college, they can pass these on to students whose parents do not have access to these norms and rules. For example, a mentor who attended college may know the importance of taking algebra early as a gateway course to college and may encourage a mentee to enroll in algebra in eighth grade, when the mentee's friends may be shying away from it. In addition, mentor-mentee discussions about college as early as elementary school can spark interest in college and begin to build those college aspirations that are an important precursor to attending college. Therefore, mentors build valuable social and cultural capital for low-income students and students of color (Laureau, 1989; Stanton-Salazar, 2001). Mentors who have gone to college can share their college experiences and help mentees explore what it means to be a college student and the benefits of attending college. With training, mentors can help mentees explore their goals, interests, values, and skills, explore information about specific colleges and various college options, and even help them complete applications (CHEPA, 2005).

One partnership strategy that counselors may utilize to foster strong positive peer relationships is a cross-age peer mentoring program. Counselors may collaborate with school personnel and community organizations to develop these programs, which pair college students (mentors) with high school students (mentees). Cross-age mentoring programs (CAMPs) have become very popular in many schools and communities, because they benefit both older and younger students and have been found to improve academic-related outcomes, such as a school connectedness and an academic self-esteem (Karcher, 2007). Mentoring works best when it is based on best practices. When evidence-based practices are utilized, such as providing student mentors with high-quality training monitoring and structuring mentor-mentee time, providing weekly group time for mentors to reflect on the experience, and parent involvement, students can benefit from being mentors and mentees in CAMPs. While mentoring may not improve academic achievement, it fosters college aspirations, is a forum for information on college-going and can encourage students to be more academically engaged (Dubois, Holloway, Valentine, & Cooper, 2002; CHEPA, 2005; Gandara & Mjorado, 2005).

Involve postsecondary education (PSE) institutions and community organizations in creating college-related experiences and rigorous academic enrichment programs, both in school and out of school, to improve students' academic achievement and college-readiness skills. Community organizations and postsecondary educational institutions such as colleges and universities are valuable resources for counselors who wish to focus on college readiness. Given that students' academic achievement is one of the strongest determinants of college application and enrollment, counselors should collaborate with college representatives and community organizations to connect students to existing early intervention and pre-college programs that focus on enhancing academic achievement and improving academic skills, especially the level of reading, writing and math skills necessary for college success (Bryan, 2005; Cabrera & LaNasa, 2000; Gandara, 2002; Tierney, 2002). Students need more rigorous coursework to be college-ready. Counselors may also reach out to PSE and community organizations to initiate school-university partnerships and create innovative programs that expose students to rigorous academic curricula and increase access to, support for and completion of rigorous coursework. These partnership programs provide students with opportunities to learn important reading, writing and math skills, as well as other college-readiness skills, such as leadership.

Early-intervention programs, pre-college programs, summer bridge and research programs, and tutoring programs can help strengthen school curriculum for low-income and minority/underrepresented students, especially in schools where rigorous coursework is missing. However, partners in these school-university/community programs must do more than supplement school curricula; they must advocate for changes to structure and curricula to increase access for low-income students and students of color to the requisite academic preparation and college information (Gandara, 2001). These partnership programs should also provide other college-readiness experiences for students by building college aspirations and college knowledge through visits to colleges, college fairs, and outreach campaigns and programs in middle and high schools at the classroom and wider school levels.

STRATEGIES AND ACTIVITIES FOR INVOLVING FAMILIES IN THE COLLEGE-READINESS PROCESS

Because research demonstrates that families of color and low-socioeconomic status (SES) families have high expectations for their children's future but lack the necessary information required to help them achieve their goals, it is vital that partnerships with parents be developed and implemented. These partnerships are additionally vital because: (1) findings from a study that explored 8,000 rural high school students' career- and college-related activities revealed that students do go to their parents for information about college and careers (Griffin, Hutchins, & Meece, 2011); (2) while parents may have high expectations for their children, teachers may not hold the same high expectations (Campbell-Whatley, & Comer, 2000; Ehrenberg, Goldhaber, & Brewer, 1995; Hughes, Gleason, & Zahang, 2005); and (3) providing information to parents can allow them to work collaboratively with school staff to make decisions that best meet the needs of their children.

It is no secret that parental involvement is linked to higher academic success (Delgado-Gaitan, 1992; Henderson & Mapp, 2002), yet families of color and low-SES families continue to remain distanced from their children's school. This poses a problem, as schools have access to information that could be beneficial to parents as they navigate the college-going process. Even parents who have attended college may have information that is no longer valid. So while partnerships with disenfranchised parents are necessary, it is also important to build relationships with parents who may also be more knowledgeable of the college-going process.

Learning ways to effectively reach and coordinate with parents is important, but challenging (Auerbach, 2004; Gandara, 2002; Swail & Perna, 2002). The involvement of racially and ethnically diverse parents may be particularly challenging due to anxiety and mistrust, often resulting from previous negative experiences or interactions with teachers and other school staff and unfamiliarity with school norms and culture. While it may be easier to work with parents who are deemed "more involved" in their children's education, schools must continue to provide outreach to parents with whom they would not normally work. This is important, as studies of African Americans demonstrate that an important strength of the African-American community is the reliance on extended relationships that can include family, friends, community members, churches, and religious leaders (Boy-Franklin, 2002; Day-Vines, Patton, & Baytops, 2003). Similarly, family and religious leaders and networks play integral roles in Latinos' lives (Suro et al., 2007).

While working with all parents is essential, African-American and Latino populations may be more difficult to reach. Indeed, these families are often deemed "uninvolved" by the school system. Below, we discuss two key components of developing relationships with African-American and Latino families, the results of three qualitative studies of African-American and Latino populations: building trust and "lazos" (Griffin, Kolb, & Tudryn, 2012). Trust, a key component for African-American families, and "lazos," a key component for Latino families, involve developing meaningful relationships as a way to foster mutual collaboration between families and schools.

BUILDING TRUST WITH AFRICAN-AMERICAN FAMILIES

Based on past experiences with schools and other formal institutions, African-American families may not trust the

school to look out for the welfare of their children. School administrators, counselors and teachers must understand that this mistrust of the school system can exist due to a parent's own negative school experiences, as well as the deficit lens through which schools tend to view them (Bryan & Henry, 2008; Harry, Klinger, & Hart, 2005). True partnerships can only begin on a foundation of trust. In order to build trust, schools should value and demonstrate respect for the values, beliefs and attitudes of African-American families. They must also understand how school systems' norms may clash with the norms of African-American families, which can lead to the labeling of African-American parents as uninvolved or disinterested in their children (Patton, 1998; Patton & Day-Vines, 2004).

To establish trust, schools must use active listening skills to hear parents' concerns and validate these concerns, feelings and experiences. Trust can be established by building rapport with families before problems arise and developing parent groups that allow these families to discuss their educational concerns regarding their children, school personnel and resources (Bradley et al., 2005; Day-Vines & Day-Hairston, 2005). To further facilitate trust, counselors should reach out to families to help celebrate their culture (Mitchell & Bryan, 2007); celebrate their children's accomplishments (Bryan & Henry, 20080; include them in decision-making (e.g., as members of counseling advisory teams) and other curriculum-related activities; engage children in enrichment activities to help their success (e.g., after-school programs, mentors); and encourage them to become active in the community by attending community events that affect children in their schools (Bradley et al., 2005; Steen & Noguera, 2010).

BUILDING "LAZOS" WITH LATINO FAMILIES

The Latino culture is about interpersonal relationships or "lazos," which means, "ties that bind lives together." To build lazos, schools must first bind with students and then use that bind to learn more about their students' families, such as parent names. During communications with students, ask them how their parents are, and use the names of their parents when asking. Call their homes, let parents know you have met their child, and discuss positive information about their child. If parents do not speak English, send a translated hand-written letter home with the child that is full of positive, glowing things about their child. Greet parents when you see them in the school, even if you cannot understand one another. Go out into the community to meet parents, go into their neighborhoods, and finally, become an advocate for this population.

Once lazo has been established, plan events that cater to this population. As the Latino culture is highly interpersonal, counselors can plan more interactive events, such as a roundtable at which parents can share their stories. Host activities just for Latino families with culturally appropriate food and themes. As demonstrated in a study on parental involvement with Latina mothers, Latina mothers love to cook and share their food and culture (Griffin, Kolb, & Tudryn, 2012). Use interpreters as last resorts, because this can negatively affect communication. If you don't speak Spanish, identify leaders, and engage them by asking for help. Be clear about what you need leaders to do. The Latino culture is highly child-oriented, so childcare is a must for all meetings. In addition, Latino parents who work or are at home with young children do not attend meetings in the morning; consider working-family friendly times. Finally, fliers, emails and information sent home with children may not be the best method of reaching out. Phones calls that require a more personal touch are more effective (Griffin, Kolb, & Tudryn, 2012).

Locating and Leveraging Resources Through Utilizing Community Asset Mapping

Only through deep immersion in the community can schools identify resources and the people within the community who can serve as valuable resources (Bryan, 2005). One way to do this is through the development and implementation of a community asset map, which provides a more detailed view of the resources available within the communities in which families live and includes a list of existing resources that can be used by all stakeholders (Griffin & Farris, 2010).

It is important to understand that all individuals, businesses and institutions can be considered community resources. There are three levels of assets to consider in community asset mapping. The first level consists of the skills, gifts and capacities of individuals living in the

community. For establishing college and career school cultures, schools can rely on any individual who attended any type or form of higher education. People who went straight to work after high school can also serve as mentors. For example, someone in the community who has a job but dropped out of school or did not attend college could talk about the need to stay in school or attend college as a way to motivate students. Indeed, in a parental involvement study of Latina mothers, findings showed that the mothers used themselves/their own stories as motivational examples to continually stress the importance of education. The Latina mothers continually told their children that they must work hard in school and get a college education so that they do not end up like their mothers (Griffin, Kolb, & Tudryn, 2012).

The second and third level of community asset mapping includes civic associations and businesses in the community. Schools wishing to develop a strong career- and college-readiness culture could establish externships and shadowing experiences with these businesses. It is important that schools rely on resources that are in their communities as a way to show students that their own communities offer resources, and that they do not have to leave their communities in order to find help. This is also empowering to parents, as it lets them know that there are resources in the community. While this may be more challenging in rural and inner-city communities, it is important to note that resources are indeed available, but may not be known or well-publicized. In a study with parents in a rural community, it was demonstrated that a plethora of resources existed in the community, but simply were not known about by the parents (Griffin & Galassi, 2010).

In sum, when developing community asset maps, it is important to include all three levels of assets, including individuals, neighborhood associations, community centers, churches, colleges and universities, and businesses and professional corporations (e.g., banks, small business) (Atkinson & Juntunen, 1994; Day-Vines, Patton, & Baytops, 2003; Bryan, 2005). Many of these resources can serve as sources of academic and career support in the form of mentors, tutors, pre-college academic preparation programs, and career information (Bryan, 2005; Griffin, Hutchins, & Meece, 2011).

IMPLEMENTING A PARTNERSHIP PROCESS MODEL FOCUSED ON COLLEGE READINESS

School counselors believe partnerships are important in delivering services to students (Bryan & Holcomb-McCoy, 2004, 2007; Bryan & Griffin, 2010). Partnership process models help schools and college counselors navigate the process of building school-family-community partnerships focused on college readiness. Building partnerships involves seven stages: (1) preparing to partner; (2) assessing needs and strengths; (3) coming together; (4) creating a shared vision and plan; (5) taking action; (6) evaluating and celebrating progress; (7) maintaining momentum. Each of these stages is important in building effective partnerships.

College Readiness Program Components:

1. Improving academic preparation

2. Building college aspirations

3. Increasing college knowledge and planning

4. Providing financial preparation and financial aid informational support

---

The model provides an organizing framework to help counselors integrate partnerships in their school counseling program in a systematic and coordinated way. To enhance college-readiness outcomes, counselors are expected, according to the American School Counselor Association model (ASCA, 2010), to be advocates, facilitators, leaders, liaisons, and initiators in partnerships. A question that often confronts counselors is: What do you do when there are few resources, no college or career counselor in your school, and/or time is very limited? This partnership process model helps counselors and educators move beyond their traditional roles and find creative ways to build partnerships. Although partnerships take time, they provide the extra resources that counselors need to effectively serve large numbers of students. Partnerships are the source of counseling, education, mentoring, and enrichment programs that meet the academic, personal-social and college-career needs of large caseload of students. The following stages comprise the main tasks

a school counselor must address to build college-readiness partnerships. (See Table 1, at the end of this chapter.)

Stage 1: Preparing to partner. The school counselor should first become familiar with the cultural groups served by the school and within the community. It is important that counselors examine their own cultural assumptions and seek to understand their assumptions about families and students—who is going to college and how families' values and experiences differ from their own in relation to college. The counselor should use current research on college readiness and access to formulate the school counseling program vision. The vision must align with the school vision, as this is how counselors can gain buy-in for partnerships form administration and staff. Sharing the vision with teachers, faculty and parents will also increase buy-in. The importance of understanding the benefits and success stories of partnerships can help school administrations embrace evidence-based programs such as school-family-community partnerships that foster college readiness and enhance the college-going culture.

Stage 2: Assessing needs and strengths. The goals of a college-readiness school-family-community partnership programs are determined by the needs of the school, families and community. In order to determine the college-readiness needs and strength of students and parents in the community, counselors can conduct needs and strengths assessment surveys and interview students, teachers, parents/families, and community members. This will assist in building relationships and incorporating diverse perspectives when developing partnership programs focused on fostering a college-going culture. These conversations will help when it is time to decide which individuals to bring together to form a partnership leadership team (PLT) (Bryan & Henry, 2012). The needs assessment helps counselors identify the students and families who may need assistance in understanding the college-going process and become aware of any barriers that may be preventing students and families from even considering college. It is important to examine the college-related data in your school (e.g., college application rates, enrollment rates) and identify the students who are less represented in college (by race/ethnicity, SES, other characteristics). The strengths assessment helps you uncover existing partnerships and seek out new partners.

Together, this relevant information helps counselors determine program goals and develop the necessary college-readiness and access programs to meet the needs of all students. The community asset map helps counselors identify valuable community resources, such as cultural brokers and persons of influence (e.g., bilingual parents and community members) who will help counselors meet their program goals (Mitchell & Bryan, 2007). This map can be built as counselors attend teacher team meetings, college and community events, parent meetings, and community meetings.

Stage 3: Coming together. The identified needs and strengths are used in bringing all partners together to form the partnership leadership team (PLT). The PLT is made up of the school counselor, administration, student services personnel (psychologist, social workers), teachers, students, parents, and community members, and should be comprised of 8–15 members. It is recommended that some members of the PLT represent the target student groups. The team should focus on college readiness and is responsible for "developing, implementing, evaluating, and maintaining the school's partnership plan and program; recruiting other partners and leaders; creating and spreading the partnership vision; and sustaining partnership programs" (Epstein, 1995; Epsein & Van Voorhis, 2010). Many of the persons who may become valuable partners are introduced to the school through the PLT. This team has the ability to empower partners by showing them how they can be of assistance to the school, families and community.

Stage 4: Creating a shared vision and plan. This stage is very critical to the success and sustenance of partnerships (Alexander et al., 2003). There should be consensus among the team, shared vision, and shared and equal decision-making. The PLT uses identified needs to create a partnership plan for college readiness. Build on existing partnerships, fill in the gaps (areas where the needs are not completely being met) and develop at least one new partnership to move close to the program's goals. Examples of partnerships may include student and parent mentoring, tutoring and college and career days, speakers who increase college aspirations, summer and after-school academic enrichment, college knowledge and planning, college visits, college preparation, and financial-aid student and parent nights. Team members determine the

goals and expected outcomes of partnership(s), as well as how they will measure the outcomes. As school personnel usually have busy schedules, it is important to schedule few meetings and hold them at convenient times for them, as well as for parents. The meetings should highlight the strengths of students, families and communities, using those strengths to build programs rather than focusing on deficits (Bryan & Henry, 2008). Counselors should manage time wisely by recognizing team members' strengths and learning to delegate small tasks accordingly, rather than always coming together in large meetings. The final draft of goals and strategies to build partnerships and programs that improve college readiness and access should be shared with school administrators and parents for feedback and ideas.

Goals/Strategies

1. Create programs to provide academic skills for college (e.g., school-college partnership program implemented in the school to improve writing among Latino students who need it).

2. Increase students' college knowledge and information.

3. Increase parents' college knowledge and information (e.g., parent education workshops).

4. Increase parents' involvement in the college process.

5. Create partnerships with colleges and universities (e.g., work with a team that includes college recruiters and admission counselors to provide and improve the four college-readiness components above).

6. Provide students with mentoring to support their college aspirations and knowledge (e.g., college students as mentors, teacher-student mentoring).

7. Provide students with college-going experiences to build their aspirations (e.g., college visits, summer college programs).

The PLT should use a logic model to create one-year and three-to-five year plans to build a college culture and improve college readiness (Kellogg, 2004). The logic model is a systematic tool that visually shows, through a graphic illustration or picture, how a program evaluation occurs through logical relationships (Rodriguez-Campos, 2005). According to the W. Kellog Foundation (2000), "Using a logic model throughout your program helps organize and systematize program planning, management, and evaluation functions" (p. 5). The logic model will help in implementation and evaluation. The partnership plan should be designed in such a way that parents who are uninvolved or have lower levels of involvement are reached (Bailey & Bradbury-Bailey, 2010; Dotson-Blakes, 2010; Moore-Thomas & Day-Vines, 2010; Suzrez-Orozco, Onaga, & de Lardemelle, 2010).

Stage 5: Taking action. Based on strengths, each member should implement the partnerships activities plan according to the timeline. PLT members should delegate to others as well, even if they are not on the team, including parents and community members. Some helpful strategies include visiting nearby colleges and postsecondary schools, college fairs, businesses, and churches. Communication should not only be written, but should also include face-to-face interaction and phone calls. Challenges and barriers will present themselves, but counselors should encourage their teams to not lose focus and to implement anyway. Small successes are still successes (Dohery & Mendenhall, 2006). At this stage, it would be beneficial to involve positive media at partnership activities, as this will publicize the school and increase opportunities for more partnerships and potential scholarships; "positive media is especially important in urban or economically depressed areas, where schools typically receive negative media attention" (Bryan & Henry, 2012).

Stage 6: Evaluating and celebrating progress. Program evaluation is an integral part of the process and should include school, family and community partners (Ryan, 2005). School counselors are challenged by the American School Counselor Association model to evaluate programs in measurable terms, to make programs accountable (ASCA, 2012). Evaluations also provide districts with credibility, as they show that the data is, in fact, linked to student achievement and college-related accomplishments.

Evaluation should follow a systematic approach, and the logic model can help guide the direction of the evaluation. This model allows counselors to examine what is relevant and useful to the partnership and to plan at what intervals they should be collecting and analyzing data. Bryan and Henry (2012) recommend using both quantitative and qualitative data in performing the evaluation, as these two methods produce rich data. Using the results, the PLT decides what should be done to improve and strengthen the partnerships and programs. Once these decisions are made, counselors should share accomplishments with administration, teachers, other staff, students, families, and the community. This can be communicated via data walls, stories, students' college acceptances, and other college-related accomplishments, newsletters, thank-you notes, letters, emails, media, school/community meetings, parent-formed support groups, and student assemblies. In particular, business and community partners appreciate thank-you cards made personally by students. Data should always be presented in such a way that all can understand it. Parents and community members may not have the data training of school personnel, but they still need to understand the outcomes of the partnerships. It is not enough to measure successes and share them; they should also be celebrated at award ceremonies, banquets and "success night" celebrations (Bryan & Henry, 2008). All those who have diligently put forth the effort to make these successes possible should be celebrated, from a custodial worker who may have cleaned the rooms for meetings to a parent who made sure her child came to tutoring sessions on a regular basis. "Feeling valued and significant may encourage partners to maintain their involvement in school-family-community partnerships" (Bryan, 2012).

Stage 7: Maintaining momentum. The final stage cannot be overlooked. It's important to keep partnerships growing from year to year and not just in the short term. A short-term donation here and there is beneficial, but a long-term partnership should be treasured. This is very significant when working with families coming from high-poverty homes, as they are accustomed to inconsistency and instability in their lives and can easily become discouraged. Long-term partners build confidence in students and parents, allowing them to believe that college access is really a possibility. Therefore, sustaining partnerships should be discussed and purposefully pursued as a team. The PLT should use evaluation results to improve its plan for college readiness and access before the next academic year. The recruitment of new partners and PLT members should also be an ongoing process for all involved in preparation for the coming school year. At the beginning of the school year, the new plan should be shared with students, teachers, families, and community partners. All partners should be contacted prior to and early in the school year, and counselors should consider beginning the year with a kick-off celebration or appreciation breakfast to welcome school personnel, teachers and community members.

CONCLUSION

School-family-community partnerships foster college readiness and can enhance the college-going culture. Success is reached when students are being academically prepared for college, there is an increase in students' college aspirations, an increase in students' and families' college knowledge, and students and their families are more knowledgeable about the college-planning and financial-aid process. It is vital that school counselors and college counselors work together to promote college readiness and college access. Further, school and college counselors must collaborate with students' families, colleges and universities, community members, and community organizations in order to make college-readiness programs effective. This chapter outlines some concrete strategies that can enhance the college-going culture in schools and delineates how to implement a partnership process model of college readiness that can be useful for school counselors as they seek to develop a comprehensive school counseling program built on a foundation of school-family-community partnerships.

ABOUT THE AUTHORS

Dr. Julia Bryan is an assistant professor in the Department of Counseling, Higher Education and Special Education at the University of Maryland at College Park. Dr. Bryan conducts research on school-family-community partnerships and the role of school counselors and other school personnel in building partnerships. Her work is based on the belief that strong partnerships enhance students' educational resilience and academic achievement,

promote social and academic supports for children, and provide opportunities and resources that help empower vulnerable children and families, especially in urban schools and communities. Dr. Bryan also conducts research on the role of school counselors, teachers and education leaders in addressing critical challenges that face children of color, such as college access, disproportionate disciplinary referrals, suspensions and expulsions, school bonding and connectedness, and educational resilience. She presents nationally and writes extensively on these topics. To date, Dr. Bryan has published 18 articles in national peer-reviewed journals such as *Journal of Counseling & Development, Counselor Education and Supervision* and *Professional School Counseling*. In addition, she has edited a special issue of *Professional School Counseling,* entitled *Collaboration and Partnerships with Families and Communities in the School Counseling Context.* Currently, Dr. Bryan enjoys working with schools to help them build school-family-community partnerships that mobilize resources to enhance achievement and resilience for minority and immigrant children, especially those from low-income backgrounds.

Dr. Dana Griffin is an assistant professor at the University of North Carolina at Chapel Hill (NC), where she teaches in the school counseling program. Dana Griffin, a Virginia native, holds degrees from the College of William and Mary (VA) and Hampton University (VA). Dr. Griffin's professional background includes working as a school counselor. While working on her doctorate, Dr. Griffin interned as a marriage and family counselor for the New Horizons Family Counseling Center on the campus of the College of William and Mary. She also worked as a community consultant, providing services to children and their families from an impoverished neighborhood in the Williamsburg area. These experiences led Dr. Griffin to pursue her research agenda: school-family-community collaboration and culturally competent parental involvement with African-American and Latino families. Dr. Griffin has presented her research data at state and national conferences and has published in counseling journals such as *Professional School Counseling, Journal of Counseling & Development,* and *The Journal for Social Action in Counseling and Psychology.* Dr. Griffin also highly values teaching future school counselors about the need for advocacy, empowerment and leadership in school counseling, especially when working with families of color and those from low-income backgrounds.

Lynette Henry is a doctoral student in counselor education and supervision with a specialty in program evaluation at the University of South Florida (FL). She holds a master's of arts degree in guidance and counselor education and a professional educator's certificate in guidance and counseling pre-K–12. She also has a graduate certificate in marriage and family therapy. She has been a school counselor since 2007 and is very passionate about making a difference in the lives of children. She believes school counselors can provide services for all children by forming school-family-community partnerships. She has also mentored new school counselors on the district's Elementary Guidance Leadership Team. She has presented at local and national conferences and is published in *Journal of Counseling & Development, Professional School Counseling* and *Journal of College Counseling.*

Additional information about the school-family-community partnership process model for promoting college readiness can be found in Julia Bryan and Lynette Henry (2012), "A Model for Building School-Family-Community Partnerships: Principles and Process," in the Journal of Counseling & Development, 90(4), pp. 408–420.

REFERENCES

American School Counselor Association (2010). *The professional school counselor and school-family-community partnerships* (Position statement). Retrieved from *http://www.schoolcousnelor.org/content.asp?contentid=178.*

Auerbach, S. (2004). Engaging Latino parents in supporting college pathways: Lessons from a college access program. *Journal of Hispanic Higher Education, 3*, 125–145.

Bailey, D.F., & Bradbury-Bailey, M.E. (2010). Empowered youth programs: Partnerships for enhancing postsecondary outcomes of African American adolescents. *Professional School Counseling, 14*, 64–74.

Bryan, J. (2005). Fostering educational resilience and academic achievement in urban schools through school-family-community partnerships. *Professional School Counseling, 8*, 219–227.

Bryan, J., & Griffin, D. (2010). A multidimensional study of school-family-community partnership involvement: School, school counselor, and training factors. *Professional School Counseling, 14*, 75–86.

Bryan, J., & Henry, L. (in press). A model for building school-family-community partnerships: Principles and process. *Journal of Counseling & Development.*

Bryan, J., & Henry, L. (2008). Strengths-based partnerships: A school-family-community partnership approach to empowering students. *Professional School Counseling, 12*, 149–156.

Bryan, J., & Holcomb-McCoy, C. (2004). School counselors' perceptions of their involvement in school-family-community partnerships. *Professional School Counseling, 7*, 162–171.

Bryan, J., & Holcomb-McCoy, C. (2007). An examination of school counselor involvement in school-family-community partnerships. *Professional School Counseling, 10*, 441–454.

Bryan, J., Holcomb-McCoy, C., Moore-Thomas, C., & Day-Vines, N. (2009). Who sees the school counselor for college information? A national study. *Professional School Counseling, 12*, 280–291.

Bryan, J., Moore-Thomas, C., Day-Vines, N., & Holcomb-McCoy, C. (2011). School counselors as social capital: The effects of high school college counseling on college application rates. *Journal of Counseling & Development, 89*, 190–199.

Cabrera, A.F., & La Nasa, S.M. (2000). Understanding the college choice of disadvantaged students. *New Directions for Institutional Research, 107*, 5–22. San Francisco: Jossey-Bass.

Cabrera, A.F., & La Nasa, S.M. (2001). On the path to college: Three critical tasks facing America's disadvantaged. *Research in Higher Education, 42*, 119–150.

Cabrera, A.F., Deil-Amen, R., Prabhu, R., Terenzini, P.T., Lee, C., & Franklin, R.E.J. (2006). Increasing the college preparedness of at-risk students. *Journal of Latinos & Education,* 5(2), 79–97.

Center for Higher Education Policy Analysis. (2005). Menotring scaffoldings: Do they promote college access? Los Angeles, CA: Center for Higher Education Policy Analysis. Retrieved from *http://www.eric. ed.gov/ERICWebPortal/detail?accno=ED499277.*

Cooper, C.R. (2002). Five bridges along students' pathways to college: A development blueprint of families, teachers, counselors, mentors, and peers in the Puente Project. *Educational Policy,* 16(4), 607–623.

Cooper C.R., Chavira, G., & Mena, D. (2005). From pipelines to partnerships: A synthesis of research on how diverse families, schools, and communities support children's pathways through school. *Journal of Education for Students Placed at Risk,* 10(4), 407–430.

Domina, T. (2009). What works in college outreach: Assessing targeted and schoolwide interventions for disadvantaged students. *Educational Evaluation and Policy Analysis,* 31, 127–152.

Dubois, D., Holloway, J., Valentine, J., & Cooper, H. (2002). Effectiveness of mentoring programs for youth: A meta-analytic review. *American Journal of Psychology*, 30(2), 157–201.

Fann, A., Jarsky, K.M., & McDonough, P.M. (2009). Parent involvement in the college planning process: A case study of P-20 collaboration. *Journal of Hispanic Higher Education,* 8, 374–393.

Gandara, P. (2002). A study of High School Puente: What we have learned about preparing Latino youth for postsecondary education. *Educational Policy,* 16(4), 474–496.

Gandara, P., & Bial, D. (1999). *Paving the way to higher education: K–12 intervention programs for underrepresented youth.* Washington, DC: National Postsecondary Education Cooperative.

Gandara, P., & Mejorado, M. (2005). Putting your money where your mouth is: Mentoring as a strategy to increase access to higher education. In W.G. Tierney, Z.B. Corwin, & J.E. Colyar (Eds.), *Preparing for college: Nine elements of effective outreach* (pp. 89–110). Albany, NY: State University of New York Press.

Gandara, P., & Moreno, J.F. (2002). Introduction: The Puente Project: Issues and perspectives on preparing Latino youth for higher education. *Educational Policy,* 16, 463–473.

Griffin, D., & Farris, A.E. (2010). School counselors in collaboration: Finding resources through community asset mapping. *Professional School Counseling*, 13, 248–256.

Griffin, D. & Galassi, J.P. (2010). Exploring parental perceptions of barriers to academic success in rural middle school: A case study. *Professional School Counseling,* 14, 87–100.

Griffin, D., & Steen, S. (2010). School-family-community partnerships: Applying Epstein's theory of the six types of involvement to school counselor practice. *Professional School Counseling,* 13, 218–226.

Griffin, D., Hutchins, B.C., & Meece, J.L. (2011). Where do rural high school students go to find information about their futures? *Journal of Counseling & Development*, 89, 172–181.

Grossman, J.B., & Tierney, J.P. (1998). Does mentoring work? An impact study of the Big Brothers Big Sisters Program. *Evaluation Review*, 22, 403–426.

Grubb, W.N., Lara, C.M., and Valdez, S. (2002). Counselor, coordinator, monitor, mom: The roles of counselors in the Puente program. *Educational Policy,* 16(4), 547–572.

Gullat, Y., & Jan, W. (2002). *How do pre-collegiate academic outreach programs impact college-going among underrepresented students?* A white paper for the Pathways to College Network. Boston: Pathways to College Network.

Holcomb-McCoy, C. (2010). Involving low-income parents and parents of color in college readiness activities: An exploratory study. *Professional School Counseling*, 14, 115–124.

Jarsky, K.M., McDonough, P.M., & Nunez, A. (2009). Establishing a college culture in secondary schools through P-20 collaboration: A case study. *Journal of Hispanic Higher Education*, 8, 357–373.

Jun, A., & Tierney, W.G. (1999). At-risk urban students and college success: A framework for effective preparation. *Metropolitan Universities: An International Forum*, 9(4), 49–60.

Karcher, M.J. (2007). Cross-age peer mentoring. *Research in Action*, 1(7), 3–17. Retrieved from *http://www.mentoring.org/downloads/mentoring_388.pdf*.

Lauland, A. (1998). *Yes you can: Establishing mentoring programs to prepare youth for college*. Washington, D.C.: Partnership for Family Involvement in Education.

Maldonado, N.L., Quarles, A., Lacey, C.H., & Thomspon, S.D. (2008). Mentoring at-risk adolescent girls: Listening to "Little Sisters." *Mentoring & Tutoring: Partnership in Learning*, 16(2), 223–234.

McDonough, P.M. (2005). Counseling matters: Knowledge, assistance, and organizational commitment in college preparation. In Tierney, W. G., Corwin, Z., & Colyar, J. E. (Eds). *Preparing for College: Nine elements of effective outreach* (pp. 69–87). Albany, NY: State University of New York Press.

McClafferty, K., McDonough, P., & Nunez, A. (2002). *What is a college culture? Facilitating college preparation through organizational change*. Paper presented at the Annual Meeting of the American Educational Research Association, New Orleans, LA. Retrieved from *http://collegetools.berkeley.edu/resources.php?cat_id=15*.

Mitchell, N.A., & Bryan, J. (2007). School-family-community partnerships: Strategies for school counselors working with Caribbean immigrant families. *Professional School Counseling*, 10, 399–409.

Militello, M., Schweid, J., & Carey, J. (2011). Si se Puede Colaboracion! Increasing college placement rates of low-income students. *Teachers College Record*, 113(7), 1435–1476.

Olivia, M. (2008). Latino access to college: Actualizing the promise and potential of K–16 partnerships. *Journal of Hispanic Higher Education*, 7(2), 119–130.

Perna, L.W. (2002). Precollege outreach programs: Characteristics of programs serving historically underrepresented groups of students. *Journal of College Student Development*, 43, 64–83.

Perna, L., Rowan-Kenyon, H., Thomas, S., Bell, A., Anderson, R., & Li, C. (2008). The role of college counseling in shaping college opportunity: Variations across high schools. *Review of Higher Education*, 31, 131–159.

Perna, L.W., & Titus, M.A. (2005). The relationship between parental involvement as social capital and college enrollment: An examination of racial/ethnic group differences. *Journal of Higher Education*, 76, 485–518.

Perna, L.W., Walsh, E., Rorison, J., & Fester, R. (2010). Understanding the involvement of volunteers in precollege outreach programs: An exploratory study. *Enrollment Management Journal*. Retrieved from *http://www.tgslc.org/pdf/emj-w10-volutneers.pdf*.

Savitz-Romer, M., Jager-Hyman, J., & Coles, A. (2009). *Removing roadblocks to rigor: Linking academic and social supports to ensure college readiness and success*. Pathways to College Network: Retrieved from *http://www.ihep.org/assets/files/programs/pcn/Roadblocks.pdf*.

Smith, M. (2008). Four steps to a paradigm shift: Employing critical perspectives to improve outreach to low-SES African-American and Latino students and their parents. *Journal of College Admission*, 201, 17–23.

Smith, M. (2009). Right directions, wrong maps: Understanding the involvement of low-SES African American parents to enlist them as partners in college choice. *Education and Urban Society*, 41(2), 171–196.

Steen, S., & Noguera, P.A., (2010). Broader and bolder approach to school reform: Expanded partnership roles for school counselors. *Professional School Counseling,* 14, 42–52.

Suro, R., Escobar, G., Livingston, G., Hakimzadeh, S., Lugo, L., Stencel, S., Green, J.C., Smith, G.A., Cox, D., & Chaudhry, S. (2007). *Changing Faiths: Latinos and the Transformation of American Religion.* Washington, DC: Pew Research Center. Retrieved from *http://www.pewhispanic.org/files/reports/75.pdf.*

Swail, W.S. (2000). Preparing American's disadvantaged for college: Programs that increase college opportunity. In A.F. Cabrera and S.M. La Nasa (Eds.), *Understanding the college choice of disadvantaged students.* San Francisco: Jossey-Bass.

Swail, W.S., & Perna, L. W. (2002). Pre-college outreach programs: A national perspective. In W.G. Tierney and L.S. Hagedorn (Eds.), *Increasing access to college: Extending possibilities for all students* (pp. 15–34). Albany, NY: State University of New York Press.

Tierney, W.G. (2002). Parents and families in precollege preparation: The lack of connection between research and practice. *Educational Policy,* 16, 588–606.

Tierney, W.G., & Auerbach, S. (2005). Toward developing an untapped resource: The role of families in college preparation. In W.G. Tierney, Z. Corwin, & J.E. Colyar (Eds.), *Preparing for College: Nine elements of effective outreach.* Albany, NY: State University of New York Press.

Torrez, N. (2004). Developing parent information frameworks that support college preparation for Latino students. *The High School Journal,* 87, 54–59.

Weinstein, L.A., & Savitz-Romer, M. (2009). Planning for opportunity: Applying organizational and social capital theories to promote college-going cultures. *Educational Planning,* 18(2), 1–11.

TABLE 1. SCHOOL-FAMILY-COMMUNITY PARTNERSHIP PROCESS MODEL FOR PROMOTING COLLEGE READINESS

Stage	Main Tasks	Questions
1. Preparing to Partner *Where do I begin?*	1. Become familiar with the cultural groups served by the school and with the community. 2. Use research on college readiness and access and your role as a school/college counselor in forming your program vision for college readiness. 3. Align your vision with the school's vision to get administration buy-in. 4. Share with administration research-based evidence of how partnerships are fostering college readiness and can enhance the college-going culture.	1. What are your college expectations for all students? What are your assumptions about the student groups who are less represented in college-going? What do you believe about parents' college knowledge and role in the college search process? 2. What is your vision for college readiness and access in the school? 3. What is the school's vision for students to be college-ready? 4. Why should administration give you the opportunity to build college-readiness partnerships?
2. Assessing Needs and Strengths *How do I identify the goals of the partnership?*	1. Conduct needs and strengths assessment surveys and interview students, school personnel, parents/families, and community members. Examine the college-related data. Identify the students who are less represented in college-going. 2. Attend college and community events and ask about cultural brokers and persons of influence. 3. Uncover existing partnerships and their effectiveness. 4. Create a community asset map for college readiness.	1. Conduct needs and strengths assessment surveys and interview students, school personnel, parents/families, and community members. Examine the college-related data. Identify the students who are less represented in college-going. 2. Attend college and community events and ask about cultural brokers and persons of influence. 3. Uncover existing partnerships and their effectiveness. 4. Create a community asset map for college readiness.
3. Coming Together *How do I bring partners together?*	1. Use identified strengths to create a partnership leadership team (PLT) with a focus on college readiness. 2. Examine identified college-readiness needs and strengths as a team. 3. Get the team's feedback and ideas. 4. Connect and share the vision and needs with identified potential partners, and help them understand how they can help increase college readiness for all students.	1. Who are potential PLT members (who has high college expectations for all students)? 2. What are the specific needs of the students, parents and community members? What are the strengths of the PLT members? 3. Whom are your identified community partners? Who are the identified cultural brokers and persons of influence? 4. Who on the PLT will share the vision and needs with which identified partners?

(continues)

TABLE 1. SCHOOL-FAMILY-COMMUNITY PARTNERSHIP PROCESS MODEL FOR PROMOTING COLLEGE READINESS *(continued)*

4. Creating a Shared Vision and Plan
 	
How do I get everyone on board and on the same page?
	1. Use identified needs to create a partnership plan for college readiness:
	   a. build on existing partnerships.
	   b. consider starting at least one new partnership.
	2. Determine the goals and expected outcomes of your partnership(s).
	3. Share the proposed plan with school administrators and parents and get their feedback and ideas.
	4. Create one-year and three-to-five-year plans to build a college culture using a logic model.
	5. Create a timeline for the year's college-readiness partnership activities.
		1. What strategies would you use to create a shared vision and plan for college readiness? What existing partnerships are already meeting identified needs? Where would new partnerships be beneficial in meeting identified needs?
		2. What are your goals and expected outcomes?
		3. How will you get buy-in from staff? How will you include parents?
		4. What is a logic model?
		5. What is your timeline, and how will you visually show progress?

5. Taking Action *What will we do and how?*	1. Delegate responsibilities for each team member based on the PLT's and your partners' strengths. 2. Implement partnership activities according to the timeline. 3. Plan for challenges you expect, but implement anyway. 4. Involve the media.	1. What strategies/ partnerships would you and the team use to implement the plan? How will you reach parents? 2. What is the timeline and implementation plan? When will you have progress meetings? 3. How will you overcome any expected barriers and challenges? 4. What are the benefits of involving the media?
6. Evaluating and Celebrating Progress *How will I measure our success?*	1. Determine how you will evaluate each partnership. 2. Measure and evaluate the results of each partnership. 3. Share accomplishments with administration, teachers, other staff, students, families, and the community. 4. Celebrate partner, student and parent accomplishments.	1. How will you measure and evaluate each partnership to show the results/ outcomes? 2. What impact did the partnership have on college readiness and access? What can be done to improve and strengthen the partnerships and programs? 3. How will you share accomplishments? 4. How will you celebrate your partner, student and parent accomplishments?

(continues)

TABLE 1. SCHOOL-FAMILY-COMMUNITY PARTNERSHIP PROCESS MODEL FOR PROMOTING COLLEGE READINESS *(continued)*

7. Maintaining Momentum *How will I sustain this partnership?*	1. Revisit your plan for enhancing college readiness and access. Use evaluation results to improve the plan. 2. Get the PLT's feedback to improve and make revisions to the plan. 3. Share the new plan with your students, teachers, families, and community partners. 4. Contact your partners prior to and early in the school year. Consider extensions of existing partnerships. 5. Identify possible new team members and new partners as new staff and parents come to the school every year.	1. What strategies will you use to improve or build on the partnerships? 2. How will you sustain the partnerships? 3. Why would you want to communicate the new plan to students, teachers, families, and community partners? 4. Who from the PLT will contact existing partners, and when will this occur? 5. Who are the new team members and partners?

Adapted from Bryan, J. and Henry, L. A model for building school-family-community partnerships: Principles and process. *Journal of Counseling & Development,* 90 (2012): 408–420.

Chapter 24: Facilitating College Participation and Success Before They Even Arrive: A Community Cultural Wealth Perspective

Raquel M. Rall, PhD

One of the gravest charges to which American society is subject is that of failing to provide a reasonable quality of educational opportunity for its youth. For the great majority of our boys and girls, the kind and amount of education they may hope to attain depends, not on their own abilities, but on the family or community into which they happened to be born or, worse still, on the color of their skin... (Zook, 1947).

Not every student who wants or has prepared to go to college will go. Though some would liken a college education to something as basic as healthcare (Weisbrod, Ballou, & Ash, 2008), this is not the reality for all students. In particular, low-income urban youth often face seemingly insurmountable challenges when trying to transition to college (Tierney & Venegas, 2006). Low-income and racial and ethnic minority students have historically encountered the greatest academic and financial barriers to gaining access to postsecondary education, yet research seldom considers the additional resources and skills they require in order to successfully navigate the educational pipeline (Miller, 2006; Welton & Martinez, 2013). Efforts have been made to counter such disparities; however, proposed solutions have disproportionately concentrated on the school environment and what happens inside of the classroom (McDonough, 2004; Tierney & Venegas, 2006). Moreover, a great deal of the work to improve college access has focused on increasing the number of college-ready students who successfully transition from high school to college, as opposed to aiding in the successful transition of those students who have already qualified for and been accepted to institutions of higher learning.

During the summer after high school graduation, many college-intending students often discover themselves to be without the crucial knowledge, resources and direction necessary to smoothly transition to college (Castleman & Page, 2011). A number of high school graduates learn firsthand that being admitted to college is not the same as going to college (Arnold, Fleming, DeAnda, Castleman, & Wartman, 2009). They find out that the college admission process has requisite, yet hidden, steps that must be completed even after getting in. Recent scholars have termed the loss of students who do not attend college in the fall after their senior year in high school—even though they have met all of the requirements for high school graduation, gained college admission and demonstrated the desire to attend college—as the "summer melt" (Arnold et

al., 2009; Castleman, Arnold, & Wartman, 2012; Castleman & Page, 2011; Castleman, Page, & Schooley, 2013; Hoover, 2009). The idea of the summer as an important time in student education is not new, but this intermediary period between high school and college has been sparsely researched as a potential focal point for increasing college access (Goldrick-Rab, Carter, & Wagner, 2007).

Pre-college experiences, such as navigating the summer between secondary and postsecondary education, play an important role in students' perception of college (Conley, 2008; Kuh, Kinzie, Bridges, & Hayek, 2007). Scholars suggest that "college culture in a high school cultivates aspirations and behaviors conducive to preparing for, applying to, and enrolling in college" (Corwin & Tierney, 2007, p. 3). Because key individuals, such as college counselors, are often the primary purveyors of college-going cultures (Corwin & Tierney, 2007; Corwin, Venegas, Oliverez, & Colyar, 2004; Venegas, 2007), the essential question addressed in this chapter is: How can college counselors facilitate and maintain a college-going culture specifically for underrepresented groups during the summer between high school and college and beyond? Moreover, how might counselors utilize the student's community cultural wealth in order to help bridge the gap between high school and college? How can college counselors establish themselves as useful institutional agents on behalf of students prior to the arrival of the students on campus? Counselors can take advantage of the short period of the summer between high school and college to help establish and/or strengthen key relationships, behaviors and patterns that will help students transition to college and remain with them once they begin their postsecondary education.

INITIATING AND SUSTAINING THE COLLEGE-GOING CULTURE OVER THE SUMMER

An integral part of the high school experience is preparing to navigate academic, cultural and social postsecondary expectations (Conley, 2005; Greene & Forster, 2003; Venezia & Kirst, 2004). Though graduation from high school is a prerequisite for immediate college enrollment, it is not by itself a sufficient indicator of successful college matriculation (Carnevale & Fry, 2002). The Immediate College Enrollment Rate (ICER) is greatly influenced by income and race/ethnicity. In each year from 1975 to

2009, this rate was worse for low-income families as compared to high-income families—in 2009, only 55 percent of low-income students enrolled in college immediately after high school versus 84 percent of high-income students (U.S. Department of Education, 2012). Additionally, in 2009, while the ICER of blacks and Latinos remained relatively unchanged from its 2003 number at approximately 60 percent, Asian and white students had increased ICERs of 90 percent and 71 percent, respectively (U.S. Department of Education, 2012).

Though not enormous in number, these students offer a finite population that practitioners can work with in order to have a considerable impact on inequitable college access and enrollment figures. With the prevalence of such disparities, every student matters, and education practitioners, especially, cannot afford to lose those who have already demonstrated the prerequisite skills and initiative for college attainment. Efforts to address the disparities in college access and transition have disproportionally focused on increasing the number of college-ready students, as opposed to helping those students who are already qualified for, gain acceptance to and send letters of commitment to institutions of higher learning successfully transition from high school to college. Moreover, the summer between high school and college is territory claimed in totality neither by practitioners at the high school level or practitioners at the college level. There has yet to be a consensus as to whether or not high schools should "stay late" or colleges should "start early" to provide guidance to high school graduates in the summer before they begin college. That said, it may prove advantageous for counselors to expand their notion of where students can get the support they need to successfully transition to college.

At present, most college-prep programs place little to no emphasis on integrating the cultural identity, needs or assets of students (Swail & Perna, 2002; Villalpando & Solórzano, 2005). This lack of consideration is a missed opportunity, as many historically underrepresented students face challenges in school that make it difficult for them to navigate the use of their school's resources (McAdoo, 2002). College counselors can work beyond school walls to establish and foster culturally integrative practices and programs that enable students to maximize their community cultural wealth. How can programs geared to improve the transition of students from high school to college better consider students' cultural identities? How might families and communities be equipped to fill the gap during this pivotal summer, during which students often feel isolated from the high school they just graduated from and the college they have yet to begin?

Summer counseling can have a strong and positive influence on on-time college enrollment (Castleman & Page, 2011). Through summer intervention, college counselors may be able to create, maintain and extend their influence in the academic success of students. To get at the deliberate actions college counselors can take to influence the academic outcomes of their students, this chapter draws on two interrelated theoretical frames—community cultural wealth (CCW) and institutional agency—best suited for highlighting the importance and strength of nontraditional networks for underrepresented and underserved students. Programs that prepare students for academic success should be delivered in culturally appropriate ways (Villalpando & Solórzano, 2005).

COMMUNITY CULTURAL WEALTH

Roderick and colleagues (2009) put forth that the academic qualifications of students could not alter the fact that they were the product of neighborhoods and families that were less able to provide them with the necessary knowledge to navigate the college admission process. In an effort to better understand why students melt and how it may be possible to reduce the failed transition to college, it is essential to recognize the strength of neighborhood and family effects on student opportunities for success (Nettles, Caughy, & O'Campo, 2008).

Yosso (2005) describes community cultural wealth as "an array of knowledge, skills, abilities, and contacts possessed and utilized by communities of color to survive and resist macro- and micro-forms of oppression" (p. 77). It is comprised of at least six types of capital—aspirational, familial, resistant, social, linguistic, and navigational capital.

1. **Aspirational capital** is the ability to safeguard hopes and dreams for the future in spite of adversity. This capital can be found in the student, the family of the student or both. Aspirational capital encompasses the possibilities for students to imagine beyond their current circumstances and aids in navigating oppressive conditions (Yosso & García, 2007).

2. **Familial capital** is the knowledge cultivated by family "that carr[ies] a sense of community history, memory and cultural intuition" (Yosso, 2005, p. 79). This form of capital is important in recognition of the family's influences on the student's emotional, educational, moral, and occupational consciousness (Listman, Rogers, & Hauser, 2011).

3. **Resistant capital** is that conglomeration of skills and knowledge that challenges inequality in society (e.g., higher education). Resistant capital also describes the ability of communities of color (COC) to maintain and pass on the various components of CCW.

4. **Social capital** alludes to the networks of people and resources that guide and support students' paths through the various institutions of society and "can provide both instrumental and emotional support to navigate through society's institutions" (Yosso, 2005, p. 79).

5. **Linguistic capital** is made up of the knowledge and skills gained from communication experiences in multiple styles and languages. It illustrates that students of color enter academic settings with multiple languages and communication skills (Yosso, 2005).

6. **Navigational capital** describes those skills that facilitate the movement through social institutions. Knowledge of how to navigate the educational system is an asset that can help a student reach his/her goal in academic settings (Listman, Rogers, & Hauser, 2011). Yosso and García (2007) stress that this ability to maneuver is especially applicable in contexts that are not created with communities of color in mind.

These six components of CCW are historically unnoticed and undervalued in academic settings (Liou, Antrop-González, & Cooper, 2009), yet possession of CCW, or "non-dominant" capital, is critical for socially marginalized groups (Carter, 2003). The importance of CCW is due to the fact that it not only combats the deficit capital perspective of communities of color, but it also highlights the strengths of these communities (Listman, Rogers, & Hauser, 2011). Using the assumption that underrepresented students, their parents and their communities value educational achievement as the foundation for facilitating the summer transition to college, it is possible to improve the immediate college matriculation rates of these under-

represented students (Villalpando & Solórzano, 2005). The involvement, support and high expectations offered by parents of students in the process of college preparation are important factors that not only enable students to graduate from high school, but also enable students to attend and succeed in college (Jun & Colyar, 2002; Hossler, Schmit, & Vesper, 1999; Tierney, 2002).

CCW offers insight into how college counselors might better provide direct support to students in academic settings and provides background on contributory aspects of the community that empower students to be successful in getting to and through postsecondary education. A focus on navigational capital, for example, may lessen the inability of some students to successfully transition from high school to college, because at this pivotal time (the summer between high school and college) in their academic trajectory, students have often relinquished key resource ties at the high school level and have yet to establish much needed connections at the college level. Counselors can step in during this time to help students navigate this gap. Counselors help students negotiate success in institutional environments by increasing the capital the students can access. Navigational capital includes those skills that facilitate the movement through social institutions. Navigational capital, in particular, elucidates how college counselors can aid students in navigating academic success through alternative social networks (Liou et al., 2009). Knowledge of how to navigate the educational system is an asset that can help a student reach his/her goal in academic settings (Listman, Rogers, & Hauser, 2011).

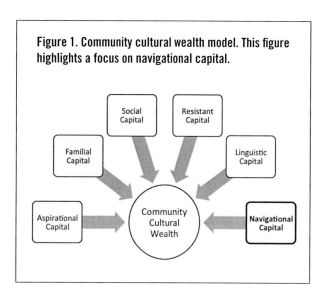

Figure 1. Community cultural wealth model. This figure highlights a focus on navigational capital.

Yosso and García (2007) stress that this ability to maneuver is especially applicable in contexts that are not created with communities of color in mind. College counselors are potentially a rich resource because their position in the institution puts them in contact with valuable resources for students. The summer offers an opportunity for college counselors to establish an authentic collection of pre-college experiences that promotes student success (Kuh, et al., 2007). Expanding intervention to include the communities from which these students come from, for example, is important

Institutional Agents

While the literature elaborately presents the idea that key personnel help students navigate academic environments and that communities of color possess forms of capital vital to their success, the research that describes how these two aspects come to be is limited. Addressing the phenomenon of the summer melt is not about academic preparation or higher education goals; to help students successfully transition to college from high school requires "aligning aspirations, knowledge, relationships, and resources so that students receive a necessary escort

Students not only need access to postsecondary education, but they also need the knowledge, skills, resources and networks necessary to continue their academic success past high school. The aim of this chapter was to elucidate options that may prove effective in helping students to successfully transition to college.

because it offers a self-perpetuating means by which we can target summer melting. Whereas "start early" programs (those that require the college to assume guidance over high school graduates immediately after graduation) and "stay late" programs (those that require the high school to maintain guidance over high school graduates until they enter college) keep much-needed college knowledge in the possession of school-based individuals, programs that train communities to know how to navigate this trajectory could have lasting effects on more than one student at a time. Younger siblings would benefit from this knowledge, and students themselves would be equipped with key skill sets that will help them act as their own guide when necessary. The knowledge garnered would remain in the community and not leave when the student matriculates into college. By providing opportunities and institutional resources, college counselors may increase the level of college-going among high school students. The goal then is for college counselors to extend their service as institutional agents on behalf of students during this summer and equip students and communities with the resources and experiences necessary to ultimately become institutional agents themselves.

into the opportunity they have prepared for, sought and won" (Arnold et al., 2009, p. 32). What can counselors do to help to bridge the gap in navigational capital that some students encounter in the summer between high school and college? They can and should enact their role as institutional agents, because they may be in the best position to help students through the high-school-to-college adjustment. College counselors who are institutional agents, for example, go beyond serving as role models or providing psychological support to students; they provide students with access to networks and knowledge bases full of resources, through a variety of forms of support (Dowd, Sawatzky, Rall, & Bensimon, 2012). College counselors possess extensive levels of social, human and cultural capital that can impact the successful college matriculation of students. College counselors are in a prime position to create meaningful change for students through actions and attitudes. Their desire and know-how to act effectively on behalf of students makes them institutional agents (Center for Urban Education, 2010).

Ricardo Stanton-Salazar (2010) describes institutional agents (IAs) as "non-kin" individuals who utilize their own status and authority, resources, and networks to service disenfranchised students. Basically, IAs serve as leaders to help students negotiate success in institutional environments by increasing the capital the students can access. Those individuals desiring to serve as IAs for underserved students need to be aware of additional forms of capital than those supported by the mainstream. Some of the various ways by which a counselor can enact his or her role as an institutional agent on behalf of students transitioning to college are provided in Table 1.

Some ways that practitioners may serve as institutional agents in order to engage students during this "forgotten" summer include phone calls, emails or texts (Castleman, Page, & Schooley, 2014; Hoover 2009). This chapter discusses how college counselors can assume the various roles of IAs and how they, as a collective entity, can broker resources to facilitate an environment that supports the success of college students.

Table 1. How a Counselor Enacts the Institutional Agent Role for Students Transitioning to College

Direct Support During the Summer Between High School and College	
A Resource Agent… …creates, provides, utilizes, or maximizes personal and positional resources on behalf of students	*A Networking Coach…* …instructs students how to network with key institutional and community agents throughout the summer …models effective networking behavior …develops relationships with important and influential people on campus, in the high schools and in the community
An Advocate… …supports and protects his or her students during the summer and beyond	
A Knowledge Agent… …accesses or provides knowledge pertinent to navigating the summer between high school and college (e.g., timelines, due dates, etc.) …knows the explicit and implicit requirements students must complete during high school and college to ensure successful matriculation	*An Advisor…* …encourages and directs productive decision-making …helps students locate and gather information …assesses potential problems and solutions in a collaborative manner …maintains open communication with the student and is accessible
Integrative Support During the Summer Between High School and College	
An Integrative Agent… …facilitates students' knowledge of, access to, and integration and participation in resource-rich professional, cultural, and academic networks and venues (professional associations, department, school, etc.)	*A Cultural Guide…* …guides students through unfamiliar social situations in a particular cultural sphere …teaches students to identify and interact with key people in a particular cultural sphere
System Developer During the Summer Between High School and College	
A Program Developer… …develops a program that embeds students in a system of agents, resources and opportunities …encourages students to perpetuate certain networks and to serve as support for others, particularly younger students …maintains notes and records that may be useful for future students	*A Political Advocate…* …is knowledgeable of, allies with or joins political action groups that advocate for social policies and institutional resources that would benefit underserved, underresourced and underrepresented student groups …stays current on policies, standards and events that directly or indirectly impact students
A Lobbyist… …lobbies for organizational resources to be directed toward student recruitment, retention and success	
System Linkage and Networking Support During the Summer Between High School and College	
A Recruiter… …actively recruits students to the institution, program, department, etc. and extends the relationship to ensure that students are actually able to matriculate	*A Bridging Agent…* …introduces students to other institutional agents …has a strong social network …knows who key players are and what they do
An Institutional Broker… …negotiates introductions and agreements between two or more parties …knows what resources are available and who controls or possesses them …serves as an intermediary between the student and the institution	*A Coordinator…* …assesses student needs (academic, cultural, etc.) …identifies resources that can address student needs …provides and accesses institutional resources on behalf of students …ensures students utilize resources effectively

Adapted from the Center for Urban Education (2010) and Stanton-Salazar (2010).

CONCLUSION

Students not only need access to postsecondary education, but they also need the knowledge, skills, resources and networks necessary to continue their academic success past high school. The aim of this chapter was to elucidate options that may prove effective in helping students to successfully transition to college. This investigation is necessary and relevant, as the triumvirate of low-income status, race and the rising cost of education creates an almost impenetrable barrier for many students (Zook, 1947). Underserved and underrepresented students seem to have the greatest need during their transition to college (Arnold et al., 2009). Educators and practitioners need to consider the impact of transition intervention on student outcomes—who benefits from such programs, the best way to design such efforts and what the key facets of the programs are. Summer intervention is but one necessary, yet insufficient, part of a comprehensive counseling regimen geared at aiding students in their transition to college.

Because the transition to college for underrepresented groups is different from the transition of their peers (Andrade, 2006), research may also expand the investigation regarding the ways in which race, ethnicity and culture affect the transition to and success in college. Though most efforts to admit and retain students of color in US higher education take place on college campuses, there are additional ways to think about how to equip students of color for collegiate success; it often begins even before they arrive on campus (Tierney, 1999). Strategies for melt-reduction may be sound investments in retention (Hoover, 2009), so rethinking the role of college counseling over the summer is integral to not only getting students to college, but also getting them successfully through college.

Those interested in improving educational outcomes can learn much from students who struggle to simultaneously preserve some and initiate other relationships. College counselors have a unique opportunity to facilitate this transition. They're able to empower students by teaching them how to navigate through college matriculation and beyond through key relationships. College counselors help students tap into their community cultural wealth through collaboration with their high school, college, community, family, mentors, and others in order to improve educational outcomes. Counselors seek-

ing to serve as institutional agents so that they can help students navigate the summer between high school and college should start with a self-assessment of the following questions:

1. How can I be proactive and consistent in helping students assess challenges, acquire information, seek assistance, stay engaged, feel supported, and make appropriate decisions during the summer they are transitioning from high school to college?

2. What resources do I have at my disposal that can benefit students as they transition from high school to college?

3. What resources do students have available to them that can benefit and support them as they transition from high school to college?

4. What are the lessons I have learned from past students that may equip me to better serve present and future students as they prepare to begin college in the fall after their high school graduation?

5. What actions can I take to ensure that a student is sufficiently supported over the summer between high school and college—that he or she either stays connected to key high school personnel or establishes a connection with key college personnel that can serve as a resource during this finite, yet pivotal, timeframe?

Prior work that has shown that underrepresented groups are particularly at risk of the summer melt would suggest that the focus on these students may actually impact the policy and practice infrastructure that contributes to students' successful transition to college. Answering these questions to assess the counselor's role as an institutional agent, and considering the community cultural wealth of students may be one step in the direction of better equipping practitioners with the resources and skills needed to facilitate college participation before students even arrive on campus.

ABOUT THE AUTHOR

Dr. Raquel M. Rall is a recent graduate of University of Southern California's Rossier School of Education (CA) where she earned her PhD in urban education policy. She obtained BA degrees in human biology and African and

African American studies from Stanford University (CA). Her research centers on identifying best practices to increase access to and success in higher education for traditionally marginalized communities and on bridging research and practice. She is dedicated to maximizing educational outcomes for communities that have traditionally had the least opportunities and uses her academic research to better understand and uncover the meanings and intricate characteristics of experiences, interactions, people, events, and environments pertaining to postsecondary access and success for underrepresented and underserved student groups. Dr. Rall aims to understand the conditions that lead to and ultimately result in widespread change in education policy and the ramifications of this transformation on student experiences and outcomes. She has presented papers at numerous national and regional conferences on her work on the transition from high school to college for low-income students of color.

REFERENCES

Andrade, M.S. (2006). International student persistence: Integration or cultural integrity? *Journal of College Student Retention: Research, Theory and Practice,* 8(1), 57–81.

Arnold, K., Fleming, S., DeAnda, M., Castleman, B.L., & Wartman, K.L. (2009). The summer flood: The invisible gap among low-income students. *The NEA Higher Education Journal,* 23–34.

Carnevale, A.P., & Fry, R.A. (2002). The demographic window of opportunity: College access and diversity in the new century. *Condition of Access: Higher Education for Lower Income Students,* 137–152.

Carter, P.L. (2003). "Black" Cultural capital, status positioning, and schooling conflicts for low-income African American youth. *Social Problems,* 50(1), 136–155.

Castleman, Arnold, K., & Wartman, K.L. (2012). Stemming the tide of summer melt: An experimental study of the effects of post-high school summer intervention on low-income students' college enrollment. *Journal of Research on Educational Effectiveness,* 5(1), 1–17.

Castleman, & Page, L.C. (2011). A trickle or a torrent? Understanding the extent of summer "melt" among college-intending high school graduates. Paper presented at the Annual Meeting of the American Educational Research Association.

Castleman, B.L., Page, L.C., & Schooley, K. (2014). The forgotten summer: Does the offer of college counseling after high school mitigate summer melt among college-intending, low-income high school graduates? *Journal of Policy Analysis and Management,* 33(2), 320–344.

Center for Urban Education. (2010). STEM Toolkit: Tools for increasing Latino and Latina STEM baccalaureates. Los Angeles, CA: Rossier School of Education.

Conley, D.T. (2005). College knowledge: What it really takes for students to succeed and what we can do to get them ready. San Francisco, CA: Jossey-Bass.

Corwin, Z.B., & Tierney, W.G. (2007). Getting there-and beyond: Building a culture of college-going in high schools. Los Angeles, CA: University of Southern California Center for Higher Education Policy Analysis.

Corwin, Z.B., Venegas, K.M., Oliverez, P.M., & Colyar, J.E. (2004). School counsel: How appropriate guidance affects educational equity. *Urban Education,* 39(4), 442–457.

Dowd, A.C., Sawatzky, M., Rall, R.M., & Bensimon, E.M. (2012). Action research: An essential practice for twenty-first century assessment. In R.T. Palmer, D.C. Maramba, & M. Gasman (Eds.), *Fostering success of ethnic and racial minorities in STEM: The role of minority serving institutions.* New York: Routledge.

Goldrick-Rab, S., Carter, D.F., & Wagner, R.W. (2007). What higher education has to say about the transition to college. *Teachers College Record,* 109(10), 2444–2481.

Greene, J.P., & Forster, G. (2003). *Public high school graduation and college readiness rates in the United States.* New York: The Center for Civic Innovation, Manhattan Institute for Policy Research.

Hoover, E. (2009). In an uncertain summer, colleges try to control enrollment "melt." *The Chronicle of Higher Education,* 55, 1.

Hossler, D., Schmit, J., & Vesper, N. (1999). *Going to college: How social, economic, and educational factors influence the decisions students make.* Baltimore, MD: Johns Hopkins University Press.

Jun, A., & Colyar, J. (2002). Parental guidance suggested: Family involvement in college preparation programs. In W.G. Tierney & L.S. Hagedorn (Eds.), *Extending their reach: Strategies for increasing access to college* (pp. 195–215). Albany, NY: State University of New York Press.

Kuh, G.D., Kinzie, J., Buckley, J.A., Bridges, B.K., & Hayek, J.C. (2007). Piecing together the student success puzzle: Research, propositions, and recommendations. *ASHE Higher Education Report*, 32(5). San Francisco, CA: Jossey-Bass.

Liou, D.D., Antrop-González, R., & Cooper, R. (2009). Unveiling the promise of community cultural wealth to sustaining Latina/o students' college-going information networks. *Educational Studies*, 45(6), 534–555.

Listman, J., Rogers, K.D., & Hauser, P.C. (2011). Community cultural wealth and deaf adolescents' resilience. In *Resilience in deaf children* (pp. 279–297). New York: Springer.

McDonough, P.M. (2004). *The impact of advice on price: Evidence from research*. Boston, MA: The Education Research Institute.

Miller, C. (2006). A test of leadership: Charting the future of US higher education. A Report of the Commission Appointed by the Secretary of Education Margaret Spellings. Retrieved from *http://www.ed.gov/about/bdscomm/list/hiedfuture/reports/final-report.pdf*

Nettles, S.M., Caughy, M.O., & O'Campo, P.J. (2008). School adjustment in the early elementary years: Toward an integrated model of neighborhood, parental, and child processes. *Review of Educational Research*, 78, 3–32.

Roderick, M., Nagaoka, J., & Coca, V. (2009). College readiness for all: The challenge for urban high schools. *The Future of Children*, 19(1), 185–210.

Stanton-Salazar, R.D. (2010). A social capital framework for the study of institutional agents & their role in the empowerment of low-status students & youth. University of Southern California.

Swail, W.S., & Perna, L.W. (2002). Pre-college outreach programs: A national perspective. In W.G. Tierney & L.S. Hagedorn (Eds.), *Increasing access to college: Extending possibilities for all students* (pp. 15–34). Albany, NY: State University of New York Press.

Tierney, W.G. (1999). Models of minority college-going and retention: Cultural integrity versus cultural suicide. *Journal of Negro Education*, 68(1) 80–91.

Tierney, W.G. (2002). Parents and families in precollege preparation: The lack of connection between research and practice. *Educational Policy*, 16(4), 588–606.

Tierney, W.G., & Venegas, K.M. (2006). Fictive kin and social capital: The role of peer groups in applying and paying for college. *American Behavioral Scientist*, 49(12), 1687–1702.

Toldson, I.A. (2008). *Breaking barriers: Plotting the path to academic success for school-age African-American males*. Washington, DC: Congressional Black Caucus Foundation.

U.S. Department of Education. (2012). The Condition of Education 2012 (NCES 2012-034), Indicator 34: National Center for Education Statistics.

Venegas, K.M. (2007). The internet and college access: Challenges for low-income students. *American Academic*, 3, 141–154.

Venezia, A., Kirst, M.W., & Antonio, A.L. (2004). *Betraying the college dream: How disconnected K–12 and postsecondary education systems undermine student aspirations*. Stanford, CA: The Stanford Institute for Higher Education Research.

Villalpando, O., & Solórzano, D.G. (2005). The role of culture in college preparation programs: A review of the research literature. In W.G. Tierney, Z.B. Corwin, & J.E. Colyar (Eds.), *Preparing for college: Nine elements of effective outreach* (pp. 13-28). Albany, NY: SUNY Press.

Weisbrod, B.A., Ballou, J.P., & Ash, E.D. (2008). The two-good framework: Revenue, mission, and why colleges do what they do. In *Mission and money: Understanding the university*. New York, NY: Cambridge University Press.

Welton, A.D., & Martinez, M.A. (2013). Coloring the college pathway: A more culturally responsive approach to college readiness and access for students of color in secondary schools. *The Urban Review*, 46(2), 197–223.

Yosso, T. J. (2005). Whose culture has capital? A critical race theory discussion of community cultural wealth. *Race Ethnicity and Education*, 8(1), 69–91.

Yosso, T.J., & Garcia, D.G. (2007). This is no slum!: A critical race theory analysis of community cultural wealth in culture clash's Chavez Ravine. *Aztlan: A Journal of Chicano Studies*, 32(1), 145–179.

Zook, G.F. (1947, December). Higher education for American democracy (Volume I: Establishing the goals): A report of the President's Commission on Higher Education. Washington, D.C.: US Government Printing Office.

Chapter 25:   The Dynamic Ecosystem of Higher Education: Implications for College Admission Counseling

William G. Tierney, PhD
@TierneyBill

A quarter of a century ago, no one predicted the challenges that higher education would face today. To be sure, throughout much of the last generation, there have been periods of optimism and periods of decline. State legislatures have, on occasion, provided less public monies than an institution's leaders and faculty may have liked, for example, but until recently, tomorrow was not that different from yesterday. Although the last quarter of a century has not seen the emergence of numerous new institutions, which occurred in the 1950s and 1960s, very few colleges or universities that existed in 1990 have died. In many respects, the majority of postsecondary institutions function much like they did a quarter of a century ago.

effort and research, however, focused on the 18–21-year-old clientele. Additional efforts were focused on increasing the participation and completion rates of underrepresented students in all sectors of higher education.

Thus, in 1990, there was little assumption that the postsecondary sector would shift from full-time teenagers to part-time adults or that the representation of students of color would still remain at alarming levels both in attendance and completion. Few predicted that some, if not many, liberal arts colleges might become an endangered species or that for-profit institutions would grow so rapidly and engender so much antipathy.

What also had not been anticipated is the disruption to how one thought about a college education. Students

If one had gone to sleep in 1990 and awakened today, there would certainly be a great deal of surprise about the changes that have occurred and the tenor of discussions about the academic environment.

In this light, the ecosystem of higher education, the various types of postsecondary institutions and how they interact with one another and the larger environment, has not changed very much. There also was not much anticipation that the ecosystem would undergo significant changes. Consider, for example, that 25 years ago the vast majority of students in the United States attended public institutions. A small, but significant, number of liberal arts colleges catered to a specific clientele that had been developed over time. Elite private and public universities were the best in the world; they received fiscal support not only from tuition, state public subsidies for the publics and largesse from donors for the privates, but also from significant federal funding of research. The for-profit sector was a tiny organism in the postsecondary ecosystem, a minor irritant for some, but ignored by most. The clientele for postsecondary education were still thought to be traditionally aged, full-time students, although by 1990, the demographic was beginning to become what it has become today—increasingly older and largely part-time. The lion's share of energy,

came to a campus. They took classes defined by "seat-time." When students had accumulated a certain number of credits, then they were ready to graduate. Full-time, tenure-track faculty were the arbiter of student quality, defined by the grade provided to the student. When students graduated from college, it was incumbent upon them to find employment; the link between curricula and jobs was indirect, at best. College completion was not a topic of conversation. Remediation was a concern, but not a crisis. Transfer between two- and four-year institutions was a nuisance, but not worthy of much effort on the state level or in policy sectors. The relationship between the secondary and postsecondary sectors was largely nonexistent.

In the larger environment, there was a general agreed-upon lament about the weaknesses of public education in the United States. The largest amount of hand-wringing and reform, however, was aimed at improving K–12 education by creating options—vouchers, charter schools and the like. Higher education received occasional commentary, but by and large, the public viewed a college education as valuable and postsecondary institutions as providing a quality product. Whereas governors, legislatures, newspapers, and think tanks had a great deal to say about schools, when it came to higher education, the same groups largely exhibited a hands-off attitude, deferring to college and university presidents and the faculty.

If one had gone to sleep in 1990 and awakened today, there would certainly be a great deal of surprise about the changes that have occurred and the tenor of discussions about the academic environment. The media offers a daily drumbeat about the weakness of the postsecondary sector and the costs of college for students and families. The cumulative amount of student loans is now more than $1 trillion—something that could not have been imagined a quarter of a century ago. Liberal arts colleges as a specific species within the general ecosystem now seem at risk for survival. The federal government is considering reducing support for basic research. For-profit institutions have become 10 percent of the marketplace (Kena et al., 2014) and, in doing so, have garnered a great deal of criticism for their often questionable recruiting practices and frequently dismal placement rates. Of consequence, all of higher education is now being assessed for the utility and quality of learning. Further, public community colleges still fail to graduate or transfer sizeable numbers of students (US Department of Education, 2012); for example, only 44 percent of the students beginning community college in 2004 who indicated that they wanted to transfer and earn a bachelor's degree did so by 2009. Rather than a nuisance, such issues are now of central concern. Policies aimed at increasing college completion and reducing remediation across all sectors are now discussed in most states and in multiple think tanks and foundations. Part-time and non-tenure-track faculty now account for the majority of the professoriate. And perhaps most importantly, the rise of social media and technology are suggesting radical changes to the structure of not only the curriculum, but also higher education itself. The end result is that many still think a college education is worthwhile (91 percent of bachelor's degree and 96 percent of graduate and professional degree holders respectively) (Pew Research Center, 2014), but the hands-off attitude that society had shown has been replaced by a demand for significant changes—although what those changes are, or should be, is entirely unclear.

Perhaps trying to chart the future is a fool's errand. And yet, systems, like organisms in an ecosystem, always evolve. At times such as these, change occurs more dramatically than during times of stability. One ought not to look to the future as if every step is certain, but based on the history of higher education and the recent trajectory of the system, there are reasonable conjectures one might make about how to think about higher education in general and college admission in particular.

Accordingly, my purpose here is neither to suggest that the challenges higher education faces are amenable to quick fixes nor to lament that they are unsolvable. However, there are four key issues that need to be dealt with over the next decade that will not only inform how to think about college admission specifically, but also higher education in general. I point out that these issues will force and enable us to think of new ways of delivering and evaluating teaching and learning and how to define postsecondary organizations in the 21st century. I conclude with what these issues might portend for college admission.

UNDERSTANDING THE VALUE OF A COLLEGE EDUCATION

The value of education has rarely been disputed in the United States. Since the time of Horace Mann in the early 19th century, the citizens of the United States have assumed that education enhances the economic and social prospects of the individual and improves the larger democratic public sphere. The importance of education has been so critical to the country's well-being that elementary and secondary education has been a free public good, and postsecondary education has been heavily subsidized through grants to public institutions and to students.

The overwhelming evidence remains that the more education one has, the greater prospects there are for better paying jobs. Earnings over a lifetime of a college graduate are nearly double that of a high school graduate. Predictions are that close to 60 percent of the workforce will have to have some form of postsecondary degree—a certificate, AA or BA degree (Lumina Foundation, 2012). Numerous studies conclude that more access to higher education is imperative for the well-being of the nation. The Georgetown Center on Education and the Workforce, the Public Policy Institute of California, the Lumina Foundation, the

Gates Foundation, and the Obama administration all have suggested that college-going and graduation rates need to be increased (Johnson & Sengupta, 2009; Lumina Foundation, 2012). The United States once ranked at the top of OECD (The Organisation for Economic Co-operation and Development) rankings for college attainment, but today, the country is ranked lower than numerous industrialized countries.

Some, but not many, have argued that the status quo is sufficient (Schalin, 2010; Vedder, Denhart, Denhart, Matgouranis, & Robe, 2010). The underpinning of the argument is that employers hire individuals with college degrees, but the job only requires a high school degree. In effect, college graduates deliver pizza because there are not enough college-degree-related jobs (Vedder et al., 2010). The assumption is that credentialing helps the higher education industry, but not the economy. The problem of such an analysis is that, for example, 60 percent of the jobs in California are expected to require what one learns in college (Lumina Foundation, 2012). California will fall short by more than one million students based on current estimates. Such a shortfall has dire consequences for the well-being of the state. The problem is that students are not learning the right sorts of skills in college in order to be ready for the job market upon graduation.

A related critique is that too many students graduate from high school and are not college-ready, and then they graduate from college and are not career-ready. The evidence seems to bear out the claims. Just under half of California State University's entering students need to take at least one remedial class. An estimated 90 percent of community college students enter the system underprepared for college-level coursework (California Legislative Analyst's Office, 2013). Students also increasingly graduate from college without the requisite job skills needed.

The challenges that the higher education sector faces are multiple. If more students need to participate in higher education, where will they go? What will they study? What sorts of relationships need to be forged between secondary and postsecondary institutions so that high school graduates are better prepared for going to, and graduating from, college? If the country accepts the status quo, then the United States will have become an island of mediocrity encumbered with an uneducated workforce.

EXAMINING THE STATE'S ROLE IN HIGHER EDUCATION

Based on the commitment to education by the citizenry, a state's role in higher education has been relatively straightforward until recently; the states had different kinds of public institutions for different kinds of students. The primary job of these institutions has been to educate individuals, and that has been defined by the attainment of a degree. The idea of education as a socializing agent, or as a way to instill civic values in individuals, has largely been downplayed for a generation.

Community colleges have always offered certificates for working-class jobs (e.g., plumbing), but they also have been frequently criticized because of their high drop-out and non-completion rates, as well as their low transfer rates to four-year institutions. The second-tier state universities also have offered master's degrees, and the research universities have focused on graduate education. Most states also have had a medical complex devoted to the training of physicians; a teaching hospital and medical complex also have contributed to the health and economic welfare of a state. Research, as an economic engine for a state, has played a significant role in some states, such as California, and much less in other states, such as Mississippi.

Although variations have occurred across states, the general principal throughout most of the 20th century was that the state funded public institutions, and a relatively small portion of a postsecondary institution's budget was dependent upon tuition or other revenue. Trends also existed by sector; virtually all of a community college's and state university's budget derived from state support, whereas the elite public research universities have a history of attracting federal research dollars, primarily for science, and foundation support for a variety of research areas.

Over the last generation, public institutions also have become involved in capital campaigns, similar to those at private universities, in order to generate revenue from alumni and wealthy philanthropists. The assumption has been, however, that if public research universities are to maintain their status as world-class institutions, then they must raise revenue from private sources insofar as the state will no longer provide enough support. Such an assumption is widespread today, whereas a generation ago, most states funded most public institutions.

One might think that a decrease in funding makes a public institution less dependent on state demands, but, as state funding has decreased as an absolute percentage of overall revenue, state regulatory control has increased. Until recently, the state had been relatively uninvolved in the regulation of postsecondary institutions. Regulation had been ceded to accrediting bodies—both institutional and professional. What a college or university offered and how quality was defined had been granted to the institution, in general, and the faculty, in particular. Regional accreditation, although critically important, simply demonstrated minimal levels of institutional competence. Without accreditation, an institution's degree was relatively worthless, although many institutions, especially for-profit institutions, have existed without it. The lack of accreditation, however, meant that the students could not receive federal or state loans and grants, and that if they wished to transfer to another institution, their degree and institutional credits would not be accepted.

challenged geographically based accrediting agencies. If a public, private or for-profit institution is based in Nebraska, but has an online master's degree that students in New York are taking, from which region of the country should the degree be given accreditation? If someone wants to be a veterinarian, is it more important for the institution to have accreditation from a state agency or one with broader reach, possibly beyond national borders? As Duderstadt and Womack (2003) have pointed out, "Higher education is breaking loose from the moorings of physical campuses, even as its credentialing monopoly begins to erode" (p. 76). The result is that, on the one hand, we are seeing the market replace regulatory control, while, on the other, the state is asking for greater oversight of those diminishing public dollars that they provide.

Higher education, then, is evolving like other deregulated industries, such as healthcare, where we see public and profit-making hospitals; we also experience all the strengths and weaknesses of the market and deregulation, such as we have recently experienced in the banking and

> *The lack of accreditation, however, meant that the students could not receive federal or state loans and grants, and that if they wished to transfer to another institution, their degree and institutional credits would not be accepted.*

Although state legislatures always have taken on hot-button curricular issues from time to time, in general, the state has stayed away from regulatory control. Presidents created budget requests, and the legislature approved all or some portion of it. Line-item vetoes or oversight on a particular course offering was generally not done. To be sure, at times, special requests occurred. The state may have decided that a particular focus was important, or a legislator simply wanted some particular center or institute at the postsecondary institution in his or her political district, but the overarching assumption was that the postsecondary institutions knew best how to lead their institutions.

Over the last generation, that assumption has gradually changed. Accreditation has come under attack as being too weak and too slow, and technological changes have

housing industries. The general winner of deregulation is for-profit companies who have viewed accrediting bodies as exclusionary gatekeepers. Critics charge, however, that the state is adding regulatory burdens to public institutions precisely at the time they are weakening their oversight capacity of other institutions. As a result, the consumer is put at risk.

The shift away from the creation, sustenance and support of a public good reflects shifts with other goods and services for the state such that the state no longer sees itself as a purveyor of public goods. A consistent and radical line of thinking is that the state and federal government's regulatory role should also be negligible. The subprime mortgage loans that contributed to the housing crisis in the United States reflect a philosophy that says markets need to be unregulated for capitalism to flourish. For-profit colleges and universities (FPCUs) have made the same sort of argument and have largely succeeded. They would argue, as most proponents of such arguments reason, that there is still too much regulation. Their argument is that if problems exist, they will fix the problems, and they do not need regulation to hamper their efforts. The consumer (the student) only buys "good" products, so it is in the organization's interest to police the quality of the product. Although there is some admitted truth to such an assertion, it also does not take into account a history of malfeasance by companies that have shown little regard or concern for the customer.

Ironically, public institutions have faced a twofold problem. They have been criticized as the opposite of consumer-friendly. Because they presumably receive a steady stream of revenue that is impervious to consumer demands, the argument has been made that they are out of touch and exist to support the faculty, rather than the students. Because of this perception, steps have been made to regulate them and to make demands with regard to admission, retention, graduation, time-to-degree, and a host of other issues.

ASSESSING PRIVATIZATION IN THE ECOSYSTEM

The shift from the idea that an organization should be the provider of a public good has opened the door to a significant increase in private providers and the privatization of public institutions.

Over the last decade, the fastest growing sector in higher education in the United States is for-profit colleges and universities (FPCUs) (Tierney & Hentschke, 2007). Because of the severe criticism the industry has experienced, it is also the fastest shrinking sector over the last two years. Although FPCUs have existed for more than a century in the United States, until recently they were relatively small companies that offered one specific skill or trade, such as cosmetology or welding. However, for-profit institutions, such as the University of Phoenix, now rank among the largest in the United States. These institutions all have a similar funding model. They outsource the vast majority of their services (such as admission) and standardize their curricula, teaching and learning across campuses. Courses are offered in areas that are convenient to students, such as shopping malls, and at convenient

times for the working adult—evenings and weekends. Faculty are part-time; in general, they do not receive health or retirement benefits, and they will be dismissed if there is a drop in enrollment in the classes that they teach or if their teaching evaluations are not excellent.

One key aspect of FPCUs is that they rely on their ability to fill out paperwork for a student to apply for grants and loans from the federal and state governments. Their admission staff can be quite large, and rather than have students wait several months from the time they apply until they are admitted and start their program, a for-profit institution may admit and enroll a student in a matter of days. The result is that more than 90 percent of the institution's income is generated from fee-paying students, and the students' fees derive from the government (Klor de Alva & Rosen, 2012) Ironically, then, the most private of our institutions thrive, and most likely could not survive, without public funding. One significant difference between FPCUs and traditional providers is that these private, for-profit companies pay taxes to the government and generate revenue for the owners or corporate boards. Students graduate with greater debt loads than at comparable public and private nonprofit institutions, the retention and graduation rates tend to be lower than at comparable institutions, and default rates on loans have been a significant issue.

The argument for for-profits has been made succinctly by Weisbrod, Ballou and Asch (2008): "Services that can be sold profitably do not need public subsidies" (p. 4). From this perspective, education, as defined as preparation for the job market, is a good that can be sold, and a for-profit college can do it as well as, or better than, a publicly subsidized institution. The alternative argument, of course, is that education is more than vocational training and that the purpose of a public university is more than simply the selling of a service.

The result is that the public landscape is significantly different in the second decade of the 21st century than it was a quarter of a century ago. Privatization also has had an impact on the working conditions of the institutions. As noted, the United States now hires more non-tenure-track faculty than tenure-track; part-time faculty are more common in many institutions than full-time (tenure-track or non-tenure-track) faculty. Because public institutions still relied on a part of their revenue from the state when the economic crisis of 2008–2009 erupted, public institutions had more significant problems than private, nonprofit institutions and especially for-profit colleges and universities. Many faculty at public institutions were furloughed, as were public employees, which resulted in a loss in many states of about 10 percent of a professor's salary (Turner, in press). The result is that private, non-profit research institutions seem to be eclipsing public research universities.

Certainly, private institutions faced economic problems; however, because their losses were largely restricted to endowment income, they did not face a crisis with regard to their operating revenue. Because for-profit institutions have a low set cost for personnel, they were not impacted. Very few of the institutions faced a decrease in applicants; the result was that those institutions that relied on tuition revenue—for-profit and private nonprofits—did better than those institutions that still existed in part through public funding. More recently, as I shall discuss below, small liberal arts colleges, as well as some public institutions, have faced enrollment declines, but that has less to do with a downturn in the economy and more to do with the changing needs and preferences of the consumer.

A consequence of privatization is greater managerial power and decision-making authority. Although private universities also function under the academic model of shared governance, it is fair to say that the diminution of the "public" nature of an institution increases the voice of administrators and decreases that of the faculty. As Douglass (2009) has observed, the consequences of globalization are "broader authority for university presidents, including greater authority in budget management and administrative authority" (p. 9). Democratic principles of decision-making are not so much eschewed or repudiated, but simply overlooked in the rush to make decisions so that the organization is more efficient.

INTERPRETING THE RISE IN DISRUPTIVE CONDITIONS WITHIN THE ECOSYSTEM

Traditional organizations, whether they are profit-making companies or nonprofit institutions, such as colleges and universities, generally try to adapt to the times and meet the needs of their customers. They do so by calling upon what Clayton Christensen has defined as "sustainable technology" (Christensen et al., 2011). A sustainable technology improves upon the current technology that exists in a traditional organization. The clearest example of a sustainable technology is when typewriter companies moved from manual to electric typewriters. Anyone who can remember the days of manual typewriters will remember the excitement of the adoption of the electric typewriter. What we were doing suddenly got easier and faster. The movement from a push lawnmower to an electric lawnmower and going from black and white television to color are additional examples of sustainable technologies that improve upon a product.

A sustainable technology improves performance for the existing market and conceivably brings in additional customers who may desire the current product. The customer has a variety of companies to choose from, and if the product does not stay up-to-date, then the company will find itself in trouble or out of business. Obviously, companies that only sold manual typewriters, black and white television sets, and push lawnmowers a decade after its competitors had introduced electric typewriters, color televisions and electric lawnmowers would find themselves in trouble.

Although public and private universities are lampooned for an inability to change, institutions have adapted within the postsecondary ecosystem by incorporating sustainable technologies throughout the 20th century. Chalkboards gave way to boards that utilized magic markers. Ancient gymnasiums morphed into student centers with multiple activities and state-of-the-art fitness centers. Slide projectors became more advanced audiovisual projectors and then PowerPoint. The faculty and administration and boards adapted to the times and their competitors by utilizing sustainable technologies.

However, the pattern is clear. The technology improves over time, the customer base expands, the cost of the invention drops, and, at some point, the disruptive technology overwhelms companies focused on sustainable technologies. Companies are focused on improving their product, not inventing a new one. Frequently, traditional companies do not see the start-ups as competitors, not only because they are miniscule, but also because they are after different markets. The result, however, is that, in a matter of years, computers make typewriters obsolete, and the telephone does the same for the telegraph. The traditional companies belatedly try to adapt, but they cannot compete. Apple and Microsoft drive Olivetti and Smith Corona out of business.

The most obvious and most recent example of a beneficiary and a casualty of disruptive technology are online social media and the newspaper industry. When outlets such as The Huffington Post began, no one really saw them as a competitor to the Washington Post. A decade later, the newspaper industry is in decline, and online media such as magazines, apps, blogs, and even Twitter and Instagram, have overwhelmed the traditional competition. Newspapers were late to utilize social media, and, although one or two, such as The New York Times, may survive, their survival will likely be as part of a social media outlet. In related fashion, print copies of books and articles have foundered to such an extent that publishing houses and bookstores are rapidly becoming artifacts of the past.

Why would anyone think that the same sorts of changes are not likely to happen in higher education? As Christensen and his colleagues (2011) point out, "the theory of disruptive innovation has significant explanatory power in thinking through the challenges and changes confronting higher education" (p. 2). The technology enabler is online learning. Again, consider how previous disruptive technologies were initially complicated, costly and of interest to a limited few. And then at one point, that technology becomes more convenient, less costly, and easy to use and customizable (Christensen, Horn, & Johnson, 2008).

How those in higher education have spoken about and used online learning up to this point is in line with initial declarations about disruptive technology. Even those people who might be thought of as proponents initially thought of online technology as a poor imitation of the "real thing," which was the model of the "sage on the stage." The users of the nascent technology were people who traditional institutions did not try to reach—perhaps the individual who was too far from a campus to take classes or the individual who worked during times that most college classes were offered. The providers were not mainstream institutions, but those on the periphery—largely for-profit providers. Initially, those higher up on the educational food chain, so to speak, suggested that the implications for distance learning were irrelevant. Just as with examples from the steel and car industry, successful organizations—in this case, the Harvards

and Stanfords of the postsecondary world—could not see how a peripheral provider had anything in common with the campus-based classroom experiences that students received.

By the second decade of the 21st century, however, online learning has followed the trajectory of other disruptive technologies. Just as computers became ubiquitous, the exponential growth in online learning underscores how the technology has improved in quality and performance, making it desirable not simply to working adults, but also to the broad panoply of postsecondary students. In 2003, about 10 percent of students took at least one online course; a decade later, the proportion is about 50 percent (Christensen et al., 2011).

If I am correct about online learning being a disruptive technology, and, like other disruptive technologies, it forces changes with other products and services, then what other changes might come about that will impact all postsecondary institutions? Online learning is a model that changes the notion of "seat-time," for example, so one might expect a greater emphasis on learning outcomes, rather than credits earned, simply because a student spent a specific amount of time attending a class once or twice a week over a set number of weeks (Tierney, 2012). Thus, inputs, such as credit hours, are likely to give way to outputs, such as what has been learned. Even degrees may become less important than what is learned. A collection of faculty assessments over a four- or five-year time horizon that attests to a student having a particular GPA has been, until now, a proxy for whether the student learned anything while attending college. Ultimately, however, the mastery of the tasks graduates undertake tells employers and others whether the student learned anything. The other possibility with online learning is that costs could come significantly down as massive numbers of students use the disruptive technology.

IMPLICATIONS FOR COLLEGE ADMISSION COUNSELING AND ACADEMIC STAFF

What might be the implications of the changing ecosystem of higher education for admission and academic staff? Although instrumental actions surely do not exist with regard to how specific grounds should act, there are issues that warrant attention if what I am suggesting is true.

CLARIFY THE NEEDS AND PREFERENCES OF THE CONSUMER

Admission offices always have been in the business of understanding how to market their institution to prospective students. What has changed is that students want different sorts of activities and timeframes in the 21st century than in the 20th. Time matters to individuals raised on social media. A four- to five-year timeframe to graduate from college may simply be too long when students want to get on with their lives. One reason that for-profit institutions have been successful is that they offer classes at convenient times and locations.

In some respects, admission officers are the front line in terms of understanding the changing nature of consumer preferences and their roles and tasks are crucial. The need for greater understanding of how to attract potential consumers to the institution is likely to engender new ways of marketing higher education. However, as much as the practices of the for-profit industry have come into criticism, it is also true that their methods raise the question about what an organization needs to know about a consumer in order to continue to attract current customers and develop new ones. Just as a "moneyball" approach to baseball introduced new ways of assessing major league talent and the tools of cyber-metrics, I am suggesting that new ways of approaching potential customers is likely to occur as the conditions change in the ecosystem.

UNDERSTAND THE CHANGING ENVIRONMENT

Not only have the preferences and needs of potential students changed, but the environment is in transition as well. Students arrive on campus more focused, but perhaps less prepared. Employers look to postsecondary institutions as training grounds in a manner that was largely unheard of a generation ago. The result is that what sorts of college knowledge students need when they enter college will change, not only because the students are different, but because the ecosystem is shifting as well. Issues such as financial literacy are now essential topics for learning, whereas only a generation ago, such topics were inconsequential. A dynamic environment suggests that what students need to be successful will be in constant flux, but it will also be of central, rather than peripheral, concern when it comes to what students learn and how to structure the curriculum.

The result is threefold. The importance of having students better prepared when they arrive on campus will engender closer working relationships between secondary and postsecondary education. A more streamlined and integrated curricula will work in consort with a tracking and monitoring system to ensure that more students graduate on time and with specific skill sets. The desire for employable job skills and gainful employment will require colleges and universities to have more well-defined relationships with employers.

Obviously, many suggestions underscore how organisms evolve. Career centers, for example, are an artifact of the second half of the 20th century. However, simply having a career center will no longer be sufficient. In a dynamic environment, discrete actions will no longer suffice, and a more concentrated, formalized approach to areas such as admission, career counseling and the like will be necessary.

CONSIDER HOW TO STREAMLINE PROCESSES

As disruptive technology takes hold, the entire system will be under pressure to compress time in a way that has not been considered in mainstream institutions. Rather than students taking classes during semesters that occur in a set time period, the learning experience will be compressed. Summers will no longer be an interlude between academic terms and instead become intense learning experiences. The assumption that students need to apply to college in November, where the start date is nine months away, will change. Those institutions that are going to be successful will find ways to start students soon after they apply, which, in turn, will change the way admission offices function. Social media has changed people's expectations of what they want and when they want it, and postsecondary institutions either will adapt or fail.

RECOGNIZE THAT CHANGE IS THE NEW NORMAL

I have suggested that one byproduct of globalization and the advent of new technologies is the speed with which change occurs. Successful administrators once were thought to be able to master a job and then improve upon it with the mastery of a specific skill set. In the 21st century, however, change occurs so rapidly that successful individuals will need to continually develop different skill sets as their jobs evolve in the new ecosystem.

Recall how important email was a decade ago and how Facebook was central for many teenagers only half a dozen years ago. But the organization that developed a Facebook page and assumed that simply updating the page was sufficient will have failed as student preferences morph away from Facebook and toward Twitter and Instagram. The question is no longer simply how to improve upon current practices. Instead, those of us in higher education need to be adept at adaptation in order for the organization to thrive in the new ecosystem.

The challenge for those of us entering academic life, in some respects, is always as it has been—to question norms, to help create the potential for students to participate in civic live and to enable them to acquire useful skills. But the 21st century also requires us to act differently to achieve those goals. The impact of globalization, the advances in social media, the transformation of the economy, the compression of time, and the privatization of what were once public goods suggest that those of us in academe have different, and potentially greater, responsibilities. The challenge is no longer to ensure that we equip individuals with this or that skill for jobs that already exist. Instead, we need to focus on enabling students and our colleagues to function in a culture that requires innovation and creativity. Rather than a commitment to improving what exists, we need to create the conditions that enable one another to build what has not yet been created.

Discussion Questions

- What are the implications of a greater need for specific skills in attracting students to your institution and ensuring they acquire them in order to find gainful employment?

- What kinds of relationships exist across institutions in the state in order to develop a synthetic, coordinated sector across all different sorts of postsecondary organizations?

- What specific regulations exist that are useful and necessary, and which are unnecessary and cumbersome?

- What are examples of sustainable technologies in your state?

- Define disruptive technology and discuss if your institution is at risk.

- If you were to forecast what the higher education ecosystem were to look like in one decade, what would you say?

- Is it possible to, in part, determine an institution's future, or is it merely buffeted about because of how the larger society changes?

About the Author

William G. Tierney is a university professor, Wilbur-Kieffer professor of higher education and co-director of the Pullias Center for Higher Education at the University of Southern California (CA). He is a past president of the American Educational Research Association (AERA). His research focuses on increasing access to higher education, improving the performance of postsecondary institutions and understanding privatization in higher education. He has had Fulbright Scholarships to Latin America and Australia and was scholar-in-residence at Universiti Sains Malaysia. He has helped develop a suite of interactive web-enhanced games for teenagers on strategies for applying to college with grant support from the Gates Foundation and the US Department of Education. His most recent books are *Urban High School Students and the Challenge of Access* and *For-profit Colleges and Universities: Their Markets, Regulation, Performance and Place in Higher Education*. He has chaired a panel for the US Department of Education and the What Works Clearinghouse that resulted in the monograph, *Helping Students Navigate the Path to College: What Schools Can Do*. He is currently involved in a life history project of low-income, first-generation high school students. He is a fellow of AERA and a member of the National Academy of Education.

References

California Legislative Analyst's Office. (2013). *Cal facts*. Sacramento, CA: Author. Retrieved from *www.lao.ca.gov/reports/2013/calfacts/calfacts_010213.pdf*.

Christensen, C.M., Horn, M.B., Caldera, L., & Soares, L. (2011, February). *Disrupting college: How disruptive innovation can deliver quality and affordability to postsecondary education*. Washington, DC: Center for American Progress. Retrieved from Innosight Institute website: *http://www.innosightinstitute.org/innosight/wp-content/uploads/2011/02/future_of_higher_ed-2.3.pdf*.

Christensen, C.M., Horn, M., & Johnson, C. (2008). *Disrupting class: How disruptive innovation will change the way the world learns.* New York, NY: McGraw-Hill.

Douglass, J.A. (2009). *Higher education's new global order: How and why governments are creating structured opportunity markets.* Berkeley, CA: Center for Studies in Higher Education.

Duderstadt, J.J., & Womack, F.W. (2003). *The future of the public university in America: Beyond the crossroads.* Baltimore, MD: The Johns Hopkins University Press.

Johnson, H., & Sengupta, R. (2009). Closing the gap: Meeting California's need for college graduates. *Public Policy Institute of California.* Retrieved from *http://www.ppic.org/content/pubs/report/R_409HJR.pdf.*

Kena, G., Aud, S., Johnson, F., Wang, X., Zhang, J., Rathbun, A., Wilkinson-Flicker, S., & Kristapovich, P. (2014). *The condition of education 2014.* Washington, DC: Department of Education.

Lumina Foundation. (2012). *A stronger nation through higher education.* Indianapolis, IN: Author. Retrieved from *http://www.luminafoundation.org/stronger_nation.*

Schalin, J. (2010). *State investment in universities: Rethinking the impact on economic growth.* Retrieved from *www.popecenter.org/acrobat/pope_articles/edreport.pdf.*

Tierney, W.G. (2012). Creativity and organizational culture. In M.N. Bastedo (Ed.), *The organization of education: Managing for a new era* (pp. 1953–1970). Baltimore, MD: Johns Hopkins University Press.

Tierney, W.G., & Hentschke, G.C. (2007). *New players, different game: Understanding the rise of for-profit colleges and universities.* Baltimore, MD: The Johns Hopkins University Press.

Turner, S.E. (in press). The impact of the financial crisis on faculty labor markets. In J.R. Brown & C.M. Hoxby (Eds.), *How the financial crisis and great recession affected higher education.* Chicago, IL: University of Chicago Press.

Vedder, R., Denhart, C., Denhart, M., Matgouranis, C., & Robe, J. (2010). *From Wall Street to Wal-Mart: Why college graduates are not getting good jobs.* Washington, DC: Center for College Affordability and Productivity. Retrieved from *http://www.centerforcollegeaffordability.org/uploads/From_Wall_Street_to_Wal-Mart.pdf.*

Weisbrod, B.A., Ballou, J.P., & Asch, E.D. (2008). *Mission and money: Understanding the university.* New York, NY: Cambridge University Press.

Further Reading

Brewer, D.C., & Tierney, W.G. (2011). Barriers to innovation in U.S. higher education. In B. Wildavsky, A. P. Kelly, & K. Carey (Eds.), *Reinventing higher education: The promise of innovation* (pp.11–40). Cambridge, MA: Harvard Education Press.

Conley, D.T. (2008). Rethinking college readiness. *New Directions for Higher Education, 144,* 3–13.

Corwin, Z.B., & Tierney, W.G. (2007). *Getting there—and beyond: Building a culture of college-going in high schools.* Los Angeles, CA: University of Southern California Center for Higher Education Policy Analysis.

Duncheon, J.C., & Tierney, W.G. (2014). Examining college writing readiness. *The Educational Forum,* 78(3), 210–230. doi:10.1080/00131725.2014.912712.

Iloh, C., & Tierney, W.G. (2013). A comparison of for-profit and community colleges' admissions practices. *College and University,* 88(4), 2–12.

Johnson, H., & Sengupta, R. (2009). *Closing the gap: Meeting California's need for college graduates.* San Francisco, CA: Public Policy Institute of California.

Jones, D., & Kelly, P. (2007). *The emerging policy triangle: Economic development, workforce development and education.* Boulder, CO: Western Interstate Commission for Higher Education. Retrieved from *http://www.wiche.edu/info/publications/EmergingPolicyTriangle.pdf.*

Klor de Alva, J., & Rosen, A. (2012). Inside the for-profit sector in higher education. *Forum for the Future of Higher Education,* 25–31.

Pew Research Center. (2014, February). *The rising cost of not going to college.* Washington, DC: Author. Retrieved from *ttp://www.pewsocialtrends. org/2014/02/11/the-rising-cost-of-not-going-to-college.*

Tierney, W.G. (2014). The disruptive future of higher education. In W.G. Tierney, Z.B. Corwin, T. Fullerton, & G. Ragusa (Eds.), *Postsecondary play: The role of games and social media in higher education* (pp 21–44). Baltimore, MD: The Johns Hopkins University Press.

Tierney, W.G., & Duncheon, J.C. (Eds.) (in press). *The problem of college readiness.* Albany, NY: SUNY Press.

U.S. Department of Education. (2012). *Community college student outcomes: 1994–2009* (NCES Report 2012-253). Washington, DC: Author.

Closing Statement

The fourth edition of *Fundamentals of College Admission Counseling* utilizes a collective, broad-base of experience and expertise, as demonstrated by the authors of the featured chapters. Consider this textbook as a tool both stewarding practice and refining professional knowledge regarding college admission counseling, and the various processes and considerations of access, enrollment and college success. We hope you have acknowledged and appreciated the historical, theoretical, research, and experiential writings provided by our authors, thus cultivating your own reflections of the current practices and recommended adaptations for the field.

The text, while thorough, is neither exhaustive in information nor action. The chapters are intended to encourage thought and discussion about the best practices and strategies that can be employed to increase inclusion and equity in college access. Practitioners, graduate students, faculty, leaders, and others should utilize this information as a precursor to continuous professional development efforts, on behalf of our work with students and families. The authors include suggested resources, discussion questions and references just for this purpose. In addition, you are encouraged to register your text, thereby joining the **Fundamentals 4th Edition List-Serve,** by visiting our online resource: *www.nacacnet.org/Fundamentals4th.* As mentioned in the introduction, this service aims to keep readers informed of new content, relevant articles and professional development opportunities provided by NACAC.

The goal of this book has been to draw the building blocks for a working knowledge of college admission counseling and create an environment in which various stakeholders are vested in helping students succeed by helping college admission practitioners succeed. We applaud the authors who have contributed to this necessary resource and who have taken steps to fortify the college admission process at their respective schools and through their academic work. Thank you for sharing your wisdom, experience and passion for this topic. We hope that this text serves as an informative resource and stands to encourage efforts to increase college access and success.

HOW TO CITE CHAPTERS FROM THE FOURTH EDITION OF FUNDAMENTALS OF COLLEGE ADMISSION COUNSELING:

Section 1:

Holocomb-McCoy, C. (2014). The counseling landscape. In J.D. Mathis, R.M. Rall & T.M. Laudino (Eds.), *Fundamentals of college admission counseling: A textbook for graduate students and practicing counselors* (pp. 4–14). Arlington, VA: NACAC.

Ware, L. & Mathis, J. D. (2014). Frameworks for college counseling: Considerations for novice and continuing professionals. In J.D. Mathis, R.M. Rall & T.M. Laudino (Eds.), *Fundamentals of college admission counseling: A textbook for graduate students and practicing counselors* (pp. 16–28). Arlington, VA: NACAC.

Hallett, R. E. & Tevis, T. (2014). Increasing access and success. In J.D. Mathis, R.M. Rall & T.M. Laudino (Eds.), *Fundamentals of college admission counseling: A textbook for graduate students and practicing counselors* (pp. 30–48). Arlington, VA: NACAC.

Mathis, J. D. & Laudino, T. M. (2014). Purpose, ethics and practice: Values, competencies and impact of NACAC. In J.D. Mathis, R.M. Rall & T.M. Laudino (Eds.), *Fundamentals of college admission counseling: A textbook for graduate students and practicing counselors* (pp. 50–60). Arlington, VA: NACAC.

Hock, P., Murphy, K. (2014). Purpose, ethics and practice: Statement of principles of good practice. In J.D. Mathis, R.M. Rall & T.M. Laudino (Eds.), *Fundamentals of college admission counseling: A textbook for graduate students and practicing counselors* (pp. 62–68). Arlington, VA: NACAC.

Section 2:

Sohmer, L. (2014). College counseling: Making it work. In J.D. Mathis, R.M. Rall & T.M. Laudino (Eds.), *Fundamentals of college admission counseling: A textbook for graduate students and practicing counselors* (pp. 98–108). Arlington, VA: NACAC.

Hugo, E. B. (2014). Counseling the crowds: Using creativity and accountability to serve large caseloads. In J.D. Mathis, R.M. Rall & T.M. Laudino (Eds.), *Fundamentals of college admission counseling: A textbook for graduate students and practicing counselors* (pp. 110–122). Arlington, VA: NACAC.

Tremblay, C. W. (2014). The college search, the college choice and applying to college: Introducing the taxonomy of applying to college. In J.D. Mathis, R.M. Rall & T.M. Laudino (Eds.), *Fundamentals of college admission counseling: A textbook for graduate students and practicing counselors* (pp. 124–138). Arlington, VA: NACAC.

Hatch, T. (2014). The use of data in college and career readiness. In J.D. Mathis, R.M. Rall & T.M. Laudino (Eds.), *Fundamentals of college admission counseling: A textbook for graduate students and practicing counselors* (pp. 140–168). Arlington, VA: NACAC.

Hawkins, D., The College Board, Habley, W. & ACT, Inc. (2014). Practical information regarding standardized assessment: Articles from The College Board and ACT, Inc. In J.D. Mathis, R.M. Rall & T.M. Laudino (Eds.), *Fundamentals of college admission counseling: A textbook for graduate students and practicing counselors* (pp. 170–172). Arlington, VA: NACAC.

The College Board. (2014). Standardized testing from The College Board. [Article within chapter: Practical information regarding standardized assessment: Articles from The College Board and ACT, Inc.] In J.D. Mathis, R.M. Rall & T.M. Laudino (Eds.), *Fundamentals of college admission counseling: A textbook for graduate students and practicing counselors* (pp. 172–186). Arlington, VA: NACAC.

Habley, W. & ACT, Inc. (2014). Using ACT's assessments in college counseling. [Article within chapter: Practical information regarding standardized assessment: Articles from The College Board and ACT, Inc.] In J.D. Mathis, R.M. Rall & T.M. Laudino (Eds.), *Fundamentals of college admission counseling: A textbook for graduate students and practicing counselors* (pp. 179–183). Arlington, VA: NACAC.

Blume, G. (2014). Academic planning for high school students: Careful choices cultivate postsecondary opportunity and success. In J.D. Mathis, R.M. Rall & T.M. Laudino (Eds.), *Fundamentals of college admission counseling: A textbook for graduate students and practicing counselors* (pp. 188–202). Arlington, VA: NACAC.

Skinner, R. (2014a). Writing an effective college recommendation letter. In J.D. Mathis, R.M. Rall & T.M. Laudino (Eds.), *Fundamentals of college admission counseling: A textbook for graduate students and practicing counselors* (pp. 204–215). Arlington, VA: NACAC.

Section 3:

O'Connor, P. (2014). Postsecondary options. In J.D. Mathis, R.M. Rall & T.M. Laudino (Eds.), *Fundamentals of college admission counseling: A textbook for graduate students and practicing counselors* (pp. 220–232). Arlington, VA: NACAC.

George Mwangi, C. A. (2014). Working with diverse student populations. In J.D. Mathis, R.M. Rall & T.M. Laudino (Eds.), *Fundamentals of college admission counseling: A textbook for graduate students and practicing counselors* (pp. 234–250). Arlington, VA: NACAC.

Venegas, K. (2014). Financial aid partnerships and possibilities. In J.D. Mathis, R.M. Rall & T.M. Laudino (Eds.), *Fundamentals of college admission counseling: A textbook for graduate students and practicing counselors* (pp. 252–262). Arlington, VA: NACAC.

Pérez, A. B. (2014). Demystifying enrollment management: How finances impact access. In J.D. Mathis, R.M. Rall & T.M. Laudino (Eds.), *Fundamentals of college admission counseling: A textbook for graduate students and practicing counselors* (pp. 264–272). Arlington, VA: NACAC.

Section 4:

Huerta, A. H. (2014). The role of counselors in facilitating college opportunities for marginalized student populations. In J.D. Mathis, R.M. Rall & T.M. Laudino (Eds.), *Fundamentals of college admission counseling: A textbook for graduate students and practicing counselors* (pp. 276–288). Arlington, VA: NACAC.

Dixon, K., Jeffers-Coly, P. & Smith, N. E. (2014). If not us, then who? Working with first-generation students. In J.D. Mathis, R.M. Rall & T.M. Laudino (Eds.), *Fundamentals of college admission counseling: A textbook for graduate students and practicing counselors* (pp. 290–314). Arlington, VA: NACAC.

Houlihan, T. J. (2014). Students with learning disabilities and the college application process. In J.D. Mathis, R.M. Rall & T.M. Laudino (Eds.), *Fundamentals of college admission counseling: A textbook for graduate students and practicing counselors* (pp. 316–334). Arlington, VA: NACAC.

Montague, P. (2014). Resources and social media for college counseling. In J.D. Mathis, R.M. Rall & T.M. Laudino (Eds.), *Fundamentals of college admission counseling: A textbook for graduate students and practicing counselors* (pp. 336–348). Arlington, VA: NACAC.

Skinner, Rod. (2014b). The college essay: Helping students find their voice. In J.D. Mathis, R.M. Rall & T.M. Laudino (Eds.), *Fundamentals of college admission counseling: A textbook for graduate students and practicing counselors* (pp. 350–366). Arlington, VA: NACAC.

Section 5:

Bardwell, R. (2014). The early years: Exploring postsecondary options in middle and elementary schools. In J.D. Mathis, R.M. Rall & T.M. Laudino (Eds.), *Fundamentals of college admission counseling: A textbook for graduate students and practicing counselors* (pp. 370–386). Arlington, VA: NACAC.

Bryan, J., Griffin, D. & Henry, L. (2014). School-family-community partnership strategies for promotion college readiness and access. In J.D. Mathis, R.M. Rall & T.M. Laudino (Eds.), *Fundamentals of college admission counseling: A textbook for graduate students and practicing counselors* (pp. 388–406). Arlington, VA: NACAC.

Rall, R. M. (2014). Facilitating college participation and success before they even arrive: A community cultural wealth perspective. In J.D. Mathis, R.M. Rall & T.M. Laudino (Eds.), *Fundamentals of college admission counseling: A textbook for graduate students and practicing counselors* (pp. 408–416). Arlington, VA: NACAC.

Tierney, W. G. (2014). The dynamic ecosystem of higher education: Implications for college admission counseling. In J.D. Mathis, R.M. Rall & T.M. Laudino (Eds.), *Fundamentals of college admission counseling: A textbook for graduate students and practicing counselors* (pp. 418–429). Arlington, VA: NACAC.